Author and journalist Pete Irvine is also Scotland's leading-edge event organizer. His company, Unique Events, created Edinburgh's annual Hogmanay Programme twelve years ago in the year that he started this book; it has become the world's biggest New Year's celebration. He's also the director of Scotland's annual contemporary-art gatherings – the Glasgow Art Fair and Glasgow International – and of the annual festival that celebrates the life and spirit of Robert Burns, Burns and a' That.

In 2000 he received the Silver Thistle Award for his 'outstanding contribution to the development of tourism in Scotland' and the MBE for services to Edinburgh.

*'Makes all other guides to Scotland redundant'*
Sunday Times

*'Infallible and quite brilliant'*
Daily Telegraph

*'The only guide to Scotland the Scots use'*
Glasgow Evening Times

*'The only guide worth a damn'*
The Scotsman

Comments from readers of previous editions of *Scotland the Best* include:

*'It's our bible!'*

*'Your book gave us the trip of a lifetime'*

*'Having this book is like having you in the car'*

*'Please do England'*

Pete Irvine is happy to receive comments about this edition and recommendations for entries for the next by post (sent c/o HarperCollins Publishers in Glasgow). He is, however, unable to reply to submissions personally.

D0533214

# Collins

# Scotland the best

## PETER IRVINE

HarperCollins Publishers
Westerhill Rd, Bishopbriggs, Glasgow G64 2QT

www.collins.co.uk

First published in Great Britain in 1993
by Mainstream Publishing Company (Edinburgh) Ltd

First published by HarperCollins Publishers in 1997

This edition published in 2005

ISBN  0 00 721673 4

A catalogue record for this book is available from the British Library


Printed in Italy by Legoprint

# Contents

# Introduction

Twelve years ago when I started doing this book it was a journey of discovery for me. I didn't know Scotland that well either! It took over two years and the book emerged as I went along. Since then, and knowing Scotland a good deal better, I've been able to rely on researchers although I've always done the bulk of it myself. However, for the 2006/07 edition I decided to go back to basics and as much as possible to visit everywhere again – myself.

I wanted to restore the high standard that I'd looked for originally. Regular readers will know that *Scotland the Best* is not a book about all the options – it only recommends the best that there is. The mediocre simply doesn't register. This applies to natural features as well as all of the areas of human endeavour that are of interest to visitors and tourists. I found as that years went by and I knew more people I was becoming lax, perhaps even generous. I was including places because I liked the people involved or because I felt that I should find somewhere to eat or stay in every town.

But it doesn't help to be anything other than totally discriminating. It's an increasingly competitive world and Scotland has to match up. Fortunately, there are loads of people who know this and are doing extraordinary things. As always, the best places are those where people really care. *Scotland the Best* is primarily about these people and places. I've always seen it as my task to find them and my duty to bring them to your attention.

It's my view that Scotland is doing better than ever and although I've tried to be more rigorous, to raise the bar (culling to be kind; perhaps losing friends in the process), there's certainly no shortage of places replacing those that have been lost.

New readers should note that every item is evaluated on the totally subjective merits of its category. Obviously fish and chip shops are considered differently to country-house dining rooms; Italian restaurants are different from trattorias. Since we all seem to be preoccupied with eating out these days I decided that I'd evaluate fine dining in a particular way. There are two chefs in Scotland who are generally considered to be at the top of their game. I agree and have given them two ticks and a small commendation (two ticks plus). Consequently I've readjusted the tick awards for other places – a chef would have to be as good as Martin Wishart or Andrew Fairlie to be given two and it's meant that many two-tick places have gone down to one, and single ticks have been removed. However, I do believe I've got this right and that this edition of *Scotland the Best* is the most accurate guide yet to what's going on in Scotland (in a world context) at the present time. I hope you agree. Please write and tell me if you think I'm wrong or if I've missed somewhere (see p. 360).

My thanks in this edition to Malcolm Gladwell, who recently published a book called *Blink*. In it he proposes that you can make up your mind about something and be invariably correct (especially if you have honed your instinct) in an instant. In short, he avows that the first impression and the snap judgment is often better that the detailed analysis. I held on to that thought as I sped around Scotland.

Don't go as quickly as I did. Happy trails.

*Pete Irvine*
*Edinburgh, October 2005*

# How To Use This Book

There are three ways to find things in this book:

1. There's an index at the back.

2. The book can be used by category, e.g. you can look up the best restaurants in the Borders or the best scenic routes in the whole of Scotland. Each entry has an item number in the outside margin. These are in numerical order and allow easy cross-referencing.

3. You can start with the maps and see how individual items are located, how they are grouped together and how much there is that's worth seeing or doing in any particular area. Then just look up the item numbers. If you are travelling round Scotland, I would urge you to use the maps and this method of finding the best of what an area or town has to offer.

   The maps correspond to the recognisable regions of Scotland. There's also an overall map to show how the regions fit together. The list of maps is on the contents pages and the map section is at the back of the book.

   All items have a code which gives (1) the specific item number; (2) the map on which it can be found; and (3) the map co-ordinates. For space reasons, items in Glasgow and Edinburgh are not marked on Maps A and B, although they do have co-ordinates in the margin to give you a rough idea of the location. City maps are readily available from any tourist office or newsagent.

A typical entry is shown below, identifying the various elements that make it up.

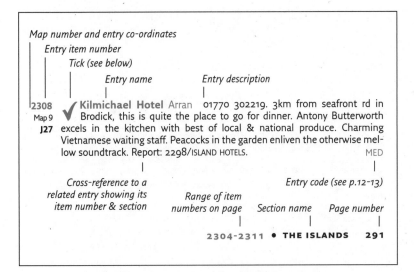

Map number and entry co-ordinates
Entry item number
Tick (see below)
Entry name          Entry description

**2308**  ✓ **Kilmichael Hotel** Arran  01770 302219. 3km from seafront rd in
Map 9      Brodick, this is quite the place to go for dinner. Antony Butterworth
**J27**  excels in the kitchen with best of local & national produce. Charming Vietnamese waiting staff. Peacocks in the garden enliven the otherwise mellow soundtrack. Report: 2298/ISLAND HOTELS.          MED

Cross-reference to a related entry showing its item number & section
Range of item numbers on page     Section name     Page number

2304-2311 ● THE ISLANDS    291

# A Note On Categories

Edinburgh and Glasgow, the destinations of most visitors and the nearest cities to more than half of the population, are covered in the substantial Sections 2 and 3. You will probably need a city map to get around, although Maps 1 and 2 should give you the rough layout.

For the purposes of maps, and particularly in Section 4 (Regional Hotels and Restaurants), I have used a combination of the subdivision of Scotland based on the current standard political regions along with the historical ones, e.g. Argyll, Clyde Valley. From Sections 5 to 12, categories are based on activities, interests and geography and refer to the whole of Scotland. Section 13 covers the islands, with a page-by-page guide to the larger ones.

Section 14 is intended to give a comprehensive and concise guide to the best of the major Scottish towns in each area. Some of the recommended hotels and restaurants will be amongst the best in the region and will have been referred to in Section

4, or even amongst the best in Scotland and referred to in Sections 5 to 13, but otherwise they have been selected because they are the best there is in the town or the immediate area.

There are some categories like Bed and Breakfasts, Fishing Beats, Antique Shops that haven't been included because they are impracticable to assess (there are too many of them, are too small, or they change hands too often).

If there are other categories that you would like to see in future editions, please let us know (see p. 360).

# Ticks For The Best There Is

Although everything listed in the book is notable and remarkable in some way, there are places that are outstanding even in this superlative company. Instead of marking them with a rosette or a star, they have been 'awarded' a tick.

 Amongst the very best in Scotland

 Amongst the best (of its type) in the UK

 A particular commendation for Andrew Fairlie and Martin Wishart, acknowledged as two of the top chefs in Scotland and the UK

Amongst the best (of its type) in the world, or simply unique

Listings generally are not in an order of merit although if there is one outstanding item it will always be at the top of the page and this obviously includes anything which has been given a tick. Hotels and restaurants are also grouped according to price and this is why a cross-marked place may appear further down the page (ticks also indicate exceptional value for money).

# The Codes

## 1. The Item Code

At the outside margin of every item is a code which will enable you to find it on a map. Thus 13 Map 5 **C20** should be read as follows: 13 is the item number, listed in simple consecutive order; Map 5 refers to the Hebrides – the map section is at the back of the book; **C20** is the map co-ordinate, to help pinpoint the item's location on the map grid. A co-ordinate such as **xA5** indicates that the item can be reached by leaving the map at grid reference **A5**.

## 2. The Hotel Code

Below each hotel recommended is a band of codes as follows:

**20RMS JAN-DEC T/T PETS CC KIDS LOTS**

**20RMS** means the hotel has 20 bedrooms in total. No differentiation is made as to the type of room. Most hotels will offer twin rooms as singles or put extra beds in doubles if required. This code merely gives an impression of size.

**JAN-DEC** means the hotel is open all year round. **APR-OCT** means approximately from the beginning of April to the end of October.

**T/T** refers to the facilities: T/ means there are direct-dial phones in the bedrooms while /T means there are TVs in the bedrooms.

**PETS** means the hotel accepts dogs and other pets, probably under certain conditions (e.g. pets should be kept in the bedroom). It's usually best to check first.

**XPETS** indicates that the hotel does not generally accept pets.

**CC** means the hotel accepts major credit cards (e.g. Access and Visa).

**XCC** means the hotel does not accept credit cards.

**KIDS** indicates children are welcome and special provisions/rates may be available.

**XKIDS** does not necessarily mean that children are not able to accompany their parents, only that special provisions/rates are not usually made. Check by phone.

**TR** Top Rooms – the best rooms in the house!

**GF** means the establishment is gay-friendly.

**LOTS** Rooms which cost more than £80 per night per person. The theory is that if you can afford over £160 a room, it doesn't matter too much if it's £160 or £185 or more.
Other price bands are:

**EXP** Expensive: £58-80 per person.

**MED.EX** Medium (expensive): £42-58.

**MED.INX** Medium (inexpensive): £35-42.

**INX** Inexpensive: £28-35.

**CHP** Cheap: less than £28.

Rates are per person per night. They are worked out by halving the published average rate for a twin room in high season and should be used only to give an impression of cost. They are based on 2005 prices. Add between £2 to £5 per year, though the band should stay the same unless the hotel undergoes improvements.

### 3. The Restaurant Code

Found at the bottom right of all restaurant entries. It refers to the price of an average dinner per person with a starter, a main course and dessert. It doesn't include wine, coffee or extras.

**EXP** Expensive: more than £32.

**MED** Medium: £22-32.

**INX** Inexpensive: £14-22.

**CHP** Cheap: under £14.

These are based on 2005 rates. With inflation, the relative price bands should stay about the same.

Where a hotel is notable also for its restaurant, there is a restaurant line below the hotel entry preceded by **EAT** and followed by a separate code in the corner.

**SD** indicates the signature dish of the chef.

**LO** means last orders at the kitchen. Some places will close earlier if they are quiet and go later on request.

**10pm/10.30pm** means usually 10pm Mon-Fri, 10.30pm at w/ends. It is v common, esp for city restaus, to open later at w/nds.

During the Festival period almost all Edinburgh restaus open later and on more days.

### 4. The Walk Code

A great number of walks are described in the book, especially in section 9. Found at bottom-right corner of item:

2-10km    CIRC    BIKE    1-A-1

**2-10km** means the walk(s) described may vary in length from 2km to 10km.

**CIRC** means the walk can be circular, while **xCIRC** shows the walk is not circular and you must return more or less the way you came.

**BIKE** indicates the walk has a path which is suitable for ordinary bikes.

**xBIKE** means the walk is not suitable for, or does not permit, cycling.

**mtBIKE** means the track is suitable for mountain or all-terrain bikes.

The **1-A-1** Code

First number (1, 2 or 3) indicates how easy the walk is.
1 the walk is easy.
2 medium difficulty, e.g. standard hillwalking, not dangerous nor requiring special knowledge or equipment.
3 difficult: care and preparation and a map are needed.

The letters (A, B or C) indicate how easy it is to find the path.
A the route is easy to find. The way is either marked or otherwise obvious.
B the route is not very obvious, but you'll get there.
C you will need a map and preparation or a guide.

The last number (1, 2 or 3) indicates what to wear on your feet.
1 ordinary outdoor shoes, including trainers, are probably okay unless the ground is very wet.
2 you will need walking boots.
3 you will need serious walking or hiking boots.

Apart from designated walks, the **1-A-1** code is employed wherever there is more than a short stroll required to get to somewhere, e.g. a waterfall or a monument.

# List of Abbreviations

As well as codes and because of obvious space limitations, a personal shorthand and ad hoc abbreviation system has had to be created. I'm the first to admit some may be annoying, especially 'restau' for restaurant, but it's a long word and it comes up often. The others which are used are ...

| | | | |
|---|---|---|---|
| Aber | Aberdeen | N | north |
| accom | accommodation | NTS | National Trust for Scotland |
| adj | adjacent | | |
| admn | admission | no smk | no smoking |
| app | approach | nr | near |
| approx | approximately | | |
| atmos | atmosphere | o/look | overlook(s)/ing |
| av | average | opp | opposite |
| AYR | all year round | o/side | outside |
| | | pl | place |
| bedrms | bedrooms | poss | possible |
| betw | between | pt | point/port |
| br | bridge | | |
| BYOB | bring your own bottle | R | river |
| | | rep | reputation |
| cl | closes/closed | r/bout | roundabout |
| contemp | contemporary | road | rd |
| cotts | cottages | refurb | refurbished/ment |
| | | restau | restaurant |
| def | definite/definitely | ret | return |
| dining-rm | dining room | rm(s) | room(s) |
| | | RSPB | Royal Society for the Protection of Birds |
| E | east | | |
| Edin | Edinburgh | rt | right |
| esp | especially | | |
| evens | evenings | S | south |
| excl | excluding or excellent | SD | signature dish |
| exhib(s) | exhibition(s) | self/c | self-catering |
| exp | expensive | sq | square |
| | | st | street |
| facs | facilities | StB | Scotland the Best |
| ft | fort | stn | station |
| | | SYHA | Scottish Youth Hostel Association |
| gdn(s) | garden(s) | | |
| GF | gay-friendly | ☕ | Worth going to for the tearoom alone |
| Gillian G | Gillian Glover, notable Scottish food critic | | |
| | | TDH | Table d'hôte |
| Glas | Glasgow | TGP | Time of going to print |
| gr | great | TIC | Tourist Information Centre |
| HS | Historic Scotland | | |
| hr(s) | hour(s) | TO | tourist office |
| | | TR | top rooms |
| incl | including | t/away | take-away food |
| inexp | inexpensive | t/off | turn off |
| info | information | trad | traditional |
| | | tratt | trattoria |
| j/tie | jacket and tie | | |
| jnct | junction | univ | university |
| Joanna B | Joanna Blythman, notable Scottish food critic | | |
| | | v | very |
| L | loch | VC | visitor centre |
| LA | last admission | vegn | vegetarian |
| LO | last orders | | |
| LO10pm/11pm | usually, last orders at 10pm during week, 11pm weekends | W | west |
| | | w/end(s) | weekend(s) |
| min(s) | minute(s) | yr(s) | years |
| mt(s) | mountain(s) | | |

# SECTION 1

*Wha's Like Us?*

# Famously Big Attractions

*Amongst the 'top 10' (paid admn) and the 'top 10' (free) visitor attractions, these are the ones really worth seeing. Find them under their item nos.*

**Edinburgh Castle; Holyrood Palace; Edinburgh Zoo; The National Gallery; Our Dynamic Earth** 388/391/390/397/396/MAIN ATTRACTIONS.

**The People's Palace, Glasgow; The Burrell Collection; Science Centre** 708/706/709/MAIN ATTRACTIONS.

**The Museum of Transport; The Glasgow Botanics; The Gallery of Modern Art** 712/713/714/OTHER ATTRACTIONS.

**The Edinburgh Botanics** 402/OTHER ATTRACTIONS.

**Culzean Castle; Stirling Castle** 1791/1788/CASTLES.

## OTHER UNMISSABLES ARE:

**1**
Map 9
**L25**
✓✓✓ **Loch Lomond** App via Stirling and A811 to Drymen or from Glas, the A82 Dumbarton rd to Balloch. Britain's largest inland waterway and a trad playground, especially for Glaswegians; jet-skis, show-off boats. **Lomond Shores** at Balloch is the new, heavily retail gateway to the loch & the **Loch Lomond National Park** which covers a vast area. Orientate & shop here.

W bank Balloch-Tarbert is most developed: marinas, cruises, ferry to Inchmurrin Island. Luss is tweeville, like a movie set (it was used in the Scottish TV soap *High Road*) but has ok tearm (1450/TEAROOMS). Rd more picturesque beyond Tarbert to Ardlui; see 1323/BLOODY GOOD PUBS for the non-tourist/real Scots experience of the Drover's Inn at Inverarnan.

E bank more natural, wooded; good lochside and hill walks (2016/MUNROS). Rd winding but picturesque beyond Balmaha towards Ben Lomond.

**2**
Map 7
**G19**
✓✓✓ **The Cuillins** Skye This hugely impressive mt range in the S of Skye, often shrouded in cloud or rain, is the romantic heartland of the Islands & was 'sold' in 2003 to a combination of public agencies so... it's ours now! The Red Cuillins are smoother and nearer the Portree-Broadford rd; the Black Cuillins gather behind and are best approached from Glen Brittle (2001/SERIOUS WALKS; 1643/WATERFALLS). This classic, untameable mt scenery has attracted walkers, climbers and artists for centuries. It still claims lives regularly. For best views apart from Glen Brittle, see 1673/SCENIC ROUTES; 1691/VIEWS. Vast range of walks and scrambles (see also 1706/PICNICS).

**3**
Map 7
**M18**
✓✓✓ **Loch Ness** Most visits start from Inverness at the N end via the R Ness. Ft Augustus is at the other end, 56km S. L Ness is part of the still-navigable Caledonian Canal linking the E and W coast at Ft William. Many small boats line the shores of the R Ness; one of the best ways to see the loch is on a cruise from Inverness (Jacobite Cruises 01463 233999 1-6 hrs, 6 options), Drumnadrochit or Fort Augustus. Most tourist traffic uses the main A82 N bank rd converging on Drumnadrochit where the L Ness Monster industry gobbles up your money. If you must, the 'official' L Ness Monster Exhibition is the one to choose. On the A82 you can't miss Urquhart Castle (1860/RUINS). But the two best things about L Ness are: the S rd (B862) from Ft Augustus back to Inverness (1678/SCENIC ROUTES; 1652/WATERFALLS); and the detour from Drumnadrochit to Cannich to Glen Affric (20-30km) (1627/GLENS; 2007/GLEN AND RIVER WALKS; 1639/WATERFALLS).

**4**
Map 10
**N25**
✓✓ **Falkirk Wheel** Falkirk 08700 500 208. Tamfourhill, halfway betw Edin & Glas, signed from M9 & M80 & locally. The splendid & deliberately dramatic massive boat-lift at the convergence of the (Millennium-funded) reinstated Union and Forth & Clyde canals – the world's first coast-to-coast ship canal (to wonder or plooter along). The 35-m lift is impressive to watch & gr to go on. Boats leave Vis Centre every 30 mins for 45-min journey. There are now 3 reasons to visit Falkirk (35/EVENTS, 1591/PARKS).

# Favourite Scottish Journeys

**5** **Wemyss Bay-Rothesay Ferry** Calmac 01475 650100. The glass-roofed
Map 9 stn at Wemyss Bay, the railhead from Glas (60km by rd on the A78), is redo-
**K25** lent of an age-old terminus. The frequent ferry (Calmac) has all the Scottish
traits and sausage rolls you can handle, and Rothesay (with its period seaside
mansions) appears out of blood-smeared sunsets and rain-sodden mornings
alike, a gentle watercolour from summer holidays past. Visit the (Victorian)
toilet when you get there and Mt Stuart (1852/HOUSES). Both are superb.

**6** **Loch Etive Cruises** 01866 822430, though booking not essential. From
Map 9 Taynuilt (Oban 20km) through the long narrow waters of one of Scotland's
**J22** most atmospheric lochs, a 3hr journey in a small cruiser with indoor and outdoor seating. Pier is 2km from main Taynuilt crossroads on A85. Easter-mid
Oct. Leaves 12-2pm (not Sat). Also **Loch Shiel Cruises**: 01687 470322. From
nr Glenfinnan House Hotel (1255/SCOTTISH HOTELS) on Rd to the Isles, A830. A
1-2-stop cruise on glorious L Shiel. Various trips avail.

**7** **Glenelg-Kylerhea** The shorter of the 2 remaining ferry journeys to Skye, and
Map 7 definitely the best way to get there if you're not pushed for time. The drive to
**H19** Glenelg from the A87 is spectacular (1667/SCENIC ROUTES) and so is this 5min
crossing of the deep Narrows of Kylerhea. Apr-Oct (frequent) 9am-5.45pm
and Sun in summer (from 10am). 01599 511302. Otter-watch hide at Kylerhea.

**8** **Corran Ferry** From Ardgour on A861-Nether Lochaber on the A82 across
Map 9 the narrows of L Linnhe. A convenient 5min crossing which can save time to
**J21** pts S of Mallaig and takes you to the wildernesses of Moidart and
Ardnamurchan. A charming and fondly regarded journey in its own rt. Runs
contin till 8.50pm summer, 7.50pm winter. Later w/ends. 01855 841243.

**9** **The Maid of the Forth Cruise to Inchcolm Island** 0131 331 4857. The
Map 10 wee boat (though they say it holds 225 people) which leaves every day at dif-
**P25** ferent times (phone for details) from Hawes Pier in S Queensferry (15km
Central Edin via A90) opp the Hawes Inn, just under the famous railway br
(389/MAIN ATTRACTIONS) & from Newhaven Harbour in town. 45min trips
under the br and on to Inchcolm, an attractive island with walks and an
impressive ruined abbey. Much birdlife and also many seals. 1hr 30mins
ashore. Tickets at pier. Mar-Oct.

**10** **The Waverley** 0845 130 4647. See the Clyde, see the world! Report:
722/GLASGOW ATTRACTIONS.

**11** **The West Highland Line** Rail info: 08457 484950. One of the most pic-
Map 9 turesque railway journeys in Europe and quite the best way to get to Skye
**J21** from the S. Travel to Ft William from Glas, then relax and watch the stunning
scenery, the Bonnie Prince Charlie country (MARY, CHARLIE AND BOB, p. 243-4)
and much that is close to a railwayman's heart go past the window. Viaducts
(incl the Harry Potter one) and tunnels over loch and down dale. Also possible to make the same journey (from Ft William to Mallaig and/or return) by
steam train June-mid-Oct (dep 10.20am). Check on 01463 239026. There's a
museum in the restored stn at Glenfinnan. Trains for Mallaig leave from Glas
Queen St, 3 times a day and take about 5hrs.

**12** **From Inverness** Info on 08457 484950. Two less-celebrated but mes-
Map 7 merising rail journeys start from Inverness. The journey to Kyle of Lochalsh
**M18** no longer has an observation car in the summer months, so get a window
seat and take an atlas; the last section through Glen Carron and around the
coast at Loch Carron is especially fine. There are 3 trains a day and it takes
2hrs 30mins. Inverness to Wick is a 3hr 50min journey. The section skirting
the E coast from Lairg-Helmsdale is full of drama, followed by the transfixing
monotony of the Flow Country. 3 trains a day in summer.

**13** **The Plane to Barra** Most of the island plane journeys pass over many
Map 5 smaller islands (e.g. Glas-Tiree, Glas-Stornoway, Wick-Orkney) and are fasci-
**C20** nating on a clear day, but BA's daily flight from Glas to Barra is doubly special
because the island's airport is on Cockleshell Beach in the N of the island (11
km from Castlebay) after a splendid app. The 12-seater Otter leaves and lands
according to the tide. 0870 8509850.

# The Best Scottish Film Locations

## ISLANDS & BEACHES

**14**
Map 5
**C20**

**Barra** *Whisky Galore* directed by Scot Sandy McKendrick (who went to Hollywood and became famous for *The Sweet Smell of Success*) was filmed on Barra. Imagine you are hiding the golden nectar from the Excise men by hanging out in the Politician (the bar named after the boat that ran aground).

**15**
Map 7
**H20**

**The Sands of Morar** The beach features in Bill Forsyth's *Local Hero* (1622/BEACHES). However, the famous phone box isn't exactly round the corner. It's actually located in Pennan on the Moray coast, one of several lovely wee villages (1607/BEACHES). The cosy hotel there was for sale at TGP.

**16**
Map 10
**R23**

**St Andrews West Sands** Run along this gr beach (1620/BEACHES) to Vangelis' *Chariots Of Fire* music in your head and take in the town's estimable qualities. You can go to the movies at the New Picture House in North St.

**17**
Map 10
**R25**

**Gullane Bents** The douce town of Gullane. Brigitte Bardot graced these sandy shores in *Two Weeks In September*.

## CASTLES & MANSIONS

**18**
Map 10
**Q27**

**Floors Castle** Kelso The gothic mansion that was the home that Tarzan (Christopher Lambert) returned to in *Greystoke – The Legend Of Tarzan* (dir. Hugh Hudson). (1859/COUNTRY HOUSES)

**19**
Map 10
**P25**
**S20**

**Blackness Castle and Dunottar Castle** Stonehaven Both were used as the home of the Danish prince in Zeffirelli's 1990 film *Hamlet*. Dunottar is dramatic on a cliff top sweeping out in to the North Sea (1811/RUINS). Eat at the Tolbooth, Stonehaven (1399/SEAFOOD RESTAURANTS) after exploring the prison cells. Dunottar also features as itself in the classic Scots novel *Sunset Song* by Lewis Grassic Gibbon (1945/LIT PLACES).

## THE GREAT OUTDOORS

**20**

**Glencoe, Rannoch Moor and Glenfinnan** Stalwart locations for their unspoilt, century-transcending qualities.
**Glencoe** There's no alternative for scale nor for conveying the passion for Scotland that Scots hero William Wallace had for his country, so Mel Gibson was to be found here of a morning, reportedly in awe of the place. *Braveheart* was shot in several locations around here (1666/SCENIC ROUTES).
**Rannoch Moor** The classic misty moor which was the end of the line for the city boys from *Trainspotting*. The Moor Of Rannoch Hotel waits for you too.
**Glenfinnan** Loch Shiel's dark beauty lent atmosphere to the *Highlander* franchise, originally starring Christopher Lambert and Sean Connery. Glencoe, Glen Nevis, Morar and Skye also featured.
**The Train from Fort William to Mallaig, the Viaduct at Glenfinnan** Memorable locations for the *Harry Potter* movies. Glen Nevis and the landscape around the Cluanie Inn (1192/INNS) were also used.

## CITY LOCATIONS

**21**

**Edinburgh** *Trainspotting* again. The film has recently won an award for best use of a location. The opening sequence with the zesty Ewan McGregor in the mad dash along Princes Street, is one to re-enact at a more leisurely pace taking in a few retail outlets.

**22**

**Edinburgh** Dame Maggie Smith encapsulated *The Prime Of Miss Jean Brodie* as her crème-de-la-crème girruls were edified in their walks about the city, most memorably down The Vennel from Heriot's School to the Grassmarket.

**23**

**Edinburgh** The Royal Mile was closed for the first time that wasn't a royal visit, to create the bustling period market scene in *Jude* where Thomas Hardy's characters, played by Christopher Eccleston and Kate Winslet, met.

**24**

**Glasgow** Doubling as Victorian-era New York in *The House of Mirth*, the Glasgow City Chambers' magnificent marbled halls and staircases were spectacular scene-setters.

# Great Ways To Get Around

**By Seaplane** Loch Lomond Seaplanes 01436 675030. See Scotland from the air, landing on land and water in the remoter parts that other transport can't reach. Most routes are West Coast but can be customised. Lunch tours drop you at a hotel/restaurant lochside location, e.g. Monchyle Mhor (1213/GETAWAY HOTELS), Ardeonaig (1214/GETAWAY HOTELS), Ardanaiseig Hotel (1137/CO HOUSE HOTELS) and the Crinan Hotel (779/ARGYLL HOTELS). Some excursions start from Culag Lochside GH at Luss on the A82. Trips start from £110 pp at TGP (£30 min flight). Max 4 adults. Mar-Oct.

**By VW Campervan** New company Scoobycampers offers VW Microbuses and Campervans on a self-drive rental basis to see Scotland at a gentle pace and save on accommodation. All vehicles are the classic version, converted with contemp comforts. Microbuses take 6 people comfortably, but you can't really sleep overnight (hire the company's camping equipment). Campervans take 4 – best suited to 2 adults/2 kids. Vehicles have CD radios/DVD machines and satellite navigation systems. They look really cool and you'll find that everyone's delighted to see you. Best contact is through www.scoobycampers.com Weekends from £220; weeks from £450 at TGP.

**By Classic Car** Choose a fabulous motor from Caledonian Classic Car Rental and take off round the by-roads, experiencing that old forgotten joy of motoring. Packages are customised, but there's unlimited mileage and free delivery/collection in central Scotland for hire of 2 days or more. Short trips come with a complimentary picnic hamper. Cars include Jaguar E-type, Porche 911, MGB Roadster and Jensen Healey Sprites. 01259 742476 for details. Prices from £120 per day/£839 per week at TGP.

**By Motorbike** Biking your way around Scotland offers a freedom often absent from driving today. scotlandbybike.com organises a range of tours and packages that combine accommodation, insurance and hire of BMW F, R & K-series bikes – or just bring along your own. There's even tuition if you want to improve your bike-riding skills *en route*. Tours are from 3-10 days and start from £220 per person at TGP. Details at scotlandbybike.com

# The Best Events

**25 Up Helly Aa** Info: 01595 693434. Traditionally on the 24th day after Christmas, but now always the last Tues in Jan. A mid-winter fire festival based on Viking lore where 'the Guizers' haul a galley thro the streets of Lerwick and burn it in the park; and the night goes on.                    JAN

**26 Celtic Connections** Glasgow Tickets and info: 0141 353 8000. A huge festival of Celtic music from round the world held in the Royal Concert Hall and other city venues over 3 weeks. Concerts, ceilidhs, workshops.                    JAN

**27 Burns Night** The National Bard celebrated with supper. No single major event (but see below).                    JAN 25TH

**28 Borders Potato Day** Galashiels Curious, but for some hundreds of people a vital event that celebrates the enduring appeal of the tattie or spud. 250 varieties on sale here (for growing). Go early to sup the specials. Run by Borders Organic Growers (BOG). Info 08700 505152.                    MAR

**29 Glasgow Art Fair** Glasgow Info: 0141 552 6027. Britain's most significant commercial art fair o/side London held in mid-April in tented pavilions in George Sq with selected galleries from Scotland and UK.                    APRIL

**30 Glasgow International** Glasgow New 'festival' presenting contemp visual art in main venues & unusual or found space thro' out city centre celebrating Glasgow's significance as a source of important contemp artists. Info: 0141 552 6027.                    MID APRIL

**31 Melrose Sevens** Info TIC 0870 608 0404. Border town of Melrose completely taken over by tournament in their small is beautiful rugby ground. 7-a-side teams from all over incl international. It's just a good place to go, fanatical or not.                    APRIL

**32 Fife Point-To-Point** Leven 01333 360229. Major 'society' i.e. county set, get-together at Balcormo Mains Farm. Sort of Scottish equivalent of Henley with horses organised by Fife Fox and Hounds. Range Rovers, hampers, Hermès and what's left of the Tories in Scotland.                    APRIL

**33 Paps of Jura Hill Race** Isle of Jura Details from the hotel 01496 820243. The amazing hill race up and down the 3 Paps or distinctive peaks (total of 7 hills altogether) on this large remote island (2276/MAGICAL ISLANDS). About 150 runners take part on the 16-mile challenge from the distillery in Craighouse, the village. Winner does it in 3 hrs!                    MAY

**34 Burns and a' That** Ayr & Ayrshire Info 01292 678100. Festival based on what he stands for rather than his work, mainly in Ayr and Alloway with flagship open-air classical concert at Culzean Castle. Programme focuses on contemporary music and theatre.                    MAY

**35 Big in Falkirk** Falkirk Info 0141 552 6027. Held mainly in Callander Park outside town centre so a delightful, almost rural setting for 'Scotland's International Street Arts Festival'. Street theatre usually incl one big finale show with fireworks. Gala-day feel to daytime family programme.                    MAY

**36 Common Ridings** Border Towns Info Jedburgh TIC 0870 608 0404. The Border town festivals. Similar formats over different weeks with 'ride-outs' (on horseback to outlying villages etc) , 'shows', dances and games, culminating on the Fri/Sat. Total local involvement. Hawick is first, then Selkirk, Peebles/Melrose, Gala, Jedburgh, Kelso and Lauder end of July.
                    MAY-JULY

**37 Flower Shows** Ingliston & Ayr Many Scottish towns hold flower shows, mainly in the autumn, but the big spring show at Gardening Scotland at the Royal Highland Centre by Edinburgh Airport (Ingliston) is well worth a look. Call 0131 333 0969 for info. Meanwhile the annual show in Ayr in early August is huge! Check local TIC for details.                    JUNE & AUG

**37A Royal Highland Show** Ingliston Showground, Edinburgh 0131 335 6200. The premiere agricultural show (over 4 days) in Scotland and for the farming world, the event of the year. Animals, machinery, food, crafts and shopping. A big day out. 150,000 attend.                    JUNE

**38** **Skye Music Festival** Broadford, Skye 2-day music fest in S of Skye in big top on the airfield. No view of the Cuillins but a mountain of music & solstice potential. Home of Mylo.Info 07092 037963.  MID JUNE

**39** **Scottish Traditional Boat Festival** Portsoy Perfect little festival in perfect little Moray coast town nr Banff over a w/end in late June/early July. Old boats in old and new harbours, open-air ceilidhs, great atmos. 01261 842951.  LATE JUNE

**40** **Mendelssohn on Mull** Classical music festival in various halls & venues around the island that celebrates the connection betw the composer & this rocky far-flung part of the world. Nice Idea, gr time to be here (see 2326/MULL). Info 01688 812377.  END JUNE

**41** **Scottish Game Conservancy Fair** Perth Held in the rural and historical setting of Scone Palace, a major Perthshire day out and gathering for the hunting, shooting, fishing and of course, shopping brigade. Details: 01620 850577.  JULY

**42** **T in the Park** Balado Airfield nr Kinross Scotland's highly successful pop festival with all that is current in Britpop and beyond. The T stands for Tennents, the sponsors who are much in evidence. Not as lifestyle-affirming as Glastonbury, but among the best fests in the UK. Expanding '06/7.  JULY

**43** **Beladrum 'Tartan Heart' Festival** nr Kiltarlity Off A862 Beauly rd W of Inverness. Good-looking 2-day music fest in terraced grounds. Expect bigger & better Highland 2007.  JULY

**44** **Hebridean Celtic Festival** Stornoway Folk-rock format festival under canvas on faraway Lewis. Celebrated 10th yr in '05 (with Van Morrison). Good music & craic. Info: 01851 621234.  MID JULY

**45** **The Great Kindrochit Quadrathlon** Loch Tay The toughest one-day sporting event – swim 1.6km across loch, run 24km (incl 7 Munros), canoe 11km & clycle 54km. Then slice a melon with a sword. Jings! Info: 01567 820409.  MID JULY

**46** **Wickerman Festival** nr Gatehouse Of Fleet New annual music fest for the SW in fields on the A755 betw Gatehouse & Kirkcudbright. Under wide skies on a cool coast. They burn a huge effigy at midnight on Sat. 01738 449430.  END JULY

**47** **Art Week** Pittenweem 01333 312168. Remarkable local event where the whole vill of Pittenweem in Fife becomes a gallery. Over 70 venues showing work incl public building & people's houses. Other events incl fireworks.  AUG

**48** **Traquair Fair** nr Traquair nr Innerleithen In grounds of Traquair House (1855/co houses), a mini Glastonbury with music, comedy & crafts. A respite from the Festival up the rd in Edin. 01896 830323.  EARLY AUG

**49** **Edinburgh International Festival** Edinburgh 0131 473 2000. The 3 week 'biggest arts festival in the world' with the Military **Tattoo** and major opera/music/drama. The **Bank of Scotland Fireworks** are on the final Saturday. Incorporates **The Fringe** Festival with hundreds of events every night; **Fringe Sunday** on the second w/end. Also the **International Film Festival**, **Jazz Festival** and (mainly for delegates on a bit of a jolly) the TV festival. Edinburgh in Aug is the best place to be in the world. (470/ESS. EDIN CULTURE)  AUG

**49A** **Edinburgh International Book Festival** 0131 228 5444. A tented village in Charlotte Sq Gardens. Same time as the above but deserving of a separate entry because it is so uniquely good. (470/ESS. EDIN CULTURE)  AUG

**50** **The World Pipe Band Championships** Glasgow 0141 221 5414. Unbelievable numbers (3-4000) of pipers from all over the world competing and seriously doing their thing on Glasgow Green.  AUG

**51** **Braemar Gathering** Braemar One of many Highland Games (Aboyne early Aug, Ballater mid Aug on Deeside alone) all over Scotland but this is where the Royals gather & prob local laird Billy Connoly & Hollywood A-list. So go ogle. Info: local TICs.  EARLY SEPT

52 **Leuchars Air Show** Leuchars nr St Andrews  Info: 01334 839000. Major air-show held over one day in RAF airfield with flying displays, exhibitions, classic cars etc.  SEPT

53 **Mountain Bike World Cup** Ft William  01397 703781. Actually held at Nevis Range 5K run, around the ski gondola. Awesome course with truly international competitors over 2 days with evening events in town. World Championships in '07.  SEPT

54 **The Ben Race** Ft William  The race over 100 yrs old up Britain's highest mt & back. Record 1hr 25 mins seems amazing. 500 runners tho curiously little national, even local interest. Starts 2pm at Claggan Park off Glen Nevis r/bout. Info: bennevisrace.co.uk  SEPT

55 **The Pedal for Scotland Glasgow-to-Edinburgh Bike Ride** Fun, chari-ty fund-raiser annual bike event. From George Sq to Meadowbank with a pasta party at the halfway point.  SEPT

56 **Merchant City Festival** Glasgow  Extended w/end of diverse 'cultural' activities that reflect the commerce & concerns of this increasingly vibrant quarter of Glas, E of George Sq. '06 will see big new venues (City Hall & Fruitmarket) back in play. Info: 0141 552 6027.  MID SEPT

57 **Tiree Wave Classic** Isle of Tiree  Windsurfing heaven of the faraway island (2281/MAGICAL ISLANDS) where beaches offer diff wind conditions & islanders offer warm hospitality. Info: 01879 220399.  EARLY OCT

58 **Tour of Mull Rally** Isle of Mull  Info Tobermory TIC 01688 302182. The high-light of the national rally calendar is this raging around Mull w/end. Though drivers enter from all over the world, the overall winner has often been a local man (well plenty time for practice). There's usually a waiting list for accom, but camping ok and locals put you up.  OCTOBER

59 **St Andrews Night** Not such a big deal, but dinners etc and cultural ID.

30 NOV

60 **Stonehaven Hogmanay** Stonehaven nr Aberdeen Since 1910 a trad fest that prob wouldn't get started nowadays for 'health & safety' reasons. 40 fireballers throw the fireballs around. We watch. Arrive early.  31 DEC

61 **Edinburgh's Hogmanay** Edinburgh  Everywhere gets booked up, but call TIC for accom, 0131 557 3990 for info. One of the world's major winter events. Launched with a **Torchlight Procession** through the city centre and with a full, largely populist programme. **Night Afore International** on 30th celebrates culture of another place (Catalonia '05, Canada '06).Main event is the **Royal Bank Street Party** on 31st; you need a wrist-band. Huge, good-natured crowd. You'll be amazed. It's the Scots at their best! (470/ESS EDIN CULTURE)  DEC/JAN

# Life-Affirming Moments

*From the first edition of* Scotland the Best *I've included a category, Seven Things To Do Before You Die. Now everybody's doing it; there's even a book called,* A Thousand Things to See Before You Die. *So it's time to move on. A few editions back travelling round Scotland to research the book with a friend, he remarked that moving so quickly, I never had time 'to smell the roses'.*

*Going around Scotland for this edition in the spring/summer/autumn of 2005 (and doing it all myself; see Introduction), it was especially difficult to smell the roses. However I realised in the middle of hectic, demanding days, or often at the end of them, that there were moments (and I'm sure this is true for everyone) when life falls into place and everything you're doing seems to have quality and purpose. These moments are rare and precious and essential. They kept me going on this sojourn that at times seemed unremitting, thankless and unhealthily obsessive.*

**The Bullers of Buchan** A hot day in the NE, I'd parked the car behind the cottage and walked the extraordinary clifftop path where you stare down into an immense rocky cavern layered in sea birds. It was the week that the BBC were doing a campaign on butterflies, how they were disappearing and how we should look out for them, recording sightings or rarities etc. When I was coming back (and I hadn't noticed it on the way in) I realised that the hedgerow was alive with butterflies, not just one variety but at least half a dozen. In a hundred metres I counted dozens. It's true of course they are precious and you don't know what you've got till it's gone. It was a natural high.

**The Birks o' Aberfeldy** These are the birch and beech woods along the gorge of the Moness Burn a short walk from Aberfeldy town centre (2028/WOODLAND WALKS). It was a day in late August and the dappled light was at its best. A young couple were having a picnic. It was so very evocative of what Robert Burns wrote:

> Now simmer blinks on flowery braes,
> And o'er the crystal streamlet plays;
> Come, let us spread the lightsome days
> In the birks of Aberfeldy.

It was extraordinary how it felt that nothing had changed. Burns himself was here on 30 August 1787 (my birthday) and a day close to this one a long time ago. Despite what concerns us in our terrified world, places like this remind us what it means to be alive.

**Arbutnott Kirkyard** I come here for each edition of the book to revisit the VC and the landscape of Lewis Grassic Gibbon (1945/LITERARY PLACES). James Leslie Mitchell was born at Bloomfield up the road and although he moved away in later years he often came back to the 'Howe of the Mearns'; his ashes are in the SW corner of this church yard. There are a few places anywhere that are as redolent of the novels in which they feature (Arundhati Roy's *The God of Small Things* comes to mind). Across from the graveyard there's a track going down to a river. You feel that nobody comes here now. There are ancient yews beside a ruined cottage and a wild meadow. It is very quiet.

*Sunset Song* is one of my favourite books (*The List*/BBC survey in August 2005 revealed that it was the nation's favourite Scottish book of all time) and somehow I feel I should check in here when I'm writing mine. On Mitchell's grave are the words:

> The kingdom of friends
> The warmth of toil
> The peace of rest

I always leave here melancholic, but restored.

**Rob Roy's Bathtub** Years ago a researcher, Graeme Kelling, who helped me on one edition discovered this amazing swimming hole below the Fallach Falls on the A82 W L Lomond rd nr the Drover's Inn (1711/SWIMMING HOLES, 1323/BLOODY GOOD PUBS). Graeme, who used to play in Deacon Blue, died a couple of years ago after a long illness which he fought with great dignity.

This was a place I had to find. It was a searing hot day; there was no one else in the river. The huge deep pool with the falls pouring in from high above you, is amazing. I thought of Graeme as the chilly water hit.

**Pete's Beach nr Durness** I know it's a bit presumptuous to call a beach after yourself but when I enquired locally some years back it didn't appear to have a name; certainly no-one else had claimed it. It's 7 km E of Durness nr where L Eriboll comes out on the sea. On a coast of many fine beaches, this to my mind is the best. They've now built a layby opp, big enough for buses; I hope I haven't spoiled this wildly beautiful spot. When I got there in early September there was nobody there but then it was an overcast afternoon with lashing rain. As I sat there, wipers going and wind whipping around the car (the road is quite high above the beach; you look down on it), there was a transformation. With uncanny suddenness the sky cleared, became blue and a perfect rainbow arched over me with one end in the sand. Minutes later a couple arrived and started taking photographs. They took one of me at that moment; it's on the inside front cover of this book.

**Brilliant Ardnamurchan** After what seemed like days of rain there were clear skies above Ardnamurchan and the supernatural landscape was in high relief. I drove down the minor rd off the A861 from Acharacle to Castle Tioram (1812/RUINS). I'd just discovered the best pork pies in Scotland at a tiny bakery which I'd missed before (1482/BAKERS). The ruins are among the most evocative of any in Scotland (there still seems to be controversy over their restoration) and they sit across a causeway from a serene beach. It was one of the warm glorious evenings of summer 2005. There were some people on the beach having a late picnic, kids running around. I'd never met them before but they called me over and I shared their wine. Just another quiet life-affirming night in Ardnamurchan. And Scotland at its best.

**Ben A'An** The Book was all but over, odyssey completed and I was back in the land of the living, ie family and friends. On a late-autumn day we climbed Ben A'an which is bloody steep to start and when you come out the woods it looks like the mountain at the beginning of the Paramount movies; but we did it. At the top there were the usual not-so-healthy snacks and wild blueberries. The view was (dare I say) to die for. Afterwards we ate somewhere that wasn't my suggestion; somewhere I didn't have to.

# SECTION 2

## *Edinburgh*

*The telephone code for Edinburgh is 0131*
*Refer to* MAP 1 *unless otherwise stated*

# The Best Hotels

**62**
**D3** ✓ ✓ **The Balmoral** 556 2414. Princes St at E end above Waverley Stn. Capital landmark with its clock always 2 min fast (except at Hogmanay) so you don't miss your train. The old pile dear to Sir Rocco Forte's heart. Exp for a mere tourist but if you can't afford to stay there's always afternoon tea in the refurbished Palm Court. Few hotels anywhere are so much in the heart of things. Good business centre, fine sports facs; luxurious and distinctive rms have ethereal views of the city, tho some don't and are simply not worth the money. Main restau, Number One Princes Street (125/BEST RESTAUS), is tops and less formal brasserie, Hadrian's (good power b/fast venue). Even the non-pretentious bar, NB, works (occ has music). **TR:** the 3 'Royal' suites: Presidential, Balmoral & Glamis. 188RMS JAN-DEC T/T PETS CC KIDS LOTS

**63**
**A4** ✓ ✓ **The Caledonian Hilton** 222 8888. Princes St, W End. Edin institution: former stn hotel built in 1903. Upgrading continues to reinforce 5-star status of Edinburgh's other landmark hotel. Good business hotel with all facs you'd expect (tho not in all rms). 'Living Well' spa with not large pool. Endearing lack of uniformity in the rms. Executive rms on fifth floor (and deluxe rms elsewhere) have gr views. Capital kind of place in every respect. Main restau, The Pompadour, for fine and très formal dining in ornate & elegant setting. Brasserie on ground floor. Cally Bar (or Chisholms) a famous rendezvous. **TR:** the 'Sean Suite'. 249RMS JAN-DEC T/T XPETS CC KIDS LOTS

**64**
**A4** ✓ ✓ **The Sheraton Grand** 229 9131. Festival Sq on Lothian Rd and Conference Centre, this city-centre business hotel won no prizes for architecture when it opened late 1980s, but now both Festival Sq & the newly emerged Conference Sq behind one part of the shiny new financial district & Edin looks like a real city at last. This is a reliable stopover with excellent service. Larger rms and castle views carry premiums, but make big difference. Terrace restau adequate, but 'The Grill' menu prepared under the supervision of Philip Garrod is elegant, with innovative Auld Alliance menu (127/BEST RESTAUS) and Santini behind the hotel also excl (178/BEST ITALIAN). The health club 'One' is routinely identified as one of the best spas in the UK, with gr pool. **TR:** the 2 'Diplomatic Suites'. 260RMS JAN-DEC T/T PETS CC KIDS LOTS

**65**
**xE5** ✓ ✓ **Prestonfield House** 668 3346. Off Priestfield Rd, 3km S of city centre. The Heilan' cattle in the 14-acre grounds tell you this isn't your average urban bed for the night. A romantic, almost other-worldly 17th-century building with period features still intact. In 2003 it was taken over by James Thomson of The Tower (121/BEST RESTAUS) and The Witchery (122/BEST RESTAUS), and he has turned this bastion of Edinburgh sensibilities into Edinburgh's most sumptuous hotel. The architecture and the detail is exceptional & romantic. All rms are highly individualistic with hand-picked antiques & artefacts. Prestonfield prob hosts more awards dinners & accommodates more celebrity guests than anywhere else in town. In summer the nightly Scottish cabaret (in the stable block) is hugely popular. House restau Rhubarb is 'an experience' (123/BEST RESTAUS) **TR:** 5/6/16/17. 28RMS JAN-DEC T/T PETS CC XKIDS LOTS

**66**
**xA3** ✓ **Channings** 315 2226. S Learmonth Gdns, parallel to Queensferry Rd after Dean Br. tasteful alternative to hotel chain hospitality. 5 period town houses joined to form a quietly elegant West End hotel. Efficient and individual service incl 24-hr rm service. Gr views from top-floor rms, incl the Prime Minister's alma mater – Fettes College. **TR:** 12/20/40, 68 good enough for Sean/Elton/David Coulthard so prob good enough for the rest of us. Restau superb under chef Hubert Lamort (remodelled at TGP) a surprising destination eating spots in this quiet corner of the W End. 45RMS JAN-DEC T/T XPETS CC KIDS TOS LOTS

**67**
**F2** **Royal Terrace** 557 3222. 18 Royal Terr. Romanesque plunge pool, other sports facs, multi-level terraced gdn out back, deceptively large number of rms and town house décor a tad on the Baroque side make this fabulous for some & a good business bet for others. Bar/restau not so notable among the natives but we could love the terrace in summer. **TR:** Aberlour Suite. 108RMS JAN-DEC T/T XPETS CC KIDS LOTS

**68** Radisson SAS 557 9797. 80 High St. Modern but sympathetic building on
**D4** the Royal Mile, handy for everything & recently refurb (taken over by
Radisson '03). Good facs but some say service lacking. Thin walls, not gr
views. Leisure facs incl small pool. Adj parking handy in a hotel so central.
238RMS JAN-DEC T/T PETS CC KIDS TOS LOTS

**69** The George 225 1251. George St (betw Hanover St and St Andrew Sq).
**B3** Recently acquired by Principal Hotel Group. Robert Adam-designed and dating back to late 18th century. Good views to Fife from the top 3 floors. Pricey,
but you pay for the location and the Georgian niceties (and extra for the
views). Carvery plus good restau, the Chambertin (225/SCOTTISH RESTAUS).
Good Festival & Hogmanay Hotel close to the heart of things (taken over by
luvvies during TV fest). **TR**: Stewart or Melville (quieter) suites.
195RMS JAN-DEC T/T PETS CC KIDS LOTS

# Individual & Boutique Hotels

**70** ✓✓ The Scotsman 556 5565. North Bridge. De-luxe boutique hotel in
**D3** landmark building (the old offices of *The Scotsman* newspaper group)
converted into chic, highly individual accom with every modern fac: internet,
flat-screen TV, privacy locker in all rms. Labyrinthine lay-out (stairs & firedoors
everywhere) & slow lifts apart, this is the convenient cool hotel in town. Nice
art, intimate dining in Vermillion (129/BEST RESTAUS) & buzzy brasserie
(137/BISTROS). Excl leisure facs – Escape – with low-lit, steel pool gr for grown-
ups. **TR**: Penthouse & Director's suites. 69RMS JAN-
DEC T/T XPETS CC KIDS LOTS

**71** ✓✓ The Howard 315 2220. 34 Gr King St in the heart of the Georgian
**C1** New Town. 3 townhouses in splendid st imbued with quiet elegance
tho only 5 mins Princes St. No bar but restful drawing rm & 15 spacious individual rms, sympatico with architecture & recently refurb. 3 new suites (**TR**) downstairs have own entrances for discreet liaisons or just convenience & own drawing rm for entertaining. 24 rm service. No leisure facs. A very Edinburgh accommodation. 18RMS+3SUITES JAN-DEC T/T XPETS CC XKIDS LOTS

**72** ✓✓ The Bonham 226 6050. 35 Drumsheugh Gdns. Discreet town-
**xA3** house in quiet W End cres. Cosmo service and ambience a stroll
from Princes St. Much favoured by visiting celebs. Owned by same people as
the Howard and Channings (66/BEST HOTELS). Rms stylish and individ (with
some bold colour schemes). Gr views outback over New Town on floors 2 and
up. Elegant dining in calm, spacious restau (esp end table by back window).
Chef Michel Bouyer forges a foody Auld Alliance of top Scottish ingredients &
French flair. No-nonsense, simple 4/5 choices described in plain English.
Nice wine-list. No bar. 48RMS JAN-DEC T/T XPETS CC XKIDS GF LOTS

**73** ✓ The Malmaison 468 5000. Tower Pl, Leith, at the dock gates. Award-
**xE1** winning, praise-laden designer chain hotel with lavish yet homely rms.
All facs we smart, young, modern people expect eg CD players in each cham-
bre (borrow CDs from reception). **TR** have harbour views & 4-poster beds.
Brasserie and café-bar have stylish ambience too (145/BEST BISTROS) and there
are many other caffs nearby in this waterfront quarter. Pity about the new
flats outfront, but Leith still onwards & upwards. 100RMS JAN-DEC T/T PETS CC KIDS EXP

**74** ✓ The Point 221 5555. 34 Bread St. You'd never guess this used to be a
**B5** Co-operative department store. Space and colour combinations manage
to look simultaneously rich and minimal; some castle views. **TR**, the suites
(LOTS), come with side-lit Jacuzzis. Once mentioned as one of the gr designery hotels in the world and on the cover of *Hotel Design*. Café-bar Monboddo
and restau have modern and spacious, mid-Euro feel. Good places to meet
Edinburgers tho food & service can be off the point. Conference Centre adj
with gr penthouse often used for cool Edin launches & parties.
140RMS JAN-DEC T/T PETS CC KIDS EXP/LOTS

**75** ✓ The Glasshouse 525 8200. 2 Greenside Pl betw Playhouse Theatre &
**E2** the Vu. First of new urban chain, this 'boutique' hotel is in many ways
more like a v upmarket travel lodge or motel. It's built above the multiplex
(rms on 2 floors) & the restaus in the mall below. Main feature is extensive

lawned garden on roof around which about half the rms look out – with patios incl their standard 'de-luxe doubles'. No restau (b/fast in rm or 'the Observatory'), honesty bar. The Mall itself is a big disappointment & the restaus within are all high st staples, but guests can use Holmes Place health facs & spa (incl 25m pool – (438/EDIN SPORTS). Interesting concept not least because of the upmarket & the downmarket juxtapositions.

65RMS JAN-DEC T/T XPETS CC KIDS LOTS

**76**
**xA3** ✓ **Edinburgh Residence** 226 3380. 7 Rothesay Terr. Another town house affair but on extravagant scale. Several Georgian town houses have been joined into an elegant apartment hotel by the Townhouse Group who own the Howard & the Bonham (above). No restau, but the Bonham do b/fasts & 24-hr room service, so a discreet & distinctive stopover in 3 diff levels of suite. Big bathrms, views of Dean Village. Drawing rm if you're feeling lonely in this quiet W End retreat but nightlife & shops a stroll away.

29RMS JAN-DEC T/T XPETS CC KIDS LOTS

**77**
**C4** ✓ **Apex City Hotel** 243 3456 & just along the **Apex International** 300 3456. Both in the middle of the Grassmarket, the picturesque but rowdy Sat night city centre. Modern, *soi-disant* – but close to castle, club life & other bits of essential Edin. Cool to roam from. Restaus called Aqua & the International Metro on street level & Heights on the 6th floor. All are good not exceptional. Some castle views (4th-floor rms at Int have balconies). Pool opened '05. There's a cheaper, more lodgy lodging just beyond the W End (91/TRAVEL LODGES). 173RMS JAN-DEC T/T XPETS CC KIDS LOTS

**78**
**C2** ✓ **Royal Garden Apartments** 625 1234. York Buildings, Queen St opp Nat Portrait Gallery (389/ATTRACTIONS) nr Playhouse Theatre and funky Broughton St. Self-cat v well turned-out apts with coffee-shop on grd floor & access to private gdns. Access to the superior leisure facs at the Scotsman Hotel (above) tho you wouldn't want to walk there in your dressing gown. Gr views esp top floor. Nightly let avail (3 days' min at peak periods).

30APTMS JAN-DEC T/T XPETS CC XKIDS MED.EX

**79**
**B2** **Rick's** 622 7800. 55 Frederick St. Very city centre hotel and bar/restau in downtown location a stone's throw from George St. By same people who have indigo yard (153/GASTROPUBS) and nearby Opal Lounge (376/COOL BARS) so the bar is full-on esp late. Restau (155/BISTROS) has (loud) contemporary dining. Rms upstairs surprisingly quiet. Modern, urban feel eg DVD players as standard. Same rate single or twin. Don't let the rms above the bar thing put you off. Go as high as you can. No longer the gr value they once were, but central & sexy. 10RMS JAN-DEC T/T XPETS CC XKIDS EXP

**80**
**xB5** **Borough** 668 2255. 72 Causewayside. V urban & self-consciously hip hotel in conversion of former snooker hall/warehouse on s side. Notable designer Ben Kelly (of the legendary Hacienda) somehow failed to warm this place up or excite. Stark look & cold lighting. Rms small & furnishings not gr, but this is still a fairly cool place to stay. They call it 'reassuringly individual'. Bar & restau are southside hang-outs. DJs till 1am w/ends.

12RMS JAN-DEC T/T XPETS CC XKIDS MED.INX

**81**
**E2** **Parliament House** 478 4000. 15 Calton Hill. Good central location, only 200m from E end of Princes St & adj to Calton Hill (430/BEST VIEWS), although tucked away. Small bar in residents lounge and restau for b/fast, even meals – but OK town house-style décor recently refurb. About half the rms have views – so you know where to go. 53RMS JAN-DEC T/T XPETS CC KIDS EXP

**82**
**xA4** **West End Hotel** 225 3656. 35 Palmerston Pl. Capital haunt for Highlanders and Islanders who feel like a blether in Gaelic or a good folk music session in the bar (decent measures). Music Sats & poss Mons. Popular with folkie nonguests too. Spacious rms – no sae cheap anymore & a bit gloomy, but real. And real Scottish b/fast. 8RMS JAN-DEC T/T XPETS CC KIDS MED.INX

**83**
**xB1** **Canon Court Apartments** 474 7000. Canonmills at foot of New Town and nr Botanics (401/ATTRACTIONS). Self-cat 1 & 2 bedrm aptms often avail for short lets, even 1 night. No café, but an inx stopover. Cable TV. Some rms o/look water of Leith. The gas station over the rd is a social hub esp middle of the night. 42APTMS JAN-DEC T/T XPETS CC KIDS MED.INX

# Most Excellent Lodgings

**84**
**C4** ✓✓ **Inner Sanctum** and the **Old Rectory** at the **Witchery** 225 5613. Castlehill. 2 highly individual rms and an apartment above the Witchery restau (122/BEST RESTAUS) at the top of the Royal Mile together with 5 sumptuous aptms across the st that put a whole new look into the Old Town. A stone's throw from the castle, few accoms anywhere are as emphatically *mise en place* as this. Prob the most exceptional and atmospheric in town – designed by owner James Thomson and Mark Rowley – fairly camp/theatrical, OTT and v sexy. B/fast & everything else you need en suite. Go with somebody good.    2+6 APT JAN-DEC T/T XPETS CC XKIDS GF LOTS

**85**
**xE5** ✓ **Southside** 668 4422. 8 Newington Rd. On main st in s side with many hotels/GH stretching halfway to Dalkeith, a surprisingly civilised haven now in new hands. Careful attention to decor & detail & excl b/fast. Nice prints, rugs, books & DVDs. Some traffic noise, but upstairs rms double-glazed. Parking nearby.    8RMS JAN-DEC T/T XPETS CC KIDS GF MED.INX

**86**
**xE1** **Ardmor House** 554 4944. 74 Pilrig St which is off Leith Walk & with lots of other B&Bs – this the top spot. Individual, contemporary and relaxed – & that's just the proprietors Colin and Robin & their gorgeous wee dog, Lola. They've also got a lovely New Town apt for short lets.    5RMS JAN-DEC X/T XPETS CC KIDS GF MED.INX

**87**
**A1** **Six St Mary's Place** 332 8965. Vegn-friendly, award-winning GH on main st of Stockbridge (St Mary's Pl part of Raeburn Pl) and busy main rd out of town for Forth Rd Br and N, this is a tastefully converted Georgian town house. Informal, friendly, well-cared-for accom popular with academics and people we like. No smk. Vegn breakfast in conservatory.    7RMS JAN-DEC T/T XPETS CC KIDS GF MED.INX

**88**
**C2** **24 Northumberland St** 556 8140. A definitive New town B&B. Georgian townhouse in mid-New Town full of antiques (owner a notable dealer). Only 3 rms so often booked. Has become a Wolsey Lodge but no dinner is served (many gr restaus nearby).    3RMS JAN-DEC T/T XPETS CC XKIDS MED.EXP

**89**
**xD1** **Stuart House** 557 9030. 12 E Claremont St. Nr the corner of main rd and pleasant walk up to Princes St (1.5km). Residential New Town st and family house decorated with taste and attention to detail – bonny flower gdn out front. Book well in advance. No smk.    5RMS JAN-DEC T/T XPETS CC KIDS MED.EXP

# The Best 'Economy' Hotels & Travel Lodges

*Hotels/B&Bs below are included on grounds of price, convenience or just because we like them for some idiosyncratic reason.*

**90**
**D4** ✔ **Ibis** 240 7000. Hunter Sq. First in Scotland of the Euro budget chain (one other in Glas 497/TRAVEL LODGES). Dead central behind the Tron so good for Hogmanay (or not). Serviceable and efficient. For tourists doing the sights, this is best bed box for location. Rates vary thro' yr.
99RMS JAN-DEC T/T PETS CC KIDS INX/MED.INX

**91**
**xA4** **Apex European** 474 3456. 90 Haymarket Terr. The western, more bedbox version of the Apex triumvirate. Apex City the grooviest (62/BOUTIQUE HOTELS) & the other, Apex International, which is adj in the Grassmarket. The European is the cheaper option. (Location! Location!)
66/168RMS JAN-DEC T/T XPETS CC KIDS EXP

**92**
**E2** **Holiday Inn Express** 558 2300 (or central reservs on 0800 434040). 16 Picardy Pl opp Playhouse Theatre. Not unpleasant converstion of several New Town houses in exceptionally convenient location. Rms all same standard (twin or double). Bar, no restau but area awash with options. This is a v clever Holiday Inn.
160RMS JAN-DEC T/T XPETS CC KIDS MED.EX

**93**
**xA4** **Hilton Edinburgh Airport** 519 4400. At the airport, 10km W of city centre. No way 'economy', but a reliable travellers' tryst. An L-shaped box high-class transit camp; charming staff. You can virtually roll out of bed and check in. That smell over the airport by the way is due to some unconscionable thing they do to chickens in the factory nearby. Living Well health club has decent pool.
150RMS JAN-DEC T/T PETS CC KIDS MED.EX

**94**
**C5** **Novotel Edinburgh Centre** 656 3500. 80 Lauriston Pl. New build nr Tollcross & Univ. No charm but functional & reasonably contemp. Small pool, bar & contemp-like brasserie. Gd beds & facs. But Premier Travel inn adj is half the price.
180RMS JAN-DEC T/T XPETS CC KIDS MED.EX

**95**
**C4** **Grassmarket Hotel** 220 2299. 94-96 Grassmarket. Basic and boisterously located accom next to Biddy Mulligan's which is open to 1am, but levels 4/5 at the back are best. The Grassmarket is fairly full-on, so good for party-animal business types on a budget.
44RMS JAN-DEC T/T XPETS CC KIDS MED.INX

**96**
**D4** **Tailors Hall** 622 6800. Cowgate. If you don't mind the racket (or want to be part of it), this is a clubby/young thing kind of hotel in the heart of the throbbing Cowgate area and above the hugely popular 3 Sisters pub. 3 bars to choose from (till 1am), 24 hr licence for residents. Can do 4 in a rm. Rms not above the huge courtyard are best.
42RMS JAN-DEC T/T PETS CC XKIDS MED.INX

**97**
**E4** **Travel Lodge** 557 6281 (or central booking 08700 850 950). 33 St Mary's St. Edin central version of national (often roadside) chain. All usual, formulaic facs but inx and nr Royal Mile (Holyrood end) and Cowgate for late-night action.
193RMS JAN-DEC T/T XPETS CC KIDS INX

**98**
**C5**
**xA4**
**xE1** **Premier Travel Inn Chain** 7 (and counting) in Edin Area. All much of a lessness. Most central is newest at 82 Lauriston Pl 0870 990 6610 nr Univ. 1 Morrison Link 0870 238 3319 is nr Haymarket Stn. The one in Newhaven/Leith (taxi/bus) 08701 977 093 is nr bars & restaus of Leith (1km) & Next Generation health club (helpfully not avail to guests). -50% rms have 'sea' views. All others are suburban.
INX

# The Best Hostels

*Edin has some YHA hostels (nae drinking) and independents (young and Hoochy, open 24 hrs), also some handy univ halls of residence to let o/side term time. With all the independent hostels, it's best to turn up around 11/11.30am if you haven't booked. The SYHA is the Scottish Youth Hostels Association. 01786 891400.*

**99**
**C4**
**D4**
✓ ✓ **Royal Mile Backpackers** 557 6120. 105 High St. On the Royal Mile, nr the Cowgate with its late-night bars. Ideal central cheap 24 hr crash-out dormitory accom with all the facs for itinerant youth seeking a capital experience. The same company (who also run Mac backpackers tours) have the original hostel, **The High St Hostel** (8 Blackfriars St): 557 3984, and the **Castle Rock**, 15 Johnston Terr (225 9666) in the old Council Environmental Health HQ. Is huge (190 beds in various dorms, but no singles/doubles) and some gr views across the Grassmarket or to the castle which is just over there. Same folk (Mr Backpacker himself, Peter Macmillan) also have places in Ft William, Inverness, Oban, Pitlochry & Skye.      CHP

**100**
**xA4**
✓ ✓ **S.Y. Hostel, Eglinton** 337 1120. 18 Eglinton Cres. From the stained glass over the main door to the tartan and wood entrance foyer, you know you're not in a typical hostel. Grand late-Victorian pile (shame about the lighting) in a quiet W End st with 150 beds – majority in dorms but some rms for 4 (single-sex dorms). Members only but you can join at reception. Booking recommended. Open 24 hrs.      CHP

**101**
**xA3**
✓ **Globetrotter Inn** 336 1030. Marine Drive, the Cramond foreshore. First venture of ambitious hostel chain. Former hotel in gr if off-centre setting. Huge no of bunks (400), excl facs (spa, gym, internet, kitchen with battery of microwaves & shop). Only drawback is distance from downtown (half hour); last bus 11.20pm & hostel runs own hourly service (till 11pm). Lawns & trees & riverside view do compensate.      CHP

**102**
**D3**
✓ **St Christopher Inn** 0207 407 1856. 9-13 Market St, behind Waverley Stn. Some good views from upper floors to Princes St. Couldn't be handier for the stn or city centre. This (with sister place in London & other Euro cultural cities) a hostel rather than hotel with bunk rms tho there are 5 tw/dbl rms. Price depends on no sharing (£16-25 at TGP). Belushi's café-bar on ground floor open till 1am. A cheap, v central option, better than most other hostels (facs are en-suite). Internet access.
29RMS JAN-DEC X/X XPETS CC XKIDS CHP

**103**
**xA3**
**D3**
✓ **Belford Hostel** 225 6209. Douglas Gdns, nr Gallery of Modern Art (excellent café, 272/BEST TEAROOMS) and quaint Dean Village, but still fairly central. Bizarre concept – 98 beds in partitioned-off (un-soundproofed) 'rms' of 6-10 in a converted church. Top-bunk berth gets you a view of the vaulted wooden ceiling way above. Nice stained glass. Games rm, bar, MTV. Sister establishment **Edinburgh Backpackers Hostel**, 65 Cockburn St (220 1717), is closer to action.      CHP

**104**
**A3**
✓ **Caledonian Backpackers** 226 2939. 3 Queensferry St. The city's biggest (accom for 300+) with a gr backpacker (live music sometimes), kitchen. Doubles, triples & quads. Good all-round Euro atmos.      CHP

**105**
**A3**
**Princes St Backpackers East** 556 6894. 5 W Register St. Behind Burger King at E end of Princes St. Incredibly central for cheap accom. Basic and attracts the usual international crowd. Nr Waverley & airport bus stops. CHP

**106**
**xB5**
**S.Y. Hostel, Bruntsfield** 447 2994. 7 Bruntsfield Cres. S of Tollcross about 10 min walk from W End. Reliable and secure hostel accom in a verdant corner of Bruntsfield. 126 beds but book 2-3 months in advance at peak times. Members only, join at reception. No doubles. Doors cl 2am (night porter). CHP

**107**
**D4**
From July-Sep, SYHA also opens 3 temporary hostels in **Royal Mile/ Cowgate** area. All offer v central, single accom – a v good bet at peak time in the city. Phone HQ for info 01786 891400.

**108**
**xB5**
**Argyle Backpackers Hotel** 667 9991. 14 Argyle Pl, in Marchmont area of up-market student flats. Quiet area though Argyle Pl the most happening st. 2 km to centre across 'The Meadows' (not advised for women at night). Some kind of gdn.      CHP

# The Best Hotels Outside Town

**110**
Map 10
R25
✓ ✓ **Greywalls, Gullane** 01620 842144. On coast 36km E of Edin off A198 just beyond golfers' paradise of Gullane. Prob best co house retreat o/side town. Full report 871/LOTHIANS.

**111**
Map 10
P25
✓ ✓ **Champany Inn** 01506 834532. On A904, 3km Linlithgow on rd to Forth Rd Bridge and S Queensferry. Exemplary restau with rms some o/looking gdn. Legendary steaks and seafood; ambience & service (257/RESTAUS FOR BURGERS AND STEAKS). B/fast in cosy dining kitchen excl with nice bacon. Extraordinary wine-list with dinner. But veggies best not venture here. 16RMS JAN-DEC T/T XPETS CC KIDS LOTS

**112**
Map 10
P25
✓ **Norton House, Ingliston** 0131 333 1275. Off A8 v close to airport, 10km W of city centre. Victorian country house in 55 acres of greenery surprisingly woody & pastoral so close to city. Highly regarded 'Hand-Picked' Hotel group. 'Exec' rms have countryside views. Labyrinthine layout with gd conference/function facs. Brasserie & small internal restau much improved of late. Good contemp (the bedrms) & trad (public rms) mix. Some rms quite swish. 47RMS JAN-DEC T/T XPETS CC KIDS LOTS

**113**
Map 10
Q26
✓ **Borthwick Castle, North Middleton** 01875 820514. On B6367, 3km off the A7, 18km bypass, 26km SE of centre. So this is a real Border castle, a big red one. Walls 30m high, this magnificent tower house knocks you off your horse with its authenticity – Mary Queen of Scots was blockaded here once and at night you expect to see her swishing up the (narrow, unavoidable) spiral stairs. 8 rms in castle, 2 in gatehouse and the (v) grand banqueting hall is impressive but you came for the decor not, I fear, the dinner. 10RMS MAR-DEC T/X PETS CC KIDS LOTS

**114**
Map 10
P25
✓ **Orocco Pier, South Queensferry** 0131 331 1298. Main St. A decent restau and boutique hotel, in tourist-thronged & Tesco-tainted South Q (which was never going to be Sausilito, but the charming Main St hasn't nearly approached its potential & the modern stuff & schemes at the road bridge app are appalling). Best to come from Edin on first t/off from dual c/way. Formerly Queensferry Arms, now substantial makeover has created a cool bistro & rms with some (5) gr views of 'the Bridge' (389/MAIN ATTRAC-TIONS). LO for food 10pm. 12RMS JAN-DEC T/T XPETS CC KIDS MED.EXP

**115**
Map 10
Q26
**Dalhousie Castle, Bonnyrigg** 01875 820153. Just off B704 2km from the A7, 15km from bypass and 23km S of centre. It looks fantastic in its setting and some bits date way back to the 13th century; a bad ersatz inside tho ideal for weddings. (Previous guests incl Edward I, Cromwell, Queen Victoria, some rock stars.) Multi-chambered Dungeon restau has 2AA rosettes. 'Aqueous spa' but no pool. 36RMS JAN-DEC T/T PETS CC KIDS TOS LOTS

**116**
Map 10
P25
**Houstoun House, Uphall** 01506 853831. On A899 at end of Broxburn/Uphall Main St, 8km from r/bout at the start of the M8 Edin–Glas motorway. Airport 10km, 18km W of centre. Bits of this tower house date to the 16th century, in sharp contrast to shiny leisure facs (inc nice pool) which attracts local patronage. 4-posters in some rooms, blazing fires and 2 restaus (main has 3 dining areas & 2 AA rosettes), all in extensive greenery. Only quite posh hotel in barren hinterland of W. Lothian. Stuffed with farmers during Royal Highland Show week. 72RMS JAN-DEC T/T XPETS CC KIDS LOTS

**117**
Map 10
P25
**Marriott Dalmahoy, Kirknewton** 333 1845. On A71 (Kilmarnock rd) on edge of town – bypass 5km, 15km W of centre, airport 6km. Georgian house with distinctive rms and big modern annexe (6 turret suites best). Two internationally rated courses make this a golfing mecca. Plenty of other sports facs to while away the hours or improve your handicaps generally incl pool, tennis & 'Lost Weekend' brasserie. Good corporate choice. 215RMS JAN-DEC T/T XPETS CC KIDS LOTS

**Open Arms, Dirleton** Report 949/LOTHIANS.

**Tweedale Arms, Gifford** Report 951/LOTHIANS.

# The Best Restaurants

**118**
**xE1** ✓ ✓+ **Martin Wishart** 553 3557. 54 The Shore. Discreet waterside frontage for Edinburgh's most notable foody experience & the standard by which other fine-dining menus in Edin & Glas can be judged. Rm designed on simple lines; uncomplicated menu & wine-list (tho no cheap plonk). 2-Michelin-star chef Martin & a clutch of awards raise expectation, but prep, cooking & presentation are demonstrably a cut above the rest. Martin just has that touch that we don't have, that brings a smile as well as saliva to the lips when the plate appears. Gr vegn menu. Mrs Wishart presides with quiet elegance. Nae nonsense (as can be the case with fine dining), only the best meal in town. *Good Food Guide* Scottish Restau of the Yr '06. Lunch Tues-Fri, Dinner Tues-Sat. LO 9.30pm                                          EXP

**119** ✓ ✓ **La Potinière, Gullane** 01620 843214. Not in town, but worth the 45-min drive to this douce golfing village on E Lothian coast. This restau has a remarkable pedigree (once the best restau in S Scotland), re-opened 2003 by Keith Marley & Mary Runciman & now La Pot is top again. Single no-smk rm, simple-choice menu & short, exemplary wine-list. Flair & integrity with market & seasonal best ingredients & quietly efficient presentation. Wed-Sun, lunch & dinner.                                          EXP

**120**
**B4** ✓ **The Atrium** 228 8882. Foyer of the Traverse Theatre (464/CULTURE), Cambridge St off Lothian Rd. Longest-standing on this page, Andrew & Lisa Radford's effortlessly stylish restau is still the best non-fussy or -fussed-over food in town. Michelin Bib Gourmand but generally underrated I say: food, wine, service always excel & a mellow ambience that gently accoms both business & romance. Often easier to get a table here than the more glam food or locations above & below – Edinburgh's all-round best bet for food to love with people you love.                                          EXP

**121**
**D4** ✓ **The Tower** 225 3003. Corner of Chambers St and George IV Br above the Museum of Scotland. Restaurant supremo James Thomson's celebrated & celebrity-strewn restau atop the distinctive 'tower' on the corner of the sandstone museum building (benefits from the much-admired grand design and detail of Gordon Benson's architectural vision). It feels that it could be anywhere, except you're looking over Edin rooftops and the castle skyline (in summer, the terrace is top). Gr private dining-rm in the tower itself. Kitchens far below in Prehistoric Scotland, but food everything one would expect – Scottish slant on modern British. The steaks are great. 7 days. Lunch and dinner. LO 11pm. Best to book. Smokers to the balcony!                                          EXP

**122**
**C4** ✓ **The Witchery** 225 5613. Castlehill. At the top of the Royal Mile where the tourists come, many will be unaware that this is one of the city's best restaus and certainly its most stylishly atmospheric. 2 salons, the upper more 'witchery'; in the 'secret gdn' downstairs, a converted school playground, James Thomson has created a more spacious ambience for the (same) elegant Scottish menu. Locals on a treat, many regulars & visiting celebs pack this place out (although they do turn round the tables), so must book. The new Witchery Apartments encapsulate this remarkable ambience (84/LODGINGS). The wine-list is exceptional. Lunch and dinner. LO a v civilised 11.30pm. (293/LATE-NIGHT RESTAUS)                                          EXP

**123** ✓ **Rhubarb @ Prestonfield** 668 3346. The restau of fabulous Prestonfield (65/HOTELS) & 1, 2, 3 in a row of gr restaus for James Thomson (see above). And as above it's the whole dining experience rather than Michelin-minded menus that drives their success. Rhubarb the most gorgeously decadent; the public rms adj for before and après are *sans pareil*, esp the upstairs drawing rms. An evening of rich romance awaits. The rhubarb desserts leave a silky aftertaste.                                          MED

**124**
**B3** ✓ **Oloroso** 226 7614. 33 Castle St. Unassuming entrance and lift to this rooftop restau renowned for its terrace with views of the castle, the New Town and Fife. Bar snacks are a gr deal – can't go wrong with 'curry of the day'. Chef/prop Tony Singh excels esp with the meatier dishes & in the main dining rm light & spacious & spilling on to the terrace, steaks are rightly popular tho there are many imaginative dishes with food & fish. After a few yrs now this is still a fashionable, foody room at the top. Excl cocktail bar. **SD** Highland beef carpaccio. Lunch and dinner 7 days. LO 10.15pm. Bar till 1am          EXP

**125**
**D3** ✓ **Number One Princes Street, Balmoral Hotel** 556 2414. Address with a certain ring for the principal restau of the Balmoral (62/BEST HOTELS) entered through lobby or off st. Opulent subterranean salons have ample space around the tables, but the lighting and lacquering do little to cosify the ritziness (and like many hotel restaus it's often not busy or buzzy – this is good to remember when other top restaus may be full). Michelin starred since 2003, Jeff Bland is one of Scotland's top chefs; creation & presentation rarely fail to please. Attentive service. **Hadrian's Brasserie**, a pastel lounge at st level, complements well. Cl Sat/Sun lunch. LO 10pm/10.30pm. EXP

**126**
**C2** ✓✓ **Fisher's In The City** 225 5109. 58 Thistle St. Uptown version of one of Leith's longest best eateries (204/SEAFOOD); this place works on all its levels (we're talking mezzanine). Fisher fan staples ('favourites') all here – the fishcakes, the soup & the blackboard specials, excl wine-list combined with gr service Some vegn & meat (steaks a special). Open all day (reduced menu late aft). **SD**: fishcakes of course, and soup! 7 days.LO 10.30pm. MED

**127**
**A4** ✓ **The Grill Room at the Sheraton** 229 9131. The fine dining rm at Edin's most corporate of top hotels. Sits alongside The Terrace which has the view (of Festival Sq) and Santini's, the Italian place out back (on Conference Sq). Not merely a 'Grill', but a serious dining-out experience with an accoladed menu by highly regarded chef Phillip Garrod. Atmos minimal, food presentation minimalist, excl service. Some grill choice but mainly Ecosse ingredients combined with French flair. Lunch Tues-Fri & LO 10.30pm (cl Sun/Mon). **SD**: Rib of beef, miniature puds. MED

**128**
**D2** ✓ **Forth Floor, Harvey Nichols** 524 8350. St Andrews Sq. On the fourth floor (through deli & furnishings & HN souvenirs) & you see the Forth from the balcony (superb outside dining on rare summer days, tho somewhat in a row). Store & restau now firmly est for ladies who lunch on the chic supper circuit; the food & service reliably spot-on. You can partake of cheaper brasserie or more exp (but similar) Mod Brit comfort-food menus either side of the glass partition – dearer dining gets the view. All Ab Fab enough for us! Lunch 7 days, dinner Tues-Sat LO 10.30pm INX/MED

**129**
**D3** **Vermillion** 622 2814. North Bridge. The fine dining rm of the urbane Scotsman Hotel (70/INDIVID HOTELS), deep in the baronial bowels of the building on N Bridge. Informal & intimate; no natural light so best for dinner à deux or a special night out. Innovative if self-conscious foody menu. Check for (classic) movie evenings combining dinner & the screening rm. Dinner only. LO 9.45pm. Wed-Sun. EXP

**130**
**B3** ✓ **Roti** 225 1233. 70 Rose St N Lane. Recently opened (they say 'not') Indian restau by Tony Singh who presided over Oloroso (above). An immediate, palpable hit! Report: 233/BEST INDIAN.

# The Best Bistros & Brasseries

**131** ✓ **First Coast** 313 4404. 99 Dalry Rd. Named after a place up N where
**xA4** brothers Hector & Alan McRae used to go their holidays, this is a v grown-up & urban restau for 2 Highland lads. Food here is simply superb value & full of integrity. They wanted to make it irresistible & impossible not to come back and they did! A wee triumph! Mon-Sat Lunch & LO 11pm.  INX

**132** ✓ **Urban Angel** 225 6215. 121 Hanover St. In a basement nr Queen St (a
**C2** long time ago the legendary Laigh). Contemp, relaxed, great value pressing all the integrity buttons. Organic where sensible & free trade (lots). Food Mod Brit but light touch. T/away counter & gr Sun brunch rendezvous (306/SUN B/FAST). All v nice without being 'nice'. 7 days lunch & dinner. LO 10pm (Suns 6pm).  INX

**133** ✓ **Blue** 221 1222. Cambridge St. Upstairs in the Traverse Theatre building.
**B4** From the makers of The Atrium (120/BEST RESTAUS), a lighter, more informal menu which continues all day till late. Still the best drop-in diner in town esp convenient for W End entertainments. The menu, which changes every 6 wks, is mix 'n' match with 'light blue' snackier options. Sound levels high; people do talk. 12noon-3pm and 6pm-10.30pm daily. Bar open to midnight (1am Sat). Cl Sun.  INX

**134** ✓ **Skippers** 554 1018. 1a Dock Pl. In a corner of Leith off Commercial Rd
**xE1** by the docks. Look for Waterfront (151/GASTROPUBS) and bear left into adj cul-de-sac. The pioneer restau in Leith before it was a restau quarter. Considered the best real bistro in town by loyal clientele. V fishy, v quayside intimate and friendly. Excl apt wine list. Lunch & dinner 7 days, LO 10pm.  MED

**135** ✓ **The Apartment** 228 6456. 7 Barclay Pl, up from the King's Theatre.
**xB5** The first of Malcolm's hugely popular contemporary eating-out experiences (see Outsider, below, & more to come), now a Bruntsfield food fixture. Big helpings of 'chunky, healthy' food, famously good salads. Some OK art. 7 days, dinner. Lunch Sat/Sun only; LO 11pm. Best to book.  INX

**136** ✓ **The Outsider** 226 3131 15 George IV Bridge. The downtown dining rm
**D4** of the Apartment (above). Malcolm Innes, the notoriously rude host, once again created a sexy, contemp & inexpensive restau which is always full. Minimalist design with surprising view of the castle. Innovative contrasts in the menu. Big helpings! 7 days, lunch & LO 10.30pm.  INX

**137** ✓ **North Bridge** 622 2900. 20 North Bridge. The brasserie of the
**D3** Scotsman Hotel (70/INDIVIDUAL HOTELS) with separate entrance directly on to main rd. Formerly the foyer & public counter of the *Scotsman* newspaper converted into excl bar/brasserie. Surrounding balcony reached by rather intrusive metal staircase, but overall v sympathetic ambience for exemplary brasserie-type menu with seasonal variations. Toilets are a find when you find them. 7 days, all day LO 10 pm/10.30pm. Bar midnight.  MED

**138** ✓ **Howie's** 221 1777. 208 Bruntsfield Pl on the way to Morningside & at
**xB5** 10 Victoria St (225 1721), certainly one of the best in this st of many
**C4** bistros. Both are flagship outposts in Howie's urban village chain which serve the locals, but are worth coming across the city for. Unpretentious, inexpensive, contemp Scottish food. Gr value lunches. Also:

**139** ✓ **Howie's Waterloo** 556 5766. 29 Waterloo Pl. 200 m E End of Princes
**D3** St (The Balmoral) in beautiful lofty rm; & **Howie's West End** 225 9594.
**A3** 1 Alva St. Like both the above, Howie has taken over locations that haven't quite worked out for others. His good value, contemp food with some flair & no-fuss formula will doubtless prevail. All open 7 days. Gr value lunch & dinner. Can BYOB. LO 10/10.30pm.  INX

**140** ✓ **Sweet Melinda's** 229 7953. 11 Roseneath St which is in deepest
**xB5** Marchmont but round the corner from Argyle Pl where some good shops are. Single not large rm on st with nice pics, catering v much for the neighbourhood clientele but famous across the city. On Tues you can pay 'what you think the meal is worth'. Mainly fish (from estimable Eddie's across the rd), but meat & vegn. Home-made bread & gr touches. Everybody goes back. Good wines & fizz. Lunch & LO 10pm. Not Mon lunch; cl Sun.  MED

**141** ✓ **The Marque Central** 229 2859. 30 Grindlay St adj (& part of) Lyceum
**B4** Theatre. Small down & mainly upstairs eaterie where you can practically
hear the applause from the circle esp when this fine city restau is often less
than full (good bet for a table at otherwise busy times). Chef/prop John Ritter
is a confident hand in the kitchen; modern Scottish good-value menu (even if
only Michelin & me have noticed). Lunch & LO 10/11pm. Cl Sun/Mon.   MED

**142** **Blonde** 668 2917. 75 St Leonard's St. Tucked away in the S side, a neigh-
**xE5** bourhood restau relaxed, inexp & simply good. Handily nr Queens Hall &
Pleasance (in Fringe time). Pale wood & spartan ie blonde set of rms & easy-
eat food with quaffable wine (several house wines under a tenner). Andy
Macgregor presides; he chefs like Jamie O. Lunch (not Mon) & LO 10pm. 7
days.   INX

**143** **Home Bistro** 667 7010. 41 W Nicolson St. Comfort food heaven in tiny &,
**E5** yes, homely bistro on S Side nr Univ. Rowland & Richard's formula of simple,
reassuring mod & trad British grub. Home-made everything should win more
recognition than it does. Lunch Mon-Fri, dinner Tues-Sat.   INX

**144** **Browns** 225 4442. 131 George St nr Charlotte Sq and **The Living Room**:
**A3** 226 0880. 113 George St. The 2 best of many bar-eateries on re-invented
George St & both northern outposts of small but carefully run UK chains that
serve the late 90s/noughties version of the Menu-U-Like. Both noisy esp
music in the L Room & both excl service. 7 days noon-10.45pm (Browns), till
11pm (LR & midnight w/ends).   INX

**145** **Malmaison Brasserie** 555 6969. Tower Pl at Leith dock gates. Restau and
**xE1** café-bar of Malmaison (73/INDIVIDUAL HOTELS). Authentic brasserie atmos and
menu, as in all Malmaisons, the still-expanding chain, with linen napkins, big
windows & Paris meets NYC menu. Prix fixé (3 courses for £12.95 at TGP) is
gr value. 7 days. Lunch and dinner. LO 10pm.   MED.INX

**146** **Le Sept** 225 5428. Hunter Sq by the Tron, just off Royal Mile. Moved 2004
**D4** from their old haunt further up Royal Mile, this long-est French bistro has a
loyal following. Friendly & real & prob busy!   INX

# Gastropubs

*It's a ghastly word, but since coined with reference to places like The Eagle or The
Well in London's emerging East End, the Gastropub at least conveys the nature
of those food destinations which are more pub than restaurant or 'café-bar'. The
implication is that you can drink without eating. Many of these Edin examples are
indeed exemplary & were here long before the word was invented.*

**147** ✓✓ **The Shore** 553 5080. 3 The Shore, Leith. Long est as a 'gastropub';
**xE1** prob one of the best in the UK – an *StB* favourite. Bar (often with live
light folk or jazz) where you can eat from the same menu as the dining-
rm/restau. Real fire and large windows looking out to the quayside – strewn
with bods on warm summer nights. Food, listed on a blackboard, changes
daily but is consistently good. Lots of fish, some meat, some vegn. 7 days
lunch & LO 10pm, bar till 12.   MED

**148** ✓✓ **King's Wark** 554 9260. 36 The Shore, on the corner of Bernard St.
**xE1** Woody, candlelit, comfortable – a classic gastropub, ie the emphasis on food. Bar & bistro dining rm. Pub-food classics & more adventurous
even menu. Tho trad & dark rather than pale, light & modern, this has long
been one of the best bets in Leith for the food under chef, Mike Greig.
Scottish slant on the menu, with excellent fish incl beer batter and chips.
Lunch and LO 10pm. Bar open to 11pm, 12midnight Fri-Sat.   INX

**149** ✓✓ **The Canny Man** 447 1484. 237 Morningside Rd (aka The
**xB5** Volunteer Arms) on the A702 via Tollcross, 7km from centre.
Idiosyncratic renowned eaterie with a certain hauteur and a true, original
'gastropub'. Carries a complement of malts as long as your arm and a serious
wine list. Excellent smorrebrod lunches (12noon-3pm) & evens 6.30-9.30pm.
Salads & desserts with Luca's ice-cream (& alcohol). No loonies or undesir-
ables are welcome (you may be tested) but this is a civilised pub; a labyrinth
of good dining & taste. Till 12midnight Mon-Thu, 1am Sat, 11.30pm Sun.
(357/REAL-ALE PUBS)   INX

**150** ✔✔ **The New Bell** 668 2868. 233 Causewayside. Way down
**xB5** Causewayside in the s side, the New Bell is upstairs from the Old
Bell; you may walk thro' the pub to find it. And it is a find! Woody, warm
pubby atmos, nice rugs etc. Richard & Michelle Heller have got the rm and
the Mod-British menu just right. Food & v decent vino well-priced for this
sound quality & smart delivery. Excl steaks & puds. Dinner only. Tues-Sun LO
10.30pm. INX

**151** ✔ **The Waterfront** 554 7427. 1c Dock Pl. Long-est wine bar in this foody
**xE1** corner of the waterfront now joined (& spilling out at the quayside) to
Skippers (134/BISTROS). The conservatory o/looks the backwater dock. It's *the*
place to head in summer, but the warren of rms is cosy in winter. Food has
wavered a bit over the yrs but v good under Skippers esp for fish & puds & of
course, wine. Site, setting and gr friendly service are mostly what you come
for. New terrace (quayside) menu 2005. 7 days, Lunch & LO 9.30/10pm. Bar
midnight. MED

**152** ✔ **Cambridge Bar** 226 2120. 20 Young St the w extension of Thistle St.
**B3** Discreet doorway to Edin institution. Sporty in a rugger kind of way &
most recently notable for its gastroburgers, thought by many to be the best
in town. Huge & huge choice incl vegn (bean burgers) & Mackies estimable
ice-cream to follow. Food 12-8.45pm. Bar 11/12 & 1am Fri/Sat. INX

**153** **indigo (yard)** 220 5603. 7 Charlotte Lane. Food in bar area and in restau up-
**A3** stairs in converted and glazed-over yard behind the W End. A 1990s' thing but
wearing well! Enormously popular, always buzzing & noisy later (you may not
hear your wine pop nor your coin drop in the condom machine). Earlier therefore better for food. Contemp comfort food better than café-bar standard. 7
days from 9am. Food all day LO 10pm. Bar till 1am. (380/COOL BARS) INX

**154** **Montpelliers** 229 3115. 159 Bruntsfield Pl. They call it 'Montpelliers of
**xB5** Bruntsfield' & it is almost an institution now S of the Meadows. Same ownership as above and similar buzz and noise levels, but more accent on food.
From b/fast menu to late supper, they've thought of everything. All the contemp faves. Gets v busy. 7 days 9am-10pm. LO 10pm. Bar till 1am. INX

**155** **Rick's** 622 7800. 55a Frederick St. Basement bar/restau of Rick's Hotel
**B2** (79/HOTELS) by same people as indigo (yard) & Montpelliers (above). Not your
av gastropub but drinking is the main activity here & they do have a well
thought-out café-bar-type menu. Later on prob too noisy to enjoy food, so
choose time & table carefully. Up-for-it crowd verging perhaps too close
these days to stag & hen nights. But good cocktails. 7 days all day. LO 10pm
(11pm w/ends). Bar 1am. Also open for b/fast from 7am. MED

**156** **The Doric** 225 1084. 15 Market St. Opp the Fruitmarket Gallery and the back
**D3** entrance to Waverley Stn. Upstairs boho bistro. Only locals know that this is
quintessential Edinburgh & tho the food is neither remarkable nor cheap, we
must still climb those creaking stairs from time to time for a civilised supper
& a v excl bottle of vino. 7 days (not Suns in winter), lunch & LO 10pm. Bar
midnight. MED

## OUTSIDE TOWN

**157** ✔ **The Waterside** Haddington 01620 825674. 28km from town off A1.
Map 10 Longest, landmark pub food watering hole. On riverside, esp ambient in
**R25** summer. Can feel just like England. Upstairs restau and labyrinthine and v pub-
like downstairs. Big helpings. Excellent food: pub menu with staples or upstairs
à la carte even better. Lunch and supper. LO 9.30pm. Bar whenever! INX

**158** **Drover's Inn** East Linton 01620 860298. 5 Bridge St. Off the A1, 35km E of
Map 10 city. Fair way to go for eats, but don't think about the A1, think about this wel-
**R25** coming pub with notable food (they run a courtesy bus if it goes on too long).
A classic village pub with warmth and delicious meals in bistro beside bar or
restau up top Thur-Sun. Beer gdn out back is o/looked and trains whoosh by,
but on a sunny day, partake their excellent lunch here. Lunch and dinner (6-
9.00pm); later w/ends. INX

# The Best French Restaurants

**159** ✓ **La Garrigue** 557 3032. 31 Jeffrey St. Airy yet intimate restau nr Royal
**D3** Mile. Chef/prop Jean Michel Ganffre brings the S of France to your plate.
More SW than Med. Simple food with flair and unusual touches. Mon-Sat,
lunch and LO 10pm                                                          MED

**160** ✓ **Café Marlayne** 226 2230. 76 Thistle St. The third in the triumvirate of
**B2** excl & authentic French eateries within 100m of another (Café St-
Honoré, La P'tite Folie), this is a wee gem (we do mean wee). Personal, inti-
mate & v v French. Food generally fab (tho not gr for veggies). Isla Fraser's in
the kitchen. This really is like a place you find in rural France on your hols.
And love that keylime pie. Lunch & LO 10pm. Cl Sun/Mon.                    INX

**161** ✓ **(The New) Café Marlayne** 225 3838. Old Fishmarket Close, off 190
**D4** High St just below the cathedral. Newer, smarter Café Marlayne with
same formula & authentic, homely French cooking (Isla's brother on the
stove). Good value. Lunch & LO 10pm. Cl Sun/Mon.                          INX

**162** ✓ **Duck's at Le Marche Noir** 558 1608. 2-4 Eyre Pl. Malcolm Duck took
**xB1** over this bistro/restau at the lower end of the v residential New Town
some yrs ago now, but this is one of the most reliable (& not so) faux French
meals in town. Some classic varitations by chef David Scoller & a gr value
wine-list le patron clearly enjoys. Dinner 7 days, lunch Tues-Fri. LO 10-
10.30pm (earlier Sun).                                                     EXP

**163** ✓ **Café Saint-Honoré** 226 2211. 34 Thistle St Lane, betw Frederick St and
**B2** Hanover St. Suits a-plenty, New Town regulars and occasional lunching
ladies all to be found in this busy, shiny bistro-cum-restau which oozes &
even smells like Paris. Go on a rainy day when it feels esp warm & sweet &
comforting. Lunch Mon-Fri, LO 10pm. Veggies phone ahead.                  EXP

**164** ✓ **Le Bistrot Des Arts** 452 8453. 19 Colinton Rd betw Bruntsfield &
**xB5** Morningside. In a city awash with credible French restaus here comes
another authentic bistro off-centre but worth finding. Chef/prop Eric Ortiz
brings Paris to the South Side, the look, the feel, the escargots. Beef mature,
fish fresh, profiteroles to die for. Short, effective wine list. Mon-Sat lunch &
dinner. Cl Sun. LO 10pm.                                                   MED

**165** ✓ **Jacques** 229 6080. 8 Gillespie Pl, Bruntsfield. Endearing French staff
**xB5** and atmos. Hard-working eaterie close to the King's Theatre. Innovative
variations on the classics. Deals thro' even mean eating here is gr value. Excl
affordable French wine list. Loyal following, book ahead. Gr steak frites &
crepes. Lunch (not Sun) LO 11pm.                                          INX

**166** ✓ **La Camargue** 554 9999. Corner at 23 Commercial St. Main rd to/from
**xE1** Leith nr 'Restaurant Row' & Dock Pl so one of many restaus to choose
from. This is surprisingly good (value & quality) v French, incl atmos, menu &
chef. Excl seafood & wine list. Cameo bar adj is popular not overly trendy Leith
hangout. 7 days, dinner only LO 9.30pm (bar till 1am).                    INX

**167** ✓ **Petit Paris** 226 2442. 40 Grassmarket (and West End 226 1890 corner
**C4** of Queensferry St & Alva St). On busy N side of st below castle, teeming
**A3** on w/end nights – get an outside table & watch: this could be Montmartre
apart from the inebriation. Good atmos & value with très typical menu. BYOB
(not w/ends). 7 days lunch & LO late. Newer W End branch upstairs, slightly
less ambient but still 'le respect de la tradition Française'. Cl Sun Cl Mon in
wint.                                                                      INX

**168** **Daniel's** 553 5933. 88 Commercial Quay, off Dock Pl. Versatile takeaway
**xE1** and bistro. Main eaterie is housed in conservatory at back of old bonded
warehouse in Leith's 'restaurant row'. Clean lines, modern look and v popular. Offers contemporary French menu with Alsace and external influences
that pack us in esp for 'tarte flambé' & casseroles (169/PIZZAS). Also tables by
the water 7 days, 10am-10pm.                                              INX

**169** **The Vintner's Room** 554 6767. 87 Giles St, Leith. Cobbled courtyard to
**xE1** wine bar, with woody ambience and open fire. Vaults, formerly used to store
claret (Leith was an important wine pt), also incl a restaurant lit by candlelight. French props Laure & Patrice. Bar and restau have same classic evening
menu. Implication is Mediterranean, but seems more Lyonnaise to me, ie not

so light! Cheaper options at lunch in the bar and less formal. Excl cheese-board & puds and top wine list. Mon-Sat lunch and 7-10pm.　　　MED

**170**　**Maison Bleue** 226 1900 at 36 Victoria St & 557 9997 at 3 Infirmary St. Two
**C4**　v Edin café-bistros different in their food offering but with a similar convivial
**E4**　ambiance. French mezze approach in Victoria St, building a meal from
　　　small/medium dishes they call bouchées. Infirmary St new '05 (was called
　　　Boudoir to start then reverted to Maison). More conventional menu with
　　　French/fusion twist. Gt clubroom downstairs. Both v friendly. Both 7 days
　　　lunch & LO 10.30pm.　　　INX

**171**　**La P'tite Folie** 225 7983. 61 Frederick St & Randolph Pl (225 7983). The
**B2**　word is unpretentious – mismatched furniture, inx French *plat du jour*.
**A3**　Relaxed eating-out in single New Town rm or Tudoresque 'maison' in W End
　　　cul de sac. Cheap lunch. 7 days. LO 10.50pm. Cl Sun lunch.　　　INX

**172**　**Café D'Odile** 225 5366. 13 Randolph Cres. A secret gdn and small cafeteria
**xA3**　downstairs at the French Institute. Lunch only but can be booked for parties
　　　at night (BYOB). Gr views over the New Town, simple French home-cooking,
　　　patronised by ladies who lunch and students. Tue-Sat.　　　CHP

　　✓ ✓+ **Restaurant Martin Wishart** 553 3557. The Shore, Leith. Best
　　　　　in show! Report: 118/BEST RESTAUS.

　　✓ ✓ **Plaisir Du Chocolat** 556 9524. Canongate. Principally a tearm,
　　　　　with chocolate! Too French not to incl here. Full Report: 271/TEA-
ROOMS.

# The Best Italian Restaurants

**173** ✓ **La Bruschetta** 467 7464. 13 Clifton Terr. Extension of Shandwick Pl
**xA4** opp Haymarket Stn. Giovanni Cariello's Italian kitchen & tiny dining rm in the W End. A modest & modern version of Cosmo (below) with a big following – so must book. The space does not cramp their style. Lunch & LO 10.30pm. Cl Sun/Mon. INX

**174** ✓ **Valvona & Crolla** 556 6066. 19 Elm Row. Cafe at the back of the leg-
**E1** endary deli, and with all the flair and attention to detail that you would expect. First-class ingredients, produce shipped in from Italy (fresh veg from Milan markets) and gr Italian domestic cooking. One of the best & healthiest b/fasts in town, fabuloso lunch & afternoon tea from 3-6 with exquisite cakes. No smk. Mon-Sat 8am-6pm. INX

**175** ✓ **Centrotre** 225 1550. 103 George St (towards W End). Fabulous conver-
**B3** sion of lofty, pillared Georgian rm by former Valvona & Crolla stalwarts Victor & Carina Contini into the most stylish Italian joint in town. Passion for food & good service always evident. Bar & central pizza oven (tho they're not thin & crispy enough for me). Top ingredients, straightforward menu. Open b/fast til LO 10pm (10.30 Fri/Sat, 5pm Sun). INX

**176** ✓ **Tinelli** 652 1932. 139 Easter Rd. Regulars still swear by Giancarlo Tinelli's
**xE1** unassuming ristorante on unfashionable st that was serving carpaccio & proper Italian food long before the pasta explosion. After almost 25 yrs it's still simple & uncompromising. Where else could you get a perfect aglio y olio & rabbit (& snails)?. Lunch (pre-book) & LO 11pm. Cl Sun/Mon. MED

**177** **Cosmo** 226 6743. 58 N Castle St (no-through rd). V much in the old, dis-
**B3** creet style for those with time & cash on their hands. Has been *the* up-market Italian restau for yrs. Lighting and music are soft, service impeccable and (Italian) wine list exemplary. Menu pragmatically brief; allow time to enjoy it in this not unpleasant time-warp. Cl Sun & Sat lunch. LO 10.45pm. EXP

**178** **Santini** 221 7788. Conference Sq by Conference Centre & back of the
**A4** Sheraton (of which it's a part, below excl health club). Business-like Italian restau & bistro created by Mr Santini himself who has brought the same clean lines & stylish eating-out experience to London & Milan tho now run by the hotel. Waiters & ingredients v Italia. Restau is refined, exp & J & T. **Santini Bis** on sq itself is still smart but casual with some staples in a lighter menu. Both lunch & dinner LO 10.30pm. Cl Sun. MED/INX

**179** **Vin Caffe** 557 0088. Multrees Walk, the recently created shopping st behind
**B2** Harvey Nix. Not sure whether this new star turn of 2004 is a tratt, a restau or a caffe after all & since opening the rest of the jury seems to be out too. Pedigrees don't come better than this because it's the downtown smart eaterie of the Valvona & Crolla dynasty (see above). But somehow it hasn't lived up to our incredibly high expectations. Café counter downstairs, restau set-up up. Interesting pastas & pizzas & other lovely creations. We love them so we'll give them the benefit of any doubt. Anyway, it's always busy. 7 days 8am-11pm (midnight Fri/Sat), Sun 11-6pm. INX

**180** **La Favorita** 554 2430. 325 Leith Walk down from Vittoria (183/TRATTS) from
**xE1** which this much-heralded offshoot came 2005. The pitch here is gourmet pasta & wood-fired pizza – 'the best in Scotland'. Well they're not bad, but somebody should go to Nice for example to see how gr pizza is done. Otherwise good Italian cooking & friendly service in contemp/retro rm with windows on 'the Walk'. 7 days, noon-11pm. INX

# The Trusty Tratts

**181** ✓✓ **La Partenhope** 347 8880. 96 Dalry Rd. A corner & cucina of
**xA4** Naples halfway up Dalry Rd (about 200m from Haymarket) where the Sartore family have created the hottest tratt in town. Big Rosario presides in the kitchen, with daily specials from market produce. Menu as long as the Amalfi coast, but fresh fish specials are tops. Even the most basic aglio y olio shows how it should be done. Despite recent extension this place fills up fast. So book. 7 days. Lunch Tue-Sat, dinner LO 10.45pm. INX

**182** ✓ **Bar Roma** 226 2977. 39 Queensferry St. One of Edin's long-standing
**A3** fave Italians, revamped so it almost looks like a Pizza Express from the
outside. Inside always bustling (this includes the menu) with Italian rudeboy
waiters as the floor show. We love it! 7 days, all day. LO 11.30pm (later
w/ends). INX

**183** ✓ **Vittoria** 556 6171. Corner of Brunswick St & Leith Walk. Recently
**E1** extended, excl tratt & caff that's a' things to a'body. Report 285/CAFÉS.

**184** ✓ **Giuliano's** 556 6590. 18 Union Pl, top of Leith Walk nr the main r/bout,
**D2** opp Playhouse Theatre. Giulli's has a new Al Fresco restau down the st
**xE1** after the t/away counter but it's the original that's usually heaving with
happy punters & their many birthdays! It's just pasta and pizza but in a no-
nonsense menu that appeals. The food is great, the din is loud. Lunch and LO
2am daily – Giuli's is always late 'n' live. **Giuliano's On The Shore**: 554
5272 on the corner of the bridge in Leith Central has recently had a makeover
but it's the same, reliable tratt menu. Some jazz & esp good for kids (263/KID-
FRIENDLY). Also 7 days, LO 10.30/11pm. INX

**185** **Lazio** 229 7788. 95 Lothian Rd. One of the prerequisites of a 'Trusty Tratt' is
**A4** that they're there where and when you want them to be. This W End stalwart
is nr Usher Hall, Filmhouse & many other destinations Best on these blocks
with post-70s makeover & open late. Narrow accom; gr service. Report
300/LATE-NIGHT RESTAUS. INX

**186** **La Lanterna** 226 3090. 83 Hanover St. One of several tratts sub street level
**C2** in this block all family-owned. But this gets our vote. For 20 yrs the Zaino family have produced this straight-down-the-line Italian menu from their open
kitchen at the back of their no-frills restau with American soundtrack. 80% of
their customers are regulars and wouldn't go anywhere else. Well chosen
wine-list. Lunch & LO10pm. Cl Sun. INX

# The Best Pizza

**187** ✓ **L'Alba D'Oro** 557 2580. 5-11 Henderson Row. The t/away pizza section
**B1** of the estimable fish 'n' chip shop, but this is def a slice above the rest.
3 sizes (incl indiv 7") & infinite toppings to go. Not thin but crispy/crunchy.
Also pasta, gr wine to go, olive oils & Luca's ice cream & fresh OJ. This is no
ordinary chip shop! 7 days lunch & LO 12. CHP

**188** **Pizza Express** 332 7229. 1 Deanhaugh St, Stockbridge. Ubiquitous nation-
**A1** al chain, same formula everywhere, but what-the-hell, it's great design & the
UK standard pizza. Stockbridge branch best; award for architecture, in
refurbed bank with Water of Leith gurgling below. Simple, no-nonsense,
affordable pizza with good service. INX

**189** **Mamma's** 225 6464. 30 Grassmarket & 229 7008 Bruntsfield Rd (home
**C4** delivery). Brash, American style. Some alternatives to pizza, eg nachos, but
**xB5** you come to mix 'n' match – haggis, calamari and BBQ sauce and 40 other
toppings piled deep and so cheap for a filling meal. 7 days till 11pm/midnight.
Delivery till 11pm (1am w/ends). INX

**190** **Daniel's Bistro** 553 5933. 88 Commercial St on 'restaurant row' in Leith.
**xE1** Gr for the Tarte Flambé – v like a thin thin pizza made from milk-bread dough
topped with onions, crème fraîche & lardons – an Alsace & house speciality.
There are other thin pizzas too (168/FRENCH RESTAUS). 7 days 10am-10pm. INX

**191** **Jolly's** 556 1588. 9 Elm Row (part of Leith Walk nr Valvona & Crolla
**E1** 1495/DELIS). Long-est (tho changed owners) tratt/ristorante well known
locally for their thinner-than-usual wood-fired pizza. Over 40 varieties. Good
family spot. Also t/away. 7 days. Lunch & LO 10.30pm. Cl Sun lunch. INX

**192** **Caprice 2 Go** 665 2991. 198 High St, Musselburgh. Number is for their
**xF2** t/away joint round the corner which delivers to this E suburb of the city &
other nearby E Lothian towns. The adj restau serves the same wood-fired
pizza & the usual Italian fare. Ask them to crisp it but pizza here still lighter
than most. 7 days LO 10/10.30pm. INX

# The Best Mediterranean Food

**193**
**D3** ✓ **Igg's** 557 8184. 15 Jeffrey St, nr Royal Mile. Since 1989 this has been a corner of Spain in Scotland. A grown-up restau for business or affairs or both. Warm south reflected in the excl wine-list, but food from well-sourced Scottish ingredients more cosmo than merely Med. Some tapas but see Barioja below. Good biz lunch spot. Lunch & LO 10.30. Cl Sun.    MED

**194**
**xE1** ✓ **Dominico** 467 7266. 30 Sandport St. Still Leith's best kept secret, this tiny restau with a loyal following has better food & is better value than most in this quarter. Gr pastas & esp fresh fish. 7 days. Lunch, dinner Mon-Sat LO 10.30pm.    INX

**195**
**C2** ✓ **Nargile** 225 5755. 73 Hanover St. Not so much Mediterranean, most definitely Turkish. This is where to go to mess with the meze. Huge choice of all East of the Med fares from houmous to shashlik with lots for veggies & good fish choice. Some tables cramped but this is a night out with the mates or mate kind of place. Buzbag as expected & fair selection of other Turkish & non Turkish wines. Lunch & LO 10.30pm (11pm Fri/Sat). Cl Sun.    INX

**196**
**D1** **Tapas Tree** 556 7118. 1 Forth St. Party night-out kind of restau with upbeat Spanish staff, gypsy/Cajun soundtrack. Starter/main/pud is the heavier option but 3 well-chosen tapas (veg, fish and something else) with some robust bread and a bottle of house red makes for a v decent meal. Snappy service. Tapas in the £2 to £5 range, so not a pocket buster. 11am-11pm. 7 days.    INX

**197**
**D3** **Barioja** 557 3622. 19 Jeffrey St. And after Igg's the restau (see above), the tapas bar next door – they are joined together in the basement. Small tables and not much room to move upstairs; more space, less ambience down. Fairly authentic tapas menu – pan con tomate, gambas pil-pil, patatas bravas, but no sideboard or counter full as in San Sebastian; Spanish waiters and vino. 11am-10pm (11pm). 7 days.    INX

**198**
**D1** **Café Mediterraneo** 557 6900. 73 Broughton St. Discreet frontage to small, bright rms on busy little Broughton St. Brazilian owner Davi Bersi keeps it fairly Mediterraneo (tho no pasta) with a mean espresso. This café/bistro/restau serves many purposes from gorging to grazing & it's nice for b/fast incl Suns (311/SUN B/FAST). 7 days 8am till 6pm, Fri-Sat LO 9pm.    INX

**199**
**D5** **Phenecia** 662 4493. 55-57 W Nicolson St, on corner nr Edin Univ. N African Mohammed Sfina's unfussy N African/Spanish eaterie with couscous, lots of grilled meats and wide vegn choice. A culinary odyssey thro' the warm south & one of the most eclectic menus in town. Poss to eat v cheaply at lunchtime. Goodly portions. Lunch Mon-Sat & LO 10.30pm. They have the Château Musar.    INX

**200**
**xB1** **Tapas Olé** 556 2754. 8-10 Eyre Pl. Tapas restau/bar. Meat/vegn/seafood menus and the usual vinos. Good value & authentic with Spanish – well, Colombian proprietor and waiters. If in doubt, let them advise & choose. Live music sometimes, live clientele always. An inx night out! 7 days, lunch and LO 10pm.    INX

**201**
**D1** **Santorini** 557 2012. 32 Broughton St. Cheap, charming, authentic – what more could you ask from the only proper Greek restau in town. Start with 'mezedes' – small portions to share, then on to mousakka, stews, souvlakis. Some sticky puds. Tues-Sun, 12-10.30pm.    CHP

# The Best Seafood Restaurants

**202**
**xE1** ✓✓ **Skippers** 554 1018. 1a Dock Pl, Leith. Bistro with truly maritime atmos; mainly seafood. Best to book. Many would argue Skippers *is* still the best place to eat seafood in this town. Small, many-chambered with conservatory & outside waterside possibilities. Full report: 134/BEST BISTROS.

**203**
**C2** ✓✓ **Fishers In The City** 225 5109. 58 Thistle St. Separate entry to sister restau (below). Bigger & buzzier & one of the best all-rounders in the aforesaid city. (126/BEST RESTAUS) MED

**204**
**xE1** ✓✓ **Fishers** 554 5666. Corner of The Shore and Tower St, Leith. At the foot of an 18th-century tower opp Malmaison Hotel and rt on the quay (though no boats come by). Seafood cooking with flair and commitment in boat-like surroundings where trad Scots dishes get an imaginative twist. Hugely popular, some stools around bar and tables o/side in summer (can be a windy corner). Often, all are packed. Cheeseboard has some gr Brits if you have rm for a third course. 7 days. 12noon-10pm. MED

**205**
**xD1** ✓✓ **Big Fish** 556 6655. 14 Bonnington Rd nr Gt Junction St. Occasional restau in 'The Commissary', James Robb's dining rm & kitchen used for private parties & to prepare outside catering for Edin's poshest parties. Big Fish an Edin secret & real treat. Windowless but light rm illuminated by projected film. Freshest of fish & personalised cooking options. Starters & puds just delicious. Alternate Fri & Sat dinner only (cl wint). Must book. MED

**206**
**D4** ✓ **Creelers** 220 4447. 3 Hunter Sq. Tim & Fran's restau & smoke house near Brodick is also called Creelers. This corner of Arran in the city behind the Tron Church is just a short cast from the Royal Mile (tables alfresco in summer). Nice wine list. Fish served pure & simple. Some supplies from their own boat & Arran (hand-dived) scallops. Nice paintings, good atmos & new chef '05. Lunch & LO 10.30/11pm (not Tues/Wed lunch in winter). MED

**207**
**B3** ✓ **The Mussel Inn** 225 5979. 61 Rose St. Popular, populist. In the heart of the city centre where parking ain't easy, a gr little seafood bistro specializing in mussels and scallops (kings and queens) which the proprietors rear/find themselves. Also catch of the day, some non-fish options & homemade puds. This formula could travel but the owners have wisely decided not to travel far – they're also in Glas (645/SEAFOOD RESTAUS). Lunch & dinner. LO 10pm. INX

# The Best Fish 'N' Chips

**208**
**B1** ✓ **L'Alba D'Oro** Henderson Row, nr corner with Dundas St. Large selection of deep-fried goodies, incl many vegn savouries. It's a lot more than your usual fry-up – as several plaques on the wall attest (incl *StB!*) & the pasta/pizza counter next door is a real winner (176/PIZZAS). Gr wine selection, olive oils, Luca's ice cream. Open till 11pm (midnight w/ends – pizza 10 & 11 w/ends). CHP

**209**
**D1** ✓ **The Rapido** 77 Broughton St. Fine chips. My local so must be loyal. Popular with late-nighters stumbling back down the hill to the New Town, and the flotsam of the 'Pink Triangle'. Open till 1.30am (3.30am Fri-Sat). CHP

**210**
**E2** ✓ **The Deep Sea** Leith Walk, opp Playhouse. Open late & often has queues but these are quickly dispatched. The haddock has to be 'of a certain size' & is famously fresh. Trad menu. Still one of the best fish suppers with which to feed a hangover. Open till 2am (-ish) (3am Fri-Sat). CHP

**211**
**xB1** **Ye Old Peacock Inn** 552 8707. Report: 265/KID-FRIENDLY & **King's Wark**
**xE1** 554 9260. Report: 148/GASTROPUBS. Both excl for fish 'n' chips. INX

**212**
**D2** **Caffe Piccante** Top of Broughton St nr Playhouse Theatre. T/away & caff with tables on the black 'n' white tiles. This is the clubbers' chippy with unhealthy lads purveying delicious unhealthy food to the nighthawks, owls and budgerigars. (It's also Irvine Welsh's 'favourite'.) Menu incl deep-fried Mars & chips (you'd need to be well out of it). Open til 2am (2 w/ends). CHP

# The Best Vegetarian Restaurants

**213**
**E5** ✓✓ **David Bann's** 556 5888. St Mary's St. Foot of St Mary's St off Royal Mile – a bit off the beaten track, but always a busy restau & not only with non-meaters. In fact this is one of the best restaus in the UK: mood lighting, non-moody staff & no dodgy stodge. A creative take on round-the-world dishes. Light meal selection; lovely tartlets & 'parcels'. Vegn & vegan (on request). 7 days, lunch & LO 10pm (later w/ends)                    INX

**214**
**E5** ✓ **Susie's Diner** 667 8729. 51-53 W Nicolson St. Cosy, neighbourhood (the univ) self-service diner. Nice people behind and in front of the counter. Mexican and Middle-Eastern dishes. Lotsa choice menu incl excl coffee. Licensed, also BYOB. 9am-9pm. Cl Sun.                    CHP

**215**
**C2** ✓ **Henderson's** 225 2131. 94 Hanover St. Edin's original and trail-blazing basement vegn self-serve café-cum-wine bar. Canteen seating to the left, candles and live piano or guitar downstairs to the rt. Happy wee wine list and organic real ales. Good cheese & some of those mains & puds will go on forever. 7.30am-10.45pm. Cl Sun (open in Fest). Also has the Farm Shop upstairs with a deli and takeaway and the more bar-like **Henderson's Bistro** round the corner in Thistle St. NOTE: Henderson's (organic) oatcakes are *the* best.                    CHP

**216**
**D4** ✓ **Black Bo's** 557 6136. 57 Blackfriars St. Long-est proper vegn restau, ie waiter service, foody approach to the food with some unpredictable often inspired vegn ideas and combos. Intimate & woody, laid-back set-up. Adj bar has been cool for yrs. Restau now with meat & fish options (on request) so you can go with all your bloody mates. Lunch Fri/Sat only. Dinner 7 days. LO 10pm.                    INX

**217**
**E5** ✓ **Kalpna** 667 9890. 2-3 St Patrick Sq. They say 'you do not have to eat meat to be strong & wise' & are they of course right. Maxim taken seriously in this long-est Indian restau on the S side. Thali gives a good overview. Lovely, light & long may it prevail. Lunch Mon-Sat, dinner Mon-Sat, LO 10.30pm. (236/INDIAN RESTAUS). No smk.                    INX

**218**
**E5** ✓ **Ann Purna** 662 1807. 45 St Patrick Sq. Excellent vegn restau nr Edin Univ with genuine Gujarati cuisine. Good atmos – old customers are greeted like friends by Mr & Mrs Pandya. Indian beer, some suitable wines. Lunch Mon-Fri, dinner 7 days, LO 10.30pm. (242/INDIAN RESTAUS)                    INX

**219**
**xE5** **Engine Shed Café** 662 0040. 19 St Leonard's Lane. Hidden away off St Leonard's St, this is a lunch-oriented vegn café where much of the work is done by adults with learning difficulties on training placements, so worth supporting. Simple, decent food and gr bread – baked on premises, for sale separately & found all over town. Nice stopping-off point after a tramp over Arthur's Seat. Lunch only. Cl Sat/Sun.                    CHP

**220**
**A3** **Cornerstone Café** 229 0212. Underneath St John's Church at the corner of Princes St and Lothian Rd. V central and PC self-service coffee shop in church vaults. Home-baking and hot dishes at lunchtime. Some seats outside in summer (in graveyard!) and market stalls during the Festival. One World Shop adj is full of Third World-type crafts and v good for presents. A respite from the fast-food frenzy of Princes St. Open 9.30am-4pm (later in Festival). Cl Sun.                    CHP

**221**
**D5** **The Forest** 220 4538. 3 Bristo Pl. Gimme Shelter campus eaterie. On one hand hippy-dippy & on the other, refreshingly non-designery retro-sixties chic. Junk furniture, cool noticeboard & people strewn around the room. Decent veggie global menu. Occ performance. 7 days, 12-late.                    CHP

**222**
**E5** **Suruchi** 556 6583. 14a Nicolson St. Excl Indian, esp good for vegn dishes. Report 235/INDIAN RESTAUS.                    INX

✓ ✓+ **Restaurant Martin Wishart** 553 3557. Not remotely a vegn restau, but does have a special vegn menu. Food, ingredients & presentation are taken seriously here, so this is where to go for *the best* vegn food in Scotland. Report: 118/BEST RESTAUS.                    EXP

# The Best Scottish Restaurants

**223**  ✓ **Off The Wall** 558 1497. 105 High St. Not so much off the wall, but in
**D3**  the wall – a doorway off the tartan & tat Royal Mile & stairs up to this
calm first-floor rm. A discreet restau often missed by the tourists but not by
locals in the know. Short, simple menu with Scottish stalwarts (quality
salmon, venison, beef, etc) all nicely concocted with contemporary ingredients and twist: the underrated accomplishments of chef David Anderson.
Mon-Sat, lunch and LO 10pm. Cl Sun. MED

**224**  ✓ **Dubh Prais** 557 5732. 123b High St. As above, slap bang (but down-
**D3**  stairs) on the Royal Mile opp the Radisson. Only 9 tables and a miniature
galley kitchen from which proprietor/chef James McWilliams and his team
produce a remarkably reliable à la carte menu & specials from sound and
sometimes surprising Scottish ingredients. Haggis is panfried, smoked haddock comes with Ayrshire bacon. Athol Brose is as good as it gets. V regular
clientele & lucked-out tourists in this outpost of culinary integrity on the
Royal Mile. Cl Sun/Mon. Lunch & LO 10.30pm. Pron 'Du Prash'. MED

**225**  **Chambertin** 225 1251. 21 George St. Despite French title, a v Taste of
**B3**  Scotland menu in discreet, v professionally run main restau of George Hotel
(69/BEST HOTELS), an opulent salon where suits dine at lunch time and other
members of the Edin establishment rub shoulders with discerning tourists.
Long-est chef Klaus Knust at the helm. More relaxed in the eves.
Knowledgeable sommelier will take you thro' excl wine list. Lunch Mon-Fri,
LO 10pm Mon-Sat. Cl Sun. EXP

**226**  **Haldane's** 556 8407. 39 Albany St. In basement of The Albany. Fine dining
**D1**  nr Brougton St and prob the best proper meal in the area. Scottish by nature
rather than hype. Everything done in a country house style, tho menu unpretentious & room far from sumptuous. We go for the excl menu of chef Steven
Falconer. Lunch Mon-Fri, dinner 7 days LO 9.30pm. MED

**227**  **Stac Polly** 229 5405. 8a Grindlay St. Opp Lyceum Theatre and not far from
**B4**  Usher Hall, Traverse and cinemas. Dark wood and tartan interior is quietly
**C2**  smart; service, too. Scottish beef, salmon, game well sourced. Haggis filo
parcels a house fave. Cheeses come from Iain Mellis. There's another **Stac
Polly** below-stairs at 29-33 Dublin St in the New Town (556 2231). Similar
menu but it feels clubbier. Both: lunch Mon-Fri. Dinner 7 days LO 10pm.
MED

**228**  **The Grain Store** 225 7635. 30 Victoria St. A long-est reliable repas in inter-
**C4**  esting Victoria St nr Royal Mile. Regulars & discriminating tourists climb the
stairs for the excl value grazing lunch menu or innovative à la carte at night.
A laid-back first-floor eaterie in a welcoming stone-walled labyrinth. Good for
groups. Perhaps more 'mod Brit' than simply 'Scottish'. Lunch and dinner LO
10 (11pm Fri/Sat). 7 days. MED

**229**  **A Room In The Town** 225 8204. 18 Howe St, corner of Jamaica St. The
**B2**  room is in the New Town for these lads (Peter Knight & John Tindal) orig from
**xA4**  the Highlands & reflects something of that legendary hospitality. So good
value, friendly service; you can BYOB (a mere £1 corkage). Predom Scottish
menu with twists. Expect haggis, game, salmon. Their wicked banoffee pie
however is as it comes. Same folk have **A Room In The West End** (226
1036) in William St with an upstairs bar **Teuchters** (Scottish word for northern, rural folk with no manners – these guys love to be outsiders) & the
restau downstairs. Similar menu. 7 days lunch & LO 10pm. INX

✓ **The Witchery** 225 5613. Top restau that really couldn't be anywhere
else but Scotland. Report 122/BEST RESTAUS. EXP

# The Best Mexican Restaurants

**230**
**D3** ✓ **Viva Mexico** 226 5145. Anchor Close, Cockburn St. Since 1984 the pre-eminent Mexican bistro in town. Judy Gonzalez's menu still throws in something innovative now and again (chilli lemon cod, prawn with tamarind), although all the expected dishes are here, genuine originals & famously good calamares. Lots of seafood choice. Reliable venue for those times when nothing else fits the mood but sour cream, fajitas & limey lager; nice atmos downstairs. Lunch (not Sun) & LO 10.30pm (Sun 10pm).    INX

**231**
**F3** **Pancho Villa's** 557 4416. 240 Canongate. This recently refurb cantina is a reliable exponent of what we've come to regard as Mexican cooking with nosh of the 'chilada, 'ajita, 'ichanga school. Contemp décor, decent edibles, happy place for parties & Royal Mile strollers. Lunch Mon-Sat (Fri/Sat 12 onwards) & dinner 7 days.    INX

# The Best Japanese & Fusion Restaurants

**232**
**E5** ✓ **Bonsai** 668 3847. 46 W Richmond St on discreet st on southside a Jap caff/bistro (good to graze) where Andrew & Noriko Ramage show a deft hand in the kitchen. Freshly made sushi/yakitori & teppanyaki. No conveyor belt in sight, just superb value in neighbourhood caff setting. Teriyaki steaks, salads & crème brûlée – actually, great crème brûlée (& banana tempura)! 7 days noon-10pm (not Sun lunch).    INX

# The Best Indian Restaurants

**233**
**B3** ✓ **Roti** 225 1233. 70 Rose St Lane North. Locations don't come more obscure/discreet than this tho it's v central (betw Frederick & Castle Sts). Simple, small rm (& bar annex), superb Indian food – tho prop Tony Singh insists this is not 'an Indian restaurant'. Chefs Segal & Kapil upstairs on the stoves. Magic combos of flavours & lots of lightness: an ethnic cuisine at its best. Tues-Sat, dinner only LO 11pm.    MED

**234**
**D5** ✓ **The Original Khushi's** 667 0888. 26 Potterow. Long regarded as the only real Indian kitchen, this basic Punjabi café has been drawing in students and others since Nehru was in his collar, or at least in the news. Though a temporary move at first, Khushi's now firmly est in larger premises closer to campus. Almost feels like a tratt but definitively Indian. May have to book. Must BYOB. 7 days lunch & dinner. LO 11pm.    INX

**235**
**E4**
**xE1** ✓ **Suruchi** 556 6583. 14a Nicolson St. Upstairs opp Festival Theatre & **Suruchi Too** at 121 Constitution St, Leith (554 3268). Owner from Jaipur Herman Rodriguez plus chefs from Bengal, Delhi & S India create eclectic Indian menu written touchingly in Scots dialect (with tatties, & nan 'het fae the tandoor'). Unfussy if somewhat worn décor & food with light touch attracts students/academics from nearby univ as well as theatregoers. Load s for veggies. Better than av wines. In Leith, the food if anything is even better: you can usually get a table in the airport-like lounge. Both Suruchis routinely praised. Don't miss the (kulfi) ice cream. Lunch (not Sun) & LO 11.30pm daily.    INX

**236**
**E5** ✓ **Kalpna** 667 9890. St Patrick Sq. The original Edin Indian veggie restau & still the business. Lighter, fluffier & not as attritional as so many tandooris. Some unique dishes. Gujarati menu. Report: 217/VEGN RESTAUS.    INX

**237**
**D5** ✓ **Namaste** 225 2000. 15 Bristo Pl on one-way system from George IV Br & nr Univ. The new place on the block for those that want care in the curry. Authentic N Indian cuisine incl currys prod in trad brass pot! Familiar faves, light nans in a rm round the corner from the rest of the crazy world. 7 days, dinner only LO 10/11pm.    MED

**238**
**xE1** **Britannia Spice** 555 2255. 150 Commercial St on developing end of Leith nr Ocean Terminal & Britannia (the **Royal Yacht**; 398/ATTRACTIONS). Widespread menu from the sub-continent served by quietly efficient waiters in modern maritime setting. Some awards, some suits. 7 days, lunch LO 11.30pm.    MED

**239** **Kebab Mahal** 667 5214. 7 Nicolson Sq. Nr Edin Univ and Festival Theatre.
**D5** Gr vegetable biryani and delicious lassi for under a fiver? Hence high cult status. Late-night Indo-Pakistani halal caff that attracts Asian families as well as students and others who know. Kebabs, curries and excellent sweets. One of Edin's most cosmopolitan restaus. 7 days noon-midnight (2am Fri/Sat). Prayers on Fri (1-2pm). No-alcohol zone. CHP

**240** **The Khukuri** 228 2085. 8 W Maitland St. The W extension of Princes St &
**xA4** Shandwick Pl before Haymarket Stn. This unassuming Nepalese restau is a quiet secret. Costumed, endlessly polite Nepali waiters. Chef Dharma Mahrajan routinely wins awards & brings the herbs himself from the mountains of Nepal. Despite massive menu & mellow atmos, meat-eaters (lamb & chicken only) will be happiest here. 7 days lunch & LO 11pm (cl Sun lunch). INX

**241** **The Raj** 553 3980. 89 Henderson St on S corner of The Shore, Leith. Nice
**xE1** location for the irrepressible Tommy Miah's airy Indian/Bangladeshi restau here some yrs now, but still bustling & still changing. Occasional events add to the jollity; jars of things available to buy and take home, also recipe books. Tables best on the raised front area. Totally Raj, in the non-Irvine Welsh sense (in-joke for Edin readers). Lunch and LO 11.30pm, 7 days. INX

**242** **Ann Purna** 662 1807. 45 St Patrick Sq. Friendly and family-run Gujarati veg-
**E5** gie restau with seriously value-for-money business lunch & lovely harmonious food at all times. Report: 218/VEGN RESTAUS. INX

**243** **Indian Cavalry Club** 228 3282. Athol Pl, W End, just off the main Glas rd,
**xA4** about 250m from Princes St the upmarket one tho'. Bargain business lunch attracts the suits. Waiters uniformed at all times in keeping with officers' club theme now retro twice-over. Good buzz here & food always pukka. An unlikely carry-out place, but they do, and it's one of the best in town. Lunch and LO 11.30pm daily. INX

**244** **Zest** 556 5028. 115 N St Andrew St, close to St Andrew Sq and Harvey Nix.
**C2** Light, modern Indian caff by the same people who have Eastern Spices (321/TAKEAWAYS). Also do home delivery (on orders above £10) so handy for New Town couch potatoes (or Aloos). 7 days lunch, LO 11pm INX

# The Best Thai Restaurants

**245** ✓ ✓ **Dusit** 220 6846. 49 Thistle St. In the proliferation of Thai restaus
**C2** in Edin, this one gets the gold orchid. Elegant interior (back from st), excl service & food good in any language that just happens to be exquisite Thai cuisine. Tantalising combinations; decent wine list. Still the tops. Lunch & dinner LO 10.30pm. Cl Sun. MED

**246** ✓ **Thai Lemongrass** 229 2225. 40 Bruntsfield Pl. Smart but intimate
**xB5** Thai eatery by the people who have the estimable Jasmine (250/BEST CHINESE). Nice, solid, woody ambience, charming waitresses (Thai & Chinese) & food that's well good enough for euro/Thai afficionados; but popular & rightly so (book w/ends). Can BYOB (£6 corkage) tho good wine list. Lunch (Fri-Sun), dinner 7 days LO 11pm. INX

**247** ✓ **Thai Me Up In Edinburgh** 558 9234. Picardy Pl by Playhouse Theatre
**D2** nr top of Broughton St. Playful title & unobtrusive entrance belies surprisingly good & innovative Thai menu under rather inspired chef, Dusadee Suwannabud. Contemporary approach retaining elegance of lofty Georgian rm. Good service. Often busy. Lunch Wed-Sat & dinner LO 10.30 (11)pm. INX

**248** ✓ **ThaisanUK** 228 8855. 21 Argyle Pl. Your classic 'tucked-away' 'wee
**xB5** gem' on residential st in student & mortgaged-to-the-hilt Marchmont. Madame Ae offers healthy, fresh & authentic Thai food & other Asian specials. This place is tiny so best book. BYOB (no wine list). 7 days dinner only. LO 10.30pm. Another not-so-cosy branch at Jock's Lodge is also open for lunch. INX

**249** **Siam Erawan** 226 3675. 48 Howe St. On corner of Stockbridge area, the
**B2** first proper Thai to arrive in Edin and still thought by many to be among the best – manages that quiet Eastern elegance v well, & those caverns have hosted many a good night on the Thai. Food varies, good atmos. Lunch & dinner, LO 10.30pm. 7 days. INX

# The Best Chinese Restaurants

**250** ✓ **Jasmine**  229 5757. 32 Grindlay St opp Lyceum. V Chinesey restau with
**B4** big local following. Pre-post-theatre menus & good service to match.
Seafood a speciality (Cantonese style). BYOB (tho exp corkage). Often may
need to book or queue in tiny doorway. Some memorable dishes await. Mon-
Fri lunch, LO 11.30pm (12.30 on w/end, 2pm-11.30pm Sun).          MED

**251** ✓ **Kweilin**  557 1875. 19 Dundas St. The here-forever New Town choice
**B1** with imaginative Cantonese cooking (and other regions); v good seafood
and genuine dim sum in pleasant but somewhat uninspired setting. Excl
wine list. No kids allowed in the evening – somewhere for grown-ups to eat
their quail & v good seafood in peace. Book. LO 10.45pm. Cl Mon.     MED

**252** ✓ **Rainbow Arch**  221 1288. 8 Morrison St nr corner with Lothian Rd.
**A5** Unprepossessing but those who know go here & it's certainly the best
real food choice adj Lothian Rd. Authentic menu, esp dim sum (dedicated
chef). This is... well, proper Chinese cuisine. Open v late. 7 days noon-3am.
                                                                   INX

**253** ✓ **Loon Fung**  556 1781. 2 Warriston Pl, Canonmills. Upstairs (and down
**xB1** when it's crowded) for 30 yrs the famous lemon chicken and crispy duck
have been signature dishes of this neighbourhood restau tho the speciality
here is Cantonese food. Now there's also crispy monkfish in honey. Good dim
sum. Mon-Thu noon-midnight, Fri/Sat till 1am, Sun 2pm-11.30pm.    INX

**254** **Joanna's Cuisine**  554 5833. 42 Dalmeny St. For yrs this was the 'Dalmeny
**xE1** St place', now it's the delightful & decorative eponymous Joanna's. Tiny dining rm on ground floor of tenement off Leith Walk, nevertheless produces a
menu of 200 Peking dishes. Home-made stocks rather than MSG & other
touches like specially imported teas make this a place people swear by, so
book. Dinner only. LO 10.30pm (11.30 w/ends). Cl Mon.            MED

**255** **Dragon Way**  668 1328. 74 S Clerk St. Décor once gloriously OTT, now just
**xE5** O in a Crouching Tiger not so Hidden Dragon kind of a way. Has spread over
yrs to Portobello, Pt Seton & t/away in Marchmont (662 8484) so the people,
they like it. Cantonese with Peking & Szechuan as we like. Seafood a speciality & vegn menu. Lunch Mon-Sat and LO 10.30.                    INX

**256** **Wok & Wine**  225 2382. 57a Frederick St next to Ricks. Find this discreet
**B2** basement restau refreshed a couple of years back. It's one of the best contemp eastern restaus in town, using all the right supplies for meat & fish &
other carefully sourced ingredients. Wok bites allow a tapas approach. This is
Edinburgh's chilled-out Chinese. 7 days. Lunch & LO 11pm (Sun from
5.30pm).                                                         INX

# The Best Restaurants For Burgers & Steaks

**257**
Map 10
**P25**
✔✔ **Champany's**  01506 834532. On A904, Linlithgow to S Queensferry rd (3km Linlithgow), but nr M9 at jnct 3. Accolade-laden restau (and 'Chop and Ale House') different from others below because it's out of town (and out of some pockets). Both surf 'n' turf with live lobsters on premises. Famously good Aberdeen Angus beef. Good service, huge helpings (Americans may feel at home). Top wine-list. Chop House 7 days, lunch and LO 10pm; restau lunch (not Sat) and LO 10pm. Cl Sun. Hotel rms adj (111/HOTELS O/SIDE TOWN)                                         INX/EXP

**258**
**A1**
✔ **Bell's Diner**  225 8116. 7 St Stephen St, Stockbridge. Edin's small, but celebrated burger joint, the antithesis of the posh nosh. Nothing has changed in 30 yrs except the annual paint job and (with an unusually low turnover) the gorgeous staff. Some people go to Bell's *every* week in life & why? For perfect burgers, steaks, shakes and coincidentally, the best veggie (nut) burger in town. Sun-Fri 6-10.30pm, Sat 12noon-10.30pm.        INX

**259**
**D3**
**A1**
✔ **Buffalo Grill**  667 7427. 12-14 Chapel St opp Appleton Tower on the univ campus, and 1 Raeburn Pl, Stockbridge (332 3864). Although this diner trades on its reputation for steaks and such-like (Scotch beef natch), there are some Mexican & Southern US variants eg jambalaya & some concessions to veggies. Both gr spots for easy-going nights out with chums & not large so book and BYOB (corkage only £1). Lunch Mon-Fri, LO 10.15pm (Sun 10pm).                                                      INX

**260**
**D1**
**xE1**
**Smoke Stack**  556 6032. 53-55 Broughton St. From the makers of The Basement (332/UNIQUE EDIN PUBS) came something equally reliably groovy across the rd – a burgundy and blue diner rather than an orange and blue bar. Modish décor complements laid-back app. Loads of burgers (Scottish beef or vegn), seared salmon, blackened tuna, corn on the cob from a corn; all jollied along by a gr staff. Lunch Mon-Sat, dinner 7 days LO 10.30pm.        INX
The Leith offshoot of the Stack at 19 Shore Pl, 476 6776 has pretty much the same menu in back courtyard warehouse kind of a rm. Open 7 days, lunch & LO 10.30pm (cl Sun lunch).                                           INX

**261**
**D4**
**Relish**  225 8770. 217 High St bang in the middle of the Royal Mile below the Cathedral. Emphatically (gastro) burger joint with no starters & limited desserts (tho Mackie's ice cream & 'chilli chocolate cake'). Towering burgers in huge variety (also vegn) & top toppings. Same people (& similar menu) have the Cambridge Bar (152/GASTROPUBS). 7 days all day, LO 9.45/10.45pm.
INX

# Kid-Friendly Places

**262**
**xB5**
✓ **Luca's**  446 0233. 16 Morningside Rd. The ice cream kings (1532/ICE CREAM) from Musselburgh opened this modern ice-creamerie and caff where kids with dads will enjoy their spag and their sundae. Big cups of capp. Crowded if not claustrophobic upstairs esp on w/ends. Excl for daytime snacks, family evening meals & gorgeous ice-cream at all times. BYOB. 9am-9.30pm. 7 days. INX

**263**
**xE1**
✓ **Giuliano's On The Shore**  554 5272. 1 Commercial St, by the br. The Leith version of 'Gulies' (184/TRUSTY TRATTS) has all the trad Italian trappings esp thro' the back (more contemp feeling front-end – same food thro'out), with cheerful pizza/pasta & waiters. Kids love it. For grown-ups nice antipasto, fish specials & decent wine list. Always a birthday party happening at w/ends. Luca's ice-cream (see above). Noon-10.30/11pm. 7 days. INX

**264**
**C4**
**Café Hub**  473 2067. Castlehill, top of Royal Mile. Tourist central roomy restau for adults that caters in a superior way for kids. This caff is within the International Festival Centre, so busy busy in Aug. Outside terrace a child-friendly zone (367/DRINKING OUTDOORS). 7 days 10am-9.30pm (Sun/Mon till 6pm). INX

**265**
**xB1**
**Ye Olde Peacock Inn**  552 8707. Newhaven Rd nr Newhaven Harbour. One of Edin's unsung all-round family eateries for yrs – you can take gran as well as the bairns. The fish here really is fresh, the menu is more adventurous than you'd think with lots that wee kids and we kids like. High tea is a treat. Pud list is a classic Scottish dietary disaster, but irresistible. Lunch and LO 9.45pm. 7 days. CHP

**266**
**E1**
**Vittoria**  556 6171. Corner of Brunswick St & Leith Walk. Excl Italian all-rounder that can seat 200 people incl outside on pavement people-watching corner. Report: 285/CAFÉS.

## OUTSIDE TOWN

**267**
**xA3**
**Cramond Brig**  339 4350. At the R Almond as you hit Edin on the dual carriageway from the Forth Rd Br. This inn has always put effort into attracting families, & altho there's no longer a kids' play area on the premises, there is one by the old brig itself, a pony field & a walk by the river. Food much better all round after recent major refurb. Lunch and LO 9pm, 7 days. Open from lunch straight through to close on Sat-Sun. INX

**268**
Map 10
**Q26**
**The Sun Inn, Lothianburn**  663 2456. On a bend of the A7 nr t/off for Newtongrange, under mega viaduct, 18km S of city centre. Happy, homely pub in the unfashionable netherlands of Midlothian. Bistro-style food more trad than fad, lunch and LO 9pm (9.30 pm w/ends). Popular family spot (book w/ends).

**269**
Map 10
**R25**
**Goblin Ha', Gifford**  01620 810244. 35km from town in neat E Lothian village. One of two hotels, this has the pub grub cornered. Lunch and supper (6-9pm, 9.30pm Fri-Sat). Gdn gets v busy in summer. Nice for kids.

**270**
Map 10
**P25**
**Bridge Inn, Ratho**  333 1320. 16km W of centre via A71, turning rt opp Dalmahoy Golf Club. Large choice of comforting food in canalside setting. Has won various awards, incl for its kids' menu. Restau, trad & basic bar food and canal cruises with nosh. Pop Inn 12noon-9pm daily. Restau lunch daily and LO 9pm Mon-Sat. Bar till 11pm, 12midnight Fri-Sat. INX

# The Best Tearooms & Coffee Shops

**271**  ✓✓ **Plaisir Du Chocolat** 556 9524. 257 Canongate at bottom end of
**F3**  Royal Mile on tourist trek, but this is a real find. Chocolate yes but
definitely for connoisseurs, and teas of which there is a huge & explicit list.
Fabulous patisserie & hot savoury menu. Tables on the terrace and inside an
Art Nouveau-ish rm. A top spot for that reviving cuppa & no coffee in sight.
7 days 10-6pm. There's a Plaisir outpost, the Patisserie, where snacks are
served, up the st at 270 Canongate (opp side). 7 days 8.30am-5.30pm.

**272**  ✓✓ **Gallery (Of Modern Art) Café** Belford Rd. Unbeatable on a fine
**xA3**  day when you can sit out on the patio by the grass, with sculptures
around, have some wine and a plate of Scottish cheese and oatcakes. Hot
dishes are excellent – always 2 soups, meat/fish/vegn dish. Coffee and cake
whenever. Art upstairs often questionable; this is always superb. 7 days
10am-4.30pm. (403/OTHER ATTRACTIONS). Lunch dishes usually gone by
2.30pm. **Café Newton** at the Dean Gallery (404/OTHER ATTRACTIONS) across
the rd & the gardens from GOMA (above) is a smaller, more interior café by
the same people. Soup, sandwiches & 2 hot lunch dishes. Coffee from mega
machine. Same hrs as GOMA.

**273**  ✓✓ **Queen Street Café** National Portrait Gallery (402/OTHER ATTRAC-
**C2**  TIONS), Queen St, betw Hanover and St Andrew's Sq. And through
the arched window ... a civil slice of old Edin gentility. Serving seriously good
light meals (same people as GOMA, above), tasteful sandwiches, coffee and
excl cake – best scones in town, exquisite salads, 2 daily soups & 2 hot mains.
Self-s but you rarely wait long. Mon-Sat 10am-4.30pm, Sun 11am-4.30pm.

**274**  ✓ **Circus Café-Bar & Deli** 220 0333. Post 20thC addition to chic New
**B1**  Town café society & no expense spared in conversion of former bank to
chrome-&-leather eaterie upstairs & surprising deli hidden in the vaults.
Grazing menu & specialising perhaps more in cocktails than cappuccino, but
perfect for the upwardly mobile of Stockbridge. 7 days 10am-10pm.

**275**  ✓ **Fruitmarket Café** 226 1843. 29 Market St. Attached to the
**D3**  Fruitmarket Gallery, a cool spacious place for coffee, pastries or a light
lunch. Big salads, home cookin', creative ciabattas & 2 daily specs. Now
looked after by the enterprising Mhairi & Roy who do gr coffee & work
damned hard. Bookshop to browse with Andy Miller's lovely shelves, big windows to look out; good mix of tourists, Edin faithfuls, art seekers and the ter-
minally unaware. Mon-Fri 11.30am-3pm, Sat till 4, Sun 12-4.

**276**  ✓ **G&T (Glass & Thompson)** 557 0909. 2 Dundas St. Patrician New
**C2**  Town coffee shop and deli with contemporary food and attitude. Many
'ladies who latte', a phrase coined by Alexander McCall Smith whom you'd
expect to see with a notepad in a corner seat. Gr *antipasti*, salads, sandwiches to go; and v fine cakes that you won't find anywhere else (cake doyenne
Sue Lawrence uses their recipes). 8.30am-6.30pm, Sun 11am-4.30pm.
(318/TAKEAWAYS)

**277**  **Made In France** 221 1184. 5 Lochrin Pl. In a side street in Tollcross behind
**B5**  the Cameo, a soupcon of France. Amanda & Graham Evans-Nash are obviously Francophiles and their café's packed with delicious tid-bits and freshly
baked baguettes, croissants and tarts. Mon-Fri 8am-4pm, Sat 10am-4pm.

**278**  **Circle Coffee Shop** 624 4666. Canonmills nr the clock. Deli/t/away
**xB1**  counter & lovely caff in the back. V quiet New Town. Salads, soups, ciabattas
& bagels. Nice place to read the papers or rendezvous. 7 days 8.30am-
5.30pm, open to 9.30pm Fri/Sat in summer. Sun 10am-5pm.

**279**  **Kaffe Politik** 446 9873. 146-148 Marchmont Rd. All black and white and
**xB5**  wood and middle-Euro chic at another converted bank in the heart of student
flat land. Taken over by Sweet Melinda's (140/BISTROS) – it's just up the rd.
Damn fine cup of coffee, sodas, juice, soup 'n' sandwiches 'n' salads. V good
breakfasts (308/SUN BREAKFAST). Some o/side tables. 7 days 10am-5pm.

**280**  **Black Medicine Coffee Shop** 622 7209. 2 Nicolson St, corner of
**D4**  Drummond St. Funky American-style coffee shop on busy Southside corner
opp Festival Theatre and Univ Old Quad. Good place to take your book from
Blackwells; get a window seat! Good smell. Big bagels, cookies & fab smooth-

ies. 7 days 8am-6pm, Sun 10am-6pm. Also at 108 Marchmont Rd in student land. 7 days 8am-5pm (till 6pm w/ends). Sun 10am-6pm.

**281** **Clarinda's** 557 1888. 69 Canongate. Nr the bottom of the Royal Mile nr the
**F3** Palace (and the new Parliament building). Small but has tearoom integrity. With hot dishes and snacks that may seem more of a sit-down stop on the tourist trail but has some of the best home-baking in town (esp the apple pie). V reasonable prices; run by good Edinburgh folk who work that tiny kitchen. T/aways poss (I know I do). 7 days 9am-4.45pm (from 10am Sun).

**282** **The Elephant House** 220 5355. 21 George IV Br. Nr libraries and Edin Univ,
**D4** a rather self-conscious but elephantine and well-run coffee shop with light
**D5** snacks and big choice. J.K. Rowling (LITERARY PLACES) once sat here. They say 'the birthplace of Harry Potter'. Counter during day, waitress service evens. Smoking section. Cakes/pastries are bought in but can be taken out. View of graveyard & castle to dream away student life in Edin. 7 days 8am-11pm. Same people have **Elephants & Bagels** at Nicolson Sq. Soup 'n' a bagel t/away and sit-in. 7 days 8.30am-6pm (w/ends 9.30am-5pm).

**283** **Botanic Gardens Cafeteria** By 'the House' (where there are regular
**xB1** exhibs), within the gdns (401/OTHER ATTRACTIONS). For café only, enter by Arboretum Pl. Disappointing catering-style food (in fact it can be ghastly) but the o/side tables & the view of the city is why we come. And the squirrels. 10am-5pm.

**284** **Police Box Coffee Bars** 228 5001. Kiosks not caffs! Rose St (behind
**C3** Jenners), Morningside Park, Hope Park Cres (E of Meadows), top of Middle
**xB5** Meadow Walk (opp Forrest Rd) and outside John Lewis' dept store and St
**D5** Andrew's Cathedral. Caffeine kiosks in former police boxes. Similar fare to
**D2** Starbucks and Costas but these are home-grown and have, in their way, reclaimed the streets. Hrs vary but early-late. Gr coffee to go.

# The Best Caffs

**285**
**E1**
✓ ✓ **Vittoria** 556 6171. Brunswick St, corner of Leith Walk. For over 30 years Tony Crolla has provided one of the best, least pretentious Scottish-Italian café-restaus in town. Great fry-ups, omelettes and full Italian menu. O/side tables on interesting corner always packed when the sun's out. 2003 extension now ensures that tho hugely popular, you can always get a table & now there's the new pizzeria further down the Walk (La Favorita 108/ITALIAN REASTAUS). 7 days. 10am-11pm.

**286**
**B5**
✓ **Ndebele** 221 1141. 59 Home St, Tollcross. The Ndebele are a southern African people, but this café has dishes from all over the continent so get your ostrich, mielie bread and moi moi here – or just have a coffee. Loads of sandwiches, light meals and a good groovalong soundtrack. Brill for vegns. Africa distant and usually hot, this delightfully chilled. Daily 10am-10pm. T/away and sit-in. Not licensed.

**287**
**D5**
✓ **Monster Mash** 225 7069. 4 Forrest Rd. Comfort-food caff nr Univ capitalising on the mash come-back of recent times. Mainly with big sausages (Crombies) & gravy; also shepherd's pie, steak pie, etc. Puds similarly retro. Vegn options. Nice idea, slightly lost in delivery. Now open in Glas (630/GLAS). 7 days 8am-10pm.

**288**
**D1**
✓ **Blue Moon Café** 557 0911. 1 Barony St on corner of Broughton St. Longest-established gay café in Scotland (1301/GAY EDIN). Straight-friendly & a good place to hang out from b/fast-late. All day b/fast. Female staff efficient, boys more spacey. Free condoms in the gents for the impecunious or impatient. 7 days 11am-1am. Food all day till 10pm (Fri/Sat till midnight), LO 15 mins before.

**289**
**xB5**
✓ **Luca's** 446 0233. 16 Morningside Rd. In town version of legendary ice cream parlour in Musselburgh (1484/ICE CREAM). Ice cream and snacks d/stairs, more family food parlour up. Cheap and cheerful. Gr for kids. Report: 262/KIDS. 7 days.

**290**
**D4**
**Spoon** 556 6922. 15 Blackfriars St off Royal Mile opp the High St Hostel (99/BEST HOSTELS). Richard & Moira's friendly, off-high st, almost neighbourhood but modern, even minimalist caff. Counters service for snacks & hot dishes using selected ingredients & more TLC than usual. Big bowls of soup, nice coffee. 9am-5pm, Sat from 10am. Cl Sun.

**291**
**D3**
**Always Sunday** 622 0667. 170 High St. At last a caff on the Royal Mile that's trying & at least reflects contemp tastes. Deli-style counter offering 'healthy' b/fasts thro lunch to afternoon 'treats'. Home baking. 7 days 8am-6pm (Sat/Sun from 9am).

**292**
**xE1**
**Café Truva** 554 5502. Cute Turkish caff on the corner in Leith & on the water (at 77 The Shore). Coffee of course & other Turkish delights, but mainly a snacky (ciabattas, panninis, couple of hot dishes like moussaka) & sit-around bolthole in Leith. 7 days 9am-6.30pm.

**Kebab Mahal** 667 5214. Nicolson Sq. Cult caff on campus. Report: 239/INDIAN.

# The Best Late-Night Restaurants

**293** ✓✓ **The Witchery** 225 5613. Castlehill, top of Royal Mile nr the Castle.
**C4** Not open v late, but does take bookings up till 11.30pm, that crucial half hr beyond 11 that allows you to eat after the movies. Special after-theatre menu from 10.30pm has 2 courses for £12.50, a v good deal from one of the best restaus in town (122/BEST RESTAUS). 7 days, lunch and **LO 11.30pm**.
MED

**294** ✓ **Pizza Express** Various branches (177/pizza) all open 11/11.30 but
**D3** North Bridge (557 6411) **open till midnight** and no booking policy, so
**xE1** a good bet. Leith branch on the shore (554 4332) is prob best chance of food after 11 in Leith. Report 188/BEST PIZZA.
INX

**295** ✓ **Giuliano's** 556 6590. 18 Union Pl, Leith walk opp Playhouse. Buzzing
**E2** Italian tratt day and night. Report 184/TRUSTY TRATTS. **Handily open till 2am (2.30 w/ends)**.
INX

**296** ✓ **Living Room** 226 0880. 113 George St. Best of many for eats on 'styl-
**B3** ish' George St & open later than similar others esp at w/ends. Full-on bar at front like Candy Bar downstairs; surprisingly large dining area at back. Mod-Brit menu with food better than you'd expect. V noisy & music too loud at w/ends, but service excl. Not a bad product from emerging UK chain. **7 days LO 11pm, midnight w/ends**.
INX

**297** ✓ **Rainbow Arch** 221 1288. 8 Morrison St. **7 days noon–3am**. Authentic
**A5** Chinese food of high standard. Report: 252/CHINESE.
INX

**298** **Favorit** 220 6880. 20 Teviot Pl and 30 Leven St (221 1800). New York diner-
**D5** type café/restau – salads, pasta, wraps, Ben and Jerry's from dawn till almost
**xB5** dawn (307/SUNDAY BREAKFAST). But many feel Favorit is not their favourite these days. **7 days till 3am**.
MED

**299** **Bar Roma** 226 2977. 39a Queensferry St, nr W End of Princes St. Buzzing
**A3** day and night. An Edin institution even better after revamp. All the old stand-bys snappily served & lots of late night Italian jive. Best wine-list you'll find in W End after midnight. (See 182/TRUSTY TRATTS). **12noon–12midnight Sun-Thu; 12.45am Fri-Sat**.
INX

**300** **Lazio** 229 7788. 95 Lothian Rd. Best of the Lothian Rd bunch by far, tho
**A4** you'd never know. Totally genuine Italian family restau (185/TRUSTY TRATTS). There's one guy always there eating at 1 in the morning when we're there. Now that's what we call 'a regular'. **Till 1.30am, 3am Fri/Sat**.
INX

**301** **Loon Fung** 556 1781. 2 Warriston Pl, Canonmills. Gr long-est reliable Chinese
**xB1** diner always open late while customers last. **Till midnight Sun-Thur, 1am Fri/Sat**. Report: 253/CHINESE.
INX

**302** **Mamma's** 225 6464. 30 Grassmarket. Open **till 11 always & midnight** if
**C4** you're lucky. Report 189/PIZZAS.
INX

# Good Places For Sunday Breakfast

**303**
**D3** ✓ **Hadrian's** 557 5000. 2 North Bridge, corner of & brasseries restau of Balmoral (62/HOTELS). Good daily (power) brunch place, but also Suns. **From 7am (Sun 7.30am)**. Not chp, but light (or lavish) & laid-back.

**304**
**D3** ✓ **The Breakfast Room @ The Scotsman Hotel** 556 5565. 20 N Bridge. B/fast in Edin's top new boutique hotel (70/HOTELS). Many refs to the morning paper this hotel replaces in the building, & this morning's is there to read. Interior rm (adj Vermillion – 129/BEST RESTAUS), but an excl, leisurely start to the day for guests & non-guests alike. **From 7-10.30am, 8-11.30 w/ends.**

**305**
**B2** ✓ **Ricks** 622 7800. 55a Frederick St. The cool café-bar (381/COOL BARS) with rooms (79/INDIVIDUAL HOTELS) opens early & late, but an excl spot for laid-back or power b/fast brunch 7 days, incl unusually early start on Suns. Eclectic, contemp menu. **Open 7 days from 7am.**

**306**
**C2** ✓ **Urban Angel** 225 6215. 121 Hanover St. Convivial, contemp b/fast from good sausages to honey & waffles. Potato scones natch! Full of bright people that can still remember their Sat night. **Open 10am.** ·

**307** **Favorit** 221 1800. 30 Leven St. The all-people all-rounder. **Open 7 days**
**xB5** **from 8am.** Report: 298/LATE-NIGHT RESTAUS.

**308** **Kaffe Politik** 446 9873. 146-148 Marchmont Rd. Good coffee in serenely
**xB5** cerebral surroundings. B/fast & other menus under review by new owners (of Sweet Melinda's) at TGP. **From 10am.** (279/BEST TEAROOMS)

**309** **City Café** Blair St. It's been here so long, it's easy to take for granted ... but
**D4** for that 'BIG' breakfast (carnivore or veggie), few places in the city beat the content or American diner atmos. Not open exactly early as most of clientele have been up v late. **From 12.30pm.**

**310** **King's Wark** 554 9260. 36 The Shore on busy corner for traffic, but calm &
**xE1** comforting inside. Dining rm or bar. No early start (**11am**), but a civilised brunch on the waterfront.

**311** **Café Mediterraneo** 557 6900. 73 Broughton St. On busy st for b/fast (see
**D1** below), this is a good choice for the non fry-up & easy start to the day. From coffee/croissants to olive oil lunch in light surroundings (198/MED RESTAUS). **From 9am (full b/fast from 10.30am).**

**312** **Black Medicine Coffee Shop** 622 7209. 2 Nicolson St. Gr atmos
**D4** American-style coffee with bagels/muffins type start to Sundays. 280/COFFEE SHOPS. **From 10am.**

**313** **Elephant House** 220 5355. 21 George IV Bridge. Another (this time exten-
**D4** sive) coffee-house nr the Univ that's open early for caffeine & sustenance. 282/COFFEE SHOPS. **From 9am.**

**314** **The Broughton St Breakfast** As well as Mediterraneo (see above), there's
**D1** lots of choice in the main st of Edin's East Village. From the top down:
**D2** **Mather's** the no-compromise drinking den does the trad fry-up from **12.30pm**, as does **The Outhouse** down the lane but with veggie variants (& outside courtyard) & until 4pm. **Baroque** also kicks in from **12.30pm** with similar nosh (slightly more expensive). **The Basement** also does Tex-Mex brex from **noon** tho it is a basement. Further down on corner with people-watching windows is **The Barony** with b/fast & the papers from 12.30-3.30 (gr live music Sun late aft).

**315** **The Olive Branch** 557 8589. Corner of Brougton St & Broughton Pl. Big
**D1** windows, o/side tables. Med menu & b/fast fry-ups. This place is strangely popular & populated 24/7. **From 10.30am.**

**316** **indigo (yard)** 220 5603. 7 Charlotte Lane. Another fashionable spot (same
**A3** org as Rick's above) & prob best brunch bet in W End. Details: 380/CAFÉ-BARS. **From 8.30am.**

**The Globe** Henderson Row branch. See 320/T/AWAY.

# The Best Takeaway Places

**317**
**B2**
✓ **Appetite** 225 3711. 42 Howe St. Formerly (the legendary) Rowlands, this son-of follows the same formula. Gr home-made food for t/away, parties or just for your own supper/picnic etc. Nearest thing in Edin to a traiteur. Daily soups/curry/quiche/pizza & specials. Good vegn & salads. Best in the Stockbridge quarter & just poss, the best in town. Janey Wright on the meatballs. Mon-Fri 8.30am-4.30pm.

**318**
**C2**
✓ **G&T (Glass & Thompson)** 557 0909. 2 Dundas St. Deli and coffee shop on main st in New Town, but also takeaway sandwiches/rolls in infinite formats using their drool-making selection of quality ingredients (breads, cheeses, salamis, etc.). V fine cakes. Take away to office, gdns or dinner party. Excellent sit-in area and small terr for whiling away Edinburgh days. Mon-Sat 8.30am-5.30pm, Sat 8.30am-5.30pm, Sun 11am-4.30pm. (276/BEST TEAROOMS)

**319**
**xE1**
✓ **Embo** 652 3880. 29 Haddington Pl. Half way down Leith Walk & one of the reasons for going that far. Mike & Erin's neighbourhood hangout & t/away now better than ever. Bespoke sandwiches, wraps, etc. Excl coffee & smoothies. 'Panino Bar' & a couple of tables o/side the door. Nice baking. This place is good to know. Mon-Fri 7.30am-4pm, from 9am on Sat. Cl Sun.

**320**
**D2**
✓ **The Globe** 558 3837. 42 Broughton St. A bright spot on the corner in the middle of the East Village. Open all day till 3/4pm for sandwiches/rolls and toasted focaccia. Big window for people-watching. Branches at 23 Henderson Row, N Castle St & Bernard St, Leith (another busy shop on the corner). Henderson Row branch the best for real b/fast & is open on Suns. But recent price hikes & thinner fillings are losing fans.

**321**
**xB1**
**Eastern Spices** 558 3609. 2 Canonmills Br, by the clock. Long on the grapevine, this place is simply better than most – phone in your order or turn up and wait. Also home delivery 2 ml radius. Full Indian menu from pakora to pasanda and meals for one. 5-11.30 7 days. New, zestier menu due at TGP.

**322**
**xB1**
**Taste Good** 313 5588. 67 Slateford Rd. At last a 21st cent Chinese t/away unfortunately far from centre (they do deliver). Contemp look & presentation. Tastes good too (also seating). 7 days 4.30-12midnight.

**323**
**B1**
**L'Alba D'Oro** 557 2580. 5-11 Henderson Row. Excl pizza, pasta, wine as well as fish 'n' chips. A v superior chippy & pizza joint. Report 187/PIZZAS.

**324**
**xE5**
**Juice Monkeys** 667 4450. Clerk St in Univ area heading S. Small internet/newspaper-reading/lecture-note-revising caff with good fresh t/away soups, juices & s/wiches. Open early. 7 days 8am-8pm (Suns 9am-8pm). Nice b/fasts.

**325**
**xB4**
**Jaspers** 229 8944. Bottom of Grove St, round corner of Morrison St nr Haymarket. Small, simple caff/t/away with home-made quiches/tartlets as well as soups/s/wiches etc. They do a nice omelette. 7.30am-3pm (Sat 8.30am). Cl Sun.

# Unique Edinburgh Pubs

**326**
**xE1**
✔✔ **Port o' Leith** 58 Constitution St. The legendary Leith bar on busy rd to what used to be the docks. The incorrigible & incorruptible Mary Moriarty still puts up the odd sailor but it's mainly the rest of us from the sea of life who frequent this unchanging neighbourhood pub full of warmth, chat, good music & all the things we left behind. DJs (gr life-affirming music) Fri/Sat night. Truly a port in the storm. Go find it. Till 12.45am.

**327**
**D2**
✔ **Café Royal** Behind Burger King at the E end of Princes St, one of Edin's longest celebrated pubs. Unrelated to the London version, though there is a similar Victorian/Baroque elegance. Through the partition is the Oyster Bar (good atmos rather than food). Central counter and often standing rm only. Open to 11pm (later at w/ends).

**328**
**xB5**
✔ **Bennet's** Leven St, by King's Theatre. Just stand at the back and watch light stream through the stained glass on a sunny day as it always did. Same era as Café Royal and similar ambience, mirrors & tiles. Decent food at lunch & early even (364/PUB FOOD). Till 12.30am Mon-Fri, 1am Sat, 11pm Sun.

**329**
**xE1**
✔ **The Pond** 467 3815. 2 Bath Rd, off Seafield Rd, Leith. Cool Edin bar on the edge of dead dockland. They don't make 'em as understated or laid-back as this anywhere except at the beach. Till 1am. (383/COOL BARS).

**330**
**D5**
✔ **Sandy Bells** 225 2751. Forrest Rd nr Univ & Greyfriars Kirk & seems like it's been there as long. Mainly known as a folky/trad music haven (live 7 nights), it reeks (& we do mean reeks) of atmos. How they'll survive the smoking ban remains to be seen. Long may it... 7 days till 1am (Suns 11pm).

**331**
**D1**
**Barony Bar** 81 Broughton St. Real-ale venue with a mixed clientele & good vibe. Belgian and guest beers. Newspapers to browse over a Sun afternoon b/fast or a (big) lunchtime pie. Bert's band on Sun aft/evens one of the best pub nights in town. Till 12midnight Mon-Thu, 12.30am Fri-Sat, 11pm Sun.

**332**
**D1**
**The Basement** 109 Broughton St. Much-imitated, still crucial, this is a chunky, happening sort of, er, basement where you can have Mex-style food during the day served by laaarvely staff in Hawaiian shirts. At night, the punters are well up for it – late, loud and still alive. Till 1am daily.

**333**
**B2**
**Kay's Bar** 39 Jamaica St. The New Town – incl Jamaica St – sometimes gives the impression that it's populated by people who were around in the late 18th century. It's an Edinburgh thing (mainly male). They care for the beer (354/REAL-ALE PUBS). Until 11.45pm (11pm Sun).

**334**
**A3**
**Mather's** 1 Queensferry St. Edin's W End has a complement of 'smart' bars that cater for people with tight haircuts and tight schedules. The alternative is here – a stand-up space for old-fashioned pubbery, slack coiffure and idle talk (340/'UNSPOILT' PUBS). Till 12midnight Mon-Thu, 1am Fri-Sat, 11pm Sun.

**335**
**xE1**
**Robbie's** Leith Walk, on corner with Iona St. Some bars on Leith Walk are downright scary – but not this one. Tolerant, good range of beer, TV will have the football on (or not). Magi mix of Trainspotters, locals and the odd dodgy character. The social workers, however, have been ousted. (344/'UNSPOILT' PUBS). Till 12midnight Mon-Sat, 11pm Sun.

**336**
**D4**
**City Café** 220 0127. 19 Blair St. Seems ancient, but 15 yrs on, the retro Americana chic has aged gracefully. Pool tables, all-day food, decent coffee. A hip Edin bar that has stood the test of mind-altering time. Music downstairs w/ends courtesy of guest DJs (309/SUNDAY BREAKFAST). 11am-1am daily.

**337**
**D4**
**Three Sisters** Cowgate. Of many booming bars in the Cowgate, we may as well select this one – one of Edinburgh's busiest. Nothing v special but good conversion of old warehouse and better than your av super bar (with vast courtyard – usually rammed). Also has rms. 7 days, 11am-1am.

**338**
**C2**
**The Dome** 624 8624. 14 George St. Edin's first megabar but not a chain. Former bank and grandiose in the way that only a converted temple to Mammon could be. Main part sits 15m under elegant domed roof with island bar and raised platform at back for determined diners. Staff impeccable; you come for the surroundings more than the victuals perhaps, but food ain't bad (MED). Lunch and LO dinner 10pm daily. Also snack menu for casual diners away from roped-off posh nosh area. Adj real-ale Art Deco bar Frazers is sep-

arate, more intimate, better for a blether. 'Garden' patio bar at back (in good weather) – enter via Rose St. Final bit, downstairs: Why Not? (494/ESS CULTURE/CLUBS), a nightclub for over-25s still lookin' for lurvv (Fri/Sat). Main bar Sun-Thu till 11.30pm, Fri-Sat till 1am.

**339** **The Doric** 225 1084. 15 Market St. More a bistro/restau than a mere pub,
**D3** but the smaller rm by the bar is Edinburgh in a nutshell (143a/BISTROS). Recent refurb downstairs but we always preferred upstairs looking over the town.

# The Best Old 'Unspoilt' Pubs

*Of course it's not necessarily the case that when a pub's done up, it's spoiled, or that all old pubs are worth preserving, but some have resisted change and that's part of their appeal. Money and effort are often spent to 'oldify' bars and contrive an atmos. The following places don't have to try.*

**340** ✓ **The Diggers** 1 Angle Park Terr. (Officially the Athletic Arms.) Jambo pub
**xA4** ✓ *par excellence*, stowed with the Tynecastle faithful before and after games. Still keeps a gr pint of McEwan's 80/-, allegedly the best in Edin. The food is basic ie pies. Till 11pm/midnight Mon-Sat, 11pm Sun.

**341** ✓ **The Royal Oak** Infirmary St. Tiny upstairs and not much bigger down.
**D4** ✓ During the day, pensioners sip their pints (couple of real ales) while the cellar opens till 2am. Music up and down. Hell for non-smokers (at least until the ban) but they definitely don't make 'em like this any more. Gold carat pubness.

**342** ✓ **Roseburn Bar** 1 Roseburn Terr, on main Glas rd out W from Haymarket
**xA4** ✓ and one of the nearest pubs to Murrayfield Stadium. Wood and grandeur and red leather, bonny wee snug, fine pint of McEwan's and wall-to-wall rugby of course. Heaving before internationals. Till 11pm (midnight w/ends).

**343** ✓ **Clark's** 142 Dundas St. A couple of snug snugs, red leather, brewery
**C2** ✓ mirrors and decidedly no frills. Good McEwan's – just the place to pop in if you're tooling downhill from town to Canonmills. A local you might learn to love. Till 11pm (11.30pm Thu-Sat).

**344** **Robbie's** Leith Walk, on corner of Iona St. Real ales and new lagers in a
**xE1** neighbourhood howf that tolerates everyone from the wifie in her raincoat to multi-pierced yoof of indeterminate gender. More rough than smooth of course, but with the footy on the box, a pint and a packet of Hula Hoops – this is a bar to save or savour life. Till 12midnight Mon-Sat, 11pm Sun. (335/UNIQUE EDIN PUBS)

**345** **Oxford Bar** 8 Young St, downhill from George St. No time machine needed
**B3** – just step in the door to see an Edin that hasn't changed since yon times. Careful what you say; this is an off-duty cop shop poss incl Inspector Rebus (& Ian Rankin fans from far & wide). Some real ales but they're as beside the point as the pies.(Actually the pies were off last time our inspector called.) Till 1am (midnight Sun).

**346** **Mather's** 1 Queensferry St. Not only a reasonable real-ale pub but almost
**A3** worth visiting just to look at the ornate fixtures and fittings – frieze and bar
**D2** esp. Unreconstructed in every sense. Pies all day. Till 12midnight Mon-Thu, 1am Fri-Sat, 11pm Sun. (334/UNIQUE PUBS) There's another, unrelated, **Mather's** in Broughton St which is managing to keep its head in the city's grooviest thoroughfare by remaining pub-like and unpretentious. Football telly.

# The Best Real-Ale Pubs

**347** ✓ **The Cumberland Bar** Cumberland St, corner of Dundonald St. After
**C1** work this New Town bar attracts its share of suits, but later the locals (&
recently droves of ya students) claim it. Camra (Campaign for Real Ale) supporters seek it out too. Av of 8 real ales on tap. Nicely appointed, decent pub
lunches (& 'curry Mondays'), unexpected beer gdn. 7 days till 1am.

**348** ✓ **Starbank Inn** 64 Laverockbank Rd, Newhaven. On the seafront rd W
**xB1** of Newhaven harbour. Usually 8 different ales on offer. Gr place to sit
with pint in hand and watch the sun sink over the Forth. The food is fine
(360/PUB FOOD). Bar till 11pm Sun-Wed, 12midnight Thu-Sat.

**349** ✓ **The Bow Bar** 80 W Bow, halfway down Victoria St. They know how to
**C4** treat drink in this excellent wee bar. Huge selection ales & whiskies – no
cocktails! One of the few places in the Grassmarket area an over 25-year-old
might not feel out of place. Bliss. Till 11.30pm Mon-Sat, 11pm Sun.

**350** ✓ **The Guildford Arms** 1 W Register St. Behind Burger King at E end of
**D2** Princes St on same block as the Café Royal (327/UNIQUE PUBS). Forever in
the same family. Lofty, ornate Victorian hostelry with loadsa good ales, typi-
cally 7 Scottish, 2 English. There are some you won't find anywhere else in
the city. Pub grub available on 'gallery' floor as well as bar. Mingin' carpet by
the way! Sun-Wed till 11pm, Thu-Sat till 12midnight.

**351** ✓ **Blue Blazer** 2 Spittal St opp Point Hotel. No frills, no pretensions, just
**B5** wooden fixtures and fittings, pies and toasties in this fine howf that carries a huge range of real ales. Regularly a CAMRA pub of the year. More soul
than any of its competitors nearby even after recent refurb. 7 days till 1am.

**352** **Bert's** 29 William St. Rare ales as well as house IPA & 80/-, suits as well as
**xA4** casual crowd in this *faux* Edwardian bar. Decent pies for carnivores or veggies
**A1** alike all day, with other pubgrub lunch till 9pm. A good place to escape from
office neurosis. Good range guest ales. Till 11pm Sun-Thu, 12midnight Fri-Sat.
More local but similar **Bert's** (with pies) at 2 Raeburn Pl, Stockbridge.

**353** **The Canny Man** 237 Morningside Rd. Officially known as the Volunteer
**xB5** Arms, but everybody calls it the Canny Man. Good smorrebrod at lunch time
& evens (149/GASTROPUBS), a wide range of real ales & myriad malts. Casual
visitors may feel that management have an attitude (problem) but this family fiefdom has been here forever.

**354** **Kay's Bar** 39 Jamaica St, off India St in the New Town. Go on an afternoon
**B2** when gentlemen of a certain age talk politics, history and rugby over pints of
real ale. The Poirot-moustached barman patiently serves. All red and black
and vaguely distinguished bar with a tiny snug – The Library. Comfort food
simmers in the window (lunch only). Till midnight (11pm Sun). (333/UNIQUE
PUBS)

**355** **Cask & Barrel** 115 Broughton St. Wall-to-wall distressed wood, gr selection
**D1** of real ales and mixed crowd at the foot of groovy Broughton St. 'Cept here
they prefer a good pint & the football. Till 12.30am Sun-Wed, 1am Thu-Sat.

**356** **Cloisters** 26 Brougham St, Tollcross. Nine real ales on tap (& 70 whiskies)
**B5** in this simple and unfussy bar with its wooden floors and laid-back app.
Same owners as Bow Bar (*see above*). Good pub grub at lunchtimes, bar clos-
es 12midnight (12.30am Fri-Sat).

**357** **Caley Sample Room** 5-8 Angle Park Terr. The CSR sells all the expected
**xA4** Caledonian real ales from nearby brewery and a couple of guests besides. A
neighbourhood bar most of the time, a haven for home and away fans before
and after games at Tynecastle/ Murrayfield. Basic pub lunches Mon-Fri, drink
served till 12midnight Sun-Thu, 1am Fri-Sat.

**358** **Black Bull** Grassmarket, below the Castle (N side). Vast woody cavern of a
**C4** pub with ales, ok food & big-screen sports. Deuchars, Caledonian 80/- & 5
guests. Daily till 1am.

# Pubs With Good Food

*Also see* Gastropubs, *p. 34-5. These below are not so high-falutin foodwise, but nevertheless are worth going to for food as well as drink.*

**359** **✓ The Compass** 554 1979. 44 Queen Charlotte St, corner of Constitution
**xE1** St opp Leith Police Station. This 'Bar & Grill' is a popular Leith haunt, maybe missed by uptown grazers. Stone & woody look with mix-match furniture; food better & more ambitious than you might first think. Staples & some Scottish cheeses. Bar kicks in later. 7 days, lunch & LO 9pm.

**360** **Starbank Inn** 552 4141. 64 Laverockbank Rd, the seafront rd in Newhaven.
**xB1** Long-est family pub with real ales (348/REAL ALE PUBS) and excl value food, with big helpings. Gr seafood salad as well as mince 'n' tatties on special. 7 days lunch and dinner LO 9pm (Sun all day menu). Bar 11pm, midnight w/ends.

**361** **Old Chain Pier** 552 1233. 1 Trinity Cres, on the Forth just W of Newhaven
**xB1** Harbour. Rt on the waterfront nr Starbank (above), both nr Ocean Terminal. Well-kept real ale, gr bar snacks and decent-value bar meals. Some delays at busy times so be prepared to watch the sunset. LO food 9.45pm. Bar 11pm, 12midnight Thu-Sat.

**362** **Sheep's Heid** 656 6951. Causeway, Duddingston Village. An 18th-century
**xE5** coaching inn 10km from centre behind Arthur's Seat and reached most easily through the Queen's Park. OK grub incl alfresco dining when poss. The village and the nearby wildfowl loch should be strolled around if you have time. Gr atmos & food improved '05. Food Lunch & 6.30-8pm, bar till 12.

**363** **Cramond Inn, Cramond Village** 336 2035. Go west and down to the sea.
**xA3** Appeal mainly as part of a stroll on the front (411/WALKS) but low ceilings, log fires, real ales make this a good escape from the city. Lotsa fish. Can snack or pack. Lunch and LO 9.30pm, 7 days. Bar open 11pm (12 w/ends).

**364** **Bennet's** 229 5143. 8 Leven St, next to the King's Theatre. An Edin stand-
**xB5** by, listed for several reasons (328/UNIQUE PUBS), not least for its honest-to-goodness (and cheap) pub lunch. À la carte (sausage, fish, steak pie, etc.) and daily specials under the enormous mirrors. Lunch & till 8.30pm (not Sun).

**365** **The Abbotsford** 225 5276. 3 Rose St. A doughty remnant of Rose St drink-
**C3** ing days of yore, and still the best pub lunch nr Princes St. Fancier than it used to be but still grills and bread & butter pudding. Huge portions. Restau upstairs serves food in evening too - LO 9.45pm. Bar till 11pm. Cl Sun.

**366** **Ecco Vino** 225 1441. 19 Cockburn St. Discreet frontage in st strewn with
**D3** pierced youth. A narrow rm where wines are supped. Med menu from tiny gantry kitchen with imaginative soups, spags & tarts. How do they do it? Food noon-10pm, bar til 12, 1am Fri/Sat.

# The Best Places To Drink Outdoors

**367** **The (Café) Hub**  473 2067. Castlehill. The café-bar of the International
**C4** Festival Centre much improved for food with & a gr enclosed terrace for people-watching. Brollies & heaters extend the possibilities.

**368** **The Shore**  553 5080. 3 The Shore, Leith. Excellent place to eat (147/GAS-
**xE1** TROPUBS), some tables just o/side the door, but it's fine to wander over to the
dock on the other side of the st and sit with your legs over the edge. Do try
not to fall in. From 11am daily.

**369** **The Waterfront**  554 7427. 1c Dock Pl. Another v good Leith eaterie
**xE1** (151/GASTROPUBS) but with waterside tables and adj pontoon for those who
fancy a float. Gr wine list. From 12noon Mon-Sat, 12.30pm Sun.

**370** **Pear Tree**  667 7533. 38 W Nicholson St. Adj to parts of Edin Univ so real
**D5** student style with big (surprisingly floral) beer gdn and refectory-style food.
From noon Mon-Sat, 12.30pm Sun. Round the corner on main drag, the
opportunistically named **Human Be-In** spills out onto the wide pavement.

**371** **The Outhouse**  557 6668. 12a Broughton St Lane. Large enclosed patio out
**D2** back, home to summer Sun afternoon barbecues. No view except of other
people. (378/COOL BARS)

**372** **The Pleasance**  In The Pleasance. Open during the Festival only, this is one
**E4** of the major Fringe venues, and has a large open courtyard. If you're here,
you're on the Fringe, so to speak.

**373** **Cargo**  659 7880. 129 Fountainbridge at the so-called 'Edinburgh Quay'.
**A5** Lofty emporium pub with over-ambitious menu, mainly distinguished by
outdoor seating on the basin of the Caledonian Canal – a surprising waterside spot in the city centre.

**374** **The Street**  556 4272. Corner of Picardy Pl & Broughton St – gr people-
**D2** watching potential. See 379/COOL BARS.

General locations: **Greenside Pl** (**Theatre Royal** and **Café Habana**), bars
in **The Grassmarket**, and **Negociants** and **Assembly** on **Lothian St**. All
make a stab at pavement café culture when the sun's out.

# Cool Bars

**375** ✓ ✓ **Dragonfly** 228 4543. West Port, the W extension of the
**B4** Grassmarket. Discreet frontage but you enter a more beautiful, more stylish world where alcohol is treated like food in a fine-dining restau & cocktails are king. Lofty rm with mezzanine. Food on way at TGP. Not too many distractions from the aesthetic. 7 days till midnight.

**376** ✓ **Opal Lounge** 226 2275. 51a George St. Basement in Edin's fashion
**B3** mile for latest and most ambitious 'lifestyle' project from the indigo (yard) stable (see below). Sunken and sexy lounges incl dancefloor and restau (fusion menu tho not what they do best). Gr staff know how to serve cocktails. Big door presence. Wills with St Andrews mates was once a regular. Admn and queue after 10pm. Open till 3am 7 days (food till 10pm).

**377** **Villager** 226 2781. 50 George IV Br. Nr Univ & Nat Library a funked-up, laid-
**D3** back place to hang out. DJs (Fri/Sat), reasonable pub food till 9.30 but mainly the right faces in a photo from 2005. Bar till 1am.

**378** **The Outhouse** 557 6668. 12a Broughton St Lane. Happily mixed & unobtru-
**D2** sive modern bar off Broughton St 'in the lane' off the Pink Triangle. Modish food 12noon-7pm (4pm w/ends) for self-conscious business diners & a regular monthly Sun barbecue on the patio (not the greatest of views). Till 1am.

**379** **The Street** 556 4272. 2 Picardy Pl. Corner glass box at the top of Broughton
**D2** St at central crossroads in the Pink Triangle; so gay-friendly. Gr people-watching spot (outside tables). DJs w/ends. Madame (Trendy) Wendy & gals in charge. 7 days till 1am.

**380** **indigo (yard)** 220 5603. 7 Charlotte Lane, off Queensferry St. Tucked away
**A3** in the W End, this long-est spacious nineties-thing café-bar offers exposed brickwork, balcony tables, booths and babes in blue of both genders serving good food and drink. More Med than Mex cuisine with flexible menu, but poss too loud later on for serious dining (153/GASTROPUBS). Bar till 1am daily. Same people have **Opal Lounge** (*above*) & **Rick's** (*below*).

**381** **Rick's** 622 7800. 55a Frederick St. New Town variant of the above. Another
**B2** café-bar-restau but this time also with rms (79/HOTELS). Same problem with the eating experience here as the others viz too much noise from the bar, tho prob best on this page. Bar service good & they know how to make cocktails. Rocks from 10 onwards (till 1am). Also good for b/fast.

**382** **Left Bank** 445 2977. 37 Guthrie St at the bend of the st in a hidden corner,
**D4** the v boho, Festival Fringe-like Left Bank. Gr atmos. Live music in cavernous 'Alba' room. Cool late-night people. 7 days 11am-3am. Go dig!

**383** **The Pond** Corner of Bath Rd & Salamander St, Leith. Turn rt at foot of
**xE1** Constitution St past the warehouses. So cool it's the opposite of a style bar, a million miles from George St (& hard to find). Run by the people who do clubs like Soft, Edinburgh Beige Cricket Team and the fanzine, *Shavers Weekly*, The Pond is where you'll find the people who don't want to be cool; they want to watch fish & swing in the basket chair. Open when you are.

**384** **Boda Bar** Corner of Leith Walk & Lorne St. Swedish import unlikely but v
**xE1** welcome on the Walk. Boda a small village in N of Sweden, & this has village
**B1** feel. Friendly staff. Well-chosen fare incl snax (moose sausages anyone?). Sister bar **Sofi's** in Henderson St, Leith. 7 days 1am (Sun midnight).

**385** **Iglu** Jamaica St off Howe St in the New Town. Surprisingly cool bar in con-
**B2** servative territory. Handily open late. Small upstairs garret with nice fish tank. Very Edinburgh, kind of lovely! 4pm-1am (Fri/Sat from 12).

**386** **Brass Monkey** 14 Drummond St. Light-touch conversion of former leg-
**E4** endary pub with younger/studenty crowd than glory days. Backroom bedouin boudoir full of cushions to lounge & big screen (movies at 3pm every day) – can hire for private functions. 7 days. LO 12.45am.

**387** **City Café** 220 0127. 19 Blair St. A true original that went from *the* hippest,
**D4** to nowhere, and now back again with cool night people. Buzzing at the w/end, downstairs the DJs play all kinds depending on the night. Pool tables never stop. 11am-1am daily. then Sundays: 309/SUN BREAKFAST.

# The Main Attractions

**388**
**B4**
✓ ✓ ✓ **Edinburgh Castle** 225 9846. Go to Princes St and look up. Extremely busy AYR and yet the city's must-see main attraction does not disappoint. St Margaret's 12th-century chapel is simple and beautiful, the rolling history lesson that leads up to the display of Scotland's crown jewels is fascinating; the Stone of Destiny is a big deal to the Scots (though others may not see why). And, ultimately, the Scottish National War Memorial is one of the most genuinely affecting places in the country – a simple, dignified testament to shared pain and loss. Last ticket 45 min before closing. Apr-Sep 9.30am-6pm, Oct-Mar 9.30am-5pm. HS

**389**
Map 10
**P25**
✓ ✓ ✓ **The Forth Bridge** S Queensferry, 20km W of Edin via A90. First turning for S Queensferry from dual carriageway; don't confuse with signs for road br. Or train from Waverley to Dalmeny, and walk 1km. Knocking on now and showing its age (& true to legend takes forever to paint), the br was 100 in 1990. But still ... Can't see too many private finance initiative wallahs rushing in to do anything of similar scope these days. And who would have the vision? An international symbol of Scotland, it should be seen, but go to the N side, S Queensferry's v crowded & sadly, very tacky these days (& shame on Tesco for spoiling the view from the road bridge approach). There is a good hotel restau in South Q (114/HOTELS OUTSIDE TOWN) with views of the bridge.

**390**
**xA4**
✓ ✓ ✓ **Edinburgh Zoo** 334 9171. Corstorphine Rd. 4km W of Princes St, buses from Princes St Gdns side. Whatever you think of zoos (see *Life of Pi*, the 2003 Booker prize winner), this one is highly respected and its serious zoology is still fun for kids (organised activities in Jul/Aug). The penguins waddle out at 2.15pm daily over summer months, and the sad, accusing eyes of the wolves connect with onlookers in a profoundly disconcerting manner. But there are many animals here to love and cherish. Open AYR 7 days, 9am-6pm Apr-Sept, 9am-4.30pm Nov-Feb, 9am-5pm Mar & Oct. (1727/KIDS) ADMN

**391**
**xF3**
✓ ✓ **Palace of Holyroodhouse** 556 5100. Foot of the Royal Mile. The Queen's N Brit time-share – she's here for a wee while late June/early July every yr. Large parts of the palace are dull (Duke of Hamilton's loo, Queen's wardrobes) and only a dozen or so rms are open, most dating from 17th century but a couple from the earlier 16th-century bit. Lovely cornices abound. Anomalous Stuart features, adj 12th-century abbey ruins quite interesting. Apr-Oct: 9.30am-5.15pm (last ticket), daily. Nov-Mar: 9.30am-3.45pm (last ticket) daily. Also... HS
**The Queen's Gallery** Recent addition to the foot of the Royal Mile (opp the Parliament building) with separate entrance & ticket from Holyroodhouse. By architect Ben Tindall (who also did the Hub at the top of the Royal Mile – this is better). Beautiful, contemp setting for changing exhibs from Royal Collection every 6 months which incl art, ceramics, tapestries, etc. Shop stuffed with monarchist mementoes. 7 days 9.30-6 (cl 4.30pm in wint).

**392**
**C4**
**D4**
**D3**
**E3**
**F3**
✓ ✓ **The Royal Mile** The High St, the medieval main thoroughfare of the capital following the trail from the volcanic crag of Castle Rock and connecting the 2 landmarks above. Heaving during the Festival but if on a winter's night you chance by with a frost settling on the cobbles and there's no one around, it's magical. Always interesting with its wynds and closes (Dunbar's Close, Whitehorse Close, the secret gdn opp Huntly House), but lots of tacky tartan shops too. Central block cl to traffic during Festival Fringe to create best street performance space in UK. See it on a walking tour – there are several esp at night (ghost/ghouls/witches, etc.). Mercat Tours (557 6464), Witchery (225 6745) and City of the Dead (225 9044) are pretty good. **Mary King's Close** is part of a medieval st actually under the Royal Mile. Tours daily 10am-9pm (last tour), till 4pm Nov-Mar. Enter thro' Warriston's Close nr City Chambers. **Scottish Poetry Library** is in Crichton's Close on right betw St Mary's St & the Parliament. Gr collections, lovely contemplative space. Endorses Edin's status as City of Literature. Mon-Fri 11am-6pm, Sat 1-5pm. Cl Sun.

**393** ✓✓ **The Scottish Parliament**  Front of the Royal Mile adj Holyrood
**F3**  (above) & Our Dynamic Earth (below). Designed by Catalan architect Enric Morales who died long before it opened, this building has been
mired in controversy since first First Minister Donald Dewar laid the first
stone. Opened finally after huge cost overruns in 2004, it is loved & hated in
equal measure but should not be missed. Guided tours & ticketed access to
the Debating Chamber. Unquestionably the finest modern building in the city
(in my view and others – it won the 2005 Stirling Prize, the UK's premier
architectural award). 0845 278 1999 or 348 5000 for details.

**394** ✓✓ **Royal Museum**  247 4422. Chambers St. From the skeletons to
**D4**  archaeological artefacts, stuffed animal habitats to all that we have
done. Humankind and its interests encapsulated (and displayed) here.
Building designed by Captain Francis Fowkes, Royal Engineers, and completed in 1888. Impressive galleried atrium (with coffee shop) often hosts dinners
and parties. Mon-Sat 10am-5pm, Sun 12noon-5pm. Open till 8pm on Tue.
FREE

**395** ✓✓ **Museum of Scotland**  247 4422. Chambers St. The story of
**D4**  Scotland from geological beginnings to Kirsty Wark's Saab
Convertible, all housed in a marvellous, honey-sandstone building by Gordon
Benson and Alan Forsyth. Opened in Dec '98, both it and the Royal (above)
had admissions abolished in April 2001. World-class space with resonant
treasures like St Filian's Crozier and the Monymusk Reliquary, said to contain
bits of St Columba. Early peoples to famous recent ones. Mon-Sat 10am-
5pm, Sun 12noon-5pm. Open till 8pm on Tue. **Tower Restaurant** (own
entrance) is on the top floor (121/RESTAURANTS). FREE

**396** ✓✓ **Our Dynamic Earth**  550 7800. Foot of Holyrood Rd. Edin's
**F3**  Millennium Dome, an interactive museum/visitor attraction, made
with Millennium money and a huge success when it opened summer '99 tho
a little less dynamic than it was. Now within the orbit and campus of the
Parliament building. Salisbury Crags rise above. Vast restau, & outside an
amphitheatre. Apr-Dec: 10am-6pm daily. Jan-Mar: 10am-5pm Wed-Sun. Last
admn 1 hr 10 mins before closing. ADMN

**397** ✓✓ **National Gallery Of Scotland**  624 6200. The Mound.
**C3**  Neoclassical buildings housing a superb collection of Old Masters in
a series of hushed salons. Many are world famous, but you don't emerge
goggle-eyed as you do from the National in London – more quietly elevated.
Many blockbuster exhibs in the pipeline. The building in front, the **Royal
Scottish Academy**, reopened in Aug '03 after a lengthy refurb. Daily 10am-
5pm, Thurs 7pm. Extended hours during Festival. FREE

**398** ✓✓ **Royal Yacht Britannia**  555 5566. Ocean Dr, Leith, in the docks,
**xE1**  enter by Commercial St at end of Gr Junction St. Berthed outside
Conran's shopping mall, the Ocean Terminal (incl famously unpopulated
shopping experience & 3 disappointing Conran food outlets). Done with rul-
ing the waves, the royal yacht has found a permanent home as a tourist
attraction (and prestigious corporate night out). Close up, the Art Deco lines
are surprisingly attractive, while the interior was one of the sets for our best-
ever soap opera. Apr-Sept 9.30am-4.30pm; Jan-Mar & Oct-Dec 10am-
3.30pm; Apr-May 9.30am-4pm. Booking advised in Aug. ADMN

**399** ✓ **Royal Commonwealth Pool**  667 7211. Dalkeith Rd. Hugely success-
**xE5**  ful pool complex which includes a 50m main pool, a gym, sauna/ steam
rm/suntan suites, children's pool & play area, and a jungle of flumes. Goes
like a fair, morning to night. Some people find the water overtreated and over
noisy, but Edin has many good pools to choose from; this is the one that
young folk prefer. Some lane swimming. Mon-Fri 6am-9.30pm (cl 9-10am
Wed), Sat-Sun 10am-9pm. Sat-Sun 10am-4.30pm.

**400** ✓✓✓ **Rosslyn Chapel, Roslin**  The ancient chapel 12km S of city,
**xE5**  made famous recently by the world bestseller, *The Da Vinci
Code*. Report: 1881/CHURCHES.

# The Other Attractions

**401**
**xB1**
✓ ✓ ✓ **Royal Botanic Garden** 552 7171. Inverleith Row, 3km Princes St. Enter from Inverleith Row or Arboretum Pl. 70 acres of ornamental gdns, trees & walkways; a joy in every season. Tropical plant houses, landscaped rock & heath gdn & space just to wander. Chinese Gdn coming on nicely, precocious squirrels everywhere. The 'Botanics' have talks, guided tours, events (info 248 2968). They also look after other imp outstanding gdns in Scotland. Gallery with occasional exhibs & café with outdoor terrace for serene afternoon teas (283/BEST TEAROOMS). Total integrity & the natural high & National Biodiversity Interpretation Centre. Open 7 days Nov-Feb 10am-4pm, Mar & Oct 10-6pm, Apr-Sept 10-7pm.    ADM for Glasshouses, otherwise FREE

**402**
**C2**
✓ ✓ **Scottish National Portrait Gallery** 624 6200. 1 Queen St. Sir Robert Rowand Anderson's fabulous & custom-built neo-Gothic pile holds paintings & photos of the good, great & merely famous. Danny McGrain hangs out next to Queen Mum and Nasmyth's familiar Burns pic is here. Good venue for photo exhibs, beautiful atrium with star-flecked ceiling & frieze of (mainly) men in Scottish history from a Stone-Age chief to Carlyle. Splendid. Gr café (273/BEST TEAROOMS). Mon-Sat 10am-5pm, 7pm on Thurs.    FREE

**403**
**xA3**
✓ **Scottish National Gallery of Modern Art** 624 6200. Belford Rd. Betw Queensferry Rd & Dean Village (nice to walk through). Best to start from Palmerston Pl & keep left or see below (Dean Gallery). Former school with permanent collection from Impressionism to Hockney & the Scottish painters alongside. An intimate space where you can fall in love (with paintings or each other). Important temporary exhibs. Excellent café (272/BEST TEAROOMS). Charles Jencks art in the landscape piece outside is stunning. Mon-Sat 10am-5pm, 7pm on Thurs. Extended hrs during Festival.    FREE

**404**
**xA3**
**Dean Gallery** 624 6200. Belford Rd. Across (busy) rd from GOMA. Relatively new addition to Edin art and life – sexy, intimate spaces, communal coffee shop, gdns to wander. Superb 20thC collection; many surreal moments. Gr way to app both galleries is by Water of Leith Walkway (409/WALKS IN THE CITY). Mon-Sat 10am-5pm, 7pm on Thurs.    FREE

**405**
**E3**
**Museum of Childhood** 529 4142. 42 High St. Local authority-run shrine to the dreamstuff of tender days where you'll find everything from tin soldiers to Lady Penelope on video. Full of adults saying, 'I had one of them!' Child-size mannequins in upper gallery can be v spooky if you're up there alone. Mon-Sat 10am-5pm. July & Aug Sun 12-5pm. (1727/KIDS)    FREE

**406**
**D4**
**St Giles' Cathedral** 225 9442. Royal Mile. Not a cathedral really, although it was once – the High Kirk of Edinburgh, Church of Scotland central and heart of the city since the 9thC. The building is mainly medieval with Norman fragments, all encased in a Georgian exterior. Lorimer's oddly ornate & chapel & the 'big new organ' are impressive. Simple, austere design and bronze of John Knox set the tone historically. Holy Communion daily & other regular services. Atmos coffee shop in the crypt. Summer: Mon-Fri 9am-7pm, Sat 9am-5pm, Sun 1-5pm. Winter: Mon-Sat 9am-5pm, Sun 1-5pm.    FREE

**407**
**A3**
**The Georgian House** 225 2160. 7 Charlotte Sq. Built in the 1790s, this town house is full of period furniture and fittings. Not many rms, but the dining-rm and kitchen are drop-dead gorgeous – you want to eat and cook there. Delightful ladies from the National Trust for Scotland answer your queries. Apr-Oct 10am-5pm, Mar, Nov & Dec 11am-3pm. Cl Jan & Feb.    NTS

**408**
**xA1**
**Lauriston Castle** 336 2060. Cramond Rd S. 9km W of centre by A90, turn rt for Cramond. Elegant architecture & gracious living. Largely Jacobean tower house set in tranquil grounds o/looking the Forth. The liveability of the house & preoccupations of the Reid family make you wish you could poke around but exquisite decorative pieces & furniture mean it's guided tours only. Continue to Cramond for the air (411/WALKS IN THE CITY). Apr-Oct 11.20am, 12.20pm, 2.20pm, 3.20pm, 4.20pm. Cl Fri. Nov-Mar 2.20pm & 3.20pm w/ends only.    ADMN

**Arthur's Seat** Report: 410/WALKS IN THE CITY.

**The Pentlands** Report: 413/WALKS OUTSIDE THE CITY.

**The Scott Monument/Calton Hill** Report: 432/430/BEST VIEWS.

**Newhailes House** Report 1856/COUNTRY HOUSES.

# The Best Walks In The City

*See p. 13 for walk codes.*

**409**
**xA2**
**A2**
**A1**
**xA1**

✓ ✓ **Water Of Leith**  The indefatigable wee river that runs from the Pentlands through the city and into the docks at Leith can be walked for most of its length, though obviously not by any circular route. (A) The longest section from Balerno 12km o/side the city, through Colinton Dell to the Tickled Trout pub car park on Lanark Rd (4km from city centre). The 'Dell' itself is a popular glen walk (1-2km). All in all a superb urban walk. The Water of Leith Visitor Centre opp the Tickled Trout is worth a look. 0131 455 7367. Open 7 days Apr-Sept 10am-4pm, Wed-Sun; Oct-Mar 10am-4pm.

**START**  (A) A70 to Currie, Juniper Green, Balerno; park by High School. (B) Dean Village to Stockbridge: enter through a marked gate opp Menzies Belford Hotel on Belford Rd (combine with a visit to the art galleries) (403/404/ATTRACTIONS). (C) Warriston, through the spooky old graveyard, to The Shore in Leith (plenty of pubs to repair to). Enter by going to the end of the cul-de-sac at Warriston Cres in Canonmills; climb up the bank and turn left. Most of the Walkway (A, B and C) is cinder track & good cycling.            12KM (OR LESS) XCIRC BIKE 1-A-1

**410**
**xF3**

✓ ✓ **Arthur's Seat**  Of many walks, a good circular one taking in the wilder bits, the lochs and gr views (431/BEST VIEWS) starts from St Margaret's Loch at the far end of the park from Holyrood Palace. Leaving the car park, skirt the loch and head for the ruined chapel. After 250m in a dry valley, the buttress of the main summit rears above you on the rt. Keeping it to the rt, ascend over a saddle joining the main route from Dunsapie Loch which appears below on the left. Crow Hill is the other peak crowned by a triangular cairn – both can be slippery when wet. From Arthur's Seat head for and traverse the long steep incline of Salisbury Crags. Paths parallel to the edge lead back to the chapel. Just cross the rd by the Palace & head up. No mt bikes. For info on the Ranger service & special events thro' the year, tel 0131 652 8150.

**PARK**  There are car parks beside the loch and in front of the palace (paths start here too, across the rd).        5-8KM CIRC MT BIKE (RESTRICTED ACCESS) 2-B-2

**START**  Enter park at palace at foot of the High St. Cross main road or follow for 1km; the loch is on the rt.

**411**
**xA1**

**Cramond**  This is the charming village (tho not the suburb) on the Forth at the mouth of the Almond with a variety of gr walks. (A) To the rt along the 'prom'; the trad seaside stroll. (B) Across the causeway at low tide to Cramond Island (1km). Best to follow the tide out; this allows 4 hrs (tides are posted). People have been known to stay the night in summer, but this is discouraged. (C) Enter estate by the East Craigie gate to west of Cramond Brig Hotel (at TGP the tiny passenger boat which used to cross the mouth of the Almond, has stopped running, but a petition is underway to resurrect it) then follow coastal path to Dalmeny House which is open to the public in the afternoons (July & Aug, Sun-Tues); or walk all the way to S Queensferry (8km). (D) Past the boathouse and up the R Almond Heritage Trail which goes eventually to the Cramond Brig Hotel on the A90 and thence to the old airport (3-8km). Though it goes through suburbs and seems to be on the flight path of the London shuttle, the Almond is a real river with a charm and ecosystem of its own. The Cramond Gallery Bistro (312 6555) on the riverside is not a bad wee bistro – its gr cakes await your return. 7 days. **Cramond Inn** (363/PUB FOOD) is another gr place to recharge.      1/3/8KM XCIRC BIKE 1-A-1

**START**  Leave centre by Queensferry Rd (A90), then rt following signs for Cramond. Cramond Rd N leads to Cramond Glebe Rd; go to end.

**PARK**  Large car park off Cramond Glebe Rd to rt. Walk 100m to sea.

**412**
**xA4**

**Corstorphine Hill**  W of centre, a knobbly hilly area of birch, beech and oak, criss-crossed by trails. A perfect place for the contemplation of life's little mysteries and mistakes. Or walking the dog. It has a radio mast, a ruined tower, a boundary with the wild plains of Africa (at the zoo) and a vast redundant nuclear shelter that nobody's supposed to know about. See how many you can spot. If it had a tearoom in an old pavilion, it would be perfect.

**START**  Leave centre by Queensferry Rd and 8km out turn left at lights, signed Clermiston. The hill is on your left for the next 2km.

**PARK**  Park where safe, on or nr this rd (Clermiston Rd).  1-7KM CIRC XBIKE 1-A-1

# Easy Walks Outside The City

**413**
Map 10
P26

✓ **The Pentlands** A serious range of hills rising to almost 600m, remote in parts and offering some fine walking. There are many paths up the various tops and round the lochs and reservoirs. (A) A good start in town is made by going off the bypass at Colinton, follow signs for Colinton Village, then the left fork up Woodhall Rd. Second left up Bonaly Rd (signed Bonaly Scout Camp). Drive/walk as far as you can (2km) and park by the gate leading to the hill proper where there is a map showing routes. The path to Glencorse is one of the classic Pentland walks. (B) Most walks start from signposted gateways on the A702 Biggar Rd. There are starts at Boghall (5km after Hillend ski slope); on the long straight stretch before Silverburn (a 10km path to Balerno); from Habbie's Howe about 18km from town; and from the village of Carlops, 22km from town. (C) The most popular start is probably from the VC behind the Flotterstone Inn, also on the A702, 14km from town (decent pub lunch and 6-10pm, all day w/ends); trailboard and ranger service. The remoter tops around Loganlea reservoir are worth the extra mile.

1-20KM CAN BE CIRC MTBIKE 2-B-2

**414** **Hermitage of Braid** Strictly speaking, still in town, but a real sense of
Map 10 being in a country glen and from the windy tops of the Braid Hills there are
Q25 some marvellous views back over the city. Main track along the burn is easy to follow and you eventually come to Hermitage House info centre; any paths ascending to the rt take you to the ridge of Blackford Hill. In winter, there's a gr sledging place over the first br up to the left and across the main rd.
**START** Blackford Glen Rd. Go S on Mayfield to main T-jnct with Liberton Rd, turn rt (signed Penicuik) then hard rt.     1-4KM CAN BE CIRC XBIKE 1-A-1

**415** **Roslin Glen** Spiritual, historical, enchanting, now v famous with the chapel
Map 10 (1915/CHURCHES), a ruined castle and woodland walks along the R Esk.
Q26 **START** A701 from Mayfield or Newington (or bypass, t/off Penicuik, A702 then fork left on A703 to Roslin). Some parking at chapel (1881/CHURCHES), 500m from corner of Main St/Manse Rd, or follow B7003 to Rosewell (also marked Rosslynlee Hospital) and 1km from village the main car park is to the left.     1-8km XCIRC BIKE 1-A-1

**416** **Almondell** A country park to W of city (18km) nr (and one of the best things
Map 10 about) Livingston. A deep, peaceful woody cleft with easy paths and riverine
P25 meadows. Fine for kids, lovers and dog walkers. VC with teashop. Trails marked.
**START** Best app from Edin by A71 via Sighthill. After Wilkieston, turn rt for Camps (B7015) then follow signs. Or A89 to Broxburn past start of M8. Follow signs from Broxburn.     2-8KM XCIRC BIKE 1-A-1

**417** **Beecraigs And Cockleroy Hill** Another country park S of Linlithgow with
Map 10 trails and clearings in mixed woods, a deer farm and a fishing loch. Gr adven-
N25 ture playground for kids. Best is the climb and extraordinary view from Cockleroy Hill, far better than you'd expect for the effort – from Ben Lomond to the Bass Rock; and the gunge of Grangemouth in the sky to the E.
**START** M90 to Linlithgow (26km), through town and left on Preston Rd. Go on 4km, park is signed, but for hill you don't need to take the left turn. The hill, and nearest car park to it, are on the rt.     2-8KM CIRC MTBIKE 1-A-1

**418** **Borthwick and Crichton Castles** Takes in 2 impressive castles, the first a
Map 10 posh hotel (113/HOTELS O/SIDE TOWN) and the other an imposing ruin on a ridge
Q26 o/looking the Tyne. A walk through dramatic Border Country steeped in lore. From Borthwick foll old railway line. The castle you're going to is always in view. Nice picnic spots nr Crichton.
**START** From Borthwick: A7 S for 16km, past Gorebridge, left at N Middleton; signed. From Crichton: A68 almost to Pathhead, signed then 3km.

7KM XCIRC XBIKE 1-B-2

# Woodland Walks Near Edinburgh

**419**
Map 10
P27

✓ **Dawyck Gardens** nr Stobo 01721 760254. 10km W of Peebles on B712 Moffat rd. Outstn of the Edin Botanics; a 'recent' acquisition, though tree planting here goes back 300 yrs. Sloping grounds around the Scrape Burn which trickles into the Tweed. Landscaped woody pathways for meditative walks. Famous for shrubs and blue Himalayan poppies. Apr-Sept 10am-6pm, Mar & Oct 10am-5pm, Feb 10am-4pm. 7 days. (Cl 17 Nov-13 Feb)     ADMN

**420**
Map 10
Q25

✓ **Dalkeith Country Park** 15km SE by A68. The wooded policies of Dalkeith House; enter at end of Main St. Along the river banks and under these stately deciduous trees, carpets of bluebells, daffs and snowdrops, primroses and wild garlic according to season. Most extensive preserved ancient oak forest in S Scotland. Excl adventure playground. Rangers 654 1666.     ADMN

**421**
Map 10
R26

**Humbie Woods** 25km SE by A68 t/off at Fala. Follow signs for church. Most open woods (beech) beyond car park. The churchyard is as reassuring a place to be buried as you could wish for; if you're set on cremation, come here and think of earth. Follow path from churchyard wall past cottage. After-hrs the sprites and the spirits must have a hell of a time.

**422**
Map 10
R25

**Smeaton Nursery and Gardens** East Linton 01620 860501. 2km from village on N Berwick rd (signed Smeaton). Up a drive in an old estate is this walled gdn going back to the early 19th century. An additional pleasure is the Lake Walk halfway down the drive through a small gate in the woods. A 1km stroll round a secret finger lake in magnificent woodland. Gdn hrs Mon-Sat 9.30am-4.30pm, Sun from 10.30am; phone for wint hrs. (2220/GARDEN CENTRES)

**423**
Map 10
R25

**Woodhall Dean** nr Dunbar From Spott r/bout on A1 by Dunbar, go to spotless Spott village then follow old road sign for Woodhall & Elmscleugh (take left halfway down main rd thro' vill, uphill then 3km. After another old roadsign to Innerwick, it's 200m. You'll see a red gash in the hillside before 'The Ford'). Damp walk to ancient oak woodland. Not many people!

**424**
Map 10
Q26

**Vogrie Country Park** nr Gorebridge 25km S by A7 then B6372 6km from Gorebridge. Small country park well organised for 'recreational pursuits'. 9-hole golf course, tearoom and country ranger staff. Busy on Sun, but otherwise a corral of countryside on the v edge of town.

**425**
Map 10
Q27

**Cardrona Forest/Glentress** nr Peebles 40km S to Peebles, 8km E on B7062 and similar distance on A72. Cardrona on same rd as Kailzie Gdn. Tearoom (Apr-Oct). Forestry Commission woodlands so mostly regimented firs, but Scots pine and deciduous trees up the burn. Glentress (on A72 to Innerleithen ) is mt bike central, but gr track also to walk. Consult at **The Hub** (01721 721736) by car park (1433/GREAT CAFÉS). See 2103/CYCLING.

# The Best Beaches

**426**
Map 10
**R25**
✓ **Seacliff** The best: least crowded/littered; perfect for picnics, beachcombing and gazing into rock pools. Harbour good for swimming. 50km from Edin, off the A198 out of N Berwick, 3km after Tantallon Castle (1824/RUINS). At a bend in the rd and a farm (Auldhame) is an unsigned rd off to the left. 2km on there's a barrier, costing £2 (2 x £1 coins) for cars. Car park 1km then walk. From A1, take E Linton t/off, go through Whitekirk towards N Berwick, then same.

**427**
Map 10
**Q25**
**Portobello** Edin's town beach, 8km from centre by London Rd. When sunny – chips, lager, bad ice cream. When miserable – soulful dog walkers. Arcades, mini-funfair, long prom and pool (439/SPORTS FACS). But with more summers like 2005, Portobello is set to come back. **Dalriada** pub is gr.

**428**
Map 10
**R25**
**Yellowcraigs** Nearest decent beach (35km). A1 or bypass, then A198 coast rd. Left o/side Dirleton for 2km, park and walk 100m across links to fairly clean strand and sea. Gets busy, but big enough to share. Hardly anyone swims, but you can. Scenic. **Gullane Bents**, a sweep of beach, is nearby and reached from village main st. Connects westwards with **Aberlady Reserve**.

**429**
Map 10
**P25**
**Silver Sands** Aberdour Over Forth Br on edge of charming Fife vill (1601/COASTAL VILLS). Can go by train from Edin. Caff and cliff walk. Those silver sands.

# The Best Views Of The City

**430**
**E2**
✓ ✓ **Calton Hill** Gr view of the city easily gained by walking up from E end of Princes St by Waterloo Pl, to the end of the buildings and then up stairs on the left. The City Observatory and the Greek-style folly lend an elegant backdrop to a panorama (unfolding as you walk round) where the view up Princes St and the sweep of the Forth estuary are particularly fine. At night, the city twinkles. Popular cruising area for gays – take care if you do.

**431**
**xF3**
✓ ✓ **Arthur's Seat** W of city centre. Best app through Holyrood Park from foot of Canongate by Holyrood Palace. The igneous core of an extinct volcano with the precipitous sill of Salisbury Crags presiding over the city and offering fine views for the fit. Top is 251m; on a clear day you can see 100km. Surprisingly wild considering proximity to city. (410/WALKS IN THE CITY)

**432**
**C3**
**Scott Monument** 529 4068. East Princes St. Design inspiration for Thunderbird 3. This 1844 Gothic memorial to one of Scotland's best-kent literary sons rises 61.5m above the main drag and provides scope for the vertiginous to come to terms with their affliction. 287 steps mean it's no cakewalk; narrow stairwells weed out claustrophobics too. Those who make it to the top are rewarded with fine views. Underneath, a statue of the mournful Sir Walter gazes across at Jenners. Apr-Sept Mon-Sat 9am-6pm, Sun 10am-6pm; Oct-Mar, Mon-Sat 9am-3pm, Sun 10am-3pm. ADMN

**433**
**C4**
**Camera Obscura** 226 3709. Castlehill, Royal Mile. At v top of st nr castle entrance, a tourist attraction that, surprisingly, has been there for over a century. You ascend through a shop, photography exhibs and interactive gallery to the viewing area where a continuous stream of small groups are shown the effect of the giant revolving periscope thingie. All Edin life is visible – amazing how much fun can be had from a pin-hole camera with a focal length of 8.6m. Apr-Oct 9.30am-6pm. Nov-Mar 10am-5pm. 7 days. ADMN

**434**
Map 10
**R25**
**North Berwick Law** The conical volcanic hill, a beacon in the E Lothian landscape. **Traprain Law** nearby is higher, tends to be frequented by rock-climbers, but has major prehistoric hillfort citadel of the Goddodin and a definite aura. BOTH 1-A-1

**The Pentlands/Hermitage** Reports: 413/414/WALKS O/SIDE CITY.

**Castle Ramparts** Report: 388/MAIN ATTRACTIONS.

# The Best Sports Facilities

## SWIMMING AND INDOOR SPORTS CENTRES

**435**
xE5
xB5
xE1
xA1

✓ ✓ **Royal Commonwealth Pool** 667 7211. Dalkeith Rd (400/MAIN ATTRACTIONS). The biggest, but Edin has many others. Recommended are **Warrender** (447 0052), Thirlestane Rd 500m beyond the Meadows S of centre; **Leith Victoria** (555 4728), in Jnct Pl off the main st in Leith complete with crèche facilities; **Glenogle** (343 6376) in Stockbridge, the New Town choice, v friendly. All these pools are old and tiled, 25yd long, seldom crowded and excellent for lane swimming – at certain times. Also all have Pulse centres & fitness classes. Different sessions, phone to check.

**436**
A4

✓ ✓ **One Spa** Sheraton Hotel 229 9131. Actually a separate 4-storey building behind hotel, offering the 'height' of luxury with usual pool & a highly unusual outdoor one dangling over Conference Sq; spa & gym. Exotic hydrotherapy, whole-body mud encasement & treatments for anything & everything. Emphasis on pampering rather than sport. Treat yourself to a day or half-day ticket.

**437**
D3

✓ **Escape** Scotsman Hotel 556 5565. Enter thro' hotel or from Market St. Metallic, modern health club with all facs & excl service. Low-lit pool, floor of machinery. Sexy, almost cruisy. Best to look good *before* you get here!

**438**
E2

✓ **Holmes Place** 550 1650. Greenside Pl, part of the 'Omnicentre' with its mediocre multiplex & tacky restaus. But Holmes Place, as elsewhere UK, has upmarket aspirations if High St realisation. This place v clean, corporate & well – cruisy. 25-lane pool, usual machinery. No day memberships, except if you're at the Glasshouse (75/INDIVIDUAL HOTELS).

**439**
xE1

**Portobello** 669 6888. Portobello Esplanade (427/BEACHES). Similar to other civic pools above. Refurbed, excellent Turkish baths still there, ladies-only, gents-only and mixed days. Phone for details.

**440**
xE1

**Ainslie Park** 551 2400. Pilton Dr, off Ferry Rd, N of centre, 5km from Princes St. Has serious keep-fit side but all the usual spa, sauna, steam too. Mon-Thu 7.30am-10pm, Fri 7.30am-9pm, Sat & Sun 8am-5.30pm.

**441**
xB1

**Next Generation** 554 5000. Newhaven Harbour. V much part of the regeneration of the waterfront, this sportsarama complex in the David Lloyd stable (in fact son of, hence naff name). Courts, gym, 2 pools incl one outdoor o/looking Forth (only in non-wet weather). Not cheap, but not as exp as some in town. 7 days till 11.30pm. Day memberships.

**442**
xF1

**Meadowbank** 661 5351. London Rd. Well-worn city athletics stadium. Courts for squash and badminton (book), Pulse centre, weights room, 13m indoor climbing wall, all-weather football/hockey pitches and velodrome. No pool.

**443**
E4

**University Gym** 650 2585. The Pleasance. No-nonsense complex, rel cheap. The best in town for weights (all the right machinery) and circuit training. Squash, badminton, indoor tennis, etc. Membership required (can be short-term) but not during the quiet vac periods. For a reasonable fee, the Fitness and Sports Injury Centre (FASIC) is an excellent alternative to the 'take 2 aspirin and go away' school of GP. Few fake suntans or lardarses here.

**444**
xA3

**Drumsheugh Baths Club** 225 2200. 5 Belford Rd, W End. Private swimming club in elegant building above Dean Village that's more exclusive than most. Gorgeous Victorian pool with rings and trapeze over the water, sauna, multigym and bistro. Frequented by the quality. Recent refurb. Go as a guest.

**445**
D3

**Balmoral Spa, Balmoral Hotel** 556 2414. Health club for residents (62/HOTELS), members and visitors (half-day tickets). Pool, sauna, steam, gym.

## GOLF COURSES

*There are several municipal courses (see phone book under City of Edin Council) & nearby, esp down the coast, some famous names not open to non-members.*

**446** **Braid Hills** 447 6666. Braid Hills app. 2 18-hole courses (no. 2 summer
**xE5** only). Thought to be the best in town. Never boring; exhilarating views. Booking usually not essential, except evenings & w/ends. Women welcome (and that ain't true everywhere round here).

✔✔ **Gullane No. 1** 01620 842255. The best of 3 courses in pretty village. Report: 2053/GOLF COURSES.

✔✔ **Glen Golf Club (aka North Berwick East)** 01620 892726. 36 km from Edin, worth the drive. Report: 2054/GOLF COURSES.

**Musselburgh** 665 5438. Original home of golf. Report: 2055/GOLF COURSES.

**Gifford** 01620 810591. Off the beaten track. Report: 2082/GREAT GOLF.

## OTHER ACTIVITIES

**447**  ✔✔ **The Adventure Centre, Ratho** 333 6333. Platt Hill, Ratho. Follow
**Map 10** signs from the M8, M9 & A71. Opened late 2003 after a long climb!
**P25** Ambitious & exciting facility designed to appeal to Joe Public & elite athletes alike. Activities incl abseils, team-building games, the Skyride (a kind of aerial assault course with ropes & trusses), a state-of-the-art adventure sports gym, not to mention the **National Rock Climbing Centre** – the best climbing arena in Europe in the roofed-off quarry. There's a 300-seater restau, 220-seater theatre, corporate facs & retail sector (incl the excl Tiso). Open 7 days.

**448**  ✔ **Skiing** Artificial slopes at **Midlothian Ski Centre (Hillend)** on A702,
**xE5** 10km S of centre. 445 4433. Excellent fac with various runs. The matting can be bloody rough when you fall & the chairlift is a bit of a dread for beginners, but once you can ski here, Vale is all yours. Tuition avail. Open 9.30am-9pm (7pm Sun in summer). Snowboarders welcome but Whistler it ain't.

**449** **Tennis** Many private clubs though only the **Grange** (332 2148) has lawn ten-
**xB5** nis & you won't get on there easily. There are places you can slip on (best not
**xE5** to talk about that), but the municipal centres (Edin residents/longer-stay visitors should get a Leisure Access card from any Edin leisure centre allowing advance reservation) are: **The Meadows** (NE corner by Univ Library). Just turn up. Many courts; **Saughton** 444 0422. Stevenson Dr. 8km W of city centre. 2 astroturf courts & one other. Also used for football & hockey, so phone to book; **Craiglockhart** 444 1969. Colinton Rd. 8km SW of centre via Morningside & Colinton Rd. 6 indoor courts, 7 outdoor & a 'centre court'. Best to check/book by phone. Other separate sports facs incl squash, badminton & gym, 443 0101. Centre open Mon-Thu 9am-11pm, Fri 10am-11 pm, Sat-Sun 9am-10.30pm.

**450** **World of Football** 443 0404. Part of the 'Newmarket Leisure Village' com-
**xA4** plex at the Corn Exchange, off Chesser Avenue. Newest of its type. 8 covered pitches. Can be booked between 9am-10.30pm daily.

**451** **Pony-trekking Lasswade Riding School** 663 7676. Lasswade exit from
**xE5** city bypass then A768, rt to Loanhead 1km and left to end of Kevock Rd. Full hacking and trekking facs and courses for all standards and ages.

**452** **Pentland Hills Trekking Centre** 01968 661095. At Carlops on A702
**Map 10** (25km from town) has sturdy, steady Icelandic horses who will bear you
**P26** good-naturedly into the hills. Exhilarating stuff. Cl Thur.

**453** **Ice-Skating** Murrayfield Ice Rink 337 6933. Riversdale Cres, just off main
**xA4** Glas Rd nr zoo. Cheap, cheerful and chilly. It has been here forever and feels like a gr 1950s B movie ... go round! Sessions daily from 2.30pm. Also ...
**Winter Wonderland** E Princes St Gardens. Big open-air ice rink in the gdns below the Scott Monument. Open late Nov-early Jan. 7 days. Mass fun!

**454** **Alien Rock** 552 7211. Old St Andrew's Church, Pier Pl, Newhaven. Indoor
**xB1** rock climbing in a converted kirk. Laid back atmos, bouldering rm & interesting 12m walls of various gnarliness to scoot up. Daily; phone for sessions. Have a pint after in **The Starbank** or **The Old Chain Pier** nearby (360/361/PUB FOOD).

# The Best Small Galleries

**455** ✓✓ **Ingleby Gallery** 556 4441. 6 Calton Terr. Important chic gallery in
**xF2** a private house backing onto Calton Hill. Shows work by significant
contemporary UK artists, eg Scotland's Callum Innes & Alison Watt.

**456** ✓✓ **The Fruitmarket Gallery** 225 2383. Market St opp City Art
**D3** Centre. Around for a while but v much on a roll these days, a smaller, warehousey space for contemporary work, retrospectives, installations;
this is the space to watch. Excl bookshop. Always interesting. Café (275/BEST
TEAROOMS) highly recommended for meeting & eating & watching the (art)
world go by.

**457** ✓ **doggerfisher** 558 7110. 11 Gayfield Sq. Susanna Beaumont's vital-to-
**E1** Edin gallery in a converted garage in the heart of the 'East Village'. Limited
wall space but always challenging new work. W/end viewing. She does good
openings.

**458** ✓ **Open Eye Gallery** 557 1020 and i2 (558 9872), both at 34 Abercromby
**C2** Pl. Excellent 2 galleries in residential part of New Town. Always worth
checking out for accessible contemporary painting and ceramics. Almost too
accessible (take cheque book) – Tom Wilson will know what you want (&
probably sell it to you).

**459** ✓ **The Printmakers' Workshop And Gallery** 557 2479. 23 Union St,
**E1** off Leith Walk nr London Rd r/bout. Workshops that you can look over.
Exhibs of work by contemporary printmakers and shop where prints from
many of the notable names in Scotland are on sale at reasonable prices. Bit
of a treasure.

**460** **The Collective Gallery** 220 1260. 22 Cockburn St. Installations of Scottish
**D3** and other young contemporary trailblazers. Members' work won't break the
bank.

**461** **The Scottish Gallery** 558 1200. 16 Dundas St. Guy Peploe's influential New
**C2** Town gallery on 2 floors. Where to go to buy something painted, sculpted,
thrown or crafted by up-and-comers or established names – everything from
affordable jewellery to original Joan Eardleys. Or just look.

**462** **Merz** 558 8778. 87 Broughton St, corner of Broughton Pl. Friendly, neigh-
**D1** bourhood (E Village) gallery, usually mixed work – a gr place to start buying
art (Wed-Sat).

**463** **Photography** Edin is blessed with 2 contemporary photo-art venues. **Stills**
**D3** 622 6200, 23 Cockburn St, with a café. **Portfolio** 220 1911, 43 Candlemaker
**C4** Row, is a small 2-floor space in what used to be the city's left-wing bookshop.

# Essential Culture

*For the current programmes of the places recommended below and all other venues, consult* The List *magazine, on sale at most newsagents.*

## UNIQUE VENUES

**464** **The Traverse** 228 1404. Small but influential, dedicated to new work (though
**B4** mainly touring companies) in modern Euro, v architectural 2-theatre premises in Cambridge St (behind Lyceum & Usher Hall). Good rendezvous café-bar upstairs (133/BEST BISTROS) plus excellent adj restau (120/BEST RESTAUS).

**465** **Dance Base** 225 5525. 14-16 Grassmarket. Scotland's award-winning
**C4** national centre for dance, in a new, purpose-built location. Classes & work-shops AYR but check *The List* for dance performance in its larger studio. State of the art building, worth a visit on its own.

**466** **The Cameo** 228 4141. Home St in Tollcross. 3 screens showing important
**B5** new films and cult classics. Some late movies at w/ends. Good snug bar.

**467** **Filmhouse** 228 2688. Lothian Rd, opp Usher Hall. 3 screens with everything
**A4** from first-run art-house movies to subtitled obscurities and retrospectives. Home of the annual Film Festival; café-bar (till 11.30pm Sun-Thu, 12.30am Fri-Sat) is a haven from the excesses of Lothian Rd. Open to non-cinephiles.

**468** **The Queen's Hall** 668 2019. Clerk St. Converted church with good atmos
**xE5** and v varied prog. Your best bet if you want to go somewhere for decent music. Café-bar & art exhibitions. Diverse (choral, jazz, art pop). Good atmos.

**469** **The Festival Theatre** 529 6000. Nicolson St. Edin's showcase theatre re-
**D4** created from the old Empire with a huge glass frontage of bars and a stage and screen dock large enough to accommodate the world's major compa-nies. Eclectic programme AYR.

## THE FESTIVALS

**470** ✓ ✓ ✓ Edinburgh invented arts festivals (more than 50 years ago) & now can truly be called a Festival City. Most of the festivals list-ed below are world leaders.

**Edinburgh International Festival** 473 2000. Last 3 weeks of Aug.

**Edinburgh Festival Fringe** 226 0026. 3 weeks in Aug.

**Edinburgh International Film Festival** 229 2550. 2 weeks in Aug.

**Edinburgh International Book Festival** 228 5444. 2 weeks in Aug.

**Edinburgh Military Tattoo** 08707 5551188. 3 weeks in Aug.

**Edinburgh International Jazz & Blues Festival** 467 5200. 1-2 weeks, end Jul/beginning Aug.

**Edinburgh International Science Festival** 220 1882. 1-2 weeks Apr.

**Scottish International Children's Festival** 225 8050. 1 week end May/beginning Jun.

**Edinburgh Mela** 557 1400. 2 days end Aug/early Sept.

**Edinburgh's Christmas** 557 3900. 4 weeks. End Nov-Christmas Eve. Mainly centred in E Princes St Gdns incl UK's biggest ice rink.

**Edinburgh's Hogmanay** 557 3990. 4 days, end of Dec-1st Jan.

*For the current programmes of the places recommended above and all other venues, consult* The List *magazine, on sale at most newsagents.*

# SECTION 3

## *Glasgow*

*The telephone code for Glasgow is 0141*
*Refer to* MAP 2 *unless otherwise stated*
*Map Codes: WE = West End; SS = South Side*

# The Best Hotels

**471**
**WE** ✓✓ **One Devonshire Gardens** 339 2001. 1 Devonshire Gdns. Off Gr Western Rd (the A82 W to Dumbarton). The original smartest hotel in town with refurbishment in progress (ask about most recent new rms) still engenders the design vision of its original owner Ken McCulloch (who went on to invent the Malmaison chain). Hotel now occupies all of the 5 townhouses on this elegant block set back from the busy rd west (house 5 is still privately occupied on the ground floor). This means that from 2006 for the first time, guests can access whole hotel without going outside – handy since b/fast is in house 5. Every rm is different but all have the things that we modern travellers look out for: DVD players, big beds, deep baths, thick carpets/towels/curtains. Many suites incl some doubles are super sumptuous. Reports on 'The Restaurant' & the jollier 'Room' (520/BEST RESTAUS) vary.

35RMS JAN-DEC T/T PETS CC KIDS LOTS

**472**
**C3** ✓✓ **Radisson SAS** 204 3333. 301 Argyle St. Bold, brash newcomer in emerging W end of Argyle St. Frontage makes major modernist statement, lifts the coolest in town. Leaning to minimalist, but rms have all you need. 2 restaus: **TaPaell'Ya** (603/SPANISH RESTAUS) more fun than Collage. **TR**: The 'Apartment' on the 6th (top) floor & corner suites on floors below. Fitness facs c/o LA Leisure Club in basement incl a pool. No parking.

247 RMS JAN-DEC T/T XPETS CC KIDS LOTS

**473**
**B2** ✓ **The Malmaison** 572 1000. 278 W George St. Sister hotel of the one in Edin & elsewhere and originally from the same stable and same team as One Devonshire (*see above*). This 'chain' of good design hotels has all the must-have features – well-proportioned rms (tho small), with CDs, cable, etc. – tho the location just off West End affords no gr views. However this is reliable, stylish & discreet. Contemp French menu sits well in the woody clubbiness of The Brasserie (565/FRENCH RESTAUS).

74RMS JAN-DEC T/T XPETS CC KIDS EXP

**474**
**C2** ✓ **The Arthouse Hotel** 221 6789. 129 Bath St (style bar street), nr Sauchiehall Centre and above Sarti (550/ITALIAN RESTAUS), so gr coffee downstairs. Smart contemp town-house hotel with wide, tiled stairwell and funky lift to 3 floors of individual rms (so size, views & noise levels vary a lot). Fab gold embossed wallpaper in the hallways, notable stained glass & nice pictures. Grill downstairs has tepanyaki and other Mod Br dishes. New owners from original vision & design but this is still the sexiest hotel stopover in town. **TR**: 129 & 204/5/6 (the Velvet Suites).

63RMS JAN-DEC T/T XPETS CC KIDS MED.EXP

**475**
**D2** ✓ **Langs** 333 1500. Port Dundas Pl nr bus station and Concert Hall. Good-looking modern high-rise hotel with designs – from lofty atrium/bar to penthouse suites on 5th floor – minimalist Japanese with more space. Glass tiles in internal bathroom wall & sunken beds (tho v comfy) won't suit everybody. Satellite TV/DVD & Playstations in all rms. Oshi restau on ground floor with oriental pretension (nice plates) & spa (no pool, but treatments). 'Californian cuisine' with good Scottish ingredients at Las Brisas on mezzanine. Langs tries v hard to please. Provided you get a rm you like, they will. **TR**: Duplexes on first floor.      100RMS JAN-DEC T/T XPETS CC KIDS LOTS

**476**
**D3** ✓ **The Millennium Hotel** 332 6711. 50 George Sq. Situated on the sq which is the municipal heart of the city and next to Queen St Stn (trains to Edin and pts N), Glasgow will be going on all about you and there's a conservatory terr, serving breakfast and afternoon tea, from which to watch. Bedrms vary. No parking or leisure facs. Busy brasserie.

117RMS JAN-DEC T/T PETS CC KIDS LOTS

**477**
**B3** ✓ **Glasgow Hilton** 204 5555. 1 William St. App from the M8 slip rd or from city centre via Waterloo St. It has a forbidding Fritz Lang/*Metropolis* appearance and entrance via underground car park is grim. But hotel is one of the best in town with good service and appointments. Japanese people made esp welcome. Huge atrium. 20 floors with top 3 'executive'. Views from here to N are stunning. Leisure facs incl pool. **TR**. Cameron's, the hotel's main restau, is present and correct, and the most highly Michelin-rated restau in town (though we don't agree). Minsky's bistro and Raffles bar are

not so special. La Primavera is excl Italian restau so all in all the best hotel food in town. 319RMS JAN-DEC T/T PETS CC KIDS LOTS

**478** ✓ **City Inn** 240 1002. Finnieston Quay by the big crane on the riverside &
**xA4** nr the SECC. Modern block makes most of Clydeside location with deck & views; rms here are a cut above the usual tho not large. Uniformity is at least thought out. City Café on ground floor takes itself seriously as a restau. Part of expanding chain, price & particularity elevate from the economy travel lodge to the designer, almost boutique hotel. The river's the thing.
164RMS JAN-DEC T/T XPETS CC XKIDS EXP

**479** **Carlton George** 353 6373. 44 W George St. Adj Queen St Stn and George
**D2** Sq, this is a smart and discreet central option and apart from parking (a hike to car park behind the stn) a decent bet in the city centre for the business traveller. It's more fun than that though, with a huge Irish bar downstairs and airy rooftop restau up top (**Windows**). Residents' lounge and drinks in rm all on the house. Good service and the usual comforts.
65RMS JAN-DEC T/T XPETS CC KIDS EXP

**480** **Glasgow Marriott** 226 5577. 500 Argyle St, nr motorway. Modern and
**B3** functional business hotel on 12 floors. Rooms recently refurb do seem small. Parking is a test for the nerves. Nevertheless, there's a calm, helpful attitude from the staff inside; for further de-stressing you can hypnotise yourself by watching the soundless traffic on the Kingston Br o/side; or there's a pool to lap and separate gym. Mediterraneo restau ain't bad. No-smk floors.
300RMS JAN-DEC T/T PETS CC KIDS LOTS

**481** **Thistle Hotel** 332 3311. Cambridge St. Opp Holiday Inn & v central. Part of
**C1** the UK chain & here in all its concrete-block anonymity for yrs (& not mentioned in *StB*) but incl now because rm rates vary hugely & if the hotel isn't busy you can get a rm v inx – so negotiate. (It is big so good chance.) Usual facs. Pool. 300RMS JAN-DEC T/T PETS CC KIDS MED.INX/LOTS

**482** **Glasgow Moat House** 306 9988. Congress Rd. Beside the SECC, on the
**xA4** Clyde, this towering, glass monument to the 1980s feels like it's in a constant state of 'siege readiness'. Science Centre & Tower gleam & twinkle on the opp bank & the new BBC HQ; there's a footbridge across. Some good river views from the 16 floors. The Marine Restau, in the lobby, has a good reputation and ring-side seating for river-gazing. Somewhat removed from city centre (about 3km, you wouldn't want to walk), it's esp handy for SECC and Armadillo goings-on. 283RMS JAN-DEC T/T PETS CC KIDS LOTS

# Individual Hotels

**483** ✓ ✓ **Saint Jude's** 352 8800. 190 Bath St. Glas first small boutique hotel
**C2** (started off as a northern Groucho Club; awaiting at TGP the arrival of The Hallion, the Edin-based equivalent, next door). All rms upstairs (no lift) retain 'original' ie 1990s design features. Restau under chef/prop Jenny Burn (519/RESTAUS) maintains fashion/foody appeal. Bar still cool; now has live music Fri/Sat. A stylee stopover. 6RMS JAN-DEC T/T XPETS CC XKIDS MED.EXP

**484** ✓ **The Pipers' Tryst Hotel** 353 5551. McPhater St. Visible from dual car-
**D1** riageway nr SMG HQ at Cowcaddens, but hard to get to the street in a car. Hotel upstairs from café-bar of the adj piping centre & whole complex a beautiful conversion of an old church & manse. Centre has courses, conferences & a museum, so staying here is to get close to Highland culture. Small restau. 8RMS JAN-DEC T/T XPETS CC KIDS MED.EXP

**485** ✓ **The Town House** 357 0862. 4 Hughenden Terr. Quiet st off Gr
**WE** Western Rd via Hyndland Rd, o/looking rugby & cricket grounds. Same area as One Devonshire (471/HOTELS) for a fraction of the price. Spacious rms faithfully restored – even if you don't happen to live in a well-appointed town house on a gracious terr yourself, you'll feel at home. Smallish bathrms & only one (rm 2) has bath. Close to the W End. Don't confuse with the Townhouse Hotel, Royal Cres. 10RMS JAN-DEC T/T XPETS CC KIDS MED.INX

**486** ✓ **Number 52 Charlotte Street** Serviced apartments in superb conver-
**F5** sion of the one remaining Georgian town house in historic (now decimated) st betw the Barrows Market and Glas Green. Tobacco Merchant's

house by Robert Adam refurb by NTS. V good rates for bedrm/lounge/kitchen; everything but breakfast. Usually by the week but shorter lets poss; units sleep 1-5.                                        6APTS JAN-DEC X/T XPETS CC KIDS MED.INX

**487** ✓ **The Brunswick Hotel** 552 0001. 104-108 Brunswick St. V contempo-
**E3** rary, minimalist hotel almost epitomises Merchant City style emerging way back in the 1990s but standing up well to time & taste. Bright and cheerful rms economically designed to make use of tight space (maybe time for plasma screens?). Bold colours. Good base for nocturnal forays into pub and club land. Restau till 8pm, breakfast pleasant. The penthouse suite is excl. No parking.                                    18RMS JAN-DEC T/T XPETS CC KIDS MED.EXP

**488** **Rab Ha's** 572 0400. 83 Hutcheson St. Rms above a pub in the urban heart
**E3** of the Merchant City. Pub goes like a fair with good food and friendly folk so noisy late night and seems permanently surrounded by building works. Cheap 'n' cheerful tho not a long-stay choice.
                                                4RMS JAN-DEC T/T PETS CC XKIDS MED.INX

**489** **Cathedral House** 552 3519. Cathedral Square opp Glasgow Cathedral on
**xF3** corner of John Knox St. A former fave, refurb has reinstated this small E End hotel in these pages. Rms above the bar, their main appeal being outlook to the edifice & the Necropolis beyond (1903/GRAVEYARDS). Functional & friendly. A walk to Merchant City.        8RMS JAN-DEC T/T PETS CC KIDS MED.INX

**490** **Babbity Bowster** 552 5055. 16-18 Blackfriars St. This late 18th-century
**F3** town house was pivotal in the redevelopment of the Merchant City and famous for its bar (681/REAL-ALE PUBS, 570/SCOTTISH RESTAUS) and beer gdn, Schottische restau upstairs & rms above with basic facs. Bathrms ensuite. No TV but nice books. A v Glasgow hostelry.
                                                6RMS JAN-DEC T/X XPETS CC XKIDS MED.INX

**491** **Kirklee Hotel** 334 5555. 11 Kensington Gate. In a city curiously short of
**WE** appealing & individual GHs here at least is one to rec – a tidy Edwardian house and most notably a tidy gdn in a leafy suburb nr Botanics and Byres Rd. Lots of pics.                          9RMS JAN-DEC T/T XPETS CC KIDS MED.INX

**492** **The White House** 339 9375. 12 Cleveden Cres. Not a hotel, but self-cater-
**WE** ing apartments nr Botanics. A friendly hame from hame in this civilised crescent & a sensible alternative, esp if there are a few of you or you are staying a week. Some quiet mews out back.
                                                32UNITS JAN-DEC T/T PETS CC KIDS MED.INX

**493** **The Victorian House** 332 0129. 212 Renfrew St. Behind Sauchiehall St &
**B1** adj School of Art (760/MACKINTOSH). One of several city-centre 'commercial' hotels in this st but prob the best appointed & tries harder than the rest. Basic facs. Pleasant front garden. Surprisingly large behind the facade.
                                                58RMS JAN-DEC T/T PETS CC KIDS CHP/INX

# Travel Lodges

**494** ✓ **Bewleys** 353 0800. 110 Bath St. In the downtown section of Bath St but
**C2** nr the style bars & designer restaus, a bed block with more taste & character than most. Thought, for example, has gone into the choice of prints in rms & halls. Loop, a credible restau on ground floor. Good accom & facs at this price.                              103RMS JAN-DEC T/T PETS CC KIDS MED.INX

**495** **Somerset Merchant City** 553 4288. Corner of Albion St & Argyle St. Large
**E4** corner-block aparthotel with modern look befitting 'Merchant City' moniker. Urban, understated, but no facs, bar or public spaces. Rms have kitchens. Comfortable enough & some human touches. Can book by night & share rms as you like.                          102RMS JAN-DEC T/T XPETS CC KIDS EXP

**496** **Premier Travel Inns** Of 16 in Glas area, most convenient prob E on corner
**E3** of Merchant City at 187 George St (0870 238 3320) & W at 10 Elmbank Gdns,
**B2** above Charing Cross Stn. Latter once an office block, now a vast city-centre budget hotel, with no frills and no pretence, but a v adequate rm for the night. Functionality, anonymity and urban melancholy may suit the lonesome traveller/family/mates packed into a rm. George St in area of many restaus, Charing Cross opp the excl Baby Grand & it's open late (540/BISTROS). Under £55 per rm at TGP.          239/278RMS JAN-DEC T/T XPETS CC KIDS MED.INX

**497** **Novotel** 222 2775. 181 Pitt St. Branch of the French bed-box empire in quiet
**B2** corner nr w end Sauchiehall St. Nothing much to distinguish, but
brass/restau is bright enough & Novotel beds are v good. Small bathrms. The
2- as opposed to the 3-star **Ibis**: 225 6000 is adj. If it's merely a bed for the
night you want, it's much cheaper & hard to see what difference a star
makes. They're both pretty soulless.

139/141RMS JAN-DEC T/T PETS CC KIDS MED.INX/CHP

**498** **Holiday Inn, City Centre** 352 8300. 161 W Nile St. Another block off the
**D2** old block. In the city centre nr Concert Hall. Gym, but no pool; restau but not
gr shakes. Holiday Inn Express adj is better value (25% less). Rm rates vary
depending on occupancy.

113/119RMS JAN-DEC T/T XPETS CC KIDS LOTS/MED.INX

**499** **Express by Holiday Inn** 548 5000. Corner of Stockwell and Clyde St (tho
**D5** only 5 rms on the river). Functional bed-box that's still a good deal. All you do
is sleep here. Nr Merchant City so plenty of restaus, nightlife and other dis-
tractions and curiously midway betw 2 of Glasgow's oldest, funkiest bars, The
Scotia and Victoria (666/665/PUBS). Another Express adj Holiday Inn (City
Centre) but this one best. 128RMS JAN-DEC T/T XPETS CC KIDS MED.INX

# The Best Hostels

*The SYHA is the Scottish Youth Hostel Association, of which you have to be a
member (or a member of an affiliated organization from another country) to stay
in their many hostels round Scotland. Phone 01786 451181 for details, or contact
any YHA hostel.*

**500** ✓ **SY Hostel** 332 3004. 8 Park Terr. Close to where the former Glas hos-
**xA1** tel used to be in Woodlands Terr, in the same area of the W End nr the
univ and Kelvingrove Park. This building was converted in 1992 from the
Beacons Hotel, which was where rock 'n' roll bands used to stay in the 1980s.
Now the bedrms are converted into dorms for 4-6 (some larger) and the public rms are common rms with TV, games, etc. You must be a member of the
YHA. *See above.* 150BEDS

**501** **Murray Hall, Strathclyde Univ** 553 4148. Cathedral St. Modern, but not
**F2** sterile block of single rms on edge of main campus and facing towards
Cathedral. Part of large complex (also some student flats to rent by the week)
with bar/shop/laundrette. Quite central, close to Merchant City bars. Vacs
only. There's also Chancellors Hall adj, 218 rms, same deal same no. 70BEDS

**502** **Euro Hostel Glasgow** 222 2828. 318 Clyde St. A v central independent hos-
**C4** tel block at the bottom of Union/Renfield St and almost o/looking the river.
Mix of single, twin or dorm accom, but all en-suite & clean. Breakfast includ-
ed in price. Kitchen & bar. Games & TV room, laundry & internet access.
Open AYR. 365BEDS

*Note: Both Strathclyde and Glasgow univs have several other halls of residence
available for short-term accom in the summer months. Phone: Glasgow 330
4116/2318 or Strathclyde 553 4148 (central booking).*

# The Best Hotels Outside Town

**503**
Map 9
**L25**
✓ ✓ **Mar Hall, Earl of Mar Estate, Bishopton** 0141 812 9999. M8 jnct 28A/29, A726 then A8 into Bishopton. 5-star luxury in not-so-rustic Renfrewshire but only 10 mins airport & 25 mins central Glas. £10M conversion of imposing, *très elegant* baronial house with grand public spaces incl the hall & rms that vary (some huge) but all with the 5-star niceties. Gr restau under Jim Kerr (fusion Scottish). Has become effortlessly the new rock 'n' roll stopover for the city. 53RMS JAN-DEC T/T XPETS CC KIDS EXP-LOTS

**504**
Map 9
**L25**
✓ **Cameron House Hotel nr Balloch Loch Lomond** 01389 755565. A82 dual carriageway through W End or via Erskine Br and M8. 45km NW of centre. Highly regarded mansion-house hotel complex with excellent leisure facs in 100 acres open grounds on the bonny banks of the loch. Sports incl 9-hole golf (& 10km L Lomond course – 2068/GOLF), good pool, tennis and a busy marina for sailing/windsurfing, etc. Notable restau (The Georgian Rm with 3 AA rosettes) and all-day brasserie. Many footballers & famous names have holed up here; it's a short helicopter hop to Glasg.
96RMS JAN-DEC T/T XPETS CC KIDS LOTS

**505**
Map 10
**L25**
**The Black Bull Hotel, Killearn** 01360 550215. 2 The Sq. A81 towards Aberfoyle, take the rt fork after Strathblane, and the hotel is at the top end of the village next to the church. Urban values, design and comforts in this restau with rms in pleasant situation. Clubby casual bistro & bar meals & finer dining conservatory restau. 12RMS JAN-DEC T/T PETS CC KIDS MED.INX

**506**
Map 9
**L25**
**Gleddoch House, Langbank nr Greenock** 01475 540711. Take M8/A8 to Greenock, then B789 signposted Langbank/Houston, then 2km – hotel is signed. 30km W of centre by fast rd. This château-like country-house hotel, formerly the home of the Lithgow shipping family, high above the Clyde estuary, was destroyed by fire early 2004. Reopen for '06 with 10 rms in rebuilt mansion, 60 in extension. Main attraction here is the 18-hole golf (751/SPORTS FACS). JAN-DEC T/T PETS CC KIDS LOTS

**507**
Map 9
**L24**
**The Lodge On Loch Lomond** 01436 860201. Edge of Luss on A82 N from Balloch. About 40 mins W End. Linear not lovely, but gr lochside setting. Rms above restau & wood-lined rms o/look the bonny banks with balconies & saunas, tho Luss is not everybody's cup of tea (and sausage roll). Restau also has the view and terrace and is surprisingly good; booking may be necessary w/ends. Rms in Munro Lodge separate, set back from lochside but v contemp boutique hotel style. 47RMS JAN-DEC T/T PETS CC KIDS MED.INX

**508**
Map 9
**L25**
**Kirkton House, Cardross** 01389 841951. A814, past Helensburgh to Cardross village then N up Darleith Rd. Kirkton House is 1km on rt. 18th-century Scottish farmhouse/GH that combines rustic charm with mod con. Nr L Lomond. 6 RMS FEB-NOV T/T PETS CC KIDS MED.INX

**509**
Map 10
**M26**
**Eglinton Arms Hotel, Eaglesham** 01355 302631. Sprawling inn in the centre of charming conservation vill of Eaglesham, a v quiet contrast to downtown Glas to the N, but with M77 improvements, surprisingly close. Only 10km to S city boundary but a diff green world & gurgling brook besides. V decent & locally popular bar/restau – Simpson's – & refurb rms for less than budget hotel rates. 35RMS JAN-DEC T/T PETS CC KIDS CHP

# The Best Restaurants

**510** ✓✓ **Étain** 225 5630. The Glass House, Springfield Court off Queen St
**D3** (enter by lift), but located in upper corner of Princes Sq, Glasgow's most interesting (small) shopping mall. This is a Conran restau & operates along with Zinc (563/BISTROS) in the new mallifying of our lives. Zinc may be more fun, but this is an elegant relaxing rm & the service is excl. Chef Geoffrey Smeddle at top of his form. Straight-talking comtemp British menu with no twiddly bits, ie refreshingly simply good. Ditto wine list. 7 days (cl Sat lunch, Sun dinner). AA Restau of the Yr '05. MED

**511** ✓ **Rococo** 221 5004. 202 W George St. corner of Wellington St and just
**C2** along from Bouzy Rouge to which it is related (526/BISTROS). But this is the upmarket, fine dining and impeccable service version. Basement but light & relaxing. Excl contemp menu has the lot in the mix. Nice private dining area and courtyard o/side for post-prandial chat and coffee. Chef Mark Tamburrini. Excl wine list; look no further than the French! Gr pre-theatre menu (till 6.30pm). **SD:** Daube of beef with horseradish pommes purée. 7 days. Lunch and LO 10pm, cl Sun. MED

**512** ✓ **Gamba** 572 0899. 225a W George St. Mellow minimalist seafood
**C2** restau in basement at corner of W Campbell St. Straight-talking menu but here good fish/seafood speaks for itself so expect prawn cocktail, sole meunière. Usually 2/3 non-fish choices. Fashionable rendezvous. Glas people love Gamba tho Michelin has failed to recognise. **SD** from chef Derek Marshall: fish soup, scallops with Thai dipping sauce & sticky rice. Lunch & dinner. LO 10 (10.30) pm. Cl Sun. MED

**513** ✓ **The Ubiquitous Chip** 334 5007. 12 Ashton Lane. A cornerstone of
**WE** culinary Glasgow & still superb. 2-storey, covered courtyard draped with vines, off a bar-strewn cobbled lane in the heart of the W End, heaped with accolades over 30 yrs in residence. The main bit is still one of the most atmospheric of rms & Ian Brown's menu is exemplary – the best of Scottish seafood, game and beef and fine, original cooking. An outstanding wine list. Chip upstairs has more bistro feel & menu which is also avail in the courtyard. **SD:** Dishes with long list of ingredients, and each Scottish provenance noted (they were about the first to do this, now everyone does), eg the black pudding is Rothesay black pudding, raspberries from Blairgowrie. Daily lunch and 6.30-11pm. EXP

**514** ✓ **Le Chardon D'Or** 248 3801. 176 W Regent St. Brian Maule's (formerly
**C2** head chef at the Roux brothers' famed Le Gavroche) Golden Thistle in French with contemp spin on Auld Alliance as far as the food's concerned – impeccable ingredients, French influence in preparation. Delightfully simple menu, tranquil rm. A temple to culinary excellence. Excl, well-priced wine list esp French. Good halves choice. **SD:** Food that is what it says on the menu. Lunch Mon-Fri, LO 9.30pm. Cl Sun. EXP

**515** ✓ **Stravaigin** 334 2665. 28-30 Gibson St. Constantly changing, innova-
**WE** tive and consciously eclectic menu from award-winning chef Colin Clydesdale. Mixes cuisines, esp Asian and Pacific Rim. 'Think global, eat local'. Excellent, affordable food without the foodie formalities and open later than most. The bar on street level has predictably excl bar food sim eclectic and at home with it. Can be cramped but nowt cramps the style. **SD:** Ever-changing with precise long list of ingredients too long to mention here. Mon-Thu 5-11pm, Fri-Sat lunch & 5pm-12midnight, Sun 5pm-12midnight. Also **Stravaigin 2** 334 7165 (see 523/BISTROS). INX/MED

**516** ✓ **The Buttery** 221 8188. 652 Argyle St. Central but curious location for
**A3** Glas's long-est and consistently top-end restau (AA Restau of the Yr 2004), still cosy & old-style after all these yrs. Prob the most gracious dining in the city. Tho tables are close, service is unobtrusive. Dining fine from start to finish; chef Willy Deans one of Scotland's star chefs, sourcing sound Scottish ingredients, presenting them with some panache. Lunch & LO 10pm (not Sat lunch). Cl Sun/Mon. EXP

**517** **Rogano** 248 4055. 11 Exchange Pl. Betw Buchanan St and Queen St. An
**D3** institution in Glas since the 1930s. Décor replicating a Cunard ship, the *Queen Mary*, is the major attraction. Long since in private hands, it's now the flagship of pub chain 'spirit' & tho restau spacious & perennially fashionable,

there's a sense of trading on fading glory, esp downstairs in 'Café Rogano', the cheaper, shabbier alternative. Restaurant: lunch and 6.30pm-10.30pm. Café Rogano: noon-11pm (Fri-Sat until 12midnight, Sun until 10pm). Upstairs for seafd esp oysters, you may even venture the lobster thermidor; some glamour still lingers. EXP.MED

**518** **La Parmigiana** 334 0686. 447 Gr Western Rd. 'Simply the best' Italian for
**WE** many a discriminating Glaswegian of the old school (convenient location nr Kelvin Br – usually parking nearby), the favourite place to eat posh pasta & vitello but that's just for starters. Main courses elaborate with Italian take on local provision. Lunch (good deal 'pre-theatre' menu). LO 10.30pm. Cl Sun. **SD**: lobster ravioli, carpaccio with rocket & parmesan. (549/ITALIAN RESTAUS)
MED

**519** **Saint Jude's** 352 8800. 190 Bath St. The restau of the boutique hotel in
**C2** fashionable Bath St (508/INDIVID HOTELS) where food & service fit the urban, urbane surroundings. Bar in basement with snackier menu till 7pm (not Suns), but restau serves modern British menu in lofty, light retro-chic rm making it easy to eat here. Chef/prop Jenny Burn now firmly in control of the kitchen. Lunch Mon-Fri, dinner 7 days. LO 10/10.30pm. MED

**520** **One Devonshire Gardens** 339 2001. Glasgow's oldest boutique hotel
**WE** (471/BEST HOTELS) has, since it opened, had one of the city's classiest dining rms. Was home to Gordon Ramsay's Amaryllis until 2004 & still repositioning at TGP. The hotel's fine dining is in newly refurbished House 5 while Amaryllis has transformed into ROOM (341 0000). A new concept & take on comfort food. 'Room cuppa soup' or 'jelly & ice cream' which come with every contemp flourish, demonstrate basic conceit of the menu. Don't expect anything wholesome old-fashioned about your fish 'n' chips. Remains at TGP to be seen whether this bold idea will catch on & overcome the drawback of this location beyond the West End. 7 days lunch & dinner. LO 10/10.30. MED

**521** **Thai Fountain** 332 2599. 2 Woodside Cres, Charing Cross. Same ownership
**A1** as Amber Regent (*see below*), this is probably Glasgow's best Asian restau. Genuinely Thai and not at all Chinese. Innovative dishes with gr diversity of flavours and textures, so sharing several is best. Of course you will eat too much. Room v interior & rather dated now. 7 days. LO 11/11.30pm. **SD**: weeping tiger beef. (585/FAR-EASTERN RESTAUS) MED

**Amber Regent** 50 W Regent St. Report: 589/FAR-EASTERN.

# The Best Bistros & Brasseries

*See also* Best Scottish Restaurants, *p. 87.*

**522**
**WE** ✓ **No. Sixteen** 339 2544. 16 Byres Rd. Mags & Ronnie's tiny restau on 2 postage stamp floors at the bottom end of Byres Rd now est as hugely pop W End haunt – so you prob have to book & squeeze in. Winning combo is good bistro food, no fuss and good value. Sublime puds.7 days. Lunch & LO 10pm, Sun 9.30pm.                                                                    INX

**523**
**WE** ✓ **Stravaigin 2** 334 7165. 8 Ruthven Lane. Just off Byres Rd thro' vennel opp underground stn. Off-shoot of **Stravaigin** (515/BEST RESTAUS), one of Glasgow's finest. Similar eclectic often inspirational but lighter menu somewhere betw the upstairs bar and downstairs finer dining of the mothership. Smallish rms (upper brighter) & couple of tables in lane; book w/ends. 7 days all day from 11/12 to 11pm.                                                           INX

**524**
**WE** ✓ **Otago** 337 2282. 61 Otago St. Charming neighbourhood restau/café with a lighter daytime menu, giving way to the full meat/fish/game after 6pm. Mediterraneo slant & excl wine-list. Service can be cool but food is somehow just what you want! Deli shelves from tasty tins to Tate & Lyle is like an art exhibit. Open 7 days 11am–10pm. LO 9pm.                              CHP

**525**
**C2** ✓ **Papingo** 332 6678. 104 Bath St. A bistro in a basement among many (in Bath St) but as many Glaswegians know, food, service & wine-list here are spot-on. Chef David Clunas's contemp Scottish menu in Michelin & AA. A perennial fave. These words haven't changed in 3 editions of *StB* but nor reassuringly has it! Lunch & LO 10/10.30pm. Cl Sun lunch.                             MED

**526**
**C2** ✓ **Bouzy Rouge** 221 8804. 111 W Regent St. Key restau in the Bouzy Rouge chain, made by the enterprising Brown family & one of the few chains we heartily endorse (it's now restricted to Glas only). An excellent bistro for eclectic, affordable contemporary food and wine. Good vegn choice. 7 days, lunch & LO 9.30pm (10.30pm w/ends). Also:                              INX

**527**
**D2** **Bouzy Rouge Seafood & Grill** 333 9725. 71 Renfield St. Diff emphasis but similar menu. Focussing both surf 'n' turf on good Scottish-sourced ingredients (Aberdeen Angus steaks, L Fyne oysters). Beautiful room. Service varies. 7 days, lunch & LO 10pm.                                                          MED

**528**
**WE** ✓ **Café Royale** 338 6606. 340 Crow Rd. West End borders (can app via Hyndland Rd – Clarence Drive to bottom then rt onto Crow Rd) but not so far to go for authentic, mainly seafood bistro that's been winning awards since it opened '04. Same family as the estimable Royal in Tighnabruich (782/BEST ARGYLL) & many fishy ingredients from out that way (sourcing noted on menu). Clair McKie on the stoves & nice Tighnabruich pics by Chris Calvarey. Tues-Sun (not Sun lunch) LO 9pm.                              INX

**529**
**WE** ✓ **Fanny Trollopes** 564 6464. 1066 Argyle St. Discreet presence on this unlovely boulevard & a narrow rm, but Fanny's was a winner when it opened a couple of yrs ago & since reopening after some fixing & furb, it's more of a dining destination than ever. Lunch & LO 10pm. Cl Sun/Mon.  INX

**530**
**C2** ✓ **48 West Regent St** 331 0303. Same address. Latest venture of the Bouzy Rouge family (see above) & poss their smartest move yet. Still in basement (like most of their establishments) but makes the most of dark, urban interior. Food 'cheap but chic' is indeed v good value. All the sophisticated staples are here. Feels like a NY or London theatre restau (say, Joe Allan). Can sip cocktails. 7 days noon-10pm. Bar 1am.                              MED

**531**
**WE** ✓ **Lux/Stazione** 576 7576. 1057 Gr Western Rd. Nr Gartnavel Hospital which for non-Glaswegians means a long way down Gr Western Rd from the Botanic corner. Informal Italian bar/bistro & the rather more formal **Lux** (upstairs) in former station. Both have relaxed ambience. O/side tables in summer. Lux quite highly rated by some (Michelin 3 forks) & more relaxed than other city centre Mod-Brit-Med eateries. 7 days, lunch and 5-11pm. Lux dinner only. Cl Sun.                                                            MED/INX

**532** **Red Onion** 221 6000. 257 W Campbell St. Chef to the stars & TV & tabloid-watchers, John Quigley will prob not speak to me again for not giving him a tick. But he does have a gr formula here with good-value Mod British menu featuring all the things we like. Informal, accessible, easy to drop in. And it buzzes. 7 days 9am-10 (10.30) pm; from noon Sat/Sun. INX

**533** **The Giffnock Ivy** 620 1003. 219 Fenwick Rd, Giffnock. Set in Glas S Side & not
**SS** London's W End, the joke is a good one (even if the name does refer to the ivy in the doorway), but this place has big local rep & at w/ends it may be just as difficult to get a table. Gr bistro atmos in small, busy rm; modest menu with blackboard specials. V Scottish. 7 days, lunch & LO 9.30pm. MED

**534** **Mitchell's** 644 2255. 107 Waterside Rd, Carmunnock, a vill to the far S of the
**SS** city (cross Albert Br, thro Gorbals & foll signs). Almost rural setting & on the rd to Cathkin Braes (733/VIEWS) so a pleasant excursion of a summer eve. Cosy suburban clientele enjoy city bistro menu in cottage-cum-brasserie setting (also o/side tables). Some delicious combos. Lunch & LO 10.30 (11) pm. Cl Mon/Tues. INX

**535** **Òran Mór; The Brasserie** 357 6226. 731 Gt Western Rd down the side of this
**WE** converted church/drink emporium at the end of Byres Rd. A one-stop celebration of the parts of Scottish culture that go well with a drink, incls food (548/GASTROPUBS), music, comedy, clubbing it & plays at lunchtime. The Brasserie is the upmarket-dining bit. Lunch Wed-Sat; dinner Mon-Sat. MED

**536** **Café Ostra** 552 4433. 15 St John St by the Italian Centre. Latest venture in this
**E3** space by notable restauranteur Alan Tomkins (Gamba 512/BEST RESTAUS & Papingo, see above). Gr lunch menu & venue (outdoor seating with heaters) & better-than-av café/bistro menu with all the faves. 7 days lunch & LO 10 (10.30) pm. INX

**537** **Zinc** 225 5620. Princes Sq. Thro' the designer shopping centre & upstairs,
**D3** o/looking the 3-floor mall. The Glas version of Conran's Zinc café-bar chain, and adj to the more formal Étain (510/BEST RESTAUS). Grazing, groovy, busy, buzzy formula pioneered at Mezzo now regionalised & in the mall rather than merely the quarter. At least the menus are not formulaic; simple, good brasserie fare. Uncle Terry still knows what we like! 7 days 11am, LO 9.45pm. INX

**538** **The Sisters** 434 1179. 1a Ashwood Gardens off Crow Rd, Jordanhill. Out of the
**WE** way but out of the ordinary, a gr Scottish eaterie run by sisters Pauline & Jacqueline O'Donnell. Gr atmos, home cooking from fine ingredients. Loyal clientele & a real find for the rest of us. Phone for directions. Tues-Sun lunch & dinner. LO 9.30pm. INX

**539** **Smith's Of Glasgow** 552 6539. 109 Candleriggs. In emerging mini theatre &
**E3** restau land, gd food in bistro/brasserie style, this more 'French'. Gt value wine list. Chef/prop Michael Smith shows flair & care that raises food from the ordinary. Coffee-shop & lighter menu avail all day. Mon 11-4pm, Tues-Sat 11am-10.30pm, cl Sun. INX

**540** **Baby Grand** 248 4942. 3-7 Elmbank Gdns. Inviting haven among high-rise
**A2** office blocks opp hotel (496/TRAVEL LODGES); a downtown-USA location. (Go behind the King's Theatre down Elmbank St, rt at gas stn and look for the hotel.) Narrow rm with bar stools and banquettes, often with background music from resident mad pianist. Char-grilled fish, steak & specials or you can graze. Best late meal in town. Daily 8am-midnight (2am on w/ends). (638/LATE RESTAUS) CHP

**541** **Cul De Sac** 334 8899. 44 Ashton Lane, the main lane off Byres Rd with
**WE** many restaus & bars & The Ubiquitous Chip (513/BEST RESTAUS). Perennially fashionable crêperie/diner now in Stefan King stable as is the more ambitious cine/restau – The Lane – next door. The atmos is relaxed and conversational, the burgers go on for ever. All day till 10pm.
CHP

✓ **Firebird** 334 0594. 1321 Argyle St. Recently more bistrotastic than only pizza, for which it's renowned, but report: 561/BEST PIZZA.

✓ **Café Gandolfi** 552 6813. 64 Albion St. Last but right up there with the best. See Report: 614/BEST TEAROOMS.

# Gastropubs

**542**
**E4** ✓✓ **Bar Gandolfi** 552 6813. 64 Albion St above Café Gandolfi (614/TEARMS). In the last edition of *StB* I suggested that if Glasgow could thole a 'gastropub', this might be it. Now I've decided there are enough pubs where food counts as much as or more than the drink to warrant a new section. Bar Gandolfi still heads it up. A foody pub wih no pretence, just gr comfort food in a light, airy upstairs garret, served all day till 11.30pm. Good veggie choice. Gr rendezvous spot. 7 days 9am-11.30pm (Sun from noon).

**543**
**WE** ✓✓ **Stravaigin** 28-30 Gibson St. Excellent pub food upstairs from one of the best restaus in town. Doors open on to sunny Gibson St & mezzanine above. Crowded maybe, but inspirational grub & no fuss. Nice wines to go with. 7 days all day & LO 10pm. Report: 515/BEST RESTAUS.

**544**
**xB1** ✓ **Liquid Ship** 331 1901. 171 Gr Western Rd. From the makers of Stravaigin (above), a new venture on the highway to the W. Eclectic menu as you'd expect from Spain to the Ukraine & lots of Stravaigin touches. Food 11am-8pm (9 sometimes) then tapas menu till 10.30pm. Bar 11 but midnight on frequent quiz/comedy/live music nights. 7 days.

**545**
**C3** **Bar Budda** 248 7881. 142 St Vincent St and Cresswell Lane, West End. 337
**WE** 6201. 2 branches of the burgeoning W coast chain, where food is surprisingly ok. I say surprising because the Budda style might be expected to triumph over content. Modern menu mix, more Thai at night. Food till the throng takes over, usually 9pm (earlier Fri/Sat St Vincent St). Bar 11/12.

**546**
**xA1** **McPhabbs** 221 0770. 22 Sandyford Pl. W of Sauchiehall St, other side of the m/way. Long-standing gr Glas pub with loyal following. Tables in front 'garden' & on narrow back deck. Standard home-made pubgrub menu. Food till 9pm. Bar 11/midnight. DJ Mark Robb from groovy Buff Club spins here.

**547**
**E4** **Tron Café-Bar** 552 8587. 63 Trongate. Attached to the important Tron Theatre, this buzzing bar/bistro is at the heart of Glas style, culture & the other things the city wants to show you. All sympatico & understated here. Bar on st & 'Victorian' rm in back. Decent house wines and an eclectic menu. Generally good vibes & good with kids. Food LO 10 (10.30) pm.

**548**
**WE** **Òran Mór** 357 6200. 731 Corner of Byres Rd & Gt Western Rd. Converted church & reverence prob due for the scale of ambition here, a paen to all things 'Scottish contemporary'. Every cloister & chapel has been turned into an albeit designery den for drinking in & the din can be hellish. However the Conservatory' to one side has a v passable gastropub-style menu & 'The Brasserie' (535/BISTROS) takes its grub quite seriously. Expect contemp versions of Scottish trad cooking. Lunch & LO 10pm.

✓ **The Goat** 357 7373. 1287 Argyle St. Report: 695/COOL BARS.

✓ **Babbity Bowsters** 552 5055. Blackfriars St. Report: 570/SCOTTISH RESTAUS.

# The Best Italian Restaurants

**549**
**WE** ✓ **La Parmigiana** 334 0686. 447 Gr Western Rd. Sophisticated ristorante that blends trad service & contemporary Italian cuisine into a seamless performance. Carefully chosen dishes and wine list; solicitous service. Milano rather than Napoli. Expect to find Italians (who consider this to be one of the city's gr restaus – 518/BEST RESTAUS). Mon-Sat lunch & 6-10.30pm. Cl Sun. MED

**550**
**C2**
**D2** ✓ **Fratelli Sarti** 248 2228, 133 Wellington St, and 204 0440 (best number for bookings), 121 Bath St. Glasgow's famed *emporio d'Italia* combining a **deli/wine shop** in Wellington St, **wine shop** in Bath St and **bistro** in each. Gr bustling atmos. Eating upstairs in deli has more atmos. Both may have queues at lunchtime. Good pizza, specials change every day, *dolci* and *gelati* in super-calorific abundance. 7 days 8am-10/11pm (Sun from noon) (563/PIZZA). The Sarti **restaurant** at 43 Renfield St (corner of W George St, 572 7000) is for finer Italian dining in elegant rm with exceptional marble tiling & wine-list. Same menu as others, but more ristorante specials. 7 days lunch & LO 10pm, 10.30/11pm. INX/MED/INX

**551**
**Map 10**
**N27** ✓ **La Vigna, Lanark** 01555 664320. 40 Wellgate. Not Glasgow, but downtown Lanark 40km away – worth the drive for the authentic ristorante, family-run for 20 yrs. 7 days, lunch & LO 10pm (Sun dinner only). MED

**552**
**D3** **L'Ariosto** 221 0971. 92 Mitchell St. Old-style ristorante (tho with new owners). Set in an indoor courtyard nr Buchanan St, this is full-blown Tuscan fare with flair & after 30 yrs still some passion & obliging staff. Notable for using only the right ingredients incl wild mushrooms. Dinner-dancing: this is old-style but real style. Gr wine list with good house. Tues-Sat. Lunch & LO 11pm. Cl Sun lunch. MED

**553**
**xA5** **La Fiorentina/Little Tuscany** 420 1585. 2 Paisley Rd W. Not far from river & motorway over Kingston Br, but app from Eglinton St (A77 Kilmarnock Rd). It's at the Y-jnct with Govan Rd. Fiorentina has absorbed trad tratt Little Tuscany from next door. Fabulous, old-style rm & service, always busy. Usually seafood specials; lighter Tuscan menu. As Italian as you want it to be, enormous menu & wine list. Mon-Sat lunch & LO 10.30pm (9.30pm Sun). MED

**554**
**B1** **Paperino's** 332 3800. 283 Sauchiehall St. Ordinary-looking though smart restau is better than the rest; down to the Giovanazzi brothers who also own La Parmigiana (*see above*) and The Big Blue (690/PUB FOOD). Perfect pasta and good service. 7 days. LO 10.50/11.30pm. INX

# The Trusty Tratts

*Old style family-run restaurants (real Italians) with familiar pasta/pizza staples & the rest. There are many of these in Glasgow as elsewhere; these are the best.*

**555**
**D2** ✓ **Ristorante Caprese** 332 3070. 217 Buchanan St. Basement café nr the Concert Hall. Glaswegians (and footballers) love this place judging by the wall-to-wall gallery of happy smiling punters. Our fave too! Checked tablecloths and crooning in the background create the authentic 'mamma mia' atmos. Friendly service, totally reliable pasta 'n' pizza joint, usually busy. The antidote to Est Est Est! LO 10/11pm. Cl Sun. Book at w/ends. INX

**556**
**WE** ✓ **Trevi** 334 3262. 526 Gr Western Rd. For 17 yrs. Tiny, even cramped, family-run tratt with celebrity photos next to cool football memorabilia on the walls. The staff can get a bit distracted on international fixture nights. Loyal clientele lap up the pasta (along with pollo, veal & other carne). Mama Donata does the sauces & the puds. Gr tiramisù. Lunch: Mon-Fri. Dinner 7 days. LO 10/10.30pm. INX

**557**
**SS** ✓ **Battlefield Rest** 636 6955. 55 Battlefield Rd. On S Side nr Victoria Park & opp Infirmary in landmark pavilion building, former tram station. Family-run with gr pasta list & home-made puds & lovely thin bread. Small but light, this place unquestionably one of the best places to eat on the S Side. 7 days 10am-10pm. Cl Sun. INX

**558**
**Map 9**
**L25**
✓ **La Scarpetta** Balloch 01389 758247 Balloch Rd nr the bridge. Not perhaps many reasons to linger in Balloch – the busy lochside (Lomond) here is not one of them, but this family-run restau is. Fave of writer A.L. Kennedy (she ain't easy to please) and now us. Gr service; integrity Italia when visiting Lomond shores (1/BIG ATTRACTIONS). 7 days LO 10.30pm.     INX

**559**
**SS**
✓ **Roma Mia** 423 6694. 164 Darnley Rd nr The Tramway on the S Side (& the best option pre-/post-theatre). Expanded, v family-friendly tratt, members of 'Ciao Italia' (denoting a 'real' Italian restau). Out of the way, but this is a backstreet of Rome, not just Glasgow. 7 days lunch & LO 10.30pm.

INX

**560**
**SS**
**Buongiorno** 649 1029. 1012 Pollokshaws Rd nr Shawlands Cross. Ronaldo follows parents' footsteps & recipe book. Pasta/pizza straight-up. Some home-made desserts. T/away menu. 7 days, lunch & LO 10/11pm.     CHP

**The Big Blue** 445 Gr Western Rd. Report: 690/PIZZA.

**Di Maggio's** Royal Exchange Sq & branches: 633/KIDS.

# The Best Pizza

**561**
**WE**
✓ **Firebird** 334 0594. 1321 Argyle St. Big-windowed, spacious bistro at the far W end of Argyle St. Mixed modern menu but notable for wood-smoked dishes, of which their light, imaginative pizzas are excellent. You'd call Firebird a popular hangout, a key Glasg spot and incidentally, a better pizza is hard to find in this town. Noon-10/10.30pm (bar midnight/1am).

INX

**562**
**WE**
✓ **Big Blue** 357 1038. 445 Gt Western Rd on corner of Kelvinbridge & with terrace o/looking river. Bar & restau together so noise can obliterate meal & conversation later on. Lots of other dishes & morsels, but the big thin pizzas here are special. 7 days lunch & LO 9.45pm (w/ends 10.30pm).   INX

**563**
**C2**
**D2**
**Fratelli Sarti** 248 2228. 133 Wellington St, 121 Bath St & 404 Sauchiehall St. Excellent, thin-crust pie, buffalo mozzarella and freshly-made *pomodoro*. 7 days, hrs vary. It's the ingredients that count here, the pizza dough still on the chunky side. Full report: 550/ITALIAN RESTAUS.     INX

# The Best French Restaurants

**564**
**C2**
✓ **Le Chardon D'Or** 248 3801. 176 W Regent St. Superlative French-style restau. Report: 514/BEST RESTAUS.

**565**
**B2**
✓ **Malmaison** 221 6401. 278 W George St. The brasserie in the basement of the hotel (473/BEST HOTELS) with the same setup as Edin & elsewhere and a v similar menu – based on the classic Parisian brasseries like La Coupole. Excellent brasserie ambience in meticulously designed woody salon. Seating layout and busy waiters mean lots of buzz; also private dining rms and the adjacent Champagne Bar which serves lite bites (oysters, burgers, eggs benedict) thro'out the day. 7 days, lunch and LO 10.30pm.     MED

**566**
**D3**
**78 St Vincent** 221 7710. 78 St Vincent St. Based on century-old Le Chartier restau in Paris (on railway carriages in fact), this restau has more of a brasserie atmos than many who aspire tho food more calculated than casual. Impressive split-level rm with a high ceiling and a big mural by Glas artist Donald McLeod. Stylish cuisine balancing the tried and tested with some originality. They say 'Scottish with a continental twist'. Slightly formal with an atmos of discreet efficiency. Not bad wines. Lunch (not Sun) and LO 10/10.30pm. Also open for b/fast Mon-Sat.     MED

# The Best Scottish Restaurants

*Restaurants where there is a conscious effort to offer traditional or contemporary Scottish dishes and/or using sourced Scottish seafood/beef/lamb etc.*

**567**
**WE**
✔ **Roastit Bubbly Jocks** 339 3355. 450 Dumbarton Rd. Far up in the W End but many beat their way to this Partick dining rm where Mo Abdulla has expanded his cosy wee empire (see Fanny Trollope's 529/BISTROS) but kept it well... cosy & excl value. Not so much 'Scottish' as Scottish sourced (ingredients) & presented (ambience). And things we Scots like incl Irish stew & pavlova. Lunch Fri-Sun. LO 10pm. Cl Mon. Can BYO.                        INX

**568**
**C2**
**E4**
✔ **Arisaig** 552 4251. 24 Candleriggs. Just off main Candleriggs corner and 140 St Vincent St (204 5399), the newer, larger, downtown version. A stylish, smartly presented Scottish bistro inspired by the area where Arisaig village lies on the Road to the Isles (1680/ROUTES). Well sourced ingredients, menu splits 'Sea and Land'. Good vegn choice. Big portions. Nice prints. More claim to be presenting contemp Scotland food, ingredients & culture than others that have clambered on bandwagon. 7 days, lunch w/ends only in E End, 7 days downtown. LO 9.30/10.30pm.                        INX

**569**
**E3**
✔ **City Merchant** 553 1577. 97 Candleriggs. One of the first restaus in the Merchant City & longevity in Glas attests to enduring appeal. 'Seafood, game, steaks' focussing on quality Scottish produce with daily & à la carte menus in warm bistro atmos. Good biz restau or intimate rendezvous. 7 days lunch & dinner (not Sun lunch).                        INX

**570**
**F3**
✔ **Babbity Bowster** 16 Blackfriars St. Already listed as a pub for real ale and as a hotel (there are rms upstairs), the food is mentioned mainly for its Scottishness (haggis and stovies) and all-day availability. It's also pleasant to eat o/side on the patio/gdn in summer. There is a restau upstairs (dinner only Tues-Sat) but we prefer down. Also breakfast served from 8am (Sun 10am). (680/REAL-ALE PUBS, 490/INDIVIDUAL HOTELS)

**571**
**D3**
✔ **The Horseshoe** 17 Drury St. This classic pub to be recommended for all kinds of reasons. But lunch is a particularly good deal with 3 courses for £2.80 (pie and beans still 80p), and old favourites on the menu like mushy peas, macaroni cheese, jelly and fruit. Lunch 12noon-2.30pm. Upstairs open all aft, then for high tea till 6.30pm (not Sun) (not quite the same atmos, but pure Glas). 4-course meal for £4.95 at TGP. All Glas faves. Pub open daily till 12midnight. (660/UNIQUE GLAS PUBS)

**572**
**WE**
**The Bothy** 334 4040. 11 Ruthven Lane. Part of Stefan King's Gl Group's takeover of the W End, this tucked-away site has housed several restaus of note. This latest reflects current return to roots, ie simpler, more comfort food from the gastrification of café-bar menus & the glorification of chefs. Contemp-retro design patchy but menu confidently conceived & presented. All Scottish fares & notable ingredients present & correct. Let's hope standards keep up. 7 days noon-10pm.                        INX

**Òran Mór** 357 6226. Corner of Byres Rd & Gt Western Rd. Reports: 548/GASTROPUBS, 662/UNIQUE PUBS.

# The Best Indian Restaurants

**573**
**E3** ✓✓ **Dakhin** 553 2585. 89 Candleriggs. Upstairs & out of sight but a must-find for lovers of Indian food. Same owners as The Dhabba (below) but menu is a subcontinent away (ie S as opposed to N India). Lighter, saucier with coconut, ginger & chilli & selection of light-as-a-feather dhosas make essential diff to the tandoori/tikka-driven menus of most other restaus on this page. 7 days. Lunch & LO 10/10.30pm. INX

**574**
**xA1** ✓✓ **Mother India** 221 1663. 28 Westminster Terr. Legendary Glas restau for Indian home-cooking in a 2-floor laid-back but stylish setting & where the food rarely lets you down. Many faves & specialities by people who know how to work the flavours & textures. House wine & Kingfisher beer but for £1 corkage you can BYOB. At w/ends & many other nights you will have to book. Take-away too. Lots of vegn choice. V relaxed neighbourhood atmos. 7 days, lunch (not Sun-Tues) & LO 10.30/11pm. INX

**575**
**WE** ✓ **Mother India Café** 339 9145. 1355 Argyle St opp Kelvingrove Museum (705/ATTRACTIONS). Recent progeny from Mother (above) & cousins to Wee Currys (below), but a distinctive twist here ensures a packed house at all times. Menu made up of 40 thali or tapas-like dishes (4/5 for a party of 2), so just as we always did, we get tastes of each other's choices – only it's cheaper! Fastidious waiters (do turn round the tables). Lunch & LO 10/10.30pm. CHP

**576**
**C1**
**WE** ✓ **The Wee Curry Shop** 353 0777. 7 Buccleuch St nr Concert Hall & STV, & upstairs (above Jinty McGinty's) in Ashton Lane (357 5280). Tiny outposts of Mother India above, 2 neighbourhood home-style cooking curry shops, just as they say. Cheap, always cheerful. Stripped-down menu in small, if not micro rms. Buccleugh St – 6 tables. House red & white & Kingfisher but can BYOB (£1.50, £2.50 West End). Lunch & LO 10.30pm. Cl Sun lunch (Buccleuch St), Mon (W End). No CC. CHP

**577**
**xC1** **Killermont Polo Club** 946 5412. 2022 Maryhill Rd. After more than a dozen yrs still one of the most refreshingly different Indian restaus in Scotland. Within a hill-top restau at the Milngavie end of Maryhill Rd, you will find courteous manners, attentive service and a clubby atmos in the front rm, which is kept as a shrine to all things polo. The food is light, often experimental and the spices are sprinkled with care. Same Dum Pukht menu (slow cooked) dishes from Uzbekistan. 7 days noon-11.30pm. INX/MED

**578** **Shish Mahal** 339 8256. 68 Park Rd. First-generation Indian restau that still,
**xA2** after 30 yrs, remains one of Glasgow's faves. Modernised some yrs back but not compromised. Still feels like it's been here forever. Menu of epic size. Many different influences in the cooking, & total commitment to the Glasgow curry. 7 days. Till 11pm/12midnight. INX

**579** **Ashoka Ashton Lane** 357 5904. 19 Ashton Lane & the **Ashoka West End**
**WE** 339 0936. 1284 Argyle St. Part of the Harlequin Restaurants chain (recently changed hands), they have always been good, simple and dependable places to go for curry but have kept up with the times. Argyle St is *the* original. Nothing surprising about the menus, just sound Punjabi via Glasgow fare. Good takeaway service (0800 195 3 195). Lunch & LO 11.30pm (not lunch W End Mon/Wed). Both 7 days, lunch and open till 12midnight (W End even later). INX

**580** **The Dhabba** 553 1249. 44 Candleriggs. Mid-Merchant City curry house
**E4** which presented itself as ground-breaking when it opened in 2003. It is at least modern & enthusiastic. N Indian cuisine in big-window diner. Complemented well by sister restau Dakhin (above), we're warming to the Dhabba. 7 days noon-10.30pm. INX

**581** **Café India** 248 4074. 171 N St. Enormous brasserie, big on a glamour that
**A2** seems a bit time-warped now, but the food is pretty good. The extensive menu is busy with herbs and spices and is not merely hot. A night on the town kind of joint. Buffet and à la carte, Sun-Mon. 7 days, lunch and LO 11.30pm/12midnight. INX

**582** **The Ashoka** 221 1761. 108 Elderslie St. Confusingly, no relation to the
**A2** Ashokas above. Designery interior but that old pink pakora sauce still runs

through the veins. Long est now but does change. The expanding 'curry karaoke nights' may stick in the throat. Persian & Indian influences. These curries will run & run! Mon-Sat lunch, 7 days dinner. LO 12.30/1am.   INX

583 **Ali Shan**   632 5294. 250 Battlefield Rd. Haven't tried but Southsiders &
SS  many from further afield swear by this Indo-Pak restau that's esp good for veggie & other diets. It's been here for nigh-on 20 yrs & hasn't changed much but honesty & integrity are v much in their mix of spices. 7 days, lunch Thur/Fri only, LO 11pm (12 midnight w/ends).   INX

# The Best Far-Eastern Restaurants

## THAI

584 ✓**Thai Lemongrass**   331 1315. 24 Renfrew St nr Bus Stn & Concert Hall.
D2  ✓ Noticing perhaps that Glas has far fewer good Thai restaus than Edin, TL has opened up here & become quite poss the best in town. Contemp while still cosy. It seems set to give old Thai Fountain (below) a run for its baht. Good service & presentation of all the new Thai faves. 7 days lunch & LO 11.30pm.   MED

585 ✓**Thai Fountain**   332 2599. 2 Woodside Cres. Charing Cross, nr M8,
A1  ✓ Mitchell Library, etc. Tho old-style now this is still one of the best Thai in Scotland. Owned by Chinese Mr Chung but the Thai chefs know a green curry from a red. Tom yam excellent and weeping tiger beef v popular with those who really just want a steak. Lots of prawn and fish dishes and real vegn choice. Lunch and LO 11pm.   MED

586 **Thai Siam**   229 1191. 1191 Argyle St (W End side). Trad homely (if dimly lit) atmos
xA2  but fashionable clientele who swear it has the prawniest crackers and greenest curry in town. Has moved on since prop/chef Pawina Kennedy sizzled the woks, but the all-Thai staff in kitchen & up front maintain authenticity. Lunch & LO 11pm. Cl Sun lunch.   MED

## CHINESE

587 ✓**Asia Style**   332 8828. 185 St George's Rd, Charing Cross. Discreet,
xA1  ✓ authentic & exceptionally good value, this was the late-night restau of choice 2005. Bright canteen with banter to match. Trad Chinese without MSG loading. Malaysian dishes. Wine comes red or white. 7 days, dinner only LO 2.30am.   CHP

588 ✓**Dragon-i**   332 7728. 311 Hope St. Refreshingly contemp Chinese-Far
D1  ✓ East fusion restau opp Theatre Royal. Thai/Malaysia & rice/noodle/pak choi dishes with sound non-MSG, often Scottish ingredients. Proper puds. Chill room & creative Chinese cuisine at last. Lunch Mon-Fri, dinner 7 days LO 11pm (10pm Suns).   MED

589 ✓**Amber Regent**   331 1655. 50 W Regent St. Elegant Cantonese restau
C2  ✓ that prides itself on courteous service and the quality of its cuisine, esp seafood. The menu is trad, the atmos too. Has v interior feel. Creditable wine list, quite romantic at night and a good business lunch spot. Only Glas Chinese restau in AA & Michelin. Lunch, LO 10.30pm w/ends 11/11.30pm. Cl Sun.   MED

590 ✓**Peking Inn**   332 8971. 191 Hope St. Smart, urban kind of Chinese restau
C2  ✓ on busy corner (with W Regent St) but light, relaxing room. Famous for its spicy, Szechuan specials as well as Beijing cuisine; and nights on town. Perenially popular. Lunch (not Sun), LO 10.30/11.30pm.   MED

591 ✓**China Town**   353 0037. 42 New City Rd. Just off centre but nr
C1  ✓ Cowcaddens, under the m/way. Here you're in Hong Kong (almost). Endless food for lunch (esp Sun) or dinner. Divine dim sum. If you love Chinese food, you must come here. 7 days, noon-11.30pm.   INX

592 **Loon Fung**   332 1240. 417 Sauchiehall St. For 35 yrs poss Glasgow's most
B1  'respected' Cantonese, the place where the local Chinese community meet for lunch on a Sun/Mon/Tue. Pace is fast and friendly while the food is fresh and authentic. Gr dim sum. Everybody on chopsticks. Even a noticeboard of Hong Kong/Beijing flights. 7 days, 12noon-11/11.30pm.   MED

**593** **Ho Wong** 221 3550. 82 York St, in city centre, betw Clyde St and Argyle St.
**C4** Unlikely location for discreet, urbane Pekinese/Cantonese restau which relies on its reputation and makes few compromises. Décor dated now, but still up-market clientele; roomful of suits at lunch and champagne list. Notable for seafood and duck. Good Szechuan. Lunch (not Sun) and LO 11/11.30pm. MED

**594** **Chow** 334 9818. 98 Byres Rd & 52 Bank St (357 6682). Away from other
**WE** Chinese restaus clustered downtown, these are the contemp, smarter & recent W End versions. Broad menu incl speciality Singapore noodles & Szechuan dishes. Good vegn choice. T/away & delivery. 7 days lunch & dinner (Sun from 4.30pm). LO 11.30pm. INX

**595** **Glasgow Noodle Bar** 333 1883. 482 Sauchiehall St. Authentic, Chinese-
**B1** style noodle bar, 100m from Charing Cross. Along with **Canton Express** opp at 407 Sauchiehall St (332 0145), two fast food joints with genuine, made on the spot – in the wok – food late into the AM. Both shabby, but groovy in a W End way. 7days, 12noon-4am. (685/684/LATE-NIGHT RESTAUS) CHP

## JAPANESE

**596** **Oko** 572 1500. 68 Ingram St. On main st of Merchant City area, out east. The
**F3** Japanese conveyor belt to the stars (local ex pop star Jim Kerr had a hand in setting this up). Reasonably authentic Japanese nibbles come past and can add up to quite a bill. Booths best. A good bet to lightly nosh when others may be booked or busy. Tues-Sun, all day. LO 11 (11.30)pm. Bar later. MED

**597** **Wagamama** 229 1468. 97 W George St. Wagamama brand & formula
**D2** comes to Scotland tho on an unprepossessing site in mid-town. If you've never been, but like Asian food that's good for you and fast, go check it out – it's a unique formula: big canteen tables, 'healthy' Japanese-based food made to order & brought when ready. Seems to work universally. 7 days 12-11pm (Sun 12.30-10pm). INX

**598** **Ichiban** 204 4200. 50 Queen St & 184 Dumbarton Rd (Partick). Noodle bar
**D3** based loosely on the Wagamama formula. Fundamental food, egalitarian
**WE** presentation, some technology. Ramen, udon, soba noodle dishes; also chow meins, tempuras and other Japanese snacks. Long tables, eat-as-it-comes 'methodology'. Light, calm, hip. Lunch and LO 10pm (w/ends 10.30pm), Sun 1-10pm. The Partick Ichiban which is nr Byres Rd is poss better of the 2; certainly the healthiest caff in the quarter. INX

## FUSION

**599** **Café Mao** 564 5161. Corner of Brunswick and Wilson St in Merchant City.
**E3** Bright, hip east-Asian restau on Merchant City corner. Indonesian, Malaysian, Korean dishes prep with varying degrees of flair & flava. Good service, right-on wine-list. Asian beers & smoothies. Nice rice. Open all day. 7 days. Lunch 12-5pm LO 10/11pm (Sun 1pm-10pm). INX

**600** **Yen** 847 0110. 28 Tunnel St in the Rotunda building nr the SECC so often busy
**xA4** with pre- or après-concert audiences. Upstairs café has Cantonese/Japanese/Thai noodle vibe, ground floor has more exp, more full-on teppanyaki restau with 8-course menus you sit & watch being prepared on the searing hobs. You might yearn for a better exchange rate. 7 days, lunch & LO 10.30pm (cl Sun lunch). INX/MED

**601** **Oshi** 333 5702. Pt Dundas Pl. The ground floor restau of Langs Hotel
**D2** (475/HOTELS) with adj spa sees itself as an 'urban retreat'. It is a v nice space, ambient & urban. This reflected in menu where Euro meets Asia on almost equal split. 7 days noon-10pm. INX

# Other Ethnic Restaurants

## SPANISH

**602**
**WE** ✓ **Café Andaluz** 339 1111. 2 Cresswell Lane off Byres Rd. Basement on corner of Cresswell (the less heaving) lane where folks gather of an evening. Nice atmos encased in ceramica with wide choice tapas & mains (incl vegn). Owned by Di Maggio (Italian) chain so authentic más o menos (we mean more or less). 7 days LO 10.30/11pm. CHP

**603**
**C3** **Tapaell'ya at the Radisson Hotel** 225 2047. Robertson St at Argyle St. The walk-in restau of the audacious new Radisson (472/HOTELS) is not often busy so who knows if this formula will remain, but the paellas (3 of), tapas & excl Spanish wine selection are refreshingly particular in a Fusion-infused world. Mon-Fri 12-10.30pm, Sat 6-10.30pm, Sun 11am-3pm. INX

## MEXICAN

**604**
**E4** **Pancho Villa's** 552 7737. 26 Bell St. Bright, colourful restau free of the cluttered cantina stereotype, run by real, live Mexican, Maira Nunez. Menu in Spanish/ingredients in English. No burritos ('an American invention'). Plenty of veggie choices but you really have to try the *albondigas en salsa* (that's spicy meatballs). Mon-Sat lunch and 6-11pm, Sun 6-10.30pm. INX

**605**
**D5** **Salsa** 420 6328. 63 Carlton Pl. On S bank of river at end of Glasgow Bridge (pedestrian), an unlikely location perhaps since bright, spicy salsa lurks in a basement here. Bar with rel small restau section but some of the best Mexican staples & lovely, imaginative mains in town. This place deserves to do well – cross that bridge when you come to it! Lunch & LO 10pm (bar later). INX

## GREEK

**606**
**xA1** **Konaki** 342 4010. 920 Sauchiehall St, w of M8 opp Kelvin Park Lorne Hotel. A paint job on the outside wouldn't go amiss here, but flaky façade is in keeping with no-frills, down-to-Greek-earth approach. This is back st Athens where the best caffs are – real, cheap, good Greek grub (incl pastas) with proper ingredients eg oregano from the home village in Crete. 7 days, lunch & dinner (not Sun lunch). LO 11pm. CHP

## MIDDLE EASTERN

**607**
**xB1** **Bay Tree Café** 334 5898. 403 Gt Western Rd nr Kelvinbridge. For yrs a veggie haven now serving lamb & chicken dishes (kept separate in the kitchen) extending Turkish, Lebanese & N African range. Diverse menu from homous (sic) to those sweet sweet desserts with many a casserole in betw. Simple caff; gr value. 7 days 9.30am-10pm (9pm-Sun). CHP

# The Best Seafood & Fish

**608**
**C2**
✓ ✓ **Gamba** 572 0899. 225a W George St, in basement at corner of W Campbell St. A seafood bistro which happens to be one of the best restaus in the city (512/BEST RESTAUS). Fashionable clientele enjoy stylish setting and snappy service, as well as excellent fresh fish unfussily presented à la mode. Exemplary wine list. Unlike many, open on Mon (cl Sun). Lunch and dinner. LO 10.30pm but may serve later so check. MED

**609**
**C2**
✓ **Mussel Inn** 572 1405. 157 Hope St. Downtown location for light, bright bistro (big windows) where seafood is serious, but fun. Mussels, scallops, oysters & vegn option, but mussels in variant concoctions & kilo pots are the thing. As in Edin (207/SEAFOOD), this formula is sound & the owners, Messrs Johansson, Spiers & Watford, are to be commended for keeping it real & for giving excl value. 7 days, lunch & dinner (not Sun lunch). INX

**610**
**WE**
**C2**
✓ **Two Fat Ladies** 339 1944. 88 Dumbarton Rd. A landmark W End restau now expanding & opening an offshoot downtown at 118 Blythswood St (847 0088) at TGP. Everything is selectively sourced & the tiny, outfront kitchen produces delicious dishes with a light touch. Lovely puds. 7 days (not Sun lunch). MED

**Café Royale** 340 Crow Rd. Report: 528/BISTROS.

**Rogano** 11 Exchange Pl. Report: 517/BEST RESTAUS.

# The Best Vegetarian Restaurants

**611**
**A1**
✓ **Grassroots Café** 333 0534. 97 St George's Rd beneath St George's Studios nr Charing Cross. This is the caff offshoot of Grassroots (the deli) round the corner at 48 Woodlands Rd (1498/DELIS): serving proper vegn & vegan food. Nutritious, worthy – all this, but round the world dishes as vegn food should be and some simply splendid salads. Calming as well as healthy despite proximity of M8. 7 days. BYO poss. 10am-10pm. CHP

**612**
**E4**
✓ **Mono** 553 2400. Kings Court opp carparks behind St Enoch's Centre. In odd no-man's land betw Merchant City & E End, a cool hangout in a forlorn mall. PC in a people's collective kind of way; the antithesis of Glas manufactured style. Gr space with art, music, occ performance & interesting vegn food served by friendly staff. Organic ales/wines. 7 days noon-10pm (bar midnight). CHP

**613**
**E4**
**The 13th Note** 553 1638. 50-60 King St. Old-style veggie hangout – a good attitude/good vibes café-bar with live music downstairs. Big range menu from excellent vegeburgers to Indian and Greek dishes. All suitable for vegans. Organic booze on offer, but also normal Glasgow bevvy. 7 days, 12noon-12midnight. Food LO 10pm.

*Restaurants serving particularly good vegn food but not exclusively vegn:*

**The Ubiquitous Chip, Thai Fountain**. Reports: 513/521/BEST RESTAUS.

**Baby Grand, St Jude's, Arthouse Grill, Arisaig** and **Tron Café-Bar**. Reports: 540/BEST BISTROS, 552/BEST RESTAUS, 547/GASTROPUBS.

**Bay Tree Café**. Report: 607/OTHER ETHNIC.

**Mother India, Dakhin**. Report: 575/INDIAN RESTAUS.

**Café Gandolfi, Tempus**. Report: 614/623/TEAROOMS.

# The Best Tearooms & Coffee Shops

**614**
**E4** ✓ ✓ **Café Gandolfi** 552 6813. 64 Albion St, Merchant City. For over 20 yrs a definitive & landmark meeting/eating place – bistro menu, but casual ambience of a tearm or coffee shop. Bohemian, Europe-somewhere atmos. Stained glass and heavy, over-sized wooden furniture create a unique ambience that has stood the fashionability test. The food is light and imaginative and served all day. You may have to queue. 7 days, 9am-11.30pm, Sun from 12noon (649/SUN BREAKFAST). The much more recent Bar upstairs (542/GASTROPUBS) has added a new rm & a new dimension.

**615**
**WE** ✓ **Tinderbox** 339 3108. 189 Byres Rd, on busy corner with Highburgh Rd. Stylish, shiny, state-of-the-art neighbourhood coffee shop. Stuff for kids, stuff to buy. Snacks and Elektra, the good-looking coffee machine. Gr people-watching potential inside and out. Better s/wiches and cakey things than others of this ilk. Tinderbox has made that huge leap to London & can be found in Upper St, Islington. 7 days, 7.45am-11pm (Sun from 8.45am).

**616**
**WE** ✓ **Kember & Jones** 337 3851. 134 Byres Rd. They call it a 'Fine Food Emporium' & it is, tho some would say 'at a price'. A deli with well-sourced nibbles & the stuff of the good life esp cheese & olives. Tables o/side & on the mezzanine. Gr sandwiches & the best tartes & tortes in town. Home-made to a high standard. The new star on the Byres Rd '05. 7 days, 9am-7pm (till 6 Sat/Sun & from 10am Suns).

**617**
**WE** ✓ **Hummingbird** 334 9699. 59 Hyndland St on corner of Chancellor St & opp the site of the Partick Farmers Market where Hummingbird was born. Adorable but unadorned tearm with exquisite home-made cakes, quiches, soups & the like. Home baking at its best. Small & perfect like a hummingbird! Tue-Sat 10am-5pm.

**618**
**C2** **Where The Monkey Sleeps** 226 3406. 182 W Regent St adj Compass Gallery & in basement below Chardon D'Or (514/BEST RESTAUS): its commercial & spiritual opposite. Exhib space ie hanging as well as hanging out. Coffee, soups & picmix s/wiches. Art students & what they turn into. 7 days. 7am-5pm. (6pm Sat). Cl Sun.

**619**
**WE** **North Star** 946 5365. 108 Queen Margaret Drive. Portuguese-cum-Iberian deli-cum-neighbourhood caff. Minimalist approach to design and product range; v laid-back in cramped surroundings. All home-made except bread. Daily specials on the tiles. Can BYOB. 7 days Mon-Sat. 8am-7/8pm. Sun 11am-6pm.

**620**
**D1** **Café Hula** 353 1660. 321 Hope St. Central, some say overlooked café opp Theatre Royal by people who have North Star (above). Simple, imaginative menu with home-made appeal; good vegn choice. Anti-style, mix 'n' match – a boho atmos rare in this town. 7 days 8.30am-10pm, Sun 11am-6pm.

**621**
**WE** **Tchai-ovna** 357 4524. 42 Otago Lane off Otago St & round the back. A 'house of tea' hidden away on the banks of the Kelvin with verandah & gdn terrace. A decidedly boho tearm which could be E Europe, N Africa or Kathmandu. 70 kinds of tea, soup, organic s/wiches & cakes. Impromptu performances likely. A real find but suits & le chic not comfortable here. 7 days 11am-11pm.

**622**
**F4** **Café Source** 548 6020. 1 St Andrews Sq. In a secret sq nr Saltmarket & Trongate below gorgeous St Andrews church, a secret caff with excl Scottish menu balancing old-style & new. 7 days lunch & dinner. LO 8.45/9.30pm.

**623**
**B1** **Tempus** 332 7959. 350 Sauchiehall St. The atrium café of the CCA, spectacularly refurbished 2002. Kind of like eating in a covered st. Stylish/contemp of course – the rm & the menu. Gd rendezvous. Always people concocting and creating or just conspiring. 11am-9pm (10pm Sat). Cl Sun.

**624**
**SS** **Art Lover's Café** 353 4779. 10 Dumbreck Rd, Bellahouston Park. On the ground floor of House for an Art Lover, a building based on drawings left by Rennie Mackintosh (768/MACKINTOSH). Bright rm, crisp presentation and a counterpoint to wrought iron, purply, swirly Mockintosh caffs elsewhere. This is unfussy & elegant. Garden views. Soup 'n' sandwiches & à la carte; a serious lunch spot. 7 days 10am-5pm.

# The Best Caffs

**625**
**WE** ✓✓ **University Café** 87 Byres Rd. 'When your granny, in the lines of the well-known song, was "shoved aff a bus", this is where she was taken afterwards and given a wee cup of tea to steady her nerves. People have been coming here for generations to sit at the "kneesy" tables and share the salt and vinegar. Run by the Verecchia family who administer advice, sympathy and pie, beans and chips with equal aplomb." ' These astute words of the late Graeme Kelling describing a real Glasgow gem, still stand 3 editions later. Daily till 10pm (w/ends till 10.30pm). Cl Tue. Takeaway open later.

**626**
**xF3** ✓ **Coia's Café** 473 Duke St. Since 1928, supplying this E End high st with ice cream, gr deal breakfasts and the kind of comforting lunch (they might call it dinner) café-bar places just cannot do. There's a telly in the corner lots of Glas chat at the tables. Sit-in or takeaway. Sweeties (tho not as evident as yore); Havana cigars. 7 days, 7.30am-9pm (LO 7.30pm); Sun from 10am.

**627**
**SS** ✓ **Brooklyn Café** 632 3427. 21 Minard Rd, corner of Frankfort St off Pollokshaws Rd. Whatever fancy café-bar Stefan King throws up on the S Side, this caff here over 70 yrs will probably outlive the lot of them. More tratt perhaps than caff with pasta/pizza, 3 risottos, 6 salads, excl puds & gr ice-cream. Recent refurb but still & forever the real thing! 7 days 9am-8pm (w/ends 10pm). Sun from 10am.

**628**
**xC1** **Café D'Jaconelli** 570 Maryhill Rd nr the Queen's Cross Church (761/MACKINTOSH). Neighbourhood caff with toasties, macaroni cheese and award-winning ice-cream to go that's been here for ever. This is the disappearing Glasgow, but used often as a film location (*Trainspotting*, *Carla's Song*). These are the real banquettes. The fish 'n' chips next door is under diff mngmt. 7 days, 10am-5pm, counter 10pm.

**629**
**C2** **Bradfords** 245 Sauchiehall St. Since 1924 the coffee shop/restau upstairs from the flagship shop of this local and estimable bakery chain. Familiar wifie waitresses, the macaroni cheese is close to mum's and the cakes and pies from downstairs represent Scottish bakery at its best. Mon-Sat 9am-5.30pm.

**630**
**WE** **Monster Mash** 339 3666. 41 Byres Rd. Self-consciously a caff but more of a meal out on the town than others on this page. British comfort food standards – sausage & mash of the day, shepherds pie, macaroni cheese, even haggis, neeps & tatties – served miraculously from tiny gantry kitchen. Small all over so may need to book or wait. 7 days 8am-10pm (Sat from 9am, Sun from 10am). Also in Edin.

**631**
**WE** **Kebabish** 334 1100. 23 Gibson St. A take & take away on the old kebab theme. Upfront you see everything being grilled, stirfried & sorted; tables at back. Like a bus-station caff on a backpacker trail, we could all happily relive our gap yrs here. Curries incl fish & vegn & unusual specials. Lassis & fresh juice. All cheap as nans (no chips!). 7 days till midnight, 1am w/ends.

**632**
**WE** **Jack McPhee's** 285 Byres Rd. Jack McPhee Fresh from the Sea it says above the door of this trad tho traded-up fish 'n' chip shop caff still frying up among the olive groves of Byres Rd. Mixed platters the thing, but a US-style Scottish b/fast (hash browns *and* potato scones) must be considered. No bad coffee. 7 days 9am-10pm.

# Kid-Friendly Places

**633**
**WE**
**SS**
**D3**
**Di Maggio's** 334 8560. 61 Ruthven Lane, off Byres Rd, W End; 632 4194, 1038 Pollokshaws Rd, on a busy corner S of the river; and 248 2111, 21 Royal Exchange Sq. 'Our family serving your family' they say & they do. Bustling, friendly pizza joints with good Italian attitude to bairns. There's a choice to defy the most finicky kid. High chairs, special menu. In summer, o/side tables in Exchange Sq so the kids can run around. 7 days.

**634**
**SS**
**Tramway Café** 422 2023. 25 Albert Drive. Caff at the back of Tramway arts venue on the S Side. Venue itself cavernous, contemporary with continuously changing programme always worth visiting. Caff well run with gr grub & facing on to 'The Secret Garden' (1568/GARDENS) so it's nice for kids. 10am-8pm, Sun 12-6pm. Cl Mon.

**635**
**SS**
**Brooklyn Café** 632 3427. 21 Minard Rd. The unassuming, long-est caff on the S Side (off Pollokshaws Rd) where families are v welcome for the carbo & the cones & the jars of sweeties on the shelf. Report: 627/CAFFS.

**636**
**SS**
**637**
**B1**
**Art Lover's Café** and **Tempus @ the CCA** 353 4779, Dumbreck Rd & 332 7959, 350 Sauchiehall St. 2 informal, light cafés with space for kids & parents not to feel confined. Reports: 624/623/COFFEESHOPS.

**Tron Café** 552 8587. The Child-friendly Bar of the Year 2003. Special family section. Report: 547/GASTROPUBS.

**Sorry there aren't more.**

# The Best Late-Night Restaurants

**638** ✓ **Baby Grand** 248 4942. Elmbank Gardens by Charing Cross Stn &
**A2** Premier Lodge skyscraper hotel (behind King's Theatre). Not easy for strangers to find, but persevere – this is a decent bar/diner at any time of day (540/BISTROS), but comes into its own after 10pm when just about everywhere that's decent is closing. Char-grilled food & grazing contemp menu. Piano player & night-time people. Daily till midnight, Fri/Sat till 2am.

**639** ✓ **Asia Style** 332 8828. 185 St George's Rd, Charing Cross. Simple,
**xA1** authentic Chinese & Malaysian café/canteen with familiar sweet 'n' sour, curry & satays & 4 kinds of noodle but exotic specials & 5 kinds of 'porridge'. Only open eves. 7 days 5pm-3am.

**640** **Spice Garden** 492 4422. 11 Clyde Pl. Just over the river, under the Glasgow
**C4** Br where trains rumble over, a restau that's long been a late-night destination. Now most definitely Indian, it's for the late & last curry craving of the day. Pleasantly light, food surprisingly good. 7 days 6pm-4am, Sun till 1am.

**641** **Gong** 576 1700. 17 Vinicombe St off N end of Byres Rd. Mezzanine bars flank
**WE** a floor of restau tables compartmentalised in a forest of bamboo. Design over dining perhaps, but late-night supper club a good call in a W End where food mostly stops at 10.30. Menu limited (nachos, goujons, chicken 'strips') but even a bowl of chips allows drinking till 2am (Fri/Sat only).

**642** **Glasgow Noodle Bar** 333 1883. 482 Sauchiehall St. Better of the 2
**B1** stripped-down noodle bars opp ea other in W Sauchiehall St (Canton Express pretty grim these days). Authentic, Chinese fast food, no frills (ticket service and eezee-kleen tables). The noodle is 'king' here; but cooking *is* taken seriously. (595/FAR-EASTERN RESTAUS) 7 days, 12noon-5am.

**643** **Stravaigin & Stravaigin 2** 334 2665 & 334 7165. Gibson St & Ruthven
**WE** Lane off Byres Rd. Worth remembering that both these excl restaus (515/RESTAUS & 523/BISTROS) serve food to 11pm.

**Ashoka West End & Ashoka Ashton Lane** 1284 Argyle St & Ashton Lane (611/INDIAN RESTAUS). 12.30am/1am w/ends.

# Good Places For Sunday Breakfast

**644** ✓ **Tinderbox** 339 3108. Corner Byres Rd & Highburgh St. Gr café/diner
**WE** open v early to late. Prob the earliest decent b/fast for out-all-nighters. Rest of the week they open 7.15am. Report: 615/COFFEE SHOPS. W/ends from 7.45am.

**645** ✓ **Babbity Bowster** 552 5055. 16 Blackfriars St. The seminal Merchant
**F3** City bar/hotel recommended for many things (570/SCOTTISH RESTAUS, 688/DRINKING OUTDOORS), but worth remembering as one of the best and earliest spots for Sun breakfast. From 8am.

**646** ✓ **Café Gandolfi** 552 6813. 64 Albion St. Atmospheric rm, with soft day-
**E4** light filtering through stained glass and the comforting, oversized wooden furniture. This is pleasant start to another Sun, that day of rest and more shopping made even better with some baked eggs, a pot of tea and the Sun papers (614/BEST TEAROOMS). Bar upstairs has all-day menu. Both from 12noon.

**647** ✓ **Coia's Café** 473 Duke St. They've been doing b/fast here for over 75 yrs
**xF3** & it's still damned good. The full-fry monty lasts all day (incl vegn option). Papers provided. The E End choice (626/BEST CAFFS). From 10am.

**648** ✓ **Stravaigin** 334 2665. 28 Gibson St. Same care & flair given to b/fast
**WE** menu as the rest (515/BEST RESTAUS). Cramped maybe, but reflects appetite for Sun b/fast from home-made granola to French toast, Ramsay's Ayrshire bacon, even a steak sandwich. Served till 5pm. From 11am.

**649** **Grassroots Café** 97 St George's Rd at Charing X. An especially calm &
**A1** healthy Sun thing incl tempeh bacon rashers (611/VEGN RESTAUS). From 10am.

**650** **Loop** 354 7705. 110 Bath St the ground floor of Bewley's Hotel (494/TRAVEL
**C2** LODGES) for whom it supplies b/fast hence early start. All the usual & some contemp twists in mod restau surroundings. B/fast menu till 11am. From 8am.

# The Best Takeaway Places

**651**
**WE** ✓ **Heart Buchanan** 334 7626. 380 Byres Rd. Deli & t/away but more what Fiona Buchanan describes as a 'traiteur', the French idea that excl food can be pre-prepared & you just take it home & reheat it. Certainly an extraordinary daily changing menu is produced in the kitchens downstairs according to a published menu of the week. Lots of other carefully selected goodies to go. Fiona puts her 'heart' into this place. Every urban neighbourhood should have a Heart & Buchanan. 7 days 8.30am-9.30pm. Suns 12-7pm.

**652**
**WE** ✓ **Delizique** 339 2000. 66 Hyndland St on corner nr Cottiers. Serving the luvvies, loaded & long-term denizens of Hyndland & beyond, more an old-fashioned provisioner than spanking new deli. Fruit/veg o/side, cheese counter; the unusual alongside the dinner-party essentials. Gorgeous food to go. 7 days 8am-8pm (Suns from 9am).

**653**
**E3** ✓ **Fresh** 552 5532. 51 Cochrane St adj George Sq. At last a t/away with integrity in the Merchant City. Hearty (& lite) healthy soups & juices. Sandwiches made up or ready-to-go. Much vegn. All dolphin-friendly. 7 days 9am-5pm (Suns from 11am).

**654**
**WE** **Naked Soup** 334 6200. 106 Byres Rd. First of the soup-to-go places. Nutritious but nice! Perhaps not best location for office lunches (new branch opening at TGP in Dumbarton Rd), but otherwise absolutely the right idea. 8 fresh (organic where poss) soups daily, gr salads (esp cous cous) & (perhaps too) thick smoothies. Sit-in or go. 7 days, 9am-5pm, Sun 11-5pm.

**655**
**WE** **Andreas Greek Deli** 576 5031. 27 Old Dumbarton Rd. W End Greek & Cypriot deli/takeaway full of treats, eg almond & rose-water shortbread, aubergine pie, as well as more predictable moussakas. Mon-Sat 9.30am-9pm. Cl Sun.

**656**
**C3**
**D2**
**D3** **Pret À Manger** 34 Sauchiehall St, St Vincent St, Bothwell St. Sad in a way that the only decent group of t/aways in Glas is the ubiquitous Pret chain. Smart, formulaic but has wiped the floor with the more trad sandwich bars. So altho we don't do many chains in this book, Pret is still as good as sandwich bars get in Glasgow. Food comes with philosophy, tho it didn't stop them selling out to McDonald's! Hrs vary.

**657**
**A1** **Grassroots** 353 3278. 20 Woodlands Rd, Charing X. Food to go, but mainly big organic deli. Vegn ready meals, bespoke s/wiches. 7 days 8am-6/7pm, Sat 9-6pm, Sun 11-5pm.

**658**
**xF3** **MacSingh's Deli** 554 5225. 330 Duke St. Along from estimable Market Gallery. Small caff, mainly t/away. Bacon rolls & s/wiches but mostly homemade pakora/samosas/chaat/daals/tikkas/jalfrezi & all things E of Glasgow. Friendly neighbourhood spot. 7 days.

**659**
**WE** **Mr India's West End** 334 0084. 11 Hyndland St, off Dumbarton Rd. Formerly Balbir's, this long est restau has gr local rep. Balti & tandoori specials & gd vegn choice. Deliver all over the posh W End (5-11pm).

**Philadelphia Fish & Chicken Bar** 445 Gt Western Rd. Report: 1418/FISH 'N' CHIPS. The old W End standby!

# Unique Glasgow Pubs

**660** ✓ ✓ **The Horseshoe** 17 Drury St. A mighty pub since the 19th cent in
**D3** the small st betw W Nile and Renfield Sts nr Central stn. Early
example of this style of pub, dubbed 'gin palaces'. Island rather than horseshoe bar ('the longest in the UK'), impressive selection of alcohols and an
upstairs lounge where they serve high tea. The food is amazing value
(571/SCOTTISH RESTAUS). All kinds of folk. Daily till 12midnight.

**661** ✓ **The Halt Bar** 160 Woodlands Rd. Edwardian pub largely unspoiled,
**xA1** unchanged tho paint job wouldn't go amiss. Original counter and snug
intact. Always gr atmos – model of how a pub should look and feel. Live
music and DJs Wed-Sun. Open mic nights. Open till 11/12pm.

**662** ✓ **Òran Mór** Corner of Byres Rd & Gt Western Rd. Huge & hugely popu-
**WE** lar pub emporium in converted church on prominent W End corner.
Drinking on all levels (& outside) but also good pub food (548/GASTROPUBS) &
separate brasserie (535/BISTROS). Big entertainment programme from DJs to
comedy & 'A Play and a Pint'. They thought of everything. 7 days till midnight.

**663** ✓ **Corinthian** 191 Ingram St. Mega makeover of impressive listed build-
**E3** ing to form cavernous bar/restau, 2 comfy lounge/cocktail bars and a
restau serving 'traditional Scottish food' (tho tapenade souffle alongside
broth & haggis). Nr George Sq and Gallery of Modern Art. Awesome ceiling in
main rm recently transformed (again) into the 'Lite Bar' – better than
megabars elsewhere. 7 days, till 12midnight. (Piano bar Thur-Sun).

**664** ✓ **Arta** Old Cheesemarket, Walls St, Merchant City. Nr & rel to Corinthian
**E4** (above) & similar scale of vision completely realised. This massive OTT
bar/restau/club somewhere betw old Madrid & new Barcelona could prob
only happen in Glasgow. 'Mediterranean' menu upstairs but also burgers (till
11pm) & down the full-on Glas drinking, dressing-up & chatting-up experience. Go thro' that curtain into a dream or just possibly a nightmare. Wed-
Sun from 5pm-1am (Thu/Fri/Sat till 3am).

**665** ✓ **Victoria Bar** 157 Bridgegate. 'The Vicky' is in the 'Briggait', one of
**D5** Glas's oldest streets, nr the Victoria Br over the Clyde. Once a pub for the
fishmarket and open odd hrs, now it's a howf for all those who like an atmos
that's old, friendly and uncontrived. Ales. Mon-Sat till 12midnight, Sun 11pm.

**666** ✓ **Scotia Bar** 112 Stockwell St. Nr the Victoria (above), late-1920s Tudor-
**D5** style pub with a low-beamed ceiling and intimate, woody 'snug'. Long
the haunt of folk musicians, writers and raconteurs. Music and poetry sessions, folk and blues Wed-Sun. Open till 12midnight.

**667** ✓ **Clutha Vaults** 167 Stockwell St. This and the pubs above are part of the
**D5** same family of trad Glas pubs. The Clutha (ancient name for the Clyde)
has a Victorian-style interior and an even longer history. Known for live music
(Wed-Sun). Mon-Sat till 12midnight, Sun till 11pm.

**668** **Bar 10** 10 Mitchell Lane, off Buchanan St. Opp new Lighthouse and nr the
**D3** Tunnel, this was one of the orig 'cool' & pre-club bars before the Glas style-
bar explosion. Dating now but remarkably resilient to fashionista trends, the
Ben Kelly interior still looks good. Food till 4.30pm, then snax. Regular DJs at
w/ends. (698/COOL BARS)

**669** **Lismore** 206 Dumbarton Rd, main rd w after Byres Rd. Lismore/Lios mor
**WE** named after the long island off Oban. Gr neighbourhood (Partick) bar that
welcomes all sorts. Gives good atmos, succour and malts. Daily till 12pm.

**670** **Ben Nevis** Argyle St. Owned by same people as Lismore & Òran Mór
**xA2** (above). An excl makeover in contemp but not faux-Scottish style. Small &
pubby, the Deuchars is spot-on & gr malt list. Live music Wed/Thu/Sun.

# The Best Old 'Unspoilt' Pubs

*The following places don't have to pretend to be old. Open till 11pm/midnight.*

**Horseshoe** 17 Drury St. Report: 660/UNIQUE PUBS.

**Halt Bar** 160 Woodlands Rd. Report: 661/UNIQUE PUBS.

**Victoria Bar** 157 Bridgegate. Report: 665/UNIQUE PUBS.

**Scotia Bar** 112 Stockwell St. Report: 666/UNIQUE PUBS.

**Clutha Vaults** 167 Stockwell St. Report: 667/UNIQUE PUBS.

671 ✓ **The Griffin (& The Griffiny & The Griffinette)** 266 Bath St. Corner
B2 of Elmbank St nr King's Theatre. Built 1903 to anticipate the completion of the theatre and offer the patrons a pre-show pie and a pint. Stand at the Edwardian Bar like generations of Glaswegians. Main bar still retains 'snug' with a posh, etched-glass partition; booths have been added but the atmos is still 'Old Glasgow'. Food till 6.30pm. Cl Sun. Amazingly cheap lunches in the bar (689/PUB FOOD).

672 **Steps** 66 Glassford St. Tiny pub & barely noticed but has the indelible marks
E3 of better by-gone days. In no way celebrated like Rogano (550/RESTAUS), but also refers to the *Queen Mary* with stained glass & gr panelling. V typical, friendly Glasgow. Often, there are free snacks on the house. A real find.

673 **M J Heraghty** 708 Pollokshaws Rd. More than a touch of the Irish here and
SS easily more authentic than recent imports. A local with loyal regulars who'll make you welcome; old pub practices still hold in this howff in the sowff. Ladies' loos introduced in 1996! Sun-Thu till 11pm, Fri-Sat till 12midnight.

674 **Brechin's** 803 Govan Rd. Nr jnct with Paisley Rd W and motorway over-
xA5 pass. Established in 1798 and, as they say, always in the same family. A former shipyard pub which is close in heart & soul to to Rangers FC. It's behind the statue of shipbuilder Sir William Pearce (which, covered in sooty grime, was known as the 'Black Man') and there's a feline 'rat-catcher' on the roof (making it a listed building). Unaffected neighbourhood atmos, some flute-playing. 7 days till 11pm, Fri/Sat midnight.

675 **The Old Toll Bar** 1 Paisley Rd W. Opp the site of the original Parkhouse Toll,
xA5 where monies were collected for use of the 'turnpikes' betw Glas and Greenock. Opened in 1874, the original interior is still intact; the *fin de siècle* painted glass and magnificent old gantry preserved under order. A 'palace pub' classic. Real ale and some single malts. 7 days till 11pm.

676 **Baird's Bar** and **The District** 2 bars from opp sides of the gr divide.
xF4 **Baird's** in the Gallowgate adj Barrowlands is a Catholic stronghold green to
xA5 the gills where, on days when Celtic play at home up the rd in Parkhead, you'd have to be in by 11am to get a drink. **The District**, 252 Paisley Rd W, Govan, nr Ibrox Park, is where Rangers supporters gather and rule in their own blue heaven. Both pubs give an extraordinary insight into what makes the Glas time-bomb tick. Provided you aren't wearing the wrong colours (or say something daft), you'll be very welcome in either.

# The Best Real-Ale Pubs

*Pubs on other pages may purvey real ale; the following take it seriously. All open 7 days till 11pm (midnight w/ends) unless stated.*

**677**  ✓ **Bon Accord**  153 N St. On a slip rd of the motorway swathe nr the
**A2**  Mitchell Library. One of the first real-ale pubs in Glas. Good selection of malts & up to 12 beers; always Theakstons, Deuchars & IPA plus many guest ales on hand pump. Food at lunchtime and light bites till 6.45pm. Light, easy-going atmos here, but they do take their ale seriously; there's even a 'tour' of the cellars if you want it. Mon-Sat till 12midnight, Sun till 11.00pm.

**678**  **Tennent's**  191 Byres Rd. Nr the always-red traffic lights at Univ Ave, a big,
**WE**  booming watering-hole of a place where you're never far away from the horseshoe bar and its several excellent hand-pumped ales, incl up to 9 guests. 'Tennent's is an institution' – some regulars do appear to live here. Basic bar meals till 9pm.

**679**  **The State**  148 Holland St off Sauchiehall St at W End. No compromising
**WE**  old-style pub: all wood & old pictures. 8 guest ales. No fancy extras. Will prob outlive the many makeovers around here. Some music. 7 days till midnight.

**680**  **Babbity Bowster**  16 Blackfriars St. In a pedestrianised part of the Merchant
**F3**  City and just off the High St, a highly successful pub/restau/hotel (490/INDI-VIDUAL HOTELS); but the pub comes first. Caledonian, Deuchars, IPA & well-chosen guests. Many malts & cask cider. Food all day (570/SCOTTISH RESTAUS), occasional folk music (esp Sun), o/side patio (688/DRINK OUTDOORS).

**681**  **Blackfriars**  36 Bell St on corner of the Merchant City. Mixed crowd in this
**E4**  a' thing to a' body kind of pub (food till 8pm, then bites, also comedy & jazz programme). Ind Coope, Burton guest beers, bottled & draught Euro beers.

**682**  **The Horseshoe**  17 Drury St. Gr for lots of reasons (660/UNIQUE GLAS PUBS),
**D3**  not the least of which is its range of beers: Caledonian, Greenmantle, Maclays and Bass on hand pump.

**683**  **Victoria Bar**  157 Bridgegate. Another pub mentioned before (665/UNIQUE
**D5**  GLAS PUBS) where IPA, Maclays and others can be drunk in a dark woody atmos enlivened by trad music (Tue & Fri-Sun).

# Places To Drink Outdoors

**684**  **Lock 27**  1100 Crow Rd. At the very N end of Crow Rd beyond Anniesland, an
**WE**  unusual boozer for Glas: a canalside pub on a lock of the Forth and Clyde Canal (724/WALKS IN THE CITY), a touch English (a v wee touch), where of a summer's day you can sit o/side. Excellent bar food, always busy.

**685**  **Cottier's**  357 5825. 93 Hyndland St. First on the left after the swing park on
**WE**  Highburgh Rd (going W) and the converted church is on your rt, around the corner. Heart of W End location. Think: a cold beer on a hot day sitting in leafy shade – it's a Hyndland kind of life!

**686**  **Ashton Lane**  As soon as the sun comes out, so do the punters. With the **Cul**
**WE**  **De Sac** & **Bar Brel** at one end & **Jinty McGinty's** at the other, benches suddenly appear & the whole lane becomes a cobbled, alfresco pub. The nearest Glas gets to Euro or even Dublin drinking. Brel has a grassy bit outback.

**687**  **Bloody Mary's**  28 Vinicombe St off Gt Western Rd end of Byres Rd. O/side
**WE**  tables have sunny aspect in this st just off busy Byres Rd & opp **Cresswell Lane** where a clutch of caffs & bars also spill outside. Ok food incl lite bites & salad menu served 11.30am-5pm. Pub till 11pm/12midnight.

**688**  **Babbity Bowster**  552 5055. 16 Blackfriars St. Unique in the Merchant City
**F3**  for several reasons (680/REAL-ALE PUBS, 570/SCOTTISH RESTAUS), but in summer certainly for its napkin of gdn in an area bereft of greenery. Though enclosed by surrounding sts, it's a concrete oasis. Feels like Soho, Soho NYC? Naw, feels like Glasgow! Always good craic.

**Big Blue**  445 Gt Western Rd. O/side terrace o/looks the murky R Kelvin. Report: 562/PIZZA.

# Pubs With Good Food

*See also* Gastropubs, *p. 84.*

**689** ✓✓ **The Griffin**  266 Bath St. On corner of Elmbank St across from
**B1** King's Theatre. The Griffin rooms have always been there on that
corner and your basic pie/chips/beans *and a pint* will not be bettered at this
price (£3.05 lunchtime, the equivalent 80 yrs ago of 8 old pence). Other staples available and a more elaborate menu in the lounge or the Griffinette next
door. Food: 12noon-2.30pm & evenings till 6.30pm (not Sun). Pub till 12mid-
night. (671/'UNSPOILT' PUBS)

**690** **The Big Blue**  445 Gr Western Rd. A modern bar/bistro in a gr uptown loca-
**WE** tion literally on the (river) Kelvinside. Drinking may drown the eating later on,
but till mid/late-evening there's excellent Italian pasta/pizza pub grub. LO
10/10.30pm. Bar 12midnight.

**691** **Blackfriars**  36 Bell St. Candleriggs is one of the focal points in the Merchant
**E4** City. Gr Glas pub for all-round ambience, provision of real ale and music, and
food available all day (meals till 8pm, then 'bites') (but drinkers are loud after
9pm). 681/REAL ALES.

**692** **Brel**  Ashton Lane. Always busy bar in often teeming W End lane so
**WE** 'Belgian'/Belgo menu can take (literally) the back seat. Still, pots of
moules/frites help the many euro brews go down. Lunch & food till 10.30pm,
bar midnight. 686/OUTSIDE DRINKING.

**693** **White Cart Inn, Busby**  644 2711. S of city 20km via M77 (Kilmarnock) or
**xA5** Albert Br thro' Gorbals to Carmunnock. Trad inn serving food on huge scale
in many-chambered bar. Pub grub (Chef & Brewer) rather than gastro standard, but hits the spot. Gd fish menu. Sunday roasts. Efficient service. 7 days.
Lunch & LO 9.30pm.

**Strata**  45 Queen St. Report: 699/COOL BARS.

# Cool Bars

**694** ✓ **Arches** 0901 022 0300 (box office). 253 Argyle St. The fab bar/café of the
**C3** fab Arches Theatre, the club & experimental theatre space refurbished
with millennium money. Design by Timorous/Taller (see Strata below), this is
an obvious pre-club pre-theatre space, but works at any time. Food & DJs &
lots going on. Even if you're only in Glas for the w/end, you should come
here.

**695** ✓ **The Goat** 357 7373. 1287 Argyle St. Up W nr Kelvingrove Gallery a com-
**WE** fortable, friendly sitting rm pub (with mezzanine & upstairs snug) known
for its excl food. Big windows & pavement terr look down Argyle St; a gr corner for people gazing & Glasgow life-affirming. 7 days. Food 12-9pm, bar midnight.

**696** ✓ **Saint Jude's** 352 8800. 190 Bath St. Another bar below stairs that
**C2** seems likely to outlive the Bath St explosion. This, the bar of Saint Jude's
(483/HOTELS, 519/BEST RESTAUS) is minimalist but still fuzzy & friendly. Good
cocktails. Food till drinking takes over & open till midnight 7 days. Being
joined adj by the bar of The Hallion (a private members' club) at TGP.

**697** ✓ **Bunker** 229 1427. 193 Bath St. Another converted basement on style
**C2** bar street, more recent than the above. Spacious & makes most of outdoor strips of terrace front & back. Food better than most around here (till
9pm). iPod kind of soundtrack, DJs & live band on Wed at TGP. 7 days. Bar
midnight.

**698** **Bar 10** 221 8353. 10 Mitchell Lane, halfway up Buchanan St pedestrian
**D3** precinct on the left in the narrow lane that also houses the Lighthouse design
centre. There's an NYC look about this joint that is so loved by its habitués,
they still pack it at w/ends 10 yrs after it arrived. Ben Kelly design has worn
well. Food, DJs & pre-club preparations. 7 days till midnight. (668/UNIQUE
PUBS)

**699** **Strata** 221 1888. 45 Queen St. Nothing hugely obvious to distinguish this
**D3** from a clutch of others, but somehow it works. Done by Timorous Beasties
& One Foot Taller (ubiquitous Glas design team), the room is not intrusive &
the food is better than most. Food till 10pm, bar midnight.

**700** **Bargo** 553 4771. 80 Albion St. In the Merchant City, this spacious, design-
**E4** er-theque is in demand for fashion shoots and, of course, high-glam posing
on a Sat night. Can be attractively, if not spookily, quiet during the week when
surprisingly OK food is served. Opens on to st in summertimes sometimes.

**701** **Cul De Sac** 649 4717. 44 Ashton Lane. The upstairs bar and **Attic** is a
**WE** perennial W End fave. Close to the underground for that last-minute dash
into town to beat club curfews.

**702** **Candy Bar** 353 7420. 185 Hope St. Still stylee after all these years (well 8), a
**C2** good place to look, linger and even eat (food till 8pm) – eclectic menu incl a
decent fish 'n' chips. Minimalist chic with the odd flourish. 7 days noon till
midnight.

**703** **Polo Lounge** 553 1221. 84 Wilson St. Urbane and stylish bar/disco by the
**E3** ubiquitous (tho hardly ever seen) Stefan King. Unmistakably gay in the heart
of the quarter (not him, it). Clubbable rather than clubby crowd (until later
on) arranged around the comfortable, now rather shabby (ok, call it lived-in)
furniture; at w/ends you go downstairs to disco. Mellow Sun afternoons;
papers and jazz. (1310/GAY GLAS)

**704** **Bar 91** 552 5211. 91 Candleriggs. A better bar among many of this ilk here-
**E3** abouts, food also is well-considered & put together, tho it stops at 6pm to
make way for pre-club ministrations (and till midnight).

# The Main Attractions

**705**
**WE** ✓ ✓ **Kelvingrove Art Gallery & Museum** 287 2699. At W end of Argyle St & Sauchiehall St by Kelvingrove Park. Huge Victorian sandstone edifice with awesome atrium. On the ground floor is a natural history/ Scottish history museum. The upper salons contain the city's superb British and European art collection. Reopening spring '06 after major refurb. FREE

**706**
**SS** ✓ ✓ **The Burrell Collection, Pollok Park & Pollok House** 287 2550. S of river via A77 Kilmarnock Rd (over Jamaica St Br) about 5km, following signs from Pollokshaws Rd. Set in rural parkland, this award-winning modern gallery was built to house the eclectic acquisitions of Sir William Burrell. Showing a preference for medieval works, among the 8500 items the magpie magnate donated to the city in 1944 are artefacts from the Roman empire to Rodin. The building itself integrates old doorways and whole rms reconstructed from Hutton Castle. Self-serve café & restau on the ground floor (Mon-Thurs, Sat 10am-5pm, Fri & Sun 11am-5pm). **Pollok House** (NTS): 616 6410 and Gdns further into the park (with works by Goya, El Greco and William Blake) is worth a detour and has, below stairs, the better tearooms & gds to the river. Both open 7 days. 10am-5pm. (725/WALKS IN THE CITY) FREE/ADM

**707**
**xF3** ✓ **Glasgow Cathedral/Provand's Lordship** 552 6891/553 2557. Castle St. Across the rd from one another they represent what remains of the oldest part of the city, which (as can be seen in the People's Palace, *see below*) was, in the early 18th century, merely a ribbon of streets from here to the river. The present Cathedral, though established by St Mungo in AD 543, dates from the 12th century and is a fine example of the v real, if gloomy, Gothic. The house, built in 1471, is a museum which strives to convey a sense of medieval life. Watch you don't get run over when you re-emerge into the 21st century and try to cross the st. In the background, the Necropolis piled on the hill invites inspection and offers a viewpoint and the full Gothic perspective (tho best not to go alone). Open 7 days. Times vary slightly. FREE

**708**
**xF5** ✓ **The People's Palace** 271 2951. App via the Tron & London Rd, then turn rt into Glas Green. This has long been a folk museum *par excellence* wherein, since 1898, the history, folklore and artefacts of a proud city have been gathered, cherished and displayed. But this is much more than a mere museum; it is the heart and soul of the city and together with the Winter Gdns adj, shouldn't be missed, to know what Glasgow's about. Tearm in the Tropics, among the palms and ferns of the Winter Gdns. Opening times as most other museums: Mon-Thurs, Sat 10am-5pm, Fri & Sun 11am-5pm. FREE

**709**
**xA5** ✓ **Glasgow Science Centre** 420 5000. On S side of Clyde opp SECC, Glasgow's newest attraction built with Millennium dosh. App via Kingston Br (from city) & Govan t/off, then rt fork at 'the angel', or walk from SECC complex by 'Bell's Bridge'. Impressive titanium-clad mall, Imax cinema & 127m-high tower. 4 floors of interactive exhibs, planetarium & theatre. Rolling story of the city with the science & the view. Separate tickets or combos (only 20 people with 2 lifts at a time for the tower). 7 days. 10am-6pm. ADM

**710**
**xF3** **St Mungo Museum Of Religious Life & Art** 553 2557. Part of the lovely & not-cherished-enough cathedral precinct (see above), this houses art and artefacts representing the world's 6 major religions arranged tactfully in an attractive stone building with a Zen gdn in the courtyard. The dramatic Dalí *Crucifixion* seems somehow lost, and the assemblage seems like a good & worthwhile vision not quite realised, but in a city where sectarianism is still an issue & a problem, this is a telling & informative display. 7 days 10am-5pm (Fri/Sun from 11am) FREE

**711**
**WE** **Hunterian Museum & Art Gallery** 330 4221/5431. Univ Ave. On one side of the st, Scotland's oldest museum with geological, archaeological & social history displayed in a venerable building. The **University Chapel** and the cloisters should not be missed. Across the st, a modern block holds part of Glasgow's exceptional civic collection – Rembrandt to the Colourists and the Glas Boys, as well as one of the most complete collections of any artist's work and personal effects to be found anywhere, viz that of Whistler. Fascinating stuff, even if you're not a fan. There's also a print gallery & the superb **Mackintosh House** (762/MACKINTOSH). Mon-Sat 9.30am-5pm. Cl Sun. FREE

# The Other Attractions

**712** ✓ ✓ **Museum Of Transport** 287 2720. Off Argyle St behind the Kelvin
**WE** Hall. May not seem your ticket to ride, but this is one of Scotland's
most fascinating museums. Has something for everybody, esp kids. The reconstruction of a cobbled Glas st c1938 is an inspired evocation. There are trains,
trams and unique collections of cars, motorbikes and bicycles. And model ships
in the Clyde rm, in remembrance of a mighty river. Make a donation and the
Mini splits in two. Mon-Thur, Sat 10am-5pm, Fri & Sun 11am-5pm.     FREE

**713** ✓ ✓ **Botanic Gardens & Kibble Palace** 334 2422. Gr Western Rd.
**WE** Smallish park close to R Kelvin with riverside walks (723/WALKS IN
THE CITY), and pretty much the 'dear green place'. Kibble Palace (built 1873) is
the distinctive domed glasshouse with statues set among lush ferns and
shrubbery from around the (mostly temperate) world. A wonderful place to
muse and wander. Gdns open till dusk; palace 10am-4.45pm (4.15pm in
wint). At TGP, closed for refurbishment but due to reopen for summer 2006.

**714** ✓ ✓ **Gallery Of Modern Art** 229 1996. Queen St. Central, controver-
**D3** sial and housed in former Stirling's Library, Glasgow's big visual arts
attraction opened in a hail of art world bickering in 1996. Main pt is: does it
reflect Glasgow's eminence as a provenance of cutting edge or conceptual
work (all those Turner & Becks Prize nominees & winners?). Murmurs stilled
of late by more representative exhibs. Leaving aside the quibbling it should
def be on your Glasgow Hit list. Smart café up top. Mon-Wed, Sat 10am-5pm,
Thu 10am-8pm, Fri & Sun 11am-5pm.     FREE

**715** ✓ **The Barrows** (pronounced 'Barras') The sprawling st and indoor mar-
**F4** ket area in the E End of the city around the Gallowgate. Even a dozen yrs
ago when I first wrote this book, the Barras was pure dead briliant, a real slab
of Glas life. Its glory days are over but, as with all gr markets, it's full of character and characters and it's still possible to find bargains and collectibles.
Everything from clairvoyants to the latest scam. Sat and Sun only 10am-5pm.

**716** **The Tenement House** 333 0183. 145 Buccleuch St. Nr Charing Cross but
**B1** can app from nr the end of Sauchiehall St & over the hill. Typical 'respectable'
Glas tenement, kept under a bell-jar since Our Agnes moved out in 1965. She
had lived there with her mother since 1911 and wasn't one for new-fangled
things. It's a touch claustrophobic when busy and is distinctly voyeuristic,
but, well... your house would be interesting, too, in 50 yrs time if the clock
were stopped. Daily, Mar-Oct 1-5pm. Reception on grnd floor.     ADMN

**717** **Sharmanka Kinetic Gallery & Theatre** 552 7080. 2nd floor, 14 King St,
**E4** Trongate. A small and intimate experience cf most others on this page, but
an extraordinary one. The gallery/theatre of Russian emigré Eduard
Bersindsky shows his meticulous & amazing mechanical sculptures.
Performances Thu 7pm, Sun 3pm & 7pm. Other times by arr.     ADMN

**718** **Greenbank Gardens** 616 5126. 10km SW of centre via Kilmarnock Rd,
**SS** Eastwood Toll, Clarkston Toll and Mearns Rd, then signposted (3km). A spacious oasis in the suburbs; formal gdns and 'working' walled gdn, parterre
and woodland walks around elegant Georgian house. V Scottish. Gdns open
AYR 9.30am-dusk, shop/tearm Apr-Oct 11am-5pm, Nov-Mar Sat & Sun 2-
4pm.     NTS

**719** **City Chambers** 287 4018. George Sq. The hugely impressive building along
**E3** the whole E end of Glasgow's municipal central sq. This is a wonderfully over-
the-top monument to the days when Glas was the second city of the empire.
Guided tours Mon-Fri 9am-4.30pm (subj to availability).     FREE

**720** **Finlaystone Country Estate** 01475 540505. 30km W of city centre via fast
Map 9 M8/A8, signed off dual carriageway just before Pt Glas. Delightful gdns and
**L25** woods around mansion house with many pottering places and longer trails
(and ranger service). Estate open AYR 10am-5pm. Visitor centre & The Celtic
Tree tearoom. Open Apr-late Sept 10am-5pm (VC also open wint w/ends).
Spectacular bluebells. Slap bang in middle of the estate is **Ferringtons**, the
largest complementary therapy centre in Scotland (0800 7837183). Sessions
& classes in pilates, massage & – well, everything you can probably think of
to feel better.     ADMN

**721** **The Pride O' The Clyde** 07711 250969. Amsterdam-style water-bus ferry-
**C4** ing passengers between Glasgow (board at Broomielaw, Jamaica Bridge) and
Braehead Shopping & Leisure Centre (board at Maritime Heritage Centre). A
35-min journey incl commentary on the sights & history of the Clyde.
Refreshments avail. AYR but no sailings Sept 05-Apr 06 due to refurb of
Finnieston Bridge. Also, while we're on the water...                    ADMN

**722** **The Waverley**   0845 130 4647. 'The World's Last Sea-going Paddle
**A4** Steamer' which plied the Clyde in the glorious 'Doon the Water' days is fresh
from its £7M lottery-funded refit. Def the way to see the W Coast. Sailings
from Glas Anderson Quay (by Kingston Br) to Rothesay, Kyles of Bute, Arran.
Other days leaves from Ayr or Greenock, many destinations. Call for complex
timetable.                                                              ADMN

**Paisley Abbey**  15km from Glas. Report: 1916/ABBEYS.

**Bothwell Castle, Uddingston**  15km E, via M74. Report: 1817/RUINS.

# The Best Walks In The City

See p. 13 for walk codes.

**723** **Kelvin Walkway** A path along the banks of Glasgow's other river, the
**WE** Kelvin, which enters the Clyde unobtrusively at Yorkhill but first meanders
through some of the most interesting parts and parks of the NW city. Walk
starts at Kelvingrove Park through the Univ and Hillhead district under Kelvin
Br and on to the celebrated Botanic Gdns (713/OTHER ATTRACTIONS). The trail
then goes N, under the Forth and Clyde Canal (see below) to the Arcadian
fields of Dawsholm Park (5km), Killermont (posh golf course) and Kirkintilloch
(13km from start). Since the river and the canal shadow each other for much
of their routes, it's possible, with a map, to go out by one waterway and
return by the other (e.g. start at Gr Western Rd, return Maryhill Rd).
**START** Usual start at the Eildon St (off Woodlands Rd) gate of Kelvingrove
Park or Kelvin Br. St parking only. 2-13+KM XCIRC BIKE 1-A-1

**724** **Forth & Clyde Canal Towpath** The canal, opened in 1790, reopened 2002
**XC1** as the Millennium Link and once a major short cut for fishing boats and trade
betw Europe and America, provides a fascinating look round the back of the
city from a pathway that stretches on a spur from Pt Dundas just N of the M8
to the main canal at the end of Lochburn Rd off Maryhill Rd and then E all the
way to Kirkintilloch and Falkirk (Falkirk Wheel: 01324 619888; 4/BIG ATTRAC-
TIONS), and W through Maryhill and Drumchapel to Bowling and the Clyde
(60km). Good option is go as far as Croy & take v reg train service back. Much
of the route is through the forsaken or redeveloped industrial heart of the
city, past waste ground, warehouses and high flats, but there are open
stretches and curious corners and, by Bishopbriggs, it's a rural waterway.
More info from British Waterways (0141 332 6936).
**START** (1) Top of Firhill Rd (gr view of city from Ruchill Park, 100m further on
– 757/BEST VIEWS). (2) Lochburn Rd (see above) at the confluence from which to
go E or W to the Clyde. (3) Top of Crow Rd, Anniesland where there is a canalside pub, Lock 27 (684/DRINK OUTDOORS), with tables o/side, real ale & food
(12noon-even). (4) Bishopbriggs Sports Centre, Balmuildy Rd. From here it is
6km to Maryhill and 1km in other direction to the 'country churchyard' of
Cadder or 3km to Kirkintilloch. All starts have some parking.
ANY KM XCIRC BIKE 1-A-1

**725** **Pollok Country Park** The park that (apart from the area around the gallery
**SS** and the house – 706/MAIN ATTRACTIONS) most feels like a real country park.
Numerous trails through woods and meadows. The leisurely guided walks
with the park rangers can be educative and more fun than you would think
(632 9299 for details). Burrell Collection and Pollok House and Gdns are obvious highlights. There's a good restau & an 'old-fashioned' tearoom in the
basement of the latter serving excellent range of hot, home-made dishes,
soups, salads, s/wiches as well as usual cakes & tasties. Open 7 days 10am-
4.30pm (616 6410). Enter by Haggs Rd or by Haggs Castle Golf Course. By car
you are directed to the entry rd off Pollokshaws Rd and then to the car park in
front of the Burrell. Train to Shawlands or Pollokshaws W from Glas Central
Stn.

**726** **Mugdock Country Park** 956 6100. Not perhaps within the city, but one of
Map 10 the nearest and easiest escapes. Park which incl Mugdock Woods (SSSI) and
**L25** 2 castles is NW of Milngavie. Regular train from Queen St Stn takes 20 min,
then follow route of W Highland Way for 4km across Drumclog Moor to S
edge of park. In summer, shuttlebus will meet the trains at Milngavie Stn and
take you right into park. By car to Milngavie by A81 park is 5km N. Well
signed. 5 car parks, main one incl Craigend Visitor Centre (9am-9pm),
Stables Tearoom (10am-5pm daily), discovery room & theatre. Many trails
marked out and further afield rambles. This is a godsend betw Glas and the
Highland hills. 5-20KM CAN BE CIRC BIKE 1-A-2

**Cathkin Braes** S edge of city with views. Report: 786/BEST VIEWS.

# Easy Walks Outside The City

*See p. 13 for walk codes.*

**727** **Campsie Fells** Range of hills 25km N of city best reached via Kirkintilloch
Map 10 or Cumbernauld/Kilsyth. Encompasses area that includes the Kilsyth Hills,
**M25** Fintry Hills and Carron Valley betw. (1) Good app from A803, Kilsyth main st
up the Tak-me-Doon (*sic*) rd. Park by the golf club and follow path by the
burn. It's poss to take in the two hills to left as well as Tomtain (453m), the
most easterly of the tops, in a good afternoon; views to the E. (2) Drive on to
the jnct (9km) of the B818 rd to Fintry and go left, following Carron Valley
reservoir to the far corner where there is a forestry rd to the left. Park here
and follow track to ascend Meikle Bin (570m) to the rt, the highest peak in
the central Campsies. (3) The bonny village of Fintry is a good start/base for
the Fintry Hills and Earl's Seat (578m). (4) Campsie Glen – a sliver of glen in
the hills. App via Clachan of Campsie on A81 (decent tearoom) or from viewpoint high on the hill on B822 from Lennoxtown-Fintry. This is the easy
Campsie intro.                                    10KM+ CAN BE CIRC XBIKE 2-B-2

**728** **Gleniffer Braes, Paisley** Ridge to the S of Paisley (15km from Glas) has
Map 10 been a favourite walking-place for centuries. M8 or Paisley Rd W to town cen-
**L26** tre then: (1) S via B775/A736 towards Irvine or (2) B774 (Causeyside St then
Neilston Rd) and sharp rt after 3km to Glenfield Rd. For (1) go 2km after last
houses, winding up ridge and park/start at Robertson Park (signed). Here
there are superb views and walks marked to E and W. (2) 500m along
Glenfield Rd is a car park/ranger centre (0141 884 3794). Walk up through
gdns and formal parkland and then W along marked paths and trails.
Eventually, after 5km, this route joins (1).    2-10KM CAN BE CIRC MTBIKE 1-A-2

**729** **Greenock Cut** 45km W of Glas. Can app via Pt Glas but simplest route is
Map 9 from A78 rd to Largs. Travelling S from Greenock take first left after IBM,
**K25** brown-signed L Thom/Cornalees. Lochside 5km up winding rd. Park at
Cornalees Br Centre (01475 521458). Walk left along lochside rd to Overton
(5km) then path is signed. The Cut, an aqueduct built in 1827 to supply water
to Greenock and its 31 mills, is now an ancient monument. Gr views from the
mast along the Cut tho it is a detour. Another route to the rt from Cornalees
leads through a glen of birch, rowan and oak to the Kelly Cut. Both trails
described on board at the car park.              15/16KM CIRC MTBIKE 1-B-2

**730** **Clyde Muirshiel** General name for vast area of 'Inverclyde' W of city, incl
Map 9 Greenock Cut (*see above*), Lochwinnoch, Castle Semple Country Park and
**K25** Lunderston Bay, a stretch of coastline nr the Cloch Lighthouse on the A770 S
of Gourock for littoral amblings. Best wildish bit is around Muirshiel Centre
itself, Muirshiel Country Park (01475 521129), with trails, a waterfall and
Windy Hill (350m). Nothing arduous, but a breath of air. The hen harrier
hunts here. From M8 jnct 29, take A737 Lochwinnoch, then B786 to top of
Calder Glen Rd. Follow brown signs.

**731** **The Whangie** On A809 N from Bearsden about 8km after last r/bout and
Map 10 2km after the Carbeth Inn, is the car park for the Queen's View (734/BEST
**L25** VIEWS). Once you get to the summit of Auchineden Hill, take the path that
drops down to the W (a half-rt-angle) and look for crags on your rt. This is the
'back door' of The Whangie. Carry on and you'll suddenly find yourself in a
deep cleft in the rock face with sheer walls rising over 10m on either side. The
Whangie is more than 100m long and at one pt the walls narrow to less than
1m. Local mythology has it that The Whangie was made by the Devil, who
lashed his tail in anticipation of a witchy rendezvous somewhere in the N, and
carved a slice through the rock, where the path now goes.
                                            5KM CIRC XBIKE XDOGS 1-A-1

**732** **Chatelhérault nr Hamilton** Jnct 6 off M74, well signposted into Hamilton,
Map 10 follow rd into centre, then bear left away from main rd where it's signed for
**M26** A723. The gates to the 'château' are about 3km o/side town. A drive leads to
the William Adam-designed hunting lodge of the Dukes of Hamilton, set amid
ornamental gdns with a notable parterre and extensive grounds. Tracks along
the deep, wooded glen of the Avon (ruins of Cadzow Castle) lead to distant
glades. Good walks and ranger service (01698 426213). House open Mon-Thur
10am-4.30pm (Sun 12-5pm), walks at all times.    2-7KM CIRC BIKE 1-A-2

# The Best Views Of The City & Beyond

**733** **Cathkin Braes, Queen Mary's Seat** The southern ridge of the city on the
**SS** B759 from Carmunnock to Cambuslang, about 12km from centre. Go S of
river by Albert Br to Aikenhead Rd which continues S as Carmunnock Rd.
Follow to Carmunnock, a delightfully rural village, and pick up the Cathkin Rd.
2km along on the rt is the Cathkin Braes Golf Club and 100m further on the
left is the park. Marvellous views to N of the Campsies, Kilpatrick Hills, Ben
Lomond and as far as Ben Ledi. Walks on the Braes on both sides of the rd.

**734** **Queen's View** Auchineden  Not so much a view of the city, more a per-
Map 10 spective on Glasgow's Highland hinterland, this short walk and sweeping vista
**L25** to the N has been a Glaswegian pilgrimage for generations. On A809 N from
Bearsden about 8km after last r/bout and 2km after the Carbeth Inn, a v
decent pub to repair to. Busy car park attests to popularity. The walk, along
path cut into ridgeside, takes 40-50 min to cairn, from which you can see The
Cobbler (1962/HILLS), that other Glas favourite, Ben Ledi and sometimes as far
as Ben Chonzie 50km away. The fine views of L Lomond are what Queen
Victoria came for. Further on is The Whangie (731/EASY WALKS).                1-A-1

**735** **Ruchill Park** An unlikely but splendid panorama from this overlooked but
**xC1** well-kept park to the N of the city nr the infamous Possilpark housing estate.
Go to top of Firhill Rd (past Partick Thistle football ground) over Forth and Clyde
Canal (724/WALKS IN THE CITY) off Garscube Rd where it becomes Maryhill Rd.
Best view is from around the flagpole; the whole city among its surrounding
hills, from the Campsies to Gleniffer & Cathkin Braes (*see above*), becomes
clear.

**736** **Bar Hill** Twechar nr Kirkintilloch  22km N of city, taking A803 Kirkintilloch
**xF1** t/off from M8, then the 'low' rd to Kilsyth, the B8023, bearing left at the
'black-and-white br'. Next to Twechar Quarry Inn, a path is signed for Bar Hill
and the Antonine Wall. Steepish climb for 2km, ignore strange dome of grass.
Over to left in copse of trees are the remains of one of the forts on the wall
which was built across Scotland in the 2nd century AD. Ground plan explained
on a board. This is a special place with strong history vibes and airy views over
the plain to the city which came a long time after.                1-A-2

**737** **Blackhill** nr Lesmahagow  28km S of city. Another marvellous outlook, but in
Map 10 the opp direction from above. Take jnct 10/11 on M74, then off the B7078
**M26** signed Lanark, take the B7018. 4km along past Clarkston Farm, head uphill for
1km and park by Water Board mound. Walk uphill through fields to rt for about
1km. Unprepossessing hill which unexpectedly reveals a vast vista of most of E
central Scotland.                1-A-2

**738** **Paisley Abbey** M8 to Paisley; frequent trains from Central Stn. Abbey Mon-
Map 10 Sat 10am-3.30pm. Every so often on Abbey 'open days', the tower of this amaz-
**L26** ing edifice can be climbed. The tower (restored 1926) is 50m high and from the
top there's a grand view of the Clyde. This is a rare experience, but phone TIC
(889 0711) or Abbey itself (889 7654, am) for details; could be your lucky day.
(1916/GREAT ABBEYS)

**739** **Lyle Hill** Gourock  Via M8 W to Greenock, then round the coast to relative-
Map 9 ly genteel old resort of Gourock where the 'Free French' worked in the yards
**K25** during the war. A monument has been erected to their memory on the top
of Lyle Hill above the town, from where you get one of the most dramatic
views of the gr crossroads of the Clyde (Holy L, Gare L and L Long). Best van-
tage-point is further along the rd on other side by trig pt. Follow British Rail
stn signs, then Lyle Hill. There's another gr view of the Clyde further down
the water at **Haylie, Largs,** the hill 3km from town reached via the A760 rd
to Kilbirnie and Paisley. The island of Cumbrae lies in the sound and the sunset.

**Campsie Fells** and **Gleniffer Braes**: 727/728/WALKS O/SIDE THE CITY.

# The Best Of The Sports Facilities

## PUBLIC SWIMMING & INDOOR SPORTS CENTRES

**740** **Whitehill Pool** 551 9969. Onslow Dr parallel to Duke St at Meadowpark St
**xF3** in the E End nr Alexandra Park (Mon-Fri 7.45am-9pm, Sat/Sun 8.30am-2pm).
25m pool with sauna/multigym.

**741** **North Woodside Leisure Centre** 332 8102. Braid Sq. Not far from St
**xB1** George's Cross nr Charing Cross at the bottom of Gr Western Rd. In a rebuilt
area; follow AA signs. Modern pool (25m) and sauna/steam/sun centre plus
the usual fitness suite & classes. Mon 10am, Tue & Thur 9.30am, Wed & Fri
7.30am all till 9pm; Sat/Sun 10am-4pm.

**742** **Pollok Leisure Centre** 881 3313. Cowglen Rd. Not a do-your-lengths kind
**SS** of a pool – more a family water outing. Plus fitness suite & classes. Mon-Fri
10am-9pm, Sat/Sun 10am-4pm.

**743** **Gourock Bathing Pool** 01475 631561. On rd S, an open-air heated pool on
**xA5** the Clyde. Gr prospect for summers like they used to be. May-Sept.
(2119/SWIMMING POOLS)

**744** **Kelvin Hall International Sports Arena** 357 2525. Argyle St by
**WE** Kelvingrove Museum (705/MAIN ATTRACTIONS). Major venue for international
indoor sports competitions, but open otherwise for weights/
badminton/tennis/athletics/climbing classes. Book hr-long sessions. No
squash. Mon-Sun 9am, Wed 10am, all to 10.30pm (6.30pm Sat).

**745** **Scotstoun Leisure Centre** 959 4000. Danes Dr. Huge state-of-the-art
**WE** sports multiplex. 10 lane pool, indoor halls and outdoor pitches. Mon, Wed,
Fri 7.30am-10pm, Tue 9am-10pm, Thur 10am-10pm, Sat 9am-5pm, Sun
9am-9pm. (2114/LEISURE CENTRES)

**746** **Tollcross Park Leisure Centre** 763 2345. Wellshot Rd, Tollcross. Another
**xF4** biggie. 10-lane pool, indoor halls, split-level fitness suite. Mon-Fri 7am (Thu
10am)-10pm, Sat 9am-5pm, Sun 9am-9pm.

**747** **Allander Sports Complex** 942 2233. Milngavie Rd, Bearsden, 16km N of
**xC1** centre via Maryhill Rd. Best by car. Squash (2 courts), sports halls, snooker,
badminton, swimming pool, fitness suite. Mon-Fri 7.30am-11pm, Sat 9am-
9pm, Sun 9am-10pm.

## GOLF COURSES

*Glas has a vast number of parks and golf courses. The following clubs are the best
open to non-members.*

**748** **Cathkin Braes** 634 0650. Cathkin Rd, SE via Aikenhead Rd/Carmunnock Rd
**SS** to Carmunnock village, then 3km. Best by car. Civilised hilltop course on the
S edge of the city. Non-members Mon-Fri (though probably not Fri am).

**749** **Haggs Castle** 427 0480. Dumbreck Rd nr jnct 22 of the M8; go straight on
**SS** to clubhouse at first r/bout. Part of the grounds of Pollok Park; a convenient
course, perhaps overplayed. Non-members Mon-Fri. (Handicap cert
required.)

**750** **Pollok Golf Club** 632 1080. Barrhead Rd. On the other side of White Cart
**SS** Water & Pollok House & rather more up-market. Well-wooded parkland course,
flat & well kept but not cheap. Women may play but call for specific timeslots!

**751** **Gleddoch** Langbank 01475 540704. Excellent 18-hole course adj and part
**xA5** of Gleddoch House Hotel (506/HOTELS O/SIDE TOWN). Restricted play.

## TENNIS

**752** Public courts (Apr-Sep), membership not required: **Kelvingrove Park** 4
**WE** courts, **Queen's Park** 5 courts, **Victoria Park** 6 courts. Mon-Fri 12noon-
**SS** 9pm, Sat 12-7pm, Sun 12-8pm.

# The Best Small Galleries

*Apart from those listed previously* (Main Attractions, Other Attractions), *the following galleries are always worth looking into. The* Glasgow Gallery Guide, *free from any of them, lists all the current exhibs.*

**753**
**E4** ✓ ✓ **Glasgow Print Studio** 552 0704. 22 & 25 King St. Influential and accessible upstairs gallery with print work on view and for sale from many of Scotland's leading and rising artists. Cl Sun & Mon. Print Shop over rd.

**754**
**E4** ✓ ✓ **Transmission Gallery** 552 4813. 28 King St. Cutting edge and often off-the-wall work from contemporary Scottish and international artists. Reflects Glasgow's increasing importance as a hot spot of conceptual art. Stuff you might disagree with. Cl Sun & Mon.

**755**
**C4** ✓ ✓ **The Modern Institute:** 248 3711. 73 Robertson St. Not really a gallery – more a concept. International rep for cutting-edge art ideas and occasional events. By appointment. Shows at London's Frieze Art Fair.

**756**
**D3** ✓ ✓ **The Glasgow Art Fair:** George Sq in tented pavilions. Held every yr in mid Apr. Some of the galleries on this page and many more are represented; selective but conventional and good fun. (2198/WHERE TO BUY ART)

**757**
**C2** ✓ **Compass Gallery** 221 6370. 178 W Regent St. Glasgow's oldest established commercial contemporary art gallery. Their 'New Generation' exhib in Jul-Aug shows work from new graduates of the art colleges and has heralded many a career. Combine with the other Gerber gallery (*see below*). Cl Sun.

**758**
**C2** ✓ **Cyril Gerber Fine Art** 221 3095. 148 W Regent St. British paintings and esp the Scottish Colourists and 'name' contemporaries. Gerber and the Compass (*see above*) have Christmas exhibs where small, accessible paintings can be bought for reasonable prices. Cl Sun.

**759**
**xF3** **Sorcha Dallas** 07812 605745. 5 St Margaret's Pl. Deep in the E End the secret salon of La Dallas where interesting new artists first come into the light. Phone first.

**Sharmanka Kinetic Gallery** 552 7080. Report: 717/OTHER ATTRACTIONS.

# The Mackintosh Trail

*The gr Scottish architect and designer Charles Rennie Mackintosh (1868–1928) had an extraordinary influence on contemporary design.*

**760**
**B1**
✔ ✔ ✔ **Glasgow School of Art**  353 4526. 167 Renfrew St. Mackintosh's supreme architectural triumph. It's enough almost to admire it from the st (and maybe best, since this is v much a working college) but there are guided tours at 11am & 2pm (Sat 10.30am, 11.30am, & many more in summer) of the sombre yet light interior, the halls and library. You might wonder if the building itself could be partly responsible for its remarkable output of acclaimed artists. Temp exhibitions in the Mackintosh Gallery. The Tenement House (716/OTHER ATTRACTIONS) is nearby.

**761**
**xC1**
✔ ✔ **Queen's Cross Church**  946 6600. 870 Garscube Rd, where it becomes Maryhill Rd (corner of Springbank St). Built 1896-99. Calm and simple, the antithesis of Victorian Gothic. If all churches had been built like this, we'd go more often. The HQ of the Charles Rennie Mackintosh Society which was founded in 1973. Mar-Oct Mon-Fri 10am-5pm, Sun 2-5pm. Nov-Feb Mon-Fri 10am-5pm. ADM

**762**
**WE**
✔ ✔ **The Mackintosh House**  330 5431. Univ Ave. Opp and part of the Hunterian Museum (711/MAIN ATTRACTIONS) within the univ campus. The Master's house has been transplanted and methodically reconstructed from the next st (they say even the light is the same). If you've ever wondered what the fuss is about, go and see how innovative and complete an artist, designer and architect he was, in this inspiring yet habitable set of rms. Mon-Sat 9.30am-5pm. Cl Sun. ADM

**763**
**xA5**
✔ ✔ **Scotland Street School Museum**  287 0500. 225 Scotland St. Opp Shields Rd u/ground and best app by car from Eglinton St (A77 Kilmarnock Rd over Jamaica St Br). Entire school (from 1906) preserved (and recently renovated) as museum of education through Victorian/ Edwardian and wartimes. Original, exquisite Mackintosh features, esp tiling, and powerfully redolent of happy school days. This is a uniquely evocative time capsule. Café and temporary exhibs. Mon-Thur, Sat 10am-5pm, Fri & Sun 11am-5pm. FREE

**764**
**D3**
✔ **The Lighthouse**  221 6362. Mitchell Lane, off Buchanan St. Glasgow's legacy from its yr as UK City of Architecture and Design. Changing exhibs in Mackintosh's 1893-5 building for *The Glasgow Herald* newspaper. Also houses a shop with cool design stuff, a café-bar & an interpretation centre on the gr architect with fantastic rooftop views from the corner tower. Mon-Sat 10.30am-5pm (Tue 11am), Sun 12-5pm. ADM

**765**
Map 9
**K25**
✔ **The Hill House** Helensburgh  01436 673900. Upper Colquhoun St. Take Sinclair St off Princes St (at Romanesque tower and TIC) and go 2km uphill, taking left into Kennedy Dr and follow signs. A complete house incorporating Mackintosh's typical total unity of design, built for Walter Blackie in 1902-4. Much to marvel over and wish that everybody else would go away and you could stay there for the night. There's even a library full of books to keep you occupied. Tearoom; gdns. Apr-Oct 1.30-5.30pm. Helensburgh is 45km NW of city centre via Dumbarton (A82) and A814 up N Clyde coast. ADMN

**766**
**C2**
**D3**
**The Willow Tea Rooms**  332 0521. Sauchiehall St & Buchanan St. A café he designed (or what's left of it); where to go for a break on the trail.

**767**
**xF2**
**Martyr's Public School**  553 2557. Parson St. Latest renovation and public access to another spectacular Mackintosh building. Check those roof trusses. Mon-Sun 2-4pm, by appt. FREE

**768**
**SS**
**House For An Art Lover**  353 4770. Bellahouston Park. 10 Dumbreck Rd. Take the M8 W, then the M77, turn rt onto Dumbreck Rd and it's on your left. These rms were designed, nearly a century ago, specifically, it would seem, for willowy women to come and go, talking of Michelangelo. Detail is the essence of Mackintosh, and there's plenty here, but the overall effect is of space and light and a complete absence of clutter. Design shop and Café (624/BEST TEAROOMS) on the ground floor. Phone for opening times. ADMN

# Essential Culture

## UNIQUE VENUES

**769**
**xF4**
✓ ✓ ✓ **Barrowland Ballroom** 552 4601. Gallowgate. When its lights are on, you can't miss it. The Barrowland is world-famous and for many bands one of their favourite gigs. It's tacky and a bit run-down, but distinctly venerable; and with its high stage and sprung dance floor, perfect for rock 'n' roll. The Glas audience is 'the best in the world'.

**770**
**xD5**
✓ ✓ **The Citizens' Theatre** 429 0022. Gorbals St, just over the river. Fabulous main auditorium and 2 small studios. Drama at its v best. One of Britain's most influential theatres, esp for design. Refurbished with lottery funds. Love the theatre? Love this theatre!

**771**
**SS**
✓ ✓ **The Tramway** 422 2023. 25 Albert Dr on S side. Studio, theatre & vast performance & exhibition space. Dynamic & influential with a varied, innovative programme from all over the world. Slated to be home of Scottish Ballet at TGP. Secret Garden behind (1568/GARDENS). Worth a visit.

**772**
**B1**
✓ **CCA** 332 7521. Centre for Contemporary Arts, 350 Sauchiehall St. Major refurb of central arts-lab complex for all kinds of performance & visual arts presentation. Impressive atrium/courtyard houses cool café/restau called Tempus. Watch press for CCA programme.

**773**
**B1**
✓ **ABC** 332 2232. Sauchiehall St. Purposeful conversion of old ABC film centre in middle of Sauchiehall St into large-capacity live-music venue with intimate ambience, clubrooms downstairs & light bar o/looking st. See *The List* for programme.

**774**
**C4**
✓ **The Arches** 221 4001. 253 Argyle St. Experimental and vital theatre on a budget in the railway arches under Central Stn. Director Andy Arnold's gong must surely be in the post! Opening times vary. W/end clubs among the best. Bar/café cool place to hang & even talk.

**775**
**E4** **The Tron Theatre** 552 4267. 63 Trongate. Contemporary Scottish theatre and other interesting performance, esp music. Gr café-bar with food before and *après* (547/GASTROPUBS).

**776**
**C1** **Glasgow Film Theatre** 332 6535. Rose St at Sauchiehall St. Known affectionately as GFT, has café/bar and 2 screens for essential art house flicks.

**777**
**B2** **King Tut's Wah Wah Hut** 221 5279. 272 St Vincent St. Every bit as good as its namesake in Alphabet City used to be; the room for interesting new bands, make-or-break atmos and cramped. Bands on the club circuit play to a damp and appreciative crowd. See flyers & *The List* for details.

## FESTIVALS

**Celtic Connections** 353 8000. 3 weeks in Jan. Fest with attitude & atmos.

**Glasgow International** 552 6027. Contemp visual arts in selected venues celebrating Glasgow's pre-eminence in producing significant contemp artists. May go biennial 2007/9 etc.

**Glasgow Art Fair** 552 6027. 4 days in Apr. (2198/WHERE TO BUY ART)

**The West End Festival** 341 0844. 2 weeks in June. Neighbourhood and arts fest that incl parade in Byres Rd and a lot of drinking.

**Glasgow International Jazz Festival** 552 3552. 1 week in July. Scotland's most credible jazz (in its widest sense) prog over diff venues.

**Merchant City Festival** 552 6027. A weekend in mid Sept in quarter to E of George Sq. Likely to step up a league in 2006.

**Glasgay** (glasgay.co.uk) Mid Nov. Modest but eclectic prog for gays & straight people alike over several days & venues.

**Radiance** Brand new & radiant at TGP. Glasgow buildings & dark corners lit up for a w/end at end of Nov.

**Hogmanay** 552 6027. 31 December. Not on the same scale as Edin. Usually a stage in George Sq (ticketed).

# SECTION 4

*Regional Hotels And Restaurants*

# The Best Hotels & Restaurants In Argyll

*See also* 2334/BEST OF OBAN.

✓ ✓ **Isle Of Eriska** 01631 720371. 20km N of Oban. Report: 1129/COUNTRY-HOUSE HOTELS.

✓ ✓ **Ardanaiseig** Loch Awe 01866 833333. Report: 1137/COUNTRY-HOUSE HOTELS.

**778**
Map 9
**J22**

✓ ✓ **Airds Hotel** Port Appin 01631 730236. 32km N of Oban 4km off A828. For a long time one of the foremost hostelries in the N & a legendary gourmet experience. Shaun & Jenny McKivragan & chef Paul Burns continue this tradition and maintain reputation in a much more competitive world. Cottagey, cosy bedrms upgrading at TGP. Conservatory restau on roadside with 3 AA rosettes firmly in place. Pt Appin one of Scotland's most charming places. Lismore passenger ferry 2km away (2287/MAGIC ISLANDS).
12RMS (+4) FEB-DEC T/T XPETS CC KIDS LOTS/MED.EX
**EAT** Always (& forever?) one of the best meals you will find in the N.     EXP

**779**
Map 9
**H24**

✓ ✓ **Crinan Hotel** Crinan 01546 830261. 8km off A816. On coast, 60km S of Oban (Lochgilphead 12km) at head of the Crinan Canal which joins L Fyne with the sea. O/side on the quay is the boat which has landed those massive prawns, sweet clams and other creatures with legs or valves, which are cooked v simply and brought on heaped tureens to your table. Stunning views o/looking canal basin (esp from the Galley bar 6.30-8.30) & from other rms, the Sound of Jura. This hotel has long housed one of the gr seafood restaus in the UK. Nick Ryan presides; his wife's (the notable artist, Frances Macdonald) pictures & those of son, Ross, are fitting & for sale.     22RMS JAN-DEC T/T PETS CC KIDS MED.EX
**EAT** Choice of 'Westward' dining rm or pub grub in bar.     EXP/CHP

**780**
Map 9
**J22**

✓ ✓ **Dun Na Mara** Benderloch 01631 720233. Off A828 Oban-Ft William rd, 12km N of Oban. Contemp conversion of seaside mansion in stunning setting, beach below & a perfect vista from all front (3) bedrms, breakfast rm & lounge. A dream GH done in immaculate (mainly white) taste retaining beautiful original features. Former architects are now your unobtrusive hosts.     7RMS JAN-DEC X/T XPETS CC KIDS MED.INX

**781**
Map 9

✓ **Balmory Hall** Ascog, Isle of Bute 01700 500669. 6km Rothesay towards Mt Stuart (1852/CO HOUSES). Grand but liveable & lived-in big hoose up rd 150m from 30mph sign. Superb appointments & they're all yours. A co house hotel with GH intimacy. Deer on the lawn. 3 excl self-cat apts all in the house. Otherwise eat at the Smiddy (1361/GASTROPUBS) 7km or The Pier at Craigmore on the way back to Rothesay (edge of town) which does gr home-cooking with big expansion afoot at TGP (01700 502867). Balmory is *the* top stay on the island. 3RMS(+3SELF-CAT) JAN-DEC X/T XPETS CC KIDS EXP

**782**
Map 9
**J25**

✓ **The Royal Hotel at Tighnabruaich** 01700 811239. Roger & Bea McKie & daughter Louise in the kitchen have transformed it into one of the best hotels in the W of Scotland. Lovely rms, many looking over to Bute, comfy furnishings & pictures. Bea leads gr out-front service & Roger & Louise toil in the kitchen. Doon the Water never as good as this. Bar meals 7 days, dining cl Sun/Mon.     11RMS JAN-DEC T/T PETS CC XKIDS MED.EX
**EAT** Dining rm & bar with conservatory restau.     MED/CHP

**783**
Map 9
**J24**

✓ **George Hotel** Inveraray 01499 302111. Main st of interesting town on L Fyne with credible attractions. Ancient inn (1770) still in the capable & friendly hands of the Clark family with real atmosphere in bar. Rms refurb tastefully in a Highland-chic kind of way. Open fire, gr grub in extensive bar. Exceptionally good value.     15RMS JAN-DEC T/T PETS CC KIDS MED.INX
**EAT** Gastropub grub in multichambered stone wood setting. Good ales, wines & eclectic menu.     CHP

**784**
Map 9
**H23**

✓ **Lerags House** nr Oban 01631 563381. 7km S of Oban. 4km from A816, a v particular GH unobtrusively brilliant (even the signage off the rd is low-key). Mansion in deep country with contemp feel & style. Charlie & Bella Miller from Oz do good rms & excl food. Cool place!
6RMS FEB-NOV X/T XPETS CC XKIDS MED.EX

**785**
Map 9
J23
**Roineabhal** Kilchrenan 01866 833207. Another hotel nr Kilchrenan (Ardanaiseig, above & Taychreggan, below) which is deep in the Loch Awe interior (10km the A85 rd to Oban, nr Taynuilt). Roger & Marion Soep call this a Highland country house & it is, tho' not a co house hotel. More like a gorgeous GH. Intimate (you eat round the same table) but all in excl taste & esp the food. You don't have to have dinner but you should (can BYO). Pron 'Ron-ay-vul'. 3RMS JAN-DEC X/T PETS CC KIDS MED.INX

**786**
Map 9
J23
**Taychreggan** Kilchrenan 01866 833211. Signed off A85 just before Taynuilt, 30km from Oban and nestling on a bluff by L Awe in imposing countryside. Quay for the old ferry to Portsonachan is nearby with boats available. With a spruce refurb & new rooms, rowan tree at the door and water lapping at gnds' edge, this hostelry looks good but suffers a tad from absentee landlord. We watch & await reports! 19RMS JAN-DEC T/T PETS CC KIDS LOTS

**787**
Map 9
J25
**Kilfinan Hotel** Kilfinan 01700 821201. 13km from Tighnabruaich on B8000. A much-loved inn on the beautiful single-track rd that skirts L Fyne. Mike & Tricia Cressdee preside over this classic, quiet getaway inn (quiet as the graveyard adj) with long-standing manager Madalon. Bar lunches & bistro dining at night. For a MED. EX retreat on a quiet peninsula, this is still a good bet. 11RMS JAN-DEC T/T PETS CC KIDS MED. EX

**788**
Map 9
J24
**Loch Fyne Hotel** Inveraray 01499 302148. Another ok hotel (tho' not aimed at individuals) in this charming town. On main A83 towards Lochgilphead o/looking loch. Part of the Crerar Group, the remains of British Trust Hotels; this one of their best. Pleasing & simple design makeover with a touch of tartan. Pool & facs. They do take coach parties.
80RMS JAN-DEC T/T PETS CC KIDS MED.INX

**789**
Map 9
H25
**Stonefield Castle Hotel** Tarbert (Argyll) 01880 820836. Just o/side town on the A83, a castle which evokes the 1970s more than preceding centuries. Splendid luxuriant gdns leading down to L Fyne. Dining-rm with baronial splendour and staggering views. Friendly, flexible staff; overall, it seems quintessentially Scottish and ok, esp for families (1150/KIDS) though the style police would have words. Most deals incl dinner too. (MED).
33RMS JAN-DEC T/T PETS CC KIDS MED.EX

**790**
Map 9
H25
**West Loch Hotel** Tarbert (Argyll) 01880 820283. Picturesque 1710 former coaching inn on the cusp of Kintyre, just o/side of Tarbert on A83. Within easy reach of ferries to Islay, Gigha and Arran. Lovely views of loch over rd, nice staff, relaxed atmos, ok food in conservatory restau. You can feel at home here; forgive the Jack Vettrianos! (1184/INNS)
8RMS FEB-DEC X/T PETS CC KIDS INX

**791**
Map 9
H25
**Columba Hotel**, Tarbert 01880 820808. Sound budget hotel on water front in this perfect Argyll town. Bar v popular with yachties and locals. Meals till 9pm. Refurb of rms in hand at TGP (to be completed '06).
10RMS JAN-DEC T/T PETS CC KIDS INX

**792**
Map 9
H23
**Glenburnie Hotel**, Oban 01631 562089. Corran Esplanade. In the middle of a broad sweep of hotels o/looking the bay, this is the best! Graeme Strachan's a natural innkeeper so everything in his seaside mansion is welcoming & easy on the eye. Gr detail. Home-made muesli; happy plants; nice furnishings. No dinner but he'll tell you exactly where to go.
12RMS MAR-OCT X/T PETS CC KIDS MED.INX

## RESTAURANTS

**793**
Map 9
J24
**Inver Cottage** Strathlachlan, Loch Fyne 01369 860537. S of Strachur on B8000, the scenic S rd by L Fyne, a cottage bar/bistro o/looking loch & ruins of Castle Lachlan. Home baking & cooking at its best. Comfort food & surroundings. Lovely walk to the ruins (40 mins ret) before or after. A real find! Apr-Oct. All-day menus till 5pm. Dinner Thu-Sun (7 days July/Aug). LO 9pm. INX

**794**
Map 9
K25
**Chatters** Dunoon 01369 706402. 58 John St. Rosie Macinnes' excellent restau in town rather than on esplanade is, by itself, a good reason for getting the ferry. The Cowal peninsula awaits your explorations (and Benmore Gdns 1543/GARDENS). Bar menu and à la carte, and a small gdn for drinks or lunch on a good day. All delightful. Wed-Sat only, lunch & dinner. MED

# The Best Hotels & Restaurants In Ayrshire & Clyde Valley

*See also* 2329/AYR.

**795**
Map 9
**K28**

✓✓ **The Westin Turnberry Resort** Turnberry 01655 331000. Not just a hotel on the Ayrshire coast, more a way of life centred on golf. Looks over the 2 courses which are difficult to get on unless you're a guest (2049/GREAT GOLF). All that should be expected of a world-class hotel except, perhaps, the buzz; but plenty of golf reminiscing and time moving slowly. The spa complex adj has state-of-the-art 'treatments', even exercise – with deals for day visitors & nice pool. Colin Montgomerie 'Golf Academy' takes all sorts. Brasserie here (The Terrace) has excl 'light' all day menus; main dining rm looks over the courses to Ailsa Craig beyond – dinner only, and epic Sun lunch. Lovely lodges down the hill. 2006 the 100th anniversary of Turnberry. Expect celebrations. 221RMS JAN-DEC T/T PETS CC KIDS LOTS
**EAT** The Terrace is the light place to eat; pastas, risottos, etc. Main restau has 2 AA rosettes. Fine dining in grand style. MED/EXP

**796**

✓✓ **Glenapp Castle** by Ballantrae 01465 831212. Discreet & immensely distinguished. A jewel in the Scottish crown goes to S Ayrshire. (Report: 1128/SUPERLATIVE COUNTRY HOUSE HOTELS.)

**797**
Map 9
**K28**

✓ **Culzean Castle** nr Maybole 01655 760615. 18km S of Ayr (coast rd most pleasant), this is accom in the suites of Culzean, the house itself (1791/CASTLES) so a bed for the night rarely comes as posh as this (includes the famous Eisenhower suite). Rates are exp, but incl afternoon tea. Dinner (incl wine) is avail. The cliff-top setting, the gdns & the vast grounds are superb. Programme of events thro'out yr incl major concert in May; many weddings. 6 SUITES APR-OCT T/T XPETS CC KIDS LOTS

**798**
Map 9
**L28**

✓ **The Ivy House** Ayr 01292 442336. North Park on the Alloway Rd, almost feels like the country. Cosy, well-appointed rms with bathrms bordering on the lavish. New ownership (no longer private) & new chef/menu so reports please; but prob still the best stopover Ayr/Alloway way. 5RMS JAN-DEC T/T PETS CC KIDS MED.EX
**EAT** One of the best meals in Ayrshire, tho at a price. EXP

**799**
Map 9
**K26**

✓ **Lochgreen House** Troon 01292 313343. Part of the Bill Costley empire in this neck of the woods, Lochgreen (adj to Royal Troon Golf Course) the most full-on upmarket – newer extension gives 40 rms. The **Brig o' Doon** at Alloway is the romance-and-Rabbie Burns hotel (01292 442466), lots of weddings but only 5 rms, while **Highgrove** (01292 312511), a bit more intimate, is just outside Troon. Recent refurb. All operate at a very acceptable standard. These Costleys also have the Ellisland Hotel in Ayr (2329/AYR) and a good roadside inn – the **Cochrane** at Gatehead, nearby (1411/PUB FOOD).
**EAT** Good restau with a Costley in the kitchen. 3 AA Rosettes. EXP

**800**
Map 10
**L27**

✓ **The Sorn Inn** 01290 551305. 35 Main St, Sorn, which is 8km E of Mauchline on the B743 off the A76. Trad inn in rural setting & pleasant vill in deepest Ayrshire. Grant family have quickly est big rep for food (Gastropub of the Year 2005) & there are 4 delightful rms which are gr value. DVD etc. 4RMS JAN-DEC T/T PETS CC KIDS MED.INX
**EAT** People travel from miles around to eat here. Restau & pub meals. See 1348/GASTROPUBS.

**801**
Map 9
**L28**

**Enterkine House** nr Annbank, by Ayr 01292 521608. 10km Ayr in beautiful grounds tho Annbank (2km) not the loveliest of vills. Self-consciously upmarket with pleasant tho' not so modern public rms. Paul Murphy presides over conservatory restau with good local rep.
6RMS JAN-DEC T/T XPETS CC XKIDS LOTS

**802**
Map 9
**K27**

**Piersland Hotel** Troon 01292 314747. Craig End Rd opp Portland Golf Course which is next to Royal Troon (2050/GREAT GOLF). Mansion house of some character & ambience much favoured for weddings. Wood-panelling, open fires, lovely gdns only a 'drive' away from the courses (no preferential booking on Royal, but Portland usually poss) & lots of gr golf nearby. 2 AA rosettes for the food. Gr whisky selection. 30RMS JAN-DEC T/T PETS CC KIDS EXP

**803** **The Park Hotel** Kilmarnock 01563 545999. Rugby Park ie adj Kilmarnock's
Map 9 football stadium. Contemp business & family hotel better than chains of
**L27** travelodge ilk. Good café/restau. Sports facs at the ground opp. Weddings &
dinner-dances.                                    50RMS JAN-DEC T/T PETS CC KIDS MED.INX

**804** **Shieldhill Castle** Quothquan nr Biggar 01899 220035. Well S of the Clyde,
Map 10 Glasgow & anywhere, a countryside retreat just off the B7016 Biggar-
**N27** Carnwath. Mostly dates from late 16thC but older bits go back to 1199.
Famous guests have included a certain Mr Mandela. Pick yr rm carefully and
you get a 4-poster and a jacuzzi. Chancellor's Restaurant has sedate dining
& an extraordinary wine-list. Gun Room menu is an option. It also has
'celebrity mussels'.            16RMS JAN-DEC T/T PETS CC KIDS EXP/LOTS

**805** **Wilding's Hotel & Restaurant** Maidens 01655 331401. Maidens is
Map 9 coastal vill in S Ayrshire, S of Maybole & lovely Culzean (1791/CASTLES), so a
**K28** good base. Run by Brian Sage, restaurateur, this is perhaps more a restau
with rms. Many o/look serene harbour but are more motel (& v basic) than
seaside inn.                          10RMS JAN-DEC T/T PETS CC KIDS MED.INX
**EAT** May be a drive for dinner, but a beautiful spot & excl gastropub-style
menu. Food LO 9pm. They come from all over the county (& Turnberry) so
book w/ends.                                                          MED

**806** **Gleddoch House** Langbank nr Greenock 01475 540711. 35km from Glas by
Map 9 fast rd – M8/A8 t/off marked Langbank/Houston after jnct 31, follow
**L25** Houston then signs. Set in extensive grounds (including 18-hole golf course),
with commanding view of Clyde by Dumbarton Rock. Leisure club adj with a
15km pool. After devastating fire, the main house re-opening spring '06.

# RESTAURANTS

**807** ✓ **Braidwoods** nr Dalry 01294 833544. First find Dalry; near the Esso
Map 9 ✓ garage take the small rd to Saltcoats and the restau is discreetly signed
**K26** around a mile out that rd. Once you find Keith and Nicola's place, you'll be
glad you made the effort. Michelin star, 3 AA rosettes, nice people, great
food. Best meal in the shire. Wed/Sun lunch and Tues-Sat dinner.     MED

**808** ✓ **MacCallums** The Harbour, Troon 01292 319339. Harbourside seafood
✓ bistro. Report: 1393/SEAFOOD.                               MED/INX

**809** ✓ **Ristorante La Vigna** Lanark 01555 664320. 40 Wellgate. For almost
Map 10 ✓ 25 yrs this famously good Italian restau in a back st in Lanark is unex-
**N27** pected, and quite a find if you're lost in the Lanarkshire badlands. Superb
Italian wine-list. This is not a tratt! Lunch Mon-Sat, dinner 7 days.    MED

**810** **Fouters** Ayr 01292 261391. 2a Academy St. Off Sandgate. Cellar bistro just
Map 9 off main st. Long-est best restau in town now under chef/prop Brian Murphy,
**L28** who has won back its reputation. Tho' locals may complain of prices, this is
prob the best meal in town (again). Contemp British.                  MED

**811** **Restaurants in Strathaven** 2 good eating places in & about this
Map 10 Lanarkshire vill (pron *Straven*) S of E Kilbride & W of Lanark & the Clyde Valley.
**M26** **Steayban**, 01357 523400, is a gastropub in Glassford, 2km from Strathaven
& serves excl suppers (Wed-Sat) & Sun lunch.                         INX
**Trattoria Da Mario**, 01357 522604, is a fine Italian tratt comparable with
any in the city. Lunch Tue-Sat, dinner Tue-Sun. Cl Mon.              INX

**812** **The Wheatsheaf** Symington, nr Ayr & Prestwick 01563 830307. Off main
Map 9 A77 (2km), just N of main Prestwick r/about. Roadside & village inn tucked
**L27** away off main rd with big local rep for wholesome pub grub. Their steak pie
is famous. No fuss, gr service. Report 1401/PUB FOOD. LO 9.30pm.

**813** **Fins** Fairlie, nr Largs 01475 568989. 8 km S of Largs on A78. Excellent
Map 9 seafood bistro. Report: 1400/SEAFOOD RESTAUS.                        MED
**K26**

# The Best Hotels & Restaurants In The South-West

*See also* 2330/BEST OF DUMFRIES.

**814**
Map 11
**J30**
✓✓ **Knockinaam Lodge** Portpatrick 01776 810471. Tucked away on dream cove, historic country house full of fresh flowers, gr food, sea air and informal, but v good service. Sian & Diana Ibbotson (2 kids, 3 black labs) balance a family home & a top-class get-away-from-it-all hotel. Refurb in progress but it's all lovely. (1131/COUNTRY-HOUSE HOTELS)

9RMS JAN-DEC T/T PETS CC KIDS LOTS

**EAT** Best meal in the S. from outstanding chef, Tony Pierce. Fixed menu – lots of unexpected treats. Michelin Star. EXP

**815**
Map 11
**J30**
✓ **Corsewall Lighthouse Hotel** Stranraer 01776 853220. A718 to Kirkcolm 3km, B738 to Corsewall 6km (follow signs). Wild location on cliff top. Cosily furnished clever but cramped (or snug) conversion. Best with a close personal friend. The adj fully functioning lighthouse (since 1817) makes for surreal evenings. 3 suites are actually o/side the lighthouse – all have the sea & sky views. Small dining rm. Food fine (& it's a long way to the chipper). 9RMS JAN-DEC T/T PETS CC KIDS EXP

**816**
Map 11
**N30**
✓ **Cavens** Kirkbean 01387 880234. 20km S Dumfries via A710, Cavens on edge & signed from Kirkbean. This elegant mansion (once home to tobacco baron Sir Richard Oswald) in 6 landscaped acres has been converted by Angus & Jane Fordyce into a homely, informal haven of peace & quiet – gr base for touring the SW. Lots of public space so you can even get away from each other. Simple, good cooking using locally sourced ingredients. The Loch Arthur granola for b/fast is *the* best.

7RMS JAN-DEC T/T XPETS CC KIDS MED.EX

**817**
Map 11
**K30**
**Kirroughtree Hotel** Newton Stewart 01671 402141. On A712. Built 1719, Rabbie Burns was once here. Extensive country house refurb with heavy drapes and plush atmos. Original panelled hall and stairs, some spacious rms. Food here gets 3 AA rosettes: Ralph Mueller's menu may be your main reason for coming. Closed mid Jan to mid Feb.

17RMS FEB-DEC T/T PETS CC KIDS LOTS

**818**
Map 11
**N31**
**Balcary Bay** Auchencairn nr Castle Douglas 01556 640311. 20km S of Castle Douglas and Dalbeattie. Off A711 at end of shore rd and as close to the water as you can get without getting wet. Ideal for walking and bird watching. Andrew Lipp in the kitchen continues a strong committment to local produce. A well-run hideaway! 20RMS MAR-NOV T/T PETS CC KIDS MED.EXP

**819**
Map 11
**N30**
**Clonyard House** Colvend nr Rockcliffe nr Dalbeattie 01556 630372. On Solway Coast rd nr Rockcliffe and Kippford (1599/COASTAL VILLAGES; 2042/ COASTAL WALKS) but not on sea. Later extension to house provides (11 of the) bedrms adj to patio gdn with own private access and ... aviary! Friendly family; decent pub grub. 17RMS JAN-DEC T/T PETS CC KIDS MED.INX

**820**
Map 11
**M31**
**Good Spots in Kirkcudbright** pronounced 'cur-coo-bree'; a gem of a town. On a street filled with posh B&Bs the **Gladstone House** stands out (High St 01557 331734). Only 3 (lovely attic) rms so book well ahead.
**Selkirk Arms** (yup, High St, 01557 330402) is much more your 'proper hotel' (a Best Western). Standard facs, no atmos & food av (but it is right central in this most interesting of SW towns).

**821**
Map 11
**N30**
**Anchor** Kippford 01556 620205. Seaside hotel in cute vill 3km off main A710. Basic accom but gr pub atmos; seafood menu (local lobster, pints of prawns). On the shore. 7RMS (+ COTT) JAN-DEC X/T PETS CC KIDS INX

## RESTAURANTS

**822**
Map 11
**M30**
✓✓ **The Plumed Horse** Crossmichael nr Castle Douglas 01556 670333. Just N of Castle Douglas on A713. Amazing find in unexpected surroundings – serious food by inimitable chef/prop/even waiter, Tony Borthwick. Firmly est on foodie map of Scotland. Michelin star & other food guides routinely praise it to the skies. Expect first-class ingredients, real flair & a change of address (tho' still in Crossmichael) 2006. Lunch Tues-Fri and Sun, dinner Tues-Sat (7 or 8pm). MED.EXP

**823**
Map 11
**N29**
✓ **The Linen Room** Dumfries 01387 255689. 53 St Michael St (direction Caerlaverock). You'd have to wish Richard (McGookin) & Michelle & chef Russell Robertson all the v best here in a town not known for its culinary highlights or demands. Easily the most considered & only fine dining around. Gr sourcing & real, imaginative cooking. Gr wine-list! Go on, Dumfries, treat yourself! Lunch & dinner Tues-Sat. MED

**824**
Map 11
**J30**
✓ **Campbells** Portpatrick 01776 810314. Portpatrick is an end-of-the-line but hugely popular destination vill with a quaint harbour & a fair few caffs & bars. This is the best and is often packed. Unpretentious fishy fare (some pork/lamb/beef/duck/chicken dishes ie something for everyone) & gr chips. 7 days lunch and LO 10pm. INX

**825**
Map 11
**M30**
✓ **The Masonic Arms** Gatehouse Of Fleet 01557 814335. Chris & Sue Walker have in 2 yrs turned 'The Masonic' into *the* place to eat hereabouts. 3 separate rms & atmos (pub/conservatory – in summer/contemp rm) but same menu featuring local produce esp fish & beef. Good vegn choices & special kids' menu. You could say they've read the market! Apr-Oct Noon-2pm, 6-9pm. Nov-Mar closed Mon-Tues. MED

**826**
Map 11
**P28**
**Lime Tree Restaurant** Moffat 01683 221654. High St. Raved about by Joanna B, Scotland's most get-around food critic, this ambitious venture has become a destination restau in this historic spa town. Mat & Artemis Seddon aim to serve good food at sensible prices. Well they do! Tues-Sat 6.30-9.30pm, Sun 12.30-2.30pm. MED

**827**
Map 11
**J30**
**The Crown** Portpatrick 01776 810261. Harbourside hotel/pub restau with better than your av pub-grub. Goes like a fair in summer. Lounge & conservatory & outside. AA Seafood Pub of the Year '05. 7 days. LO 10pm. Competition next door from the **Waterfront** 01776 810800. Crown is the better pub, newcomer has more modern rms. INX

**828**
Map 11
**M31**
**The Auld Alliance** Kirkcudbright 01557 330569. Solway scallops and salmon, etc. 7 nights. Franco-Scottish flavour. Open Easter-Oct for dinner only (and Sun lunch) but the quieter it gets, the less they open & soon they may not open at all. For sale at TGP. MED

**829**
Map 11
**M30**
**Carlo's** Castle Douglas 01556 503977. 211 King St. Curiously, Castle Douglas is Scotland's food town even tho' there are virtually no good restaus. Carlo's is your nearest best option. Bustling tratt atmos & offering. It is said that Carlo's is the best Italian food in S. Open Tues-Sun 6-9pm. INX

**830**
Map 11
**N29**
**Hullabaloo** Dumfries 01387 259679. At the Robert Burns Centre, W side of the river and which also houses the local art-house cinema. Wraps, steaks, burgers & superior soup; oh and sandwiches. Cl time varies acc to movie times, but usually 11am-9/10pm (wint Tues-Sat only). INX

**831**
Map 11
**M31**
**Kirkpatrick's** Kirkcudbright 01557 330888. Scottish restau opened in 2002 & highly regarded by locals despite unprepossessing frontage (upstairs & round corner from Main St). Dinner is where Tom Kirkpatrick shows his stuff. Open 7 days lunch & LO 9pm. Cl Jan.

# The Best Hotels & Restaurants In Central Scotland

*See also* 2236/BEST OF STIRLING.

**832**
Map 10
M24

✓ ✓ **The Roman Camp** Callander  01877 330003. Nothing has changed here since last edition in this exemplary hotel. Behind the main st (at E or Stirling end), away from the tourist throng and with extensive gdns on the R Teith; another, more elegant world. Roman ruins nearby, but the house was built for the Dukes of Perth and has been a hotel since the war. Rms low-ceilinged and snug; period furnishings; some rms small, many magnificent. In the old building corridors do creak. Delightful drawing rm and conservatory. Oval dining-rm v sympatico. Private chapel should a prayer come on and, of course, many weddings. Rods for fishing – the river swishes past the lawn.  14RMS JAN-DEC T/T PETS CC KIDS LOTS
**EAT** Dining rm effortlessly the best food in town & country with a gr chef – Ian McNaught.  EXP

**833**
Map 10
L23

✓ ✓ **Monachyle Mhor** nr Balquhidder  01877 384622. Along the ribbon of rd that skirts Loch Voil 7 km beyond the vill (which is 4km) from the A84 Callander-Crianlarich rd. Rel remote (1213/GET AWAY FROM IT ALL) & splendid location for this informal farmhouse hotel with gr food, contemp rms & altogether good vibes. 10RMS+2COTT JAN-DEC T/T PETS CC KIDS MED.EX
**EAT** It's a long way to go for dinner, but I would.  MED

**834**

✓ ✓ **Cromlix House** Dunblane  01786 822125. 3km from A9 & 4km from town on B8033; foll signs for Perth, then Kinbuck. A leisurely drive thro' old estate with splended mature woodlands to this spacious country mansion both sumptuous & homely. New ownership autumn '05 but no immediate changes planned. 3000 acres of meadows & fishing lochs (Home L v serene) but no leisure facs.  14RMS(8SUITES) JAN-DEC T/T PETS CC KIDS LOTS
**EAT** Chef Steven MacCallum, gr conservatory & cosy dining rms  EXP

**835**
Map 10
M24

✓ **The Inn at Kippen** Kippen  01786 871010. Middle of vill on rd in from L Lomond direction. Thoroughly good village-inn experience with some style. Real chef, real nice people. Rms are good value.  4RMS JAN-DEC X/T XPETS CC KIDS MED.INX
**EAT** Arnmore Restau or lighter/cheaper in 'Glen Tirran Bar'. Both under Richard Truesdale. Excl options.  MED/INX

**836**
Map 10
N24

**Queens Hotel** Bridge Of Allan  01786 833268. Main st of pleasant town (good shops & restaus). Surprisingly & self-consciously 'stylish' & modern with cool interiors & art (tho' main picture odd choice). Groovy restau (Jekyll's) & bars. O/side terrace.  10RMS JAN-DEC T/T XPETS CC KIDS MED.EXP

**837**
Map 10
M23

**Creagan House** Strathyre  01877 384638. End of the village on main A84 for Crianlarich (as above). Creagan House is the place to eat in Rob Roy & Callander country (one of only 4 Michelin Bib Gourmand restaus in Scotland & the only one with accom). They have 5 inexp rms and the Gunns are a congenial bunch. You eat in a pleasant baronial dining rm. There are many hills to walk & forest trails that start in the garden (1964/HILLS). Cl Feb.  5RMS JAN-DEC T/T PETS CC KIDS MED.EX

**838**
Map 10
M24

**Lake Hotel** Port Of Menteith  01877 385258. A v lake-side hotel on the Lake of Menteith in the purple heart of the Trossachs. Good centre for touring and walking. The Inchmahome ferry leaves from nearby (1930/MARY, CHARLIE AND BOB). 5 rms o/look lake (and are more exp, but worth the extra). Conservatory for sunset supper. Recently taken over by partnership which incl TV chef Nick Nairn, so reasonable to expect high-calibre cooking. Rolling refurb over 06/07 but for clean air and/or dirty w/end, this is a romantic spot.  16RMS JAN-DEC T/T PETS CC KIDS MED.EX

**839**
Map 10
M25

**Black Bull** Killearn  01360 550215. In this good-looking village, 30mins N of Glasgow betw L Lomond (Drymen) and the Campsies, a good conversion of an old inn & a testament to the good taste of the previous owners. Conservatory dining rm & bar/bistro menus. Rms simple & decent value (505/HOTELS OUTSIDE TOWN). In Killearn check also **The Old Mill** (1363/GASTROPUBS).  12RMS JAN-DEC X/T PETS CC KIDS MED.INX

**840** **Hilton Dunblane Hydro** Dunblane 01786 822551. One of the huge hydro
Map 10 hotels left over from the last health boom, recently sold by Hilton to... some
**M24** other company. Refurb likely – you could spend a lot of money here. Nice
views for some and a long walk down corridors for most. Leisure facs incl
pool. Whatever improvements are made it's likely to remain a dinner-dance
and wedded world. 210RMS JAN-DEC T/T PETS KIDS CC EXP

**841** **Inverarnan Hotel/The Drover's Inn & The Stagger Inn** Inverarnan
Map 9 01301 704234. N of Ardlui on L Lomond and 12km S of Crianlarich on the A82.
**K23** Much the same as it was when it began in 1705; bare floors, open fires and
heavy drinking (1323/BLOODY GOOD PUBS). Highland hoolies here much recommended. Bar staff wearing kilts look like they mean it. Rms not Gleneagles
but highly individual. A wild place in the wilderness. Expect atmos not service. They also own the Stagger Inn across the road (704274). 16 en suite rms
& restau – the rms more standard here with 4-posters. Neither places have
phones nor TV & mobiles prob don't work. Hey, you're away!
12+16RMS JAN-DEC X/X PETS CC KIDS CHP

**842** **3 Great B&Bs in Callander: Leny House** 01877 331078. On estate on
Map 10 edge of town (off main rd N to Crianlarich) & far from the madd(en)ing crowd.
**M24** Gorgeous house, luxuriously appointed bedrms, brilliant b/fast. A v superior
billet for the night. 4RMS MAY-SEPT X/T XPETS CC XKIDS EXP
**The Priory** 01877 330001. Bracklinn Rd off Main St (500m). Victorian mansion in nice garden (one of many, but much better than most). Gets Michelin
mention. Teddy bears & attentive hosts.
8RMS APR-OCT X/T PETS CC KIDS MED.INX
**Arden House** 01877 330235. Bracklinn Rd same as The Priory (above), further up. Similar set-up: superior B&B in elegant mansion. This one used to
be featured in that seminal Sunday night series, *Dr Finlay's Casebook*. It is
redolent of Tannochbrae. 6RMS MAR-NOV X/T XPETS CC KIDS INX

✓✓ **Mar Hall** Bishopton 0141 312 9999. Opulent co house on big scale
nr Glasgow & airport. Report: 503/OUTSIDE TOWN HOTELS.

✓ **Cameron House** Loch Lomond 01389 755565. Report: 504/OUTSIDE
TOWN HOTELS.

✓ **Lodge on Loch Lomond** 01436 860201. Report: 507/OUTSIDE TOWN
HOTELS.

## RESTAURANTS

**843** ✓ **Unicorn** Kincardine 01259 739129. Excise St but follow signs. Real find
Map 10 in Forth shores wasteland, a bistro with gr food & seafood dining
**N25** upstairs in the Red Room. Tony & Liz Budde run a tight & classy shop. Go
find! Cl Mon & Sun evens. Red Room Fri/Sat dinner only. INX/MED

**844** ✓ **The Allan Water Café** Bridge of Allan Caff that's been here for ever at
Map 10 end of the main st in Bridge of Allan now has big brassy, glassy extension
**N24** & it occupies the whole block. Original featues & clientele still remain in the
old bit. It's all down to fish 'n' chips and the ice cream (1430/CAFÉS). 7 days,
8am-9pm. CHP

**845** **Glenskirlie House** Banknock 01324 840207. On A803 Kilsyth-
Map 10 Bonnybridge rd, J4 off A80 Glas-Stirling rd, not far (15 mins) Stirling or Falkirk.
**N25** Edwardian elegant mansion house serving bar lunches and serious dining in
stylish surroundings. Mod British menu with good Scottish ingredients. 7
days lunch & LO 9.30pm (not Mon dinner). CHP/EXP

**846** **Atrium** Callander 01877 331611. Main St above CCW (Caledonian) outdoor
Map 10 shop. Unprepossessing approach thro' shop & upstairs to light, spacious
**M24** mezzanine self/s restau prob best choice in stopover town. Home-made
comfort food. Daytime only (till 5pm). CHP

# The Best Hotels & Restaurants In The Borders

See also 2333/BEST OF THE BORDER TOWNS.

**847**
Map 10
**S27**
✓ **Roxburghe Hotel** nr Kelso 01573 450331. *The* best country-house hotel in the Borders. Owned by the Duke and Duchess of Roxburghe, who have a personal input. Rms distinctive, all light with garden views. Reliable wine list (by the Duke) and Keith Short's safe hands in the kitchen. The 18-hole golf course has broadened appeal – it's challenging and championship standard and in a beautiful riverside setting. Non-res can play (2069/GOLF). 'Health & Beauty Suite' for golf widows. Compared with other country-house hotels, the Roxburghe is good value. Personal, not overbearing service.     22RMS JAN-DEC T/T PETS CC KIDS EXP
**EAT** Where to go for fine dining and wining in the E Borders. Chef Keith Short. Also Fairways Brasserie o/looking golf course open w/ends.     EXP

**848**
Map 10
**Q27**
✓ **Cringletie House** Peebles 01721 730233. Country house 5km from town just off A703 Edin rd (35km). Late 19th-century Scottish baronial house in 28 acres. Recent new owners making many improvements. Comfortable & civilised. Restful garden view from every rm. Top disabled facs incl a lift! Conservatory does light lunches and nice aft tea (reservations only). Walled gdn. Tennis.     14RMS JAN-DEC T/T PETS CC KIDS LOTS
**EAT** Gracious dining (o/looking) conservatory & gdn.     EXP

**849**
Map 10
**P27**
✓ **Skirling House** Skirling 01899 860274. On A72. 3km from Biggar as you come into Skirling vill. In an Arts & Crafts house (by Ramsay Traquair, brother of Phoebe), Bob & Isobel Hunter have created the definitive rural GH. All aspiring couples go see! From the toiletries (Arran Aromatics) to the white doves in the doocot & the hens from which your b/fast eggs come, it's just perfect. Bob cooks, Isobel waits (& then goes to work). B/fast a model of its kind; didn't have dinner – I imagine it was rather good.     5RMS MAR-DEC X/T PETS CC KIDS MED.INX

**850**
Map 10
**R27**
✓ **Burts** Melrose 01896 822285. In Market Sq/main st, some (double-glazed) rms o/look. Busy bars, esp for food, The dining-rm is *where to eat* in this part of the Borders. Trad, but comfortably modernised small town hotel, though some rms also feel small. Convenient location. Good service (1921/ABBEYS; 1980/HILL WALKS; 1558/GARDENS). Where to stay for the Sevens, but try getting in!     20RMS JAN-DEC T/T PETS CC KIDS MED.EX
**EAT** Bar gastropub standard; more refined dining rm has 2 AA rosettes. EXP

**851**
Map 10
**R27**
✓ **The Townhouse** Melrose 01896 822645. Burts (above) has now spawned a more fashion-conscious little sister across the st. Charming, contemp & almost boutiqueish, tho' only one rm (room 11) had been given the full modern makeover at TGP. Others more than comfortable. Dining rm & busy brasserie confidently positioned betw Burts' fine dining & its bar.     11RMS JAN-DEC T/T PETS CC KIDS EXP

**852**
Map 10
**S27**
✓ **Edenwater House** Ednam nr Kelso 01573 224070. Find Ednam on Kelso-Swinton rd B6461, 4 km. Discreet manse-type house beside old kirk and o/look graveyard and tranquil green countryside. You have the run of the home of Jeff & Jacqui Kelly & Jacqui's superb cooking. Good wines, good life & a gorgeous garden.     4RMS JAN-DEC X/T XPETS CC KIDS MED.INX

**853**
Map 10
**R26**
**Lodge At Carfraemill** nr Lauder 01578 750750. On A68 r/bout 8km N of Lauder. Old coaching type lodging. This sure beats a motel! Old-style cooking, a good stop on the rd for grub ('Jo's Kitchen') & a gateway to the Borders. Nice for kids.     10RMS JAN-DEC T/T PETS CC KIDS MED.INX-EXP

**854**
Map 10
**R27**
**Dryburgh Abbey Hotel** nr St Boswells 01835 822261. Secluded, elegant 19thC house in abbey grounds banking R Tweed. Peaceful & beautiful location; good tho' small swimming pool. No atmos, average dining. Lovely riverside walks. Abbey pure romance by moonlight.     38RMS JAN-DEC T/T PETS CC KIDS EXP

**855**
Map 10
**Q27**
**Philipburn Selkirk** 01750 720747. 1km from town centre on A707 Peebles Rd. Excl hotel for families, walkers, weekend away from it all. Selkirk is a good Borders base. Restaurant and bar-bistro and rare outdoor pool (with 2 family

rms o/looking). Comfy rms, some luxurious. Best vegn food for miles around here.         17RMS JAN-DEC T/T PETS CC KIDS EXP

**856** **Jedforest Country Hotel** nr Jedburgh  01835 840222. On A68 about 12km
Map 10    from the border at Carter Bar (the first hotel in Scotland!) and 5km from
**R28**    Jedburgh, my home town. New owners at TGP but French chef remains –
food notable hereabouts. Also a cottage. The Jed gurgles nearby.
8RMS JAN-DEC T/T XPETS CC KIDS MED.INX

**857** **Ednam House** Kelso 01573 224168. Just off town sq o/look R Tweed; majes-
Map 10    tic Georgian mansion with v old original features incl some of the guests!
**S27**    Dated in a comfy way, fishing regalia dotted around; the restau's river view is,
however, the main attraction. Only half the bedrms have view. *The* place to
stay when fishing these parts.         32RMS JAN-DEC T/T PETS CC KIDS MED.INX

**858** **Clint Lodge** St Boswells 01835 822027. On B6356 (1713/SCENIC ROUTES) betw
Map 10    Dryburgh Abbey (1918/ABBEYS) & Smailholm Tower (1918/MONUMENTS). Small
**R27**    country GH in gr border country with tranquil views from rms. V good home-
cooking & service from Bill & Heather Walker with splendid Border b/fast.
5RMS JAN-DEC X/T PETS XCC KIDS MED

**859** **Caddon View** Innerleithen  01896 830208. Pirn Rd. Hotel in the doctor's
Map 10    house, comfy & tasteful rms. Excl restau dinner & b/fast from French chef/
**Q27**    prop tho' changing hands at TGP. 8RMS EASTER-DEC X/T PETS CC KIDS MED.INX

**860** **Fauhope** Melrose 01896 823184. Borders house in sylvan setting o/looking
Map 10    Tweed. Only 3 rms but run by Sheila Robson who also has Marmions (see
**R27**    below), so worth a stopover. Highly awarded.
3RMS JAN-DEC T/X PETS CC KIDS INX

**Hart Manor** Eskdalemuir  01387 373217. Report: 1230/GET-AWAY HOTELS.

**Wheatsheaf** Swinton 01890 860257. (1354/GASTROPUBS)

**Auld Crosskeys Inn** Denholm  01450 870305. (1374/GASTROPUBS)

**Traquair Arms** Innerleithen  01896 830229. (1193/ROADSIDE INNS)

**Gordon Arms** Yarrow Valley  01750 82222. (1199/ROADSIDE INNS)

**The Craw Inn** Auchencrow 01890 761253. (1181/ROADSIDE INNS)

## RESTAURANTS

**861** ✓**Marmion's** Melrose  01896 822245. Buccleuch St nr the abbey. Local
Map 10   ✓ fave bistro, now going a long time, but on our last visit it was just as
**R27**    good food-wise & facing up to the new competition in Melrose, the Borders'
food capital. Lunch and dinner. Cl Sun.         INX

**862** ✓**Chapters** Gattonside nr Melrose 01896 823217. Over the R Tweed (you
Map 10   ✓ could walk by footbridge as quick as going round by car). Kevin & Nicki
**R27**    Winsland's surprising bistro – a bit of a find. Huge choice from à la carte and
specials. Tues–Sat dinner only.         MED

✓**Burts** Melrose and **Cringletie** Peebles (*see above*): Burts for best dining
✓ hereabouts, Cringletie for country treat (Cringletie is nr Peebles).

**863** ✓**Halcyon** Peebles  01721 725100. Main St of cosy town adj fab Eastgate
Map 10   ✓ Theatre (2268/THEATRES). Chef Ali McGrath & a small team in a small rm
**Q27**    above (estimable) Villeneuve Wines bring this part of Scotland the simply
bloody good restau it has always deserved. No-nonsense 3 choices. Tues–Sat
lunch & 6–9pm.         INX

**864** ✓**King's Arms** Melrose  01896 822143. High St. Excl bar food in 17th cent
Map 10    coaching inn. The locals' choice. LO 9pm (10pm Sat).
**R27**

**865** **The Hoebridge Inn** Gattonside nr Melrose  01896 823082. At Earlston end
Map 10    of vill, signed to rt. Under new management at TGP but a long rep for supe-
**R27**    rior & imaginative pub fd with flair. Seems likely to continue. Book for w/end.
INX

**866** **Monte Cassino** Melrose  01896 820082. Occupying old station building just
Map 10    up from main sq. Cheerful, non-pretentious & locally popular Italian with
**R27**    pasta/pizza staples & the odd ok special. Cl Mon.         INX

**867** **Queens Bistro** Kelso 01573 228899. Bridge St nr Sq opp Ednam House
Map 10 Hotel (above). Finally tians, risottos & the like have landed in the E Borders
**S27** courtesy of Gary Moore who provides v similar fare to the denizens of Melrose
(where there's a lot more competition – see above). Here it's where locals go
for contemp bistro fare. 7 days, lunch & LO 9.30/10pm. INX

**868** **Sunflower Restaurant** Peebles 01721 722420. Bridgegate off Main St at
Map 10 Veitches corner. Long-standing spot for restau, a local fave. Café menu dur-
**Q27** ing day & nice for kids. Thu/Fri/Sat for dinner 7–9 pm. Cl Suns. INX

**869** **Lazel's** Peebles 01721 730233. Restaurant in the bowels of the Hydro
Map 10 (1148/FAMILY HOTELS), but real chef so good for lunch if passing thro' or Fri/Sat
**Q27** dinner. Modern makeover & menu, but well below stairs. INX/MED

**870** **Giacopazzi's & Oblo's** Eyemouth 01890 752527. Gr fish 'n' chips & ice-
cream plus new upstairs bistro nr harbour of this fishy & friendly town.
1422/FISH 'N' CHIPS. INX

# The Best Hotels & Restaurants In The Lothians

*See Section 2 for Edin.*

**871** ✓ ✓ **Greywalls** Gullane 01620 842144. On the coast, 36km E of Edin
Map 10 off A198 just beyond Gullane towards N Berwick. O/looks Muirfield,
**R25** the championship course (no right of access but some 'golf packages' avail)
and nr Gullane's 3 courses and N Berwick's 2 (2053/2054/GREAT GOLF). No
grey walls here but warm sandstone and light, summery public rms in this
Lutyens-designed manor with gdns attributed to Gertrude Jekyll. It's the look
that makes it special and the roses are legendary. Sculpture from Edin's
Scottish Gallery occ in summer. Lovely dining rm; indeed all the public rms
are homely & full of nice books & things. A brilliant summer house hotel – it
seems a pity to waste it on golfers! 23RMS APR-OCT T/T PETS CC XKIDS LOTS
**EAT** Fine and subtle dining in elegant rm adj the course; chef David Williams
is a confident player. Wine list has depth and character. EXP

**872** ✓ ✓ **Champany Inn** nr Linlithgow 01506 834532. Excl restau with rms
Map 10 nr M9 jnct 3 (Edinburgh-Stirling), 30rms Edin city centre, 15 mins
**P25** airport. Convenient high standard hotel adj nationally famous restau
(111/EDIN RESTAUS) esp if you love your meat well-hung & properly presented.
Separate b/fast rm. Superlative wine-list, esp S African vintages.
16RMS JAN-DEC T/T XPETS CC XKIDS LOTS
**EAT** As much mentioned, the best meal in West Lothian. INX/EXP

**873** **Kilspindie House** Aberlady 01875 870682. Old-style village inn taken over
Map 10 by Edin restauranteur of repute, Malcolm Duck. Rms perfectly adequate, but
**Q25** hotel excels not surprisingly in the food dept. Bar & proper dining. Excl wine
list. 26RMS JAN-DEC T/T PETS CC KIDS MED.EX
**EAT** The new place to eat on the coast. Revising menu at TGP.

**874** **Open Arms** Dirleton 01620 850241. Dirleton is 4km from Gullane towards
Map 10 N Berwick. Comfortable, pricey and rather country-set hotel in centre of vil-
**R25** lage, opp ruins of castle. Location means it's a golfers' haven and special
packages are available. Deveaus Restau has one wee AA rosette (LO 9pm).
Nice public rms. 10RMS JAN-DEC T/T PETS CC KIDS LOTS

**875** **The Rocks** Dunbar 01368 862287. At the E (ie Edin) & John Muir Park end
Map 10 of Dunbar with gr views across to the rocky harbour area, a made-over hotel
**R25** with big local rep for food. Rms vary – you would want 'the view'. Big beds,
all the mod cons. Big food operation downstairs.
12RMS JAN-DEC T/T PETS CC KIDS INX
**EAT** They do come from far & wide (phone for directions). Seafood & the rest.

**876** **Nether Abbey** North Berwick 01620 892802. 20 Dirleton Ave on way in on
Map 10 'Coastal Trail' from Gullane. Long-est family 'seaside' hotel with recent
**R25** makeover incl major bar/restau operation – the Fly-Half Bar & Grill. So, busy
downstairs! 13RMS JAN-DEC T/T XPETS CC KIDS MED.EX

**877**
Map 10
**R26**
**Tweedale Arms** Gifford 01620 810240. One of two inns in this heart of E Lothian village 9km from the A1 at Haddington, within easy reach of Edin. Set among rich farming country, Gifford is conservative and couthy. Some bedrms small, but public rms pleasant & comfy in a country way. Has been here forever, like some of the guests.
16RMS JAN-DEC T/T PETS CC KIDS MED.INX

**878**
Map 10
**R25**
**Marine Hotel** North Berwick 01620 892406. The old seaside hotel of N Berwick undergoing long & extensive re-fit at TGP. Will re-emerge as Spa Conference Centre courtesy of Macdonald Hotels. Report next edition (probably!).

## RESTAURANTS

**879**
Map 10
**R25**
✓ ✓ **La Potinière** Gullane 01620 843214. Main St of E Lothian golfing mecca, a once-legendary restau with new owners completely restoring its rep. A top meal on this coast & the city from where we come! Report: 119/EDIN RESTAUS.

**880**
Map 10
**N25**
✓ **Livingston's** Linlithgow 01506 846565. Thro arch at E end of High St opp PO. Cottage conversion with conservatory and gdn – a quiet bistro with imaginative modern Franco-Scottish cuisine. 2 AA rosettes. Polite and formal; easily the best in town but see below. Good vegn. Tues-Sat, lunch and dinner. Cl Jan.
INX

**881**
Map 10
**N25**
**Marynka** Linlithgow 01506 840123. Couple of doors down from 4 Marys pub (1340/REAL ALE PUBS), not far from Livingston's (see above), so not bad choice in old Linlithgow. This is a stylish, bright, modern town restaurant with bistro-cool lunches and serious dinners. Small New World wine list & Iain Mellis cheese. Tues-Sat 12-2pm, 6-9.30pm.
INX-MED

**882**
Map 10
**R25**
**The Waterside** Haddington 01620 825674. 1-5 Waterside. On the river, opp side of the pedestrianised old br from St Mary's (1898/CHURCHES). Upstairs restau is more of a pink-napkin affair, bistro/bar down has various rms. Separate vegn menu. This was the pioneer bistro in these parts, now owned by major brewery. Daily lunch/supper, LO 10pm (Sun 9pm).
INX

**883**
Map 10
**R25**
**Drover's Inn** East Linton 01620 860298. Bridge St, middle of neat vill just off A1. Pub with good atmos; bistro downstairs and more elaborate dining up. Beer gdn out back. Lunch and dinner all areas, LO 8.45pm Pub till 11pm, 1am w/ends. Under new ownership at TGP.
INX/MED

**884**
Map 10
**P26**
**The Old Bakehouse** West Linton 01968 660830. Jens and Anita Steffen – no strangers to this book – opened this place early in 2000. Just a place that feels really cared for. Everything made on the premises, and a nice line in smorrebrod too. Lunch (w/ends) and dinner, Wed-Sun. LO 9pm.
MED

**885**
Map 10
**R25**
**Bonar's** Haddington 01620 822100. Douglas Bonar's smart E Lothian dining rm & adj brasserie Poldrates in the old mill on the road out to Gifford. Accomplished and polite. Well-priced & thought-out wine list.Wed-Sun, lunch and dinner.
MED/EXP

**886**
Map 10
**R25**
**Creel** Dunbar 01368 863279. In Lamer St by harbour. New prop since early '03: Gavin Howat, formerly at Greywalls (871/BEST LOTHIAN HOTELS). Still small & intimate. Well-sourced & local suppliers. Specials!. Tues-Sun lunch & dinner.
INX-MED

**887**
Map 10
**R25**
**The Old Clubhouse** Gullane 01620 842008. E Links Rd behind main st, on corner of Green. Large woody clubhouse; a bar/bistro serving food all day till 9.45pm. Gr busy atmos. Gr busy menu. Surprising wine selection.
INX

**888**
Map 10
**Q25**
**Dragon Way** Port Seton 01875 813551. 27C Links Rd. E Lothian country cousin of the DW in town (255/BEST CHINESE). Near the local caravan park and often packed. This is the E Lothian t/away (& they deliver). 7 days 5-11pm.
CHP

# The Best Hotels & Restaurants In Fife

See also 2331/BEST OF DUNFERMLINE & KIRKCALDY; 2340/BEST OF ST ANDREWS.

**889**
Map 10
R23
✓✓ **Old Course** St Andrews 01334 474371. This world-famous hotel is the one you come to first on the A91 from N or W. Unlike many de luxe UK hotels, this has a lightness & accessibility – surrounded by greens & full of golfers coming & going. Most rms o/look the famous course & sea (immaculate & tastefully done with no fac or expense spared), as do the Sands Brasserie and less informal Road Hole Grill up top. Bar here also for lingering views. Truly gr for golf, but anyone could unwind here, towelled in luxury. Spa well appointed. Small beautiful pool. 144RMS JAN-DEC T/T PETS CC KIDS LOTS
**EAT** Rd Hole Grill for spectacular dinner esp in late light summer. Sands on ground floor for lighter and later food. Both excl. EXP/MED

**890**
Map 10
Q24
✓ **Balbirnie House** Markinch 01592 610066. Signed from the rd system around Glenrothes (3km) in surprisingly sylvan setting of Balbirnie Country Park. One of the most sociable & comfortable co-house hotels in the land, with high standards in service and décor that's easy to be at home with. Library Bar leads on to tranquil gdn. Orangery restau has 2 AA rosettes with chef Ian Macdonald & good wine list. Their 'pamper breaks' – incl tea on arrival – are a gr deal à deux. No leisure facs, but good golf in the park. Wake to the thwack of balls! 30RMS JAN-DEC T/T PETS CC KIDS LOTS
**EAT** An elegant hotel for lunch and dinner. 2 AA rosettes. EXP

**891**
Map 10
R23
✓ **Rufflets** St Andrews 01334 472594. 4km from centre via Argyle St opp W Pt along Strathkinness Low Rd past univ playing fields. Serene feel to this co-house hotel on edge of town. The celebrated gdns are a joy. Garden restau fine dining with 2 AA rosettes and more informal bar/brasserie. Cosy rms incl garden suites. 24RMS JAN-DEC T/T PETS CC KIDS EXP

**892**
Map 10
R23
✓ **St Andrews Bay** nr St Andrews 01334 837000. 8km E on A917 to Crail o/looking eponymous bay. Modern edifice in rolling greens. Soulless perhaps but every fac a golfing family could need. Brasserie-type restau in immense atrium. Fine dining in 'Esperante' up top – Mediterranean menu with chef Scott Dougal (cl Mon/Tues). 209RMS JAN-DEC T/T PETS CC KIDS EXP

**893**
Map 10
R23
✓ **Old Station** nr St Andrews 01334 880505. On B9131 (Anstruther rd) off A917 from St Andrews. Individualist makeover of old station with contemp look by previous owners. Design foibles remain in almost boutique rms. New owners Colin & Fiona Wiseman (of milk dynasty) welcome you to their home. Conservatory dining rm, comfy lounge with log fire. 2 'suites' in a railway carriage in the garden! B&B only. 8RMS JAN-DEC X/T PETS CC XKIDS MED.INX

**894**
Map 10
Q24
**Kilconquhar Castle Estate** nr Elie 01333 340501. On B942 nr Colinburgh, 3km from Elie (that famously nice town). Mainly time-share villas (newer ones seem esp naff), but 'club rms' & suites avail in castle itself with access to all facs incl pool, tennis, golf & esp riding. 2-night min. Bistro & posher dining rm in baronial setting. 15RMS JAN-DEC T/T PETS CC KIDS MED.INX

**895**
Map 10
R24
**Cambo Estate** nr Crail 01333 450313. 2km E of Crail on A917. Huge country pile in glorious gdns on the coastal rd betw St Andrews and Crail. Only few flats (and 2 cotts), but this is self/c in the grand if quirky manner. Rms vary greatly. Grds are always superb; gr walks & Kingsbarns golf & beach adj (2062/GOLF). Rattle around, pretend you're house guests and be grateful you don't have to pay the bills. 4&2COTTS JAN-DEC X/X PETS CC KIDS MED.INX

**896**
Map 10
R24
**The Ship Inn** Elie 01333 330246. 6 basic rms in Rock View adj pub notable for food and good life (1360/GASTROPUBS) close to beach in an excellent neuk of Fife. Summer only. 5RMS JAN-DEC X/X PETS CC KIDS MED.INX

**897**
Map 10
P25
**Woodside Hotel** Aberdour 01383 860328. Refurb inn in main st of pleasant village with prize-winning rail stn, castle and church (1890/CHURCHES), coastal walk and nearby beach. This is where to come from Edin (by train, of course) with your bit on the side. 20RMS JAN-DEC T/T PETS CC KIDS MED.INX

**898**
Map 10
R23
**Inn On North Street** St Andrews 01334 474664. 127 North St. Corner of Murray park where there are numerous GH options. This a hipper, younger alternative to the stalwart, elegant but exp offerings above. Lizard bar in base-

ment, the Oakrooms on street level is quite civilised café-bar. Comfy, contemporary rms best for students & their mates, rather than their parents (perhaps!).

13RMS JAN-DEC T/T PETS CC KIDS MED.EX

**2 Good Guest Houses, St Andrews: 18 Queens Terrace** 01334 478849. Highly individual, boho, homely & **5 Pilmour Place** 01334 478665. Contemp & stylish nr Old Course. Reports: 2320/ST ANDREWS.

**Sandford Hill** 01382 541802. 7km S of Tay Br. Underrated co-house hotel in N Fife nr Dundee. Report: 1139/COUNTRY-HOUSE HOTELS.

## RESTAURANTS

**899**
Map 10
**R24**

✓ ✓ **The Cellar** Anstruther 01333 310378. This classic bistro serves some of the best fish you'll eat in Scotland or anywhere. Off courtyard behind Fisheries Museum in this busy E Neuk town (1600/COASTAL VILLAGES) – you'd never think this was a restau from the entrance but inside is a welcoming oasis of epicurean delight. Peter Jukes sources only the best produce & he does mean *the best*. Even the crabs want to crawl in here. One meat dish, excl complementary wine-list. Pure, simple food & gr atmos. Wed-Sun lunch, 6.30-9.30 7 days. Times may change. (1388/SEAFOOD RESTAUS)    MED

**900**
Map 10
**Q23**

✓ **Ostler's Close** Cupar 01334 655574. Down a close (Temperance Close) of the main st, Amanda and Jimmy Graham run a bistro/restau that has Cupar on the gastronomic map (for over 20 yrs). Intimate, cottagy rms. Amanda out front also does puds, Jimmy a star in the kitchen. Often organic, big on mushrooms and other wild things. Sat lunch & Tues-Sun 7-9.30pm. Must book.    MED

**901**

✓ **The Seafood Restaurants** St Andrews 01334 479475 & St Monans 01333 730327. Both excl, unpretentious restaus by the Butler family in perfect, if v diff, settings. Reports: 1391/1392/SEAFOOD RESTAUS.    INX

**902**
Map 10
**R24**

✓ **Sangster's** Elie 01333 331001. Main St of a favourite town. Bruce Sangster has impressive form & all in evidence here. Welcome, stripped-down menu with impeccable ingredients. Simple, divine food & excl value at this level. Lunch Wed-Fri & Sun. Dinner Tues-Sat.    MED

**903**
Map 10
**Q24**

**The Greenhouse** Falkland 01337 858400. St on corner of main st of delightful mid-Fife vill (1792/CASTLES). Light and friendly cafe-bistro serving supper (Tues-Sun) & big Sun brunch (in many formats) to walk off (1979/HILL WALKS, 2012/GLEN WALKS). All home-made, some organic (incl wine-list). LO 9pm.    INX

**904**
Map 10
**Q24**

**Old Rectory** Dysart 01592 651211. 2km E of Kirkcaldy (5km centre); still worth the drive from town or anywhere W Fife. Loyal regulars wouldn't go anywhere else but this 18thC inn with 3 separate dining areas. Tues-Sun lunch and dinner (not Sun eve).    MED

**905**

**Fish 'n' Chips In Fife** Valente's Kirkcaldy, **The Anstruther Fish Bar, The Pittenweem Fish & Chip Bar** 3 gr fish 'n' chip shops with queues every day. Famously good, that's why! (1412/1420/FISH AND CHIPS).    CHP

**906**
Map 10
**R24**

**Wok & Spice** St Monans 01333 730888. On main A917 rd turning past St Monans. Not a caff but a takeaway. Sizzling woks, proper rice, a taste of real Malaysian food (please don't have the chips). This would work in Edin or Glas. When in Fife, order here (they deliver betw Largo & Crail). 7 days 4.30 til whenever.    CHP

**907**
Map 10
**Q24**

✓ ✓ **The Peat Inn** nr Cupar & St Andrews 01334 840206. Legendary restau (with rms) at eponymous crossroads of Fife. For sale at TGP so gr chef David Wilson moving on to pastures new where he doesn't have to farm & cook. Report next time.

**The Grange Inn** St Andrews 01334 472670. Report: 1352/GASTROPUBS.

**The Ship Inn** Elie 01333 330246. Report: 1360/GASTROPUBS.

# The Best Hotels & Restaurants In Perthshire & Tayside

*See also* DUNDEE HOTELS & RESTAURANTS, *p. 147–148*; 2335/CENTRES: PERTH *and* 2338/HOLIDAY CENTRES: PITLOCHRY.

**908**
Map 10
P22
✓ ✓ **Kinloch House** nr Blairgowrie 01250 884237. 5km W on A923 to Dunkeld. The Allen family, formerly at Airds Hotel, Port Appin, have been much praised in this book. They've now established Kinloch as the premier hotel in this country quarter with comfy rms, informal but sure service, excl food (Graeme Allen often in the kitchen) & a top wine list (esp French). Fine S-facing views. Surprising pool. Enjoy!
18RMS JAN-DEC T/T PETS CC KIDS LOTS

**909**
Map 10
M22
✓ ✓ **Ardeonaig** South Shore, Loch Tay 01567 820400. This lochside inn ain't easy to get to (midway Killin & Kenmore on bumpy rd) but that's what it's about (1214/GET AWAY HOTELS). A real stylish haven when you get there. Gr views of loch & ben (Lawyers), no TV but books & excl food & service. A rising star in the north. 20RMS JAN-DEC T/X XPETS CC XKIDS MED.EX-LOTS
**EAT** Pete Grottgens: hot chef, hot kitchen. Gr service out front. EXP

**910**
Map 10
M23
✓ **Royal Hotel** Comrie 01764 679200. Central sq of cosy town, a sympathetic and stylish if trad small-town hotel. Excellent restau with good light and superb pub out back with real ale and atmos (1339/REAL ALES). Nice rugs and pictures. A pleasing bit of style in the county bit of the country. Delightful restau & bar meals. Gr value. 11RMS JAN-DEC T/T XPETS CC KIDS MED.EX

**911**
Map 10
Q22
✓ **Castleton House** Eassie nr Glamis 01307 840340. 13km W Forfar, 25km N of Dundee. App from Glamis, 5km SW on A94. Family-run co-house hotel with excl restau. Castleton House piling up the accolades now has 3 AA rosettes for food. Best Angus option. 6RMS JAN-DEC T/T PETS CC KIDS EXP
**EAT** Pleasing conservatory restau; chef Andrew Wilkie on top form. MED

**912**
Map 10
R22
✓ **Ethie Castle** nr Arbroath 01382 808808. 12km N on the small country rd to Lunan Bay (1615/BEACHES). Proximity to beach not the only spectacular aspect here. This is real (sandstone) lived-in castle with fabulous appointments, some good taste & a ghost (Cardinal Beaton!). Kirstin de Morgan is a friendly & fastidious host (also cooks) but informality prevails – you have the run of the place. Dinner on request. Lots of public space. No telly. 3RMS JAN-DEC X/X XPETS CC XKIDS MED.EX

**913**
Map 10
P22
✓ **(Hilton) Dunkeld House** Dunkeld 01350 727771. Former home of Duke of Atholl, a v large impressive country house on the banks of the R Tay in beautiful grounds (some time-share) just outside Dunkeld. Leisure complex with good pool etc and many other activities laid on. V decent menu. Fine for kids. Pleasant walks. Not cheap but often good deals available. Hilton have it on the market at TGP but it prob won't change much.
96RMS JAN-DEC T/T PETS CC KIDS LOTS

**914**
Map 10
P22
✓ **Ballathie House** nr Perth 01250 883268. 20km N of Perth and also reported in the town section (2352/PERTH), but a true co house hotel on the Tay that you fall in love with, esp if you hunt/shoot/fish/lounge around. Good dining, gr fishing; good for the w/end away. Riverside rms are removed & uniform but you taste the Tay. 42RMS JAN-DEC T/T PETS CC KIDS LOTS
**EAT** Award-winning chef Kevin MacGillivray. Gr local produce esp beef/lamb.
EXP

**915**
Map 10
N22
**Farleyer Restaurant & Rooms** nr Aberfeldy 01887 820332. Same road from town as Castle Menzies (1802/CASTLES). Jake & Kim Schamrel have transformed this bit next to the big house (which curiously you never see) into a smart 2-rm restau with bar & 6 smart rms above. Lunch & LO 9pm. Unusually cool for round here & nr fabulous Glen Lyon (1628/GLENS).
6RMS JAN-DEC T/T XPETS CC KIDS MED.EX

**916**
Map 10
P23
**Huntingtower Hotel** nr Perth 01738 583771. 3km from town, 1km ring rd (direction Crieff). Serviceable, good looking hotel (part of small chain) in gdns close to Perth and the rds N & W. Report: (2335/PERTH).
34RMS JAN-DEC T/T XPETS CC KIDS EXP

**917 Pine Trees Hotel** Pitlochry 01796 472121. A safe haven in visitor-ville – it's
above the town and above all that (there are many mansions here). Take
Larchwood Rd off W end of main st. Woody gdns, woody interior. Scots owners. With some taste (nice rugs). 20RMS JAN-DEC T/T XPETS CC KIDS MED.EX

Map 10
N21

**918 East Haugh House** nr Pitlochry 01796 473121. On S approach to Pitlochry
from A9, a mansion house built 18thC; part of the Atholl estate. Family run &
notable for hunting/shooting & esp fishing hols & for v decent food in dining rm or bar. Nice rms esp up top, romantic with it (8 rms have 4-posters).
13RMS JAN-DEC T/T PETS CC KIDS MED.EX

Map 10
N21

**919 Killiecrankie Hotel** Killiecrankie 01796 473220. 5km N of Pitlochry.
Village inn ambience; cosy rms of individual character. Carefully run but food
not what it used to be. Nevertheless pop for bar meals in the conservatory &
also the dining rm. Gr wine list. 10RMS MAR-DEC T/T PETS CC KIDS EXP

Map 10
N21

**920 Kenmore Hotel** Kenmore 01887 830205. Ancient coaching inn (16thC) in
quaint conservation village. Excellent prospect for golfing (at Taymouth
Castle adj, 2081/GOLF IN GREAT PLACES) and fishing. On river (Tay) itself with terrace and restau o/looking. Layout bitty, food so-so but real fires (& Robert
Burns wuz here). 40RMS JAN-DEC T/T PETS CC KIDS MED.INX

Map 10
M22

**921 Glen Clova Hotel** 01575 550350. Nr end of Glen Clova, one of the gr Angus
Glens (1632/GLENS), on B955 25km N of Kirriemuir. A walk/climb/country
retreat hotel; v comfy. Superb walking nearby. Often full. Also CHP bunkhouse
accom behind. This place a v civilised Scottish inn in the hills & gr value. The
lovely Claire is everywhere. 10RMS JAN-DEC T/T XPETS CC KIDS MED.INX

Map 10
Q21

**922 Coll Earn House** Auchterarder 01764 663553. Signposted from main st.
Extravagant Victorian mansion with exceptional stained glass. Comfy rms,
huge beds. Pleasant gdn. 8RMS JAN-DEC T/T XPETS CC KIDS EXP

Map 10
N23

**923 Cairn Lodge** Auchterarder 01764 622634. Ochil Rd (on way in to vill from
M9 S or Gleneagles). Privately owned mansion-house hotel. Recent major
refurb of public rms. Capercaillie Restaurant & bar. Good rep.
10RMS JAN-DEC T/T XPETS CC KIDS EXP-LOTS

Map 10
N23

**924 Dalmunzie House** Spittal O' Glenshee nr Blairgowrie 01250 885224. 3 km
from Perth-Braemar rd close to Glenshee ski slopes & good base for Royal
Deeside without Deeside prices. 9 hole golf-course for fun. Food improving of
late. Hills all around. Fire to come home to. Under new ownership with major
refurb underway at TGP. 16RMS JAN-DEC T/T PETS CC KIDS MED.INX

Map 10
P21

**925 The Bield at Blackruthven** Tibbermore nr Perth 01738 583238. Take
Crieff rd (A85) from Perth & A9/ring rd past Huntingtower then left for
Tibbermore. 2km. More perhaps 'a retreat' than a conventional GH. Certainly
staying here is to be part of a Christian community. But it is beautiful, peace-
ful & all v tasteful. High standard of facs incl pool, tennis court & a chapel.
Meals & self-cat. Serenity! 9RMS JAN-DEC X/X XPETS CC XKIDS INX

Map 10
P23

**926 Craigatin House** Pitlochry 01796 472478.The houSe (& courtyard) built
1820s is now a stylish GH on rd N out of Pitlochry. Aspiring perhaps to be part
of the cool/hip hotels network, this is contemp first for the area & tho' modest in facs (more GH than hotel) it's good value & a refreshing find.
13RMS JAN-DEC T/T XPETS CC XKIDS INX

Map 10
N21

**927 Dunalastair Hotel** Kinloch Rannoch 01882 632323. Dominates one side
of cute Vict village sq on this rd (B8019) that stabs into the wild heart of
Scotland. 30km Pitlochry on A9 (station for Edin train) and 30km Rannoch
station further up (station for Glas train). Schiehallion overlooks and must be
climbed (1985/MUNROS); many other easy hikes. Big refurb underway by guy
who owns Hotel-Review internet hotel company (so take awards with a pinch
of something). Newer rms on tartan edge and pics needs radical rethink, but
on the whole pleasant hotel with good bar for locals and activity prog.
28RMS JAN-DEC T/T PETS CC KIDS MED.INX

✓ ✓ ✓**Gleneagles** 01764 662231 (1127/COUNTRY-HOUSE HOTELS).

✓ ✓**Kinnaird House** 01796 482440 (1130/COUNTRY-HOUSE HOTELS).

✓ ✓**Crieff Hydro Crieff** 01764 655555. Superb for many reasons, esp
kids. Quintessentially Scottish (1141/KIDS).

# RESTAURANTS

**928**
Map 10
**N24**
✓ ✓+ **Andrew Fairlie at Gleneagles** 01764 694267. The 'other' restau apart from main dining rm in this de-luxe resort hotel (1127/CO HOUSE HOTELS) & comfortably the best meal to be had in this & many other counties. Mr Fairlie comes with big rep, a Michelin star & good PR. Understated opulence in interior rm and confident French food of a v superior nature. Andrew, who stares from the wall while generally keeping to the kitchen, has recently lambasted the parlous state of Scottish cooking – come spot the difference. Mon-Sat dinner only. LO 10 pm.                    EXP

**929**
Map 10
**P23**
✓ ✓ **Let's Eat** Perth 01738 643377. Corner of Kinnoull St. Tony Heath and Shona Drysdale's perfect county town eaterie. Cuisine without the trappings, but all the rt trimmings. Extremely good value and many accolades. Tues-Sat lunch & LO 9.30pm.                    MED

**930**
Map 10
**P23**
✓ ✓ **63 Tay Street** Perth 01738 441451. 63 Tay St on the new riverside rd and walk. Award winning chef Jeremy Wares in kitchen, Shona out front running a small tight ship. Contemp light rm and Modern Brit cuisine with hand-picked ingredients. This place is perfect for Perth. Tues-Sat lunch, LO 9 pm. Book w/ends.                    MED

**931**
Map 10
**Q22**
✓ ✓ **Lochside Lodge** Bridgend of Lintrathen 01575 560340. 9km from Alyth towards Glenisla on B954 past Reekie Linn (1649/WATERFALLS), or via Kirriemuir. Deep in watery countryside. Converted stone steading nr loch; gr setting, decent accom (6 rms, 2 new 2005) & notable esp for food. Joint prop/chef Graham Riley is a 'Master Chef of Gr Britain' & it shows. The best meal you'll get for a long country mile. Fine ingredients that look great on the plate. Lunch/dinner LO 9pm. Cl Sun even & Mon.                    MED

**932**
Map 10
**R22**
✓ **Gordon's** Inverkeilor nr Arbroath 01241 830364. Halfway betw Arbroath and Montrose on the main st. A restau with rms (3) which has won loadsa accolades for Gordon, now son Gary in the kitchen. It's been here for more than 20 years! Splendid people doing good Franco-Scot cooking. What it lacks in atmos more than made up for by what's on the plate. Lunch Tues-Fri & Sun; dinner Tues-Sat LO 8.45pm. Advisable to book.    .MED

**933**
Map 10
**R22**
✓ **The But 'N' Ben** Auchmithie nr Arbroath 01241 877223. 2km off A92 N from Arbroath, 8km to town or 4km by cliff-top walk. Village perched on cliff top where ravine leads to small cove and quay. Adj cottages converted into cosy restau. Cl Tues all day and Sun eve but otherwise 11am-9.30pm for lunches, high tea & dinner. Menus vary but all v Scottish and informal with emphasis on fresh fish/seafood. Brilliant value – 30 yrs on Margaret Horn continues to provide a Scottish experience for her ain folk and all others (hub out front, son Angus in the kitchen): an amazing output all day long.    INX

**934**
Map 10
**R22**
**Taste** Arbroath 01241 878104. 59 Ladybridge St, a st off the harbour. Now I don't know but I've been told, this is a gr new place to eat (in a part of the world that needs one). Haven't eaten but the menu looks good & the word is out. Reports, please.                    INX

**935**
Map 10
**P22**
**Cargills** Blairgowrie 01250 876735. Cosy wine bar ambience, busy à la carte menu and blackboard. Serviceable, reliable; def the best bet in Blairgowrie tho' not perhaps what it was! Unprepossessing frontage, but on river side. Adj coffee shop/gallery. Mon-Sat lunch & dinner until 10pm, Sun 12.30-9pm. Cl Tues.                    INX

**936**
Map 10
**N21**
**Old Armoury** Pitlochry 01796 474281. On rd from main st that winds down to Salmon Ladder attraction. Old Black Watch armoury gives spacious, light bistro ambience and nice terrace/tea gdn. All things to all people: morning coffee, lunches, outdoor tables, afternoon tea & 2 even menu (LO 8.30pm). Mar-Oct; wint hrs vary.                    INX/MED

**937**
Map 10
**N21**
**The Loft** Blair Atholl 01796 481377. Off the A9, in vill turn left at Bridge of Tilt Hotel. Odd location (corner of a caravan park) & totally unprepossessing entrance for this solidly reputable restau which has 2 AA rosettes. Hearty food with a good combo of new and traditional touches in lofty setting. Bistro & finer dining menus. New chef at TGP. Lunch and LO 9pm. Cl Mon.    INX

**938** **The Bank** Crieff 01764 656575. 32 High St. Go to the landmark opp TIC and
Map 10 town clock. A real meal out in cosy Crieff (you may want a meal out from the
**N23** Hydro) in former bank. Chef/prop Bill McGuigan's modern Scottish cooking.
Good atmos, gr food. Lunch & dinner Tues-Sat. MED

**939** **The Red Onion** Crieff 01764 654407. W end of main st. Contemp new
Map 10 restau for Crieff. Chef/prop Martin Lutri (Studleigh Park & others) creates nice
**N23** ambience (esp lunch times) & Mod Brit/Scottish menu. Tues-Sat, lunch & LO
9pm. INX

**940** **Port-na-Craig** Pitlochry 01796 472777. Just by the Pitlochry Theatre, new
Map 10 owners in '02 and now a bright, modern bistro in a 17thC inn. Informal and
**N21** friendly with a mod-Euro menu.

**941** **Deil's Cauldron** Comrie 01764 670352. 27 Dundas St on bend of A85 main
Map 10 rd thro' town and rd to Glen Lednock. Cottage restau with simple, effective
**M23** menu incl staples like haggis and neeps or tiger prawns & eclectic tapas early
evens. Lunch Tues-Sun, dinner Tues-Sat. INX

**Keracher's** Perth 01738 449777 (2325/PERTH) MED

# The Best Hotels & Restaurants In The North-East

*Excludes city of Aberdeen (except Marcliffe). Speyside listings on p. 134. For the rest, see pp. 143–46 and 2341/ROYAL DEESIDE.*

**942** ✓✓ **Marcliffe Of Pitfodels** 01224 861000. N Deeside Rd (en route to
Map 8 Royal Deeside 5km from Union St). On the edge of town, a suc-
**S20** cessful mix of the intimate and the spacious, the old (mansion house) and
the new (1993 refurb). Personally run by the Spence family, the sort of hoteliers whom no detail or guest's face escapes. 2 excellent restaus, breakfast in
refurb light conservatory. Nice courtyard & terrace o/looking gardens. New
spa '05 but no pool. New honeymoon suites are fab (I had one tho' not a honeymoon) & there are more than a few weddings but this understated hotel
caters for all sorts not least the gr & good of Aberdeen.
42RMS JAN-DEC T/T PETS CC KIDS LOTS

**943** ✓✓ **Darroch Learg** Ballater 01339 755443. On main A93 at edge of
Map 8 town. The Franks maintain high standards at this Deeside mansion
**Q20** esp for food. With a relaxed ambience and an excellent dining-rm, it is the
best in this hotel-studded town & on Deesdie. Three AA rosettes.
Comfortable, informal with attentive and considerate staff. Some gr views of
grounds & Grampian hills. No bar, but civilised drinks before and *après*. Good
base for touring. They also run the Station Restau in Ballater itself which,
oddly, is a bit of a disappointment. 17RMS FEB-DEC T/T PETS CC KIDS LOTS
**EAT** Conservatory dining-rm and one of best restaus in NE; chef David
Mutter was Hotel Chef of the Yr '05. Nice gdn view, fab food. EXP

**944** ✓✓ **Raemoir House** Banchory 01330 824884. 5km N from town via
Map 8 A980 off main st. Mansion in the country just off the Deeside con-
**R20** veyor belt; quirky, romantic – it has something which sets it apart. Old-fashioned v individual comfy rms given contemporary details. Flowers everywhere, candles at night. 9-hole golf and tennis. Stable annex and self-cat
apts. Extensive grounds (helicopter pad). Chef is Grant Walker; dinner a treat
& lots of public space to slouch about in. Event prog incl theatre on the lawn
& recitals by top artists. And there's a spa in the attic. Girls from Banchory,
light from God. Bliss! 20RMS & SELF-CAT JAN-DEC T/T PETS CC KIDS LOTS

**945** ✓ **Pittodrie House** Pitcaple 01467 681444. Large 'family' mansion
Map 8 house on estate in one of the best bits of Aberdeenshire with Bennachie
**R19** above. 40km Aber but 'only 30mins from airport' via A96. Follow signs off
B9002. Lots of activities available on the estate, croquet lawn, billiards, many
comfortable rms. Exquisite walled gdn 500m from house. Now a Macdonald
hotel (& poss their best), a major extesnion is planned – presumably the car-
destroying driveway will be repaired then too. Hopefully the ambience, the
pictures & the gr whisky bar will not be lost.
27RMS JAN-DEC T/T PETS CC KIDS LOTS

**946** ✓ **Udny Arms** Newburgh 01358 789444. A975 off A92. Village pub with
Map 8 gr food and character run by the Craig family for a long time now. Rms
**T19** tasteful and individually furnished. Folk come from far & wide to eat here.
Golf course Cruden Bay (2058/GREAT GOLF) 16km N and walks beside Ythan
estuary (1779/WILDLIFE).     27RMS JAN-DEC T/T XPETS CC KIDS MED.INX
**EAT** Excellent grub in bar or dining-rm. Good ambience. Formidable chef
team incl French guys with Michelin credentials. Lunch; LO 9.30pm. This was
where Sticky Toffee Pudding was launched on an unsuspecting & highly sus-
ceptible Scottish public – the rest is culinary history.     MED

**947** ✓ **Hilton Craigendarroch** Ballater 013397 55858. On the Braemar rd
Map 8 (A93). Part of a country-club/time-share operation with elegant dining,
**Q20** good leisure facs and discreet resort-in-the-woods feel. 2 restaus: an infor-
mal one by the pool (like a leisure-centre caff) and the self-conscious Oaks.
J/t if you please. Lodges can be available on short lets, a good idea for a group
holiday or w/end.     45RMS JAN-DEC T/T XPETS CC KIDS LOTS

**948** **Meldrum House** Oldmeldrum 01651 872294. 1km from village, 30km N of
Map 8 Aber via A947 Banff rd. Immediately impressive and solid establishment –
**S18** Scottish baronial style. Set amid new 18-hole golf course (private membership, but guests can use) landscaped & managed to high standard (gr practice range). Rms large with atmos & nice furnishing – many orig antiques &
chosen pictures. New lodge had added bedspace and new mngm will hopefully attend to the detail (better extractor fans in the kitchen, flowers & lighting etc). This hotel could be truly great. Many weddings.
    14RMS (5 IN LODGE) JAN-DEC T/T PETS CC KIDS LOTS

**949** **The Red Garth** Oldmeldrum 01651 872353. Oddly enough there is a hotel
Map 8 in Oldmeldrum that really has its act together (4 Star Tourist Board, Meldrum
**S18** House only 3), a third of the price of the above. This inn (signed from main rd
system) only has 3 rms but it's gr value; bar meals on the premises. Nice
flowers.     3RMS JAN-DEC T/T PETS CC KIDS INX

**950** **Lys-na-Greyne House** Aboyne 01339 887397. Off main A93 rd out of
Map 8 Abone towards Ballater, 400m on left down Rhu-na-Haven rd. Edwardian
**R20** mansion on the Dee, the private home of the Whites. This B&B with only 3
rms is too good not to mention. Sauna, snooker table, fabulous gardens,
plush rms. Dinner by apt but good options nearby (see below).
    3RMS JAN-DEC X/X XPETS CC XKIDS MED.INX

**951** **Seafield Hotel** Cullen 01542 840791. On the main Brae; an activity-orient-
Map 8 ed hotel with lots to do on nearby Seafield estate (hunt, shoot, fish). Single
**R17** rms can be a bit pokey but there's a comfortable lounge with a fair range of
malts. Restau not rec. Mr and Mrs Cox run an enduring and friendly family
hotel.     21RMS JAN-DEC T/T PETS KIDS CC MED.INX

**952** **Castle Hotel** Huntly 01466 792696. Behind Huntly Castle ruin; app from
Map 8 town through castle entrance and then over R Deveron up impressive drive.
**R18** Former dowager house of the Dukes of Gordon, family-run by the
Meiklejohns. Not bad value for the grandeur/setting – tourists and business
travellers keep it busy.     18RMS JAN-DEC T/T XPETS CC KIDS MED.EX

**953** **Waterside Inn** Peterhead 01779 471121. Edge of town on A952 to
Map 8 Fraserburgh on tidal R Ugie. Standard, well-run modern hotel, recommend-
**T18** ed for its service and convenience and because it's the best option around.
Karen Home was Grampian Chef of the Yr '05. Good for kids (1161/KIDS).
    109RMS JAN-DEC T/T PETS CC KIDS MED.EX

**954** **Grant Arms** Monymusk 01467 651226. The village inn on a remarkable
Map 8 small square, a good centre for walking, close to the 'Castle Trail' (1805/CAS-
**R19** TLES; 1862/COUNTRY HOUSES) and with fishing rts on the Don. Rms in hotel &
round courtyard have recently been refurb (now all ES) but the food, esp in
the bar, is why folk find the GA.     17RMS JAN-DEC T/T PETS CC KIDS INX
**EAT** Best pub food for miles, and dining. Daily lunch, 6.30-9pm.     INX

# RESTAURANTS

**955** ✓ **Lairhillock** nr Stonehaven  01569 730001. 15km S of Aber off A92. Excellent country pub and restau, good for kids. Full report 1054/ABER RESTAUS; 1353/GASTROPUBS.

**956** ✓ **Tolbooth** Stonehaven  01569 762287. Excl location on Stonehaven Harbour gives great lobster. Report: 1399/SEAFOOD RESTAUS.

**957**
Map 8
S20
✓ **The (Art Deco) Carron Restaurant** Stonehaven  01569 760460. 20 Carron St off main st nr the sq. They use 'art deco' in the title, but you couldn't miss the reference in this fantastic period piece faithfully restored & embellished. Run by Robert Cleaver who has the Tolbooth (1399/SEAFOOD RESTAUS), this is becoming one of the top dining-out experiences in the NE. Cl Sun/Mon.                                                                                        MED

**958**
Map 8
S20
✓ **Milton Restaurant**  01330 844566. On main A93 Royal Deeside rd 4km E of Banchory opp the entrance to Crathes (1545/GARDENS; 1863/COUNTRY HOUSES). Roadside and surprisingly contemporary restau in old steading adj craft vill of varying quality. Light and exceedingly pleasant space. Menu from brunch-lunch-aft tea (till 5pm)-supper, then dinner so they cater for everything (& rather well). Tues-Sat LO 9pm, Sun & Mon lunch/tea till 7pm. A contemp corner of Deeside.                                                      INX

**959**
Map 8
T18
✓ **Eat On The Green** Udny Green nr Ellon  01651 842337. Former pub now restau on green of cute vill in deepest Aberdeenshire. Craig Wilson (formerly cheffing at Cromlix & Ballathie) & his missus made a lifestyle choice, returning from S to open their own place in this obscure corner Rm & menu all simply done & it's always busy. Guess they made the right choice: the days of working for others behind & the Green in front. Wed-Sun lunch, LO 9pm.                                                                                        INX

**960**
Map 8
Q20
**The Green Inn** Ballater  01339 755701. Victoria Rd. Small frontage, surpris- ingly opens out at back. Long-est restau in this town has good rep again under the O'Halloran family with son Chris in the kitchen. 2 INX rms upstairs. Dinner only Mon-Sat 7-9pm.

**961**
Map 8
R20
**White Cottage** nr Aboyne  01398 885757. On the main A93 outside Abyone from Aberdeen. John Inches's (formerly of the long-estimable Faradays at Cults) roadside white cottage (conservatory attached) serving Mod Brit menu to loyal locals & travellers. Wed-Sat dinner only & Sun lunch. LO 8.30pm. INX

**962**
Map 8
R20
**The Candlestick-Maker** Aboyne  01339 886060. Just off A93 in Deeside, middle of Aboyne by the PO & o/look the green. Haven't tried but George & Judith Anderson's simple, clean rm is building local rep. Everybody says, 'go there,' so reports please. Dinner only Wed-Sat.                                      INX

**963**
Map 8
R17
**The County Hotel** Banff  01261 815353. Francophile dining options in dear sleepy Banff. Bistro & bar downstairs (lunches & bar suppers Mon-Sat); posh evening meals upstairs (daily 7-9pm, booking advisable). Quite a find and there's a beer garden with an apple tree.                                       CHP/EXP

**The Black-Faced Sheep** Aboyne  01339 887311. Report: 1442/TEARMS.

**The Creel Inn** Catterline  01569 750254. Report: 1371/GASTROPUBS.

**The Raemoir Garden Centre**  Report: 2218/GARDEN CENTRES.

**The Falls of Feugh** Banchory  01330 822123. Report: 1443/TEARMS.

# The Best Of Speyside

**964**
Map 8
**Q18**
✓ **Craigellachie Hotel** Craigellachie 01340 881204. The quintessential Speyside hotel, off A941 Elgin to Perth and Aber rd by the br over Spey. Esp good for fishing, but well placed for walking (Speyside Way runs along bottom of gdn, see 1998/LONG WALKS) and distillery visits (1537/WHISKY). Informal; some fab rms. The food is well regarded but the bar could keep a whisky lover amused for years. Simply one of the best places in Scotland for a dram. 25RMS JAN-DEC T/T XPETS CC KIDS MED.EX

**965**
Map 8
**P18**
✓ **Minmore House** Glenlivet 01807 590378. Adj Glenlivet Distillery (1536/WHISKY TOURS) so signed from all over, but on the B9008 off the A95 betw Keith & Grantown. The former home of the distillery founder now a comfortable, not overly dressed-up co house hotel with an excl rep for food. This extends from their sumptuous dram-driven dinners to top b/fast & an aft tea, which is a local event in its own right. This is a v Speyside experience.
11RMS MAR-JAN T/T PETS CC KIDS MED.EX
**EAT** A long way for dinner, non-res make do with tea – a fine ritual.    MED

**966**
Map 8
**P17**
**The Mansion House** Elgin 01343 548811. Sits discreetly under the monument to the last Duke of Gordon & nr the big Tesco store. Comfortable and elegant town house in a comfortable and gentle town with 'leisure facs', incl small pool/gym and drop-in (v small) bistro. Nice dining-rm.
23RMS JAN-DEC T/T XPETS CC KIDS EXP

**967**
Map 8
**P18**
**Delnashaugh Inn** Ballindalloch nr Grantown On Spey 01807 500255. Road-side and Speyside (actually the Avon, pron 'Arn') inn, comfy, unpretentious. On bend of A95 betw Craigellachie and Grantown nr confluence of main rds and rivers. Laura Ashley/Sarah Churchill décor, not minimalist, but simple. Food also. Much ado about fishing, and golf.
9RMS JAN-DEC T/T PETS CC KIDS MED.INX

**968**
Map 8
**P18**
**Archiestown Hotel** Archiestown 01340 810218. Main st of small village in heart of Speyside nr Cardhu Distillery (1539/WHISKY). A village inn with comfortable rms and celebrated food in bistro setting (LO 8.30pm). Fishers and locals. 11RMS JAN-DEC T/T PETS CC KIDS MED.EX
**EAT** Bistro here (& it's not a gastropub – there's no bar) is local destination.
INX

**969**
Map 8
**Q18**
**Tannochbrae** Dufftown 01340 820541. 22 Fife St. Twee by name (older readers will remember *Dr Finlay's Casebook*) & twee by nature (from Scotty-dog doorstops to Jack Vettriano) GH in Speyside centre. Conscientiously run accom & à la carte restau & a good dram selection. This place, tho' tartan-tastic, gets away from it. 6RMS JAN-DEC X/T XPETS CC KIDS INX
For the complete over-indulgent dose you might want to experience **The world-famous, award-winning Glenfiddich Restaurant** nr to town clock. Enough to send a modern Scot gibbering into his irn bru cocktail, others may be in their unreconstructed heaven. The food is ghastly! 7 days (LO 9pm, wint hrs vary). CHP

## RESTAURANTS

**970**
Map 8
**Q18**
**La Faisanderie** Dufftown 01340 821273. The Whisky Trail with a French twist. A small Franco-Scots affair, corner of The Square and Balvenie St, nr the TIC. A welcome departure for these parts – and well known as *the place*. Lunch & dinner daily LO 9pm (except cl all day Tues & Wed lunch). INX

# The Best Hotels & Restaurants In The Highlands

*See also* Inverness, *p. 149-50*; Ft William, *p. 311*; Skye, *p. 297*; Outer Hebrides, *p. 298*.

**971**
Map 9
**K21**

✓ ✓ **Inverlochy Castle** Fort William  01397 702177. 5km from town on A82 Inverness rd, Scotland's flagship Highland hotel filled with sumptuous furnishings, elegant decor and occasional film stars, luminaries and royalty. As you sit in the atrium after dinner marvelling at the ceiling & stylish people swish up & down the staircase, you know this is no ordinary co house hotel. And it has everything you expect of a 'castle' ; the epitome of grandeur and service. Huge colourful, comfortable bedrms, set in acres of rhododendrons with trout in the lake, tennis & a lovely terrace. The big Ben is over there.  17RMS JAN-DEC T/T PETS CC KIDS LOTS
**EAT** Not a drop-in dining rm, but non-res can book. Long-serving chef Matthew Gray makes this a destination in its own right (3 AA rosettes).

**972**
Map 7
**H16**

✓ ✓ **Pool House Hotel** Poolewe  01445 781272. Formerly owned by Osgood MacKenzie who founded the gdns up the road (1544/ GARDENS). The Harrisons have transformed with immaculate style & sheer determination this Highland home into one of the must-do stopovers in the land. Only 6 but fabulously themed suites. Huge bathrooms. Gr dining with chef John Moir; bar has great malt collection. Simultaneously special & personable. The new destination hotel in the N.  7RMS MAR-DEC T/T XPETS CC XKIDS LOTS

**973**
Map 8
**N17**

✓ ✓ **The Boath House** Auldearn nr Nairn  01667 454896. Signed from the main A96 3km E of Nairn. A small country-house hotel in a classic & immaculately restored mansion – Don & Wendy Matheson's family home; well chosen pics for sale. Add chef Charlie Lockley (3AA) & you're in for a memorable stay. Sometimes you think: getting it right in the hotel biz can't be that difficult. Don & Wendy started from scratch. You budding hoteliers – come here, see what they've done in 10 yrs. Spa/gym in basement, massage on hand & delightful grounds with walled garden in restoration (& beautiful Brodie nearby; 1790/CASTLES) with a lake. 7RMS JAN-DEC T/T PETS CC KIDS LOTS
**EAT** Mr Lockley: intuitive, unassuming, gr judgement. 'Local ingredients' a matter of course incl the kitchen garden. Bistro 'Orangerie' also open for lunch, you lucky Nairn- & Elginites.

**974**
Map 9
**J22**

✓ ✓ **Ballachulish House** Ballachulish  01855 811266. On A828 Ft William/Glencoe-Oban rd just S of br. Brilliant dining in historic house with 9-hole golf course o/looking loch. Report: 1252/SCOTTISH HOTELS.
8RMS JAN-DEC T/X XPETS CC KIDS EXP/LOTS

**975**
Map 7
**M18**

✓ ✓ **Glenmoriston Townhouse** Inverness  01463 223777. 20 Nessbank along riverside opp Edin Court Theatre. No expense spared in the conversion of this long-reputed hotel (& the one next door) into a chic boutique & v urban hotel in the energising city of Inverness. Rms split 50/50 betw main hotel & adj annex. All the latter refurb & most of main house at TGP to high standard. 'Piano' bar & top restau 'Abstract'. Def the most *au courant* stay in the N.  30RMS JAN-DEC T/T PETS CC KIDS LOTS
**EAT** Rm could be Edin/NY/London. Gr staff (mainly French), reasonable wine list & Loic Lefebvre's signature on every dish is reaching for the stars.

**976**
Map 7
**M18**

✓ **Culloden House** Inverness  01463 790461. 5km E of town nr A9, follow signs for Culloden village, not the battlefield. Hugely impressive, Georgian mansion and lawn a big green duvet on edge of suburbia and, of course, history. The most conscientiously de luxe hotel hereabouts. Lovely big bedrooms o/looking the policies. Some fab gdn suites, and elegant dining.  28RMS JAN-DEC T/T PETS CC KIDS LOTS

**977**
Map 7
**M20**

✓ **The Cross** Kingussie  01540 661166. Off main st at traffic lights, 200m uphill then left into glen. Tasteful hotel & superb restau in converted tweed mill by river which gurgles o/side most windows. David & Katie Young in full swing with Becca (from the previous regime who did put The Cross on the map) still in the kitchen.  8RMS MAR-OCT T/T XPETS CC KIDS EXP
**EAT** To stay, you're expected to eat; you'd be mad not to. Open non-res for the best restau in the region. 3 choices ea course. Fixed price incl all the tastery bits a steal at £35. Cl Sun/Mon.

**978**
Map 7
**L17**

✓ **Dower House** nr Muir Of Ord  01463 870090. On A862 between Beauly & Dingwall, 18km NW of Inverness & 2km N of village. Charming, personal place; you are a house guest so best to fit in. Cottagey-style nay, stylish small country house, with comfy public rms. Also self-cat lodge house. Robyn (in the kitchen) & Mena Aitchison are consummate hosts & here a long time. Let's hope they stay. 5RMS JAN-DEC T/T PETS CC XKIDS EXP
**EAT** Robyn Aitchison's cooking: simple, sophisticated. Fixed menu.    MED

**979**
Map 7
**M18**

✓ **Dunain Park** Inverness  01463 230512. 6km SW town on A82 Ft William rd. Mansion-house just off the rd, a lived-in, civilised and old-style alternative to hotels in town for those on business or pleasure. Some good deals out of season. Nice gdns, small pool and sauna; real countryside beyond. Notable restau in various cosy dining rms with sound Scottish menu; lots of creamy puds. Excellent wine and malt list. Nice people who care, and enviro-friendly gdn.    11(+2 COTT)RMS JAN-DEC T/T PETS CC KIDS EXP
**EAT** Ann Nicholl's no-nonsense menu and sideboard of delicious puds. MED

**980**
Map 7
**N16**

✓ **Glenmorangie House at Cadboll** nr Fearn  01862 871671. S of Tain 10km E of A9. Old whisky mansion in open grounds o/look sea recently taken over by Louis Vuitton Moët Hennessy so expect some luxury (tho' everything is understated). No leisure facs but no shortage of distraction around. Return to comfy rms, open fires & communal, house-party atmos. Fixed dinner round one table, honesty bar, gr service.
6RMS (+3COTT) JAN-DEC T/T XPETS CC KIDS EXP

**981**
Map 6
**J15**

✓ **The Summer Isles Hotel** Achiltibuie  01854 622282. 40km from Ullapool with views over the isles; Stac Polly and Suilven are close by to climb. For over 20 years Mark & Gerry Irvine's famous for dining romantic retreat enduring & endearing. Adj pub offers similar quality food at half the price (1351/GASTROPUBS). 2 gr suites & a fab crofter's cott nearby.
13RMS APR-OCT T/X PETS CC XKIDS EXP
**EAT** Formal dining: don't be late! Fixed (truly individual) menu, trolleys of puds & cheese: the big moment. Sunsets. Bar gr value.    MED.EX

**982**
Map 7
**J17**

✓ **Loch Torridon Hotel** Loch Torridon nr Kinlochewe  01445 791242. At the end of Glen Torridon in immense scenery. Highland Lodge atmos, big hills to climb. Now with adj **Ben Damph Lodge** (INX with bar & bistro). Report: 1215/GET-AWAY HOTELS.    20RMS JAN-DEC T/T XPETS CC XKIDS LOTS

**983**
Map 6
**N15**

✓ **Royal Marine Hotel** Brora  01408 621252. Golf Rd. O/looks golf course so find that first. Major overhaul of turn-of-cent house by Robert Lorimer incl adj apt block '05. Ambition to be on par with gr golf hotels else-where. Contemp public rms. Bedrms vary. Spa has good pool.
22RMS JAN-DEC T/T PETS CC KIDS EXP

**984**
Map 6
**P12**

✓ **Forss House Hotel** nr Thurso  01847 861201. 8km W on A836. The MacGregor's family home (of Ackergill Tower, 1267/HOUSE PARTIES) set in 20 woodland acres by the sea is the best quality hotel for miles. Popular restau (you should book), nearly 300 malts in the bar, comfortable spacious rms and 3 chalets in the grounds too. Breakfast in the conservatory then birds, walks, old mill and waterfall. Good fishing.
8RMS+5COTTS JAN-DEC T/T PETS CC KIDS MED.EX

**985**
Map 9
**J21**

✓ **Lodge On The Loch** Onich  01855 821237. The best hotel in this strip S of Ft William (16km) back in private ownership at TGP. Notable relaxed ambience, furnishings etc. Beautiful contemp bedrooms, many o/look loch. Open AYR but Nov-Feb weekdays only. Most deals incl (v good) dinner.
15RMS JAN-DEC T/T PETS CC XKIDS EXP

**986**
Map 7
**M18**

**Bunchrew House** nr Inverness  01463 234917. On A862 Beauly rd only 5km from Inverness yet completely removed from town; on the wooded shore of the Beauly Firth. Almost completely positioned as a wedding hotel, but there may be midweek poss. It's an atmos place.
14RMS JAN-DEC T/T PETS CC KIDS EXP

**987**
Map 7
**L17**

**Coul House Contin** nr Strathpeffer  01997 421487. Comfortable country-house hotel on the edge of the wilds with some elegant public rms, partic the octagonal dining rm. Well-kept lawns. Comfortable rms; an accessible not-too-posh country-house retreat. Trad music on Fri in summer. Didn't dine but menu looks interesting.    21RMS JAN-DEC T/T PETS CC KIDS MED.EX

**988** **Golf View** Nairn 01667 452301. Seafront on Inverness side of town. Not so
Map 7 much golf, more beach view but nr the famous course (2059/GOLF). Well
**N17** appointed, refurb rms with conservatory restau & leisure facs incl good pool
for kids. Out of private hands '05: Swallowed up (as it were).
44RMS JAN-DEC T/T PETS CC KIDS MED.EX

**989** **Royal Golf** Dornoch 01862 810283. Sits on golf course nr small town sq.
Map 6 Refurb has brought up to scratch with nice sunny dining rm. Recently
**N16** become part of the gr northern Swallow chain (as above). But gr malts & of
course... gr golf (2060/GOLF). 24RMS JAN-DEC T/T PETS CC KIDS MED.EX

**990** **Polmaily House** Drumnadrochit, Loch Ness 01456 450343. 5km from
Map 7 Drumnadrochit on A831 to Cannich in Glen Urquhart and nr awesome Glen
**L18** Affric (1627/GLENS). Unpretentious country-house retreat in lived-in unman-
icured grounds. Many walks; tennis, riding and covered-in pool. Small, comfy
public rms, individual bedrms. Sensible dinner and wine list. Lots on hand for
kids (1147/KIDS), but ok for those without. The house and the glen are yours.
10RMS(+2SELF-CAT) JAN-DEC T/T PETS CC KIDS EXP

**991** **Onich Hotel** Onich by Fort William 01855 821214. As above 16km S on
Map 9 main A82, one of many roadside and in this case, lochside hotels which are
**J21** more attractive than those in Ft William. Onich is good value with excl public space; some bedrms o/look L Linnhe. Busy bars, grassy terrace & nice garden. 27RMS JAN-DEC T/T PETS CC KIDS MED.EX

**992** **Holly Tree** Kentallen Argyll 01631 740292. On A828 Ft William
Map 9 (Ballachulish)–Oban rd, 8km S of Ballachulish Bridge. On road & sea & once the
**J22** railway; formerly a station. A slightly idiosyncratic hotel with decor of mixed
taste (incl Mockintosh), but fab views from bdrms & dining rm. Superb location, gd surf 'n' turf restau. Nice for kids. 10RMS JAN-DEC T/T PETS CC EXP

✓ ✓ **Ackergill Tower** nr Wick 01955 603556 (1267/HOUSE PARTIES).

✓ ✓ **House Over-By** Skye 01470 571258 (2289/ISLAND HOTELS).

✓ **Eilean Iarmain** Skye 01470 833332 (2294/ISLAND HOTELS).

✓ **Kinloch Lodge** Skye 01470 833333 (2291/ISLAND HOTELS).

✓ **Scarista House** S Harris 01859 550238 (2295/ISLAND HOTELS).

# RESTAURANTS

✓ ✓ **Three Chimneys** Skye 01470 511258. Report: 2304/ISLAND RESTAUS.

**993** ✓ **2 Quail Restaurant** Dornoch 01862 811811. Castle St. Unassuming
Map 6 townhouse on rd into centre conceals best restau NE of Inverness. Tiny
**N16** rms (lounge & library/dining rm). 4 tables so book! 3-choice menu. Ooh:
lovely wines! The Carrs do everything to make you feel comfortable. Rms
above (1001/LESS EXP HOTELS). Dinner only Tues-Sat. MED

**994** ✓ **The Glass House** Grantown On Spey 01479 872980. Grant Rd (paral-
Map 8 lel to Main St). Newish venture at TGP by prop/chef Stephen Robertson
**P18** (ex Cromlix etc) quickly finding a relieved local clientele. Built with conserva-
tory, the light is nice, the noise maybe not. But no argument from regulars
about the food. Aviemore environs has a good restau at last. No-nonsense
Mod Brit menu. Cl Sun even & Mon/Tues lunch. MED

**995** ✓ **The Quiet Piggy** Brora 01408 622011. Station Sq. With 2 Quail (above),
Map 6 it's now poss to eat your way to John o' Groats. Lovely, woody rm in quiet
**N15** old Brora with chef Lindsay Mackay cooking up a quietly Mod Brit menu with
some flair, no fuss. Lunch & LO 8.30pm. Cl Mon. MED

*Best Restaurants In Inverness* see pp. 149–150. Especially:

**Abstract At Glenmoriston Hotel** 01463 223777. Ness Bank.

**Rocpool** 01463 717274 Ness Walk, corner of main bridge.

**Café One** 01463 226200 Castle St.

**The Mustard Seed** 01463 220220 Bank St.

# Good Less Expensive Hotels In The Highlands

**996**
Map 6
**K15**

✓✓ **The Ceilidh Place** Ullapool · 01854 612103. Jean Urquhart's oasis of hospitality, craic & culture in the Highlands. What started out in the 1970s as a coffee/exhibition shop in a boat shed, has spread along this row of cottages now comprising a restau, bookshop, café/bar (& performance) area, and bdrms upstairs. In winter food is served in front of the roaring fire in the Parlour Bar. Bunkhouse across the rd offers cheaper accom: stay 'luxuriously rough'. Live music and events throughout the yr, or you can simply sit in the lounge upstairs with honesty bar or on the terrace overlooking Ullapool. We come back! 11RMS+BUNKS JAN-DEC T/X PETS CC KIDS EXP
**EAT** Restau & coffee shop/bistro 8am-LO9pm. Restau service sometimes slips when busy. We forgive. MED

**997**
Map 6
**J14**

✓✓ **The Albannach** Lochinver · 01571 844407. 2km up rd to Baddidarach as you come into Lochinver on the A837 at the br. Lesley & Colin have created a unique and comfortable haven in their 18thC house. The suite adj used to be a byre & looks over 'the croft' with Stac Polly peeping over. Moves afoot at TGP to make more rms into suites together with expansion of dining rm allowing more non-res to sample excl 5-course dinner using impeccable ingredients & incl Colin's perfect puds. Suilven over there from a rel midge-free terrace. 5RMS MAR-DEC T/X XPETS CC XKIDS EXP
**EAT** When in farflung Assynt, you must eat at the Albannach. MED

**998**
Map 8
**N18**

✓ **Auchendean Lodge** Dulnain Bridge nr Grantown On Spey · 01479 851347. An urbane enclave in an area of stunning scenery nr Aviemore skiing and Whisky Trail. Tastefully and cosily furnished Edwardian lodge with log fires, good malts and cellar, and books. Food with flair and imagination with many ingredients from the kitchen gdn. Esp good with mushrooms. Home-made everything. Intimate dinner can turn into a house party as Ian patiently serves: Eric takes care of the kitchen.
5RMS (& FLAT) MAR-OCT X/T PETS CC KIDS GF MED.EX
**EAT** Most imaginative menu in wide area of S Speyside, incl Aviemore. MED

**999**
Map 5
**M20**

✓ **Coig na Shee** Newtonmore · 01540 670109. Rd out of Newtonmore (which is just off the A9) for Ft William. Mansion house with light, contemp feel & furnishings. Nr where they filmed *Monarch of the Glen* & some of the principals stayed here (one of them wrote to me about this 'stunning' GH). B&B only. Friendly folk. You'll be back.
5RMS (& FLAT) MAR-OCT X/T PETS CC KIDS GF MED.EX

**1000**
Map 8
**N19**

✓ **Boat Hotel** Boat Of Garten · 01479 831258. Centre of vill o/looking the steam train line & golf course (2102/GOLF). Gr old style (Victorian/ 1920s) hotel good refurb & good restau, The Capercaillie, where chef Tony Allcott has 2 AA rosettes. Bar the locals use & hotel bar with good bar meals. This hotel way better than anything in Aviemore. 32RMS JAN-DEC T/T PETS CC KIDS MED.INX

**1001**
Map 6
**N16**

✓ **2 Quail** Dornoch · 01862 811811. Castle St as you arrive from S. Rms above restau (993/HIGHLAND RESTAUS, 1208/RESTAUS WITH RMS), only 3 but every bit as much detail & elegance as the food below. The Carrs run a tight but small, elegant ship. 3RMS JAN-DEC T/T XPETS CC XKIDS MED.INX

**1002**
Map 9
**J20**

✓ **Glenfinnan House Hotel** Glenfinnan · 01397 722235. Victorian mansion with lawns down to L Shiel and the Glenfinnan Monument over the water. No shortbread-tin twee or tartan carpet here; instead a warm welcome from the MacFarlanes & managers the Gibsons (everything just gets better here). Refurbed bar has not lost its gr atmos. A cruise on this stunning loch or your own rowboat a must (01687 470322 for cruise)! (1255/SCOTTISH HOTELS). 13RMS MAR-NOV X/X PETS CC KIDS MED.INX-EXP

**1003**
Map 9
**K20**

✓ **Corriechoille Lodge** by Spean Bridge · 01397 712002. 4 (riverside) kms out of Spean Bridge on the small rd by the station. Justin & Lucy Swabey's hideaway house facing the mountains. Beautiful corner of the country with spectacular views towards the Grey Corries & Aonach Mor. Lovely dinner, cosy rms. 2 turf-roofed self-cat chalets over by. Gt walks begin here. Also 1223/GET AWAY HOTELS. 5RMS MAR-OCT X/T XPETS CC KIDS INX

**1004** ✓ **Mackays** Durness 01971 511202. An unlikely gorgeous restau with rms in the far N. Report: 1221/GET AWAY HOTELS.

**1005** **Glengarry Castle** Invergarry 01809 501254. A family-run hotel in the
Map 7 Highlands for over 40 yrs, now in the charge of young Donald MacCallum.
**K20** Rhodies, honeysuckle as you walk to the loch. Magnificent trees and a ruined castle in the grounds. Romantic in every way. Big rms. Food reports please.
26RMS MAR-NOV T/T PETS CC KIDS MED.EX

**1006** **Kinkell House** nr Dingwall 01349 861270. 15 km n of Inverness, 2km from
Map 7 main A9 taking B9169 E signed Easter Kinkell. Mansion house in farming
**M17** country (the Black Isle) with rms o/look the Firth & Ben Wyvis. Gr local rep for food being built again by newish owner James MacLennan.
9RMS JAN-DEC T/T PETS CC KIDS MED.INX
**EAT** Dining being improved at TGP. Expect destination food 2006. Book w/ends.                                                                            MED

**1007** **The Plockton Inn** Plockton 01599 544222. Neat village inn and seafood
Map 7 restau in neat little seaside vill (1592/COASTAL VILLAGES). Some good cask ale in
**H18** bar. Simple, quiet tasteful rms. Bar & bistro, mainly seafood. Tables on terrace in summer, back gdn for kids. 9RMS JAN-DEC T/T PETS CC KIDS MED.INX

**1008** **The Plockton Hotel** Plockton 01599 544274. The other Plockton hotel (of
Map 7 3) to rec. This by the water's edge. Busier, buzzier; pub & pub meals seem
**H18** always packed. Maybe noisy w/ends (1183/INNS)/ Rms nice.
11RMS JAN-DEC T/T PETS CC KIDS MED.EX

**1009** **Old Pines** nr Spean Bridge 01397 712324. 3km Spean Br via B8004 for
Map 9 Garlochy at Commando Monument. New owners the Dalleys replace the
**K20** award-winning Barbours & are rebuilding the rep. Open-plan pine cabin with log fires, neat bedrooms and a huge new polytunnel (where bits of yr dinner come from).                                    8RMS JAN-DEC T/T XPETS CC KIDS MED.INX

**1010** **Old Mill Highland Lodge** 01445 760271. On A832 15km S of Kinlochewe,
Map 7 the rd that follows L Maree. Across rd from loch in woody, as they say,
**J17** Highland situation. Family house/GH; 3 rms in newer section are more uniform. Deal incl dinner which comes highly rec by readers. Many pinemartins also come to the kitchen. 6RMS MAR-OCT X/X XPETS XCC XKIDS INX

**1011** **Carnegie Lodge** Tain 01862 894039. At 'top' of the town signed from A9
Map 7 (ring rd). It's a Tain thing, but the Wynes sold Morangie House to Swallow &
**N16** moved over here, quickly building the rep they had for food (INX). Motel-type rms on edge of town & easy dining. Good value.
6RMS JAN-DEC T/T PETS CC KIDS INX

**1012** **Tongue Hotel** Tongue 01847 611206. One of 2 hotels in Tongue at the cen-
Map 6 tre of the N coast, where Ben Loyal presides. This the most presentable tho'
**M13** more exp. Nicely turned-out rooms. Same menu bar & dining rm. V Highland. Other hotel, the Ben Loyal: front rms best.
19RMS APR-NOV T/T PETS CC KIDS MED.EX

**1013** **Tigh-an-Eilean** Shieldaig 01520 755251. Lovely freshly furnished hotel on
Map 7 waterfront o/look Scots Pine island on loch. The Fields run a pleasant house
**H17** – the locale has that serene otherness. Chris is a folk-buff so poss music in the adj pub. Dinner or seafd supper in bar. The view remains fab, like a Colin Baxter postcard.                              11RMS APR-OCT X/X PETS CC KIDS EXP

**1014** **The Anderson** Fortrose 01381 620236. Main St of town in the middle of the
Map 7 Black Isle. Restau, bar & reasonable rms in v individual hotel notable esp for an
**M17** extraordinary whisky collection.       9RMS JAN-DEC X/T PETS CC KIDS MED.INX

**1015** **Lovat Arms** Beauly 01463 782313. Best hotel of many in main st of market
Map 7 town 20km from Inverness. Relaxed, welcoming family-run hotel with good
**L18** bar meals and comfy public rms. Much tartan upstairs. Locals also rec the Priory for bar meals.                      28RMS JAN-DEC T/T PETS CC KIDS MED.INX

**1016** **Tomich Hotel** Tomich nr Drumnadrochit 01456 415399. The inn of a quiet
Map 7 conservation village, part of an old estate on the edge of Guisachan Forest.
**K18** Nr fantastic Plodda Falls (1639/WATERFALLS) & Glen Affric (1627/GLENS). Basic facs, but use of pool nearby in farm steading (9am-9pm); esp good for fishing holidays. 25km drive from Drumnadrochit by A831. Nice bar.
8RMS JAN-DEC T/T PETS CC KIDS MED.INX

## FOUR GREAT HIGHLAND B&Bs

**1017** **The Old Smiddy** Laide  01445 731425. This book doesn't feature many
Map 6  B&Bs, but readers' letters sent us here. New landlady Julie Clements keeping
**J16**  the place on the map (Gruinard Bay, Wester Ross on the A832). She's a fine
cook and does serious dinners (book then BYO) incl non-res.
3RMS JAN-NOV X/T PETS XCC XKIDS MED.EX

**1018** **Port-Na-Con** nr Durness 01971 511367. Ken & Lesley Black's guesthouse on
Map 6  this idyllic shore is gr value. Conservatory v pleasant for browsing the extensive
**L12**  library or just gazing at Ben Hope & other bens. Seafood from the loch often
on the dinner menu (INX). Non-residents should book. If they're full, Lesley
knows somewhere nice in Durness.    4RMS JAN-DEC X/X PETS CC KIDS CHP

**1019** **Tanglewood House** Ullapool  01854 612059. Just outside town on A835 S
Map 6  o/look L Broom. Family GH v personally run by Anne Holloway who is an excl
**K15**  cook. Can do dinner for non-res. BYO. Dining & all rms have gr view.
3RMS JAN-DEC X/T PETS XCC KIDS MED.INX

**1020** **Feorag House** Glenborrodale, Ardnamurchan   01972 500248. Modern-
Map 5  build GH in secluded, spectacular location o/looking a faraway cove in
**G21**  Ardnamurchan. Off B8007 8km W of Salen. All rms o/look shoreline. All-in
rate incl B&B, tea & dinner. BYO wine.
3RMS APR-OCT X/X PETS CC XKIDS MED.EX

**Glenelg Inn** Glenelg  01599 522273 (1178/INNS).

# Good Inexpensive Restaurants In The Highlands

**1021**
Map 5
**M17**
✓ **Sutor Creek** Cromarty  01381 600855. 21 Bank St nr the seafront. Run by a local collective in true '60s style, a '00s lifestyle restau at the end of the rd (in the Black Isle) that's as good as anywhere similar in yr town or mine. Woodfired oven turning out gr crispy pizza & lots more; many specials Gr craic. Don Coutts you have partaken of another slice of life! Wed-Sun. LO 9/10pm.  INX

**1022**
Map 7
**H18**
✓ **The Seafood Restaurant** Kyle Of Lochalsh  01599 534813. Gt atmos bistro nr (and still an actual station platform) the busy port, off the rd to Skye and with that bridge in the distance. Seafood from Kyle/Mallaig/Skye ie v local, and vegn selection. Apr-Oct. Dinner 7 days 6.30-9pm. V popular. Phone to book & check opening hrs (may vary edge of season).  MED

**1023**
Map 7
**H18**
✓ **Off The Rails** Plockton  01599 544423. On the platform of this working railway stn; but no droopy sandwiches here, just good home cooking. Snacks in the day then blackboard specials and evening menu later. 10am-9.30pm in summer. Weekends only in winter. Brilliant faraway bistro atmos. Take the trail or the train! (Also 1592/COASTAL VILLAGES).  INX

**1024**
Map 6
**P15**
✓ **La Mirage** Helmsdale  01431 821615. Dunrobin St nr the Br Hotel. A little piece of Las Vegas in Sutherland; a homage to Barbara Cartland, the romantic 'novelist', who once lived nr in this wee village by the sea. Snacks of every kind all day; with life-size photos of the once proprietor Nancy Sinclair and various celebs gracing the walls. Now owned by the Wakefields but Nancy pops in most evens. Great fish and chips. Open all day.  INX

**1025**
Map 5
**N19**
**The Einich** Coylumbridge by Aviemore  01479 812334. Discreetly lodged in the Rothiemurchus VC on the A951 Cairngorm rd 5km Aviemore. Nice old rm doing daytime snacks & specials & dinner w/ends. Best choice in the ski zone. 7 days 9.30-5pm, dinner Wed-Sat LO 9pm.  INX

**1026**
Map 9
**K20**
**Russell's @ Smiddy House** Spean Bridge  01397 712335. Nr jnct of A82 for Skye on A86 for Laggan, a GH more a restau with rms. Good, unpretentious fare all home-made building solid local rep. Best to book. Cl Nov. 7 days in summer, lunch & LO 9.30pm. Wint: Wed-Sun.

**1027**
Map 7
**N19**
**The Boathouse** Kincraig  01540 651394. 2km from village towards Feshiebridge along L Insh. Part of L Insh Water sports (2133/WATER SPORTS), a balcony restau o/look beach and loch. Fine setting and ambience, friendly young staff (but they come and go). Some vegn. Salmon from the loch. You're in competition with the ospreys. Bar menu and home-baking till 6pm; supper till 9pm, bar 11pm. Apr-Oct. Check wint opening hrs.  CHP

**1028**
Map 9
**H22**
**Whitehouse** Lochaline, Ardnamurchan  01967 421777. Sits above the ferry port as the boats come in from Mull, a restau adj the vill shop with all the right/best intentions (local produce, organic, simple & slow cooking). I say intend because I haven't been. All reports glowing. Yours please. Apr-Dec. 11.30am-aft tea-dinner LO 8.30pm. Cl Sun.  MED

**1029**
Map 6
**L15**
**Carron Restaurant** Strathcarron  01520 722488. On A890 rd round L Carron (joins A87 Kyle of Lochalsh rd) just S of Strathcarron. Peter & Michelle Teago's roadside diner & grill a destination in these parts. Local seafood, good rep for steaks, home-made bread, puds etc. All-day menu. Apr-Nov, 10.30am-9pm. Cl Sun.  INX

**1030**
Map 6
**K13**
**Old School** Inshegra nr Kinlochbervie  01971 521383. B801 Betw Rhiconich and Kinlochbervie. Not exactly converted but *adapted*, which gives it some atmos. The world map from 1945 is not the only nostalgia. Gourmet it is not, but this is the best foodstop hereabouts – Margaret's home-cooking (they also have 6 decent rms). Dinner daily 6-8pm, Easter-Sept.  INX

**1031**
Map 7
**N17**
**The Classroom**, Nairn  01667 455999. Cawdor St – ask directions. Ambitious, stylish makeover in this conservative, golfy town. Contemp bar/restau menu. Lunch & LO 9.30pm. Nice room. 7 days.

**1032**
Map 6
**J14**
**Riverside Bistro** Lochinver  01571 844356. On way into town on A837. Self-serve during day; vast array of Ian Stewart's home-made pies and calorific cakes. You can eat in or take away. Conservatories out front & back. Bistro on riverside serves v popular meals at night; using local seafood, venison, vegn

– something for everyone incl, apparently, Michael Winner (though don't let that put you off). Food 10am-8pm although bistro menu kicks in even, LO 7.45pm.                                                                                                    MED

**1033  The Oystercatcher** Portmahomack nr Tain 01862 871560. On promonto-
Map 7  ry of the Dornoch Firth (Tain 15km) this hidden seaside village (the only E
**M16**  coast vill that faces W) could bring back childhood memories. Restau (more a caff during the day – they switch rms) is a destination in itself. The wine list & malt choice are truly extraordinary. Food is inventive, multi-ingredient, somewhat rich, but always interesting. Michael Winner was here too! Café dining during day 11.45am-4.15pm (from 12.45 Sun) & dinner 6.15pm (LO 9.30pm). Cl Nov-Feb & Mon/Tues. Dinner: best book.                             CHP

**1034  The Point** Ullapool 01854 612836. W Shore St, W from ferry terminal. A nice
Map 7  upstairs dining rm above a pub o/looking the water. Here for a while but
**K15**  much improved '05. Dinner only Tues-Sat. LO 9pm.                                   INX

**1035  Blueprint Café** Gairloch 01445 712397. Main part of strung-out vill opp
Map 6  Mountain Restaurant (daytime only, see 1380/VEGN). Contemp café/restau
**H16**  with mixed menu incl ok pizza, pasta & specials. 'Café' LO 4pm, even menu LO 8.45pm. Cl Jan/Feb.                                                                    INX

**1036  Falls of Shin Visitor Centre**  Self-serve café/restau in VC & shop across rd
Map 6  from Falls of Shin on the Achany Glen rd 8km S of Lairg (1653/WATERFALLS).
**M15**  Excl home-made food better than it prob has to be in an unlikely emporium of Harrods (Mohammed al Fayed's Highland estate is here). Somebody in that kitchen cooks like your mum. They come from miles at Xmas for hampers! 9.30am-6pm AYR. Food LO 4.30pm.

**1037  Kylesku Hotel** nr Kylestrome 01971 502231. On A894; tucked down beside
Map 6  L Glencoul where the boat leaves to see Britain's 'highest waterfall'
**K14**  (1644/WATERFALLS). Small quayside pub/hotel (8 rms) serving gr seafood in seafood setting with mighty Quinag behind. Noon-9pm AYR (see also 1359/GASTROPUBS). Expect improvements from switched-on new owners. INX

**1038  Delny House** nr Invergordon 01862 842678. On A9 N of Inverness, S of
Map 5  Tain, a mansion house GH with increasing rep for food at TGP. Readers have
**N17**  raved, I haven't eaten. 3 rms.                                                       INX

**1039  Mustn't Grumble** Melvich nr Gairloch 01445 771212. On B8021 N of
Map 7  Gairloch (rd to the lighthouse) 12km. Just when you're losing it on that windy,
**H16**  pictuesque rd: mustn't grumble (signed The Grumble Inn). Far-away but vibrant café-bar: contemp feel in pebble-dash bungalow, big stoves, big TV, odd animals incl emus (sic), not v good food & erratic service but worth a visit for individuality alone. Open AYR 11am-11pm.                                       INX

*Good Inexpensive Restaurants In Inverness* see pp. 149-150. Especially:

**La Tortilla Asesina**  01463 709809. Castle St. (1126/INVERNESS RESTAUS.)

**River Café**  01463 714884. Bank St. (1123/INVERNESS RESTAUS.)

**Castle Restaurant**  The legendary caff. Castle St. (1427/CAFÉS.)

*Other Inexpensive Restaurants In The North*

**Lochbay Seafood, Skye**  01470 592235 (1397/SEAFOOD RESTAUS).

**Thai Café, Stornoway**  01851 701811 (2325/WESTERN ISLES).

**Tigh Mealros, Lewis**  01851 621333 (2325/WESTERN ISLES).

**Applecross Inn, Applecross**  01520 744262 (1222/GET AWAY HOTELS).

**Glenelg Inn, Glenelg**  01599 522273 (1178/INNS).

**Crannog At The Waterfront, Ft William**  01397 705589 (1404/SEAFOOD RESTAUS).

# The Best Places To Stay In & Around Aberdeen

**1040**
Map 8
**S20**
✔✔ **Marcliffe Of Pitfodels** 01224 861000. N Deeside Rd (en route to Royal Deeside 5km from Union St). Unquestionably Aberdeen's premiere hotel – nothing else is remotely close for comfort, service & detail. Full report: 942/HOTELS NE. 42RMS JAN-DEC T/T PETS CC KIDS LOTS

**1041**
Map 8
**S20**
**Maryculter House Hotel** Maryculter 01224 732124. Out-of-town hotel, in the same direction as Ardoe below but 7km further on. Excellent situation on banks of Dee with river side walks & an old graveyard & ruined chapel. Newer annex; 8/9 rms o/look river (with another 18 in 2006). Poacher's Bar is special, dining rm not. Many weddings here, so be prepared if over w/end. Hotel on site of 13thC preceptory. 23+18RMS JAN-DEC T/T XPETS CC KIDS EXP

**1042**
Map 8
**S20**
**Ardoe House** Blairs 01224 867355. 12km SW of centre on S Deeside (poss to turn off the A92 from Stonehaven & the S at the first br & get to the hotel avoiding the city). The Dee is nearby on other side of rd from hotel. A granite chunk of Scottish Baronial with few, but more individual (they call them 'feature') rms & an annex where most rms are featureless but have pleasant country views. Restau gets 2 AA rosettes. Leisure facs adj this corporate but all-round, fairly reliable biz hotel. 110RMS JAN-DEC T/T PETS CC KIDS LOTS

**1043** **The Patio Hotel** 01224 633339. Beach Boulevard. Accom in the Beach pleasure zone, slightly apart from both the dire mall-type development & the beautiful long seafront that it dominates. Serviceable biz hotel wins no architectural plaudits from the o/side, but is comfortable and contemporary in its inner courtyard. Lightsome though bedrms have curiously wee windows. Own pool etc. Not far to Silver Darling for dinner (1064/ABER RESTAUS). 124RMS JAN-DEC T/T PETS CC KIDS EXP/ LOTS

**1044** **Thistle Caledonian Hotel** 01224 640233. Victorian edifice on Union Terr. Of several city centre hotels just off Union St, this always somehow seems the easiest to deal with; the most likely to be calm and efficient. Dining rm & refurb bar/brasserie. Some nice suites o/looking the Gardens. 77RMS JAN-DEC T/T PETS CC KIDS LOTS

**1045** **Simpson's Hotel** 01224 327777. 59 Queen's Rd. V late 90s hotel (peach & turquoise thro' out) which tries hard to please. Huge bar & brasserie/restau adj is hugely pop: they say it 'evokes a Roman bath house'. 'Classic', 'Executive' rms & suites have same decor but diff sizes. Some people will prob like all this; take your sunglasses. 50RMS JAN-DEC T/T XPETS CC KIDS MED.EXP/LOTS

**1046** **Atholl Hotel** 01224 323505. 54 King's Gate, a busy rd in W towards Hazelhead. An Aberdeen stalwart, the sort of place you sort out for your rellies and join them for dinner or a bar meal. I've never stayed, but people say this is the best among many mansions. The Atholl people say it's 'in a class of its own'. 34RMS JAN-DEC T/T XPETS CC KIDS MED.EX

**1047** **The Brentwood Hotel** 01224 595440. 101 Crown St. In an area of many hotels and guesthouses to the S of Union St, this one's somewhat garish tho flower-covered appearance belies a surprisingly commodious hostelry that is a better prospect than most. An adequate business hotel on a budget. Close to Union St and bars/restaus. Bar meals in subterranean 'Carriages' recommended; the ale is real. 65RMS JAN-DEC T/T PETS CC KIDS MED.INX

**1048** **Express by Holiday Inn** 01224 623500. Chapel St in the middle of W end nightlife zone. The title's a mouthful – what they mean is a better than av bedbox in a central location for, say, urban w/end breakers. Contemp & convenient. You'd eat out (& there's plenty to choose from) tho' not perhaps the legendary all-night bakery opp. 155RMS JAN-DEC T/T XPETS CC KIDS MED.INX

**1049** **The Globe Inn** 01224 624258. 15 Silver St. Rms above the Globe pub, the civilised pub in a st off Union St (1078/ABERDEEN PUBS). Pub has good rep for ales, food (& does live music, so no early to bed). The recently created accom is chp, v serviceable & good value. 7RMS JAN-DEC T/T XPETS CC XKIDS CHP

**1050** **Travelodge** 01224 584555. 9 Bridge St o/looking central Union St which is why it's here. Usual conversion of office block to serviceable bedbox, but given Abd prices, a v reasonable billet. 97RMS JAN-DEC T/T XPETS CC KIDS CHP

1051 **Hostels  SYHA**  8 Queen's Rd, an arterial rd to W. Grade 1 hostel 2km from centre (plenty buses). No café. Rms mainly for 4-6 people. You can stay out till 2am. Other hostels & self-catering flats c/o Univ, of which the best is the **Robert Gordon**, 01224 262134. Campus in Old Aberdeen is good place to be tho' 2km city centre has univ halls accom 01224 273444. Both these vacs only.

# The Best Places To Eat In Aberdeen

## BISTROS & CAFÉ-BARS

1052 ✓ **Café 52**  01224 590094. 52 The Green. Not easy for a non-Aberdonian to find but v close – in fact below – E end of Union St. Go down steps or app via Market St. They'd say this place was 'a little bit different'. It has a boho, verging on chaotic buzz. A sliver of a cosy bistro with outside tables & light, contemp food incl tapas (4-7pm). Chef David Littlewood doing gr stuff in the frenzied galley kitchen. 12-9.30pm (bar midnight). Till 6pm Suns. Cl Mon. CHP

1053 ✓ **The Foyer**  01224 582277. 82a Crown St. Remarkable in that this busy, contemporary restau with good mod-British seasonal menu & gr service is part of a local charity org who help homeless & disadvantaged people. No hint of charity surfaces, but you can satisfy your conscience as well as your appetite for food & tasteful surroundings. Can't help thinking there should be more places like this. Lunch onwards LO 9.30pm. Cl Sun/Mon.      INX

1054 ✓ **The Lairhillock Inn**  01569 730001. Not in the city at all, but a road-
Map 8   side inn at a country crossroads to the S, reached from either the rd to
S20   Stonehaven or the S Deeside Rd W. Easiest is: head S on main A92, turn off at 'Durris' then 5km. Famous for its pub food (1353/GASTROPUBS), informal atmos. Restau adj called **Crynoch** with more ambitious menu, excl cheese-board & malt selection. Both are worth the drive from town. Restau: dinner & Sun lunch. Cl Tues. LO 9.30pm. Inn: 7days lunch and LO 10pm.   MED/INX

1055 **Olive Tree**  01224 208877. 32 Queen's Rd. Off-centre but a significant part of smart dining in the Granite City. From the start Mike Reilly certainly made sure it had the look & the good management. Fine dining bistro & **Black Olive** brasserie in conservatory annex. Tangible diff in offering – brazz fairly av, restau pretty good. Service and presentation tip-top in both. The Olive Branch adj is curiously more Spar than special. Mon-Sat L and LO 10pm, BO till 11pm & on Sun.      EXP

1056 **The Square**  01224 646362. 1 Golden Sq, enter by S Silver St off Union St nr Music Hall. Well-liked, family-run restau in a spacious, modern rm (nice win-dows), contemp menu (3 diff thro' day), consistently good service & relaxing ambience. Expanding to the revamped, no, fabulous His Majesty's Theatre glass house at TGP. Lunch & dinner LO 10/11pm. Cl Sun/Mon.      INX

1057 **Howie's**  01224 639500. 50 Chapel St. Foll successful formula in Edin (138/BISTROS) & elsewhere in classic/contemp bistro style, this discreetly fronted restau presses all the right Aberdonian buttons (yes, incl the price!). 7 days, lunch & LO 10pm.      INX

1058 **Bistro Verde**  01224 586180. The Green (down steps from Union St at Virgin megastore). Hard to find in a car but off Market St. Unpretentious fish restau (one steak, one chicken dish) with blackboard daily catch. Nice place. Lunch & LO 10pm. cl Sun/Mon.      INX

1059 **La Bonne Baguette**  01224 644445. Off Union St down steps at side of graveyard. Très popular and quite French café. Pâtisserie, snacks (baguettes, etc) and specials. 7 days till 5pm & dinner Thu-Sat LO 9pm.      CHP

1060 **The Eating Room**  01224 212125. 239 Gt Western Rd, the front end of the Clubhouse Hotel. '05 addition to smart dining in Aberdeen. Chris Wills in kitchen & Jackie Spence (of the Spences who run the Marcliffe, above) on the tables. Haven't eaten at TGP but building a rep for a menu that's as straight-talking as the title.      MED

1061 **Beautiful Mountain**  01224 645353. 11 Belmont St. In area of many bars & eateries, this unpretentious caff stands out. T/away & tables jammed togeth-er in 2 rms upstairs. Gr combos & ingredients – just better & prob healthier! 7 days till 5pm (Sun 4.30pm).      CHP

**1062  Moonfish** 01224 644166. 9 Correction Wynd. Round corner from La Bonne Baguette (above), this funkier foodwise tho' flatter in atmos. Light food Euro-style: meze, tapas, salads etc. Lunch Tues-Sat, dinner Thur-Sat. Cl Sun.  CHP

**1063  ✓ The Victoria** 01224 621381. Upstairs at 140 Union St. Not a bistro or café-bar as such, more a luncheon & tearm, but too good not to incl here. Same staircase & foyer as adj jewellery & gift emporium so an odd alliance. Gr light menu, everything home-made & terribly well incl the bread & the biscuits & in July (actually AYR), a lemonade. Soup & Eve's Pudding for a fiver – perfect! 9am-5pm (6.30pm Thur). Cl Sun.  INX

## SEAFOOD

**1064  ✓ ✓ Silver Darling** 01224 576229. Didier Dejean's breakthrough bistro still going strong in this perfect spot poss the most dynamic location of any seafood (or other) restau in the land. Not so easy to find – head for Beach Esplanade, the lighthouse & harbour mouth (Pocra Quay). The light winks & boats glide past. Upstairs dining rm not large (best to book) & you so want to be by the window. Mostly chargrilled; the smell pleasantly pervades. Different menu for lunch & dinner, depends on the catch & season. Apposite wines, wicked desserts. Mon-Fri lunch, Mon-Sat dinner 7-9.30pm.  EXP

**1065  ✓ Atlantis at the Mariner Hotel** 01224 591403. 349 Gr Western Rd. Those that know where to go in Aber for excellent fish and seafood may not necessarily go to Silver Darling, but come here off centre & in a hotel but always busy. Hotel dining-rm atmos is not too evident (tables in conservatory) and the fish v good. Bar menu also avail. Moderately priced wines. Lunch (not Sat) and dinner LO 9pm.  MED

## ITALIAN

**1066  ✓ Rustico** 01224 658444. Corner of Union Row & Summer St 50m from Union St. If this were French I'd say it had the *je ne sais quoi*, but it is most definitely Italian (Sicilian actually). Tony & Niko's love for Sicily evident (their brill photos on the walls) tho' Niko's Greek. And the food well above the tratt av. As good as anywhere in Edin or Glas. Lunch & LO 10.30pm. Cl Sun.  INX

**1067  Carmine's Pizza** 01224 624145. 32 Union Terr. This tiny slice of a rm for *the* best pizza in town & behind, slaving over a hot stove, the eponymous, much-loved chef. Take away (to the Gardens opp). Real authentic pasta in basic spag/tag & penne variants. Noon-6.45pm. Cl Sun.  CHP

## EASTERN

**1068  The Royal Thai** 01224 212922. Crown Terr (off Crown St which is off Union St). The first and still one of the best of the late-20thC Asian invasion. 'Banquets' with sample dishes are a good idea. Good service, moody lighting. Daily lunch & LO 11pm.  MED

**1069  Saigon** 01224 213212. Also in Crown Terr adj Royal Thai. Vietnamese obviously & long-est (7+ yrs). Refreshing, Asian, intimate. Daily lunch & LO 10.30pm.  INX

**1070  Jewel In The Crown** 01224 210288. Way down (145) Crown St, on corner with Affleck. Gr N Indian food all home-made & authentic. Prob best curry in town – always arguments about that, natch, tho' not from the 4 sons of Farooq Ahmed who work like a football team to make this place a top spot. Expanding at TGP. Lunch & LO 11pm. 7 days.

**1071  Blue Moon** 01224 589977. 11 Holburn St. Contemp curry house, long thin & quite blue. Also **Blue Moon 2**, a blue replica denoted by their rude pepper motif over the rd in Alford Lane. Good curries in cool surroundings. Trad menu incl kids'. 7 days, lunch & LO 12am (a good late bet in a city that tucks up early).

**1072  Nargile** 01224 636093. 77 Skene St. Turkish survivor that has made its regulars happy for 20 yrs. Turkish owner, who also spawned the **Meze Café** at 3 Rose St. Under new ownership at TGP (gr t/away & open v late ie 3/4am) & has another **Nargile** in Edin (195/BEST MED FOOD). Doric staff, reliable meze, kebabs, swordfish etc & good puds. Dinner only LO 11pm. Cl Sun.  MED

# The Best Pubs In Aberdeen

## PUBS WITH ATMOSPHERE (& FOOD)

1073 ✓ **The Prince Of Wales** 7 St Nicholas Lane, just off Union St at George St. An all-round gr pub always mentioned in guides and one of the best places in the city for real ale: Old Peculier, Caledonian 80/- and guest beers. V cheap self-service **food** at lunchtime. Lots of wood, flagstones, booths. Large area but gets v crowded. 7 days, 11am-midnight (11pm Sun).

1074 ✓ **Under The Hammer** 11 N Silver St. Basement bar along the st from above, v intimately Aberdonian and a good place to meet them. Slightly older and mixed crowd. Only open evenings (till midnight) and best late on. My kind of place. Every time I go there seems to be a single, beautiful girl reading a book tho' last time (10pm on a Fri), it was a boy: a v civilised bar!

1075 **The Lemon Tree** 5 W North St. A theatre (upstairs) and a spacious bar/restau on st level where there's lunchtime **food** (Thur-Sun) and a mixed programme of entertainment. Phone (01224 642230) or watch for fliers, but prog will include comedy, jazz, folk, pop and cabaret. This is one of the best live rooms in the land.

1076 **The Blue Lamp** Gallowgate. Snug pub with nice ambience and long-established clientele and up the st large stone-floored lounge (The Blue Lampie) with gr atmos and often gr live music w/ends (so open 1am). Pub has pics of that '83 team and a jukebox unchanged forever.

1077 **Ma Cameron's Inn** Little Belmont St. The 'oldest pub in the city' (though the old bit is actually a small portion of the sprawling whole – but there's a good snug). No nonsense oasis in buzzy street. **food** from a huge menu incl all (we mean all) the pub staples: lunch and early evening.

1078 **The Globe** 13 N Silver St. Urban and urbane bar in single rm – a place to drink coffee as well as lager, but without self-conscious, pretentious 'café-bar' atmos. Known for its **food** at lunch and 5-7.45pm (not w/ends) and for live music – jazz and blues in the corner. The Globe Inn now has rms upstairs (1049/ABER HOTELS) so not a bad place to base a w/end in Aberdeen.

## CONTEMPORARY PUBS

1079 **College** Alfred Pl at W end of Union St. Hugely popular 'sports' and MTV kind of bar with stylish interior. Screens hanging everywhere for the footie, boxing, and other bodies disporting and competing as they do around the bar.

1080 **The Priory** Belmont St. Excl conversion of town centre church. If churches were like this we might go back (actually no we wouldn't).

1081 **Paramount** Bon Accord St. Designer café-bar looking a little worn now, but v popular and gr place to check out the club scene (flyers etc). Till midnight.

1082 **Blue** Bon Accord St. In the mini-shopping mall behind Pancho Villa's (bouncers at the entrance on the st). They'd hate it, but you could call it trendy. Certainly it is blue. They do cocktails. 7 days till midnight.

1083 **Justice Mill Lane and Windmill Brae** Many pubs to choose from. JM Lane has bigger selection and slightly older age group. All loud and lively. For the up-for-it crowd swilling thro' the Sat night streets of Aberdeen.

# The Best Places To Stay In & Around Dundee

**1084** ✓ **The Apex** 01382 202404. West Victoria Dock Rd. I have perhaps been overly modest in my rec of the Apexs in Edin (77/EDIN INDIVID) where there is a slew of top hotels to compare. Here in Dundee this 21stC edifice is in a league of its own. It's really the only place to stay! O/looking both the bridge & the new waterfront & with good detail in the v modern facs (incl a spa & pool), Apex show every evidence of rolling out a chain (one in London now) in the niche only occupied by Malmaison. Not chp (for Dundee) but not exp for what you get – it is a v civilised stopover. Metro restau also one of the city's reliably good eats.

153RMS JAN-DEC T/T XPETS CC KIDS MED.INX/MED.EXP

**EAT** V acceptable brasserie & grazing menu in Metro o/looking the waterfront.

**1085** **Hilton** 01382 229271. On riverside adj Olympic Centre nr Discovery Point. Serviceable, mainly business hotel with little charm but reasonable facs. Tired now cf Apex (above). Living Well leisure centre with ok pool. The rms facing south have some great Tay views.

128RMS JAN-DEC T/T PETS CC KIDS EXP

**1086** **The Queen's Hotel** 01382 322515. 160 Nethergate. Not much charm but convenient location now finding itself in the middle of 'the Cultural Quarter' (adj DCA, the Arts Centre). Some back rms o/looking distant R Tay are best.

52RMS JAN-DEC T/T PETS CC KIDS MED.EX

**1087** **The Shaftesbury** 01382 669216. 1 Hyndford St just off Perth Rd (about 3km from city centre). A suburban (jute baron's) mansion converted into a comfortable hotel with neat back gdn (tho' the kitchen pervades). All rms different; loungeable lounge. Decent food courtesy of chef Bill Morrison in one of 2 restaus, the 3 Olives. Chinese chefs in the other, the Royal China.

12RMS JAN-DEC T/T PETS CC KIDS MED.INX

**1088** **Fisherman's Tavern** 01382 775941. Broughty Ferry, Fort St nr the river/sea. 17thC fisherman's cottage converted to a pub in 1827. Rms much more recent! Excl real ales, but also nearby Ship Inn (1100/DUNDEE RESTAUS) preferred for eats (Tavern does lunch only).

11RMS (9 EN-SUITE) JAN-DEC X/X PETS CC KIDS INX

**1089** **Woodlands** Broughty Ferry 01382 480033. In the 'burbs between BF and Monifieth, signposted up Abercromby St opp the Esso garage. High-falutin' house in substantial acreage. Good disabled access. Popular out-of-town wedding venue quite complete with small swimming pool and gym.

38RMS JAN-DEC T/T PETS CC KIDS MED.INX

**1090** **Sandford Hill** 01382 541802. Excellent rural retreat over the water 7km S of Tay Br via A92/914 (1139 /COUNTRY-HOUSE HOTELS).

**Hostels** There is no S.Y.H. in the area, although in summer months univ hall accom is available – info from TIC. 01382 527527.

The nearest really good hotel to Dundee is:

✓ **Castleton House** nr Glamis 01307 840340. 28km N. Report: 911/TAYSIDE HOTELS.

# The Best Places To Eat In & Around Dundee

**1091** ✓ **Jute at Dundee Contemporary Arts** 01382 909246. Perth Rd. Jute, the downstairs bar/restau of Dundee's acclaimed art centre, DCA, is the most convivial place in town to eat – no contest. Chef Chris Wilson offers a menu far superior to any old arts venue esp one which is all things to all people. Bar & restau: your rendezvous in Dundee. All day LO 9.30pm.                    CHP

**1092** ✓ **The Agacan** 01382 644227. 113 Perth Rd. Fabled bistro for Turkish eats and wine. OTT frontage and much art on the walls. Bohemian ambience & you smell the meat (veggies go meze). Cl Mon.                    INX

**1093** ✓ **Fisher & Donaldson** Whitehall St off Nethergate. Trad bakers the v best in Scotland (1475/BAKERS) with elevated tearm. Snacks & all their fine fare. Mon-Sat LO 4.45pm.                    CHP

**1094** ✓ **The Parrot Café** 01382 206277. 91 Perth Rd. In an emerging café zone, Val Ireland holds her own coz she makes her own (cakes, scones, soups, blackboard specials) with a reg following of students & ladies who lunch & tea. No cellophaned muffins in sight. Tues-Sat 10am-5pm.                    CHP

**1095** **The Italian** 01382 206444. 36 Commercial St. 2-floored restau in city centre aptly named – it is *the* Italian. Somewhere between a tratt & a restau with well-chosen wine list & excl service. Look no further than this. 7 days lunch & LO 10pm.                    INX

**1096** **Visocchi's** 01382 779297. 40 Gray St, Broughty Ferry. More of a café than the original Kirriemuir branch caff (1489/ICE CREAM). After 70 yrs they're still making mouthwatering Italian flavoured ice creams (*amaretto, cassata* etc.) alongside home-made pasta and snacks. Til 8pm (10pm Fri/Sat). Cl Mon.
                    CHP

**1097** **Bon Appétit** 01382 809000. Exchange St nr corner with Commercial St. Haven't tried here but good rep & esp dear to Dundonians because the props Audrey & John Batchelor spent 16 yrs in France then came back to Dundee to 'make a difference'. Bloody good luck to them! Lunch & LO 10pm.                    INX

**1098** **Mandarin Garden** 01382 227733. 40 Tay St. V acceptable Chinese. Low key décor, peaceful atmos; food is the thing. Excellent seafood and different meats covered sauce-u-like but also MSG. Dinner only 5-11pm.                    INX

**1099** **Dil Se** 01382 221501. 99-101 Perth Rd. Bangldeshi restau; on two floors and food from all over the subcontinent but it's for curries ain't it? Rel to Balaka in St Andrews, this is just a bit smarter than the competition. Lunch & dinner Sun-Thurs, open all day Fri & Sat. Until late!                    MED

**1100** **The Ship Inn** 01382 779176. On front at Broughty Ferry. Weathered by the R Tay since the 1800s, this cosy pub has sustained smugglers, fishermen & foody folk alike. Bar & upstairs restau; no-nonsense Scottish menu & picture windows o/look the Tay. Lunch & bar food till 7.30pm, restau 8.30/9pm.                    CHP

# The Best Places To Stay In & Around Inverness

**1101** ✓ ✓ **Glenmoriston** 01463 223777. Ness Bank. The smart stay & fabulous food experience in the N. Report: 975/HIGHLAND HOTELS.
15RMS(+15 ADJ) JAN-DEC T/T XPETS CC KIDS LOTS

**1102** ✓ ✓ **Boath House** Auldearn 01667 454896. Half an hour E on A96. Report: 973/HIGHLAND HOTELS.

**1103** ✓ **Culloden House** 01463 790461. 5km E nr (but not adj) battlefield. Report: 976/HIGHLANDS HOTELS.
LOTS

**1104** ✓ **Dunain Park Hotel** 01463 230512. 6km SW on A82 Ft William rd. Report: 979/HIGHLANDS HOTELS.
EXP

**1105** **Royal Highland Hotel** 01463 231926. Academy St. Formerly the Station Hotel but big refurb & new owners. Nice staircase. Rather av rms. A surreal start to the day in the b/fast rm. V much in the centre of things but otherwise av.
70RMS JAN-DEC T/T PETS CC KIDS EXP

**1106** **The Heathmount** 01463 235877. Kingsmills, then centre (from Eastgate Mall). Fiona Newton's surprisingly groovy boutique-style hotel with popular bar/restau. High standard of mod-con. Famously, some rms have TVs in the shower. Good value at the price. 7RMS JAN-DEC T/T XPETS CC XKIDS MED.EX

**1107** **Marriott Hotel** 01463 237166. Culcabock Rd. In suburban area S of centre nr A9. Modern, v well-appointed with pleasant gdn. Best of the chain hotels. Leisure facs incl pool
82RMS JAN-DEC T/T PETS CC KIDS EXP

**1108** **Ramada Jarvis** 08457 303040 (central booking). Church St. V central & some rms o/look river. Better than your av bunk for the night. Ok restau & bar. Leisure facs with pool. 106RMS JAN-DEC T/T XPETS CC KIDS MED/INX

**1109** **The Alexander/Felstead** 01463 231151/712266/231634. 2 hotels on Ness Bank, along the river opp Eden Court and v central. Alexander (formerly Ardmuir) new owners & shiny (well, the floors) new makeover '05. Nice uniformity in block out back. Other rms bigger but some contemp look. Felstead old-style comfort. Belongings belong. Both B&B only. Many other hotels in this st. These ones are good value. 11/8RMS VARIES X/T PETS CC KIDS MED.INX

**1110** **Moyness House** 01463 233836. 6 Bruce Gardens. Accolade-gathering suburban GH over br S of river but 10 mins' walk to centre & on-street parking. Friendly family house. B&B only. The writer Neil Gunn used to live here!
7RMS JAN-DEC X/T PETS CC KIDS MED.INX

**1111** **3 Good Hostels: SY Hostel** 01463 231771. Victoria Drive; Large official hostel. More funky are the **Student Hostel** 236556. 8 Culduthel Rd, and 3 doors down **Bazpackers** 717663.

**1112** **Camping & Caravan Parks** Most central (2km) at **Bught Park** 01463 236920. Well-equipped and large-scale site on flat river meadow. Many facs. App via A82 Ft William rd.

# The Best Places To Eat In Inverness

**1113** ✓ ✓ **Boath House** Auldearn 01667 454896. Well out of town, but worth drive. Just off A96 3km E of Nairn. 30mins from Inverness. Chef Charlie Lockely accumulating AA rosettes & rep. A fine-dining night out. Report: 1041/HIGHLAND HOTELS.
MED

**1114** ✓ ✓ **Abstract @ The Glenmoriston** 01463 223777. 20 Nessbank along the river. The top-end restau in town part of Barry Larsen's Gllenmoriston Hotel. Chef Loic Lefebvre v French, v imaginative, v likely to get noticed. Tasting menu & à la carte.
EXP

**1115** ✓ **Rocpool** 01463 717274. Ness Walk. Corner of main br over river. Excl modern diner with accent on tapas-grazing daytime & eclectic even menu. Joanna B once gave it 9/10! We'd say it is the consistently good place to eat in the centre. 7 days. Cl Sun lunch.
INX

1116  ✓ **Café One** 01463 226200. 10 Castle St nr the Castle. Contemporary décor and cuisine in hands of good team. Menu changes monthly, carefully sourced ingredients – salmon wild all summer – reasonably priced for this standard of food and service. Express menu a good deal. Another restau for Inverness to be pleased about. Lunch, dinner LO 9.30pm. Cl Sun.   MED

1117  ✓ **The Mustard Seed** 01463 220220. 16 Fraser St. Catriona Bissett's cool restau in spectacular riverside rm attests (with Rocpool above) to Inverness's new confidence & city status. Contemp menu, ok wine. Service can vary, but a restau that would not be out of place in any European city. Expansion plans across the river should see spectacular new place '06. 7 days 12-4pm, 6-10pm.   INX

1118  ✓ **Dunain Park Hotel** As above. 3 adj elegant dining-rms; drawing rm for avant/après. The country-house hotel on the L Ness edge of town where the good burghers come for Ann Nicholl's honest-to-goodness cookery and wish they'd left more rm for the puds. Excl wines; & malt list.   MED

1119  ✓ **Castle Restaurant** Castle St. Legendary caff of the Highlands. Hardest-working tearm in the N turns out all the things with (crinkly) chips. Report: 1427/CAFÉS.   CHP

1120  **Chez Christophe** 01463 717126. 16 Ardross St. The restau of small Craignay House hotel in street off 'rive gauche' of R Ness run by Christophe Magie & his wife Carol. Authentic French cuisine and gr French wine list. Regret to say I hadn't eaten here at TGP but most definitely will soon (because I'm going to be in Inverness a lot & everyone recs). Dinner only LO 10pm. Cl Sun.   MED

1121  **Riva & Pazzo's** 01463 237377. 4 Ness Walk. Prominent (adj main br) central Italian restau & (upstairs) tratt. Prob best in town. Contemp rm o/looking riverside. Decent Italian menu with clear distinction betw treat and tratt. Riva lunch & LO 9.30pm, Pazzo's evens only.   MED/INX

1122  **Riverhouse Restaurant** 01463 222033. Greig St, over the pedestrian bridge. Intimate restaurant with contemp food from Alan Little's open kitchen. Gets busy so can feel cramped but good rep. Lunch Thur-Sat, LO 10pm.   MED

1123  **River Café** 01463 714884. Bank St on town side of river nr pedestrian br. Small, friendly café/restau. Solid & unpretentious even menu. Ladies who lunch. 7 days LO 9pm (Sun/Mon 7.30pm).   INX

1124  **Shapla** 01463 241919. 2 Castle Rd on town side of main rd br. Indian restau with the usual UK curryhouse menu served in upstairs lounge with river views. Open late (LO 11pm). Some say **Rajah**, 01463 237190 downstairs in Post Office Lane (betw Church St & Academy St, behind Queensgate) is the better curry. But most are agreed **The Beauly Tandoori**, 01463 782221 20km away in Beauly High St is the best Indian restau in the area.   INX

1125  **Red Pepper** 01463 237111. 74 Church St. The cooler coffee-shop by the people that brought us the Mustard Seed (above). Daytime caffeine hit with bespoke s/wiches etc. 7.30am-4.30pm. Cl Sun.   INX

1126  **La Tortilla Asesina** 01463 709809. Top of Castle St nr castle & hostels (see above). Reasonably authentic Spanish restau serving the UK version of tapas ie 2/3 portions as a meal. All the faves & some variants are here. 'Scotland's only' sherry bar upstairs with surprising range. Otherwise the Rioja. Also open Spanish hrs (till midnight/1am).   INX

**Kinkell House** 01349 861270. Off A9N. Report 1006/LESS EXP. HIGHLAND HOTELS.

**Delny House** 01862 842678. Off A9N. Report 1038/INEXP. HIGHLAND RESTAUS.

# SECTION 5

*Particular Places To Eat And Stay
In Scotland*

# Superlative Country-House Hotels

**1127** ✓ ✓ ✓ **Gleneagles** Auchterarder 01764 662231. Off A9 Perth-
Map 10 Stirling rd and signposted. Scotland's truly luxurious resort
**N24** hotel. For facs on the grand scale others pale into insignificance; it is an inter-national destination. More famously fabulous than ever since the G8 Summit '05. All sport & leisure activities you could want incl shooting, riding, fishing, off-roading (even jeeps for kids), 2 pools with outdoor tub. Spa for ladies. Oh & the world-renowned golf (3 courses). Refurb rms by Amanda Rosa & the new wing 'Braid House' contemp & remote (in the 'handset to control temp, lights, curtains & fireplace' sense). Strathearn Restau is a foodie heaven but expensive. Club bistro lighter and brighter & there are 2 other restaus on the estate. Andrew Fairlie's intimate dining rm is considered by many to offer the best dining in Scotland. Report 928/PERTHSHIRE RESTAUS. Gleneagles could be anywhere but it is quintessentially Scottish. It has airs & graces but it's a friendly old place too. 271RMS JAN-DEC T/T PETS CC KIDS LOTS

**1128** ✓ ✓ **Glenapp Castle** nr Ballantrae 01465 831212. Luxury manor S of
Map 11 Ballantrae. V discreet entrance (first rt turn after vill – no sign;
**J29** entryphone system). Home of Inchcape family for most of 20thC, opened as a hotel in first year of 21st. Run by Graham and Fay Cowan (Fay's family has other hotels in the SW). Fabulous restoration on a house that fell into disuse in the 1990s. Excellent and studied service, good food (3 AA rosettes), impec-cable environment. The rms are all individually beautful; the suites are enor-mous. Quality costs but the price is inclusive of just about everything, so relax and join this effortless house party. Tennis, lovely walks. A southern secret! 17RMS EASTER-OCT T/T PETS CC KIDS LOTS AND LOTS

**1129** ✓ ✓ **Isle Of Eriska** Ledaig 01631 720371. 20km N of Oban (signed from
Map 9 A85 nr Benderloch Castle). As you drive over the Victorian iron br
**J22** onto the isle (a real island), you enter a more tranquil and gracious world. Its 300 acres are a sanctuary for wildlife; you are not the only guests. The famous badgers come almost every night to the door of the bar for their milk. Comfortable baronial house with fastidious service and facs. The picturesque 9-hole golf, gr 17m pool should be open at last (and gym) (excl in summer when it opens on to the gdn). Also putting, tennis and clay shooting; it's all there if you feel like action, but it's v pleasant just to stay still. Spa suites with many treatments avail. Dining, with a Scottish flavour and impeccable local ingredients from a rich backyard and bay, has 3 AA rosettes under chef Robert MacPherson. 5 new rms by the spa incl 3 with own outside hot tubs.
22RMS FEB-DEC T/T PETS CC KIDS LOTS

**1130** ✓ ✓ **Kinnaird** Dunkeld 01796 482440. 12km N of Dunkeld (Perth
Map 10 35km) via A9 and B898 for Dalguise. In Kinnaird estate, a bucolic
**N22** setting beneath woody ridge of Tay Valley, this country house envelops you with good taste and comfort. Good, unobtrusive service from friendly arrival to sad departure. You get a teddy on your bed and there's a stylish 'K' on everything. Gr snooker rm and drawing rm warmed by open fires. J/T pre-ferred. V fine dining in v fine dining room. Some management changes since last edition but prop Constance Ward allows nothing to falter & long-stand-ing chef Trevor Brooks is superb. 'The Retreat' upstairs does 'treatments'. Silently beyond the grounds and river, endless traffic ploughs N and S on the A9. One day you'll have to join it again. Until then, live Kinnaird. There are individual cottages (esp rec 'Castle Peroch') for more privacy – 2 in the near-by courtyard. 9RMS (8 COTT) JAN-DEC T/T PETS CC KIDS LOTS

**1131** ✓ ✓ **Knockinaam Lodge** Portpatrick 01776 810471. An ideal place to
Map 11 lie low; an historic Victorian house nestled on a cove. The Irish
**J30** coastline is the only thing on the horizon, apart from discreet service and excellent food (Michelin chef Tony Pierce excels with a fixed menu which is full of surprises). Winston Churchill was once v comfortable here, too! Superb wine & whisky lists. 15km S of Stranraer, off A77 nr Lochans. Report 814/SOUTH-WEST HOTELS. 9RMS MAR-DEC T/T PETS CC KIDS LOTS

**1132** ✓ ✓ **Greywalls** East Lothian 01620 842144. Close to Edinburgh & adj
the rarified world of Muirfield, but one of the most homely & aes-thetically pleasing co-house hotels in the UK in an Edwardian summerhouse

built by the humanist genius architect Lutyens. Fabulous gardens. Report: 110/HOTELS OUTSIDE TOWN.

**1133** ✓ ✓ **Cromlix House** Dunblane 01786 822125. Nr A9 N of Perth, 4km Dunblane. New owners autumn '05 for this quintessential co house hotel in beautiful grounds. Report: 834/CENTRAL HOTELS.

**1134** ✓ ✓ **Raemoir House** Banchory 01330 824884. 5 km N from town via A980. A gem in the NE. Historical with contemp comforts & excl dining. Report 944/NE HOTELS.

**1135** ✓ ✓ **Ballachulish House** Ballachulish 01855 811266. Report: 1252/SCOTTISH HOTELS.

**1136** ✓ **The Roxburghe Hotel** nr Kelso 01573 450331. The pre-eminent hotel in the green, rolling Borders. Fewer facs than some on this page, but excl golf course. Report: 847/BORDERS.

**1137** ✓ **Ardanaiseig** Loch Awe 01866 833333. 16km from Taynuilt signed from
Map 9 main A85 to Oban down beautiful winding rd and 7km from Kilchrenan.
J23 In sheltered landscaped gdns dotted with ongoing sculpture project to complement this rambling gothic mansion's collection of selected antiques (prop owns antique biz in London) o/looking an enchanting loch. Peaty water on tap & all amongst gr trees. Genuine 'faux' grand that works. O/side by the loch, deer wander and bats flap at dusk. Pure romance. Chef Gary Goldie deserves more credit perhaps, than he gets.

16RMS MAR-DEC T/T PETS CC KIDS LOTS

**1138** **Ballathie House** Kinclaven nr Blairgowrie & Perth 01250 883268. Superb situation on R Tay. Handy for Perth and probably the best place to stay nr the town; full report and codes: 2335/BEST PERTH.

**1139** **Sandford Hill** nr Wormit (nr Dundee & St Andrews) 01382 541802. 7km S
Map 10 of Tay Bridge via A92 and A914, 100m along B946 to Wormit. In an unpromis-
Q23 ing landscape of quarries and pigfarms, a civilised withdrawal from the jams of Dundee and bunkers of St Andrews. An austere mansion with unusual layout and mullioned windows looking out to gorgeous gdns. Wild but romantic tennis court (someday they must get it back in use), pub lunches. 750 acres adj farmland of 'activities' – clay-pigeon shooting, fishing in Farm Loch, off-road driving. 16RMS JAN-DEC T/T PETS CC KIDS EXP

**1140** **Corrour House** Aviemore 01479 810220. Small country house 3km from
Map 7 Aviemore on Coylumbridge rd, handy for the ski slopes. Without airs but not
N19 without graces, this family-run hotel is decent value. More like a GH with chef. Young deer in the gdn at daybreak, fine-size rms. Has changed hands a bit since original vision. 8RMS JAN-DEC T/T PETS CC KIDS MED.EX

# Hotels That Welcome Kids

**1141**
Map 10
N23
✔✔ **Crieff Hydro** Crieff 01764 655555. A national institution & still a family business; your family is part of theirs. App via High St, turning off at Drummond Arms Hotel uphill then follow signs. Vast Victorian pile with activities for all from bowlers to babies. Still run by the Leckies from hydropathic beginnings but with continuous refurbs, incl the fabulous winter gdns moving graciously with the times (fine coffee shop: freshly squeezed OJ & big donuts). Formal dining rm & the Brasserie (best for food Med-style; open all day). Gr tennis courts, riding school, Lagoon Pool. Tiny cinema shows family movies; nature talks, donkey rides. Kids endlessly entertained (even while you eat). Chalets in grounds are among the best in Scotland. Gr for family get-togethers. 213RMS(+SELF-CAT) JAN-DEC T/T PETS CC KIDS MED.INX

**1142**
Map 9
J22
✔ **Isles Of Glencoe Hotel** Ballachulish 01855 811602. Beside the A82 Crianlarich to Ft William: a modern hotel and leisure centre jutting out onto L. Leven. Adventure playground o/side and nature trails. Conservatory restau o/looking the water. Lochaber Watersports next door have all kind of boats from pedalos to kayaks & bikes. Hotel has pool. 2 diff standards of family rms. Snacks in the restau all day. Glencoe and 2 ski areas nearby. 59RMS JAN-DEC T/T PETS CC KIDS MED.INX/EXP

**1143**
Map 7
E15
✔ **Scarista House** Harris 01859 550238. 20 mins S of Tarbert on W coast of S Harris, 45 mins Stornoway. Big, comfortable farmhouse o/looking amazing beach (1614/BEACHES); also golf course (2078/GOLF). Lots of other gr countryside around. The Martins have 3 school-age kids & yours may muck in with them (incl 6pm supper). Laid-back but civilised ambience. 5RMS JAN-DEC X/X PETS CC KIDS EXP

**1144**
Map 7
E14
✔ **Baile-Na-Cille** Timsgarry, Lewis 01851 672242. Far far into the sunset on the W of Lewis 60km Stornoway so a plane/ferry & drive to somewhere you & the kids can leave it all behind. Exquisite, vast beach, garden, tennis, games rm. No TV/phone/mobile/smoking. Plenty books. The kids will never forget it. 7RMS APR-OCT X/X PETS CC KIDS MED.INX

**1145**
Map 9
J20
✔ **Glenfinnan House** Glenfinnan 01397 722235. Just off the 'Road to the Isles' (the A830 from Ft William to Mallaig). V large Highland 'hoose' with so many rms and such large gdns you can be as noisy as you like. Great intro to the Highland heartland; music, scenery and local characters. Cruise of the loch leaves from the foot of the lawn. Midge-eater in the garden. (1002/INEXP HIGHLAND HOTELS). 13RMS MAR-NOV X/X PETS CC KIDS MED.INX-EXP

**1146**
Map 9
K20
**Old Pines** nr Spean Bridge 01397 712324. 3km Spean Br via B8004 for Gairlochy at Commando Monument. A ranch-like hotel in a good spot N of Ft William. Previous owners the Barbours forged a big rep not only for food but for a hotel that welcomed kids. New owners the Dalleys have (little) kids too & seem set to continue the laid-back & accommodating app. Separate mealtimes & with real food for kids. 8RMS JAN-DEC X/X XPETS CC KID MED.INX

**1147**
Map 7
L18
**Polmaily House** nr Drumnadrochit 01456 450343. 5km from main L Ness rd at Drumnadrochit via A831 to Cannich (& glorious Glen Affric; 1627/GLENS), a good co-house hotel for adults that is excellent for kids. Lots to do in the gdns: trout pond where older kids can fish, pet rabbit run, bikes, indoor swimming pool, pool room. Tree house & swing up the back esp popular. Separate kids' meal time; special rates. 10RMS + 2SUITES JAN-DEC T/T PETS CC KIDS MED.EX

**1148**
Map 10
Q27
**Peebles Hydro** Peebles 01721 720602. Innerleithen Rd. One of the first Victorian hydros, now more Butlins than Bath. Huge grounds, corridors (you get lost) and floors of rms where kids can run around. Pool & leisure facs. Entertainment and baby-sitting services. V traditional and refreshingly untrendy. Rms vary. Dining rm is vast and hotel-like. Lazels bistro downstairs is light, contemp and unnecessarily good (869/BORDER EATS). Many family rms. 128RMS JAN-DEC T/T PETS CC KIDS MED.INX/EXP

**1149**
Map 11
M30
**The Cally Palace** Gatehouse Of Fleet 01557 814341. The big all-round family & golf hotel in the SW in charming vill with walks & beaches nearby. Leisure facs incl pool & tennis. 500 acres of forested grounds. 9 family rms. 56RMS JAN-DEC T/T PETS CC KIDS MED.EX

**1150** **Stonefield Castle Hotel** Tarbert 01880 820836. O/side Tarbert on A83 on slopes of L Fyne with wonderful views. A real castle with 60 acres of woody grounds to explore. Full report and codes: 789/ARGYLL HOTELS.

**1151**
Map 7
**N19**
**Hilton Coylumbridge** nr Aviemore 01479 810661. 8km from Aviemore Centre on B970 rd to ski slopes and nearest hotel to them. 2 pools of decent size, sauna, flume, etc. Plenty to do in summer and winter (1747/KIDS) and certainly where to go when it rains. Best of the often-criticised Aviemore concrete blocks, the most facs, huge new shed with kids' play area (the 'Funhouse'), staff wandering around in animal costumes, kids' mealtimes & even prog. 175 (INCL FAMILY)RMS JAN-DEC T/T PETS CC KIDS LOTS

**1152** **Calgary Hotel** nr Dervaig, Mull 01688 400256. 20km S Tobermory (& a long way from Balamory), a roadside farmhouse/bistro/gallery, ie v laid-back place. Main features are beautiful wood out back (with art in it, but an adventure land for kids) & Mull's famously fab beach adj. 2 gr family rms. 2297/ISLAND HOTELS. 9RMS MAR-NOV X/X PETS CC KIDS MED.INX

**1153**
Map 8
**T18**
**Waterside Inn** Peterhead 01779 471121. Edge of town on A952 to Fraserburgh. Modern hotel with pool etc and some activities for kids. Aden Country Park nearby (1746/KIDS). Kids' meal and playrm 7-9pm while you eat, and family rms. Ugie and Deedee (the bears) are a gr success, but you wouldn't want to take them to bed. Adventure playground. Go-karts. Sometimes special family w/ends. 109(16FAMILY)RMS JAN-DEC T/T PETS CC KIDS MED.EX

**1154** **Philipburn** Selkirk 01750 720747. 1km town centre on Peebles Rd. Main attraction is open-air pool; 2 family rms o/look. Also easy-eat bistro restau. Report: 855/BORDER HOTELS.

## The Best Hostels

*For hostels in* Edinburgh, *see p. 31; for* Glasgow, *see p. 78. SYHA Info: 01786 891400. Central reservations (SYHA) 01541 553255.*

**1155**
Map 6
**L15**
✓ ✓ ✓ **Carbisdale Castle** Culrain nr Bonar Bridge 01549 421232. The flagship hostel of the SYHA, an Edwardian castle in terraced gdns o/looking the Kyle of Sutherland on the edge of the Highlands. Once the home of the exiled King of Norway, it still contains original works of art (nothing of gr value though the sculptures are elegant). The library, ballrm, lounges are all in use and it's only a few quid a night. Shared dorms as usual but no chores. Kitchens and café. Bike hire in summer; lots scenic walks. Stn (from Inverness) 1km up steep hill. Buses: Inverness/Thurso/Lairg. 75km Inverness, 330km Edin. 189 beds. You can have the whole place (1271/HOUSE PARTIES).

**1156**
Map 10
**N24**
✓ **Stirling** 01786 473442 Fax 445715. Modern conversion in gr part of town, close to castle, adj ancient graveyard and with fine views from some rms. One of the new hotel-like hostels with student-hall standard and facs. Many oldies & internat tourists. B'fast incl or self-catering. Access till 2am. 126 beds.

**1157**
Map 9
**L25**
✓ **Loch Lomond SYH** 01389 850226 Fax 850623. Alexandria, Dumbarton. Built in 1866 by George Martin, the tobacco baron (as opposed to the other one who produced the Beatles), this is hostelling on the grand scale. Towers and turrets, galleried upper-hall, space for banqueting and a splendid view across the loch, of where you're going tomorrow. 30km Glas. Stn (Balloch) 4km. Buses 200m. Access till 2am. 160 beds.

**1158**
Map 7
**N19**
✓ **Aviemore Bunkhouse** Aviemore 01479 811181. Nr main rd into Aviemore from S (A95) off Coylumbridge rd to Cairngorm & by the river. Part of Old Inn (1358/GASTROPUBS) so gr food adj. En-suite rms for 6/8 & family rms avail. AYR.

**1159**
Map 6
**K14**
✓ **Inchnadamph Lodge** Assynt 01571 822218. 25km N Ullapool on A837 rd to Lochinver & Sutherland. Well appointed mansion house for individs or groups in geologist-gazing, hill-walking, mountain-rearing Assynt. Kitchen, canteen (dinner not provided but self/s b/fast), annex with smoking rm, DVDs. Some twins.

**1160**
Map 7
**M20**
✓ **Pottery Bunkhouse** Laggan Bridge nr A9 01528 544231. On A889 E-W nr L Laggan, 12km from A9 at Dalwhinnie. Homely bunkhouse & gt home-bake caff (1446/TEARMS). Lounge o/look hills, wood stove, hot tub on deck. AYR (tearm Easter-Oct).

**1161**
Map 7
**N19**
✓ **Glen Feshie** nr Aviemore 01540 651323. Privately run hostel in farmhouse by the rd-side in Glen Feshie, signed Achlean from Feshiebridge on the B970. A walkers' refuge which has a genuine, friendly atmos. Store sells basics; free porridge, but also meals provided. Good base for Cairngorm walking (2005/SERIOUS WALKS). 4 places incl 3 rms for 4. Open AYR.

**1162**
Map 10
**Q27**
**R27**
**The Borders** *There are some ideal wee hostels in this hill-walking tract of Scotland (where it all began). These 2 are esp good, one grand, one very small.*
**Melrose** 01896 822521. Grade 1, 90 beds, v popular. Well-appointed mansion on Meadow 250m by riverside from the Abbey.
**Broadmeadows** 8km from Selkirk off A708, the first hostel in Scotland (1931) is a cosy howff with a stove and a view.

**1163**
Map 7
**M18**
**Inverness Student Hostel** 01463 236556. Indep hostel at 8 Culduthel Rd opp the SYH, uphill from town centre (some dorms have views). Run by same folk who have the great Edin one (99/HOSTELS), with similar laid-back atmos and camaraderie. **Bazpackers** 100m downhill, same vibe.

**1164**
Map 9
**L24**
**Rowardennan** Loch Lomond 01360 870259. The hostel at the end of the rd up the E (less touristy) side of L Lomond from Balmaha and Drymen. Large, well managed and modernised and on a water-side site. On W Highland Way and obvious base for climbing Ben Lomond (1984/MUNROS). Good all-round activity centre and lawns to the loch of your dreams. Rowardennan Hotel boozer nearby.

**1165**
**Hostelling In The Hebrides** Simple hostelling in the crofting communities of Lewis, Harris and the Uists. Run by a trust to maintain standards in the spirit of Highland hospitality with local crofters acting as wardens. Lewis, Harris and one each in N and S Uist. No advance bookings necessary or accepted (suggests they will always fit you in). No smk and no Sun arrival or departure. Check local TICs for details (2325/WESTERN ISLES). Also:

**1166**
Map 5
**E16**
**Am Bothan** Harris 01859 520251. At Leverburgh in the S of S Harris a bunkhouse handbuilt & personally run – a bright, cool building with contemp feel. Good disabled facs. Caff, shop nearby. 18 spaces & camping nearby. One of 8 hostels in Scotland given 5 Stars by visitscotland. Also **Na Gearrannan** nr Carloway, N Lewis. The remarkable hostel in a village of Blackhouses. An idyllic spot. 2226/MUSEUMS.

**1167**
Map 9
**F23**
**Iagandorain** Iona 01681 700781. Bunkhouse at N tip of island on John Maclean's farm. This feels like the edge of the world looking over to Staffa and beyond on the spiritual isle. Open AYR.

**1168**
Map 9
**G22**
**Tobermory** Mull 01688 302481. Looks out to Tobermory Bay. Central rel high standard hostel v busy in summer. 39 places 7 rms (4 on front). Kitchen. Internet. Nr ferry to Ardnamurchan main Oban ferry 35km away (1597/VILLS). Mar-Oct. Door 11.45pm.

**1169**
Map 9
**J26**
**Lochranza Youth Hostel** Lochranza 01770 830631. On left app vill from S – Vict house o/looking fab bay & castle ruins. Swans dip at dawn. Full self-cat facs. Comfortable sitting rm & lots of local books. Mar-Nov.

**1170**
Map 9
**J21**
**Glencoe** 01855 811219. Deep in the glen itself, 3km off A82/4km by back rd from Glencoe village and 33km from Ft William. Modern timber house nr river; especially handy for climbers and walkers. Clachaig pub, 2km for good food and craic. (Also 1666/SCENIC ROUTES; 1950/SPOOKY PLACES; 1925/BATTLE-GROUNDS; 1326/PUBS; 2091/SKIING; 2002/SERIOUS WALKS.)

**1171**
Map 7
**J19**
**Ratagan** 01599 511243. 29km from Kyle of Lochalsh, 3km Shiel Br (on A87). A much-loved Highland hostel on the shore of L Duich and well situated for walking and exploring some of Scotland's most celebrated scenery e.g. 5 Sisters of Kintail/Cluanie Ridge (2004/SERIOUS WALKS), Glenelg (1667/SCENIC ROUTES; 1845/PREHISTORIC SITES), Falls of Glomach (1638/WATERFALLS). From Glenelg there's the short and dramatic crossing to Skye through the Kylerhea narrows (continuous, summer only), quite the best way to go. Mar-Oct.

**1172**
Map 7
**F20**
**Kinloch Castle** Rum 01687 462037. The hostel below stairs in one of the most opulent castle-fantasies in the Highlands. Currently subject to grant-aid to restore to former glory, the hostel operates to allow visitors to experience the rich natural wildlife, grandeur & peace of Rum. Self-cat. For ferry details see Rum: 2280/ISLANDS.

**1173**
Map 7
**G17**
**Dun Flodigarry** nr Staffin, Skye 01470 552212. In far N 32km from Portree beside Flodigarry Country-House Hotel, which has a decent pub (more for visitors than locals), and amidst big scenery. O/looks sea. Bunkrms for 2-6 & 4 singles (holds up to 54) and great refectory. Open AYR.

**1174**
Map 7
**H18**
**Skye Backpackers Guest House** Kyleakin 01599 534510. Convenient GH with mainly 4-bunk rms and smallish gantry/lounge nr br for last/ first stop on what used to be the island. Open AYR. There are many other independent hostels on Skye incl 2 in Portree. This has laundry service & internet.

**1175**
Map 10
**Q24**
**The Burgh Lodge** Falkland 01337 857710. Back Wynd behind main st of Fife's most charming inland village (1792/PALACE, 2012/WALKS). Refurb, friendly, linen provided, log fire. Gr organic restau round corner (903/RESTAU). Run by local community. Ideal for walking in Lomond Hills. 9 rms incl 2 twins.

**1176**
Map 10
**S26**
**Mount Coldingham Sands Youth Hostel** Coldingham off A1 01890 771298. Impressive position & views over N Sea, N of Berwick. Usual ascetics of hostel life (SYH) but vill has some facs. Gr surfing & kayaking spot. An easy walk to the beach for the rest of us & Coldingham is a gr old cove. Cl Oct-Mar.

# The Best Roadside, Seaside & Countryside Inns

**1177**
Map 7
**F18**
✓ ✓ **The Three Chimneys** Colbost, Skye 01470 511258. 7km W of Dunvegan on B884 to Glendale. Rms in a new build across the yard from the excl, long-established and much-awarded Three Chimneys restau (2304/ISLAND RESTAU) called **The House Over-by**. Roadside tho few cars and within sight and smell of the sea. Good standard split-level rms with own doors to the sward. Breakfast lounge, s/serv v healthy buffet. A model of its kind in the Highlands, hence often full. And be sure to book for dinner!
8RMS JAN-DEC T/T PETS CC KIDS LOTS

**1178**
Map 7
**H19**
✓ **Glenelg Inn** Glenelg 01599 522273. At the end of that gr rd over the hill from Shiel Br on the A87 (1667/SCENIC ROUTES)...well, not quite the end because you can drive further round to ethereal L Hourn, but this halt is the civilised hostelry of the irrepressible Chris Main. Decent food, good drinking, snug lounge. Gdn with tables and views. Charming rms. Chris's wife's pictures adorn the walls & his boat *Blossom* may take you to Sandaig or elsewhere on this mystic coast. Yvonne cooks Tues-Sat. Adj cottage (rm7) avail. From Glenelg, take the best route to Skye (7/FAVOURITE JOURNEYS).
6RMS (+1) JAN-DEC X/X PETS XCC KIDS MED.EXP

**1179**
Map 9
**F23**
✓ **Argyll Hotel** Iona 01681 700334. On beautiful, turquoise bay betw Iona & Mull on rd betw ferry & abbey. Daytrippers come & go but stay! This is a charming hotel & a remarkable island. Cosy rms (1 suite), good food (esp vegn) fresh from the organic garden. The real peace & quiet and that's just sitting on the bench outside – it's Colourist country & this is where they would have stayed too.
16RMS EASTER-NOV X/X PETS CC KIDS MED.INX

**1180**
✓ **The Applecross Inn** 01520 744262. The legendary end of the rd, seaside inn on the shore opp Applecross. Report: 1222/GET AWAY HOTELS.
15RMS JAN-DEC T/T PETS CC KIDS MED.INX

**1181**
Map 10
**S26**
**Craw Inn** Auchencrow nr Reston 01890 761253. 5 km A1 and well worth short detour into Berwickshire countryside. Quintessential inn with cosy pub & dining rm. Funky furniture, simple rms. Food decent, wines extraordinary.
3RMS JAN-DEC X/X PETS CC XKIDS INX

**1182**
Map 7
**F17**
**The Stein Inn** Waternish, Skye 01470 592362. Off B886 the Dunvegan-Portree rd, about 10km Dunvegan. In row of cottages on waterside. The 'oldest inn on Skye' with gr pub (open fire, good grub) & comfortable small rms above. Gr value in a special spot. Excl seafood restau adj (1397/SEAFOOD RESTAUS).
5RMS JAN-DEC X/X PETS CC KIDS CHP

**1183** **Plockton Hotel** Plockton 01599 544274. On shoreline of one of Scotland's
Map 7   most picturesque vills (1592/COASTAL VILLS). Dreamy little bay. Many visitors &
**H18**   this pub gets busy, but food is great & rms upstairs are recently refurb & not
without charm.                        11RMS JAN-DEC T/T XPETS CC KIDS MED.INX

**1184** **West Loch Hotel** Tarbert 01880 820283. Beside A83 just W of Tarbert; rea-
Map 9   sonable inx stopover en route to the islands. Comfortably furnished; with
**H25**   some original features. Board games and books dotted around, children welcome in relaxed, friendly atmos. Good value, but roadside rms may be noisy.
8RMS JAN-DEC X/T PETS CC KIDS MED.INX

**1185** **Old Inn** Gairloch 01445 712006. Southern app on A832, tucked away by
Map 7   river and 'old bridge'. Excl pub for food, music (trad & contemp nights
**H16**   Tue/Fri). A recent 'pub of the year'. Nice, simple rms (tho' the pub goes like
a fair). Routinely rec in pub guides.
15RMS JAN-DEC T/T PETS CC KIDS MED.INX

**1186** **Kilberry Inn** nr Tarbert, Argyll 01880 770223. Half-way round the Knapdale
Map 9   peninsula on the single-track B8024 (1682/SCENIC ROUTES), the long way to
**H26**   Lochgilphead. Homely roadside inn with simple inex rms & excl cooking
(1369/GASTROPUBS). A gem.        3RMS MAR-DEC X/T PETS CC KIDS MED.INX

**1187** **Cairnbaan Hotel** Cairnbaan nr Lochgilphead 01546 603668. Main attrac-
Map 9   tion here is the location o/looking lochs of the Crinan Canal – nice to watch
**H25**   or walk (all the way to Crinan) if not messing about on a boat yourself. Decent
pubgrub in or out & less successful dinner menu. Some ales.
12RMS JAN-DEC T/T PETS CC KIDS MED.INX

**1188** **Pier House** Port Appin 01631 730302. An inn at the end of the rd (the minor
Map 10  rd that leads off the A828 Oban to Ft William) and at the end of the 'pier',
**M24**   where the tiny passenger ferry leaves for Lismore (2287/MAGIC ISLANDS). Bistro
restau with decent seafood (1408/SEAFOOD RESTAUS) in gr setting. Comfy
motel-type rms (more exp o/look the sea & island) & conservatory restau &
lounge. Gr place to take kids.
12RMS JAN-DEC T/T XPETS CC KIDS MED.INX/MED.EX

**1189** **Glenisla Hotel** Kirkton Of Glenisla 01575 582223. 20km NW of Kirriemuir
Map 10  via B951 at head of this secluded story-book glen. A home from home: hearty
**P21**   food, real ale & local colour. Fishers, stalkers, trekkers & walkers all come by.
Miles from the town literally and laterally. Neat rms; convivial bar (sometimes
live music).                        6RMS JAN-DEC X/X PETS CC KIDS MED.INX

**1190** **Meikleour Hotel** Meikleour 01250 883206. Just off the A93 Perth-
Blairgowrie rd (on the B984) by the famously high beech hedge (a Perthshire
icon). Roadside inn with quiet accom & food in dining rm or (more atmos) the
bar. Deals going.                   5RMS JAN-DEC X/T PETS CC KIDS MED.EX

**1191** **Bridge Of Orchy Hotel** Bridge Of Orchy 01838 400208. Unmissable on
Map 9   the A82 (the rd to Glencoe, Ft William and Skye) 11km N of Tyndrum. Old inn
**K22**   extensively refurbished and run as a stopover hotel. Simple, quite stylish rms.
A la carte menu & specials in pub/conservatory. Good spot for the malt on
the W Highland Way (1996/LONG WALKS). Also 54-bed bunkhouse (v chp).
10RMS JAN-DEC T/T PETS CC KIDS MED.INX

**1192** **Cluanie Inn** Glenmoriston 01320 340238. On main rd to Skye 15km before
Map 7   Shiel Br, a trad inn surrounded by the mt summits that attract walkers and
**J19**   travellers – the 5 Sisters, the Ridge & the Saddle (2004/SERIOUS WALKS). Club
house adj has some group accom while inn rms can be high-spec – one with
sauna, one with jacuzzi! Bar food LO 9pm. New management finding its feet
might review bunkhouse prices & rms do vary. Friendly staff.
12RMS+BUNKHOUSE JAN-DEC T/X PETS CC KIDS INX-MED.EX

**1193** **Traquair Arms** Innerleithen 01896 830229. 100m from the A72
Map 10  Gala–Peebles rd towards Traquair, a popular village and country inn that
**Q27**   caters for all kinds of folk (and, at w/ends, large numbers of them). Notable
for bar meals, real ale and family facs. Rms refurb. Nice gdn out back. All food
v home-made. New owners at TGP & additional rms imminent.
20RMS JAN-DEC T/T PETS CC KIDS MED.INX

**1194** **The Kames Hotel** Tighnabruaich 01700 811489. Frequented by passing
Map 9   yachtsmen who moor alongside and pop in for lunch. Good base for all things
**J25**   offshore; marine cruises or a nostalgic journey on a 'puffer', with a gr selec-

tion of malts to warm you up before or after. Hotel on a rolling refurb, keen to be seen as an inn with rms. Great bar tho' the famous lock-ins are over.

10RMS JAN-DEC X/T PETS CC KIDS MED.INX

**1195** **Bridge Of Cally Hotel** Bridge Of Cally 01250 886231. Wayside pub on a
Map 10 bend of the road betw Blairgowrie and Glenshee/Braemar (the ski zone and
**P22** Royal Deeside). Cosy and inexpensive betw gentle Perthshire and the wilder Grampians. Rms quiet & pleasant & good value. Restau & bar meals till 9pm.

18RMS JAN-DEC X/T PETS CC KIDS MED.INX

**1196** **Clachaig Inn** Glencoe 01855 811252. Basic accom but you will sleep well,
Map 9 esp after walking/climbing/drinking, which is what most people are doing
**J21** here. Gr atmos both inside and out. Food avail bar/lounge and dining rm. 4 lodges out back. Harry Potter & film crew was once here.

23RMS JAN-DEC X/T XPETS CC KIDS INX

**1197** **Moulin Hotel** Pitlochry 01796 472196. Kirkmichael Rd; at the landmark
Map 10 crossrds on the A924. Basic rms above and beside notable pub for excl pub-
**N21** food and esp ales – they brew their own out the back. (1338/REAL ALES). They have an annexe across the street. 16RMS JAN-DEC T/T MED.INX

**1198** **Glenmoriston Arms Hotel** Invermoriston Loch Ness 01320 351206. On
Map 7 main A82 betw Inverness (45km) and Ft Augustus (10km) at the Glen
**L19** Moriston corner, and a worthwhile corner of this famous loch side to explore. Busy local bar, fishermen's tales. Bistro over-by (LO 8.30pm – 7 days summer, Thu-Sat in wint) tables o/side in summer. Bar meals look ok and extensive malt list – certainly a good place to drink them. Inn-like bedrms.

8RMS JAN-DEC T/T PETS CC KIDS MED.INX

**1199** **Gordon Arms Hotel** Yarrow Valley 01750 82222. Old Borders coaching inn
Map 10 at historic crossroads deep in James Hogg country (1947/LITERARY PLACES) –
**Q27** there's a letter above the mantlepiece. Recent refurb has brought this place to comfortable as well as cosy. Reasonable accom & decent meals (till 9/10pm). 5RMS (& BUNKHOUSE) JAN DEC X/X PETS CC KIDS INX

✓✓ **Ardeonaig** Loch Tay 01567 820400. On tiny lochside rd, a haven with superb dining. Report: 1214/GET AWAY FROM IT ALL.

✓ **The Harbour Inn** 01496 810330, **The Port Charlotte Hotel** 01496 850360, Islay Reports: 2293/2292/ISLAND HOTELS.

✓ **The Royal At Tighnabruaich** 01700 811239. More hotel perhaps than inn (tho gr pub meals), but top service & attention to detail in glorious seaside setting. Report: 781/ARGYLL HOTELS.

✓ **The Sorn Inn** Sorn, Ayrshire 01290 551305 Report: 1348/GASTROPUBS.

**Anchor Hotel** Kippford 01556 620205. Report: 821/SW HOTELS/RESTAUS.

# The Best Restaurants With Rooms

**1200** ✓✓ **The Sorn Inn** Sorn 01290 551305. 8km E of Mauchline on the B743, half an hour from Ayr. Report: 800/AYRSHIRE HOTELS.

**1201** ✓✓ **The Peat Inn** nr Cupar 01334 840206. At eponymous Fife cross-rds. Long-est brilliant restau tho, gulp! for sale at TGP. Report: 907/FIFE RESTAUS.

**1202** ✓✓ **The Three Chimneys** Colbost Skye 01470 511258. State-of-the-art dining & contemp rms far away in the W. Nr Dunvegan. Report: 2289/ISLAND HOTELS.

**1203** ✓ **Lochside Lodge** Bridgend of Lyntrathen nr Alyth 01575 560340. 9km from Alyth towards Glenisla. Excl food. Reports: 931/PERTH HOTELS.

**1204** ✓ **Mackays** Durness 01971 511202. Contemporary make-over of long-established hotel in the far NW. Report: 1221/GET AWAY FROM IT ALL.

**1205** ✓ **The Inn At Kippen** Kippen 01786 871010. Excl bar and restau in cen-tre of vill just off the rd from Stirling to Loch Lomond. Report: 835/CEN-TRAL HOTELS.

1206 ✓ **2 Quail** Dornoch 01862 811811. Centre of town. Small & beautiful. Report: 993/HIGHLAND HOTELS.

1207 **Kilspindie House** Aberlady 01875 870682. Main St of E Lothian Village. Report: 873/LOTHIAN HOTELS.

1208 **The Rocks** Dunbar 01368 862287. At E end of town. O/looking harbour area. Report: 875/LOTHIAN HOTELS.

1209 **Farleyer Restaurant & Rooms** nr Aberfeldy 01887 820332. On the Weem/Glenlyon Rd. A lovely bistro/restau with quite large rms above. Report: 915/PERTH HOTELS.

1210 **Creagan House** Strathyre 01877 384638. Rob Roy & Trossachs country. On the road W and to the islands. Report: 837/CENTRAL HOTELS.

1211 **The Creel Inn** St Margaret's Hope, Orkney 01856 831311. Report: 2327/ORKNEY.

# The Great Get-Away-From-It-All Hotels

1212 ✓ ✓ ✓ **The Carnegie Club** Skibo Castle, Dornoch 01862 894600.
Map 6 Not a hotel, they stress, but listen up! Just over Dornoch Br on
M16 A9 at Clashmore. A vast estate once home to the formidable Carnegies (those halls in NYC, Dunfermline, etc.). They declared it to be 'heaven on earth' which may be your sentiment too. Now it's a club for members only; however you can sample the atmos once, say for a w/end, but to return you join the club. Some club! The sumptuous castle retains its original furnishings (silk wallpaper, panelling, etc.) and the service from your discreet 'hosts' is exemplary. Lodges in the grounds offer more privacy, with the obligatory 2 golf courses (which are solely for guests), spa, gym, pool and 'beach', all oases of relaxing indulgence – vintage Rolls Royces take you around. Many dining options. Everything here has a plus factor.
21RMS(11LODGES) JAN-DEC T/T XPETS CC KIDS LOTS AND LOTS

1213 ✓ ✓ **Monachyle Mhor** nr Balquhidder 01877 384622. Not so very
Map 10 remote, but seems so once you've negotiated the thread of rd
L23 alongside Loch Voil from Balquhidder (only 11km from the A84 Callander-Crianlarich rd) and Rob Roy's now famous grave (1911/GRAVEYARDS). Farmhouse o/looking L Voil from the magnificent Balquhidder Braes. Friendly, cosy and inexp; a place to relax in summer or winter. Rms in courtyard annex are best (5), but all have character. Fishing. Food fairly fab, well-sourced ingredients, 2 AA rosettes. Tastefully done, gr informal atmos.
5+5RMS+2 COTT JAN-DEC T/T PETS CC KIDS MED.INX

1214 ✓ ✓ **Ardeonaig** Loch Tay 01567 820400. On narrow and scenic S Loch
Map 10 Tay rd midway betw Kenmore and Killin. An airy roadside inn by the
M22 water opp Ben Lawers. South African chef/prop making the most of this perfectly remote location. Stylish rms, gr bar & excl dining with top urban standard of service. And friendly! See also 909/BEST TAYSIDE. Upstairs library with cool books and dreamy view of the Ben. Love that loch!
20RMS JAN-DEC T/X PETS CC KIDS MED.EX-LOTS

1215 ✓ ✓ **Loch Torridon** Glen Torridon nr Kinlochewe 01445 791242.
Map 7 Impressive former hunting lodge on lochside, surrounded by
J17 majestic mts. A comfortable but cosy family-run baronial house with very relaxed atmos. For all that, it also focuses on outdoor activities like clay-pigeon shoots, mountain bikes or fishing. Lots of walking possibilities and Diabeg nearby (1602/COASTAL VILLAGES). This gr hotel has now spawned a cheaper travel lodge in the outdoors kind of option: **The Ben Damph Lodges** in adj block with own bar & bistro. Excl budget choice (12 rms, MED.INX). Gr malts in the dwindling day (WHISKY, p. 193).
19RMS JAN-DEC T/T XPETS CC XKIDS LOTS

1216 ✓ **Tiroran House** Isle Of Mull 01681 705232. SW corner on rd to Iona
Map 9 from Craignure then B8035 round Loch na Keal. 1 hr Tobermory. Family-
G22 friendly small co house in fabulous gdns by the sea, being refurb under new

owners Laurence Mackay & Katie Munro (Katie a Cordon Bleu cook). Nr Iona & Ulva ferry; you won't miss Tobermory. Excl food from sea & kitchen gdn. Lovely rms. Sea eagles fly over, otters in the bay.

6RMS+2COTT MAR-NOV X/T XPETS CC KIDS EXP

**1217**
Map 9
**F23**
✓ **Argyll Hotel** Iona 01681 700334. Quintessential island hotel on the best of small islands just large enough to get away for walks & explore (2277/ISLANDS). You can hire bikes (or bring). Abbey is nearby (1914/ABBEYS). 3 lounges (1 with TV, 1 with sun) & 1 lovely suite (with wood-burning stove). Gd home-grown/made food. 15RMS(1SUITE) APR-NOV X/X PETS CC KIDS MED.INX

**1218**
Map 9
**L22**
✓ **Moor Of Rannoch Hotel** Rannoch Station 01882 633238. Beyond Pitlochry and the Trossachs and far W via L Tummel and L Rannoch (B8019 and B8846) so a wonderful journey to the edge of Rannoch Moor & adj station so you could get the sleeper from London & be here for b/fast. 4 trains either way ea day via Glasgow. Literally the end of the road but an exceptional find in the middle of nowhere. Cosy, wood-panelled rms, great restau (open to non-residents). Quintessential Highland Inn. Gr walking.

5RMS JAN-DEC X/X PETS CC KIDS MED INX

**1219**
Map 10
**Q21**
✓ **Glen Clova Hotel** nr Kirriemuir 01575 550350. Well, not that nr Kirriemuir; 25km N to head of glen on B955 and once you're there there's nowhere else to go except up. Rms all en-suite & surprisingly well appointed. Climbers' bar (till all hrs). Superb walking hereabouts (e.g. L Brandy and the classic path to L Muick). A laid-back get-away tho lots of families drive up on a Sun for lunch. Also has (CHP) bunkhouse. Gr value.

10RMS JAN-DEC T/T XPETS CC KIDS MED.INX

**1220**
Map 11
**J30**
✓ **Corsewall Lighthouse Hotel** nr Stranraer 01776 853220. Only 15mins from Stranraer (via A718 to Kirkcolm) and follow signs, but way up on the peninsula and as it suggests a hotel made out of a working lighthouse. Romantic and offbeat, decent food too, and there are attractions nearby esp at Portpatrick 30 mins away thro the maze of quiet backroads.

7RMS (+ SUITES IN GROUNDS) JAN-DEC T/T PETS CC KIDS EXP

**1221**
Map 6
**L12**
✓ **Mackays** Durness 01971 511202. Remote from rest of Scotland (the top NW corner) but actually in centre of township. Many interesting distractions nearby (2085/GOLF, 1872/MONUMENTS, Smoo Cave, etc). A comfortable, contemp restau with rms. Wood & slate: the coolest retreat in the N. Gr food.

7RMS JAN-DEC X/T XPETS CC KIDS MED.INX

**1222**
Map 7
**H18**
✓ **Applecross Inn** Applecross 01520 744262. At the end of the rd (the Pass of the Cattle which is often snowed up in winter, so you can really disappear) N of Kyle of Lochalsh and W of Strathcarron. After a spectacular journey, this waterside inn is a haven of hospitality. Buzzes all seasons. Rms small (1+7 best). Judy Fish & a gr team & a real chef look after you. Poignant VC (2232/HERITAGE), walled garden, lovely walks and even a real pizza hut in summer (1459/COFFEE SHOPS) to keep you happy in Applecross for days.

7RMS JAN-DEC X/X PETS CC KIDS INX

**1223**
Map 9
**K20**
✓ **Corriechoille Lodge** by Spean Bridge 01397 712002. 3km from S Bridge via rd by station. Lovely rd & spectacularly situated; it's great to arrive. Justin & Lucy share their perfect retreat with you in house & chalets outs back. Report 1003/HIGHLAND HOTELS.

5RMS MAR-OCT X/T XPETS CC KIDS INX

**1224**
Map 7
**N16**
✓ **Glenmorangie House** Cadboll by Fearn nr Tain 01862 871671. On the little peninsula E of Tain off A9 (10km). Comfortable mansion once owned by distillery, now by LVMH. Chef has good rep. Class not just in the glass. Report: 980/HIGHLAND HOTELS. 9RMS JAN-DEC T/X XPETS CC XKIDS EXP

**1225**
Map 7
**K20**
**Tomdoun Hotel** nr Invergarry 01809 511218. 20km from Invergarry, 12km off the A87 to Kyle of Lochalsh. A 19th-century coaching inn that replaced a much older one; off the beaten track but perfect (we do mean perfect) for fishing & walking (L Quoich and Knoydart, the last wilderness, have been waiting a long time for you). Superb views over Glengarry and Bonnie Prince Charlie's country. House-party atmos, mix-match furniture & nice dogs. Real chef with meticulously sourced seafd menu.

10RMS JAN-DEC X/X PETS CC KIDS INX

**1226** **The Pier House** Inverie, Knoydart 01687 462347. Currently the only restau
Map 7 on this far-away peninsula, though good grub at the pub nearby
**H20** (1325/BLOODY GOOD PUBS). Accessible on foot (sic) from Kinlochourn (25km) or
Bruce Watt's boat from Mallaig (Mon-Fri summer; Mon, Wed, Fri wint. 01687
462320). Friendly couple offer warm hospitality in their home and surprisingly good cooking for somewhere so remote; rovers often return.
4RMS MAR-OCT X/X XPETS XCC KIDS CHP

**1227** **Doune Stone Lodge** Knoydart 01687 462667. As above, on this remote
Map 7 peninsula & this gr spot on the W tip o/looking a bay on the Sound of Sleat.
**H20** They have own boats so pick you up from Mallaig & drop you round the inlets
for walking. Otherwise 8km from Inverie. Rms & lodge for 12. Own restau.
Only lodge avail in wint. 6RMS(+12) APR-SEP X/X XPETS CC KIDS MED.INX

**1228** **Tomich Hotel** nr Cannich 01456 415399. 8km from Cannich which is 25km
Map 7 from Drumnadrochit. Fabulous Plodda Falls are nearby (1639/WATERFALLS).
**K18** Cosy country inn in conservation village with added bonus of use of swim-
ming pool in nearby steading. Faraway feel, surprising bar round the back.
Good base for outdoorsy w/end. Glen Affric across the way.
8RMS JAN-DEC T/T PETS CC KIDS MED.INX

**1229** **Cape Wrath Hotel** nr Durness 01971 511212. 3km S Durness just off A838; on
Map 6 rd to Cape Wrath Ferry (2040/COASTAL WALKS) which takes you to Britain's farthest-
**L12** flung corner and the Cliffs of Clo Mor. O/looking the loch, the sparsely furnished
hotel is popular with fishermen. Fishing on 2 rivers including the celebrated
Dionard and lochs. Durness Golf nearby (2085/GOLF) and there's some of Britain's
most spectacular and undisturbed coastline to wander. Excl views from some
rms down Kyle of Durness but it is like a setting for something rather morose:
think Ibsen. 14RMS JAN-DEC X/X PETS CC KIDS MED.INX

**1230** **Hart Manor** Eskdalemuir nr Langholm 01387 373217. From N, jnct 17 of
Map 11 M6 (Lockerbie). From S, jnct 44 (Langholm, 25km). A pleasant old house out-
**P29** side the village with views along the valley. Clean, fresh, calm & home-made
– that nice pastry. 6RMS JAN-DEC X/T PETS CC KIDS MED.INX

## ALSO ...

✓ ✓ **Knockinaam Lodge** nr Portpatrick 01776 810471. Report:
814/SOUTH WEST HOTELS

✓ ✓ **Glenapp Castle** Ballantrae 01465 831212. Report: 1128/CO HOUSE
HOTELS

✓ ✓ **Three Chimneys** Skye 01470 511258. Report: 1177/ROADSIDE INNS,
2304/ISLAND RESTAU.

✓ ✓ **Ackergill Tower** nr Wick 01955 603556. Report: 1267/HOUSE PAR-
TIES.

✓ **Glenelg Inn** Glenelg 01599 522273 (Report: 1178/ROADSIDE INNS).

**Stein Inn** Skye 01470 59232 (Report: 1182/ROADSIDE INNS).

# Great Wild Camping Up North

*In Scotland the Best we don't do caravan life style. In fact, because we spend a lot of time behind them on Highland roads, WE HATE CARAVANS, but wild camping is a different matter. Although probably irresponsible to encourage it, it's a good and inexp way to experience Scotland, provided you are sensitive to the environment and respect the rights of farmers and other landowners.*

**1231** **Kintra Islay** Bowmore-Port Ellen rd, take Oa turn-off then follow signs 7km.
Map 9 Long beach one way, wild coastal walk the other. Camping (room also for a
**F26** few caravans) on grassy strand looking out to sea; not a formal site but facs available.

**1232** **Lochailort** A 12km stretch S from Lochailort on the A861, along the south-
Map 9 ern shore of the sea loch itself. A flat, rocky and grassy foreshore with a
**H21** splendid seascape and backed by brooding mtns. Nearby is L nan Uamh where Bonnie Prince Charlie landed (1937/MARY, CHARLIE AND BOB). Once past the salmon farm laboratories, you're in calendar scenery; the Glenuig Inn at the southern end is the pub to repair to. No facs except the sea.

**1233** **Mull** Calgary Beach 10km from Dervaig, where there are toilets; also S of
Map 9 Killiechronan on the gentle shore of L na Keal where there is nothing but the
**F22** sky and the sea. Ben More is in the background (1990/MUNROS). Both sublime!

**1234** **Glen Etive** nr Ballachulish & Glencoe One of Scotland's gr unofficial camp-
Map 9 ing grounds. Along the rd/river side in a classic glen (1630/GLENS) guarded
**K22** where it joins the pass into Glencoe by the awesome Buachaille Etive Mor. Innumerable grassy terraces and small meadows on which climbers and walkers have camped for generations, and pools to bathe in (1707/SWIMMING HOLES). The famous Kingshouse Pub is 2km from the foot of the glen for sustenance, malt whisky and comparing midge bites.

**1235** **Glenelg** Nr the vill of Glenelg itself which is over the amazing hill from Shiel
Map 7 Bridge (1667/SCENIC ROUTES). Vill has gr pub, the Glenelg Inn (1178/INNS) & cof-
**H19** fee shop (1454/COFFEE SHOPS) for sustenance & a shop. Best spots 1km from vill on rd to Skye ferry (1667/SCENIC ROUTES) on the strand.

**1236** **Oldshoremore** nr Kinlochbervie 3km from vill and supplies. Gorgeous
Map 6 beach (1610/BEACHES) & **Polin**, next cove. On the way to **Sandwood Bay**
**K13** where the camping is legendary (but you have to carry everything 7km).

**1237** **Achmelvich** nr Lochinver Signed off the fabulous Lochinver to Drumbeg rd
Map 6 (1674/SCENIC ROUTES) or walk from vill 3km via Ardroe (& a gr spot to watch
**J14** otters that have been there for generations). There is an official campsite adj horrible caravan park, but walk further N towards Stoer. The beach at Alltan na Bradhan with the ruins of the old mill is fabulous. Best seaswimming on this coast.

**1238** **On The Road To Applecross** The rd that winds up the mountain from the
Map 7 A896 that takes you to Applecross (1668/SCENIC ROUTES) is one of the most
**H18** dramatic in Scotland or anywhere. At the plateau before you descend to the coast, the landscape is lunar & the views to die for. Camp here (wind permitting) with the gods. Lay-by & Applecross Inn (1180/INNS) 8km downhill & proper campsite with caff (see next page).

**1239** **Barra** Lots of quiet places but you may as well be next to an amazing beach
Map 5 – one by 'the airport' where the little Otters come & go has added interest (&
**C20** mobile phone reception – unlike rest of the island) but the twin crescent beaches on **Vatersay** are prob too beautiful to miss (1618/BEACHES).

**1240** **Harris** W coast S of Tarbert where the boat comes in. 35km to Stornoway.
Map 5 Follow rd & you reach some truly splendid beaches (eg Scarista 1614/BEACH-
**E16** ES). Bring on your own private sunset.

# Camping With The Kids

*Caravan sites and camp grounds that are especially kid-friendly, with good facilities and a range of things to do (incl a good pub).*

*Key:* HIRE *Caravans for rent* XHIRE *No rental caravans available*
X CVAN *Number of caravan pitches* X TENT *Number of tent pitches*

**1241** **Glen More Camp Site** nr Aviemore  01479 861271. 9km from Aviemore on
Map 7  the road to the ski slopes, the B970. Across the road from the Glen More Visitor
**N19**  Centre and adj to L Morlich Watersports Centre (2134/WATER SPORTS). Extensive
grassy site on loch side with trees and views of the mountains. Loads of activities include watery ones esp the reindeer (1747/KIDS) and at the Coylumbridge
Hotel (1151/HOTELS THAT WELCOME KIDS) where there' s a pool and The Fun House
– a separate building full of stuff to amuse kids of all ages (soft play, mini golf,
etc). Well stocked shop at site entrance.          DEC-OCT XHIRE 240TENT

**1242** **Carfraemill Camping & Caravanning Site** 01578 750697. Just off A697
Map 10  where it joins the A68 near Oxton. Small, sheltered and friendly campsite in
**R26**  the green countryside with trickling burn. 4 chalets for hire on site. Good
gateway to the Borders (Melrose 20km). The Lodge (or Jo's Kitchen as it is
also known) adj has gr family restau where kids made v welcome (play area
and the food they like, etc).          MAR-OCT XHIRE 60TENT

**1243** **Applecross Campsite** 01520 744268. First thing you come to as you app
Map 7  the coast afther your hair-raising drive over the bealach, the mountain pass.
**H18**  Grassy meadow in farm setting 1km sea. Usual facs & Flower Tunnel bakery
& café (1459/COFFEE SHOPS) Apr-Oct. Safe haven.      APR-OCT XHIRE CVAN/TENT

**1244** **Sands Holiday Centre** Gairloch  01445 712152. 4km Gairloch (rd to
Map 7  Melvich) with views to the islands, a large park with its own sandy beach.
**H16**  Kids' play area but plenty to do & see in Gairloch itself – a gr pub, the Old Inn,
for adults (1185/ROADSIDE INNS) & another up the rd to the lighthouse: Mustn't
Grumble (1039/INX HIGHLAND RESTAUS) with adj zoo (sic) – plus walking, fishing,
etc.          JAN-DEC HIRE 100CVAN MANY TENT

**1245** **Boat Of Garten Caravan Park** 01479 831652. In vill itself, a medium-
Map 8  sized, slightly regimented site tailored to families with play area for the kids
**N19**  and even cots available to rent for the very wee. Cabins if the Scottish weather gets too much. Not the most rural or attractive site in the Highlands, but
lots on doorstep to keep the kids happy, incl brilliant Landmark Centre
(1749/KIDS) and Loch Garten ospreys (1765/BIRDS).          AYR HIRE 37TENT

**1246** **Oban Divers Caravan Park** Oban  01631 562755. 1.5 miles out of Oban.
Map 9  Quiet, clean and friendly ground with stream running through. All sorts of
**H23**  'extras' such as undercover cooking area, BBQ, adventure playground. No
dogs. A good base for day trips incl Rare Breeds Farm and Sealife Sanctuary
(1755/1754/KIDS).          MAR-OCT XHIRE 30CVAN 32TENT

**1247** **Shieling Holidays** Craignure, Mull  01680 812496. 35km from Tobermory but
Map 9  right where the ferry comes in. Gr views and a no-nonsense, thought-of-every-
**H22**  thing camp park. Self-catering 'shielings' (carpeted cottage tents with heaters
& en-suite facs) or hostel beds if you prefer. Loads to do & see, incl nearby
Torosay & Duart Castles (1799/1798/CASTLES); the fun & novel Mull Light
Railway.          APR-OCT XHIRE 30CVAN 30TENT

**1248** **Cashel Caravan & Campsite** Rowardennan  01360 870234. Forestry
Map 9  Commission site on the quieter shores of L Lomond in Queen Elizabeth Forest
**L24**  Park. Excellent facilities and tons to do in the surrounding area which incl Ben
Lomond and plootering by the loch.      MAR-OCT XHIRE 100CVAN 135TENT

**1249** **Scoutscroft Holiday Centre** Coldingham  01890 771338. Massive coastal
Map 10  park with every fac under the sun, incl restau, burger bar, cabaret bar, sports
**S26**  bar. Not everyone's cup of tea. It's 1km from lovely Coldingham Sands (wild
camping poss) and kids will love it.          MAR-NOV HIRE 30CVAN 60TENT

# The Best Very Scottish Hotels

**1250**
Map 6
**K15**
✓✓ **The Ceilidh Place** Ullapool 01854 612103. Off main st near pt for the Hebrides. Inimitable Jean Urquhart's place which more than any other in the Highlands, encapsulates Scottish trad culture & hospitality & interprets it in a contemporary manner. Caters for all sorts: there's an excellent hotel above (with a truly comfortable lounge – you help yourself to drinks) & a bistro/bar below with occasional live music & performance (ceilidh-style). A bunkhouse across the way with cheap & cheerful (tho' thin-walled) accom & a bookshop where you can browse through the best new Scottish literature. Scottish-ness is all here & nothing embarrassing in sight. These comments unchanged in 3 editions: that says it all.    23RMS JAN-DEC T/X PETS CC KIDS EXP/CHP

**1251**
Map 6
**J14**
✓✓ **The Albannach** Lochinver 01571 844407. 2km up rd to Baddidarach as you come from S into Lochinver on A837, at the br. Lovely 18thC house in one of Scotland's most scenic areas, Assynt, where the mtns can take your breath away even without going up them (1959/1960/ FAVOURITE HILLS). Colin & Lesley have created an exceptional Highland retreat. The outbuilding o/looking the croft gives extra privacy & space. Rms being turned into gorgeous suites at TGP. You unwind in tasteful, informal surroundings. Food is the best for miles. Gr walk behind house to Archemelvich beach – otters on the way. Non-res can eat.    5RMS MAR-DEC T/X XPETS CC XKIDS MED.INX

**1252**
Map 9
**J22**
✓✓ **Ballachulish House** Ballachulish 01855 811266. On A828 to Oban nr south side of the bridge, not to be confused with the nearby Ballachulish hotel. The house is thro' the golf course which it now owns. Marie McLaughlin in charge will make you v welcome & chef Allan Donald goes from strength to strength winning all awards going, now heading up a v strong team in the kitchen. Gr b/fast to fuel Glencoe walking. Sometimes piper with dinner. This small co house hotel has become a W of Scotland destination. House v Scottish and makes much more of its historical background (Appin murder, Glencoe etc) – tasteful update of 17thC laird's lair.    8RMS JAN-DEC T/X XPETS CC KIDS EXP/LOTS

**1253**
Map 8
**Q19**
✓ **Kildrummy Castle Hotel** nr Alford, Aberdeenshire 01975 571288. 60km W of Aberdeen via A944, through some fine bucolic scenery & the green Don valley to this spectacular location with real Highlands aura. Well placed if you're on the 'Castle Trail', this comfortable chunk of Scottish Baronial has the redolent ruins of Kildrummy Castle on the opposite bluff & a gorgeful of gdns betw. Some rms small, but all v Scottish. Romantic in autumn when the gdns are good. J/tie for dinner.    16RMS FEB-DEC T/T PETS CC KIDS LOTS

**1254**
Map 7
**H19**
✓ **Eilean Iarmain** Skye 01471 833332. Sleat area on S of island, this snug Gaelic inn nestles in the bay and is the classic island hostelry. A dram in your rm awaits you; from the adj whisky company. Bedrms in hotel best but cottage annex quieter. New suites in adj steading more exp but nice. Food real good in d-rm or pub. Mystic shore walks. Gallery with selected exhibs and shop nearby.    12RMS+4SUITES JAN-DEC T/T PETS CC KIDS EXP/LOTS

**1255**
Map 9
**J20**
✓ **G lenfinnan House** Glenfinnan 01397 722235. Off the Road to the Isles (A830 Ft William to Mallaig). The MacFarlanes have been running their legendary hotel in this historic house for 30 yrs (1938/MARY, CHARLIE AND BOB). Ongoing refurb under the Gibsons retains its charm; the huge rms remain intimate & cosy with open fires. Impromptu sessions & ceilidhs wherever there's a gathering in the bar. Solitude still achievable in the huge grounds, or fishing or dreaming on L Shiel (boat avail 01687 470322). Day trips to Skye & small islands nearby. Quintessential!    17RMS APR-OCT X/X PETS CC KIDS MED.INX-EXP

**1256**
Map 9
**L28**
**Savoy Park** Ayr 01292 266112. 16 Racecourse Rd. In a street and area of many indifferent hotels this one, owned and run by the Henderson family for over 40 yrs, is a real Scottish gem. Many weddings here. Period features, lovely gdn, not too much tartan, but a warm cosy lived-in atmos. Round one of the fireplaces, 'blessed be God for his giftis'. Good place to stop for the Burns Festival (34/EVENTS).    15RMS JAN-DEC T/T PETS KIDS MED.INX

**Crieff Hydro** Crieff 01764 655555. The quintessential Scottish family hotel. (1141/HOTELS FOR KIDS).

**Stonefield Castle** Tarbert 01880 820836 (789/ARGYLL HOTELS).

# Real Retreats

**1257**
Map 11
P29

✓ ✓ ✓ **Samye Ling** Eskdalemuir nr Lockerbie/Dumfries 01387 373232. Bus or train to Lockerbie/Carlisle then bus (Mon-Sat 0870 6082608) or taxi (01576 470480). 2km from village, community consists of an extraordinary and inspiring temple incongruous in these border parts. The complex comprises main house (with some accom), dorm and guesthouse blocks many single rms, a café (open 7 days 9am-5pm) and shop. Further up the hill, real retreats – months and years – in some annexes. Much of Samye Ling, a world centre for Tibetan Buddhism, is still under construction under the supervision of Tibetan masters, but they offer daily and longer stays (£15-25) and courses in all aspects of Buddhism, meditation, tai chi, yoga, etc. Daily timetable, from prayers at 6am and work period. Breakfast/lunch and soup, etc. for supper at 6pm; all vegn. Busy, thriving community atmos; some space cases and holier-than-thous, but rewarding and unique and thriving. This is Buddhism with no celebrity, pure & simple. See also World Peace Centre (below).

**1258**
Map 8
P17

✓ ✓ **Pluscarden** betw Forres & Elgin Fax: 01343 890258. Signed from the main A96 (11km from Elgin) in a sheltered glen S-facing with a background of wooded hillside, this is the only medieval monastery in the UK still inhabited by monks. It's a deeply calming place. The (Benedictine) community keep walled gdns and bees. 8 services a day in the glorious chapel (1915/ABBEYS) which visitors can attend. Retreat for men (14 places) and women (separate, self-catering) with 2 week max and no obligatory charge. Write to the Guest Master, Pluscarden Abbey, by Elgin IV30 8VA; no telephone bookings. Men eat with monks (mainly vegn). Restoration/building work always in progress (of the abbey and of the spirit).

**1259**
Map 8
P17

✓ ✓ **Findhorn Community** Findhorn nr Forres 01309 690311. The world-famous spiritual community (now a foundation) begun by Peter Caddy and Dorothy Maclean in 1962, a village of mainly caravans and cabins on the way into Findhorn on the B9011. Open as an ordinary caravan park and visitors can join the community as 'short-term guests' eating and working on-site but probably staying at recommended B&Bs. Full programme of courses and residential workshops in spiritual growth/dance/healing, etc. Accom mainly at Cluny Hill College in Forres. Many other aspects and facs available in this cosmopolitan and well-organised new-age township. Excl shop (1504/DELIS) and cafe – the Green Room (1377/VEGN).

**1260**
Map 10
L24

✓ **Lendrick Lodge** Brig O' Turk 01877 376263. On A821 scenic rd thro' the Trossachs, 15km from Callander. Nr rd but in beautiful grounds with gurgling river. An organised retreat & get away from it all 'yoga and healing' centre. Yoga/reiki & shamanic teaching thro'out yr. Indiv rms & full board if reqd. New 'River Retreat' being built at TGP will have ensuite rms.

**1261**
Map 10
L23

✓ **Dhana Kosa** Balquhidder 01877 384213. 3km vill on L Voilside 9km from A84 Callander-Crianlarich rd. Gentle Buddhist place with ongoing retreat programmes (1 wk or w/ends in wint). Guidance & group sessions. Dorms hold 3/4. Vegn food. Beautiful setting.

**1262**
Map 9
J27

✓ **The World Peace Centre** Holy Island 01770 601100. Take a ferry from Lamlash on Arran (ferry 01770 600349/600998) to find yourself part of a Tibetan (albeit contemporary) mystery. Escape from the madding crowd on the mainland and compose your spirit or just refresh the parts that need it. Built by Samye Ling Abbots on this tiny Celtic refuge, the centre offers a range of activities to help purge the soul or restore the faith. Day trippers to the island welcome. Can accommodate 60 & has conference/gathering centre. Do phone ahead. Ferries v limited in wint.

**1263**
Map 9
K26

**College Of The Holy Spirit** Millport, Island of Cumbrae 01475 530353. Continuous ferry service from Largs (hourly in winter), then 6km bus journey to Millport. Off main st through gate in the wall, into grounds of the Cathedral of the Isles (1886/CHURCHES) and another more peaceful world. A retreat for the Episcopal Church since 1884, there are 16 comfortable rms, all renovated 2003, some ensuite, in the college next to the church with B&B (around £20). Also half/full board. Morning and night prayer each day, Eucharist on Sun and occasional concerts in summer. Warden available for direction and spiritual counselling. Fine library. Bike hire available on island. Phone the warden. Try the island's gr café (1431/CAFÉS).

**1264** **Carberry Towers** Musselburgh nr Edinburgh 0131 665 3135. Sitting in
Map 10 extensive, well-kept grounds 3km S of Musselburgh, parts of this fine old
**Q25** house date back to the 15th century. Now a Christian residential and conference centre, most accom is in new block 50m away; student-hall standard. Courses for church workers/group weekends which visitors may sometimes join. Not a quiet retreat but inexp for a break; high on 'renewal', low on rock 'n' roll. But they receive 'everyone'.

**1265** **Nunraw Abbey** Garvald nr Haddington 01620 830228. Cistercian com-
Map 10 munity earning its daily bread with a working farm in the land surrounding
**R25** the abbey – but visitors can come and stay for a while and get their heads together in the Sancta Maria Guesthouse (a house for visitors is part of their doctrine). Payment by donation. V Catholic monastic ambience throughout. Guesthouse is 1km from the monastery, a modern complex built to a trad Cistercian pattern. Services open to visitors. Charge by donation.

**1266** **Camas Adventure Centre** Mull 01681 700404. Part of Iona Community
Map 9 near to Fionnphort in S of island. Good bus service then a yomp over the
**F23** moor. On a rocky coast with no electricity, cars, TV or noise except the waves and the gulls. Outdoor activities (e.g. canoeing, hillwalking). 2 dorms; share chores. Week-long stays. You'll probably have to relate but this spiritual place while invoking the simple life & the outdoor life also enjoins the life where you're not alone. May-Sept.

# For The Best House Parties

*Places you can rent for families or friends & have to yourselves.*

**1267** ✓ ✓ **Ackergill Tower** nr Wick 01955 603556. Deluxe retreat in distant
Map 6 north. Totally geared for parties & groups (mostly corporates). 5
**Q13** times a year, eg Valentines/Hogmanay, you can join their 'House Parties'. Fixed price (3 nights minimum stay) all inclusive – this means fab atmos dinners (huge fires & candlelight) but you may not eat in the same place twice. Host of activities (there's even an 'Opera House') & outside, the wild coast. A perfect treat/retreat. Indiv prices on request. You'll prob have to mingle.

**1268** ✓ **Myres Castle** 01337 828350. 2 km Auchtermuchty on Falkland rd. Well-
Map 10 preserved castle/family home in stunningly beautiful gdns. High country
**P24** life though at a price. 9 rms individually & recently refurb to exceptional standard. Formal dining rm, funky kitchen & impressive billiard rm. The perfect setting for a murder mystery shindig. Central to all Fife attractions esp Falkland & St Andrews. £250 per person per night, can take 18. Dinners up to 20.

**1269** ✓ **Glenn House** Traquair 01896 830210. On A709 4km from vill in stun-
Map 10 ning Border scenery, the notable family home of the Tennants (Colin
**Q27** Tennant the man who made Mustique and host to royalty). House reeks of atmosphere and echoes of swinging parties gone by. Hire complete (incl Princess Margaret's bedroom), ballroom, snooker room, etc. Lots of public space & grounds but family don't want to install firedoors in this fab property so only 6 people can stay o/night. £4-5K per w/end. Meals extra but you can BYO. Live like they did!

**1270** ✓ **Drynachan Lodge** nr Nairn 01667 402402. This fab 19thC hunting
Map 8 lodge is on the Cawdor Estate S of Nairn. The castle is signed from all
**N17** over (1794/CASTLES). While there are many cotts here for let this is the big house (sleeps 20) & was personally decked out by Lady Isabella Cawdor. Like all things on the estate it's done with gr taste. Fully staffed, it's like a hip shooting lodge. But it'll cost ya.

**1271** **Carbisdale Castle** Culrain nr Bonar Bridge 01549 421232. Another castle
Map 6 and hugely impressive but on a per head basis, v inexpensive. Carbisdale is
**L15** the flagship hostel of the SYHA (1155/BEST HOSTELS gives directions). From Nov-Feb you can hire the whole place so big Highland hoolies over Xmas/Hogmanay are an option. More than 150 people can be accom in the 32 rms (varying from singles to 12-bed dorms). Per-night price around £1500.

Bring your own chef or muck in. You get the whole place to yourself. Other SYHA hostels can be hired Oct-May. Check 0870 1553255.

**1272** **Glen Feshie Hostel** nr Aviemore 01540 651323. At other end of scale from
Map 7 above, a friendly, independent hostel in the superb walking countryside nr
**N19** Cairngorm and Aviemore. A max of 15 people in dorms of 4, twins and a sin-
gle. Meals provided or self-cater. Main report: 1161/BEST HOSTELS.

**1273** **Cavens, Kirkbean** nr Dumfries 01387 880234. Off A710, the Solway Coast
Map 11 rd 20km S Dumfries. Well-appointed mansion in gorgeous grounds nr the
**N30** beach. Up to 12 guests accom with exclusive use & service. (816/SW HOTELS).

**1274** **Castle Lachlan** Loch Fyne 01369 860669. For directions see Inver Cottage,
Map 9 the tearm on the estate (793/ARGYLL RESTAUS). Stunning setting in heart of
**J24** Scotland scenery, the 18thC ancestral home of the Clan Maclachlan. Beautiful
library, snooker rm – you are guests of Lisa & Ewan Maclachlan. Sleeps 13 (22
for dinner). £2-3K per week. Sumptuous surroundings for rock stars & the rest
of us.

**1275** **Rua Reidh Lighthouse** Melvaig nr Gairloch 01445 771263. End of the rd
Map 6 20km from Gairloch but yes, you can have this lighthouse to yourself. Sleeps
**H16** up to 24 in 8 bedrms (£500 for 2 nights low season, £1600 7 nights New Year
at TGP). Mustn't Grumble pub experience nearby (1039/HIGHLAND INX) &
Gairloch has good food/pub options. Plus the sea & the scenery!

**1276** **Amhuinnsuidhe Castle** Harris 01859 560200. N from Tarbert then W into
Map 5 the faraway strand (for directions see Lost Glen 2313/FANTASTIC ISLAND WALKS).
**E15** Fully staffed, fab food & gothic Victorian castle/shooting & fishing lodge (the
salmon arrive in a foaming mass at the adj river mouth). 12 bedrms can take
20 guests: mainly corporate groups but individs can join at certain times for
a mixed house party. Grand interiors & top fishing on 9 lochs & rivers. This
info supplied by Vivienne Devlin who stayed there – me not!

**National Trust for Scotland** *have many interesting properties they rent out
for w/ends or longer. 0131-243 9331 for details.*

# Scotland's Great Guesthouses

**1277** ✓ ✓ **Balmory Hall** Isle Of Bute 01700 500 669. In Ascog, 6km from Rothsay towards Mount Stuart. Report: 781/ARGYLL HOTELS.

**1278** ✓ ✓ **Dun Na Mara** Benderloch 01631 720 233. Off the A828 Ft William rd. 12 km N of Oban. Report: 780/ARGYLL HOTELS.

**1279** ✓ ✓ **Skirling House** Skirling nr Biggar 01899 860 274. On the A72 3km from Biggar. Report: 849/BORDERS HOTELS.

**1280** ✓ **Ethie Castle** nr Arbroath 01382 808 808. 12km N on rd to Lunen Bay. Report: 912/TAYSIDE HOTELS.

**1281** ✓ **Lerags House** nr Oban 01631 563 381. 7km S of Oban and 4 km from the main A816. Report: 784/ARGYLL HOTELS.

**1282** ✓ **Edenwater House** Ednam nr Kelso 01733 22 4370. On the Kelso-Swinton Rd B6461. 4km from Kelso. Report: 852/BORDERS HOTELS.

**1283** ✓ **Coig Na Sheen** Newtonmore 01540 670 109. Just outside the village towards Ft William, just off the A9. Report: 999/HIGHLAND HOTELS.

**1284** ✓ **Roineabhal** nr Kilchrenan, Loch Awe 01866 833 207. 10km from the A85 rd to Oban nr Taynuilt. Report: 785/ARGYLL HOTELS.

**1285** **Clint Lodge** nr St Boswells 01899 860 274. Near Dryburgh Abbey in Scott country. Report: 858/BORDERS HOTELS.

**1286** **Old Station** nr St Andrews 01334 880 505. On B9131, the Anstruther rd off the A917 St Andrews-Crail (3km). Report: 893/FIFE HOTELS.

**1287** **Lys-Na-Greyne House** Aboyne 01339 887 397. Just off main A93 Deeside rd to Ballater. Report: 950/NE HOTELS.

**1288** **The Bield At Blackruthven** Tibbermore nr Perth 01738 583 238. Crieff rd, from Perth off the ringrd. Report: 925/PERTHSHIRE HOTELS.

**1289** **Craigatin House** Pitlochry 01796 472 478. Surprisingly stylish gh in this traditional tourist town. Report: 926/PERTHSHIRE HOTELS.

**1290** **Tanglewood House** nr Ullapool 01854 612 059. Beautiful house overlooking Loch Broom. Bedrooms and dining have the view. Report: 1019/INX HIGHLAND HOTELS.

**1291** **Feorag House** Glen Borrodale, Ardnamurchan 01972 500 248. Highland house overlooking cove in siren scenery. Report: 1020/INX HIGHLAND HOTELS.

**1292** **Ptarmigan House** Tobermory, Mull 01688 302 863. Modern house with swimming pool high above the village. Report: 2326/MULL.

**1293** **Leny House** Callander 01877 331078: House in its own estate just outside town in the midst of the Trossachs. Report: 842/CENTRAL HOTELS.

**1294** **Doune Stone Lodge** Knoydart 01687 462 667. Remote but comfy house on this faraway peninsula. Will collect from Mallaig. Boat excursions & wonderful walks. Report: 1227/GETAWAY HOTELS.

# Gay Scotland The Best!

## EDINBURGH
### BARS & CLUBS

**1295**
Map 1
**D2**
✓ **New Town Bar** 538 7775. 26 Dublin St. Basement and underground club. Tends to be watering hole for older crowd. No twinkies. Downstairs bar open weekend nights for more shady corners and dance action. Open 7 days till 12/1am, w/ends 2am. Mixed crowd.

**1296**
Map 1
**E1**
✓ **Planet Out** 524 0061. Greenside Pl. Traditionally the pre-club, pre-CCs hangout. Now has loyal following of bright-er, younger things. Handy too for the Hill later on. It has an unthreatening vibe (except for the door dykes). 7 days till 1am. LA 12.45am.

**1297**
Map 1
**E2**
✓ **CC Bloom's** 556 9331. Next to Playhouse. Bar up, (too small) disco down. Now an institution, this is where everybody eventually ends up. Busy bar with karaoke upstairs & club below. It's well... impossibly crowded at weekends. 7 days 7pm-3am (your second-last chance!). LA 1.45am.

**1298**
Map 1
**E2**
**Habana** 558 1270. 22 Greenside Pl adj CCs above. Banging music. Young crowd. Always seems about to lead to trouble but rarely does. 7 days till 1am.

**1299**
Map 1
**B3**
**Frenchie's** 225 7651. Rose St Lane N nr Castle St. Intimate bar quite removed from the East End Pink Triangle. Hence more intimate but no less trashy. Age before beauty so suits all. 7 days till 1am. (Sun midnight.)

**1300**
Map 1
**F2**
**The Regent** 661 8198. Corner of Abbeyhill adj well-known cruising area ('The Gardens of Fun'.). Friendly locals, relaxed, straight-friendly. Even have ales (Deuchars, Cally 80/- & guests). 7 days till 1am.

### OTHER PLACES

**1301**
Map 1
**D1**
✓ **Blue Moon Café** 556 2788. 36 Broughton St. Always busy, the boys and girls serve quick & cool in this all-day café. Attracts lively mixed (& earnest) crowd for food & drink and chat. Exhibitions and 'Out of the Blue' gay accessories shop next door in Barony St. If you are arriving in Edin and don't know anybody, come here first. Food 7 days till 10ish; bar 11/11.30pm. (288/CAFÉS)

**1302**
Map 1
**D1**
✓ **Sala** 478 7069. 60 Broughton St. Tapas bar & restau run by Spanish gels. Hence the bravas & chorizo autentico & atmos Euro – kind of place you do have to fit in. Open Tues-Sun 11am-11pm.

**1303**
Map 1
**D1**
**Claremont Bar & Restaurant** 556 5662. 133 East Claremont St. Small and cheery wee bar. Regular crowd and occasional fetish nights. Bulkies, bears and furries have own nights. Food 7 days till 10pm. Bar 7 days till 1am.

**1304**
Map 1
**D1**
**No. 18** 553 3222. 18 Albert Pl. Sauna for gentlemen (mainly older). Discreet doorway halfway down Leith Walk. Dark rm. Mon-Sat 12noon-10pm. Sun 2-10pm.

**1305**
Map 1
**D1**
**Steamworks** 477 3567. Broughton Market which is at the end of Barony St off Broughton St at the Blue Moon. Modern, Euro-style wet & dry areas. Cubies. Café. Mixed crowd. 7 days 11am-10pm.

### GUESTHOUSES

**1306**
Map 1
**E1**
✓ **Ardmor House** 554 4944. 74 Pilrig St. Quiet mix of contemporary & original design meet in this stylish GH run by nice boys (in the media) who have a gorgeous wee dog called Lola. Family room so straight-friendly. No smk.
5RMS JAN-DEC X/T PETS CC KIDS MED.EXP

**1307**
Map 1
**E1**
**Acorn GH** 554 2187. 70 Pilrig St nr Ardmor (above) & Garlands (below) & the scene (tho' it is a stroll). No twins. Contemp; not gay only. No smk.
5RMS JAN-DEC X/T XPETS CC KIDS MED.INX

**1308**
Map 1
**E1**
**Garlands** 554 4205. 48 Pilrig St. The 3rd of the 3 GH on Pilrig St, Garlands predates others; more old-style here. Prob most gay.
6RMS JAN-DEC X/T PETS CC KIDS CHP

# GLASGOW
## BARS & CLUBS

**1309** ✓ **Delmonica's** 552 4803. 68 Virginia St. Glasgow-stylish pub with long
Map 2 bar and open plan in quiet lane in Merchant City gay quarter. Pleasant
E3 and airy during day but busy and 'sceney' at night, esp w/ends. As they say
in Scots Gay – 'nice if your face fits'. 7 days till 12midnight.

**1310** ✓ **Polo Lounge** 553 1221. 84 Wilson St. Now long-est venue with stylish
Map 2 refurb decor, period furnishings. Something like gents' club meets Euro-
E3 lounge. Downstairs disco (Fri-Sun) with 3am licence; otherwise till 1am (one
of the few pubs in town serving after midnight). (703/GLAS COOL BARS)

**1311** **Waterloo Bar** 229 5891. 306 Argyle St. Scotland's oldest gay bar and it tells.
Map 2 But an unpretentious down-to-earth vibe so refreshing in its way. Old-estab-
C3 lished bar and clientele. Not really for trendy young things. You might not
fancy anybody but they're a friendly old bunch. 7 days till 12 midnight.

**1312** **Court Bar** 552 2463. 69 Hutcheson St, centre of Merchant City area. Long-
Map 2 going small bar that's straight till mid-evening then turns into a fairy. 7 days
E4 till midnight.

**1313** **Bennet's** 552 5761. 80 Glassford St. In the beginning & in the end...
Map 2 Bennet's. Relentless, unashamed disco fun without attitude on 2 floors.
E4 Wed-Sun 11pm-3am, Tue is 'traditionally' straight night.

**1314** **Revolver** 553 2456. 6a John St in basement opp Italian Centre. Civilised
Map 2 subterranea. Gr free juke box, pool, ale. Some uniform nights. 7 days all day
E3 to midnight.

## OTHER PLACES

**1315** **GGLC (Glasgow Gay & Lesbian Centre)** 221 7203. 11 Dixon St in a car-
Map 2 park zone. Café-bar drop-in centre with newspapers, info, 'garden of reflec-
D4 tion', art gallery. Good spot! Daily 11am-midnight.

**1316** **Club Eros** 0845 4562310. 1 Bridge St, first building on left crossing the
Map 2 Jamaica St Br. 3-floor sauna, spa & caff. Dark room. 7 days till 10pm.
C4

**1317** **The Lane** 221 1802. 60 Robertson St, nr Waterloo (*see above*) opp side of
Map 2 Argyle St, lane on rt. You 'look for the green light'. Sauna and private club. You
C4 wouldn't call it upmarket, that cabin fever! 7 days, afternoons till 8/9pm.

**1318** **Belhaven Hotel** 339 3222. 15 Belhaven Terr in heart of W End nr Byres Rd
WE so nr restaus/bars but 15min taxi from gay scene. Gay-friendly rather than
gay. 18RMS JAN-DEC T/T PETS CC KIDS INX

# ABERDEEN

*Gay scene in Aberdeen still in disarray at TGP.*

**1319** **Bar Indigo** 01224 586949. 20 Adelphi Lane off Market St. Bar & disco. Quite
Map 8 friendly – just as well, it's all there is. Call for opening.
T19

# DUNDEE

**1320** **Out** 01382 200660. 124 Seagate. Bar and dancefloor. Everybody knows
Map 10 everybody else, but not you. This may have its advantages. Wed-Sun till
Q23 2.30am. Also ...

**1321** **Brooklyn Bar** 01382 200660. St Andrews Lane. Behind and above Out.
Map 10 Small bar, a pre-club bar on disco nights (reduced tickets avail at bar). Wed-
Q23 Sun till midnight (11pm Sun).

# HOTELS ELSEWHERE

*Not many, but Auchendean more than just 'gay-friendly'.*

**1322** **Auchendean Lodge** Dulnain Bridge 01479 851347. A Highland retreat in an
Map 8 area with lots of outdoorsy things to do. Innovative cooking from their kitchen
N18 garden (35 varieties of potatoes, 10 of basil). (Eric and Ian well on the case;
998/INEXP HIGHLAND HOTELS). This is still the place to take your other half away
from it all. Romance & more. 7RMS MAR-OCT X/T PETS CC KIDS MED.EX

# SECTION 6

*Good Food And Drink*

# Bloody Good Pubs

*Pubs in* Edinburgh, Glasgow *and* Aberdeen *are listed in their own sections.*

**1323**
Map 9
**K23**
✓ ✓ **Drover's Inn** Inverarnan  A famously Scottish drinking den/hotel on the edge of the Highlands just N of Ardlui at the head of L Lomond and 12km S of Crianlarich on the A82. Smoky, low-ceilinged rooms, open ranges, whisky in the jar, stuffed animals in the hall and kilted barmen; this is nevertheless the antithesis of the contrived Scottish tourist pub. Also see 841/HOTELS CENTRAL.

**1324**
Map 9
**G22**
✓ ✓ **The Mishnish** Tobermory  The family-run Mish has always been the real Tobermory. 7 days till late. Often live music from Scot trad to DJs and indie esp Sats. Diff rms, nooks & crannies. Gr pub grub, open fire. Something, as they say, for everybody.

**1325**
Map 7
**H20**
✓ **Old Forge** Inverie Knoydart  01687 462267. A warm haven for visitors to this remote peninsula. Suddenly you're part of the community, real ales and real characters, excl pub grub. Lunch & LO 9pm. Stay along the rd. (1227/GET-AWAY-FROM-IT-ALL)

**1326**
Map 9
**J21**
✓ **Clachaig Inn** Glencoe  01855 811252. Deep in the glen itself down the rd signed off the A82, 5km from Glencoe village. Both the pub with its wood-burning stove and the lounge are woody and welcoming. Real ale and real climbers and walkers. Handy for hostel 2km down rd. Decent food (in bar/lounge and good, inexp accom incl 4 lodges. Clachaig now deep in Harry Potter country. They have beerfests – Oct one a biggie.

**1327**
Map 9
**H23**
**Tigh-An-Truish** Clachan, Isle Of Seil  01852 300242. Beside the much-photographed 'Bridge over the Atlantic' which links the 'Isle' of Seil with the 'mainland'. On B884, 8km from B816 & 22km S of Oban. Country pub with 2 apartments above (with views of br). A place where no one cares how daft your hair looks after a hard day's messing about on boats. Food LO 8.30pm (Mar-Oct).

**1328**
Map 5
**C20**
**Castlebay Bar** Barra · Adj Castlebay Hotel. Brilliant bar. All human life is here. More Irish than all the Irish makeovers on the mainland. Occasional live music incl The Vatersay Boys; conversations with strangers.

**1329**
Map 10
**Q23**
**Taybridge Bar** Dundee  129 Perth Rd. Legendary drinking place. Est 1867: the smoke-filled gloom of a Dundee afternoon. When Peter Howson runs out of Glaswegian gnarled heads, he might come here. Women are present, but usually accompanied by their 'man'.

**$1330**
Map 7
**J19**
**Cluanie Inn** Loch Cluanie  01320 340238. On A87 at head of L Cluanie 15km before Shiel Br on the long rd to Kyle of Lochalsh. A wayside inn with good pub food, a restau and the accom walkers want. Good base for climbing/walking (esp the Five Sisters of Kintail, 2034/SERIOUS WALKS). A cosy refuge. LO 9pm for food.

**1331**
Map 10
**L27**
**Poosie Nansie's** Mauchline  Main St of this Ayrshire vill where Burns lived in 1788. This pub there then, those characters still there at the bar. 4 of his children buried (yes, 4) in the churyard opp. A room in the pub left as was. Living heritage at its most real! Lunch & 6-8 Fri/Sat. Otherwise just the ale.

**1332**
Map 10
**P27**
**Tibbie Shiels Inn** Borders  Off A708 Moffat-Selkirk rd. Occupies its own particular place in Scottish culture, esp literature (1947/LITERARY PLACES) and in the Border hills SW of Selkirk where it nestles between 2 romantic lochs. On Southern Upland Way (1647/WATERFALLS) a good place to stop and refuel.

**1333**
Map 11
**M30**
**The Murray Arms & The Masonic** Gatehouse Of Fleet  2 adj unrelated pubs that just fit perfectly into the life of this gr wee town. The Masonic is the gastropub of the region with gr atmos. Masonic symbols still on the walls of the upstairs rms. Murray Arms has Burns connection. Their food rms go like a fair.

**1334**
Map 7
**L19**
**Lock Inn Fort** Augustus  Busy canalside (Caledonian Canal which joins L Ness in the distance) pub for locals and visitors. Good grub (you should book for the upstairs restau) The Gilliegorm, reasonable malts. Food LO 9.30pm. Some live music. Seats on the canal in summer.

**1335**
Map 11
**L31**
**The Steampacket Inn** Isle of Whithorn  01988 500334. The hub of atmos wee vill at the end of the rd (1603/COASTAL VILLS) south. On harbour that fills & empties with the tide. Gr for ales & food (brunch & LO 9pm AYR).

# Great Pubs For Real Ale

*For pubs in* Edinburgh, *see p. 57–61,* Glasgow *p. 98–102.*

**1336**
Map 10
**Q23**
✓ **Fisherman's Tavern** Broughty Ferry In Dundee, but not too far to go for gr atmos and the best collection of ales in the area. In Fort St near the seafront. Regular ales and many guests. Low-ceilinged and friendly. Inx accom adj (1088/DUNDEE HOTS).

**1337**
Map 10
**R25**
✓ **The Pheasant** Haddington On corner where main st divides. Old-style, real-ale howff claiming to have the best selection in E Lothian. No arguments from us. Rare guests on tap, and local Belhaven brewed along the road in Dunbar. Busy market-town atmos; pool and frequent live music. Mind the parrot and 'spirited' locals at weekend.

**1338**
Map 10
**N21**
✓ **Moulin Inn/Hotel** Pitlochry 4km uphill from main st on rd to Br of Cally, an inn at a picturesque crossrds since 1695. Some rms and big rep for pubgrub, but also for cosy (smoky) bar and brewery out back from which comes 'Moulin Light', 'Ale of Atholl' & others. Live music some Sun. Food LO 9.30pm.

**1339**
Map 10
**M23**
✓ **Royal Hotel** Comrie Main sq; public bar is behind hotel. Distressed-wood & stone-walled howf behind hotel on main st (910/PERTHSHIRE HOTELS). Cask ales & beer garden. Food till 9pm. Good stop, v good in summer.

**1340**
Map 10
**N25**
✓ **The Four Marys** Linlithgow Main st nr rd up to palace so handy for a pint after schlepping around the historical attractions. Mentioned in most beer guides. Half a dozen ales on tap incl various guests. Beer festivals May and Oct. Notable malt whisky collection and popular locally for lunches (daily) and evening meals (Thurs-Sat, LO 8.45pm). Open 7 days.

**1341**
Map 9
**J26**
✓ **The Port Royal** Port Bannatyne nr Rothesay Seafront on Kames Bay in Bute. A 'Russian' tavern with latkas & sauerkraut with your stroganoff. Some live music. 5 rms upstairs & a gr selection of ales. Brill atmos.

**1342**
Map 10
**M24**
**The Tappit Hen** Dunblane By the cathedral. Good ales (usually Deuchars & 4 guests & many malts) , atmos and live music (well, once a month). A good find in these parts.

**1343**
Map 10
**S20**
**Marine Hotel** Stonehaven Popular local on great harbour front with seats o/side; juke box and bar meals inside. Youngish crowd. Has won awards for its cask ales – various on tap. Lounge/restau upstairs. Open all day.

**1344**
Map 10
**N24**
**The Woolpack** Tillicoultry Via Upper Mill St (signed 'Mill Glen') from main st on your way to the Ochils. They come far and wide to this ancient pub. Bar food and a changing selection of ales which they know how to keep. Sup after stroll.

**1345**
Map 7
**M18**
**Clachnaharry Inn** Inverness On A862 Inverness-Beauly rd just outside Inverness o/looking firth & railway, with beer gdn. Long list of regulars posted, 5/6 on tap incl Clachnaharry Village Ale. Local fave for pub food. Friendly, let's say harmonious.

**1346**
Map 8
**R17**
**The Shore Inn** Portsoy Down at the harbour good atmos (& ales). Food all day in summer, weekends only in winter. A central plank & seat at the Trad Boats fest (39/EVENTS). May be quiet other times, but a gr pub.

**1347**
Map 7
**H16**
**The Old Inn** Gairloch Southern app on A832 nr golf course, an 'old inn' across an old br; a goodly selection of malts. Some real ales in the cellar. Tourists and locals mix in season, live music some nights. Tasteful Solas Studio Gallery adj (2190/ART). Rms above make this an all-round good reason to stop in Gairloch (1185/ROADSIDE INNS).

**The Masonic Arms** Gatehouse of Fleet 825/SW RESTAUS; **The Steam Packet** Isle of Whithorn 1335/BLOODY GOOD PUBS. The 2 pubs in the SW that look after their ale (& their drinkers).

# The Best Gastropubs

*Gastropubs in* Edinburgh *&* Glasgow *are listed in their own sections.*

**1348**
Map 10
**L27**
✓ ✓ **The Sorn Inn** Sorn 01290 551305.Main St of vill, 8km E of Mauchline 25 km Ayr. Pub with rms & big rep for food. Restaus & tables in bar. Family-run (the Grants with chef Craig Grant). Gastropub of the Yr 2005 & Michelin Bib Gourmand. Everything just so. Lunch & LO 9pm (8pm in bar).

**1349**
Map 10
**M24**
✓ ✓ **The Inn At Kippen** Kippen 01786 871010. The newer place in town (well, village) & country, but this place is significantly on the foodie map. Gr value & excl special menu for kids. Suddenly Kippen is the village pub destination of central Scotland (see also below). 4 rms (report: 835/CENTRAL HOTELS). 7 days, lunch & LO 9pm.

**1350**
Map 10
**R26**
✓ ✓ **Black Bull** Lauder 01578 722208. Main St of ribbon town on the A68 betw Edin & the Borders, but nr enough the city to be a destination meal. 7 individ rms above, diverse rms below. Some gr Mod Brit cooking with excl wine list. 7 days. LO 9pm.

**1351**
Map 6
**J15**
✓ ✓ **The Summer Isles Hotel Bar** Achiltibuie 01854 622282. The adj bar of this long-est romantic hotel on the foreshore facing the isles & the sunset (981/HIGHLAND HOTELS). All the superior qualities of their famous (Michelin) food operation avail at less than half the price in the cosy bistro-like bar. Gr seafd & vegn. Apr-Oct, lunch & LO 8.30pm.

**1352**
Map 10
**R23**
✓ ✓ **The Grange Inn** St Andrews 01334 472670. 4km out of town off Anstruther/Crail rd A917. Perenially pop. Mike & Lena Singer have built on long rep of this almost Englishy pub with cosy rms & comfort food with flair. Lunch & dinner (not Sun even or Mon) LO 8.30pm. Must book w/ends.

**1353**
Map 8
**S20**
✓ **Lairhillock** nr Netherley, Stonehaven 01569 730001. Known forever for gr pubfood (7 days lunch & dinner) more informal and downright friendly. Fine for kids. Superb cheese selection, notable malts and ales. Can app from S Deeside Rd, but simplest direction for strangers is: 15km S of Aber by main A92 towards Stonehaven, then signed Durris, go 5km to country crossrds. **The Crynoch Restaurant** is adj (1054/ABER RESTAUS).

**1354**
Map 10
**S26**
✓ **The Wheatsheaf** Swinton betw Kelso & Berwick 01890 860257. A hotel pub in an undistinguished village about halfway betw the 2 towns (18km) on the B6461. In deepest, flattest Berwickshire, newish owners Chris & Jan Winson serve up the best pub grub you've had since England. 7 rms adj. An all-round good hostelry. Lunch, 6-9.30pm. Cl Mon.

**1355**
Map 9
**L26**
✓ **Fox And Hounds** Houston On B790 village main st in Renfrewshire, 30km W of Glasgow by M8 jnct 29 (A726), then cross back under motorway on B790. Village pub home to Houston brewery with gr ales, excl pubfood and dining-rm upstairs for family meals and suppers. Folk come from miles around. Sunday roasts. Fine for kids. Lunch and 6-10pm (all day w/ends). Restau 01505 612448. Bar till midnight.

**1356**
Map 10
**M24**
✓ **The Cross Keys** Kippen 01786 870293. Here forever in this quiet backwater town off the A811 15km W of Stirling. Bar meals by coal fire, à la carte and family restaus. An old-style pub food stop, for a'body. LO 9pm.

**1357**
Map 9
**L27**
✓ **Wheatsheaf Inn** Symington nr Ayr 01563 830307. 2km A77. Pleasant village off the unpleasant A77 with this busy coaching inn opposite church. Folk come from miles arouné to eat (book at w/ends) honest-to-goodness pub fare in various rms (roast beef every Sunday). Menu on boards. Beer gdn. LO 9.30pm.

**1358**
Map 7
**N19**
✓ **Old Bridge Inn** Aviemore Off Coylumbridge rd at S end of Aviemore as you come in from A9 or Kincraig. 100m main st but sits in hollow. An old inn like it says with basic à la carte and more interesting blackboard specials. Three cask ales on tap. Kids' menu that is not just pizza & chips, ski-bums welcome. Lunch & 6-9pm. In summer, tables over rd go down to river. New hostel adj (1158/HOSTELS). LO 9.30pm.

**1359**
Map 6
**K14**
✓ **Kylesku Hotel** Kylesku 01971 502231. Off A894 betw Scourie & Lochinver in Sutherland. A hotel & pub with a gr quayside location on L Glencoul where boats leave for trips to see the 'highest waterfall in Europe'

(1644/WATERFALLS, 1037/INEXP HIGHLAND RESTAUS). Friendly atmos with local fish, seafood (esp with legs: the prawn thing!) & yummy desserts. Noon-9pm.

**1360** ✓**Ship Inn** Elie Pub on the bay at Elie, the perfect toon in the picturesque
Map 10 East Neuk of Fife (1600/COASTAL VILLAGES). In summer a huge food opera-
R24 tion: bar, back rm, next door & upstairs (latter has good view, book w/ends).
Same menu throughout and blackboard specials. Real popular place esp in
summer when terrace o/looking the beach goes like Bondi. LO 9pm. Also has
5 chp rms adj in summer (01333 330246).

**1361** ✓**Smiddy Bar at the Kingarth Hotel** Isle of Bute 01700 831662. 13 km
Map 9 Rothesay 24km after Mt Stuart (1852/CO HOUSES). Good, friendly old inn
J26 prob serving the best food on the island. Blackboard menu. The atmos is just
right. Open AYR. LO for food 8pm.

**1362** ✓**Cochrane Inn** Gatehead 01563 570122. Part of the Costley hotel empire
Map 9 (875/HOTELS IN AYRSHIRE). A trim & cosy ivy-covered, v inn-like inn – most
L27 agreeable. On A759 Troon to Kilmarnock & 2km A71 Kilmarnock-Irvine rd. Excl
gourmet pub with huge local rep – must book w/ends. Lunch & LO 9pm.

**1363** ✓**Old Mill** Killearn 01360 550068. Main St. More than one notable inn in
Map 10 this village but this is cosy, friendly, all an old pub should be (old here is
M25 from 1774). Pub & restau. Log fires, nice for kids. Garden. Oh & the chef
worked with Marco Pierre White & the brothers Roux: try the specials! 7 days
12-9.30pm, Sun from 12.30.

**1364** **Hunting Lodge Hotel** Falkland 01337 857226. Main st of much visited
Map 10 town in central Fife, opp the fabulous Palace (1792/CASTLES). All day menu of
Q24 mainly stalwarts like 80/- ale steak pie and macaroni cheese. Lounge &
restau in back. Open 7 days. LO 8pm.

**1365** **Lion & Unicorn Thornhill** Trossachs 01786 850204. On A873 off A84 rd
Map 10 betw the M9 and Callander & nr Lake of Menteith. On main rd thro' nonde-
M24 script vill. They come from mls around for pubgrub & sizzling steaks. Cosy
dining areas & gdn. Changing menu, not fancy. 7 days. LO 9pm.

**1366** **Goblin Ha' Hotel** Gifford 01620 810244. Twee village in the boondocks;
Map 10 one of 2 hotels (877/LOTHIANS HOTELS). This, the one with the gr name, serves
R26 a decent pub lunch and supper (6-9pm; 9.30pm on Fri and Sat) in lounge and
more basic version in the pub. Conservatory and 'Biergarten'; kids' play area.

**1367** **The Byre** Brig O' Turk 01877 376292. Off A821 at Callander end of the village
Map 10 adj Dundarroch Hotel and L Achray. Ann Parks back in this country inn in
L24 deepest Trossachs. More change of ownership, we don't know what to say.
Good o/side deck? Reports please!

**1368** **Drover's Inn** East Linton 01620 860298. A village off A1, 35km from Edin.
Map 10 A notable & hospitable E Lothian hostelry within reach of city. Restau
R25 upstairs, bistro with blackboard specials down. Can eat alfresco in summer
with trains whooshing by (158/EDIN PUBS WITH GOOD FOOD). LO 9.30pm.

**1369** **Kilberry Inn** nr Tarbert, Argyll 01880 770223. On the single-track B8024
Map 9 that follows the coast of the Knapdale peninsula betw Lochgilphead &
H26 Tarbert, this is out on its own. Fortunately Clare Johnson (formerly the
Anchorage, Tarbert) is a gr cook & the bar has a lovely ambience. So make the
journey (1682/SCENIC ROUTES) for lunch or dinner. Cl Mon. Mar-Dec.

**1370** **Archiestown Hotel** Archiestown 01340 810218. On square of small
Map 8 Speyside vill, more a bistro perhaps than a mere pub (in fact there's no bar at
P18 all) but mentioned here because it is top quality, unpretentious pub-type grub
& so you don't miss it. See also 968/SPEYSIDE. 7 days, LO 9pm; big Sun lunch.

**1371** **The Creel Inn** Catterline nr Stonehaven 01569 750254. 2km from main
Map 10 A92 Arbroath-Stonehaven rd 8km S Stonehaven (signed) perching above the
S21 bay from where the lobsters come. And lots of other seafd. Gd wine & huge
beer selection. Cove itself a bit spooky. Catterline is Joan Eardley (the notable
artist) territory. 7 days lunch & LO 9pm.

**1372** **The Crown** Portpatrick 01776 810261. Hugely popular pub on harbour with
Map 11 tables o/side in summer. Light, airy conservatory at back serving freshly
J30 caught fish. 12rms above. Locals & Irish who sail over for lunch (sic). LO
10pm.

**1373** The Ship Inn Broughty Ferry Excellent seafront (Tay estuary – last time we
Map 10 saw dolphins outside) snug pub with food upstairs and down (best tables at
**Q23** window upstairs). Famous for clootie dumpling. 7 days, lunch and 5-9pm
(1100/DUNDEE EAT).

**1374** The Auld Cross Keys Inn Denholm nr Hawick 01450 870305. Not a lot to
Map 10 recommend in Hawick, so this village pub with rms is worth the 8km journey
**R28** on the A698 Jedburgh rd. On the Green, with pub and dining lounges through
the back. Blackboard menu, heaps of choice. Curries on Mon/Tues at TGP.
Real fire & candles. Sun carvery. Open late Thur-Sat (Sun 11pm). 3 rms if you
want to stay (CHP).

Moulin Inn Pitlochry 01796 472196. Report: 1197/ROADSIDE INNS.

Old Clubhouse Gullane 01620 842008. Report: 887/LOTHIANS HOTELS.

Old Inn Gairloch 01445 712006. AA Pub of the Year 2003. Report:
1118S/ROADSIDE INNS.

The Masonic Gatehouse Of Fleet 01557 814335. Report: 825/SW RESTAUS.

# The Best Vegetarian Restaurants

*Not surprisingly, perhaps, there are precious few completely vegetarian restaus in
Scotland. But there are lots in* Edinburgh *(see p. 44) & some in* Glasgow *(see p.
92).*

**1375** ✓ Kilmartin House Café Kilmartin 01546 510278. Attached to early-
Map 9 ✓ peoples' museum (2238/MUSEUMS) in Kilmartin Glen & on main rd N of
**H24** Lochgilphead. Organic garden produce incl tisanes for the revitalising that
the gr range of home-made lunches (& dinners) don't fix. Not 100% vegn but
as nr as dammit. 7 days, hot food till 3pm, cakes till 5pm & dinner Thur-Sat
in summer. CHP

**1376** ✓ Pinto's Lochgilphead 01546 602547. So unlikely (in Lochgilphead!) this
Map 9 ✓ has to be a gr find – 1 Argyll St nr main rd thro' town. Chef/prop Ian Ward
**H25** bravely bringing vegn food to the wild west. Gr Sun brunches (all vegn) &
special menus eg Mezze, Spanish. Somebody should give this man an award!
Vegan options. Tues-Sat, Lunch & LO 9pm.

**1377** ✓ Green Room at Findhorn Community Findhorn You will go a long
Map 8 ✓ way in the N to find real vegn food, so it may be worth the detour from
**P17** the main A96 Inverness-Elgin rd, to Findhorn and the famous commune
(1259/RETREATS) where there is a gr deli (1504/DELIS) and a pleasant caff by the
'Hall'. 7 days till 5pm and evens if event in the hall. (Hot food till 3pm.) CHP

**1378** ✓ Musicker Rothesay 01700 502287. On High St opp castle. Gr pastries,
Map 9 ✓ paninis & soups, range of coffee (soya milk if you want). Nice books,
**J26** newspapers, bluesy – jazz CDs for sale. Friendly, relaxed. All this info supplied
by Leslie Hills who is v often right. Tues-Sat 10am-5pm. CHP

**1379** An Tuireann Portree, Skye Off Uig (then Struan) rd (at the Co-op). Excl gallery
Map 7 cafe & restau with contemp menu; salads, hot meals, snacks. Some bacon
**G18** creeps in, but mostly vegn. 10am-4.30pm. Tues-Sat. Changing exhibs. CHP

**1380** The Mountain Restaurant Gairloch 01445 712316. Vegn-friendly restau
Map 7 with conservatory and tables outside with mt view. Bookshop and adj Nature
**H16** Shop with every kind of spiritual whatsits you may want. We've had com-
plaints about the price of tea and scones – but look at the size of them! Self-
serv food all day. All seems kinda American & v welcome this far N. Mar-Nov
till 6pm (later July/Aug). INX

# The Best Vegetarian-Friendly Places

### 1381 HIGHLANDS
Map 7

**The Ceilidh Place** Ullapool  01854 612103 (996/INEXP HIGHLAND HOTELS).

**Café Number One** Inverness  01463 226200 (1116/INVERNESS).

**Three Chimneys** Skye  01470 511258 (2304/ISLAND RESTAUS).

**The Seafood Restaurant** Kyle of Lochalsh  (1022/INEXP HIGHLAND RESTAUS).

**Riverside Bistro** Lochinver  01571 844356 (1032/INEXP HIGHLAND RESTAUS).

**Plockton Hotel**  01599 544274 (1183/ROADSIDE INNS).

**Off the Rails** Plockton  01599 544423 (1023/INEXP HIGHLAND).

**Summer Isles Hotel Bar**  01854 622282 (1351/GASTROPUBS).

### 1382 NORTH EAST
Map 8

**The Foyer** Aberdeen  01224 582277 (1053/ABER RESTAUS).

**Beautiful Mountain** Aberdeen  01224 645353 (1061/ABER RESTAUS).

**Milton Restaurant** Crathes  01330 844566 (958/NE HOTELS)

### 1383 ARGYLL
Map 9

**Argyll Hotel** Iona  01681 700334 (1179/SEASIDE INNS).

**Inver Cottage**  01369 860537 (793/ARGYLL RESTAUS).

**The Green Welly Stop** Tyndrum  01838 400271.

**The Royal At Tighnabruaigh**  01700 811239 (782/ARGYLL HOTELS).

**Julie's Coffee House** Oban  01631 565952. (2334/OBAN).

### 1384 FIFE & LOTHIANS
Map 3

**Pillars Of Hercules** nr Falkland  01337 857749 (1448/BEST TEARMS).

**Ostler's Close** Cupar  01334 655574 (900/FIFE RESTAUS).

**The Vine Leaf** St Andrews  01334 477497 (2340/ST ANDREWS).

**Waterside Bistro** Haddington  01620 825674 (882/LOTHIANS RESTAUS).

**Old Clubhouse** Gullane  01620 842008 (887/LOTHIANS RESTAUS).

**Drover's Inn** East Linton  01620 860298 (158/EDIN GASTROPUBS).

**Livingston's** Linlithgow  01506 846565 (880/LOTHIAN RESTAUS).

### 1385 CENTRAL
Map 10

**Let's Eat** Perth  01738 643377 (929/PERTHSHIRE RESTAUS).

**Monachyle Mhor** nr Balquhidder  01877 384622 (1213/GET-AWAY-FROM-IT-ALL).

**The Old Armoury** Pitlochry  01796 474281 (936/PERTHSHIRE RESTAUS).

### 1386 SOUTH & SOUTH WEST:
Map 10

**Marmions** Melrose  01896 822245 (861/BORDERS EATS).

**Philipburn** Selkirk  01750 20747 (855/BORDERS HOTELS).

**The Masonic** Gatehouse Of Fleet  01557 814335. Report: 825/SW RESTAUS.

### 1387 ORKNEY
Map 3
Q10

**Woodwick House** Evie, Orkney  01856 751330. B&B, seals, music and woodland. (2327/ORKNEY)

# The Best Seafood Restaurants

*For seafood restaus in* Edinburgh, *see p. 44; for* Glasgow, *see p. 92.*

**1388**
Map 10
**R24**
✓ ✓ **The Cellar** Anstruther 01333 310378. For many yrs now the best seafood restau in Scotland. Behind Fisheries Museum in busy East Neuk of Fife town. Fish & shellfish from only the best waters, some meat options. Cosy French bistro atmos. Report: 899/FIFE RESTAUS. **MED**

**1389**
Map 6
**P12**
✓ ✓ **The Captain's Galley** Scrabster 01847 894999. The place to eat on the N coast. A rep built on total integrity. All local produce (from 50 ml radius). No tuna here, just what they catch (conservation ethos in menu). Tho' menu rel short (4 choices), it's come straight off a boat. Nice rm, nice guy (Jim Cowie): even the fish would approve. Home-made bread, ice-cream, everything. Other restaurantiers take note: this is the future for food we want. 7 days dinner 2 sittings (but check). **MED**

**1390**
Map 8
**T19**
✓ ✓ **Silver Darling** Aberdeen 01224 576229. Down by harbour. For many yrs one of the best restaus in the city and the NE. Exquisite chargrilled seafood. Report: 1164/ABER RESTAUS. **MED**

**1391**
Map 10
**R23**
✓ ✓ **The Seafood Restaurant** St Andrews 01334 479475. Opened autumn '03 & effortlessly became the top spot in town. Landmark position (o/looking Old Course) & building – glass-walled pavilion. Chef/prop Craig Millar is brilliant with (esp) white fish & the little things that make it zing. Gr wines, rich puds but mainly fish pure & simple. 7 days lunch & dinner LO 10pm. **MED**

**1392**
Map 10
**R24**
✓ ✓ **The Seafood Restaurant** St Monans, Fife 01333 730327. W end of East Neuk Village. As St Andrews (above), Butler family offer simple title & no fuss in menu either. Conservatory & terrace o/looks sea, waves lap, gulls mew etc. Bar menu lunch & dinner LO 10pm Cl Mon/Tues in wint. **MED**

**1393**
Map 9
**K27**
✓ ✓ **MacCallum's Of Troon Oyster Bar** 01292 319339. Right down at the quayside, so follow the signs for Seacat & go the extra mile. 3km from centre. Red brick building with discreet sign, so eyes peeled. Lovely fish, great atmos, unpretentious and worth the trip even from Glasgow. Tues-Sat lunch and LO 9.30pm. Sun lunch only. **MED**

**1394**
Map 9
**H25**
✓ **The Anchorage** Tarbert 01880 820881. Discreet, quayside bistro in quintessential Argyll port. We haven't tried since previous owners put this firmly on the seafood map, when it was the best place to eat in these peninsulas. Reports please. **MED**

**1395**
Map 9
**H23**
✓ **The Waterfront Oban** 01631 563110. On the waterfront at the station and upstairs from unimposing entrance a light, airy rm which nevertheless is poss serving the best seafood around in authentic setting. Blackboard specials change daily. The fish leap upstairs & onto your plate. somewhere in Oban to linger on the way to the ferry. Mar-Dec. L & LO 9pm. **MED**

**1396**
Map 9
**H23**
✓ **Ee-usk Oban** 01631 565666. New build on the north pier by the indefatigable Macleod's (adj an Italian restau in a similar building which they also run). Seafront caff with urban bistro feel, gr views & fish from that sea. Good wee wine list. 7 days lunch & LO 9.30pm. **MED**

**1397**
Map 7
**F17**
✓ **Lochbay Seafood Skye** 01470 592235. 12km N Dunvegan; A850 to Portree, B886 Waternish peninsula coastal route. A scenic Skye drive leads you to the door of this small cottage at end of the village row. O/looks water where your scallops, prawns & oysters are surfaced. Main dishes served unfussily with puds like clootie dumpling. Simply v good – you'll need to book. Apr-Oct; lunch & LO 8.30ish. Cl Sun & Sat (except Sat dinner in season). **MED**

**1398**
Map 9
**K23**
✓ **Loch Fyne Seafood & Smokery** 01499 600264. On A83 the L Lomond to Inveraray rd, 20km Inveraray/11km Rest and Be Thankful. Landmark roadside restau and all-round seafood experience on the way out west. Tho now a huge UK chain this is the original. This restau not actually in the chain – a separate entity after management buy-out. People come from afar for the oysters & the smokery fare, esp the kippers. Spacious, & recent re-arrangements have opened it out more. House white (other whites & whisky) well chosen. Same menu all day; LO 8.30pm. Shop sells every conceivable packaging of salmon & other Scots produce; shop 8pm. **INX**

**1399**
Map 10
S20
✓ **The Tolbooth** Stonehaven 01569 762287. On corner of harbour, long one of the best restaus in the area in a great setting – oldest building in town. Upstairs bistro with owner Robert Cleaver who also has the Art Deco restau in town (956/NE RESTAUS) v on the case here. Reliably fresh & simple. Gr lobster. Wed-Sun lunch & dinner, LO 9pm.                                    MED

**1400**
Map 9
K26
✓ **Fins** Fairlie nr Largs 01475 568989. On main A78 S of Fairlie a seafood bistro, smokery (Fencebay), shop and craft/cookshop. Roadside fish farm bistro, best place to eat for miles in either direction. Chefs Jane, Paul & Gary use exemplary restraint and the wine list is similarly to the point. Nice conservatory with geraniums. Lunch & dinner LO 8.30/9pm. Cl Mon.          INX

**1401**
Map 9
L26
✓ **Creelers** Brodick, Arran 01770 302810. Just outside Brodick on rd N to castle in uninspiring plastic gift plaza tho' the cheese shop is nice (1528/CHEESES). Excl seafood bistro – gr food, fun staff tho' as always on islands they come & go. Phone ahead, to be sure. Easter-Oct. Cl Mon.   MED

**1402**
Map 11
J30
✓ **Campbell's** Portpatrick 01776 810314. Friendly, harbourside restau in immensely popular Portpatrick. Some meat dishes, but mainly seafood. Sardines were nice. 7 days lunch & LO 10pm. Cl Jan-Mar & Mons.          MED

**1403**
Map 10
P23
**Keracher's** Perth 01738 449777. Corner of South St & Scott St. Fish counter at street level, designery restau upstairs. Keracher's are major fish wholesalers & supply most of the best hotel dining rms in Perthshire, so they know their mullet. Lunch Tues-Sat, dinner Mon-Sat LO 10pm.       INX/MED

**1404**
Map 9
K21
**Crannog at the Waterfront** Fort William 01397 705589. Crannog for many yrs on the pier downtown, now moved to Waterfront development on lochside to N. Nice bright contemp setting, not only gr seafood but the best restau in this rainy town. 7 days, lunch & LO 9pm (later w/ends).   MED

**1405**
Map 8
S17
**The Harbour Restaurant & Café** Gardenstown nr Banff 01261 851690. Tiny caff right on the harbour in one of many enchanting Moray Coast vills (1593/COASTAL VILLS), this the only caff. Handful of tables in & out. Simple fish preps & home-baking. Charly & Fiona Pretorians, a long way from S Africa. April-end Sept 12-9pm. 7 days.                                    CHP

**1406**
Map 6
K13
**Seafood Café** Tarbet nr Scourie 01971 502251. Charming conservatory restau on cove where boats leave for Handa Island bird reserve (1758/BIRDS). Julian catches your seafood from his boat & Jackie cooks it; they have the Rick Stein seal of approval. Cheesecake for dessert. Located at end of unclassified rd off the A894 between Laxford Br & Scourie; best phone to check openings. Apr-Sept: Mon-Sat 12-8pm. Some Sun in summer. Licensed.             INX

**1407**
Map 7
H18
**Kishorn Seafood Bar** 01520 733240. On A896 at Kishorn on rd betw Lochcarron (Inverness) and Sheildaig nr the rd over the hill to Applecross (1668/ROUTES). Fresh local seafood in a roadside diner: Kishorn oysters, Applecross crab; lobsters in a tank out back. Light, bright and a real find in the middle of beautiful nowhere courtesy of the enthusiastic Viv Rollo. Apr-Oct daily 10-5pm (9pm July/Aug). Sun 12-5pm.                    MED

**1408**
Map 9
J22
**The Pierhouse** Port Appin 01631 730302. At the end of the minor rd and 3km from the A828 Oban-Ft William rd in Pt Appin village rt by the tiny 'pier' where the passenger ferry leaves for Lismore. Locally caught seafood (Lismore oysters, Mallaig flatfish, hand-dived shellfish) is handed over fresh to the door by boat. Lively atmos, wine and wonderful view. (1188/INNS)  INX

**1409**
Map 9
J26
**The Seafood Cabin** Skipness 01880 760207. Adj Skipness Castle, signed from Claonaig where the CalMac ferry from Lochranza arrives. Cabin, outdoor seating & indoor options in perfect spot for their fresh & local seafood snacks & cakes. Mussels come further (L Etive). Smoked stuff from Creelers in Arran. June-Sept. 11-6pm. Cl Sat.                                    CHP

**1410** **Applecross Inn** 01520 744262. The inn at the end of the rd with excl fresh seafd & classic fish 'n' chips. Report: 1222/GETAWAY HOTELS.

# The Best Fish & Chip Shops

**1411**
Map 1
**B1**
✓✓ **L'Alba D'Oro** Edinburgh Henderson Row, nr corner with Dundas St. Large selection of deep-fried goodies, incl many vegn savouries. Inexpensive proper pasta, real pizzas and superb, surprising Italian wine to go. This is still the chip shop of the future. Open until midnight. (187/EDIN PIZZA)

**1412**
. Map 10
**Q24**
✓✓ **Valente's** Kirkcaldy 01592 651991. 73 Overton Rd (not downtown version). Ask directions to this superb chippy in E of town; worth the detour and worth the queue when you get there. Phone if you're lost. Lard used. Till 11pm. Also branch at 73 Henry St 01592 203600. Cl Wed.

**1413**
Map 8
**P17**
**S19**
**T19**
Map 10
**R21**
✓ **The Ashvale** Aberdeen, Elgin, Inverurie, Ellon, Brechin Original restau (1985) at 46 Gt Western Rd nr Union St, and 2 other city branches. Restau and takeaway complex à la Harry Ramsden (they stick to dripping but . veg oil supplied on request). Various sizes of haddock, sole, plaice. Home-made stovies, etc., all served fresh so you may wait. Main branch open 7 days, noon-1am; restau noon-11pm Sun-Thu; till midnight Fri/Sat. Others vary.

**1414**
Map 8
**T19**
✓ **The New Dolphin** Aberdeen Chapel St. Despite the pre-eminence of the Ashvale in Aberdeen, many would rather swear by this small, always busy place just off Union St. They both swear by lard. Till 1am; 3am w/ends.

**1415**
Map 1
**D1**
✓ **The Rapido** Edinburgh 77 Broughton St. Legendary chippie. Popular with late-nighters stumbling back down the hill to the New Town, incl the flotsam of the 'Pink Triangle.' 1.30am (3.30am Fri/Sat).

**1416**
Map 1
**E1**
✓ **The Deep Sea** Edinburgh Leith Walk, opp Playhouse. Open late and often has queues (which are quickly dispatched). The haddock has to be 'of a certain size'. Trad menu. Still one of the best fish suppers with which to feed your hangover. 2am-ish (3am Fri/Sat).

**1417**
Map 10
**Q23**
✓ **Deep Sea** Dundee 81 Nethergate at bottom end of Perth Rd; v central. The Sterpaio family have been serving the Dundonians excellent fish 'n' chips since 1939; gr range of fish in groundnut (the most expensive) oil. Café with aproned waitress service is a classic. so v trad, so very tasty. Mon-Sat, 11.30am-6.40pm (7pm carry-out).

**1418**
**WE**
✓ **Philadelphia** Glasgow 445 Gt Western Rd. Adj Big Blue (562/PIZZA) & La Parmagiana (518/BEST RESTAUS), owned by same family. Since 1930, a Glas fixture & fresher fryer than most. 7 days noon-12 (Fri/Sat 3am).

**1419**
Map 10
**R22**
✓ **Peppo's** Arbroath 53 Ladybridge St next to the harbour where those fish come in. Fresh as that and chips in dripping. Peppo has been here since 1951; John and Frank Orsi are carrying on the gr family trad and feeding the hordes. 7 days 4pm-8pm (it's a teatime thing). **Marco's** further along opens earlier & later & uses vegetable oil.

**1420**
Map 10
**R24**
✓ **The Anstruther Fish Bar** On the front in Fife seaside town (1600/COASTAL VILLAGES). They say best F&C UK 2000; the continuous queue suggests they may be right but that was then. Locals prefer **The Pittenweem Fish & Chip Bar**. Tiny door in the wall in Main St of next town along. So we say, go west!. Lard used. Eating-in at Anstruther is cramped (cardboard trays etc) so takeaway best. 7 days 11.30-10.30pm.

**1421**
Map 9
**J26**
✓ **West End** Rothesay 1 Gallowgate. Winner of awards (tho' it's time to get their former glories off the windows) & poss a must-do if you're on Bute, despite their ticket system. Only haddock, but wide range of other fries & fresh pizza. We can't make head nor tail of their hrs, but they're mostly open!

**1422**
Map 10
**T26**
✓ **Giacopazzi's** Eyemouth Harbour by the fishmarket (or what's left of it). A caff & takeaway with the catch on its doorstep. Dispensing excl F&C & their award-winning ice-cream quietly here in the far-flung SE corner of Scotland since 1900. 7 days 11am-9pm. Upstairs to **Oblo's Bistro** 01890 752527. Sun-Thur 10am-midnight, Fri & Sat 10am-1am.

**1423**
Map 10
**S20**
**S21**
**The Bervie Chipper** Inverbervie, Arbroath & Stonehaven   Main st Inverbervie. Sit-in area up and downstairs and take-away. Gets through enormous amounts of haddock and cod. Lard used. In Stoney it's on David St, the rd to Aberdeen – here it competes with Sandy's (see below) & in Arbroath, Peppos. All open noon-10pm 7 days.

**1424**
Map 11
**N29**
**Balmoral** Dumfries   Balmoral Rd. Seems as old and essential as the Bard himself. Using groundnut oil, it's the best chip in the south. Out the Annan rd heading E, 1km from centre. Daily.

**1425**
Map 9
**G22**
**Fish & Chip Van** Tobermory   Parked on Fisherman's Pier by the clock, this van has almost achieved the status of a destination restau. Always a queue. Fresh & al fresco. Apr-Dec 12-9pm.

**1426**
Map 10
**S20**
**Sandy's** Stonehaven   Market Sq. The established Stoney chipper, & always busy despite interlopers (*see above*). Daily, LO 10pm, 9pm Sun. Big haddock like the old days.

## Great Cafés

*For cafés in* Edinburgh, *see p. 53,* Glasgow, *p. 94.*

**1427**
Map 7
**M18**
✓✓ **The Castle Restaurant** Inverness   On rd that winds up to the castle from the main st, nr the TIC and the hostels. No pandering to tourists here, but this great caff has been serving chips with everything for 40 years (crinkle cuts). Pork chops, prawn cocktail, perfect fried eggs. They work damned hard. In Inverness or anywhere nearby, there is no better deal than this! 9am-8.25pm (sic). Cl Sun.

**1428**
Map 9
**K23**
✓✓ **The Real Food Café** Tyndrum   Created from a Little Chef on the main A82 just before the jnct Oban/Fort William & what a difference. Excl food for the rd, conscientiously prepared, seriously sourced, the antitheses of frozen, fast & couldn't-care-less. Fish 'n' chips, burgers, b/fasts, pies – all home-made. The new destination on the way NW. 7 days 12-10pm.

**1429**
Map 6
**K15**
✓ **The Tea Store** Ullapool   Argyll St parallel to & one up from the waterfront. Excl, unpretentious café serving all-day fry-ups & other snacks. Gr home baking incl strawberry tarts in season. Best in Ullapool (or Lewis where you might be heading). AYR. 8am-8pm (wint hrs vary).

**1430**
Map 10
**N24**
✓ **Allan Water Café** Bridge Of Allan   Henderson St (main st) beside the eponymous br. Real whiff of nostalgia along with the fish'n'chips and the ice cream, which are the best around. Worth coming over from Stirling (8km) for a takeaway or a seat in the comforting woody caff – 'and a reminisce of the life before the mall and the burgering of your high st'. Well, that's what I said last time – now the've gone & gotten a steel/glass mall-like extension. I still like the chips & the ice cream! 7 days, 8am-9pm.

**1431**
Map 9
**K26**
✓ **The Ritz Café** Millport   See Millport, see the Ritz. Since 1906 and now in its fourth generation, the classic café on the Clyde. Once overshadowed by Nardini's and a short ferry journey away (from Largs, continuous; then 6km), it should be an essential part of any visit to this part of the coast, and Millport is not entirely without charm. Toasties, rolls, the famous 'hot peas' Excl home-made ice cream (esp with melted marshmallow). Something of 'things past'. 7 days, 10am-9pm in season. Other hrs vary.

**1432**
Map 9
**K27**
✓ **Togs** Troon   Templehill nr main crossrds. There are more caffs in Troon than you could shake a golf club at (the pleasingly named Venice Café is also good, tho' it has turned into a bistro – with home-baking & good ice cream), but this is the one that did it for me – it even smells like a café should. Fairy drops & vanilla fudge & the rest! 7 days 9am-6 or 8pm (from 10am on Sun). Cl Wed.

**1433**
Map 10
**Q27**
✓ **The Hub** Glentress nr Innerleithen   01721 721736. At entranceway to Glentress Forest Park on A72 5km from Peebles. Glentress is mt bike mecca so this US-style caff in a shack serves shorts- & lycra-clad allsorts with big appetites. Frys & baking & cheap nosh for energy. Outdoor terrace. Cool spot. 7 days till 6pm (7pm Sat/Sun) & till 10pm Wed (night biking!).

**1434**
Map 10
**M24**
✓ **Ben Ledi Café** Callander Main st nr sq (rd to Monachyle Mhor 833/CENTRAL HOTELS). New owners take on a legend! But they know what they're doing! Fish teas, and a sq meal. Unprepossessing frontage, but here is the genuine, ungentrified article – who needs an internet cafe? Take away or sit in. Gr chips & the Rocky Road is another killer. 7 days till 10pm.

**1435**
Map 10
**L24**
**The Café In Brig O' Turk In The Trossachs** 01877 376267. Hanging baskets of flowers o/side this shack are what you notice from the rd (the A821 12km W of Callander) in the heart of the afternoon tea belt of the Trossachs. Restau rather than snack menu. V Scottish feel (Polish waiters natch!). 7 days in summer till 8pm.

**1436**
Map 9
**K27**
**The Melbourne** Saltcoats 72 Hamilton St. A tatty 1950s leftover with good coffee, good panini, breakfasts, filled rolls etc. Juke box nearly as cool as the lassies behind the counter! Used as a film location (*Late Night Shopping*). Damned fine! Daily until 5pm.

# The Best Tearooms & Coffee Shops

*For* Edinburgh, *see p. 51; for* Glasgow, *p. 93.*

**1437**
Map 1
**F2**
✓ ✓ **Plaisir Du Chocolat** Edinburgh All other Edin places on p. 50, but this must feature here. A tribute to tea, France & the good life. Report 271/TEARMS.

**1438**
Map 2
**F4**
✓ ✓ **Café Gandolfi** Glasgow Glas's definitive tearoom, long-standing & a formula that has not been bettered. Report 614/TEARMS. Also in Glasgow the more recent and decidedly boho **Tchai-Ovna**. No chintz nor cream teas here, just good tchai and chat. Report 621/TEARMS.

**1439**
Map 10
**P24**
✓ ✓ **The Powmill Milkbar** nr Kinross On the A977 Kinross (on the M90, jnct 6) to Kincardine Br rd, a real milkbar and a real slice of Scottish craic and cake. Apple pie and moist fly cemeteries – an essential stop on any Sunday run (but open every day). The paper plates do little justice to the confections they bear, but they are part of the deal, so don't complain! Hot meals and salads. Good place to take kids. 7 days, 9am-5pm (6pm summer). (2009/GLEN AND RIVER WALKS)

**1440**
Map 10
**P23**
✓ ✓ **Gloagburn Farm & Coffee Shop** Tibbermore nr Perth Off A85 Perth-Methven & Crieff rd from A9 & ring rd at Huntingtower, signed Tibbermore. Thro vill, 2nd farm on rt – a real farm shop on the verandah with excl fresh produce & inside a deli & café where the food (hot dishes, cakes etc) is exemplary. A destination place only 15 mins from Perth. Open AYR. 9am-5pm (4pm wint). 7 days.

**1441**
Map 9
**K23**
✓ ✓ **The Green Welly Stop** Tyndrum On A82, a strategically placed pit-stop on the drive to Oban or Ft William (just before the rd divides), with a Scottish produce shop and the gas stn (open later). Self-service comfort food to break the journey. Much home-made, v Scottish & a whole lot better than you'd expect. Shop stuffed with everything you don't & do need (incl this book). 7 days, 8.30am-5.30pm.

**1442**
Map 8
**R20**
✓ ✓ **The Black-Faced Sheep** Aboyne 01339 887311. Nr main Royal Deeside rd through Aboyne (A93) and TIC, this excellent coffee shop/gift shop is well-loved by locals (and regulars from all over) but is thankfully missed by the bus parties hurtling towards Balmoral. Home-made breads and cakes, light specials; good coffee (real capp & espresso from Elektra machine). 10am-5pm, Sun from 11am.

**1443**
Map 8
**S20**
✓ ✓ **The Falls of Freugh** Banchory 01330 822123. Over br S from town, the B974 for Fettercairn (signed), a restau-cum-tearoom by a local beauty spot, the Tumbling Falls. Ann Taylor's labour of love with à la carte menu, specials & gr bakes. A model of how it should be done, here on the Deeside teaside where there are more than a few to choose form. AYR. 7 days till 4.30pm.

**1444**
Map 9
**L28**
✓ **Tudor Restaurant** Ayr 8 Beresford Terr, nr Odeon & Burns Monument Sq. High tea from 3.15pm, breakfast all day. Roomy, well-used, full of life. Bakery counter at front (fab cream donuts & bacon butties as they're supposed to be) & locals from bairns to OAPs in the body of the kirk. 10am-9pm Mon-Sat, 12-8pm Sun.

**1445**
Map 10
**S22**

✓ **The Watermill** Aberfeldy 01887 822896. Mill St off Main St direction Kenmore nr the Birks (2028/WOODLAND WALKS). V civilised gallery, book-shop & downstairs caff on riverside in conserved mill. Excl book choice. Home-baking & snacks. 9.30am-4.30pm (Suns from 12). Times may change.

**1446**
Map 7
**M20**

✓ **Laggan Coffeeshop** nr Laggan On A889 from Dalwhinnie on A9 that leads to A86, the rd W to Spean Bridge & Kyle. Former pottery. Craft shop & bunkhouse (1160/HOSTELS) but gr home baking, esp carrot cake & lemon driz-zle & Queen Mary's Tart (a Claire Macdonald recipe). Nr gr spot for forest walks & river swimming (1710/PICNICS). Easter-Oct 7 days till 5.30pm.

**1447**
Map 8
**R18**

✓ **The Tearoom at Clatt** nr Alford & Inverurie In the village hall in the hamlet of Clatt where local ladies display gr home-made Scottish baking – like a weekly sale of work. Take A96 N of Inverurie, then B9002 follow sign for Auchleven, then Clatt. Gr countryside. W/ends May-Sept 1pm-5pm. One of the gr tea & scone experiences in the world (I hope you see what I mean).

**1448**
Map 10
**Q24**

✓ **The Pillars Of Hercules** nr Falkland 01337 857749. Tearoom on organic farm on A912 rd 2km from vill towards Strathmiglo & m/way. Excl, homely place & fare & all PC. Home-made cakes, soup etc. See also 1516/DELIS. 7 days 10am-5.30pm.

**1449**
Map 11
**M29**

✓ **Kitty's Tearoom** New Galloway Main St of town in the forest. Absolutely splendid. Sylvia Brown's steady hand in the kitchen, great cakes, good tea, and conversations between local ladies, it's an Alan Bennett kind of place. 11am-7pm, Easter-Oct. Tues-Sun.

**1450**
Map 9
**L24**

✓ **The Coach House** Luss, Loch Lomond In the heart of Take The High Road country & this vill still throngs with visitors. Gary & Rowena Grove's much (self) publicised success story also goes like the proverbial fair. Not all home-made but they'd need v big ovens. Nice loos, some o/side seat-ing. 7 days 10am-5pm.

**1451**
Map 9
**J22**

✓ **Castle Stalker View** Portnacroish nr Port Appin On main A828 Oban-Ft William about half-way. Modern-build café/gift shop with contemp snack menu & home cooking. Nice people so a pop local rendezvous as well as you & me just passing thro'. The main thing is the extraordinary view. Mar-Oct 9.30am-5.30pm, wint Wed-Sun 10-4pm.

**1452**
Map 9
**H27**

✓ **North Beachmore Farm Restaurant** nr Muasdale on A83 Tarbert–Campbeltown rd. Signposted up a steep track, 2km off the rd and into the hills. Matt and Eileen McInnes' home-cooking is hugely popular locally; you see why. Stunning views of the Sound of Gigha, (and on a clear day Ireland). Food excl too tho' some talk of retirement '06 (phone first 01583 421328).10am-10pm. Cl in wint.

**1453**
Map 8
**R20**

✓ **Raemoir Garden Centre** Banchory On A980 off main A93, the Deeside rd thro' town, about 3km. You have to beat a path thro' the gar-den (centre) to the tearoom, tho' it's a good 'un (2218/GARDEN CENTRES). The caff is superb with excl home-baking & a full hot-meal menu. Gr quality stuff, the way it used to be. Then shop! 7 days till 5pm (Sun 4.30pm). Centre till 5.30pm.

**1454**
Map 7
**H19**

✓ **Glenelg Candles** Glenelg As you come into the vill after the spectac-ular mountain pass rd from Shiel Bridge, a candle-making studio & craft shop (2169/SHOPPING) & café/restau in fab modern, woody conservatory with grass roof. All home-made; garden. Apr-Oct 9.30-5pm.

**1455**
Map 9
**G22**

✓ **Glengorm Farm Coffee Shop** nr Tobermory 01688 302321. First right on Tobermory-Dervaig rd. Organic food served in well refurbed stable block. Soups, cakes, venison burgers... all you need after a walk in the grounds of this gr estate (2326/MULL HOTELS) & gr ceramics adj (2175/SHOP-PING). Open Easter-Oct LO 4.30pm.

**1456**
Map 9
**H26**

✓ **The Lighthouse** Pirnmill, Arran 01770 850240. On rd W looking on to Mull of Kintyre. Perfect pit-stop for home-cooking looking over bay. Full menu avail in curiously contemp decor. 7 days 10am-9pm Jan-Dec.

**1457**
Map 10
**L23**

✓ **Library Tearoom** Balquhidder Centre of vill opp church (1911/GRAVE-YARDS) where many walks start incl gr view (1699/VIEWS) & nr long walk to Brig o' Turk (2008/GLEN WALKS). Excl bakes: carrot cake, cheese scones, soup & BLT. Only 4 tables. Apr-Oct, 10am-4.30pm.

**1458** ✓ **Kind Kyttock's Kitchen** Falkland  Folk come to Falkland (1792/CASTLES;
Map 10  1979/HILL WALKS) for many reasons, not least for afternoon tea. Several
Q24  choices, this the longest established and most regarded. Omelettes, toasties,
baked potatoes, baking. Good service. 10.30am-5.30pm. Cl Mon.

**1459** **The Flower Tunnel** Applecross  In campsite (1243/CAMPING WITH KIDS) as
Map 7  you arrive in Applecross after amazing journey (1668/SCENIC ROUTES). Coffee-
H18  shop in greenhouse full of plants & outdoor seating. Famous pizzas, tho' bak-
ery cl '05. Apr-Oct. 7 days, supper only high season.

**1460** **Bridge Cottage** Poolewe  In vill & nr Inverwere Gardens (1544/GARDENS),
Map 7  cottage right enough with crafts/pictures up stairs & parlour teashop down.
H16  Salads, big cakes; local produce. 7 days till 4.30pm (wint hrs vary). Cl Nov.

**1461** **Robin's Nest** Taynuilt  Main St off the A85 (leading to Bonawe 2246/MUSE-
Map 9  UMS & Glen Etive Cruises). Tiny home-baking caff wtih unusual soups &
J23  snacks as well as the good WRI cake. Easter-Oct 7 days 10am-5pm, Thur-Sun
in wint.

**1462** **Crinan Coffee Shop** Crinan  Run by the hotel people (779/BEST HOTELS
Map 9  ARGYLL) up the rd – I guess they opened this because Crinan had to have a
H25  good coffee shop. Now it does. Fascinating vill for yachties & anyone with
time to while, this place o/looks the busy canal basin where boats are always
going thro'. Good cakes. Easter-Oct 9am-5.30pm.

**1463** **Tully Bannocher Farm Restaurant**  2km W on A85 to Lochearnhead.
Map 10  Recommended roadside coffee shop/self-service diner with fairly trad hot
M23  dishes, salads, some baking. Home-made chips. Handy for the delights of
Comrie. Tables o/side. LO 7.15pm. W/ends only in deep wint.

**1464** **Flat Cat Gallery Coffee Shop** Lauder  2 Market St opp Eagle Hotel.
Map 10  Speeding thro' Lauder (note speed camera at Edinburgh end) you might miss
R26  this cool coffee spot & serious gallery. Always interesting work & ethnic
things. Home-baking natch. 7 days till 5pm.

**1465** **Silver Spoon** Peebles  Innerleithen Rd at end of main st adj Green Tree
Map 10  hotel. Mumsy, definitely not funky tearoom, but with good attitude to baking
Q27  (& mums). Perfectly Peebles! 7 days. 9-4.30pm (Sun 11-4pm).

**1466** **The Riverside & Abbey Artefacts** Abbey St Bathans  01361 840312. By
Map 10  the trout farm, nr R Whiteadder in the middle of this rustic hamlet on the
S26  Southern Upland Way. A welcome place for a restau & gallery. They do insist
they're not a tearoom but it feels like a tearoom. Seasonal menu. Light or 3-
course lunches incl savoury flans, steaks, local seafood. Puds. Tues-Sun
11am-5pm (4pm Oct-Easter). Cl Mons.

**1467** **Logie Steading** nr Forres  S of town towards Grantown (A940) – 10km. Or
Map 8  from Carrbridge via B9007. See 2022/WOODLAND WALKS (**Randolph's Leap**).
N17  In a lovely spot nr the R Findhorn, a courtyard of fine things (2159/SHOPPING)
& a superior tearoom – home-bakes & snacks. & days. 10.30am-5pm (wint
hrs may vary).

**1468** **The Waterfront** Rothesay  01700 505166. E Princes St on the front (turn
Map 9  left off the ferry). Small, hard-working caff/restau with local rep & big por-
J26  tions. They say 'real food for real money', ie no CC. Newish so still fixing open-
ing but cl Mon/Tues.

**1469** **Garden Room Teashop** Rockcliffe  On main rd in/out of this seaside cul de
Map 11  sac. Best on sunny days when you can sit in the gdn. Snacks and cakes
N30  (though not all home-made). 10.30-5pm. Cl Mon & Tues.

**1470** **The Ariundle Centre** Strontian  At beginning of walk in Ariundle Woods
Map 9  (2026/WOODLAND WALKS) in wonderful Ardnamurchan. Bungalow tearoom
H21  with knits & nick nacks. Hot dishes, home bakes. AYR incl (candlelit) dinner
in summer.

**1471** **Crafty Kitchen** Ardfern  Down the Ardfern B8002 rd (4km) from A816
Map 9  Oban-Lochgilphead rd, the yachty seafaring nice manna port of the Craignish
H24  peninsula. A book & crafty shop right enough and a kitchen out back from
which gr home-made cakes & special hot dishes emerge along with superi-
or burgers & fries. Tues-Sun 10am-5.30pm. W/ends only Nov/Dec. Cl Jan-
Mar.

**1472** **Horsemill Restaurant** Crathes Castle, nr Banchory  01330 844525. Adj
Map 8  magnificent Crathes (1863/COUNTRY HOUSES; 1545/GARDENS) so lots of reasons
**S20**  to go off the Deeside rd (A93) & up the drive. More tearoom than restau but
some hot dishes eg haggis tart with red-onion marmalade and excl home-
baking mm ... meringues. Open AYR lunch/aft tea till 5pm.                    INX

**1473** **The Pantry** Cromarty  In great wee town in Black Isle 45km NE of Inverness
Map 7  (1595/COASTAL VILLAGES) on corner of Church St. Good home baking and a
**M17**  decent cup of coffee. Easter-end Oct. 10.30am-4pm. Cl Fri.

**1474** **Dun Whinny's** Callander  Off main st at Glas rd, a welcoming wee (but not
Map 10  twee) tearoom; not run by wifies. Banoffee pie kind of thing and clootie
**M24**  dumpling. There's a few naff caffs in Callander. This one still OK (2006) in my
book. 7 days till 5pm.

# The Best Scotch Bakers

**1475**  ✓ ✓ **Fisher & Donaldson** Dundee, St Andrews, Cupar  Main or origi-
Map 10          nal branch in Cupar and 3 in Dundee. Superior contemporary bak-
**Q23**  ers along trad lines (born 1919) – surprising (and a pity) that they haven't gone
**R23**  further, although they do supply selected outlets (e.g. Jenners in Edin with
pastries and the most excellent Dr Floyd's bread which is as good as anything
you could make yourself). Main sq, Cupar; Church St, St Andrews; Whitehall
St, 300 Perth Rd and Lochee, Dundee, which is v well served with decent bak-
ers (*see below*). Dundee Whitehall & Cupar have good tearms (1093/DUNDEE).

**1476**  ✓ **Bradford's** 245 Sauchiehall St, Glas, & suburban branches in selected
Map 2     areas, i.e. they have not over-expanded; for a bakery chain, some lines
**B1**  seem almost home-made. Certainly better than all the industrial 'home'-
bakers around. Individual fruit pies, for example, are uniquely yummy, and
the all-important Scotch pie pastry is exemplary. (629/TEAROOMS.)

**1477**  ✓ **Alexander Taylor's** Strathaven nr Lanark 01357 521260. Specialising
Map 10     in huge array of savoury breads: sunflower, Bavarian, sourdough, black
**M27**  bun and, at Christmas, stollen. Also make all their shortbreads and oatcakes.
Good & wholesome! Mon-Sat 7.30am-5.30pm (Sat from 8.30am!).

**1478**  ✓ **Riverside Bistro** Lochinver  On way into town from Ullapool etc, not
Map 6     a baker's as such but rightly famous for their brilliant pies from t/away
**J14**  counter. Huge variety of savoury & fruit from trad to exotic. And irresistible
puds. Sustenance for the hills or just indulge. 7 days.

**1479**  ✓ **Scotch Oven** Callander  W end of main st in busy touristy town and
Map 10     one of the best things about it. Good bread, rolls, cakes, the biggest,
**M24**  possibly the best, tattie scones and sublime doughnuts. Also featuring what
may be the perfect Scotch pie pastry. Adj caff at side much less convincing.
Better to picnic on the Braes or by the river. Open 7 days till 5pm.

**1480** **Goodfellow & Steven**  The other bakers in the Fife/Dundee belt (not a
Map 10  patch on Fisher & Donaldson; but hey). G&S have several branches in
**Q23**  Dundee, Perth and Fife. Good Scotch baking with the kind of cakes your mum
used to have for a treat.

**1481** **Cromarty Bakery** Bank St. One of the many reasons to visit this pic-
Map 7  turesque seaside town. Abundance of speciality cakes, organic bread, rolls &
**M17**  pies, baked daily on premises. Also tea, coffee, hot savouries & takeaway.
Mon, Tue, Thu, Fri 8.30am-5.30pm; Wed/Sat till 4 pm.

**1482** **The Bakehouse** Acharacle in Arnamurchan  Helen Macgillvray's roadside
Map 9  bakery unprepossessing, tiny inside but gr bakes incl bread, pastries & esp
**H21**  savouries. Top pork pie in Scotland. Stock up for picnics at Singing Sands
(2044/COASTAL WALKS)or Castle Tioram shoreline (1812/RUINS). AYR. Cl Suns.

**1483** **McLaren's** Forfar  Town centre next to Queens Hotel and in Kirriemuir. The
Map 10  best in town to sample the famous Forfar bridie, a meaty shortcrust pastie
**Q22**  hugely underestimated as a national delicacy. They're so much better than
the gross & grossly overblown Cornish pasty but have never progressed
beyond this part of Perthshire. As it happens, one of the best examples is the
home-made bridie can be found in the café at Glamis (1796/CASTLES).
**Saddler's** in North St Forfar do them too.

# The Best Ice-Cream

**1484** ✓ ✓ **Luca's** Musselburgh nr Edinburgh (& Edinburgh)  32 High St.
Map 10   Queues out the door in the middle of a Sun afternoon in February are
**Q25** testament to the enduring popularity of this almost-legendary ice-cream parlour. 3 classic flavours (vanilla, choc and strawberry) & now a plethora of sorbets. Pure ingredients attract folk from Edin (14km) though there is now a
branch in Edin at 16 Morningside Rd, a more designery Italian version (289/
CAFÉS). In café thro' the back, still basic after recent refurb, sundae, snacks, &
you might have to wait. In Edin café upstairs more pizza/pasta & smart sandwiches. Mon-Sat 9am-10pm, Sun 10.30am-10pm. Edin hrs: 7 days 9am (10.30
Sun)-10pm. Luca's (wholesale) spreading everywhere so look out for the sign.

**1485** ✓ ✓ **Mancini's, The Royal Café** Ayr  11 New Rd, the rd to Prestwick. Ice
Map 9   cream that's taken seriously, entered for competitions & usually wins.
**L28** Best UK Vanilla 2001 & '03. Family biz for aeons. Massive no. of flavours at their
disposal, always new ones. Home-made ice-cream cakes. Café recent refurb &
newer caff in Prestwick on the esplanade. Their sorbets taste better than the
fruit they're made from. They were first with ice-cream toasties & diabetic ice-
cream. These Mancinis are surely the kings of ice cream. 7 days till 10.30pm.

**1486** ✓ **Cream O' Galloway** Rainton nr Gatehouse Of Fleet  01557 814040.
Map 11   A75 take Sandgreen exit 2km, then left at sign for Carrick. Originally a
**M30** dairy farm producing cheese, now you can watch them making the creamy
concoctions which you find all over. Nature trail, absolutely fab kids adventure
play area (1739/KIDS) & decent organic-type café. AYR 10am-6pm.

**1487** ✓ **Janetta's** St Andrews  31 South St. Family firm since 1908. There are two
Map 10   Janetta's, but the one to adore is top end South St. Once only vanilla,
**R23** Americans at the Open asked for other flavours. Now there are 52 (2 vanillas),
& numerous awards. Also frozen yogs. Janetta's is another good reason for
being a student at St Andrews. Good café adj, family fare, o/side tables. LO 5pm
& t/away. 7 days till 5pm, 10.30pm in summer.

**1488** ✓ **Caldwell's** Innerleithen  On the High St in this ribbon of a town
Map 10   between Peebles and Gala they've been making ice cream since 1911.
**Q27** Purists may bemoan the fact that they've exploded into flavours in the 21stC,
but their vanilla is still best. The shop still sells everything from Blue Nun to
bicycles. Mon-Fri till 8.30pm, Sat/Sun 7.30pm.

**1489** **Visocchi's** Broughty Ferry, Kirriemuir  Orig from St Andrews; ice-cream
Map 10   makers for 75 years and still with the café they opened in Kirriemuir in 1930.
**Q22** On the main drag of the Angus town (1632/GLENS), it's the local caff (v basic
**Q23** menu, no chips). Broughty Ferry (Dundee's seaside suburb) more middle-
class, with a contemp menu; home-made pasta as well as the peach melba.
7 days (1096/DUNDEE EAT & DRINK).

**1490** **The Allan Water Café** Bridge Of Allan  An old-fashioned café in an old-fash-
Map 10   ioned town, near the eponymous br in the main st since 1902. Fabulously good
**N24** fish 'n' chips and ice cream. Now with a new-fashioned metal extension. And
many new flavours. I don't know what to think! 7 days, 8am-8pm.

**1491** **Cones & Candies** Biggar  Main St. There's always been a thing about ice-
Map 11   cream in Biggar. Let's not go into the local history. This is where you get
**P27** Taylor's perfect vanilla. Nuff said. 7 days till 5.30pm (6pm Sats).

**1492** **Colpi's** Milngavie, Glasgow  Opp Marks & Spencer in Milngavie centre (pron
Map 10   Mullguy) and there since 1928. Many consider this to be Glas's finest. Vanilla
**L25** at the cone counter, other flavours to take home. Till 9pm, 7 days.

**1493** **Drummuir Farm** Collin nr Dumfries  5km off A75 (Carlisle/Annan) rd E of
Map 11   Dumfries on B724 (nr Clarencefield). A real farm producing real ice cream –
**P30** still does supersmooth original and honeycomb, seasonal specials; on a fine
day, sit out and chill. Indoor & outdoor play areas. Easter-Sept daily to
5.30pm; Oct-Dec & Mar Sat-Sun until 5pm; Jan/Feb closed.

**1494** **Capaldi's** Brora  Rosslyn St. Here since 1936 & recntly bought out so expect
Map 6   to see more on the streets of the N. Inventive flavours incl the fab puff candy
**N15** (or honeycomb) & rhubarb & custard. Daily until 8pm. Avail locally at many
outlets & at the beach in Dornoch.

# The Really Good Delis

**1495**
Map 1
E1

✔ ✔ ✔ **Valvona & Crolla** Edinburgh  19 Elm Row, nr top of Leith Walk. Since 1934, an Edin institution, the shop you show visitors. Full of smells, genial, knowledgeable staff and a floor-to-ceiling range of cheese (Ital/Scot, etc.), meats, oils, wines and more. Fresh veg trucked in from Milan markets, on-premises bakery, great café/bar (174/ITALIAN RESTAUS). Also demos, tastings, Fringe venue. Valvona's an Edin landmark & a national treasure. 8am-6.30pm (Sun 11-5pm). Gr website (valvonacrolla.com).

**1496**
Map 1
C4
xB5
A1
Map 2
WE

✔ ✔ **I.J. Mellis** Edinburgh, Glasgow & St Andrews  3 branches in Edin - Victoria St, Morningside & Stockbridge; Kelvinbridge in Glas & St Andrews. Started out as the cheese guy, now more of a v select deli for food that's good & 'slow'. Coffees, hams, sausages, olives & seasonal stuff like apples & mushrooms (branches vary), so smells mingle. Irresistible! 7 days tho' times vary. See also 1525/CHEESES.

**1497**
Map 1
A2

✔ **Glass & Thompson** Edinburgh  2 Dundas St. Exemplary and contemporary New Town provisioner. Selective choice of Mediterranean – style goodies to eat or take away and bread/pâtisserie; also those all-important New Town dinner party essentials. Report: 276/TEAROOMS.

**1498**
Map 1
A1

✔ **Grassroots Organic** Glasgow  48 Woodlands Rd, nr Charing Cross. First-class vegn food and provisions store, everything chemically unaltered and environmentally-friendly. Gr breads and sandwiches for lunch and the best organic fruit/veg range in town. Vegn restau round the corner (611/GLAS VEGN). 7 days 8am-8pm (Sat 9am-6pm, Sun 11am-5pm).

**1499**
Map 10
Q27

✔ **Cook's Fine Foods** Peebles  25 High St in midst of Peebles where people like a good bit of cheese. Here they take it seriously & they make bread, savouries & continental-type bakes. Sit-in for snacks; they also do outside catering. A place you'd expect to find in Edinburgh New Town; they have *the* best brie. Tues-Sat 10am-6pm.

**1500**
WE

✔ **Delizique** Glasgow  66 Hyndland St nr Cottier's bar & theatre. Excl neighbourhood deli for the affluent Hyndlanders & others who roam & graze round here. Gr prepared meals (in-house chef) & hand-picked goodies incl oils, hams, flowers & Mellis cheeses. 7 days 9am-8pm.

**1501**
WE

✔ **Heart Buchanan** Glasgow  380 Byres Rd. Gr deli & first-rate t/away. Report 651/T/AWAY.

**1502**
Map 1
A1

✔ **Herbie** Edinburgh  66 Raeburn Pl & t/away at 7 William St. Notable mainly for cheese & other cold-counter irresistibles (1526/CHEESES).

**1503**
Map 10
N24

✔ **Clive Ramsay** Bridge Of Allan  Main St. Here for yrs, but just gets better. New café/restau adj with gr coffee & eats. Deli gr for fruit/veg, cheese, olives, seeds & well-chosen usuals incl own-brand. Methinks the deli better than the caff. 7 days 7am-7pm.

**1504**
Map 8
P17

✔ **Phoenix Findhorn Community** Findhorn  Serving the new age township of the Findhorn Community and therefore pursuing a conscientious app, this has become an exemplary and v high quality deli, worth the detour from the A96 Inverness-Elgin rd even if you have apprehensions about their 'thing'. Packed and carefully selected shelves; as much for pleasurable eating as for healthy. Till 6pm (w/ends 5pm).

**1505**
Map 8
Q18

✔ **Spey Larder** Aberlour  In deepest Speyside. Main St. Beautiful old shop (1864) spacious & full of gr, often local produce (honeys, bread, game in wint, Speyside chanterelles & of course whisky). AYR. Cl Suns. 9am-5.30pm.

**1506**
Map 7
M18

**Gourmet's Lair** Inverness  81 Union St. Inverness is a city & now it has delis of which this is the best. Huge selection of cheeses. Shelves & baskets & cold counter all stuffed with good things. 8am-5pm (6pm w/ends).

**1507**
Map 1
A1

**The Store** Edinburgh  Raeburn Pl, the main st in Stockbridge. Modern, stylish presentation of vicuals, wine, bread but most notably vacuum-packed meat from the family's own farm in Aberdeenshire. A big hit with New Town ladies who DP. 7 days 10am-8pm (9am-6pm Sat, 11am-5pm Sun).

**1508**
Map 1
**B5**
Map 2
**WE**
**Lupe Pintos** Edinburgh & Glasgow  24 Leven St nr King's Theatre & 313 Gt Western Rd. Unusual Latin deli (ie Mexican, Central American, Spanish). Where to go for chorizo, manchego and 20 kinds of tequila. T/away incl home-made burritos and the usual Tex-Mex. Every kind of chili & gr Riojas. 10am-6pm. Cl Suns.

**1509**
Map 2
**F4**
**Garlic** Glasgow  793 Shettleston Road. 0141 763 0399. A foody oasis in the unfashionable E End, the fame of this little emporio Italiano has spread to the Merchant City and beyond. The usual meats and cheeses are represented, with a gr Italian wine range (incl org) and beer, and a superb choice of home-made and fresh foods. Giovanna's pasta dishes supply city-centre restaurants, but the shop offers a wider and ever-changing range, such as pumpkin risotto, and a daily special. Have a coffee while you peruse.

**1510**
**WE**
Map 2
**E3**
Map 1
**A1**
**Peckham's** Glasgow (inc Lenzie & Newton Mearns) & Edinburgh  Scotland's most prolific deli chain, but ea shop individually run. Hyndland (43 Clarence Dr) & Merchant City (61 Glassford St) are the best of them. Expensive but always serviceable & loads of choice from staples to wines and cheeses, and a good range of up-market nibbles. The Edin branch is at 155 Bruntsfield Pl which is has tables o/side in summer.

**1511**
Map 10
**R23**
**Butler & Co** St Andrews  10 Church St. Excl deli by the people who have the seafood restaus here & in St Monans (1391/1392/SEAFOOD RESTAUS). Good range of Scottish and other cheeses. Till 5.30pm.

**1512**
Map 8
**P17**
**Gordon & MacPhail** Elgin  South St. Purveyors of fine wines, cheeses, meats, Mediterranean goodies, unusual breads and other epicurean delights to the good burghers of Elgin for nigh on a century. Traditional shopkeeping, in the style of the 'family grocer'. G & M are widely known as bottlers of lesser-known high-quality malts ('Connoisseurs' range) – on sale here as well as every other whisky you've ever heard of & many you ain't. Some rare real ales by the bottle too. Mon-Sat 9am-5.15pm.

**1513**
Map 10
**Q27**
**The Olive Tree** Peebles  7 High St. Small emporium packed with wide selection of European groceries plus local delicacies: beer, honey, cheese ad infinitum – specialises in farmhouse and unpasteurised cheeses.

**1514**
Map 11
**L13**
**Ravenstone Deli** Whithorn  01988 500329. Main St up from Whithorn Story VC. New good food & coffeestop in faraway Whithorn. Good cheese & olive selection, local produce, some organics, excl daily bread (baked on premises). 8am-5pm (Sun 9am-3pm). Cl Tues/Wed & poss wint months.

**1515**
Map 10
**N22**
**Dows** Aberfeldy  01887 829616. Main St, Grantully direction nr sq. People who had the estimable Lurgan Farm shop now in town with tratteur range of ready-to-go meals & selected packet things. Till 5pm. Cl Suns.

**1516**
Map 10
**Q24**
**The Pillars of Hercules** nr Falkland  01337 857749.On A912 2km from town towards Strathmiglo & m/way. Completely organic grocers with tearm (1448/TEAROOMS) on farm/nursery where you can PYO herbs & flowers. Always fruit/veg & gr selection of dry goods that's a long way from Sainsburys. 7 days 10am-6pm.

**1517**
Map 10
**P23**
**Provender Brown** Perth  01738 587300. 23 George St. As we might expect, a decent deli in the town/city where several good restaus reside, there's a big farmers' market (first in Scotland) & many folk aren't short of a bob or two. P&B are good for olives, vacuum-packed products & esp cheese. 9am-5.30pm. Cl Sun.

# Scottish Cheeses

**1518** **Mull or Tobermory Cheddar**  From Sgriob-Ruadh Farm (pron 'Skibrua'). Comes in big 50lb cheeses and 1lb truckles. Good, strong cheddar, one of the v best in the UK.

**1519** **Dunsyre Blue/Lanark Blue**  Made by Humphrey Errington at Carnwath. Next to Stilton, **Dunsyre** (made from the unpasteurised milk of Ayrshire cows) is the best blue in the UK. It is soft, rather like Dolcelatte. **Lanark,** the original, is Scotland's Roquefort and made from ewes' milk. Both can vary but are excellent. Go on, live dangerously – unpasteurise your life.

**1520** **Locharthur Cheese**  Anything from this SW creamery is worth a nibble: the cheddar, **Criffel** (mild), **Kebbuck** (shaped like a dinosaur's tooth, semi-soft).

**1521** **Bonnet**  Hard goat's milk cheese from Anne Dorwood's farm at Stewarton in Ayrshire. Also a v good cheddar (& sheep's-milk cheddar).

**1522** **Wester Lawrenceton Farm Cheeses** Forres  Pam Rodway's excl organic cheeses: **Carola**, **Califer** (goat's milk) & the hard-to-get **Sweetmilk Cheddar**. On sale Findhorn shop & Gordon & MacPhail (1512/DELIS).

**1523** **Highland Fine Cheeses**  From the Stone family in Tain. 6 cheeses incl **Crowdie** (trad curd cheese), **Caboc** & **Strathdon Blue** (award winner).

**1524** **Cairnsmore**  A hard, tangy, cheddary cheese from Sorbie in Wigtownshire surprisingly made from ewes' milk, smoked or unsmoked.

## AND WHERE TO FIND THEM

*The delis on pp. 188-189 will have good selections (esp Valvona's and Delizique). Also:*

**1525**
Map 1
C4
xB3
A1
& WE
✓ ✓ **I.J. Mellis** Edinburgh, Glasgow & St Andrews  30a Victoria St, far end of Morningside Rd and Baker's Pl, Stockbridge (Edin), 492 Gr Western Rd (Glas), 149 South St, St Andrews. A real cheesemonger. Smell and taste before you buy. Cheeses from all over the UK in prime condition. Daily and seasonal specials. (1496/DELIS)

**1526**
Map 1
A1
✓ **Herbie** Edinburgh  66 Raeburn Pl & William St. Excellent selection – everything here is the right stuff. Gr bread, bagels etc from independent baker, home-made hummus & with Scottish cheeses, it's practically impossible here to find a Brie or a blue in less than perfect condition. William St (W End is the t/away of choice hereabouts.

✓ **Cook's Fine Foods** Peebles  Report: 1499/DELIS

**1527**
Map 10
P22
✓ **MacDonald's Cheese Shop** Rattray nr Blairgowrie  01250 872493. 2km Blairgowrie on rd to Glenshee and Braemar. Discreet 'shack' you could easily miss, but don't! Extraordinary selection of cheese esp Scottish and Swiss. Veg & other market produce. 10am-5pm. Cl Mon. Sun 10am-4pm.

**1528**
Map 9
J27
**Island Cheeses** Arran  5km Brodick, rd to castle and Corrie. Excellent selection of their own (the well-known cheddars but many others esp crowdie with garlic and hand-rolled cream cheeses) and others. See them being made. 7 days. 9.30am-5.30pm. Sun 10am-4.30pm.

**1529**
Map 7
H18
**West Highland Dairy** Achmore nr Plockton  01599 577203. Mr and Mrs Biss still running their great farm dairy shop selling their own cheeses (ewe and cow milk), yoghurt, ice cream and cheesecake. Mar-Dec dawn to dusk! Signed from village. If you're making the trip specially, phone first to check they're open.

**House Of Bruar** nr Blair Atholl  Roadside emporium (2161/SHOPPING).

**Falls Of Shin Visitor Centre** nr Lairg  The Harrods of the North (2163/SHOPPING).

**Peter MacLennan** Fort Willaim  28 High St.

**Scottish Speciality Food** North Ballachulish  By Leven Hotel.

**Jenners Department Store** Edinburgh  Princes St, top-floor.

**Corner on the Square** Beauly  Main St.

# Whisky: The Best Distillery Tours

*The process is basically the same in every distillery, but some are more atmospheric and some have more interesting tours, like these:*

**1530** ✓ ✓ **The Islay Malts** Plenty to choose from incl, in the N, **Caol Ila** (by
Map 9 appointment 01496 302760), the wholly independent **Bruich-**
**F25** **laddich** (3 tours daily Mon-Fri, twice daily on Sat, 01496 850221). In the S nr
**F26** Port Ellen, 3 of the world's gr malts are in a row on a mystic coast. The distilleries here look like distilleries ought to. **Lagavulin** (01496 302730) and
**Laphroaig** (01496 302418) offer fascinating tours where your guide will lay on
the anecdotes as well as the process and you get a feel for the life and history
as well as the product of these world-famous places. At Laphroaig you can join
their 'Friend' scheme (free) and own a piece of their hallowed ground. Lagavulin
tours Mon-Fri only, Laphroaig same. **Ardbeg** is perhaps the most visitor-oriented and has a really good café (2323/ISLAY RESTAUS) where if you blunder in at
mid morning and ask for toast, they make you some toast (302244). All these
distilleries are in settings that entirely justify the romantic hyperbole of their
advertising. Worth seeing from the o/side as well as the floor. **Bowmore**
(810441) has professional, more commercial, 1hr tours regularly (incl video
show & the usual dram) & perhaps the most convenient.

**1531** **Strathisla** Keith 01542 783044. The oldest working distillery in the
Map 8 Highlands, literally on the strath of the Isla river and methinks the most
**Q17** evocative atmos of all the Speyside distilleries. The refurb made this an even
classier halt for the malt. Used as the 'heart' of Chivas Regal, the malt not
commonly available is still a fine dram. You wait for a tour group to gather;
there's a dram at the beginning & the end. Mar-Oct 10am-4pm (Sun from
12.30).

**1532** **Talisker** Carbost, Isle Of Skye From Sligachan-Dunvegan rd (A863) take
Map 7 B8009 for Carbost and Glen Brittle along the S side of L Harport for 5km.
**F18** Skye's only distillery; since 1830 they've been making this classic after-dinner
malt from barley and the burn that runs off the Hawkhill behind. A dram
before the informative 40min tour. Good VC. Apr-Oct 9.30am-5pm (2-5pm
wint by apt only, 01478 614308). Gr gifts nearby (2167/CRAFT SHOPS).

**1533** **Glenkinchie** Pencaitland nr Edinburgh 01875 342004. Only 25km from
Map 10 city centre (via A68 and A6093 before Pathhead), signposted & so v popular.
**Q25** Founded in 1837 in a peaceful, pastoral place (it's 3km from the village) with
its own bowling green; a country trip as well as a whisky tour. State-of-the-
art VC. Summer daily till 5pm (cl 4pm in wint). Wint cl w/ends.

**1534** **Edradour** nr Pitlochry Claims to be the smallest distillery in Scotland, pro-
Map 10 ducing single malts for blends since 1825 and limited quantities of the
**N21** Edradour (since 1986) as well as the House of Lords' own brand. Guided tour
of charming cottage complex every 20min. 4km from Pitlochry off
Kirkmichael rd, A924; signed after Moulin village. Complex opening hrs tho'
open AYR, 7 days.

**1535** **Highland Park** Kirkwall, Orkney 01856 874619. 2km from town on main
Map 3 A961 rd S to S Ronaldsay. The whisky is great (the 18 Year Old won The Best
**Q10** Spirit in the World '05) and the award-winning tour one of the best. The most
northerly whisky in a class and a bottle of its own. You walk through the floor
maltings and you can touch the warm barley and fair smell the peat. Good
combination of the industrial and trad. Tours every half hour. Open AYR
10am-5pm (Sun from 12pm).

**The Best Of The Speyside Whisky Trail** *Well signposted but bewildering
number of tours, though by no means at every distillery. Many are in rather featureless industrial complexes & settings. These are the best, with Strathisla
(above):* ·

**1536** **The Glenlivet** Minmore 01542 783220. Starting as an illicit dram celebrat-
Map 8 ed as far S as Edin, George Smith licensed the brand in 1824 and founded this
**P18** distillery in 1858, registering the already mighty name so that anyone else had
to use a prefix. After various successions and mergers, independence was lost
in 1978 when Seagrams took over. Now owned by Pernod Ricard. The famous
Josie's Well, from which the water springs, is underground and not shown, but
small parties and a walk-through which is not on a gantry make the tour as

satisfying and as popular, esp with Americans, as the product. Excellent reception centre with bar/restau & shop. Mar-Oct, 10am-4pm. Sun 12.30-4pm.

**1537 Glenfiddich** Dufftown  O/side town on the A941 to Craigellachie by the
Map 8 ruins of Balvenie Castle. Well-oiled tourist operation and the only distillery
**Q18** where you can see the whisky bottled on the premises; indeed, the whole
process from barley to bar. Also the only major distillery that's free (incl
dram). Also now runs own artists-in-residence scheme with changing shows
over the summer in gallery adj carpark: 01340 821565 for details. AYR
9.30am-4.30pm not w/ends in winter. On the same rd there's a chance to
see a whisky-related industry/craft that hasn't changed in decades. The
**Speyside Cooperage** is 1km from Craigellachie. You watch those poor guys
from the gantry (no chance to slack). AYR Mon-Fri 9.30am-4.30pm. (Good
coffee shop.)

**1538 Glen Grant** Rothes  In Rothes on the A941 Elgin to Perth rd. Not the most
Map 8 picturesque but a distillery tour with an added attraction viz the gdns and
**Q17** orchard reconstructed around the shallow bowl of the glen of the burn that
runs through the distillery: there's a delightful Dram Pavilion. The French
own this one too: reflect as you sit in the library & listen to the founder before
you leave. Apr-Oct 10-4pm, from 12.30pm on Sun.

**1539 Cardhu (or Cardow)** Carron  Off B9102 from Craigellachie to Grantown
Map 8 through deepest Speyside, a small if charming distillery with its own com-
**P18** munity, a millpond, picnic tables, etc. Owned by United Distillers, Cardhu is
the 'heart of Johnnie Walker' (which, amazingly, has another 30 malts in it).
July-Sept daily 10am-5pm Mon-Sat, 12-4pm Sun. Otherwise open at least
weekdays – call 01340 872555 for details.

**1540 Ben Romach** nr Forres  Smallest working distillery so no bus tours or big
Map 8 tourist operation. Human beings with time for a chat. Rescued by Gordon &
**P17** MacPhail (1512/DELIS) & reopened 1999. 'Malt Whisky Centre' a good intro:
you may need no other tour even if you've never heard of the brand. Apr-Sept
9.30am-5pm (Suns in June-Aug only 12-4pm). Wint 10-4pm.

**1541 Dallas Dhu** nr Forres  Not really nr the Spey (3km S of Forres on B9010) and
Map 8 no longer a working distillery (ceased 1983), but instant history provided by
**P17** HS and you don't have to go round on a tour. The wax workers are a bit
spooky; the product itself is more life-like. Apr-Sept 9.30-6.30, restricted hrs
in wint (01309 676548).                                                          HS

**1542 Scotch Whisky Heritage Centre** Edinburgh  0131 220 0441. On Castlehill
Map 1 on last stretch to castle (you cannot miss it). Not a distillery of course, but a
**D4** visitor attraction to celebrate all things a tourist can take in about Scotland's
main export. Shop has huge range. 7 days 10-5pm (extended hrs in summer).

**Promotional Tours: Glenturret nr Crieff, and Aberfeldy** A recent and
not entirely welcome trend has been to makeover distilleries into interactive
ads for certain brands of blends. The quaint old Glenturret distillery by Crieff
is now the Famous Grouse Experience (daily AYR 08450 451800) while
Aberfeldy distillery is now Dewar's World of Whisky (AYR, call for times 01887
822010) tho' it also incls Aberfeldy (the whisky, not the town or the band).
The branding density is tiresome but the production tours are super-profes-
sional.

# Whisky: The Best Malts Selections

## EDINBURGH

✓ ✓ **Scotch Malt Whisky Society** The Vaults, 87 Giles St, Leith & 28 Queen St. Your search will end here. More a club (with membership); visitors must be signed in.

✓ **Royal Mile Whiskies** 379 High St. *Whisky Magazine* Retailer of the Yr. Also in London.

**Bennet's** 8 Leven St by King's Theatre.

**Kay's Bar** 39 Jamaica St.

**The Bow Bar** 80 West Bow.

**Cadenhead's** 172 Canongate. The shop with the lot.

**Canny Man's** 237 Morningside Rd.

**Blue Blazer** Corner Spittal & Bread St (351/REAL ALE PUBS).

## GLASGOW

✓ ✓ **The Pot Still** 154 Hope St. 450 diff bottles of single malt. And proud of it.

**The Bon Accord** 153 North St (677/REAL ALE).

**The Lismore** 206 Dumbarton Rd (691/UNIQUE PUBS).

**Ubiquitous Chip** Ashton lane. Restau, bistro & gr bar on the corner.

**Ben Nevis** Argyle St (far W end) (670/UNIQUE PUBS).

## REST OF SCOTLAND

✓ ✓ **Lochside Hotel** Bowmore, Islay More Islay malts than you ever imagined in friendly local near the Bowmore Distillery.

✓ ✓ **Loch Torridon Hotel** nr Kinlochewe Classic Highland hotel & 300 malts shelf by shelf. And the mountains! 1215/GET AWAY HOTELS.

✓ ✓ **Clachaig Inn** Glencoe Over 100 malts to go with the range of ales & the range of folk that come here to drink after the hills (1326/BLOODY GOOD PUBS).

✓ ✓ **The Drover's Inn** Inverarnan Same as above, with around 75 to choose from and the rt atmos to drink them in (1323/BLOODY GOOD PUBS).

✓ ✓ **The Oystercatcher** Portnahomack Gordon Robertson's exceptional malt (& wine collection) in quality restau in far-flung vill (1033/HIGHLAND RESTAUS).

✓ ✓ **Forss House** nr Thurso Hotel bar on N coast. Often a wee wind outside. Warm up with one of the 300 well-presented malts. (984/HIGHLAND.)

✓ **The Bar At The Craigellachie Hotel** Whiskies arranged around cosy bar of this essential Speyside hotel & the river below (964/SPEYSIDE).

✓ **Knockinaam Lodge** Portpatrick Comfortable country-house hotel; esp good lowland selection incl the (extinct) local Bladnoch (814/SW HOTELS).

✓ **The Piano Bar at the Glenmoriston Hotel** Inverness Easy-to-decipher malt list in superior, stylish surroundings (975/HIGHLAND HOTELS).

✓ **The Alexander** Fortrose Amazing collection of malts (& beers) in town hotel bar. (1014/LESS EXP HIGHLANDS.)

✓ **Ardanaiseig Hotel** Loch Awe A dram's a must after dinner in the bar o/looking the loch where the bats come in.

✓ **Dunain Park Hotel** Inverness After dinner in one of the best places to eat hereabouts, there's a serious malts list to mull over (979/HIGHLAND HOTELS).

**✓ Hotel Eilean Iarmain** Skye  Also known as the Isleornsay Hotel (2294/ISLAND HOTELS); not the biggest range but one of the best places to drink (it).

**Kinloch House Hotel** nr Blairgowrie (908/PERTHSHIRE BEST HOTELS).

**Fox & Hounds** Houston  1355/GASTROPUBS.

**Oban Inn** Oban  Good mix of customers, whisky and ale.

**Fisherman's Tavern** Broughty Ferry  (1088/DUNDEE EAT AND DRINK).

**Lock Inn** Fort Augustus  Canalside setting, good food & plenty whisky.

**Sligachan Hotel** Skye  01478 650204. On A87 (A850) 11km S of Portree. 71 malts in Seamus' huge cabin bar. Good ale selection; Apr/Sept festivals.

**Pittodrie House Hotel** Pitcaple  In the snug (945/NE HOTELS).

**The Lairhillock** nr Stonehaven  Public bar (1353/PUB FOOD).

**Gordon & MacPhail** Elgin  The whisky provisioner and bottlers of the Connoisseurs brand you see in other shops and bars all over. From these humble beginnings over 100yrs ago, they now supply their exclusive and rarity range to the world. Mon-Sat till 5.15pm (5pm Wed). Cl Sun.

**The Whisky Shop** Dufftown  The whisky shop in the main st (by the clock-tower) at the heart of whisky country. Within a few miles of numerous distilleries and their sales operations, this place stocks all the product (incl many halfs). 10am-5pm Mon-Sat, 2-4pm Sun.

**Loch Fyne Whiskies** Inverary  Beyond the church on the A83 a shop with 400 malts to choose from in various sizes & disguises; and whisky ware.

# SECTION 7

*Outdoor Places*

# The Best Gardens

☕ signifies **notable tearoom**.

**1543**
Map 9
**K25**

✓ ✓ **The Younger Botanic Garden** Benmore 12km Dunoon on the A815 to Strachur. An 'outstation' of the Royal Botanic in Edin, gifted to the nation by Harry Younger in 1928, but the first plantations dating from 1820. Walks clearly marked through formal gdns, woody grounds and the 'pinetum' where the air is often so sweet and spicy it can seem like the elixir of life. Redwood avenue, terraced hill sides, views; a gdn of different moods and fine proportions. Good walk, 'Puck's Glen', nearby (2024/WOODLAND WALKS). Café. Mar-Oct 10-6pm (5pm Mar & Oct). ☕         ADMN

**1544**
Map 7
**H16**

✓ ✓ **Inverewe** Poolewe on A832, 80km S of Ullapool. The world-famous gdns on a promontory of L Ewe. Begun in 1862, Osgood Mackenzie made it his life's work in 1883 and it continues with large crowds coming to admire his efforts. Helped by the ameliorating effect of the Gulf Stream, the 'wild' gdn became the model for many others. The guided tours (1.30pm Mon-Fri Apr-Sept) are probably the best way to get the most out of this extensive gdn. Gardens AYR till dusk – go in the evening when it's quiet! Shop, VC till 5pm. ☕         ADMN

**1545**
Map 8
**S20**

✓ ✓ **Crathes** nr Banchory Royal Deeside 25km W of Aber and just off A93. One of the most interesting tower houses (1897/COUNTRY HOUSES) surrounded by exceptional topiary and walled gdns of inspired design and tranquil atmos. Keen gardeners will be in their scented heaven. The Golden Garden (after Gertrude Jekyll) works particularly well and there's a wild gdn beyond the old wall that many people miss. All in all, a v *House and Garden* experience tho' in summer it's stuffed with people as well as plants. Grounds open AYR 9am-sunset. ☕         NTS ADMN

**1546**
Map 10
**P26**

✓ ✓ **Little Sparta** nr Dunsyre 01899 810252. Nr Biggar SW of Edin off A702 (5km), go thro vill then signed. House in bare hill country the home of conceptual artist & national treasure, Ian Hamilton Finlay. Gardens lovingly created over yrs, full of thought-provoking art/sculpture/perspectives. Unike anywhere else. A privilege to visit. June-Sept, Fri & Sun 2-5pm only.

**1547**
Map 10
**N23**

✓ ✓ **Drummond Castle Gardens** Muthill nr Crieff Signed from A822, 2km from Muthill then up a long avenue, the most exquisite formal gdns viewed first from the terrace by the house. A boxwood parterre of a vast St Andrew's Cross in yellow & red (esp antirrhinums & roses), the Drummond colours, with extraordinary sundial centrepiece; 5 gardeners keep every leaf in place. 7 days May-Oct 2-5pm (last adm). House not open to public.     ADMN

**1548**
Map 11
**K31**

✓ ✓ **Logan Botanical Gardens** nr Sandhead S of Stranraer 16km S of Stranraer by A77/A716 and 2km on from Sandhead. Remarkable outstation of the Edin Botanics amongst sheltering woodland in the mild SW. Compact and full of pleasant southern surprises. Less crowded than other 'exotic' gdns. Their 'soundwands' giving commentary on demand make it all v interesting. Salad bar not bad. The Gunnera Bog is quite extraterrestrial. Mar-Oct; 7 days, 10am-5pm (6pm Apr-Sept). ☕         ADMN

**1549**
Map 9
**J24**

✓ ✓ **Crarae** Inverary 16km SE on A83 to Lochgilphead. Famed & fabulous. Recntly taken over by NTS so difficulties in staying open resolved. The wooded banks of L Fyne with gushing burn are as lush as the jungles of Borneo. AYR. Dawn till dusk. Vis centre till 5pm.         NTS

**1550**
Map 6
**N15**

✓ ✓ **Dunrobin Castle Gardens** Golspie On A9 1km N of town. The Versailles-inspired gardens that sit below the opulent Highland chateau of the Dukes of Sutherland (1808/CASTLES). Terraced, parterred & immaculate, they stretch to the sea. 30 gardeners once tended them, now there are 4 but little has changed since they impressed a more exclusive clientele. Apr-Oct. 10.30am-LA 4pm (5pm June-Sept).

**1551**
Map 11
**M30**

✓ **Threave** nr Castle Douglas 64 acres of magnificent Victorian landscaping in incomparable setting overlooking Galloway coastline. Gardeners shouldn't miss the walled kitchen garden. Horticulturally inspiring; and daunting. Open Feb-Dec 10-dusk. ☕

**1552**
Map 10
**P27**

✓ **Dawyck** Stobo nr Peebles On B712 Moffat rd off the A72 Biggar rd from Peebles, 2km from Stobo. Another outstation of the Edin Botanics; a 'recent' acquisition, though tree planting here goes back 300 yrs. Sloping grounds around the gurgling Scrape burn which trickles into the Tweed. Landscaped woody pathways for meditative walks. Famous for shrubs, blue Himalayan poppies & 'the azalea terrace'. Gr walk on Drovers rd, 2km on Stobo Rd before entrance. Tiny basic tearoom. Mar-Oct 10am-5pm.    ADMN

**1553**
Map 9
J23
✓ **Angus' Garden** Taynuilt 7km from village (which is 12km from Oban on the A85) along the Glen Lonan rd. Take first rt after Barguillen Gdn Centre. A gdn laid out by the family who own the centre in memory of their son Angus, a soldier, who was killed in Cyprus. On the slopes around a small loch brimful of lilies and ducks. Informal mix of tended and uncultivated (though wild prevails), a more poignant remembrance is hard to imagine as you while an hr away in this peaceful place. Open AYR.    HONESTY BOX

**1554**
Map 9
H24
✓ **Arduaine Garden** nr Kilmelford 28km S of Oban on A816, one of Argyll's undiscovered arcadias gifted to the NTS and brought to wider attention. Creation of the microclimate in which the rich, diverse vegetation has flourished, influenced by Osgood Mackenzie of Inverewe and its restoration a testimony to 20 yrs hard labour by the Wright brothers (still not happy with the NTS). Enter/park by L Melfort hotel, gate 100m. Until dusk.    NTS

**1555**
Map 9
G26
✓ **Achamore Gardens** Isle of Gigha 1km from ferry. Walk or cycle from ferry (bike hire at post office at top of ferry rd); an easy day trip. The 'big house' on the island set in 65 acres. Lush tropical plants mingle with early-flourishing rhodies (Feb-March): all due to the mild climate & the devotion of only 2 gardeners. 2 marked walks (40mins/2hrs) start from the walled gdn (green route takes in the sea view of Islay & Jura). Density & variety of shrubs, pond plants & trees revealed as you meander in this enchanting spot. Leaflet guides at entrance. Open AYR dawn to dusk. (2282/MAGICAL ISLANDS)    ADMN

**1556**
Map 8
S20
✓ **Drum Castle Rose Garden** nr Banchory 1km from A93, the Deeside rd. In the grounds of Drum Castle (the Irvine ancestral home – tho' nothing remotely to do with my family) a superb walled garden paying homage to the rose & encapsulating 4 cents of its horticulture. 4 separate areas (17th-20thC). Fabulous, July/Aug esp. Open 10-6pm.

**1557**
Map 9
J26
**Ascog Hall Fernery** Rothesay Outside town on rd to Mt Stuart (1852/CO HOUSES), worth stopping at this small garden & v small Victorian Fern House. Green & lush & dripping! Easter-Oct, 10-5pm. Cl Mon/Tues. (& don't miss Rothesay's Victorian men's loos (women can visit); they are not small.) ADMN

**1558**
Map 10
R27
**Priorwood** Melrose Next to Melrose Abbey, a tranquil secret gdn behind high walls which specialises in growing flowers and plants for drying. Picking, drying and arranging is continuously in progress. Samples for sale. Run by enthusiasts on behalf of the NTS, they're always willing to talk stamens with you. Also includes an historical apple orchard with trees through the ages. Heavenly jelly on sale. Mon-Sat 10am-5pm; Sun 1.30-5pm. Cl 4pm wint. Dried flower shop.    NTS ADMN

**1559**
Map 10
Q27
**Kailzie Gardens** Peebles On B7062 Traquair rd. Informal woodland gdns just out of town; not extensive but eminently strollable. Old-fashioned roses and wilder bits. Some poor birds in cages and the odd peacock. Courtyard teashop. Kids' corner. Fishing pond popular. Apr-Oct 11am-5.30pm (restricted access in wint).    ADMN

**1560**
Map 10
R27
**Monteviot House Garden & Woodside Nursery** nr Ancrum and Jedburgh Off A68 at Ancrum, the B6400 to Nisbet (3km), first there's Woodside on left (the Victorian walled garden for the house – now separate) & the terraced to the river (Teviot), mainly formal gardens of the house (the home of the Tory Nicholas Soames, now Lord Lothian). V pleasant to amble. Woodside has organic demonstarations section & is mainly a garden centre. House: Apr-Oct 12-5pm. Nursery: Mar-Oct 9.30am-5.30pm.    ADMN

**1561**
Map 8
S18
**Pitmedden Garden** nr Ellon 35km N of Aber & 10km W of main A92. Formal French gdns recreated in 1950s on site of Sir Alex Seaton's 17thC ones. The 4 gr parterres, 3 based on designs for gdns at Holyrood Palace, are best viewed from the terrace. Charming farmhouse 'museum' seems transplanted. For lovers of symmetry & an orderly universe only (but there is a woodland walk with wildlife garden area). May-Sept 10am-5.30pm.    NTS ADMN

**1562**
Map 8
R19
**Pittodrie House** nr Inverurie An exceptional walled gdn in the grounds of Pittodrie House Hotel at Chapel of Garioch in Aberdeenshire (945/NE HOTELS). Diff gardens compartmentalised by hedges. 500m from house & largely unvisited by most of the guests, this secret & sheltered haven is both a kitchen gdn & a place for meditations and reflections (& possibly wedding photos).

**1563** **Ardkinglas Woodland** Cairndow  Off the A83 L Lomond to Inveraray rd.
Map 9  Through village to signed car park and these mature woodlands in the
**K24**  grounds of Ardkinglas House on the southern bank nr the head of L Fyne.
Fine pines include the 'tallest tree in Britain'. Magical at dawn or dusk. 2km
Loch Fyne Seafood (1398/SEAFOOD RESTAUS) where there is also a tree-shop
gdn centre esp for trees & shrubs (2233/GARDEN CENTRES).          ADMN

**1564** **Jura House Walled Garden** Ardfin, Jura  Around 8km from the ferry on
Map 9  the only rd. Park opp & follow track into woods. Walled garden only part of
**G26**  walk that takes you to coast & ultimately (tho steep) to the beach & the
'Misty Pools'. Beautiful in rain (frequent) or shine! Open AYR.          ADMN

**1565** **Attadale Gardens** Strathcarron  On A890 from Kyle of Lochalsh & A87 just S
Map 7  of Strathcarron. Lovely W Highland house & gardens nr L Carron. Exotic spe-
**J18**  cials, water gardens, sculpture, gr rhodies May/June. Nursery & kitchen gdn.
Good restau nearby (1091/HIGHLAND RESTAUS). Apr-Oct 10am-5.30pm.          ADMN

**1566** **The Hydroponicum** Achiltibuie  The 'Garden of the Future'; a weird
Map 6  glasshouse waterworld where a huge variety of plants thrive without soil in
**J15**  their various microclimates. Apr-Sep. Tours: hourly. Limited hrs in Oct. Growing
kits to buy (strawberries at Christmas?). Lovely 'Lily Pond' café round a pool
using produce grown here. Gr salads! Café 10am-6pm. 01854 622202.  ADMN

**1567** **Ard-Daraich Hill Garden** Ardgour  3 km S Ardgour at Corran Ferry (8/JOUR-
Map 9  NEYS) on A861 to Strontian. Private, labour of love 'hill' and wild gdn which
**J21**  you are at liberty to wander in. Specialising in rhodies, shrubs, trees.
Nursery/small gdn centre. 01855 841248. Open AYR, 7 days.

**1568** **The Hidden Gardens** Glasgow  This garden oasis in the asphalt jungle of
Map 2  Glasgow's S side opened in the disused wasteland behind The Tramway per-
**xA5**  formance & studio space in 2003. A project of environmental theatre group
nva working with landscape architects City Design Co-operative, this is a v
modern approach to an age-old challenge – how to make & keep a sanctuary in the city! It works so far. Open 10am-8pm (wint hrs vary). Cl Mon.

**Royal Botanic Garden** Edinburgh  401/OTHER ATTRACTIONS.

**Botanic Garden & Kibble Palace** Glasgow  713/ATTRACTIONS.

# The Best Country Parks

**1569**  ✓ ✓ **Drumlanrig Castle** Thornhill nr Dumfries  01848 330248. On
Map 11  A76, 7km N of Thornhill in the W Borders in whose romance and
**N29**  history it's steeped, much more than merely a country park; spend a good
day, both inside the castle and in the grounds. Apart from THAT art collection
(Rembrandt, Holbein, alas no longer the Leonardo) and the Craft Courtyard
(2180/CRAFT SHOPS), the delights include: a stunning tearoom, woodland and
riverside walks, an adventure playground, the 'Working Forge' and bike hire
for further afield explorations along the Nith etc. Open Apr-Sept 11-5pm.
(House: May-late Aug 12-4pm.)

**1570**  ✓ **Muirshiel nr Lochwinnoch** Via Largs (A760) or Glas (M8, jnct 29 A737
Map 9  then A760 5km S of Johnstone). N from village on Kilmacolm rd for 3km
**L26**  then signed. Muirshiel is name given to wider area, but park proper begins
6km on rd along the Calder valley. Despite proximity of conurbation (Pt Glas
is over the hill), this is a wild and enchanting place for walking/picnics etc.
Trails marked to waterfall and summit views. Extensive 'events' programme:
www.clydemuirsheil.co.uk Go look for hen harriers. See also 730/GLAS WALKS.
Escape!

**1571** **John Muir Country Park** nr Dunbar  Named after the 19th-century conser-
Map 10  vationist who founded America's National Parks (and the Sierra Club) and
**R25**  who was born in Dunbar. This swathe of coastline to the W of the town
(known locally as Tyninghame) is an important estuarine nature reserve but
is good for family walks and beachcombing. Can enter via B6370 off A198 to
N Berwick or by 'cliff-top' trail from Dunbar (1781/WILDLIFE).

**1572** **Strathclyde Park** betw Hamilton & Motherwell  15km SE of Glas. Take
Map 10  M8/A725 interchange or M74/jnct 5 or 6. Scotland's most popular country
**M26**  park, esp for water sports. From canoeing to parascending; you can hire the
gear (2138/WATER SPORTS). Also: excavated Roman bath house, playgrounds,
sports pitches and now that the trees are maturing, some pleasant walks.

Nearby Baron's Haugh and Dalzell Country Park more notable for their nature trails and gdns. 'Scotland's Theme Park' & the horrid Alona Hotel remind us what country parks should not be about. (1868/MONUMENTS.)

**1573** **Finlaystone Estate** Langbank nr Greenock  A8 to Greenock, Houston
Map 9  direction at Langbank, then signed. Grand mansion home to Chief of Clan
**L25**  Macmillan set in formal gdns in wooded estate. Lots of facs ('Celtic' tearm, craft shop etc), leafy walks, walled gdn. Rare magic. Oct-Mar w/ends only, Apr-Sep daily until 5pm. ☕

**1574** **Almondell** nr East Calder  12km from Edin city bypass. Well-managed park
Map 10  in R Almond valley set amidst area of redundant industry. If you've just spent
**P26**  light yrs trying to exit from Livingston's notorious rd system, you'll need this green oasis with its walks in woods, meadows and along cinder tracks. Picnic sites, VC with refreshments, kids' areas. From Edin take A71 from bypass (Kilmarnock rd), then B7015 (Camps) for 7km. Park on rt just into E Calder. Walk ahead to woods.

**1575** **Hirsel Country Park** Coldstream  On A697, N edge town (direction Kelso).
Map 10  3000 acres the grounds of Hirsel House (not open public). 2-4km walks thro'
**S27**  farmland & woods incl lovely languid lake. Museum, tearm & nice pottery shop (Abbey Ceramics).

**1576** **Muiravonside Country Park**  4km SW of Linlithgow on B825. Also sign-
Map 10  posted from J4 of the M9 Edin/Stirling. Former farm estate now run by the
**N25**  local authority providing 170 acres of woodland walks, parkland, picnic sites and a VC for school parties or anyone else with an interest in birds, bees and badgers. Ranger service does guided walks Apr-Sep. Gr place to walk off that lunch at the not-too-distant Champany Inn (257/BURGERS).

**1557** **Eglinton** nr Irvine  Beside main A78 Largs to Ayr rd signed from
Map 9  Irvine/Kilwinning intersection. Spacious lungful of Ayrshire nr new town
**K27**  nexus and traffic tribulations. Visitor centre with interpretation of absolutely everything. Much made of the Eglintons' place in Scottish history. Park open all the time, VC Easter-Oct. Network of walks.

✓✓**Culzean Castle Park**  Superb & hugely pop (1791/CASTLES).

✓**Haddo House** Aberdeenshire  Beautiful grounds (1851/CO HOUSES).

**Mugdock Country Park** nr Milngavie  Marvellous park close to Glas (5 car parks around the vast site). Report 726/CITY WALKS.

**Tentsmuir** nr Tayport  Estuarine; John Muir, on Tay (1784/WILDLIFE).

**Kelburne Country Centre** Largs  1733/KIDS.

# The Best Town Parks

**1578** ✓✓**Princes St Gardens** Edinburgh  S side of Princes St. The greenery
Map 1  that launched a thousand postcards (tho' now under threat from a
**C3**  thousand events). This former loch – drained around the time the New Town was built – is divided by the Mound. The eastern half has pitch and putt, Winter Wonderland and the Scott Monument (432/BEST VIEWS), the western has its much-photographed fountain, open-air café and space for locals and tourists to sprawl on the grass when sunny. You'll also find the the Ross Bandstand here – heart of Edinburgh's Hogmanay (61/BEST EVENTS) and the International Festival's fireworks concert (470/ESSENTIAL CULTURE). Louts with lager, senior citz on benches, dazed tourists: all our lives are here. Till dusk.

**1579** ✓✓**Hazelhead Park** Aberdeen  Via Queens Rd, 3km centre. Extraor-
Map 8  dinary park where the Aberdonians' mysterious gardening skills are
**T19**  magnificently in evidence. Many facs incl a maze, pets' corner, wonderful tacky tearoom & there are lawns, memorials & botanical splendours aplenty esp azalea gdn in spring and roses in summer. Gr sculpture.

**1580** ✓**Duthie Park** Aberdeen  Riverside Dr along R Dee from the br carrying
Map 8  main A92 rd from/to Stonehaven. The other large well-kept park with
**T19**  duck pond, bandstand, hugely impressive rose gdns in summer, carved sculptures and the famous, now renamed 'David Welch' (a former Director of Parks) Winter Gdn of subtropical palms/ferns etc; under restoration (9.30am-7.30pm summer, wint at dusk).

**1581** ✓ **Pittencrieff Park** Dunfermline  The extensive park alongside the
Map 10   Abbey and Palace ruins gifted to the town in 1903 by Carnegie. Open
P25   areas, glasshouses, pavilion (more a function rm) but most notably a deep
verdant glen criss-crossed with pathways. Gr kids' play area. Lush, full of
birds, good after rain.

**1582** **Beveridge Park** Kirkcaldy  Also in Fife, another big municipal park with a
Map 10   duck and boat pond, wide-open spaces and many amusements (e.g. bowling,
Q24   tennis, putting, plootering). Ravenscraig a coastal park on the main rd E to
Dysart is an excellent place to walk. Gr prospect of town and Firth, coves and
skerries.

**1583** **Macrosty Park** Crieff  The park you see on your left as you're leaving Crieff
Map 10   for Comrie & Crianlarich, but for parking ask locally. A perfect green place on
N23   sloping ground down to the R Earn (good level walk – Lady Mary's Walk) with
tearms/kids' area, mature trees & a superb bandstand.

**1584** **Wilton Lodge Park** Hawick  Hawick not overfull of visitor attractions, but
Map 10   it does have a nice park with facs and diversions enough for everyone e.g. the
R28   civic gallery, rugby pitches (they quite like rugby in Hawick), a large kids' playground, a seasonal café and lots of riverside walks by the Teviot. Lots of my
school friends lost their virginity in the shed here. All-round open-air recreation centre. S end of town by A7.

**1585** **Station Park** Moffat  On your rt as you enter the town from the M74. Well-
Map 11   proportioned people's park; boating pond (with giant swans) main feature.
P28   Annan water aldongside offers nice walking. Notable also for the monument
to Air Chief Marshall Hugh Dowding, Commander in Chief during the Battle
of Britain. 'Never... was so much owed so many to so few'.

**1586** **Dean Castle Park** Kilmarnock  A77 S first t/off for Kilmarnock then signed;
Map 9   from Ayr A77 N, 3rd t/off. Surprising green & woody oasis in suburban
L27   Kilmarnock; lawns & woods around restored castle & courtyard. Riding cen-
tre. Burns Rose Garden.

**1587** **Garries Park** Gatehouse of Fleet  Notable for its tiny perfect garden which
Map 11   you enter under an arch from the main st of this SW vill. A wee gem esp for
the roses. Leads to bigger public space, but pause in the garden & smell
those roses. There are 2 seats.

**1588** **Rouken Glen & Linn Park** Glasgow  Both on S side of river. Rouken Glen
Map 2   via Pollokshaws/Kilmarnock rd to Eastwood Toll then rt. Good place to park
xC5   is second left, Davieland Rd beside pond. Across park from here (or beside
main Rouken Glen rd) is main visitor area with info centre, gdn centre, a
Chinese restau, kids' play area and woodland walks (0141 577 3913 for info).
Linn Park via Aikenhead and Carmunnock rd. After King's Park on left, take rt
to Simshill Rd and park at golf course beyond houses. A long route there, but
worth it; this is one of the undiscovered Elysiums of a city which boasts 60
parks. Ranger Centre (0141 637 1147) – activities, wildlife walks, kids' nature
trails, horse-riding (0141 637 3096) and Alexander 'Greek' Thomson's
Holmwood House; open Easter-Oct 12-5pm (NTS).

**1589** **Camperdown Park** Dundee  Calling itself a country park, Camperdown is
Map 10   the main recreational breathing space for the city and hosts a plethora of dis-
Q23   tractions (a golf course, a wildlife complex, mansion house etc). Situated
beyond Kingsway, the ring-route; go via Coupar Angus rd t/off. Best walks
across the A923 in the Templeton Woods. **Balgray Park** also excl.

**1590** **Grant Park** Forres  Frequent winner of the Bonny Bloom competitions (but
Map 8   not recently, so spruce up, Forres!) with its balance of ornamental gdns, open
P17   parkland and woody hill side, this is a carefully tended rose. Good municipal
facs like pitch and putt, playground. Cricket in summer and topping topiary.
Through woods at top of Cluny Hill, a tower affords gr views of the Moray and
Cromarty Firths and surrounding forest.

**1591** **Callander Park** Falkirk  Park on edge of town centre, signed from all over.
Map 10   O/looked by high-rise blocks & nr busy rd system, this is nevertheless a
N25   beautiful green space with a big hoose (heritage museum), woods & lawns.
Comes alive in May as venue for Big in Falkirk (35/EVENTS).

# The Most Interesting Coastal Villages

**1592**
Map 7
**H18**
✓ **Plockton** nr Kyle of Lochalsh  A Highland gem of a place 8km over the hill from Kyle, clustered around inlets of a wooded bay on L Carron. Cottage gdns down to the bay and palm trees! Some gr walks over headlands. Plockton Inn prob best bet for reasonable stay and eats (1007/LESS EXP HIGH-LAND HOTELS). Plockton Hotel (1183/ROADSIDE INNS CHP, pub grub). It's not hard to feel connected with this village (& so many people do).

**1593**
✓ **Moray Coast Fishing Villages**  From Speybay (where the Spey slips into the sea) along to Fraserburgh, some of Scotland's best coastal scenery and many interesting villages in cliff/cove and beach settings. Esp notable are **Portsoy** with 17thC harbour – and see 39/EVENTS & 346/PUBS; **Sandend** with its own popular beach & a fabulous one nearby (1609/BEACH-ES); **Pennan** made famous by the film *Local Hero* (the hotel/pub for sale at TGP; 01346 561201); **Gardenstown** (has a gr café/restau at the harbour 1405/SEAFOOD) with a walk along the water's edge to **Crovie** (pron 'Crivee') the epitome of a coast-clinging community; and **Cullen**, which is more of a town and has a gr beach. (951/NE HOTELS.)

**1594**
Map 3
**Q10**
✓ **Stromness** Orkney Mainland  24km from Kirkwall and a different kettle of fish. Hugging the shore and with narrow streets and wynds, it has a unique atmos, both maritime and European. Some of the most singular shops you'll see anywhere and the Orkney folk going about their business. Park nr harbour and walk down the cobbled main st if you don't want to scrape your paintwork (2327/ORKNEY; 2261/GALLERIES).

**1595**
Map 7
**M17**
✓ **Cromarty** nr Inverness  At end of rd across Black Isle from Inverness (45km NE), does take longer than you think (well, 30 mins). Village with dreamy times-gone-by atmos, without being twee. Lots of kids running about and a pink strand of beach. Delights to discover include: the east kirk, plain and aesthetic with countryside through the windows behind the altar; Hugh (the geologist) Miller's cottage/Courthouse museum (2240/BEST HISTO-RY AND HERITAGE); The Pantry (1473/TEAROOMS); Cromarty Bakery (1481/BEST SCOTCH BAKERS); the fab new restau Sutor Creek (1021/INX HIGHLANDS); the shore and cliff walk (2046/COASTAL WALKS); the Pirates' Cemetery and of course the dolphins (1777/DOLPHINS).

**1596**
Map 10
**N25**
**Culross** nr Dunfermline  By A994 from Dunfermline or jnct 1 of M90 just over Forth Rd Br (15km). Old centre conserved and being restored by NTS. Mainly residential and not awash with craft and coffee shops. More historical than merely quaint; a community of careful custodians lives in the white, red-pantiled houses. Footsteps echo in the cobbled wynds. Palace and Town House open Easter-Oct 10-6pm, w/ends only Oct. Interesting back gdns and lovely church at top of hill (1891/CHURCHES). Pamphlet by Rights of Way Society available locally, is useful.

**1597**
Map 9
**G22**
**Tobermory** Mull  Not so much a village or setting for a kids' TV show (the brilliant *Balamory*), rather the main town of Mull, set around a hill on superb Tobermory Bay. Ferry pt for Ardnamurchan, but main Oban ferry is 35km away at Craignure. Usually a bustling harbour front with quieter streets behind; a quintessential island atmos. Some good inexp hotels (and quayside hostel) well situated to explore the whole island. (2326/MULL; 2296/ISLAND HOTELS; 1168/BEST HOSTELS.)

**1598**
Map 9
**F26**
**Port Charlotte** Islay  A township on the 'Rhinns of Islay', the western peninsula. By A846 from the pts, Askaig and Ellen via Bridgend. Rows of white-washed, well-kept cottages along and back from shoreline. On rd in, there's an island museum and a coffee/bookshop. Also a 'town' beach and one between PC and Bruichladdich (and esp the one with the war memorial nearby). Quiet and charming, not merely quaint. (2323/ISLAY; 2292/ISLAND HOTELS; 1786/WILDLIFE CENTRES)

**1599**
Map 11
**N30**
**Rockcliffe** nr Dumfries  25km S on Solway Coast rd, A710. On the 'Scottish Riviera', the rocky part of the coast around to Kippford (2042/COASTAL WALKS). A good rock-scrambling foreshore tho not so clean, and a village with few houses and Baron's Craig hotel; set back with gr views (27 MED.EX rms) but a somewhat gloomy presence. Tearm in vill (1469/TEAROOMS).

**1600**
Map 10
**R24**
**East Neuk Villages** The quintessential quaint wee fishing villages along the bit of Fife that forms the mouth of the Firth of Forth, **Crail, Anstruther, Pittenweem, St Monans** & **Elie** all have different characters & attractions esp Crail & Pittenweem harbours, Anstruther as main centre & home of Fisheries Museum (see also 1420/FISH AND CHIPS; FIFE HOTELS; 1761/BIRDS) and perfect Elie (2147/WINDSURFING; 895/896/FIFE HOTELS; 1360/GASTROPUBS; 2064/GREAT GOLF). Or see ST ANDREWS. Cycling good, traffic in summer not.

**1601**
Map 10
**P25**
**Aberdour** Betw Dunfermline and Kirkcaldy and nr Forth Rd Br (10km E from jnct 1 of M90) or, better still, go by train from Edin (frequent service: Dundee or Kirkcaldy); delightful station. Walks round harbour and to headland, Silver Sands beach 1km (429/EDIN BEACHES), castle ruins. (1890/CHURCHES; 897/FIFE HOTELS.)

**1602**
Map 7
**H17**
**Diabeg Wester Ross** On N shore of L Torridon at the end of the unclassi-fied rd from Torridon on one of Scotland's most inaccessible peninsulas. Diabeg is simply beautiful (tho' pity about those fish cages). Fantastic rd there and then walk! PS: there's no pub.

**1603**
Map 11
**L31**
**Isle of Whithorn** Strange faraway village at end of the rd, 35km S Newton Stewart, 6km Whithorn (1842/PREHISTORIC SITES). Mystical harbour where low tide does mean low, saintly shoreline, a sea angler's pub, the Steam Packet – v good pubgrub (1335/BLOODY GOOD PUBS). Ninian's chapel round the headland not so uplifting but en route you'll see the *Solway Harvester* memorial by the white building. Everybody visiting Whithorn seems to walk this way.

**1604**
Map 9
**J27**
**Corrie** Arran Last but not least, the bonniest bit of Arran (apart from Kildonan & the glens, etc), best reached by bike from Brodick (01770 302460 or 302868). Many walks from here incl Goat Fell but nice just to sit or potter on the foreshore. Hotel has never lived up to expectations but the vill shop is fab. I'd like a memorial bench on that shoreline.

# Fantastic Beaches & Bays

**1605**
Map 6
**L12**
✓✓ **Pete's Beach** nr Durness The One of many gr beaches on the N coast (see below) that I've called my own. The hill above it is called 'Ceannabeinne'; you find it 7km E of Durness. Coming from Tongue it's just after where L Eriboll comes out to the sea & the rd hits the coast again (there's a layby opp). It's a small perfect cove flanked by walls of coral-pink rock and shallow turquoise sea. Splendid from above (land rises to a bluff with a huge boulder) & from below. There's a bench – come sit by me then leave your footprints in the sand. Excl inx GH nearby – Port-Na-Con (1018/INX HIGHLAND HOTELS).

**1606**
Map 9
**F24**
✓✓ **Kiloran Beach** Colonsay 9km from quay and hotel, past Colonsay House: parking and access on hill side. Often described as the finest beach in the Hebrides, it does not disappoint tho' it has changed character in recent yrs (a shallower sandbar traps tidal run-off). Craggy cliffs on one side, negotiable rocks on the other and, in betw, tiers of grassy dunes. Do go to the end! The island of Colonsay was once bought as a picnic spot. This beach was probably the reason why.

**1607**
✓✓ **Moray Coast** Many gr beaches along coast from Spey Bay to Fraserburgh, notably **Cullen** and **Lossiemouth** (town beaches) and **New Aberdour** (1km from New Aberdour village on B9031, 15km W of Fraserburgh) and **Rosehearty** (8km W of Fraserburgh) both quieter places for walks and picnics. One of the best-kept secrets is the beach at Sunnyside where you walk past the incredible ruins of Findlater Castle on the cliff top (how did they build it? A place, on its grassed-over roof, for a pic-nic) and down to a cove which on my sunny day was simply perfect. Take a left going into Sandend 16km W of Banff, follow rd for 2km, turn rt, park in the farmyard. Walk from here past dovecote, 1km to cliff. Also signed from A98. *See also* 2045/COASTAL WALKS.

**1608**
Map 9
**G28**
✓✓ **Macrihanish** At the bottom of the Kintyre peninsula 10km from Campbeltown. Walk N from Macrihanish village or golf course, or from the car park on the main A83 to Tayinloan and Tarbert at pt where it hits/leaves the coast. A joyously long strand (8km) of unspoiled orange-pink sand backed by dunes and facing the 'steepe Atlantic Stream' all the way to Newfoundland (2071/GOLF IN GREAT PLACES).

**1609**
MAP 6
**K12**
✓✓ **Sandwood Bay** Kinlochbervie  This mile-long sandy strand with its old 'Stack', is legendary, but therein lies the problem since now too many people know about it and you may have to share in its glorious isolation. Inaccessibility is its saving grace, a 7km walk from the sign off the rd at Balchrick (nr the cattle grid), 6km from Kinlochbervie or cut a third of the distance in a 4-wheel drive; allow 3hrs return plus time there. More venturesome is the walk from the N and Cape Wrath (2040/COASTAL WALKS). Managed by John Muir Trust. Go easy & go in summer! Also

**1610**
Map 6
**K13**
✓ **Oldshoremore**  The beach you pass on the rd to Balchrick, only 3km from Kinlochbervie. It's easy to reach and a beautiful spot: the water is clear and perfect for swimming, and there are rocky walks and quiet places. **Polin**, 500m N, is a cove you might have to yourself. (1236/CAMPING)

**1611**
Map 9
**F26**
✓ **Islay  Saligo, Machir Bay & The Big Strand**  The first two are bays on NW of island via A847 rd to Pt Charlotte, then B8018 past L Gorm. Wide beaches; remains of war fortifications in deep dunes, Machir perhaps best for beach bums. They say 'no swimming' so paddle with extreme prejudice. The Big Strand on Laggan Bay: along Bowmore-Pt Ellen rd take Oa t/off, follow Kintra signs. There's camping and gr walks in either direction, 8km of glorious sand and dunes (contains the Machrie Golf Course). An airy amble under a wide sky. (2070/GOLF IN GREAT PLACES; 2038/COASTAL WALKS.)

**1612**
Map 9
**J25**
✓ **Ostal Beach/Kilbride Bay** Millhouse nr Tighnabruaich   3km from Millhouse on B8000 signed Ardlamont (not Portvadie, the ferry), a track to rt before white house (often with a chain across to restrict access). Park and walk 1.5km, turning rt after lochan. You arrive on a perfect white sandy crescent known locally as Ostal and, apart from the odd swatch of sewage, in certain conditions, a mystical secret place to swim and picnic. The N coast of Arran is like a Greek island in the bay.

**1613**
Map 5
**D18**
✓ **South Uist**  Deserted but for birds, an almost unbroken strand of beach running for miles down the W coast; the machair at its best early summer. Take any rd off the spinal A865; usually less than 2km. Good spot to try is t/off at Tobha Mor; real black houses and a chapel on the way to the sea.

**1614**
Map 5
**E15**
✓ **Scarista Beach** South Harris  On main rd S of Tarbert (15km) to Rodel. The beach is so beautiful that people have been married there. Hotel over the rd is worth staying just for this, but is also a gr retreat – also 2 excl self-cat cotts 2295/ISLAND HOTELS. Golf course on links (2078/GOLF IN GREAT PLACES). Fab in early evening. The sun also rises.

**1615**
Map 10
**R22**
✓ **Lunan Bay** nr Montrose  5km from main A92 rd to Aber and 5km of deep red crescent beach under a wide northern sky. But'n'Ben, Auchmithie, is an excellent place to start or finish (933/PERTHSHIRE EATS) and good app (from S), although Gordon's restau at Inverkeilor is closer (932/PERTHSHIRE EATS). Best viewpoint from Boddin Farm 3km S Montrose and 3km from A92 signed 'Usan'. Often deserted.

**1616**
Map 6
**J14**
✓ **The Secret Beach** nr Achmelvich  Can app from Archmelvich car park going N (it's the next proper bay round) or from Lochinver-Stoer/Drumbeg rd (less walk, layby on rt after Archmelvich t/off). Called **Alltan na Bradhan**, it's the site of an old mill (griding wheels still there), perfect for camping & the best sea for swimming. Sorry Colin & Leslie – hope you still have it to yourselves next summer.

**1617**
Map 9
**G25**
**Jura** Lowlandman's Bay  Not strictly a beach (there is a sandy strand before the headland) but a rocky foreshore with ethereal atmos; gr light and space. Only seals break the spell. Go rt at 3-arch br to first group of houses (Knockdrome), through yard on left and rt around cottages to track to Ardmenish. After deer fences, bay is visible on your rt, 1km walk away.

**1618**
Map 5
**C20**
**Vatersay Outer Hebrides**  The tiny island joined by a causeway to Barra. Twin crescent beaches on either side of the isthmus, one shallow and sheltered visible from Castlebay, the other an ocean beach with rollers. Dunes/machair; safe swimming. There's a helluva hill betw Barra and Vatersay if you're cycling.

**1619**
Map 5
**C20**
**Barra** Seal Bay  5km Castlebay on W coast, 2km after Isle of Barra Hotel through gate across machair where rd rt is signed Taobh a Deas Allathasdal. A flat, rocky Hebridean shore and skerries where seals flop into the water and eye you with intense curiosity. The better-beach beach is next to the hotel.

**1620** **West Sands** St Andrews  As a town beach, this is hard to beat; it dominates
Map 10  the view to W. Wide swathe not too unclean and sea swimmable. Golf cours-
**R23**  es behind. Consistently gets 'the blue flag', but beach buffs may prefer
Kinshaldy (1785/WILDLIFE), Kingsbarns (10km S), or Elie (28km S).

**1621** **North Coast**  To the W of Thurso, along the N coast, are some of Britain's
Map 6  most unspoiled and unsung beaches. No beach bums, no Beach Boys. There
are so many gr little coves, you can have one to yourself even on a hot day,
but those to mention are: **Strathy** and **Armadale** (35km W Thurso), **Farr**
and **Torrisdale** (48km) and **Coldbackie** (65km). My favourite is elevated to
the top of this category.

**1622** **Sands Of Morar** nr Mallaig  70km W of Ft William & 6km from Mallaig by
Map 7  newly improved rd, these easily accessible beaches may seem overpopulated
**H20**  on summer days and the S stretch nearest to Arisaig may have one too many
caravan parks, but they go on for miles and there's enough space for everybody. The sand's supposed to be silver but in fact it's a v pleasing pink. Lots
of rocky bits for exploration. One of the best beachy bits (the bay before the
estuary) is 'Camusdaroch', signed from the main rd (where *Local Hero* was
filmed), further from rd, is quieter and a v good swathe of sand. Traigh, the
golf course makes good use of the dunes (2087/GOOD GOLF).

**1623** **The Bay At The Back Of The Ocean** Iona  Easy 2km walk from frequent
Map 9  ferry from Fionnphort, S of Mull (2277/MAGICAL ISLANDS) or hire a bike from the
**F23**  store on your left as you walk into the village (01681 700357). Paved rd most
of way. John Smith, who is buried beside the abbey, once told me that this
was one of his favourite places. There's a gr inx hotel on Iona, The Argyll
(1217/GET AWAY FROM IT ALL).

**1624** **Dornoch (& Embo Beaches)**  The wide and extensive sandy beach of this
Map 6  pleasant town at the mouth of the Dornoch Firth famous also for its golf
**N16**  links. 4km N, Embo Sands starts with ghastly caravan city, but walk N
towards Golspie. Embo is twinned with Kaunakakai, Hawaii!

**1625** **Port of Ness** Isle Of Lewis  Also signed Port Nis, this is the beach at the end
Map 5  of the Hebrides in the far N of Lewis. Just keep driving. There are some inter-
**G12**  esting stops on the way (2196/ART, 2226/2227/MUSEUMS) – until you get to
this tiny bay & harbour down the hill at the end of the rd. Anthony Barber's
Harbour View Gallery full of his own work (which you find in many other gal-
leries & even postcards) is worth a visit (10am-5pm, cl Sun).

**1626** **2 Beaches in the far SW** **Killantringan Bay nr Portpatrick**  Off A77
Map 11  before PP signed 'Dunskey Gardens' in summer, foll rd signed Killantringan
Lighthouse (dirt track). Park 1km before lighthouse. Beautiful bay for explo-
ration. **Sandhead Beach**  A716 S of Stranraer. Shallow, safe waters of Luce
Bay. Perfect for families. And thanks to Alison.

# The Great Glens

**1627**  ✔ ✔ ✔ **Glen Affric**  Beyond Cannich at end of Glen Urquhart A831,
Map 7  20km from Drumnadrochit on L Ness. A dramatic gorge that
**K18**  strikes westwards into the wild heart of Scotland. Superb for rambles
(2007/GLEN AND RIVER WALKS), expeditions, Munro-bagging (further in, beyond
L Affric) and even just tootling through in the car. Shaped by the Hydro Board,
L. Benevean nevertheless adds to the drama. Cycling good (bike hire in
Cannich 01456 415251 & at the campsite) as is the detour to Tomich and
Plodda Falls (1639/WATERFALLS). Stop at Dog Falls (1714/PICNICS).

**1628**  ✔ ✔ ✔ **Glen Lyon nr Aberfeldy**  One of Scotland's crucial places
Map 10  both historically and geographically, much favoured by fish-
**M22**  ers/walkers/Munro-baggers. Wordsworth and Tennyson, Gladstone and
Baden Powell all sang its praises. Site of ground-breaking theatre 'The Path'
in 2000. The Lyon is a classic Highland river tumbling through corries, gorges
and riverine meadows. Several Munros are within its watershed and rise gloriously on either side. Rd all the way to the loch side (30km). Eagles soar over
the remoter tops at the head of the glen. The Post Office coffee shop does a
roaring trade.

**1629**
Map 9
**K21**
✓ ✓ **Glen Nevis** Fort William Used by many a film director; easy to see why. Ben Nevis is only part of magnificent scenery. Many walks and convenient facs (1645/WATERFALLS; 2003/SERIOUS WALKS). W Highland Way emerges here. Vis centre & cross river to climb Ben Nevis. Good caff in season (2332/FT WILLIAM). This woody dramatic glen is a national treasure.

**1630**
Map 9
**K22**
✓ ✓ **Glen Etive** Off from more exalted Glencoe (and the A82) at Kingshouse, as anyone you meet in those parts will tell you, this truly is a glen of glens. And, as my friends who camp and climb here implore, it needs no more advertisement. (1234/CAMPING, 1707/POOLS)

**1631**
Map 6
**L15**
**Strathcarron** nr Bonar Bridge You drive up the N bank of this Highland river from the br o/side Ardgay (pron 'Ordguy') which is 3km over the br from Bonar Br. Rd goes 15km to Croick and its remarkable church (1896/CHURCHES). The river gurgles and gushes along its rocky course to the Dornoch Firth and there are innumerable places to picnic, swim and stroll further up. Quite heavenly on a warm day.

**1632**
Map 10
**Q21**
**The Angus Glens** Glen Clova/Glen Prosen/Glen Isla. All via Kirriemuir. Isla to W is a woody, approachable glen with a deep gorge, on B954 nr Alyth (1649/WATERFALLS) and the lovely Glenisla Hotel (1189/INNS). Others via B955, to Dykehead then rd bifurcates. Both glens stab into the heart of the Grampians. 'Minister's Walk' goes betw them from behind the kirk at Prosen village over the hill to B955 before Clova village (7km). Glen Clova is a walkers' paradise esp from Glendoll 24km from Dykehead; limit of rd. Viewpoint. 'Jock's Rd' to Braemar and the Capel Mounth to Ballater (both 24km). Good hotel at Clova (921/PERTHSHIRE HOTELS) and famous 'Loops of Brandy' walk (2hrs, 2-B-2); stark and beautiful.

**1633**
Map 9
**J25**
**Glendaruel** The Cowal Peninsula on the A886 betw Colintraive and Strachur. Humble but perfectly formed glen of R Ruel, from Clachan in S (a kirk and an inn) through deciduous meadowland to more rugged grandeur 10km N. Easy walking and cycling. W rd best. Kilmodan carved stones signed. Inver Cottage on L Fyne a gr coffee/food stop (793/ARGYLL RESTAUS).       2-B-2

**1634**
Map 9
**J23**
**Glen Lonan** nr Taynuilt Betw Taynuilt on A85 and A816 S of Oban. Another quiet wee glen, but all the rt elements for walking, picnics, cycling and fishing or just a run in the car. Varying scenery, a bubbling burn (the R Lonan), some standing stones and not many folk. Angus' Garden at the Taynuilt end should not be missed (1553/GARDENS). No marked walks; now get lost!       2-B-2

**1635**
Map 11
**L29**
**Glen Trool** nr Newton Stewart 26km N by A714 via Bargrennan which is on the S Upland Way (1997/LONG WALKS). A gentle wooded glen within the vast Galloway Forest Park (one of the most charming, accessible parts) VC 5km from Bargrennan. Pick up a walk brochure. Many options. (1939/MARY, CHARLIE, BOB.) Start of the Merrick climb (1969/HILLS).

**1636**
Map 10
**N23**
**The Sma' Glen** nr Crieff Off the A85 to Perth, the A822 to Amulree and Aberfeldy. Sma' meaning small, this is the valley of the R Almond where the Mealls (lumpish, shapeless hills) fall steeply down to the rd. Where the rd turns away from the river, the long distance path to L Tay begins (28km). Sma' Glen, 8km, has good picnic spots, but they get busy and midgy in summer.

**1637**
Map 7
**L18**
**Strathfarrar** nr Beauly or Drumnadrochit Rare unspoiled glen accessed from A831 leaving Drumnadrochit on L Ness via Cannich (30km) or S from Beauly (15km). Signed at Struy. Arrive at gatekeeper's house. Access restricted to 25 cars per day (Cl Tue & till 1.30pm on Wed). For access Oct-Mar 01463 761260; you must be out by 6pm. 22km to head of glen past lochs. Good climbing, walking, fishing. The real peace & quiet!

# The Most Spectacular Waterfalls

*One aspect of Scotland that really is improved by rain. All the walks to these falls are graded 1-A-1 unless otherwise stated (see p. 13 for walk codes).*

**1638**
Map 7
**J18**

✓✓ **Falls of Glomach** 25km Kyle of Lochalsh off A87 nr Shiel Br, past Kintail Centre at Morvich then 2km further up Glen Croe to br. Walk starts other side; there are other ways, (e.g. from the SY Hostel in Glen Affric), but this is most straightforward. Allow 5/7 hrs for the pilgrimage to one of Britain's highest falls. Path is steep but well trod. Glomach means gloomy and you might feel so, peering into the ravine; from precipice to pool, it's 200m. But to pay tribute, go down carefully to ledge. Vertigo factor and sense of achievement both fairly high. (1171/HOSTELS.) Consult *Where to Walk in Kintail, Glenelg & Lochalsh*, sold locally for the Kintail Mt Rescue Team. 2-C-3

**1639**
Map 7
**K18**

✓✓ **Plodda Falls** nr Tomich nr Drumnadrochit A831 from L Ness to Cannich (20km), then 7km to Tomich, a further 5km up mainly woodland track to car park. 200m walk down through woods of Scots Pine and ancient Douglas Fir to one of the most enchanting woodland sites in Britain and the Victorian iron br over the brink of the 150m fall into the churning river below. The dawn chorus here must be amazing. Freezes into winter wonderland (ice climbers from Inverness take advantage). Good hotel in village (1016/HIGHLANDS HOTELS).

**1640**
Map 10
**N21**

✓ **Falls Of Bruar** nr Blair Atholl Close to the main A9 Perth-Inverness rd, 12km N of B Atholl nr House of Bruar shopping experience. (2161/SCOT-TISH SHOPPING). Consequently, the short walk to lower falls is v consumer-led but less crowded than you might expect. The lichen-covered walls of the gorge below the upper falls (1km) are less ogled and more dramatic. Circular path is well marked but steep and rocky in places. Tempting to swim on hot days (1753/SWIMMING HOLES). ☕

**1641**
Map 9
**J27**

✓ **Glenashdale Falls** Arran 5km walk from br on main rd at Whiting Bay. Signed up the burn side, but uphill and further on than you think, so allow 2hrs (return). Series of falls in a rocky gorge in the woods with paths so you get rt down to the brim and the pools. Swim here, swim in heaven! 1-B-1

**1642**
Map 9
**G22**

**Eas Fors** Mull On the Dervaig to Fionnphort rd 3km from Ulva Ferry; a series of cataracts tumbling down on either side of the rd. Easily accessible. There's a path down the side to the brink where the river plunges into the sea. On a warm day swimming in the sea below the fall is a rare exhilaration.

**1643**
Map 7

**Lealt Falls** Skye Impressive torrent of wild mt water about 20km N of Portree on the A855. There's a car park on a bend on rt (going N). You can walk to grassy ledges & look over or go down to the beach.
**Kilt Rock**, a viewpoint much favoured by bus parties, is a few km further (you look over & along the cliffs). Also...
**Eas Mor** Glen Brittle nr end of rd. 24km from Sligachan. A mt waterfall with the wild Cuillins behind and views to the sea. App as part of a serious scramble or merely a 30-min Cuillin sampler. Start at the Memorial Hut, cross the rd, bear rt, cross burn and then follow path uphill. 2-C-2

**1644**
Map 6
**L14**

**Eas A' Chual Aluinn** Kylesku 'Britain's highest waterfall' nr the head of Glencoul, is not easy to reach. Kylesku is betw Scourie and Lochinver off the main A894, 20km S of Scourie. There are 2hr cruises at 11am/3pm May-Sept (and 2pm Fri) outside hotel (1037/INEXP HIGHLAND RESTAUS). Falls are a rather distant prospect, but you may be able to alight and get next boat. Baby seals an added attraction June-Aug. (Another boat trip from the same quay goes to **Kerracher Gardens**, a lochside labour of love that's worth seeing – boats 1pm every day in summer or phone 01971 502345). There's also a track to the top of the falls from 5km N of the Skiag Br on the main rd (4hrs return), but you will need to take directions locally. The water freefalls for 200m, which is 4 times further than Niagara (take pinch of salt here). There is a spectacular pulpit view down the cliff, 100m to rt. 2-C-3

**1645**
Map 9
**K21**

**Steall Falls** Glen Nevis, Fort William Take Glen Nevis rd at r/bout o/side town centre and drive 'to end' (16km) through glen. Start from the second & final car park, following path marked Corrour, uphill through the woody gorge with R Ness thrashing below. Glen eventually and dramatically opens out and there are gr views of the long veils of the Falls. Precarious 3-wire br for which you will also need nerves of steel. Always fun to see the macho types bottle out of doing it! I never have (you can cross further down). 3-A-3

**1646** **Corrieshalloch Gorge/Falls of Measach** Jnct of A832 and A835, 20km S
Map 7 of Ullapool; possible to walk down into the gorge from both rds. Most dra-
**K16** matic app is from the car park on the A832 Gairloch rd. Staircase to swing br
from whence to consider how such a wee burn could make such a deep gash.
V impressive. A must-stop on the way to/from Ullapool.

**1647** **The Grey Mare's Tail** On the wildly scenic rd betw Moffat and Selkirk, the
Map 10 A708. About halfway, a car park and signs for waterfall. 8km from Tibby Shiels
**P28** Inn. The lower track takes 10/15mins to a viewing place still 500m from falls;
the higher, on the other side of the Tail burn, threads betw the austere hills
and up to L Skene from which the falls overflow (45/60mins). Mountain
goats.

**1648** **The Falls Of Clyde** New Lanark nr Lanark Dramatic falls in a long gorge of
Map 10 the Clyde. New Lanark, the conservation village of Robert Owen the social
**N27** reformer, is signed from Lanark. It's hard to avoid the 'award-winning' tourist
bazaar, but the riverbank has... a more natural appeal. The path to the Power
Station is about 1km, but the route doesn't get interesting till after it, a 1km
climb to the first fall (Cora Linn) & another 1km to the next (Bonnington Linn).
Swimming above or below them is not advised (but it's gr). Certainly don't
swim on an 'open day', when they close the station and divert all the water
back down the river in a mighty surge; submerged rocks are another hazard
(details from VC: 01555 665262). There is a gr Italian restau in Lanark and one
of the mills is now a hotel. The strange uniformity of New Lanark is better
when the other tourists have gone home.

**1649** **Reekie Linn** Alyth 8km N of town on back rds to Kirriemuir on B951 betw
Map 10 Br of Craigisla and Br of Lintrathen. A picnic site and car park on bend of rd
**Q22** leads by 200m to the wooded gorge of Glen Isla with precipitous viewpoints
of defile where Isla is squeezed and falls in tiers for 100ft. Can walk further
along the glen. Lochside restau nearby (931/PERTHSHIRE EATS).

**1650** **Falls of Acharn** nr Kenmore Loch Tay 5km along S side of loch on unclass
Map 10 rd. Walk from nr bridge in township of Acharn; falls are signed. Steepish start
**M22** then 1km up side of gorge; waterfalls on other side. Can be circular route.

**1651** **Falls of Rogie** nr Strathpeffer Car park on A835 Inverness-Ullapool rd, 5km
Map 7 Contin/10km Strathpeffer. Accessibility makes short walk (250m) quite pop-
**L17** ular to these hurtling falls on the Blackwater R. Br (built by T Army) and
salmon ladder (they leap in summer). Woodland trails marked, include a circular route to Contin (2035/WOODLAND WALKS).

**1652** **Foyers** Loch Ness On southern route from Ft Augustus to Inverness, the
Map 7 B862 (1678/SCENIC ROUTES) at the village of Foyers (35km from Inverness). Park
**L19** next to shops and cross rd, go through fence and down steep track to viewing places (slither-proof shoes advised). R Foyers falls 150m into foaming
gorge below and then into L Ness throwing clouds of spray into the trees (you
may get drenched).

**1653** **Falls Of Shin** nr Lairg, Sutherland 6km E of town on signed rd, car park &
Map 6 falls nearby are easily accessible. Not quite up to the splendours of others on
**M15** this page, but an excellent place to see salmon battling upstream (best June-
Aug). VC with extensive shop; the café/restau is excl (1036/INX RESTAUS) &
there's an adventure playground & other reasons to hang around. ☕

# The Lochs We Love

**1654** ✓ ✓ **Loch Maree** A832 betw Kinlochewe and Gairloch. Dotted with
Map 7 islands covered in Scots pine hiding some of the best examples of
**J16** Viking graves and apparently a money tree in their midst. Easily viewed from
the rd which follows its length for 15km. Beinn Eighe rises behind you and
the omniscient presence of Slioch is opposite. Aultroy Vistor Centre (5km
Kinlochewe), fine walks from car park further on, good accom nr lochside
(1010/ INX HIGHLAND HOTELS).

**1655** ✓ ✓ **Loch An Eilean** An enchanted loch in the heart of the
Map 7 Rothiemurchus Forest (2025/WOODLAND WALKS *for directions*).
**N19** There's a good VC. You can walk rt round the loch (5km, allow 1.5hrs). This is
classic Highland scenery, a calendar landscape of magnificent Scots pine.

**1656** ✓ **Loch Arkaig** 25km Ft William. An enigmatic loch long renowned for its
Map 7 fishing. From the A82 beyond Spean Br (at the Commando Monument)
**J20** cross the Caledonian Canal, then on by single track rd through the Clune
Forest and the 'Dark Mile' past the 'Witches' Pool' (a cauldron of dark water
below cataracts), to the loch. Bonnie Prince Charlie came this way before and
after Culloden; one of his refuge caves is marked on a trail.

**1657** **Loch Lubhair** nr Crianlarich The loch you pass (on the rt) on the A85 to
Map 9 Crianlarich (4km), in Glen Dochart, the upper reaches of the Tay water sys-
**L23** tem. Small, perfect, with bare hills surrounding and fringed with pines and
woody islets. Beautiful scenery that most people just go past in the car heading for Oban or Ft William.

**1658** **Loch Achray** nr Brig O' Turk The small loch at the centre of the Trossachs
Map 10 betw **Loch Katrine** (on which the *SS Sir Walter Scott* makes 4/5 sailings a
**L24** day – some stop at end of loch: 01877 376316) and **Loch Venachar**. The
A821 from Callander skirts both Venachar and Achray (picnic sites). Ben
Venue and Ben An rise above: gr walks (1963/HILLS) and views. A one-way for-
est rd goes round the other side of L Achray thro Achray Forest (enter and
leave from the Duke's Pass rd betw Aberfoyle and Brig O' Turk). Details of
trails from forest VC 3km N Aberfoyle. Bike hire at L Katrine/Callander/
Aberfoyle – it's the best way to see these lochs.

**1659** **Glen Finglas Reservoir** Brig O' Turk And while we're on the subject of
Map 10 lochs in the Trossachs (see above) here's a hidden gem. Although it's man-
**L24** made it's a real beauty surrounded by soft green hills & the odd burn bubbling in. App 'thro' Brig O'Turk houses (past the caff; 1435/CAFFS) and park
2km up road or from new car park 2km before Brig o' Turk from Callander.
Walk to right (not 'the Dam' rd although this an interesting 1km diversion on
the way back). 5 km walk to head of loch or poss make the loop round it &
back to dam (no path, lots of scrambling, boots only) or go further to
Balquhidder – a walk across the heart of Scotland (2008/GLEN WALKS).

**1660** **Loch Muick nr Ballater** At head of rd off B976, the S Dee rd at Ballater.
Map 10 14km up Glen Muick (pron 'Mick') to car park, VC and 100m to loch side.
**Q20** Lochnagar rises above (1992/MUNROS) and walk also begins here for Capel
Mounth and Glen Clova (1632/GLENS). 3hr walk around loch and any number
of ambles. The lodge where Vic met John is at the furthest pt (well it would
be). Open aspect with grazing deer and not too much forestry.

**1661** **Loch Eriboll North Coast** 90km W of Thurso. The long sea loch that
Map 6 indents into the N coast for 15km and which you drive rt round on the main
**L13** A838. Deepest natural anchorage in the UK, exhibiting every aspect of loch
side scenery including, alas, fish cages. Ben Hope stands nr the head of the
loch and there is a perfect beach (my own private Idaho) on the coast
(1621/BEACHES). Walks from Hope. Good GH on shore.

**1662** **Loch Trool nr Newton Stewart** The small, celebrated loch in a bowl of
Map 11 the Galloway Hills reached via Bargrennan 14km N via A714 and 8km to end
**L29** of rd. Woodland VC/café on the way. Get Galloway Forest Park Brochure.
Good walks but best viewed from Bruce's Stone (1939/MARY, CHARLIE AND BOB)
and the slopes of Merrick (1969/HILLS). An idyllic place.

**1663**
Map 7
**H20**

**Loch Morar** nr Mallaig 70km W of Ft William by the A850 (a wildly scenic & much improved route). Morar village is 6km from Mallaig & a single track rd leads away from the coast to the loch (only 500m but out of sight) then along it for 5km to Bracora. It's the prettiest part with wooded islets, small beaches, loch side meadows & bobbing boats. The rd stops at a turning place but a track continues from Bracorina to Tarbet & it's poss to connect with a post boat & sail back to Mallaig on L Nevis around 3.30pm (check TIC). L Morar, joined to the coast by the shortest river in Britain, also has the deepest water. There is a spookiness about it and just possibly a monster called Morag.

**1664**
Map 10
**N22**

**Loch Tummel** nr Pitlochry W from Pitlochry on B8019 to Rannoch (and the end of the rd), L Tummel comes into view, as it did for Queen Victoria, scintillating beneath you, and on a clear day with Schiehallion beyond (1698/VIEWS). This N side has good walks (2032/WOODLAND WALKS), but the S rd from Faskally just o/side Pitlochry is the one to take to get down to the lochside to picnic etc.

**1665**
Map 9
**K21**

**Loch Lundavra** nr Fort William Here's a secret loch in the hills, but not far from the well-trodden tracks through the glens and the sunny streets of Ft William. Go up Lundavra Rd from r/bout at W end of main st, out of town, over cattle grid and on (to end of rd) 8km. You should have it to yourself; good picnic spots and gr view of Ben Nevis. W Highland Way comes this way (1996/LONG WALKS).

**Loch Lomond** The biggest, maybe not the bonniest (1/BIG ATTRACTIONS) with major VC & retail experience, **Lomond Shores**, at S end nr Balloch.

**Loch Ness** The longest; you haven't heard the last of it (3/BIG ATTRACTIONS).

# The Scenic Routes

**1666**
Map 9
**J21**

✓ ✓ ✓ **Glencoe** The A82 from Crianlarich to Ballachulish is a fine drive, but from the extraterrestrial L Ba onwards, there can be few rds anywhere that have direct contact with such imposing scenery. After Kingshouse and Buachaille Etive Mor on the left, the mts and ridges rising on either side of Glencoe proper are truly awesome. The new VC, more discreet than the former nr Glencoe village, sets the topographical and historical scene. (1326/BLOODY GOOD PUBS; 2002/SERIOUS WALKS; 1925/BATTLEGROUNDS; 1950/SPOOKY PLACES; 1170/HOSTELS.)                               NTS

**1667**
Map 7
**H19**

✓ ✓ **Shiel Bridge-Glenelg** The switchback rd that climbs from the A87 (Ft William 96km) at Shiel Br over the 'hill' and down to the coast opp the Sleat Peninsula in Skye (short ferry to Kylerhea). As you climb you're almost as high as the surrounding summits and there's the classic view across L Duich to the 5 Sisters of Kintail. Coming back you think you're going straight into the loch! It's really worth driving to Glenelg (1454/COFFEE SHOPS, 1235/CAMPING, 1178/INNS) and beyond to Arnisdale & ethereal L Hourn (16km).

**1668**
Map 7
**H18**

✓ ✓ **Applecross** 120km Inverness. From Tornapress nr Lochcarron for 18km. Leaving the A896 seems like leaving civilisation; the winding ribbon heads into monstrous mts and the high plateau at the top is another planet. It's not for the faint-hearted and Applecross is a relief to see with its campsite/coffee shop and a faraway inn: the legendary Applecross Inn. 1222/GET-AWAY-FROM-IT-ALL. Also see 1459/COFFEE SHOPS, 1238/1243/CAMPING. This hair-raising rd rises 2000' in 6 mls. See how they built it at the Applecross Heritage Centre (2232/HERITAGE).

**1669**
Map 7
**J17**

✓ ✓ **Glen Torridon** The A896 which follows the glen to Kinlochewe. Starting in delightful Diabeg (1602/COASTAL VILLS) allows views of staggering Ben Alligin, but either side of L Torridon is impressive. Excl hotel (982/HIGHLAND HOTELS). Towards Kinlochewe there's Liatach & Beinn Elghe (1687/VIEWS). Much to climb, much to merely amaze.

**1670**
Map 9
**J26**

✓ ✓ **Rothesay-Tighnabruaich** A886/A8003. The most celebrated part of this route is the latter, the A8003 down the side of L Riddon to Tighnabruaich along the hill sides which give the breathtaking views of Bute & the Kyles, but the whole way, with its diverse aspects of lochside, riverine and rocky scenery, is supernatural. Includes short crossing betw Rhubodach and Colintraive. Gr hotel/retau at Tighnabruaich (782/ARGYLL HOTELS).

**1671**
Map 5
E16
✓ **The Golden Road** South Harris  The main rd in Harris follows the W coast, notable for bays & beaches (1614/BEACHES). This is the other one, winding round a series of coves and inlets with offshore skerries & a treeless rocky hinterland – classic Hebridean landscape, esp Finsbay. Good caff in the middle (2325/HEBRIDES). Tweed is woven in this area; you can visit the crofts but it seems impolite to leave without buying some (2208/TWEED).

**1672**
Map 6
J14
✓ **Lochinver-Drumbeg-Kylestrome**  The coast rd N from Lochinver (35km) is marvellous; essential Assynt. Actually best travelled N-S so that you leave the splendid vista of Eddrachilles Bay and pass through lochan, moor and even woodland, touching the coast again by sandy beaches (at Stoer a rd leads 7km to the lighthouse and the walk to the Old Man of Storr, 2041/COASTAL WALKS) and app Lochinver (poss detour to Auchmelvich and beaches) with one of the classic long views of Suilven. Excl caff at Drumbeg half-way round: **Drumbeg Designs & Little Tea Garden**. Open 7 days, Easter-Oct till 4.45pm.

**1673**
Map 6
J14
**Lochinver-Achiltibuie**  And S from Lochinver Achiltibuie is 40km from Ullapool; so this is the route from the N; 28km of winding rd/unwinding Highland scenery; through glens, mts and silver sea. Known locally as the 'wee mad rd' (it is maddening if you're in a hurry). Passes Achin's Bookshop (2172/CRAFT SHOPS), the path to Kirkaig Falls and the mighty Suilven.

**1674**
Map 7
G19
**Sleat Peninsula, Skye**  The unclassified rd off the A851 (main Sleat rd) esp coming from S, i.e. take rd at Ostaig nr Gaelic College (gr place to stay near-by: 2324/SKYE); it meets coast after 9km. Affords rare views of the Cuillins from a craggy coast. Returning to 'main' rd S of Isleornsay, pop into the gr hotel pub there (2294/ISLAND HOTELS).

**1675**
Map 10
R27
**Leaderfoot-Clintmains** nr St Boswells  The B6356 betw the A68 (look out for Leaderfoot viaduct & signs for Dryburgh) & the B6404 Kelso-St Boswells rd. This small rd, busy in summer, links Scott's View and Dryburgh Abbey (1918/ABBEYS; find by following Abbey signs) and Smailholm Tower, and passes through classic Border/Tweedside scenery. Don't miss Irvine's View if you want to see the Borders (1695/VIEWS). Nice GH (849/BORDER HOTELS).

**1676**
Map 10
P20
**Braemar-Linn Of Dee**  12km of renowned Highland river scenery along the upper valley of the (Royal) Dee. The Linn (rapids) is at the end of the rd, but there are river walks and the start of the gr Glen Tilt walk to Blair Atholl (2005/SERIOUS WALKS). Deer abound.

**1677**
Map 8
Q20
**Ballater-Tomintoul**  The ski road to the Lecht (2092/SKIING), the A939 which leaves the Royal Deeside rd (A93) W of Ballater before it gets really royal. A ribbon of road in the bare Grampians, past the sentinel ruin Corgarff (open to view, 250m walk; extensive repairs '05) & the valley of the trickling Don. Rd proceeds seriously uphill & main viewpoints are S of the Lecht. There is just nobody for miles. Walks in Glenlivet estates S of Tomintoul.

**1678**
Map 7
L19
**Fort Augustus-Dores** nr Inverness  The B862 often single-track rd that follows and latterly skirts L Ness. Quieter & more interesting than the main W bank A82. Starts in rugged country & follows the straight rd built by Wade to tame the Highlands. Reaches the lochside at Foyers (1652/WATERFALLS) & goes all the way to Dores (15km from Inverness). Paths to the shore of the loch. Fabulous untrodden woodlands nr Errogie (marked) & the spooky graveyard adj Boleskin House where Aleister Crowley did his dark magic and Jimmy Page of Led Zeppelin may have done his. 35km total; worth taking slowly.

**1679**
Map 10
L24
**The Duke's Pass** Aberfoyle-Brig O' Turk  Of the many rds through the Trossachs, this one is spectacular though gets busy; numerous possibilities for stopping, exploration & gr views. Good viewpoint 4km from L Achray Hotel, above rd & lay-by. One-way forest rd goes round L Achray. Good hill walking starts (1963/1964/1965/FAVOURITE HILLS) & L Katrine Ferry (2km) 4/5 times a day Apr-Oct (01877 376316). Bike hire at L Katrine, Aberfoyle & Callander.

**1680**
Map 9
J20
**Glenfinnan-Mallaig**  The A830, Road to the Isles. Through some of the most impressive and romantic landscapes in the Highlands, splendid in any weather (it does rain rather a lot) to the coast at the Sands of Morar (1622/BEACHES). This is deepest Bonnie Prince Charlie country (1938/MARY, CHARLIE AND BOB) and demonstrates what a misty eye he had for magnificent settings. A full-throttle bikers' dream. The rd is shadowed for much of the way by the West Highland Railway, which is an even better way to enjoy the scenery (11/FAVOURITE JOURNEYS). Rd recently improved, esp Arisaig-Mallaig.

**1681** **Lochailort–Acharacle** Off from the A830 above at Lochailort and turning
Map 9  S on the A861, the coastal section of this gr scenery is superb esp in the set-
**H21**  ting sun, or in May when the rhodies are out. Glen Uig Inn is rough & ready!
This is the rd to the Castle Tioram shoreline, which should not be missed
(1812/RUINS), & glorious Ardnamurchan.

**1682** **Knapdale** Lochgiphead– Tarbert Argyll B8024 off the main A83 follows the
Map 9  coast for most of its route. Views to Jura are immense. Not much happens
**H25**  here but in the middle in exactly the right place is a superb inn (1186/ROAD-
SIDE INNS, 1369/GASTROPUBS). Take it easy on this v Scottish 35kms of single
track.

**1683** **Amulree–Kenmore** Unclassified single-track & v narrow rd from the hill-
Map 10  country hamlet of Amulree to cosy Kenmore signed Glen Quaich. Past L
**N22**  Freuchie, a steep climb takes you to a plateau ringed by magnificent (far) mts
to L Tay. Steep descent to L Tay and Kenmore. Don't forget to close the gates.

**1684** **Pure Perthshire** Muthill–Comrie A route which takes you thro some of the
Map 10  best scenery in central Scotland & ends up (best this way round) in Comrie
**N23**  with teashops & other pleasures (1463/TEAROOMS; 1715/PICNICS). Leave Muthill
by Crieff rd turning left (2km) into Drummond Castle grounds up a glorious
avenue of beech trees (gate open 2-5pm). Visit gdn (1547/GARDENS); continue
through estate. At gate, go rt, following signs for Strowan. V quiet rd; we have
it to ourselves. First jnct, go left following signs (4km). At T-jnct, go left to
Comrie (7km). Best have a map, but if not, who cares – it's all bonny!

**1685** **The Heads Of Ayr** The coast rd S from Ayr to Culzean (1791/CASTLES) &
Map 9  Turnberry (795/AYRSHIRE HOTELS) incl these headlands, gr views of Ailsa Craig
**K28**  & Arran & some horrible caravan parks. The Electric Brae S of Dunure vill is
famously worth stopping on (your car runs the opp way to the slope). Culzean
grounds are gorgeous.

# The Classic Views

*For views of and around Edinburgh and Glasgow see p. 69 and p. 108. No views
from hill or mt tops are included here.*

**1686** ✓ ✓ ✓ **The Quirang** Skye Best app is from Uig direction taking the
Map 7  rt-hand unclassified rd off the hairpin of the A855 above and
**G17**  2km from town (more usual app from Staffin side is less of a revelation). View
(and walk) from car park, the massive rock formations of a towering, con-
torted ridge. Solidified lava heaved and eroded into fantastic pinnacles. Fine
views also across Staffin Bay to Wester Ross. (2318/ISLAND WALKS.)

**1687** ✓ ✓ ✓ The views of **An Teallach** and **Liathach** An Teallach, that gr
Map 7  favourite of Scottish hill walkers (40km S of Ullapool by the
**J16**  A835/A832), is best viewed from the side of Little L Broom or the A832 just
before you get to Dundonald.
The classic view of the other great Torridon mts (**Beinn Eighe**, pron 'Ben A',
& **Liathach** together, 100km S by rd from Ullapool) in Glen Torridon (1669/
SCENIC ROUTES) 4km from Kinlochewe. This viewpt is not marked but it's on the
track around L Clair which is reached from the entrance to the Coulin estate
off the A896, Glen Torridon rd (be aware of stalking). Park o/side gate; no cars
allowed, 1km walk to lochside. These mts have to be seen to be believed.

**1688** ✓ ✓ From **Raasay** There are several fabulous views looking over to Skye
Map 7  from Raasay, the small island reached by ferry from Sconser (2275/
**G18**  MAGICAL ISLANDS). The panorama from Dun Caan, the hill in the centre of the
island (444m) is of Munro proportions, producing an elation incommensurate
with the small effort required to get there. Start from the rd to the 'N End' or
ask at the Activity Centre in the big house: the Dolphin Café (& bar).    2-B-2

**1689** ✓ ✓ **The Summer Isles** Achiltibuie The Summer Isles are a scattering
Map 6  of islands seen from the coast of Achiltibuie (and the lounge of the
**J15**  Summer Isles Hotel 981/HIGHLANDS HOTELS) and visited by boat from Ullapool.
But the best place to see them, and the stunning perspective of this western
shore is on the road to Altandhu, possibly to the pub there. On way to
Achiltibuie, turn rt thro Polbain, thro' Allandhu, then on 500m past turning
for Reiff. There's a bench. Sit on it. You're alive! And further on, 500m round
the corner, the distant mts of Assynt all in a row.

**1690** ✓✓ **The Rest And Be Thankful** On A83 L Lomond-Inveraray rd where
Map 9 it's met by the B828 from Lochgoilhead. In summer the rest may be
**K24** from driving stress and you may not be thankful for the camera-toting mass-
es, but this was always one of the most accessible, rewarding viewpoints in
the land. Surprisingly, none of the encompassing hills are Munros but they
are nonetheless dramatic. Only a few carpets of conifer to smother the
grandeur of the crags as you look down the valley.

**1691** ✓ **Elgol** Skye End of the rd, the B8083, 22km from Broadford. The classic
Map 7 view of the Cuillins from across L Scavaig and of Soay & Rum. Cruises
**G19** (Apr-Oct) in the *Bella Jane* (0800 731 3089) or *The Misty Isle* (May-Sept, not
Sun 01471 866288) to the famous corrie of L Coruisk, painted by Turner,
romanticised by Walter Scott. A journey you'll remember.

**1692** **Camas Nan Geall** Ardnamurchan 12km Salen on B8007. 4km from
Map 9 Ardnamurchan's Natural History Centre (1756/KIDS) 65km Ft William. Coming
**G21** esp from the Kilchoan direction, a magnificent bay appears below you, where
the rd first meets the sea. Almost symmetrical with high cliffs and a perfect
field (still cultivated) in the bowl fringed by a shingle beach. Car park viewpoint and there is a path down. Amazing Ardnamurchan!

**1693** **Glengarry** 3km after Tomdoun t/off on A87, Invergarry-Kyle of Lochalsh rd.
Map 7 Lay-by with viewfinder. An uncluttered vista up and down loch and glen with
**K20** not a house in sight (pity about the salmon cages). Distant peaks of Knoydart
are identified, but not L Quoich nestling spookily and full of fish in the wilderness at the head of the glen. Gaelic mouthfuls of mts on the orientation
board. Bonnie Prince Charlie passed this way.

**1694** **Scott's View** St Boswells Off A68 at Leaderfoot Br nr St Boswells, signed
Map 10 Gattonside. 'The View', old Walter's favourite (the horses still stopped there
**R27** long after he'd gone), is 4km along the rd (Dryburgh Abbey 3km further;
1918/ABBEYS). Magnificent sweep of his beloved Border country, but only in
one direction. If you cross the rd & go through the kissing gate and head up
the hill towards the jagged standing stone that comes into view, you reach ...

**1695** **Irvine's View** The full panorama from the Cheviots to the Lammermuirs.
Map 10 This, the finest view in southern Scotland, is only a furlong further (than
**R27** Scott's View, above) – cross rd from layby, go thro' kissing gate & climb thro'
rough pasture; mind the livestock. On first rise, you'll see the spiky standing
stone – head for it; about 15 mins' walk). This is where I'd like my bench –
unfortunately some bastard has erected a horrible phone mast up there (not
that I go anywhere without a moby myself). Turn your back on it & gaze into
the beautiful Borders.

**1696** **Penielheugh** nr Ancrum While we're on the subject of gr views in the
Map 10 Borders, you may look no further than this – the sentinel Borders symbol.
**R27** Report: 1869/BEST MONUMENTS.

**1697** **The Law** Dundee Few cities have such a single good viewpoint. To N of the
Map 10 centre, it reveals the panoramic perspective of the city on the estuary of the
**Q23** silvery Tay. Best to walk from town; the one-way system is a nightmare, tho
there are signposts.

**1698** **Queen's View** Loch Tummel nr Pitlochry 8km on B8019 to Kinloch Rannoch.
Map 10 Car park and 100m walk to rocky knoll where pioneers of tourism, Queen
**N22** Victoria & Prince Albert, were 'transported into ecstasies' by view of L Tummel
& Schiehallion (1664/LOCHS; 2032/WOODLAND WALKS). Their view was flooded by
a hydro scheme after WW2; more recently it has spawned a whole view-driven
visitor experience (& it costs a quid to park). It all... makes you wonder.

**1699** **The Rallying Place Of The Maclarens** Balquhidder Short climb from
Map 10 behind the church (1911/GRAVEYARDS), signed Creag an Tuire, steep at first.
**L23** Superb view down L Voil, the Balquhidder Braes and the real Rob Roy Country
& gr caff with home-baking on your descent (1457/COFFEE SHOPS).

**1700** **Califer** nr Forres 7km from Forres on A96 to Elgin, turn rt for 'Pluscarden',
Map 8 follow rd for 5km. Viewpoint is on rd & looks down across Findhorn Bay & the
**P17** wide vista of the Moray Firth to the Black Isle & Ben Wyvis. Fantastic light.

**1701** **The Malcolm Memorial** Langholm 3km from Langholm and signed from
Map 11 main A7, a single-track rd leads to a path to this obelisk raised to celebrate
**Q29** the military and masonic achievements of one John Malcolm. The eulogy is
fulsome esp compared with that for Hugh MacDiarmid on the cairn by the

stunning sculpture at the start of the path (1877/MEMORIALS). Views from the obelisk, however, are among the finest in the S, encompassing a vista from the Lakeland Fells and the Solway Firth to the wild Border hills. Path 1km.

**1702** **Duncryne Hill** Gartocharn nr Balloch  Gartocharn is betw Balloch and
Map 9  Drymen on the A811, and this view, was recommended by writer and out-
L25  doorsman Tom Weir as 'the finest viewpoint of any small hill in Scotland'. Turn up Duncryne rd at the E end of village and park 1km on left by a small wood (a sign reads 'Woods reserved for Teddy bears'). The hill is only 470ft high and 'easy', but the view of L Lomond and the Kilpatrick Hills is superb.

**1703** **Blackhill** Lesmahagow nr Glasgow  28km S of city. Another marvellous out-
Map 10  look, but in the opp direction from above. Take jnct 10/11 on M74, then off
N27  the B7078 signed Lanark, take the B7018. 4km along past Clarkston Farm, head uphill for 1km & park by Water Board mound. Walk uphill through fields to rt for about 1km. Unprepossessing hill which unexpectedly reveals a vast vista of most of E central Scotland (& most of the uphill is in the car).   1-A-2

**1704** **Tongue**  From the causeway across the kyle, or better, follow the minor rd to
Map 6  Talmine on the W side, look S to Ben Loyal or north to the small islands off
M13  the coast.

**1705** **Cairnpapple Hill** nr Linlithgow  Volcanic geology, neolithic henge, E
Map 10  Scottish agriculture, the Forth plain, the Bridges, Grangemouth industrial
N25  complex & telecoms masts: not all pretty, but the whole of Scotland at a glance. For directions see 1837/PREHISTORIC SITES.

# Summer Picnics & Great Swimming Holes

*Care should be taken when swimming in rivers; don't take them for granted. Kids should be watched. Most of these places are trad local swimming and picnic spots where people have swum for yrs, but rivers continuously change their course and their nature. Wearing sandals or old sports shoes is a good idea.*

**1706** ✓✓ **The Fairy Pools** Glen Brittle, Skye  On that rare hot day, this is one
Map 7  of the best places on Skye to head for; swimming in deep pools with
G19  the massif of the Cuillins around you. One pool has a stone br you can swim under. Head off A863 Dunvegan rd from Sligachan Hotel then B8009 and Glenbrittle rd. 7km down just as rd begins to parallel the glen itself, you'll see a river coming off the hills. Park in lay-by on rt. 1km walk, follow this up. Lady Clair Macdonald recs also, the pools at Torrin nr Elgol.

**1707** ✓✓ **The Pools In Glen Etive**  Glen Etive is a wild, enchanted place
Map 9  where people have been camping for yrs to walk and climb in the
K22  Glencoe area. There are many grassy landings at the river side as well as these perfect pools for bathing. The first is about 5km from the main Glencoe rd, the A82 at Kingshouse, but just follow the river and find your own. Take midge cream for evening wear. Lots.

**1708** ✓✓ **Feshiebridge**  At the br itself on the B970 betw Kingussie and
Map 7  Inverdruie nr Aviemore. 4km from Kincraig. Gr walks here into Glen
N19  Feshie and in nearby woodland, but under br a perfect spot for Highland swimming. Go down to left from S. Rocky ledges, clear water. One of the best but cold even in high summer. Further pools nearby, up river.

**1709** ✓✓ **Rumbling Bridge & The Braan Walk** nr Dunkeld  Excl stretch of
Map 10  cascading river with pools, rocky banks & ledges. Just off A9 head-
P22  ing N opp first turning for Dunkeld, the A822 for Aberfeldy, Amulree. Car park on rt after 4km. Connects with forest paths (the Braan Walk) to the Hermitage (2029/WOODLAND WALKS) – 2km. Fab picnic & swimming spot tho take gr care. This is the nearest Highland-type river to Edin (about 1 hr).

**1710** ✓✓ **Strathmashie nr Newtonmore**  On A86 Newtonmore-
Map 7  Dalwhinnie (on A9) to Ft William rd 7km from Laggan, watch for
M20  Forest sign. Car parks on either side of the rd; the Druim an Aird car park has finder boards. Gr swimming spot, but often campers. Viewpoints, waterfall, pines. If people are here don't despair – there are gr forest walks & foll river, there are many other gr pools. Gr café with home-baking 5km towards A9 (1446/TEAROOMS).

**1711**
Map 9
**K23**
**Rob Roy's Bathtub** The Fallach Falls nr Inverarnan  A82 N of Ardlui and 3 km past The Drover's Inn (1323/BLOODY GOOD PUBS). Sign on the rt (Picnic Area) going N. Park, then follow the path. Some pools on the rocky river course but 500m from car park you reach the main falls & below a perfect round natural pool 30m across. There's an overhanging rock face on one side and smooth slabs at the edge of the falls. Natural suntrap in summer, but the water is 'Baltic' at all times.

**1712**
Map 10
**Q27**
**Neidpath** Peebles  2km from town on A72, Biggar rd; sign for castle. Park by Hay Lodge Park or poss the lay-by past the castle track (some- times by the castle itself). Idyllic setting of a broad meander of the Tweed, with medieval Neidpath Castle, a sentinel above. Two 'pools' (3m deep in av summer) linked by shallow rapids which the adventurous chute down on their backs. Usually a rope-swing at upper pool. TAKE CARE. Also see (2015/GLEN AND RIVER WALKS).

**1713**
Map 8
**N17**
**Randolph's Leap** nr Forres  Spectacular gorge on the mythical Findhorn which carves out some craggy scenery on its way to a gentle coast. This secret glade and fabulous swimming hole are behind a wall on a bend of the B9007 (see 2026/WOODLAND WALKS for directions) S of Forres and Nairn and nr Logie Steading, a courtyard of good things (a board there maps out walks). One Randolph may have leapt here; we just bathe & lie under the trees dreaming of gods (and satyrs).

**1714**
Map 7
**K18**
**Dog Falls** Glen Affric  Half-way along Glen Affric rd from Cannich before you come to the loch, a well-marked picnic spot and gr place to swim in the peaty waters surrounded by the Caledonian Forest (with trails). Birds well sussed to picnic potential – your car covered in tits & finches – Hitchcock or what? (2007/GLEN AND RIVER WALKS).

**1715**
Map 10
**M23**
**Nr Comrie**  2 great pools of different character nr the neat little town in deepest Perthshire. **The Linn**, the town pool: go over humpback br from main A85 W to Lochearnhead, signed The Ross. Take left fork then after 2km there's a parking place on left. River's relatively wide, v pleasant spot. For more adventurous, **Glenartney**, known locally as 'the cliffs', is past Cultybraggan training camp (no longer in use), (5km) and then MoD range on left until a ruined cottage on rt. Park and walk down to river in glen. What with the twin perils of the Army and the Comrie Angling Club, you might feel you have no right to be here, but you do and this stretch of river is marvel- lous. Respect the farmland. Follow rd further for more gr picnic spots. Comrie has gr pub/hotel bistro (910/PERTHSHIRE HOTELS) & tearm (1463/TEAROOMS).

**1716**
Map 9
**J27**
**North Sannox Burn** Arran  Park at the North Sannox Bridge on the A841 (rd from Lochranza to Sannox Bay) and follow the track W to the deer fence and treeline (1km). Just past there you will find a gt pool with small waterfall, dragonflies and perhaps even an eagle or two wheeling above.

**1717**
Map 10
**N21**
**Falls of Bruar** nr Blair Atholl  Just off A9, 12km N of Blair Atholl. 250m walk from **House of Bruar** car park & shopping experience (2161/SHOPPING) to lower fall (1640/WATERFALLS) where there is an accessible large deep pool by the br. Cold, fresh mt water in a woody gorge. The proximity of the 'retail experience' can make it all the more... naturally exhilirating.

**1718**
Map 10
**M24**
**The Scout Pool & The Bracklinn Falls** Callander  The latter are a Callander must-see-easy-to-find (signposted from S end of Main St, up hill to golf course then next car park up – from there it's a 10min walk). The Scout Pool is a traditional swimming hole on same river so a summer thing only. Foll rd further – 5km from Bracklinn car park till rd goes on thro' iron gate. Park on rt. Downhill 150m cross wooden br then foll river path to rt 250m. Access to huge pool dammed by giant boulders, made less easy by storms 2005, but a beautiful secret spot in the woods.

**1719**
Map 11
**L30**
**The Otter's Pool New Galloway Forest**  A clearing in the forest reached by a track, 'The Raider's Rd', running from 8km N of Laurieston on the A762, for 16km to Clatteringshaws Loch. The track, which is only open Apr-Oct, has a toll of £2 and gets busy. It follows the Water of Dee and halfway down the rd – the Otter's Pool. A bronze otter used to mark the spot (it got nicked) and it's a place mainly for kids and paddling; but when the dam runs off it can be deep enough to swim. Rd closes dusk. (2033/WOODLAND WALKS.)

**1720**
Map 10
**R27**
**Ancrum**  A secret place on the quiet Ale Water (out of village towards Lilliesleaf, 3km out 250m from farm sign to Hopton – a recessed gate on the rt before a bend & a rough track that locals know). A meadow, a Border burn,

a surprisingly deep pool to swim. Go to left of rough vegn – defile, downhill foll fence on your right. Cross further gate at bottom (100m from rd). Arcadia!

**1721**
Map 10
**S28**
**Towford** nr Hounam & Jedburgh Another Border burn with a surprising pool. This one legendary but hard to find. Deep in the Cheviots, nobody else for miles. It's where I went as a kid. Only the intrepid may venture here. Ask a local.

**1722**
Map 10
**N24**
**Paradise** Sheriffmuir nr Dunblane A pool at the foot of an unexpected leafy gorge on the moor betw the Ochils and Strathallan. Here the Wharry Burn is known locally as 'Paradise', and for good reason. Take rd from 'behind' Dunblane or Br of Allan to the Sheriffmuir Inn; head downhill (back) towards Br of Allan and park 1km after the hump back br. Head for the pylon nearest the river & you'll find the pool. It can be midgy and it can be perfect.

**1723**
Map 8
**Q20**
**Potarch Bridge & Cambus O' May** On The Dee 2 places on the 'Royal' Dee, the first by the reconstructed Victorian br (and nr the hotel) 3km E of Kincardine O'Neill. Cambus another stretch of river E of Ballater (6km). Locals swim, picnic on rocks, etc, and there are forest walks on the other side of rd. The brave jump off the bridge at Cambus (& in wetsuits) – best just to watch. Gr tearm nearby – The Black Faced Sheep in Aboyne (1442/TEAROOMS).

**1724**
Map 7
**L19**
**Invermoriston** On main L Ness rd A82 betw Inverness and Ft Augustus, this is the best bit. R Moriston tumbles under an ancient br. Perfectly Highland. Ledges for picnics, invigorating pools, ozone-friendly. Nice beech woods. Follow signs 'To the Falls' or go opp side rd. Tavern/bistro nearby (1198/INNS).

**1725**
Map 8
**N18**
**Dulsie Bridge** nr Nairn 16km S of Nairn on the A939 to Grantown, this locally revered beauty spot is fabulous for summer swimming. The ancient arched br spans the rocky gorge of the Findhorn (again – see Randolph's Leap, above) and there are ledges and even sandy beaches for picnics and from which to launch yourself or paddle into the peaty waters.

**1726**
Map 6
**Q13**
**The Trinkie** Wick On S edge of town, foll cliff walk up from harbour or car thro' housing estate. 2km. Not a river spot of course, but a pool sluiced & filled by the sea within a natural formation of rocks. A bracing stroll, never mind immersion.

**Strathcarron** nr Bonar Bridge Pick your spot (1631/GLENS).

# Good Places To Take Kids

## CENTRAL

**1727**
Map 1
**xA4**
✓ ✓ ✓ **Edinburgh Zoo** 0131 334 9171. Corstorphine Rd. 4km W of Princes St. A large and long-established zoo, where the natural world from the poles to the plains of Africa is ranged around Corstorphine Hill. Enough huge/exotic/ghastly creatures and friendly, amusing ones to fill an overstimulated day. The penguins and the seals do their stuff at set times. More familiar creatures hang out at the 'farm'. The koalas are cool as... Café and shop stocked with PC toys and souvenirs. Open AYR 7 days. Apr-Sept 9am-6pm, Nov-Feb 9am-5pm, Mar & Oct 9am-5.30pm.

✓ ✓ **Our Dynamic Earth** Edinburgh 0131 550 7800. Holyrood Rd. Edinburgh's major kids' attraction. Report 396/ATTRACTIONS.

✓ ✓ **Museum of Childhood** Edinburgh 0131 529 4142. 42 High St. An Aladdin's cave of toys for all ages. 405/ATTRACTIONS.

**1728**
Map 10
**Q25**
✓ **Edinburgh Butterfly Farm & Insect World** nr Dalkeith & Edinburgh 0131 663 4932. On A7, signed Eskbank/Galashiels from ring rd (1km). Part of a gdn centre complex. As for the bugs, the butterflies are delightful but kids will be far more impressed with the scorpions, locusts and other assorted uglies on show. Red-kneed tarantula not for the faint-hearted. 7 days, 9.30am-5.30pm (10am-5pm in winter).

**1729**
Map 2
**xA5**
✓ **Glasgow Science Centre** 0141 420 5000. Glasgow's newest and most flash attraction. State-of-the-art interactive, landmark tower & Imax. Report: 709/MAIN ATTRACTIONS.

**1730**
Map 1
**Gorgie City Farm** Edinburgh 0131 337 4202. 57 Gorgie Rd. A working farm on busy rd in the heart of the city. Friendly domestic animals, garden & café. AYR 9.30m-4.30pm (4pm in wint). Free.

**1731** **The Edinburgh Dungeon** 0131 240 1000. 31 Market St. Multimillion très
Map 1 contrived experience takes you thro a ghoulish history of Scottish nasties.
**D3** Hammy of course, but kids will love the monorail. 7 days 10am-5pm.

**1732** **Auchingarrich Wildlife Centre** nr Comrie 4km from main st turning off
Map 10 at br then signed. Sympathetic corralling in picturesque Perthshire Hills. Excl
**M23** for kids. Huge playbarn. Daily hatchings & lots of baby fluffy things, some of
which you can hold. Don't ask what happens to them when they grow up!
Good place to start sex education. Meerkats especially wonderful. Apr-Oct(ish)
10am-dusk. Coffee shop till 5pm.

**1733** **Kelburn Country Centre** Largs 2km S of Largs on A78. Riding school,
Map 9 gdns, woodland walks up the Kel Burn and a central visitor/consumer sec-
**K26** tion with shops/exhibits/cafés. Wooden stockade for clambering kids; indoor
playbarn with quite scary slides. Falconry displays (and long-suffering owl).
'The Plaisance' indeed a pleasant place. Stock up at Nardini's caff nr the
Cumbrae ferry. 7 days 10am-6pm. Apr-Oct. Grounds only in wint 11-dusk.

✓ ✓ **Falkirk Wheel** Falkirk Report: 4/MAIN ATTRACTIONS.

## FIFE & DUNDEE

**1734** ✓ **Deep Sea World** N Queensferry 01383 411411. The aquarium in a
Map 10 quarry which may be reaching its swim-by date. Park'n'ride system and
**P25** buses from Edin, or better still by *Maid of the Forth* from S Queensferry
(9/FAVOURITE JOURNEYS). Habitats are viewed from a conveyor belt where you
can stare at the fish and diverse divers teeming around and above you.
Maximum hard sell to this all-weather attraction 'the shark capital', but kids
like it even when they've been queueing for aeons. New cute seals '05. Cafe
is fairly awful, but nice views. Open AYR 7 days 10am-6pm; wint till 5pm.

**1735** ✓ **Sensation** Dundee 01382 228800. Greenmarket across r/bout from
Map 10 Discovery Pt and adj DCA (2254/GALLERIES). Purpose-built indoor kids
**Q23** info-tainment attraction. With basis in Dundee's 'Discover Yourself' &
'Scientific Centre of Excellence' claims, this is an innovative and v interactive
games room with a message. We all learn something. 7 days 10am-closing
varies.

**1736** ✓ **Verdant Works** Dundee 01382 225282. West Henderson's Wynd nr
Map 10 Westport. Heritage museum that recreates workings of a jute mill. Sounds
**Q23** dull, but brilliant for kids and grown-ups. Report: 2225/MUSEUMS. ☕

**1737** ✓ **Craigton Park** St Andrews 01334 473666. 3km SW of St Andrews on
Map 10 the Pitscottie rd. An oasis of fun: bouncy castles, trampolines, putting,
**R23** crazy golf, boating lake, a train thro the grounds, adventure playgrounds and
glasshouses. A perfect day's amusement esp for nippers. 10.30am-5.30pm
(wint: park only, attractions cl).

**1738** **Camperdown Park** Dundee The large park just off the ring-road system
Map 10 (the Kingsway and via A923 to Coupar Angus) with a wildlife centre and a
**Q23** nearby play complex. Animal-handling at w/ends. 'Over 80 species' bears,
bats & wolves! Open AYR, but centre 10am-4.30pm, earlier in winter
(1589/TOWN PARKS).

## SOUTH & SOUTH WEST

**1739** ✓ ✓ **Cream O' Galloway** Rainton There is something inherently good
Map 11 about a visitor attraction that is based on the incontrovertible fact
**M31** that human beings love ice cream. Esp when it's presented with a 'pure &
simple' message, an organic café, a herb garden & a fab adventure playground in the woods, part of 5km of child-friendly nature trails. Let's hear it
for cows! AYR 10am-6pm. Report: 1486/ICE CREAM.

**1740** ✓ **Kidz Play** Prestwick 01292 475215. Off main st at Station rd, past stn
Map 9 to beach and to rt. Big shed soft play area for kids. Everything that the
**L27** little blighters will like in the throwing-themselves-around department.
Shriek city. Sun-Thur 9.30am-7pm. Fri-Sat 9.30am-7.30pm.

**1741** ✓ **Loudoun Castle** nr Galston Theme park with big ambitions S of Glas.
Map 10 Off A71 Kilmarnock-Edin rd (go from Glas via A77 Kilmarnock rd). Behind
**L27** the ruins of the said Loudon Castle (burned out in 1941), a fairground which
includes the 'largest carousel in Europe' and 'chairy plane', has been trans-

planted in the old walled gdn. 'Farm' area & birds of prey demos. Nice setting. Open Easter-Sep.

**1742** **Palacerigg Country Park** Cumbernauld  01236 720047. 6km E of
Map 10  Cumbernauld. 740 acres of parkland; ranger service, nature trails, picnic area
**M25**  and kids farm. 18-hole golf course and putting green. Exhib area with changing exhibits about forestry, conservation etc. Open AYR: 7 days; daylight hrs. Visitor centre and tearm.

✓✓ **Drumlanrig Castle** nr Dumfries 1569/COUNTRY PARKS.

## NORTH EAST

**1743** ✓ **Macduff Marine Aquarium** On seafront E of the harbour, a family
Map 8  attraction for this under-rated Moray Firth port. Under-rated perhaps
**R17**  because neighbouring Banff gets more attention from tourists, but Duff House (2259/GALLERIES) gets fewer visitors than this user- and child-friendly sea-life centre. All the fish seem curiously happy with their lot and content to educate and entertain. Open AYR 10-5pm (LA 4.15pm).

**1744** ✓ **Storybook Glen** nr Aberdeen Fibreglass fantasy land in verdant glen
Map 8  16km S of Aber via B9077, the S Deeside rd, a nice drive. Characters from
**S20**  every fairy tale and nursery story dotted around 20-acre park. Their fixed manic stares give them a spooky resemblance to people you know. Older kids may find it tame – no guns, no big technology but nice for little 'uns. Indoor play area. 7 days, 10am-6pm (5pm in wint), weather permitting. Apart from anything kids like, there are wonderful gdns.

**1745** ✓ **Satrosphere** Aberdeen Nr beach (off Beach Boulevard, nr Patio Hotel),
Map 8  Scotland's 'original interactive science centre'. Hands on, it is! Granny
**T19**  will learn as much as she can take in. AYR. 7 days 10am-5pm.

**1746** **Aden** Mintlaw nr Peterhead  (pron 'Ah-den'). Country park just beyond
Map 8  Mintlaw on A950 16km from Peterhead. Former grounds of mansion with
**T18**  walks and organised activities and events. Farm buildings converted into Heritage Centre (kids free), café etc. Adventure playground. AYR.

## HIGHLANDS & ISLANDS

**1747** ✓ **The Cairngorm Reindeer Herd** nr Aviemore 01479 861228. Stop at
Map 7  Centre (shop, exhibition) to buy tickets and follow the guide in your vehi-
**N19**  cle up the mountain. From here, 20 min walk. At Glenmore Forest Park on rd from Coylumbridge 12km from Aviemore. Real reindeer aplenty in authentic free-ranging habitat (when they come down off the cloudy hillside in winter with snow all around). They've come a long way from Sweden (in 1952). 1hr 30min trip. They are so ...small. 11am AYR plus 2.30pm in summer. Wear appropriate footwear and phone if weather looks threatening.

**1748** ✓ **Leault Farm** nr Kincraig On the main A9, but easier to find by looking
Map 7  for sign 1km S of Kincraig on the B9152. Working farm with daily sheep-
**N19**  dog trials where Neil Ross demonstrates his extraordinary facility with dogs and sheep (and ducks). A gr spectacle and totally authentic in this setting. Usually 4pm (poss other times, check TIC). Cl Sat.

**1749** ✓ **Landmark Centre** Carrbridge 01479 841614. A purpose-built tourist
Map 7  centre with audiovisual displays and a gr deal of shopping. Gr for kids
**N19**  messing about in the woods on slides, in a 'maze' etc, in a large adventure playground, Microworld or (esp squealy) the Wildwater Coaster. The Tower may be too much for Granny but there are fine forest views. Open AYR 7 days till 6pm (5pm in wint, 7pm mid July-mid Aug).

**1750** **The Highland Wildlife Park** Kincraig On B9152 betw Aviemore and
Map 7  Kingussie. Large drive-through 'reserve' run by Royal Zoological Society with
**N19**  wandering herds of deer, bison etc and pens of other animals. 'Habitats', but mostly cages. Must be time to bring back bears, let the wolves go free and liven up the caravan parks. Open 10-6pm (July/Aug 7pm, wint 4pm).

**1751** **Islay Wildlife Info & Field Centre** Port Charlotte  01496 850288.
Map 9  Fascinating wildlife centre, activities and day trips. (1786/WILDLIFE;
**F26**  2323/ISLAY). Excl for getting kids interested in wildlife. Then go find it! Apr-Oct 10am-3pm. Cl Sat (July/Aug 7 days 10am-5pm).

1752 **Wings Over Mull** nr Craignure, Mull 01680 812594. Off main rd S of Duart
Map 9 (1798/CASTLES). Whatever you think about falconry, this is a wonderful place
**H22** for the Balamory bairns to see these elusive birds of prey up close & over 20
other species incl all the native owls. Regular flying displays and birds on
perches – they squawk & cheep & mainly sleep; happy enough I suppose &
at least 'conserved'. Meanwhile swallows soar above. Apr-Oct 7 days.

1753 **Mull Railway & Torosay Castle** 01680 812494. See it as the Balamory Ex-
Map 9 press? Well: this is a long-est chugalong train from the ferry at Craignure to
**H22** Torosay Gardens & Castle. 20min journey. Lovely when you get there. Apr-Oct.

1754 **The Scottish Sealife Sanctuary** Oban 01631 720386. 16km N on the
Map 9 A828. On the shore of L Creran this one of the oldest of a number of UK
**H23** waterworlds still the best (another non-rel in **St Andrews**). Environmentally
conscientious they 'rescue' seals and house numerous aquatic life. The new,
multi-level viewing otter enclosure is spectacular. Café/shop/adventure
playground. Open summer, 10am-6pm. Call for winter hrs.

1755 **Rare Breeds Farm** Oban 4km from town via Argyll Sq, then S (A816), bear-
Map 9 ing left at church, past golf course. Weird and wonderful collection of animals
**H23** in hill side pens and runs and a touchy-feely barn, who seem all the more
peculiar because they're versions of familiar ones. Leaving the caging ques-
tions aside, it's a funny farm for kids and the creatures seem keen enough for
the attention and crumbs from the tearoom table. 7 days in season.

1756 **Natural History Centre** Ardnamurchan 01972 500209. A861 Strontian,
Map 9 B8007 Glenmore 14km. Photographer Michael McGregor's award-winning
**G21** interactive exhib; under new owners. Kids will enjoy, adults may be
impressed. A walk-thro' of wildlife incl live pine martins (if you're lucky) &
CCTV of more cautious creatures. Tearoom. Mon-Sat; 10.30am-5.30pm. Sun;
12-5.30pm.

1757 **Highland Folk Museum** Kingussie and Newtonmore 01540 661307. Final
Map 7 word in this section to Calum (6½) & Katie (2) who loved this place (they vis-
**M20** ited the latter). 'Brilliant play park, old school'. Katie liked the chickens & the
waterwheel. They spent 5hrs there. What do I know? The sites are separate.
Hrs changing '06 but 7 days Mar-Sept.

# The Best Places To See Birds

*See p. 222 for* Wildlife Reserves, *many of which are good for bird-watching.*

**1758** ✓✓ **Handa Island** nr Scourie Sutherland  Take the boat from Tarbet
Map 6  Pier 6km off A894 5km N of Scourie and land on a beautiful island
**K13** run by the Scottish Wildlife Trust as a nature reserve. Boats (Apr-early Sept though fewer birds after Aug) are continuous depending on demand (01971 502347). Crossing 30mins. Small reception hut and 2.5km walk over island to cliffs which rise 350m and are layered in colonies from fulmars to shags. Allow 3 to 4hrs. Though you must take care not to disturb the birds, you'll be eye to eye with seals and bill to bill with razorbills. Eat at the seafood café on the cove when you return (1406/SEAFOOD RESTAUS). Mon-Sat only (some Suns in summer). Last ret 5pm.

**1759** ✓✓ **Caerlaverock** nr Dumfries  17km S on B725 nr Bankend, signed
Map 11  from rd. The WWT Caerlaverock Wetlands Centre (01387 770200) is
**P30** an excellent place to see whooper swans, barnacle geese and more (countless hides, observatories, viewing towers). Has Fair Trade café as well as farmhouse-style accom for up to 14 (INX). More than just birds too: natterjack toads, badgers so not just for twitchers. Eastpark Farm, Caerlaverock. Centre open daily AYR 10am-5pm. ADMN

**1760** ✓✓ **Lunga & The Treshnish Islands**  Off Mull. Sail from Iona or
Map 9  Fionnphort or Ulva ferry on Mull to these uninhabited islands on a
**F22** 5/6hr excursion which probably takes in Staffa and Fingal's Cave. Best months are May-July when birds are breeding. Some trips allow 3hrs on Lunga. Razorbills, guillemots & a carpet of puffins oblivious to your presence. This will be a memorable day. Boat trips (01688 400242) or ring Tobermory TIC (01688 302182) who will advise of other boatmen. All trips dependent on sea conditions.

**1761** ✓✓ **Isle Of May** Firth Of Forth  Island at mouth of Forth off Crail/
Map 10  Anstruther reached by daily boat trip from Anstruther Harbour
**R24** (01333 310103), May-Oct 9am-2.30pm depending on tides. Boats hold 40-50; trip 45mins; allows 3hrs ashore. Prob is you can't book by phone & CC & often by the time you get to Anstruther, it's full. Island (including isthmus to Rona) 1.5km x 0.5km. Info centre and resident wardens. See guillemots, razorbills and kittiwakes on cliffs and shags, terns and thousands of puffins. Most populations increasing. This place is strange as well as beautiful. The puffins in early summer are, as always, engaging.

**1762** ✓ **The Lagoon** Musselburgh  On E edge of town behind the racecourse
Map 10  (follow rd round, take turn-off signed Race-Course Parking), at the estu-
**Q25** arine mouth of the R Esk. Waders, sea birds, ducks aplenty & often interesting migrants on the mudflats & wide littoral. The 'lagoon' itself is a man-made pond behind with hide & attracts big populations (both birds and binocs). This is the nearest diverse-species area to Edin (15km) & in recent yrs has become one of the most significant migrant stopovers in the UK.

**1763** ✓ **Fowlsheugh** nr Stonehaven  8km S of Stonehaven & signed from A92
Map 10  with path from Crawton. Sea-bird city on 2km of red sandstone cliffs up
**S21** to 200' high; take gr care. 80,000 pairs of 6 species esp guillemots, kittiwakes, razorbills & also fulmar, shag, puffins. Poss to view the birds without disturbing them & see the 'layers' they occupy on the cliff face. Best seen May-July.

**1764** ✓ **Loch Of The Lowes** Dunkeld  4km NE Dunkeld on A923 to Blairgowrie.
Map 10  Properly managed (Scottish Wildlife Trust) site with double-floored hide
**P22** (always open) & new hide (same hrs as VC) and permanent binocs. Main attractions are the captivating ospreys (from early Apr-Aug). Nest 100m over loch and clearly visible. Their revival (now over 260 pairs in UK) is well documented, including diary of movements, breeding history etc. Also the near-at-hand endless fascination of watching wild birds incl woodpeckers, & red squirrels feeding outside the picture window is a real treat.

**1765** ✓ **Loch Garten** Boat of Garten  3km village off B970 into Abernethy Forest.
Map 8  Famous for the ospreys and so popular that access may be restricted until
**N19** after the eggs have hatched. 2 car parks: the first has nature trails through Scots pine woods and around loch; other has VC with the main hide 250m away: TV screens, binocs, other wild-bird viewing & informed chat. This one pair has done wonders for local tourism. Och, but they are magnificent.

**1766** ✓ **Islay** Loch Gruinart, Loch Indaal RSPB reserve. Take A847 at Bridgend
Map 9 then B8017 turning N and rt for Gruinart. The mudflats and fields at the
**F25** head of the loch provide winter grazing for huge flocks of Barnacle and
Greenland geese. They arrive, as do flocks of fellow bird-watchers, in late Oct.
Hides and good vantage points near rd. The Rhinns and the Oa in the S sus-
tain a huge variety of bird life.

**1767** ✓ **Marwick Head** Orkney Mainland 40km NW of Kirkwall, via Finstown
Map 3 and Dounby; take left at Birsay after L of Isbister cross the B9056 and
**P10** park at Cumlaquoy. Spectacular sea bird breeding colony on 100m cliffs and
nearby at the Loons Reserve, wet meadowland, 8 species of duck and many
waders. Orkney sites include the Noup cliffs on Westray, North Hill on Papa
Westray and Copinsay, 3km E of the mainland. The remoter, the merrier.

**1768** **Isle of Mull**   Sea eagles. Since the reintroduction of these magnificent
eagles, there is now a hide with CCTV viewing. By appt only. Site changes
every yr. Contact Forest Enterprise (01631 566155) or ask at TIC.

**1769** **Orkney Puffins** 'Wildabout' tour's dusk puffin patrol (01856 851011). Or go
solo at Costa Head, Brough of Birsay and Westray; check Kirkwall TIC for latest.

**1770** **The Bass Rock** off North Berwick 01620 892838. 'Temple of gannets'. A
Map 10 guano encrusted massif sticking out of the Forth and where Davie Balfour
**R25** was imprisoned in RLS's *Catriona* (aka *Kidnapped II*). Weather-dependent
boat trips available May-Sep courtesy of Fred Marr & the *Sula II*, from N
Berwick harbour (also to nearby Fidra). Phone for details.

**1771** **Scottish Seabirds Centre** North Berwick 01620 890202. Award-winning,
Map 10 interactive visitor attraction nr Harbour o/looking Bass Rock and Fidra. Video
**R25** and other state-of-the-art technology makes you feel as if the birds are next
to you. Viewing deck for dramatic perspective of gannets diving (140kmph!)
Excl teashop (seafood esp). 10am-6pm (4pm wint/5.30pm w/ends).

**1772** **Montrose Basin Wildlife Centre** 1.5km south of Montrose on the A92 to
Map 10 Arbroath. V accessible Scottish Wildlife Trust centre overlooks the estuarine
**S22** basin that hosts various residents and migrants. Good for twitchers and kids.
And autumn geese. Apr-Oct daily 10.30am-5pm. Wint hrs, ring 01674
676336.

**1773** **Forsinard Nature Reserve** By road, 44km from Helmsdale on the A897,
Map 6 or the train stops on route to Wick/Thurso. RSPB (proposed World Heritage
**N13** Site) reserve, acquired in '95 following public appeal. 17, 500 acres of the
'Flow Country' and the birds that go with it: divers, plovers, merlins and hen
harriers (CCTV pics). Guided walks avail. Reserve open AYR; VC Apr-Oct daily
9am-6pm. 01641 571225.

**1774** **Loch of Kinnordy** Kirriemuir 4km W of town on B951, an easily accessible
Map 10 site with 3 hides o/look loch and wetland area managed by RSPB. Geese in
**Q22** late autumn, gulls aplenty; always tickworthy. You may see the vanishing
ruglet butterfly.

**1775** **Piperdam Golf & Country Park** Fowlis by Dundee 01382 581374. This
Map 10 expensive housing development o/looking loch also attracts the upwardly
**Q23** mobile osprey. Gd viewing centre. Other upmarket residents inc short-eared
owls & reed buntings. All enjoy our suburbias.

**1776** **Strathbeg** nr Fraserburgh 12km S off main Fraserburgh-Peterhead rd, the
Map 8 A952 and signed 'Nature Reserve' at Crimond. Wide, shallow loch v close to
**T17** coastline, a 'magnet for migrating wildfowl' and from the (unmanned) reception centre at loch side it's poss to get a v good view of them. Marsh/fen,
dune and meadow habitats. In winter 30,000 geese/widgeon/mallard/
swans and occasional rarities like cranes and egrets. Binocs in centre and
other hides (Towerpool hide is 1km walk).

# Where To See Dolphins, Whales, Porpoises & Seals

1777 ✓ ✓ *The coast around the N of Scotland offers some of the best places in Europe from which to see whales and dolphins and, more ubiquitously, seals. You don't have to go on boat trips, though of course you get closer, the boatman will know where to find them and the trip itself can be exhilarating. Good operators are listed below. Dolphins are most active on a rising tide esp May-Sept.*

## MORAY & CROMARTY FIRTHS nr INVERNESS & CROMARTY

The best area in Scotland. The population of bottlenose dolphins in this area well exceeds 100 and they can be seen AYR (tho' mostly June-Sept).

**The Dolphins & Seals Of The Moray Firth Centre** 01463 731866. Just N of the Kessock Br on the A9 and adj the TIC (01463 731701). Underwater microphones pick up the chatterings of dolphins and porpoises and there's always somebody there to explain. They keep an up-to-date list of recent sightings and all cruises available. Summer only Mon-Sat 9.30am-4.30pm.

**Cromarty** Any vantage around the town is good esp S Sutor for coastal walk and an old lighthouse cottage has been converted into a research station run by Aberdeen Uni. **Chanonry Point, Fortrose,** E end of pt beyond lighthouse is the *best* place to see dolphins from land in Britain. Occasional sightings can also be seen at **Balintore,** opp Seaboard Memorial Hall; **Tarbert Ness** beyond **Portmahomack,** end of path through reserve further out along the Moray Firth poss at **Burghead, Lossiemouth** and **Buckie, Spey Bay** and **Portknockie.**

## NORTH WEST

On the W coast, esp nr Gairloch the following places may offer sightings of orcas, dolphins and minke whales mainly in summer.

**Rubha Reidh** nr Gairloch 20km N by unclassified rd beyond Melvaig. Nr the Carn Dearg Youth Hostel W of Lonemore where rd turns inland is good spot.

**Greenstone Point** N of Laide on the A832 nr Inverewe Gardens and Gruinard Bay. Harbour porpoises here Apr-Dec and minke whales May-Oct.

**Red Point Of Gairloch** by unclassified rd via Badachro. High ground looking over N Minch & S to L Torridon. Harbour porpoises often along this coast.

**Rubha Hunish** Skye The far NW finger of Skye. Walk from Duntulm Castle or Flodigarry (2324/SKYE). Dolphins & mink whales in autumn.

## OTHER PLACES

**Mousa Sound** Shetland 20km S of Lerwick (1833/PREHISTORIC SITES).

**Ardnamurchan** The Point The most westerly point (and lighthouse) on this wildly beautiful peninsula. Go to end of rd or park nr Sanna Beach and walk round. Sanna Beach worth going to just to walk the strand. VC; tearm.

**Stornoway** Isle of Lewis Heading out of town for Eye Peninsula, at Holm nr Sandwick S of A866 or from Bayble Bay (all within walking distance).

# Best Sealife Cruises

**Eco Ventures** Cromarty 01381 600323. Intimate and informative tours, but pricey. 2 trips per day AYR. Booking essential.

**Moray Firth Cruises** Inverness 01463 717900. 4 trips per day Mar-Oct.

**Summer Isles Cruises** 01854 622200. Seals & seabirds abound round these beautiful islands. 2 trips per day plus all day special.

**Hebridean Wildlife Cruises** Oban 01680 814260. 3 cruise vessels out of Oban for big range of island destinations incl St Kilda. Food & accom. Max 12.

**Wildlife Cruises** John O' Groats 01955 611353. Puffins, seabirds, seals. 2.30pm daily June-Sept. Large panoramic boat. Also all-day trips to Orkney from John o' Groats & Inverness.

**Sea.Fari Adventures** Based in **Edinburgh** (0131 331 4857), **Oban** (01852 300003) & **Skye** (01471 833316). Sealife adventure boating specialists. Range of eco-tours & trips in fast, inflatable boats. Sailing out of **Easdale, Isle of Seil** 25km S Oban.

## ON THE ISLANDS

**Sea-Life Surveys** Tobermory, Mull 01688 400223. Various packages from relaxed half-hr trip to the more intense eight hour. Small groups on comfortable boat & high-speed bts. Good percentage of porpoise, dolphin & whale sightings.

**Turus Mara** Mull 08000 858786. Daytrips from Ulva Ferry. Various itineraries taking in bird colonies of Treshnish Isles, Staffa & Iona. Dolphins, whales, puffins & seals.

**Whale Watching** Dervaig, Mull 01688 400264. 12-passenger MV *Flamer* leaves dailyl from Croig 5km Dervaig. Full day at sea.

**Shetland Wildlife & The Company of Whales** Shetland 01950 422483. From day trips to 7-day wildlife holidays. Sealife, birds, whales & otters.

**Bressaboats** Shetland 01595 693434. Award-winning wildlife adventure cruises.

**Island Cruising** Lewis 01851 672381. Wildlife, birdwatching and diving cruises around the Western Isles and St Kilda.

**Seatrek** Uig, Lewis 01851 672464. 2.5hr excursions from 3 western berths destinations. A purist experience.

**Islay Marine Charters** Islay 01496 850436. Trips on Sound of Islay, round Jura, Colonsay. Fishing & whale watching.

**Strond Wildlife Charters** Harris 01859 520204. From 1 hour to full day boat trips to see seals & birdlife of the Sound of Harris. Pay per boat, not per person.

There are two glass-bottom boat companies offering trips in **Skye**. **Family's Pride II** (0800 7832175) operate from Broadford Pier and concentrate on the reefs round the local islands. **Seaprobe Atlantis** (0800 9804846) based on the mainland at Kyle (over the bridge), stays around Kyle of Lochalsh (conservation) area. Sit underwater in the 'gallery' so better viewing advantage.

## WILDLIFE TOURS

**Island Encounter Wildlife Safaris** Mull 01680 300441. All-day tour with local expert. Possible sightings of otters, eagles, seals and falcons. Numerous pick-up points incl ferry terminals.

**Isle of Mull Wildlife Expeditions** Mull 01688 500121. Long-est personal day-long trips (collected from ferry). Nice.

**Wildabout** Orkney 01856 851011. Various trips with experienced guides. Wildlife plus history & folklore. Interactive.

**Out & About Tours** Lewis 01851 612288. Former countryside ranger leads groups of all sizes on guided walks and day trips of Lewis and Harris. Experience the landscape, culture and wildlife of the islands.

*Otters can be seen all over the NW Highlands in sheltered inlets, esp early morning and late evening and on an ebb tide. Skye is one of best places in Europe to see them. Go with:*

**International Otter Survival Fund** Broadford 01471 822487 organise courses & trips for all wildlife and might pt you in the rt direction.

**Otter Haven** Kylerhea Basically a viewing hide with CCTV, binoculars and a knowledgeable warden (not always there). Seabirds & seals too and a forest walk. 500m walk along a track from car park signposted on road out of Kylerhea (& from the ferry from Glenelg – 7/JOURNEYS).

# Great Wildlife Reserves

*These wildlife reserves are not merely bird-watching places. Most of them are easy to get to from major centres; none requires permits.*

**1778**
Map 10
**S25**
✓ ✓ **St Abb's Head** nr Berwick 22km N Berwick, 9km N Eyemouth & 10km E of main A1. Spectacular cliff scenery (2043/COASTAL WALKS), a huge sea bird colony, rich marine life & varied flora. Good view from top of stacks, geos and cliff face full of serried ranks of guillemot, kittiwake, razorbill etc. Hanging gdns of grasses & campion. Behind cliffs, grassland rolls down to the Mire L & its varied habitat of bird, insect, butterfly life & vegetation. The coffeeshop at the car park does a mean scone-stock for the walk!

**1779**
Map 8
**T19**
✓ ✓ **Sands Of Forvie & The Ythan Estuary** Newburgh 25km N Aber. Cross br o/side Newburgh on A975 to Cruden Bay & park. Path follows Ythan estuary, bears N & enters the largest undisturbed dune system in the UK. Dunes in every aspect of formation. Collieston, a 17/18thC fishing vill, is 5km away. These habitats support the largest population of eiders in UK (esp June) & huge numbers of terns. It's easy to get lost here, so get lost!

**1780**
Map 7
**J17**
✓ **Beinn Eighe** Bounded by the A832 & A896 W of Kinlochewe, this first National Nature Reserve in Britain includes a remaining fragments of old Caledonian pinewood on the S shore of L Maree & rises to the rugged tops with their spectacular views & varied geology. Excellent wood & mountain trails. Best app via Glen Torridon (1669/SCENIC ROUTES). Start from roadside car park (on A832 beyond L Clair). 3km nearer the village on this road is a VC.

**1781**
Map 10
**R25**
**John Muir Country Park** Dunbar Vast park betw Dunbar & N Berwick named after the Dunbar-born father of the Conservation movement. Includes estuary of the Tyne (park also known as Tyninghame), cliffs, sand spits & woodland. Many bird species. crabs, lichens, sea and marsh plants. Enter at E extremity of Dunbar at Belhaven, off the B6370 from A1; or off A198 to N Berwick 3km from A1. Or better, walk from Dunbar by 'cliff top trail' (2km).

**1782**
Map 9
**L26**
**Lochwinnoch** 30km SW of Glas via M8 jnct 28A then A737 past Johnstone onto A760. Also from Largs 20km via A760. Reserve just o/side village on lochside & comprises wetland & woodland habitats. A serious 'nature centre' incorporating an observation tower. Hides & marked trails; & a birds-spotted board. Shop & coffee shop. Good for kids. VC open daily 10am-5pm (cl Thurs).   RSPB

**1783**
Map 7
**M20**
**Insh Marshes** Kingussie 4km from town along B970 (past Ruthven Barracks, 1825/RUINS), 2500 acres of Spey floodplain run by RSPB. Trail (3km) marked out through meadow & wetland & a note of species to look out for (incl 6 types of orchid, 7 'red list' birds & half the UK population of goldeneye). Also 2 hides (250m & 450m) high above marshes, vantage points to see waterfowl, birds of prey, otters & deer. Declared a National Nature Reserve in 2003.

**1784**
Map 10
**R23**
**Tentsmuir** betw Newport & Leuchars N tip of Fife at the mouth of the Tay, reached from Tayport or Leuchars via the B945. Follow signs for Kinshaldy Beach taking rd that winds for 4km over flat then forested land. Park (car park closes 9pm in summer) & cross dunes to broad strand. Walks in both direction: W back to Tayport, E to Leuchars. Also 4km circular walk of beach & forest. Hide 2km away at Ice House Pond. Seals often watch from waves & bask in summer. Lots of butterflies. Waders aplenty and, to E, one of UK's most significant populations of eider. Most wildfowl offshore. Ranger 01334 473047.

**1785**
Map 10
**P24**
**Vane Farm** RSPB reserve on S shore of L Leven, beside & bisected by B9097 off jnct 5 of M90. Easily reached & v busy VC with observation lounge & education/orientation facs. Hide nearer loch side reached by tunnel under rd. Nature Trail on hill behind through heath & birchwood (2km circ). Good place to introduce kids to nature watching. Events: 01577 862355. ☕

**1786**
Map 9
**F26**
**Islay Wildlife Info & Field Centre** Port Charlotte Jam-packed info centre that's v 'hands-on' & interactive. Up-to-date displays of geology, natural history (rocks, skeletons, sealife tanks). Recent sightings of wildlife, flora and fauna lists, video rm, reference library. Kids' area & activity days. Gr for kids. Apr-Oct 10am-3pm. Cl Sat (July/Aug 10am-5pm 7 days).

**1787**
Map 5
**C17**
**Balranald** North Uist, Western Isles W coast of N Uist reached by the rd from Lochmaddy, then the Bayhead t/off at Clachan Stores (10km N). This most western, most faraway reach is one of the last redoubts of the disappearing corncrake. Catch its twitter while you can.

# SECTION 8

*Historical Places*

# The Best Castles

NTS: *Under the care of the National Trust for Scotland. Hrs vary.* HS: *Under the care of Historic Scotland. Standard hrs are: Apr-end Sept Mon-Sat 9.30am-6.30pm; Sun 2-6.30pm. Oct-Mar Mon-Sat 9.30am-4.30pm; Sun 2-4.30pm.*

**1788**
Map 10
**N24**
✓ ✓ ✓ **Stirling Castle** Dominating the town and the plain, this like Edin Castle is worth the hype and the history. And like Edin, it's a timeless attraction that can withstand waves of tourism as it survived the centuries of warfare for which it was built. Despite this primary function, it does seem a v civilised billet, with peaceful gdns and rampart walks from which the views are excellent (esp the aerial view of the Royal Gdns, 'the cup and saucer' as they're known locally). Incls the Renaissance Palace of James V and the Great Hall of James IV restored to full magnificence. Some rock legends also play here in summer (Wet Wet Wet in 2005). The Costa caff is a bit of a letdown in these historical circumstances (but it does hot food).     HS

**1789**
Map 1
**B4**
✓ ✓ ✓ **Edinburgh Castle** City centre. Impressive from any angle and all the more so from inside. Despite the tides of tourists and time, it still enthralls. Superb perspectives of the city and of Scottish history. Stone of Destiny & the Crown Jewels are the Big Attractions. Café and restau (superb views) with efficient, but uninspiring catering operation; open only castle hrs and to castle visitors. Report: 388/MAIN ATTRACTIONS.     HS

**1790**
Map 8
**N17**
✓ ✓ **Brodie Castle** nr Nairn 6-7km W of Forres off main A96. More a (Z-plan) tower house than a castle, dating from 1567. In this century & like Cawdor nearby, the subject of family feuding. With a minimum of historical hocum, this 16/17th-century, but mainly Victorian, country house is furnished from rugs to moulded ceilings in the most excellent taste. Every picture (v few gloomies) bears examination. The nursery and nanny's rm, the guest rms, indeed all the rms, are eminently habitable. I could live in the library. There are regular musical evenings and other events (01309 641371 for event programme). Tearoom and informal walks in grounds. An avenue leads to a lake; in spring the daffodils are famous. Mar-Sept 12-4pm (cl Fri/Sat May, June, Sept); Sun 1.30-5.30pm. W/ends in Oct. Grounds open AYR till sunset.     NTS

**1791**
Map 9
**K28**
✓ ✓ **Culzean Castle** Maybole 24km S of Ayr on A719. Impossible to convey here the scale and the scope of the house and the country park. Allow some hrs esp for the grounds. Castle is more like a country house and you examine from the other side of a rope. From the 12th century, but rebuilt by Robert Adam in 1775, a time of soaring ambition, its grandeur is almost out of place in this exposed cliff-top position. It was designed for entertaining, and the oval staircase is magnificent. Wartime associations (esp with President Eisenhower) plus the enduring fascination of the aristocracy. 560 acres of grounds including cliff-top walk, formal gdns, walled gdn, Swan Pond (a must) and Happy Valley. Harmonious home farm is VC with café, exhibits and shop etc. Open Apr-Oct 11am-5.30pm. Many special 'events'. Culzean is pron 'Cullane'. And you can stay (797/AYRSHIRE HOTELS). ☕     NTS

**1792**
Map 10
**Q24**
✓ ✓ **Falkland Palace** Falkland Middle of farming Fife, 15km from M90 jnct 8. Not a castle at all, but the hunting palace of the Stewart dynasty. Despite its recreational rather than political role, it's one of the landmark buildings in Scottish history and in the 16th century was the finest Renaissance building in Britain. They all came here for archery, falconry and hunting boar and deer on the Lomonds; and for Royal Tennis which is displayed and explained. Still occupied by the Crichton-Stewarts, the house is dark and rich and redolent of those days of 'dancin and deray at Falkland on the Grene'. Mar-Oct 10-6pm. Sun 1-5.30pm. Plant shop & events programme. 979/FIFE RESTAUS. Gr walks from village (1979/HILL WALKS). (2012/GLEN WALKS).
NTS

**1793**
Map 6
**Q12**
✓ ✓ **Castle of Mey** nr Thurso Actually nr John o' Groats (off A836), castles don't get further-flung than this. Stunted trees, frequent wind & a wild coast but the Queen Mother famously fell in love with this dilapidated house in 1952, filled it with things she found & was given & turned it into one of the most human & endearing of the Royal (if not all aristocratic) residences. Guides in every rm tell the story & if you didn't love her already, you will when you leave. Charles & Camilla still visit. May-July, mid Aug-Sept but check (01847 851473). Cl Fri.

**1794** ✓ **Cawdor Castle** Cawdor nr Nairn & Inverness The mighty Cawdor of
Map 7  Macbeth fame. Most of the family clear off for the summer and leave their
**N17**  romantic yet habitable & yes... stylish castle, sylvan grounds and gurgling
Cawdor Burn to you. Pictures from Claude to Craigie Aitcheson, a modern
kitchen as fascinating as the enormous one of yore. Even the 'tartan passage'
is nicely done. The burn is the colour of tea. An easy drive (25km) to Brodie
(above) means you can see 2 of Scotland's most appealing castles in one day.
Gdns are gorgeous. May-early Oct, 7 days, 10am-5.30pm, 9-hole golf.

**1795** ✓ **Blair Castle** Blair Atholl Impressive from the A9, the castle and the
Map 10  landscape of the Dukes of Atholl (present duke not present); 10km N of
**N21**  Pitlochry. Hugely popular; almost a holiday camp atmos. Numbered rms
chock-full of 'collections': costumes, toys, plates, weapons, stag skulls, walking sticks – so many things! Upstairs, the more usual stuffed apartments
including the Jacobite bits. Walk in the policies (incl 'Hercules Gdn' with tranquil ponds). Mar-Oct 9.30am-4.30pm (LA) daily.

**1796** ✓ **Glamis** Forfar 8km from Forfar via A94 or off main A929, Dundee-Aber
Map 10  rd (t/off 10km N of Dundee, a picturesque app). Fairy-tale castle in
**Q22**  majestic setting. Seat of the Strathmore family (Queen Mum spent her childhood here) for 600 yrs; every rm an example of the interior of a certain period. Guided tours (continuous/50mins duration). Restau/gallery shop haven
for tourists (& for an excl bridie 1483/BAKERS). Easter-mid Oct, 10.30am. Last
admn 4.45pm. Italian Gdns & nature trail well worth 500m walk.

**1797** ✓ **Brodick Castle** Arran 4km from town (bike hire 01770 302868).
Map 9  Impressive, well-maintained castle, exotic formal gdns and extensive
**J27**  grounds. Goat Fell in the background and the sea through the trees. Dating
from 13th century and until the 1950s the home of the Dukes of Hamilton.
An over-antlered hall leads to liveable rms with portraits and heirlooms, an
atmos of long-ago afternoons. Tangible sense of relief in the kitchens now all
the entertaining is over. Robert the Bruce's cell is not so convincing. Easter-
Oct daily until 4pm (last adm). Marvellous grounds open AYR. NTS

**1798** ✓ **Duart Castle** Mull 13th-century ancestral seat of the Clan Maclean &
Map 9  home to Sir Lachlan & Lady Maclean. Quite a few modifications over the
**H23**  centuries as methods of defence grew in sophistication but with walls as thick
as a truck and the sheer isolation of the place it must have made any prospect
of attack seem doomed from the outset. Now a happier, homlier place, the
only attacking that gets done these days is on scones in the superior tearoom.
April Sun-Thur 11-4pm. May-Oct 10.30am-5.30pm. 🍵

**1799** **Torosay Castle** Mull 3km from Craignure and the ferry. A Victorian *arriviste*
Map 9  in this strategic corner where Duart Castle has ruled for centuries. Not many
**H23**  apartments open but who could blame them – this is a family home, endearing and eccentric esp their more recent history (like Dad's Loch Ness Monster
fixation). The heirlooms are valuable because they have been cherished and
there's a human proportion to the house and its contents which is rare in
such places. The gdns, attributed to Lorimer, are fabulous, esp the Italianate
Statue Walk, and are open AYR. The Mull Light Railway from Craignure is one
way to go (1753/KIDS), woodland walk another. Tearoom. Mar-Oct 10.30am-
5pm. Gardens AYR 9am-7pm.

**1800** **Dunvegan Castle** Skye 3km Dunvegan village. Romantic history and set-
Map 7  ting, though more baronial than castellate, the result of mid-19th-century
**F18**  restoration that incorporated the disparate parts. Necessary crowd management leads you through a series of rms where the Fairy Flag, displayed above
a table of exquisite marquetry, has pride of place. Lovely gdns down to the
loch; boats leave the jetty 'to see the seals'. Busy café and gift shop at gate
side car park. Open Mar-Oct 10am-5.30pm, wint 11-4pm.

**1801** **Eilean Donan** Dornie On A87, 13km before Kyle of Lochalsh. A calendar
Map 7  favourite, often depicted illuminated; and once, with the balloon hovering
**J18**  above, an abiding image from the BBC promo. Inside it's a v decent slice of
history for the price. The Banqueting Hall with its Pipers' Gallery must make
for splendid dinner parties for the Macraes. Much military regalia amongst
the bric-a-brac, but also the impressive Raasay Punchbowl partaken of by
Johnson and Boswell. Mystical views from ramparts. Mar-Nov, 10-5.30pm.

**1802  Castle Menzies Weem** nr Aberfeldy  In Tay valley with spectacular ridge
Map 10  behind (**Walks In The Weem Forest**, part of the Tummel Valley Forest
N22  Park; separate car park). On B846, 7km W of Aberfeldy, through Weem. The
16th-century stronghold of the Menzies (pron 'Ming-iss'), one of Scotland's
oldest clans. Sparsely furnished with odd clan memorabilia, the house nevertheless conveys more of a sense of Jacobite times than many more brimful
of bric-a-brac. Bonnie Prince Charlie stopped here on the way to Culloden.
Open farmland situation, so manured rather than manicured grounds. Apr-
Oct 10.30am-5pm, Sun 2-5pm.

**1803  Scone Palace** nr Perth  On A93 rd to Blairgowrie and Braemar. A 'great
Map 10  house', the home to the Earl of Mansfield and gorgeous grounds. Famous for
P23  the 'Stone of Scone' on which the Kings of Scots were crowned, and the
Queen Vic bedroom. Maze and pinetum. Many contented animals greet you
and a plethora of peacocks. Easter-Oct 7days 9.30am-4.45pm (last adm.) Fri
only in wint 10am-5pm.

**1804  Kellie Castle** nr Pittenweem Fife  Major castle in Fife. Dating from 14th
Map 10  century restored by Robert Lorimer, his influence evidenced by magnificent
R24  plaster ceilings and furniture. The gdns, nursery and kitchen recall all the old
Victorian virtues. The old-fashioned roses still bloom for us. May-Sept 1-5pm.
Grounds open AYR.                                                          ADMN

**1805  Craigievar** nr Banchory 15km N of main A93 Aber-Braemar rd betw Banchory
Map 8  and Aboyne. A classic tower house, perfect like a porcelain miniature. Random
R19  windows, turrets, balustrades. Set amongst sloping lawns & tall trees. Limited
access to halt deterioration (only 8 people at a time) means you are spared the
shuffling hordes, but don't go unless you are respecter of the NTS conservation
policy. Apr-Sept, Fri-Tues only 12-5.30pm (last adm 4.45pm).               NTS

**1806  Drum Castle** (the Irvine Ancestral Home) nr Banchory  Please forgive this,
Map 8  the longest entry in the book! 1km off main A93 Aberdeen-Braemar rd betw
S20  Banchory and Peterculter and 20km from Aberdeen centre. For 24 generations this has been the seat of the Irvines. Our lot! Gifted to one William De
Irwin by Robert the Bruce, it combines the original keep, a Jacobean mansion
and Victorian expansionism. I have twice signed the book in the Irvine Rm
and wandered through the accumulated history hopeful of identifying with
something. Hugh Irvine, the family 'artist' whose extravagant self-portrait as
the Angel Gabriel raised eyebrows in 1810, seems more interesting than most
of my soldiering forebears. Give me a window seat in the library! Grounds
have a peaceful & exceptional walled rose gdn (Apr-Sept 10-6pm; 1556/GAR-
DENS). House: Easter-Sept 12.30-5.30 (from 10am June-Aug). Tower can be
climbed for gr views. I thought the Old Wood of Drum was a bit of a swizz ie
not old at all.                                                            NTS

**1807  Balmoral** nr Ballater  On main A93 betw Ballater and Braemar. Limited
Map 8  access to the house (i.e. only the ballrm - public functions are held here
Q20  when they're in residence & new corporate thrust '05) so grounds (open Apr-
July) with Albert's wonderful trees are more rewarding. For royalty rooters
only, and if you like Landseers ...Crathie Church along the main rd has a good
rose window, an altar of Iona marble. John Brown is somewhere in the old
graveyard down track from VC, the memorial on the hill is worth a climb for
a poignant moment and the view of the policies. The Crathie services have
never been quite the same Sunday attraction since Di and Fergie on a
prince's arm. Daily 10-5pm, Easter-July.

**1808  Dunrobin Castle** Golspie  The largest house in the Highlands, the home of
Map 6  the Dukes of Sutherland who once owned more land than anyone else in the
N15  British Empire. It's the first Duke who occupies an accursed place in Scots
history for his inhumane replacement, in these vast tracts, of people with
sheep. His statue stands on Ben Bhraggie above the town (1873/MONUMENTS).
Living the life of English grandees, the Sutherlands transformed the castle
into a *château* and filled it with their obscene wealth. Once there were 100
servants for a house party of 20 and it had 30 gardeners. Now it's all just history. The gdns are still fabulous (1550/GARDENS). The castle and separate
museum are open Apr-mid Oct. Check 01408 633177 for times.               ADMN

**Crathes** nr Banchory 1545/GARDENS; 1863/COUNTRY HOUSES.

**Fyvie** Aberdeenshire 1862/COUNTRY HOUSES.

# The Most Interesting Ruins

HS: *Under the care of Historic Scotland. Standard hrs are: Apr-end Sept 7 days 9.30am-6.30pm. Oct-Mar Mon-Sat 9.30am-4.30pm, Sun 2-4.30pm. Some variations with individual properties; call 0131 668 8831 to check. 'Friends of Historic Scotland' membership: 0131 668 8600 or any of the manned sites (annual charge but then free admn).*

**1809**
Map 10
**N25**
✓ ✓ ✓ **Linlithgow Palace** Impressive from the M9 and the S app to this the most agreeable of W Lothian towns, but don't confuse the magnificent Renaissance edifice with St Michael's Church next door, topped with its controversial crown and spear spire. From the Gr Hall, built for James I, King of Scots, with its huge adj kitchens, & the North Range with loch views, you get a real impression of the lavish lifestyle of the court. Apparently 'underperforms' as an attraction for Historic Scotland, but fabulous King's Fountain has reemerged from restoration to add to the Palace appeal.                                                                    HS

**1810**
Map 10
**P30**
✓ ✓ **Caerlaverock** nr Dumfries 17km S by B725. Follow signs for Wetlands Reserve (1795/BIRDS), but go past rd end. Fairy-tale fortress within double moat and manicured lawns, the daunting frontage being the apex of an uncommon triangular shape. Since 1270, the bastion of the Maxwells, the Wardens of the W Marches. Destroyed by Bruce, besieged in 1640; now with siege engine and AV voiced by Time Team's Tony Robinson. The whole castle experience.                                           HS

**1811**
Map 10
**S20**
✓ **Dunnottar Castle** nr Stonehaven 3km S of Stonehaven on the coast rd just off the A92. Like Slains further N, the ruins are impressively and precariously perched on a cliff top. Historical links with Wallace, Mary Queen of Scots (the odd night) and even Oliver Cromwell, whose Roundheads besieged it in 1650. Mel Gibson's *Hamlet* was filmed here (bet you don't remember the film) and the Crown Jewels of Scotland were once held here. 400m walk from car park. Can walk along cliff top from Stonehaven (2km). Mar-Oct 9am-6pm, Sun 2-5pm. Nov-Mar weekdays only 9-dusk.

**1812**
Map 9
**H21**
✓ **Castle Tioram** nr Acharacle Romantic ruin where you don't need the saga to sense the place, and maybe the mystery is better than the history. 5km from A861 just N of Acharacle signed 'Dorlin'. 5km then park by Dorlin Cottage. Serenely beautiful shoreline then walk across a short causeway. Future of this ruin still under review at TGP. Pron 'Cheerum'. Musical beach at nearby Kentra Bay (2044/COASTAL WALKS).

**1813**
Map 8
**P17**
✓ **Elgin Cathedral** Elgin Follow signs in town centre. Set in a meadow by the river, a tranquil corner of this busy market town, the scattered ruins and surrounding graveyard of what was once Scotland's finest cathedral. The nasty Wolf of Badenoch burned it down in 1390, but there are some 13thC and medieval renewals. The octagonal chapterhouse is especially revered, but this is an impressive and evocative slice of history. HS have made gr job of recent restorations. Now tower can be climbed. Around the corner, there's now a biblical gdn planted with species mentioned in the Bible. (May-Sept, 10am-7.30pm daily).                                                    HS ADMN

**1814**
Map 8
**Q19**
✓ **Kildrummy Castle** nr Alford 15km SW of Alford on A97 nr the hotel (1253/SCOTTISH HOTELS) and across the gorge from its famous gdns. Most complete 13th-century castle in Scotland, an HQ for the Jacobite uprising of 1715 and an evocative and v Highland site. Here the invitation in HS advertising to 'bring your imagination' is truly valid. Apr-Sep 9.30am-6.30pm. Now head for the gardens (500m).                                                         HS

**1815**
Map 5
**C20**
✓ **Kisimull Castle** Isle of Barra The medieval fortress, home of the MacNeils that sits on a rocky outcrop in the bay 200m offshore. Originally built in the 11th century, it was burnt in the 18th and restored by the 45th chief, an American architect, but was unfinished when he died in 1970. An essential pilgrimage for all MacNeils, it is fascinating and atmospheric for the rest of us, a grim exterior belying an unusual internal layout – a courtyard that seems unchanged and rms betwixt renovation and decay. Open every day in season & has a gift shop. You phone or flip board when you want to visit & they come in the boat (01871 810313). Phone for wint hrs or enq adj TIC.                                                                       HS

**1816** **Edzell Castle** Edzell  2km village off main st, signed. Pleasing red sandstone
Map 10  ruin in bucolic setting – birds twitter, rabbits run. Notable walled parterre gdn
**R21**  created by Sir David Lindsay way back in 1604. The wall niches are nice. Lotsa
lobelias! Mary Queen of Scots was here (she so got around).  HS

**1817** **Bothwell Castle** Uddingston, Glasgow  15km E of city via M74, Uddingston
Map 10  t/off into main st and follow signs. Hugely impressive 13th-century ruin, the
**M26**  home of the Black Douglas, o/look Clyde (with fine walks). Remarkable considering proximity to city that there is hardly any 21st-century intrusion except
yourself. Pay to go inside or just sit and watch the Clyde go by.  HS

**1818** **Fort George** nr Inverness  On promontory of Moray Firth 18km NE via A96
Map 7  by village of Ardersier. A vast site and 'one of the most outstanding artillery
**M17**  fortifications in Europe'. Planned after Culloden as a base for George II's army
and completed 1769, it has remained unaltered ever since and allows a v
complete picture. May provoke palpitations in the Nationalist heart, but it's
heaven for militarists and altogether impressive. It's hardly a ruin of course,
and is still occupied by the army.  HS

**1819** **Dunollie Castle** Oban  Just o/side town via Corran Esplanade towards
Map 9  Ganavan. Best to walk to or park on Esplanade and then walk 1km. (No park-
**H23**  ing on main rd below castle.) Bit of a scramble up and a slither down (& the
run itself is note 'safe'), but the views are superb. More atmospheric than
Dunstaffnage and not commercialised. You can climb one flight up, but the
ruin is only a remnant of the gr stronghold of the Lorn Kings that it was. The
Macdougals, who took it over in the 12th century, still live in the house below.

**1820** **Tarbert Castle** Tarbert, Argyll  Strategically and dramatically o/look the shel-
Map 9  tered harbour of this epitome of a West Highland pt. Unsafe to clamber over,
**H25**  it's for the timeless view rather than an evocation of tangible history that it's
worth finding the way up. Steps up from Harbour Rd next to dental surgery.

**1821** **Kilchurn Castle** Loch Awe  The romantic ruin at the head of L Awe, visited
Map 9  either by a short walk (1km) from car park off the main A85 5km E of Lochawe
**J23**  village (betw the Stronmilchan t/off and the Inveraray rd) or by a fetching wee
steamboat from Loch Awe Pierhead (by the station) – call 01838 200440 for
details. Pleasant spot for loch reflections. If you go by boat, take tea in the
railway carriage cafe while you're waiting.

**1822** **St Andrews Cathedral**  The ruins of the largest church in Scotland before
Map 10  the Reformation, a place of gr influence and pilgrimage. St Rule's Tower and
**R23**  the jagged fragment of the huge W Front in their striking position at the convergence of the main streets and o/look the sea, are remnants of its gr glory.
7 days 9.30-6.30pm (wint 4pm). Suns 2-4.30pm.

**1823** **Crichton Castle** nr Pathhead  6km W of A68 at Pathhead (28km S Edin) or
Map 10  via A7 turning E, 3km S of Gorebridge. Massive Border keep dominating the
**Q26**  Tyne valley. Open Apr-Sept. Nearby is the 15thC collegiate church. Summer
Suns only, 2-5pm. They record Radio 3 religious music here. 500m walk from
Crichton village. Good picnic spots below by the river. See 419/EASY WALKS.
ADMN HS

**1824** **Tantallon Castle** North Berwick  5km E of town by coast rd; 500m to dra-
Map 10  matic cliff top setting with views to Bass Rock. Dates from 1350 with massive
**R25**  'curtain wall' to see it through stormy weather and stormy history. The Red
Douglases and their friends kept the world at bay. Wonderful beach nearby
(426/BEACHES).  ADMN HS

**1825** **Ruthven Barracks** Kingussie  2km along B970 and visible from A9 esp at
Map 7  night when it's illuminated, these former barracks built by the English
**M20**  Redcoats as part of the campaign to tame the Highlands after the first
Jacobite rising in 1715, were actually destroyed by the Jacobites in 1746 after
Culloden. It was here that Bonnie Prince Charlie sent his final order, 'Let every
man seek his own safety', signalling the absolute end of the doomed cause.
Life for the soldiers is well described and visualised. Open AYR.  HS

**1826** **Urquhart Castle** Drumnadrochit, Loch Ness  28km S of Inverness on A82.
Map 7  The classic Highland fortress on a promontory o/look L Ness visited every yr
**L18**  by bus loads and boat loads of tourists. Photo opportunities galore amongst
the well-kept lawns and extensive ruins of the once formidable stronghold of
the Picts and their scions, finally abandoned in the 18th
century. New visitor facs to cope with demand.  ADMN HS

**1827**   **Doune Castle** Doune   Follow signs from centre of village which is just off
Map 10   A84 Callander-Dunblane rd. O/look the R Teith, the well-preserved ruin of a
**M24**   late 14th-century courtyard castle with a Gr Hall and another draughty rm
where Mary Queen of Scots once slept. Nice walk to the meadow begins on
track to left of castle.         ADMN   HS

**1828**   **Slains Castle** nr Cruden Bay   32km N of Aber off the A975 Meikle Partens car
Map 8   park then 1km perched on the cliffs (1.5km vill). Obviously because of its loca-
**T18**   tion, but also because there's no reception centre/postcard shop or proper
signposts, this is a ruin that talks. Your imagination, like Bram Stoker's (who
was inspired after staying here, to write Dracula), can be cast to the winds. The
seat of the Earls of Errol, it has been gradually disintegrating since the roof was
removed in 1925. Once, it had the finest dining rm in Scotland. The waves
crash below, as always. Be careful!

# The Best Prehistoric Sites

**1829**   ✓ ✓ ✓ **Skara Brae** Orkney Mainland   32km Kirkwall by A965/B9655
Map 3            via Finstown and Dounby. Can be a windy walk to this remark-
**P10**   able shoreline site, the subterranean remains of a compact village 5,000 yrs
old. It was engulfed by a sandstorm 600yrs later and lay perfectly preserved
until uncovered by another storm in 1850. Now it permits one of the most
evocative glimpses of truly ancient times in the UK.       ADMN   HS

**1830**   ✓ ✓ **The Standing Stones Of Stenness** Orkney Mainland   Together
Map 3        with the Ring of Brodgar and the great chambered tomb of Maes
**Q10**   Howe, all within walking distance of the A965, 18km from Kirkwall, this is as
impressive a ceremonial site as you'll find anywhere. From same period as
Skara Brae. The individual stones and the scale of the Ring are v imposing
and deeply mysterious. The burial cairn is the finest megalithic tomb in the
UK. Seen together, they will stimulate even the most jaded sense of wonder.
        HS

**1831**   ✓ ✓ **The Callanish Stones** Isle Of Lewis   24km from Stornoway. Take
Map 5        Tarbert rd and go rt at Leurbost. The best preserved and most
**F14**   unusual combination of standing stones in a ring around a tomb, with radi-
ating arms in cross shape. Predating Stonehenge, they were unearthed from
the peat in the mid-19th century and have become the major historical
attraction of the Hebrides. Other configurations nearby. At dawn there's
nobody else there (except camping New-Agers). VC out of sight is a good one
with a nice caff. Cl Sun. Free. 🍵          HS

**1832**   ✓ **The Clava Cairns** nr Culloden nr Inverness   Here long before the most
Map 7   infamous battle in Scottish and other histories; another special atmos.
**N17**   Not so well marked but continue along the B9006 towards Cawdor Castle,
that other gr historical landmark (1794/CASTLES), taking a rt at the Culloden
Moor Inn and follow signs for Clava Lodge (holiday homes), picking up HS
sign to rt. Chambered cairns in grove of trees. Really just piles of stones, but
the death rattle echo from 5,000 yrs ago is perceptible to all esp when no one
else is there. Remoteness prob inhibits new age attentions and allows more
private meditations in this extraterrestrial spot.         HS

**1833**   ✓ **The Mousa Broch** Shetland   On small island of Mousa, off Shetland
Map 4   mainland 20km S of Lerwick, visible from main A970; but to see it prop-
**V5**   erly, take boat (01950 431367). Isolated in its island fastness, this is the best
preserved broch in Scotland. Walls are 13m high (originally 15m) and galleries
run up the middle, in one case to the top. Solid as a rock, this example of a
uniquely Scottish phenomenon would once have been a v des res. Also
Jarlshof in the far S next to Sumburgh airport has remnants and ruins from
Neolithic to Viking times – 18thC, with esp impressive 'wheelhouses'.
        ADMN

**1834**   ✓ **Crannog Centre** Aberfeldy   Adj Croft-Na-Caber Water Sports Centre on
Map 10   L Tay (2135/WATER SPORTS). Superb reconstruction of iron-age dwelling
**M22**   (there are several under the loch). Credible and worthwhile archeological project now gr for kids & conveys history well. Displays in progress and human
story told by pleasant humans. Open Apr-Oct 10am-5.30pm, wint hrs vary.

**1835**
Map 9
**H24**
✓ **Kilmartin Glen** nr Lochgilphead, Templewood  2km S of Kilmartin and 1km (signed) from A816 and across rd from car park, 2 distinct stone circles from a long period of history betw 3000-1200 BC. Story and speculations described on boards. Pastoral countryside and wide skies. There are other sites in the vicinity, and an excl museum/café (2238/MUSEUMS).                    HS

**1836**
Map 3
**Q10**
**Tomb Of The Eagles** Orkney Mainland  33km S of Kirkwall at the foot of S Ronaldsay; signed from Burwick. A 'recent' discovery, the excavation of this cliff cave is on private land. You call in at the VC first and they'll tell you the whole story. Then there's a 2km walk. Allow time; ethereal stuff. Open AYR, Apr-Oct 9.30am-6pm, Nov-Mar 10am-noon.                    ADMN

**1837**
Map 10
**N25**
**Cairnpapple Hill** nr Linlithgow, West Lothian  App from the 'Beecraigs' rd off W end of Linlithgow main st. Go past the Beecraigs t/off and continue for 3km. Cairnpapple is signed. Astonishing Neolithic henge & later burial site on windy hill with views from Highlands to Pentlands. Atmos even more strange by the very 21st-century communications mast next door. Cute VC! Summer only 9.30am-6.30pm but can be accessed any time.                    ADMN HS

**1838**
Map 11
**L30**
**Cairnholy** betw Newton Stewart & Gatehouse Of Fleet  2km off main A75. Signed from rd. A mini Callanish of standing stones around a burial cairn on v human scale and in a serene setting with another site (with chambered tomb) 150m up the farm track. Excellent view – sit and contemplate what went on 4000-6000 years ago. There will be nobody else around.

**1839**
Map 10
**R21**
**The Brown And White Caterthuns** Kirkton Of Menmuir, nr Brechin  5km uphill from war memorial at Menmuir, then signed 1km. Lay-by with obvious path to both on either side of the rd. White easiest (500m uphill). These iron-age hill top settlements give tremendous sense of scale and space and afford an impressive panorama of the Highland line. Colours refer to the heather-covered turf and stone of one and the massive collapsed ramparts of the White. Sit here for a while & picture the Pict.

**1840**
Map 6
**Q13**
**The Grey Cairns Of Canster** nr Wick  20km S of Wick, a v straight rd (signed for Cairns) heads W from the A9 for 8km. The cairns are instantly identifiable nr the rd and impressively complete. The 'horned cairn' is the best in the UK. In 2500 BC these stone-piled structures were used for the disposal of the dead. You can crawl inside them if you're agile (or at night, brave). Nearby, also signed from A9 is:

**1841**
Map 6
**Q13**
**Hill O' Many Stanes** nr Wick  Aptly named place with extraordinary number of small standing stones; 200 in 22 rows. If fan shape was complete, there would be 600. Their v purposeful layout is enigmatic and strange.

**1842**
Map 11
**L31**
**The Whithorn Story** Whithorn  Excavation site (tho' no longer active), medieval priory, shrine of St Ninian, VC & café. More than enough to keep the whole family occupied – enthusiastic staff. Christianity? Look where it got us. This is where it started. (Also 1603/COASTAL VILLS). Easter-Oct 10.30-5pm daily.

**1843**
Map 11
**N30**
**The Motte Of Ur** nr Dalbeattie  Off B794 N of Dalbeattie and 6km from main A75 Castle Douglas to Dumfries rd. Most extensive bailey earthwork castle in Scotland dating from 12th century. No walls or excavation visible but a gr sense of scale and place. Go through village of Haugh and on for 2km S. Looking down to rt at farm buildings the minor rd crosses a ford; park here, cross footbridge and head to rt – the hillock is above the ford.

**1844**
Map 10
**M25**
**Bar Hill** nr Kirkintilloch  A fine example of the low ruins of a Roman fort on the Antonine Wall which ran across Scotland for 200 yrs early ad. Gr place for an out-of-town walk (736/VIEWS).

**1845**
Map 7
**H19**
**The Brochs** Glenelg  110km from Ft William. Glenelg is 14km from the A87 at Shiel Br (1705/SCENIC ROUTES). 5km from Glenelg village in beautiful Glen Beag. The 2 brochs, Dun Trodden and Dun Telve, are the best preserved examples on the mainland of these mysterious 1st-century homesteads. Easy here to distinguish the twin stone walls that kept out the cold and the more disagreeable neighbours. Free.                    HS

**1846**
Map 5
**D17**
**Barpa Lanyass** North Uist  8km S Lochmaddy, visible from main A867 rd, like a hat on the hill (200m away). A 'squashed' beehive burial cairn dating from 1000 BC, the tomb of a chieftain. It's largely intact and the small and

nimble can explore inside, crawling through the short entrance tunnel and down through the yrs.

**1847** **Sueno's Stone** Forres  Signposted from Grant Pk (1590/TOWN PARKS). More
Map 8  late Dark Age than prehistoric, a 9th or 10th C carved stone, 6m high in its
**P17**  own glass case. Pictish, magnificent; arguments still over what it shows.

**1848** **Aberdeenshire Prehistoric Trail: East Aquhorthies Stone Circle** nr
Map 8  Inverurie Aberdeenshire  Signed from B993 from Inverurie to Monymusk. A
**S19**  circle of pinkish stones with 2 grey sentinels flanking a huge recumbent
stone set in the rolling countryside of the Don Valley. Bennachie over there,
then as now! (1976/HILLS).

**1849** **Loanhead Of Daviot Stone Circle** nr Inverurie Aberdeenshire  Head for
Map 8  the village of Daviot on B9001 from Inverurie; or Loanhead, signed off A920
**S18**  rd betw Oldmeldrum and Insch. The site is 500m from top of village.
Impressive and spooky circle of 11 stones and one recumbent from
4000/5000 BC. Unusual second circle adj encloses a cremation cemetery
from 1500 BC. Remains of 32 people were found here. Obviously, an important place. God knows what they were up to.

**1850** **Archaeolink** nr Insch Aberdeenshire  Geographically betw the 2 sites above
Map 8  and within an area of many prehistoric remnants, a more recent interpreta-
**R18**  tive centre. Impressively modern app to history both from exterior and within, where interactive and audiovisual displays bring the food hunter-gatherer past into the culture hunter-gatherer present. Up the hill, 3 adaptable staff
members alternate as Iron/Bronze/Stone Age natives or visiting Romans.
Easter-Nov 10am-5pm. Wint 11am-4pm.                                    ADMN

# Great Country Houses

**1851**    ✓ ✓ **Haddo House**  Tarves, by Ellon. 01651 851440. Designed by
Map 8    ✓ ✓  William Adam for the Earl of Aberdeen, the Palladian-style man-
**S18**  sion well known for its musical evenings. Not so much a house, more a
leisure land in the best poss taste, with country park to wander, a pleasant
café, estate shop and gentle education. Grand, full of things, but the base-
ments are the place to ponder. The window by Burne-Jones in the chapel is
glorious. Excl programme of events, both NTS and Haddo House Trust. ☕
NTS

**1852**    ✓ ✓ **Mount Stuart** Bute  01700 503877. Unique Victorian Gothic
Map 9    ✓ ✓  house; echoes 3rd Marquis of Bute's passion for mythology,
**J26**  astronomy, astrology and religion. Amazing splendour and scale, but atmos
intimate and romantic. Beautiful Italian antiques, notable paintings and fascinating attention to detail with surprising humourous touches. Equally
grand gdns, with fabulous walks and sea views. Stylish VC – straight out of
*Wallpaper* magazine with restau/coffee shop & notable, well-curated gallery
space. May-Sept 11am-5pm. Coffeeshop by the house less impressive (Sat till
2.30pm). Grounds 10am-6pm. *Spend the best part of a day here!* ☕

**1853**    ✓ ✓ **Fasque betw** Stonehaven & Montrose  W of A92 at Laurencekirk
Map 10   ✓ ✓  and through Victorian Fettercairn to Fasque, one of the most fasci-
**R21**  nating old houses you'll ever be permitted to wander through. Home of
Gladstone (4 times Prime Minister). Shut down in 1939 till the 1970s, the
world before and betw the wars was preserved and is still there for faded-
grandeur connoisseurs to savour and all of us to sense. Best is below stairs.
Open by appointment only for groups – 01561 340569.

**1854**    ✓ ✓ **Manderston** Duns  Off A6105, 2km down Duns-Berwick rd.
Map 10   ✓ ✓  Described as the swan-song of the Gr Classical House, one of the
**S26**  finest examples of Edwardian opulence in UK. *The* Edwardian CH of TV fame.
All the more fascinating because the family still live there. Below stairs as
fascinating as up; sublime gdns (don't miss the woodland gdn on other side
of the lake, or the marble dairy). Open May-end Sept, Thu/Sun 2-5pm.

**1855**    ✓ ✓ **Traquair** Innerleithen 01896 830323. 2km from A72 Peebles-Gala
Map 10   ✓ ✓  rd. Archetypal romantic Border retreat steeped in Jacobite history
**Q27**  (ask about the Bear gates). Human proportions, liveability and lots of atmos.
An enchanting house, a maze (20th cent) and tranquil duck pond in the gdn.
Traquair ale still brewed. 1745 cottage tearoom, pottery and candlemaking.

Apr-Oct House 12.30-5.30pm (grounds 10.30am-5.30pm June-Aug). Crafty, folky fair in Aug & other events. Apr-Oct (w/ends Nov). Woodland walks.

**1856** ✓✓ **Newhailes** Musselburgh nr Edinburgh 0131 653 5599. Newhailes
Map 10 Rd, well signed from Portobello end of Musselburgh (3km). NTS
Q25 flagship project 'stabilising' the microcosm of 18thC history encapsulated here & uniquely intact. Gr rococo interiors, v liveable, esp library. A rural sanctuary nr the city & unlikely outdoor pop venue '05. May-Sept, Thur-Mon, 12-5pm. NTS

**1857** ✓ **Paxton** nr Berwick 01289 386291. Off B6461 rd to Swinton and Kelso
Map 10 about 6km from A1. Country park & Adam mansion with Chippendales,
T26 Trotters and a picture gallery which is an outstation of the National Gallery. They've made a very good job of the wallpapering. 80 acres woodland to walk. Good adventure playground. Restored Victorian boathouse and salmon fishing museum on the R Tweed. Red-squirrel hide. Ambitious summer music prog in July augurs gr things for Paxton. Tours (1hr) every 45mins, Apr-Oct 11.15am-4.15pm. Garden 10am-sunset.

**1858** **Gosford House** nr Aberlady East Lothian On A198 betw Longniddry and
Map 10 Aberlady, the Gosford estate is behind a high wall and strangely stunted veg-
Q25 etation. Imposing house with centre block by Robert Adam and the wing you visit by William Young who did Glas City Chambers. The Marble Hall houses the remarkable collections of the unbroken line of the Earls of Wemyss. Priceless art, informally displayed. Superb grounds avail with a 'permit' (£5 annually or by the day 01875 870201). Mid June-early Aug, Fri-Sun 2-5pm.

**1859** **Floors Castle** Kelso 01573 223333. More vast mansion than old castle, the
Map 10 ancestral home of the Duke of Roxburghe, o/look with imposing grandeur
S27 the town and the Tweed. 18th-century with later additions. You're led round lofty public rms past family collections of fine furniture, tapestries and porcelain. Priceless; spectacularly impractical. Good gdn centre (2235/GARDEN CENTRES). Annual event prog (phone for details) or floorscastle.com Excl tearm. Apr-Oct 10am-4.30pm. ☕

**1860** **Mellerstain** nr Gordon/Kelso 01573 410225. Home of the Earl of
Map 10 Haddington, signed from A6089 (Kelso-Gordon) or A6105 (Earlston-
R27 Greenlaw). One of Scotland's gr Georgian houses, begun by Wm Adam in 1725, completed by Robert. Outstanding decorative interiors esp the library & spectacular exterior 1761. Easter w/end plus May-Sept 12.30-5pm (not Tue or Sat) & Oct (Suns only). Café/shop 11.30am-5.30pm.

**1861** **Thirlestane** Lauder 01578 722430. 2km off A68. A castellate/baronial seat
Map 10 of the Earls and Duke of Lauderdale and family home of the Maitlands; it
R26 must take some upkeeping. Extraordinary staterooms, esp plaster work; the ceilings must be seen to be believed. In contrast, the nurseries (with toy collection), kitchens and laundry are more approachable. Easter & May-mid Sept Wed-Fri & Sun. July/Aug Sun-Fri. 10.30am-2.30pm (LA).

**1862** **Fyvie** Aberdeenshire 40km NW Aber, an important stop on the 'Castle Trail'
Map 8 which links the gr houses of Aberdeenshire. Before opulence fatigue sets in,
S18 see this pleasant baronial pile first (13 rms on show). It was lived-in until the 1980s so feels less remote than most. Fantastic roofscape and ceilings. The *best* tearoom. Tree-lined acres; loch side walks. July/Aug 11am-5pm. Other mths vary. NTS

**1863** **Crathes** nr Banchory 25km W of Aber on A93. Amidst superb gdns
Map 8 (1545/GARDENS) a 'fairy-tale castle', a tower house which is actually interest-
S20 ing to visit. Up and down spiral staircases and into small but liveable rms. The notable painted ceilings and the Long Gallery at the top are all worth lingering over. 350yrs of the Burnett family are ingrained in this oak. Apr-Oct 10am-5.30pm. Big event prog; from International Orienteers (when I was there – boy, they're a weird bunch) to concerts & craft fairs. Grounds open AYR 9.30am-dusk. Excl tearm (958/NE RESTAUS). ☕

**Abbotsford** nr Melrose Home of Walter Scott (1948/LITERARY PLACES).

# Great Monuments, Memorials & Follies

*These sites are open at all times and free unless otherwise stated.*

**1864**
Map 9
F27
✓ ✓ **The American Monument** Islay  On the SW peninsula of the island, known as the Oa (pron 'Oh'), 13km from Pt Ellen. A monument to commemorate the shipwrecks nearby of 2 American ships, the *Tuscania* & the *Ontranto*; both sank in 1918 at the end of the war. The obelisk o/look this sea – which is often beset by storms – from a spectacular headland, the sort of disquieting place where you could imagine looking round & finding the person you're with has disappeared. Take rd from Pt Ellen past Maltings marked Mull of Oa 12km, through gate and left at broken sign. Park & walk 1.5km steadily uphill to monument. Bird life good in Oa area.   1-A-2

**1865**
Map 10
N24
✓ **Wallace Monument** Stirling  Visible for miles and with gr views, though not as dramatic as Stirling Castle. App from A91 or Br of Allan rd. 150m walk from car park (or minibus) and 246 steps up. Victorian gothic spire marking the place where Scotland's gr patriot swooped down upon the English at the Battle of Stirling Br. Mel Gibson's *Braveheart* increased visitors though his face on the Wallace statue is thanks too far. In the 'Hall of Heroes' the new heroines section requires a feminist leap of the imagination. The famous sword is v big. Cliff top walk through Abbey Craig woods is worth detour. Monument open daily AYR. 01786 472140 for details; hrs vary. ADM

**1866**
Map 7
F17
**The Grave Of Flora Macdonald** Skye  Kilmuir on A855, Uig-Staffin rd, 40km N of Portree. A 10ft-high Celtic cross supported against the wind, high on the ridge o/look the Uists from whence she came. Long after the legendary journey, her funeral in 1790 attracted the biggest crowd since Culloden. The present memorial replaced the original, which was chipped away by souvenir hunters. Dubious though the whole business may have been, she still helped to shape the folklore of the Highlands.

**1867**
Map 10
M26
**Carfin Grotto** Motherwell  Between Motherwell & the M8, take the B road into Carfin and it's by Newarthill Rd. Gardens & pathways with shrines, pavilion, chapel & memorials. Latest statues: St Peregrine (patron saint of cancer sufferers) & one for the Lockerbie victims. A major Catholic centre and never less than thought-provoking as the rest of us go station to station. Carfin Pilgrimage Centre adj open daily, 10am-5pm AYR. Grotto open at all times.

**1868**
Map 10
M26
**Hamilton Mausoleum** Strathclyde Park  Off (and visible from) M74 at jnct 5/6, 15km from Glas (1572/COUNTRY PARKS). Huge, over-the-top/over-the-tomb (though removed 1921) stone memorial to the 10th Duke of Hamilton. Guided tours Wed/Sat/Sun 3pm in summer, 2pm in wint. Eerie and chilling and with remarkable acoustics – the 'longest echo in Europe'. Give it a shout or take your violin. Info and tickets from Hamilton Museum: 01698 328232.

**1869**
Map 10
R27
**Peniel Heugh** nr Ancrum/Jedburgh  (pron 'Pinal-hue'.) An obelisk visible for miles and on a rise which offers some of the most exhilarating views of the Borders. Also known as the Waterloo Monument, it was built on the Marquis of Lothian's estate to commemorate the battle. It's said that the woodland on the surrounding slopes represents the positions of Wellington's troops. From A68 opposite Ancrum t/off, on B6400, go 1km past Monteviot Gardens up steep, unmarked rd to left (cycle sign) for 150m; sign says 'Vehicles Prohibited, etc'. Park, walk up through woods.

**1870**
Map 10
R25
**The Hopetoun Monument** Athelstaneford nr Haddington  The needle atop a rare rise in E Lothian (Byres Hill) and a gr vantage point from which to view the county from the Forth to the Lammermuirs and Edinburgh over there. Off A6737 Haddington to Aberlady rd on B1343 to Athelstaneford. Car park and short climb. Tower usually open and viewfinder boards at top but take a torch; it's a dark climb. Good gentle 'ridge' walk E from here.

**1871**
Map 10
N25
**The Pineapple** Airth  From Airth N of Grangemouth, take A905 to Stirling & after 1km the B9124 for Cowie. It sits on the edge of a walled gdn at the end of the drive. 45ft high, it was built in 1761 as a gdn retreat by an unknown architect & remained 'undiscovered' until 1963. How exotic the fruit must have seemed in the 18thC, never mind this extraordinary folly. Grounds open AYR; oddly enough, you can stay here (2 bedrms, 01628 825925).

**1872** **John Lennon Memorial** Durness  In garden created 2002 (a BBC
Map 6 Beechgrove project) amazing in itself surviving these harsh, v northern con-
**L12** ditions, an inscribed slate memorial to JL who for many yrs as a child came
here with his aunt for the hols. 'There are places I'll remember all my life'
from *Rubber Soul*. Who'd have thought that song (*In My Life*) was about here.

**1873** **The Monument On Ben Bhraggie** Golspie  Atop the hill (pron 'Brachee')
Map 6 that dominates the town, the domineering statue and plinth (over 35m) of
**N15** the dreaded first Duke of Sutherland; there's a campaign group that would
like to see it demolished, but it survives yet. Climb from town fountain on
marked path. The hill race go up in 10mins but allow 2hrs return. His private
view along the NE coast is superb (1808/CASTLES; 2230/MUSEUMS).

**1874** **McCaig's Tower or Folly** Oban  Oban's gr landmark built in 1897 by
Map 9 McCaig, a local banker, to give 'work to the unemployed' and as a memorial
**H23** to his family. It's like a temple or coliseum and time has mellowed whatever
incongruous effect it may have had originally. The views of the town and the
bay are magnificent and it's easy to get up from several points in town centre. (*See* OBAN, p. 314.)

**1875** **The Victoria Memorial To Albert** Balmoral  Atop the fir-covered hill
Map 8 behind the house, she raised a monument whose distinctive pyramid shape
**Q20** can be seen peeping over the crest from all over the estate. Desolated by his
death, the 'broken-hearted' widow had this memorial built in 1862 and spent
so much time here, she became a recluse and the Empire trembled. Path
begins at shop on way to Lochnagar distillery, 45mins up. Forget Balmoral
(1807/CASTLES), all the longing and love for Scotland can be felt here, the gr
estate laid out below.

**1876** **The Prop Of Ythsie** nr Aberdeen  35km NW city nr Ellon to W of A92, or
Map 8 pass on the 'Castle Trail' since this monument commemorates one George
**S18** Gordon of Haddo House nearby, who was prime minister 1852-55 (the good-
looking guy in the first portrait you come to in the house). Tower visible from
all of rolling Aberdeenshire around and there are reciprocal views should you
take the easy but unclear route up. On B999 Aber-Tarves rd (Haddo-
Pitmeddon on Castle Trail) and 2km from entrance to house. Take rd for the
Ythsie (pron 'icy') farms, car park 100m. Stone circle nearby.

**1877** **The Monument To Hugh MacDiarmid** Langholm  Brilliant piece of mod-
Map 11 ern sculpture by Jake Harvey rapidly rusting on the hill above Langholm 3km
**Q29** from A7 at beginning of path to the Malcolm obelisk from where there are gr
views (1701/VIEWS). MacDiarmid, our national poet, was born in Langholm in
1872 and, though they never liked him much after he left, the monument
was commissioned and a cairn beside it raised in 1992. The bare hills surround you. The motifs of the sculpture were used by Scotland's favourite
Celtic rock band, Runrig, on the cover of their 1993 album, *Amazing Things*.

**1878** **Memorial to Norman MacCaig** nr Lochinver  Foll directions for the
Map 6 remarkable Achin's bookshop (2172/SHOPPING) which is at the start of the gr
**J14** walk to Suilven (1959/HILLS). Simple memorial of Torridon sandstone to
Scotland's gr poet who wrote so much about this landscape he loved: Assynt.
Some words writ here to guide us on the way, metaphorically speaking.

**1879** **Murray Monument** nr New Galloway  Above A712 rd to Newton Stewart
Map 11 about halfway betw. A fairly austere needle of granite to commemorate a
**L29** 'shepherd boy', one Alexander Murray, who rose to become a professor of
Oriental Languages at Edinburgh Univ in early 19th century. 10min walk up
for fine views of Galloway Hills; pleasant waterfall nearby. Just as he, bare-
foot ...

**1880** **Smailholm Tower** nr Kelso & St Boswells  The classic Border tower; plen-
Map 10 ty of history and romance and a v nice place to stop, picnic whatever. Good
**R27** views. Nr main rd B6404 or off smaller B6937 - well signposted. Open Apr-
Sept 9.30am-6.30pm. For hrs outwith, 01573 460365. But fine to visit at any
time (1675/SCENIC ROUTES).

**Scott Monument** Edinburgh  432/VIEWS.

# The Most Interesting Churches

*All 'generally open' unless otherwise stated; those marked * have public services.*

**1881**
Map 10
Q26

✓ ✓ ✓ **\*Rosslyn Chapel** Roslin  12km S of Edin city centre. Take A702, then A703 from ring-route rd, marked Penicuik. Roslin village 1km from main rd and chapel 500m from village crossroads above Roslin Glen (416/WALKS OUTSIDE THE CITY). Here since the 15thC but firmly on the world map in recent times because of the *Da Vinci Code*. Grail seekers have been coming forever but now so many, it's guided tours only in summer. No doubting the atmos in this temple to the Templars & all holy meaningful stuff in a *Foucault's Pendulum* sense. But a special place. In restoration till 2010. Episcopalian. Mon-Sat 10-5pm, 12-4.45pm Sun. Coffee shop.

**1882**
Map 9
J23

✓ ✓ **\*St Conan's Kirk** Loch Awe  A85 33km E of Oban. Perched amongst trees on the side of L Awe, this small but spacious church seems to incorporate every ecclesiastical architectural style. Its building was a labour of love for one Walter Campbell who was perhaps striving for beauty rather than consistency. Though modern (begun by him in 1881 and finished by his sister and a board of trustees in 1930), the result is a place of ethereal light and atmos, enhanced by and befitting the inherent spirituality of the setting. There's a spooky carved effigy of Robert the Bruce, a cosy cloister and the most amazing flying buttresses. A place to wander and reflect.

**1883**
Map 3
R12

✓ ✓ **The Italian Chapel** Orkney Mainland  8km S of Kirkwall at Lamb Holm and the first causeway on the way to St Margaret's Hope. In 1943, Italian PoWs brought to work on the Churchill Barriers transformed a Nissen hut, using the most meagre materials, into this remarkable ornate chapel. The meticulous *trompe l'œil* and wrought-iron work are a touching affirmation of faith. At the other end of the architectural scale, **St Magnus Cathedral** in Kirkwall is a gr edifice, but also filled with spirituality.

**1884**
Map 2
xC1

✓ ✓ **Queen's Cross Church** Glasgow  870 Garscube Rd where it becomes Maryhill Rd at Springbank St. C R Mackintosh's only church. Fascinating and unpredictable in every part of its design. Some elements reminiscent of The Art School (built in the same year 1897) and others, like the tower, evoke medieval architecture. Bold and innovative, now restored and functioning as the headquarters of The Mackintosh Society. Mon-Fri 10am-5pm, Sun 2pm-5pm. Cl Sat. No services. (761/MACKINTOSH.)

ADM

**1885**
Map 11
N28

✓ **\*Durisdeer Parish Church nr Abington & Thornhill**  Off A702 Abington-Thornhill rd and nr Drumlanrig (1569/COUNTRY PARKS). If I lived nr this delightful village in the hills, I'd go to church more often. It's exquisite and the history of Scotland is in the stones. The Queensberry marbles (1709) are displayed in the N transept (enter behind church) and there's a cradle roll and a list of ministers from the 14th century. The plaque to the two brothers who died at Gallipoli is especially touching. Covenanter tales are writ on the gravestones.

**1886**
Map 9
K26

✓ **\*Cathedral Of The Isles** Millport On The Island Of Cumbrae  Frequent ferry service from Largs is met by bus for 6km journey to Millport. Lane from main st by Newton pub, 250m then through gate. The smallest 'cathedral' in Europe, one of Butterfield's gr works (other is Keble Coll, Oxford). Here, small is outstandingly beautiful & absolutely quiet. (1263/RETREATS; 1431/CAFÉS.)

**1887**
Map 5
E16

✓ **St Clements** Rodel South Harris  Tarbert 40km. Classic island kirk in Hebridean landscape. Go by the Golden Road (1671/ROUTES). Simple cruciform structure with tower, which the adventurous can climb. Probably influenced by Iona. Now an empty but atmospheric shell, with blackened effigies and important monumental sculpture. Goats in the churchyard graze amongst the headstones of all the young Harris lads lost at sea in the Gr War. There are other fallen angels on the outside of the tower.

**1888**
Map 5
D19

**\*St Michael's Chapel** Eriskay nr South Uist/Barra  That rare example of an ordinary modern church without history or grand architecture, which has charm and serenity and imbues the sense of well-being that a religious centre should. The focal pt of a relatively devout Catholic community who obviously care about it. Alabaster angels abound. O/look Sound of Barra. A real delight whatever your religion.

**1889** **\*St Athernase Leuchars** The parish church on a corner of what is essen-
Map 10 tially an Air Force base spans centuries of warfare and architecture. The
**Q23** Norman bell tower is remarkable.

**1890** **\*St Fillan's Church** Aberdour Behind ruined castle in this pleasant seaside
Map 10 village (1601/COASTAL VILLAGES), a more agreeable old kirk would be hard to
**P25** find. Restored from a 12th-century ruin in 1926, the warm stonework and
stained glass create a v soothing atmos (church open at most times, but if
closed the graveyard is v fine).

**1891** **\*Culross Abbey Church** Top of Forth-side village full of interesting build-
Map 10 ings and windy streets (1596/COASTAL VILLS). Worth hike up hill (signed 'Abbey',
**N25** ruins are adj) for views and this well-loved and looked-after church. Gr
stained glass (see Sandy's window), often full of flowers.

**1892** **\*Dunblane Cathedral** A huge nave of a church built around a Norman
Map 10 tower (from David I) on the Allan Water and restored 1892. The wondrously
**M24** bright stained glass is mostly 20th-century. The poisoned sisters buried
under the altar helped change the course of Scottish history. HS

**1893** **\*St Machar's Cathedral** Aberdeen The Chanonry in 'Old Aberdeen' off St
Map 8 Machar's Dr about 2km from centre. Best seen as part of a walk round the
**T19** old 'village within the city' occupied mainly by the university's old and modern buildings. Cathedral's fine granite nave and twin-spired W Front date
from 15th century, on site of 6th-century Celtic church. Noted for heraldic
ceiling and 19/20th-century stained glass. Seaton Park adj has pleasant Don-
side walks and there's the old Brig o' Balgownie. Church open daily 9am-
5pm.

**1894** **\*The East Lothian Churches At Aberlady, Whitekirk &**
Map 10 **Athelstaneford** 3 charming churches in bucolic settings; quiet corners to
**Q25** explore and reflect. Easy to find. All have interesting local histories and in the
**R25** case of Athelstaneford, a national resonance – a 'vision' in the sky nr here
**R25** became the flag of Scotland, the saltire. The spooky Doocot Heritage Centre
behind the church explains. Aberlady my favourite.

**1895** **Abercorn Church** nr S Queensferry Off A904. 4 km W 11th cent kirk
Map 10 nestling among ancient yews in a sleepy hamlet, untouched since
**P25** Covenanter days. St Ninian said to have preached to the Picts here and
Abercorn once on a par with York and Lindisfarne in religious importance.
Church always open.

**1896** **Croick Church nr** Bonar Bridge 16km W of Ardgay, which is just over the
Map 6 river from Bonar Br and through the splendid glen of Strathcarron
**L15** (1631/GLENS). This humble and charming church is chiefly remembered for its
place in the history of the Highland clearances. In May 1845, 90 folk took
shelter in the graveyard around the church after they had been cleared from
their homes in nearby Glencalvie. Not allowed even in the kirk, their plight
did not go unnoticed and was reported in *The Times*. The harrowing account
is there to read, and the messages they scratched on the windows. Sheep
graze all around.

**1897** **\*Thomas Coates Memorial Church** Paisley Built by Coates (of thread
Map 10 fame), an imposing edifice, one of the grandest Baptist churches in Europe.
**L26** A monument to God, prosperity and the Industrial Revolution. Opening hrs,
check TIC – 0141 889 0711. Service on Sun at 11am.

**1898** **\*The Lamp Of The Lothians St Mary's Collegiate** Haddington Follow
Map 10 signs from E main st. At the risk of sounding profane or at least trite, this is
**R25** a church that's really got its act together, both now and throughout ecclesiastical history. It's beautiful and in a fine setting on the R Tyne, with good
stained glass and interesting crypts and corners. But it's obviously v much at
the centre of the community, a lamp as it were, in the Lothians. Guided
tours, brass rubbings (Sat). Monthly summer recitals (Sun afternoon). Coffee
shop and gift shop. Don't miss Lady Kitty's gdn nearby, including the secret
medicinal gdn, a quiet spot to contemplate (if not sort out) your condition.
Daily 11am-4pm.

**1899**
Map 10
**P22**
**\*Dunkeld Cathedral** In town centre by lane to the banks of the Tay at its most silvery. Medieval splendour amongst lofty trees. Notable for 13th-century choir and 15th-century nave and tower. Parish church open for edifying services and other spiritual purposes. Lovely summer recitals.

**1900**
Map 11
**P30**
**Ruthwell Church** Ruthwell 10 miles SE Dumfries, B724 nr Clarencefield. Collect keys from Mrs Coulthard, Kirkyett House (bungalow where you turn off the main rd); she's the fount of all knowledge concerning this important building. Unique 18ft Runic Cross within Church, dating from 7th century. Carvings depict Biblical scenes with monk's inscription of 'The Holy Rood' poem. Fascinating history of its creation, preservation during the religious troubles of 1640, and subsequent restoration in 1823 by the community. Buy the guidebook from Mrs C, 01387 870249. And some postcards!

**1901**
Map 9
**J20**
**St Mary & St Finnan Church** Glenfinnan On main A830 Ft William-Mallaig rd (the Road to the Isles, 1680/SCENIC ROUTES), a beautiful (tho' inside a bit crumbly) Catholic church in a spectacular setting. Queen Vic said she never saw a lovelier or more romantic spot. Late 19thC. Always open for quiet meditations.

**1902**
Map 9
**H25**
**Keills Chapel** S Of Crinan The chapel at the end of nowhere. From Lochgilphead, drive towards Crinan, but before you get there, turn S down the B8025 and follow it for nearly 20km to the end. Park at the farm then walk the last 200m. You are 7km across the Sound from Jura, at the edge of Knapdale. Early 13thC chapel houses some remarkable cross slabs, a 7thC cross & ghosts. HS

**St Giles Cathedral** Edinburgh 406/OTHER ATTRACTIONS.

**Glasgow Cathedral/University Chapel** 707/711/MAIN ATTRACTIONS.

# The Most Interesting Graveyards

**1903**
Map 2
**xF2**
✓✓ **Glasgow Necropolis** The vast burial ground at the crest of the ridge, running down to the river, that was the focus of the original settlement of Glas. Everything began at the foot of this hill and, ultimately, ended at the top where many of the city's most famous (and infamous) sons and daughters are interred within the reach of the long shadow of John Knox's obelisk. Generally open (official times), but best if you can get the full spooky experience to yourself. Check with TIC 0141 204 4400. (707/MAIN ATTRACTIONS.)

**1904**
Map 1
**F2**
**F3**
**C4**
**B1**
**A2**
✓ **Edinburgh Canongate** On left of Royal Mile going down to Palace. Adam Smith and the tragic poet Robert Fergusson revered by Rabbie Burns (who raised the memorial stone in 1787 over his pauper's grave) are buried here in the heart of Auld Reekie. Tourists can easily miss this one. **Greyfriars** A place of ancient mystery, famous for the wee dog who guarded his master's grave for 14yrs, for the plundering of graves in the early 18th century for the Anatomy School and for the graves of Allan Ramsay (prominent poet and burgher), James Hutton (the father of geology), William McGonagall (the 'world's worst poet') and sundry serious Highlanders. Annals of a gr city are written on these stones. **Warriston** Warriston Rd by B&Q or end of cul-de-sac at Warriston Cres (Canonmills), up bank and along railway line. Overgrown, peaceful, steeped in atmos. Gothic horrorland (some of those cruising guys may like that sort of thing). **Dean** is an Edinburgh secret.

**1905**
Map 9
**G25**
✓ **Isle Of Jura** Killchianaig graveyard in the N. Follow rd as far as it goes to Inverlussa, graveyard is on rt, just before hamlet. Mairi Ribeach apparently lived until she was 128. In the south at Keils (2km from rd N out of Craighouse, bearing left past Keils houses and through the deer fence), her father is buried and he was 180! Both sites are beautiful, isolated and redolent of island history, with much to reflect on, not least the mysterious longevity of the inhabitants & that soon we may all live this long.

**1906**
Map 7
**L18**
✓ **Chisholm Graveyard** nr Beauly Last resting place of the Chisholms and 3 of the largest Celtic crosses you'll see anywhere, in a secret and atmospheric woodland setting. 15km W Beauly on A831 to Struy after Algas dam & golf course, 1km before Cnoc Hotel opp Erchless Estate and through a white iron gate on rt. Walk 150m.

**1907** **Campbeltown Cemetery** Campbeltown. Odd, but one of the nicest things
Map 9 about this end-of-the-line town is the cemetery. It's at the end of a row of
H28 fascinating posh houses, the original merchant and mariner owners of which
will be interred in the leafy plots next door. Still v much in use after centuries
of commerce and seafaring disasters, it has crept up the terraces of a steep
and lush overhanging bank. The white cross and row of WW2 headstones are
particularly affecting.

**1908** **Kirkoswald Kirkyard** nr Maybole & Girvan  On main rd through village
Map 9 betw Ayr and Girvan. The graveyard around the ruined Kirk and famous as the
K28 burial place of the characters in Burns' most famous poem, *Tam o' Shanter*.
A must for Burns fans and famous-grave seekers with Souter Johnnie and
Kirkton Jean buried here.

**1909** **Humbie Churchyard** Humbie, E Lothian 25km SE of Edin via A68 (t/off at
Map 10 Fala). This is as reassuring a place to be buried as you could wish for; if you're
Q26 set on cremation, come here and think of earth. Deep in the woods with the
burn besides; after-hrs the sprites and the spirits must have a hell of a time.

**1910** **Ancrum Churchyard nr Jedburgh**  The quintessential country church-
Map 10 yard; away from the village (2km along B6400), by a lazy river (the Ale Water)
R27 crossed to a farm by a humpback br and a chapel in ruins. Elegiac and deeply
peaceful (1720/PICNICS).

**1911** **Balquhidder Churchyard** Chiefly notable as the last resting place of one
Map 10 Rob Roy Macgregor who was buried in 1734 after causing a heap of trouble
L23 hereabouts and raised to immortality by Sir Walter Scott and Michael Caton-
Jones. Despite well-trodden path, setting is poignant. For best reflections
head along L Voil to Inverlochlarig. Beautiful Sunday evening concerts in kirk
July/Aug. (check with local TICs). Nice walk from back corner signed
'Waterfall' & gr long walk to Brig O' Turk (2008/GLEN WALKS). Tearoom in **Old
Library** in vill is cosy & couthie, with v good cakes (1457/TEAROOMS).

**1912** **Logie Old Kirk** nr Stirling  A crumbling chapel and an ancient graveyard at
Map 10 the foot of the Ochils. The wall is round to keep out the demons, a burn gur-
N24 gles beside and there are some fine and v old stones going back to the 16th
century. Take rd for Wallace Monument off A91, 2km from Stirling, then first
rt. The old kirk is beyond the new. Continuing on this steep narrow rd (then
rt & the T-jnct) takes you onto the Ochils (1981/HILL WALKS).

**1913** **Tout-Na-Qual** Dunbeath  An enchanting cemetery 5km from Dunbeath,
Map 6 Neil Gunn's birthplace, and found by walking up the 'Strath' he describes in
P14 his book *Highland River* (1946/LITERARY PLACES). With a white wall around it,
this graveyard, which before the clearances once served a valley community
of 400 souls, can be seen for miles. Ask at Heritage Centre for route.

# The Great Abbeys

**1914** ✔✔ **Iona Abbey** This hugely significant place of pilgrimage for new age
Map 9 and old age pilgrims and tourists alike is reached from Fionnphort,
F23 SW Mull, by frequent Calmac Ferry (5min crossing). Walk 1km. Here in 563 BC
St Columba began his mission for a Celtic Church that changed the face of
Europe. Cloisters, graveyard of Scottish kings and, marked by a modest stone,
the inscription already faded by the weather, the grave of John Smith, the
patron saint of New Labour. Regular services. Good shop (2173/CRAFT SHOPS).
Residential courses and retreats (MacLeod Centre adj, 01681 700404) include
a 'Christmas house party' (2277/MAGICAL ISLANDS).                    HS

**1915** ✔✔ **Pluscarden Abbey** betw Forres & Elgin  The oldest abbey monas-
Map 8 tic community still working in the UK (1258/RETREATS) in one of the
P17 most spiritual of places. Founded by Alexander II in 1230 and being restored
since 1948. Benedictine services (starting with Vigil & Lauds at 4.45am
through Prime-Terce-Sext-None-Vespers at 5.30pm and Compline at 8pm)
open to public. The ancient honey-coloured walls, the brilliant stained glass,
the monks' Gregorian chant: the whole effect is a truly uplifting experience.
The bell rings down the valley. Services aside, open to visitors 9am-5pm.

**1916**
Map 10
**L26**
✓ ✓ **Paisley Abbey** Town centre. An abbey founded in 1163, razed (by the English) in 1307 and with successive deteriorations and renovations ever since. Major restoration in the 1920s brought it to present-day cathedral-like magnificence. Exceptional stained glass (the recent window complementing the formidable Strachan E Window), an impressive choir and an edifying sense of space. Sunday Services (11am, 12.15pm, 6.30pm) are superb, esp full-dress communion and there are open days; phone 0141 889 7654 for dates. Otherwise Abbey open AYR Mon-Sat 10am-3.30pm. Café/shop.

**1917**
Map 10
**R28**
✓ ✓ **Jedburgh Abbey** The classic abbey ruin; conveys the most complete impression of the Border abbeys built under the patronage of David I in the 12th century. Its tower and remarkable Catherine window are still intact. Excavations have unearthed example of a 12th-century comb. It's now displayed in the excellent VC which brilliantly illustrates the full story of the abbey's amazing history. Best view from across the Jed in the 'Glebe'. May-Sep 9.30am-6.30pm, Oct-Mar until 4.30pm.                                    HS

**1918**
Map 10
**R27**
✓ **Dryburgh Abbey** nr St Boswells One of the most evocative of ruins, an aesthetic attraction since the late 18th century. Sustained innumerable attacks from the English since its inauguration by Premonstratensian Canons in 1150. Celebrated by Sir Walter Scott, buried here in 1832 (with his biographer Lockhart at his feet), its setting, amongst huge cedar trees on the banks of the Tweed is one of pure historical romance. 4km A68. (1694/VIEWS.) Apr-Sept 9.30-6.30, Oct-Mar till 4.30, Sun 2-4.30.                              HS

**1919**
Map 9
**K28**
**Crossraguel Abbey** Maybole 24km S of Ayr on A77. Built 1244, one of first Cluniac settlements in Scotland, an influential and rich order, stripped in the Reformation. Now an extensive ruin of architectural distinction, the ground plan v well preserved and obvious. Poss place to go to relieve the stress of driving on the A77 under those predatory speed cameras.                              HS

**1920**
Map 11
**N30**
**Sweetheart** New Abbey nr Dumfries 12km S by A710. The endearing and enduring warm red sandstone abbey in the shadow of Criffel, so named because Devorguilla de Balliol, devoted to her husband (he of the Oxford College), founded the abbey for Cistercian monks and kept his heart in a casket which is buried with her here. No roof, but the tower is intact. OK tearoom (& 'orrible gift shop) adj, you can sit out and gaze at the ruins while eating your fruit pie.                                                            HS

**1921**
Map 10
**R27**
**Melrose Abbey** Another romantic setting, the abbey seems to give an atmos to the whole town. Once again built by David I (what a guy!) for Cistercian monks from Rievaulx from 1136, there wasn't much left, spiritually or architecturally, by the Reformation. Once, however, it sustained a huge community, as evinced by the widespread excavations. There's a museum of abbey, church and Roman relics; soon to include Robert the Bruce's heart, recently excavated in the gdns. Nice Tweed walks can start here. Same hrs as Jed.                                                                        HS

**1922**
Map 10
**R22**
**Arbroath Abbey** 25km N of Dundee. Founded in 1178 and endowed on an unparalleled scale, this is an important place in Scots history. It's where the Declaration was signed in 1320 to appeal to the Pope to release the Scots from the yoke of the English (you can buy facsimiles of the yellow parchment; the original is in the Scottish Records Office in Edin – oh, and teatowels). It was to Arbroath that the Stone of Destiny (on which Scottish kings were traditionally crowned) was returned after being 'stolen' from Westminster Abbey in the 1950s and is now at Edinburgh Castle. Gr interpretation centre before you tour the ruins.                                                     HS

# The Great Battlegrounds

**1923**
Map 7
**M18**
**Culloden** Inverness  Signed from A9 and A96 into Inverness and about 8km from town. New VC & parking opening early '07 will give more prominence, accuracy & scale to the battle (2km walk round site). Positions of the clans and the troops marked out across the moor; flags enable you to get a real sense of scale. If you go in spring you see how wet and miserable the Moor can be (the battle took place on 16 April 1746). No matter how many other folk are there wandering down the lines, a visit to this most infamous of battlefields can still leave a pain in the heart. Centre 9am-6pm (winter 11am-4pm). New hrs may vary. Ground open at all times for more personal Cullodens.  NTS

**1924**
Map 7
**F18**
**Battle Of The Braes** Skye  10km Portree. Take main A850 rd S for 3km then left, marked 'Braes' for 7km. Monument is on a rise on rt. The last battle fought on British soil and a significant place in Scots history. When the clearances, uninterrupted by any organised opposition, were virtually complete and vast tracts of Scotland had been depopulated for sheep, the Skye crofters finally stood up in 1882 to the Government troops and said enough is enough. A cairn has been erected nr the spot where they fought on behalf of 'all the crofters of Gaeldom', a battle which led eventually to the Crofters Act which has guaranteed their rights ever since. At the end of this rd at Peinchorran, there are fine views of Raasay (which was devastated by clearances) and Glamaig, the conical Cuillin, across L Sligachan.

**1925**
Map 9
**J21**
**Glencoe**  Not much of a battle, of course, but one of the most infamous massacres in British history. Much has been written (John Prebble's *Glencoe* and others) and the new VC provides audiovisual scenario. There's the Macdonald monument nr Glencoe village and the walk to the more evocative Signal Rock where the bonfire was lit, now a happy wood-land trail in this doom-laden landscape. Many gr walks. (1950/SPOOKY PLACES, 1326/PUBS)

**1926**
Map 3
**Q11**
**Scapa Flow** Orkney Mainland & Hoy  Scapa Flow, surrounded by various of the southern Orkney islands, is one of the most sheltered anchorages in Europe. Hence the huge presence in Orkney of ships and personnel during both wars. The Germans scuttled 54 of their warships here in 1919 and many still lie in the bay. The *Royal Oak* was torpedoed in 1939 with the loss of 833 men. Much still remains of the war yrs (especially if you're a diver, 2145/DIVING): the rusting hulks, the shore fortifications, the Churchill Barriers and the ghosts of a long-gone army at Scapa and Lyness on Hoy. Excl 'tour' on MV Guide with remote controlled camera exploring 3 wrecks. 01856 811360.

**1927**
Map 10
**R27**
**Lilliard's Edge** nr St Boswells  On main A68, look for Lilliard's Edge Caravan Park 5km S of St Boswells; park and walk back towards St Boswells to the brim of the hill (about 500m), then cross rough ground on rt along ridge, following tree-line hedge. Marvellous view attests to strategic location. 200m along, a cairn marks the grave of Lilliard who, in 1545, joined the Battle of Ancrum Moor against the English 'loons' under the Earl of Angus. 'And when her legs were cuttit off, she fought upon her stumps'. An ancient poem etched on the stone records her legendary ... feet.

**1928**
Map 10
**N21**
**Killiecrankie** nr Pitlochry  The first battle of the Jacobite Risings where, in July 1689, the Highlanders lost their leader Viscount (aka Bonnie) Dundee, but won the battle, using the narrow Pass of Killiecrankie. One escaping soldier made a famous leap. Well-depicted scenario in VC; short walk to 'The Leap'. Battle viewpoint and cairn is further along rd to Blair Atholl, turning rt and doubling back nr the Garry GH and on, almost to A9 underpass (3km from VC). You get the lie of the land from here. Many good walks.

**1929**
Map 10
**N24**
**Bannockburn** nr Stirling  4km town centre via Glas rd (it's well signposted) or jnct 9 of M9 (3km), behind a sad hotel & car-rental centre. Some visitors might be perplexed as to why 24 June 1314 was such a big deal for the Scots and, apart from the 50m walk to the flag-pole and the huge statue, there's not a lot doing. But the 'Heritage Centre' does bring the scale of it to life, the horror and the glory. The battlefield itself is thought to lie around the orange building of the High School some distance away, and the best place to see the famous wee burn is from below the magnificent Telford Br. Ask at centre (5km by road). NTS arrange mega reenactments in mid Sept.

# Mary, Charlie & Bob

## MARY, QUEEN OF SCOTS 1542-87

**Linlithgow Palace** Where she was born (1809/RUINS).

**Holyrood Palace** Edinburgh And lived (391/MAIN ATTRACTIONS).

**1930** **Inchmahome Priory** Port Of Menteith The ruins of the Priory on the island
Map 10 in Scotland's only lake, where the infant Queen spent her early years in the
**M24** safe keeping of the Augustinian monks. Short journey by boat from quay nr
lake hotel. Signal the ferryman by turning the board to the island, much as
she did. Apr-Oct. 7 days. Last trip 5.15pm (3.15 Oct). Delights of the Trossachs
surround you. Good pub fd on way home (1365/GASTROPUBS).                                   HS

**1931** **Mary Queen Of Scots' House** Jedburgh In gdns via Smiths Wynd off main
Map 10 st. Historians quibble but this long-standing museum claims to be 'the'
**R28** house where she became ill in 1566, but somehow made it over to visit the
injured Bothwell at Hermitage Castle 50km away. Tower house in good con-
dition; displays and well-told saga. Mar-Nov 10am-4.30pm (4.30 June-Aug),
Sun 11am-4.30pm. Wint hrs vary slightly.

**1932** **Loch Leven Castle** nr Kinross Well-signed! The ultimate in romantic pen-
Map 10 itentiaries; on the island in the middle of the loch and clearly visible from the
**P24** M90. Not much left of the ruin to fill out the fantasy, but this is where Mary
spent 10 months in 1568 before her famous escape and her final attempt to
get back the throne. Sailings Apr-Sept, 9.30am-6.30pm (last outward
5.15pm) from pier at National Game Angling Academy (Pier Bar/café serves
while you wait) in small launch from Kirkgate Park. 7min trip, return as you
like.

**1933** **Dundrennan Abbey** nr Auchencairn & Kirkcudbright  Mary Queen of
Map 11 Scots got around and there are innumerable places, castles and abbeys
**M31** where she spent the night. This, however, was where she spent her last one
on Scottish soil. She left next day from Pt Mary (nothing much to see there
except a beach – it's 2km along the rd that skirts the sinister MoD range – the
pier's long gone and ... well, there's no plaque). The Cistercian abbey of
Whitemonks (established 1142), which harboured her on her last night, is
now a tranquil ruin.                                                                           HS

'In my end is my beginning,' she said, facing her execution which came 19 yrs
later.

**1934** Her 'death mask' is displayed at **Lennoxlove House** nr Haddington; it does
Map 10 seem on the small side for someone who was supposedly 6 feet tall!
**R25** Lennoxlove on rd to Gifford open Easter-Oct 1.30-4pm.

**1935** **Blair Museum** nr Peterculter Aberdeen  Scotland's 'Catholic treasury' in
Map 8 college at Blairs on the S Deeside Rd. Massive & austere former pile cl 1986,
**S20** with adj chapel a repository for religious artefacts, history of the seminary &
the 'official' memorial portrait of the recently dead queen – the start of the
legend. Apr-Sept, Sat/Sun till 5pm. A lock of Bonnie Prince Charlie's hair is
also here (but no T-shirts).

## BONNIE PRINCE CHARLIE 1720-88

**1936** **Prince Charlie's Bay (or Strand)** Eriskay  The uncelebrated, unmarked
Map 5 and quietly beautiful beach where Charlie first landed in Scotland to begin
**D19** the Jacobite Rebellion. Nothing much has changed and this crescent of sand
with soft machair and a turquoise sea is still a secret place. 1km from township heading S adj pier for Barra ferry. (2284/MAGICAL ISLANDS.)

**1937** **Loch Nan Uamh nr Arisaig, The Prince's Cairn**  7km from Lochailort on
Map 7 A830 (1680/SCENIC ROUTES), 48km Ft William. Signed from the rd (100m layby),
**H20** a path leads down to the left. This is the 'traditional' spot (pron 'Loch Na
Nuan') where Charlie embarked for France in Sept 1746, having lost the battle and the cause. The rocky headland also o/look the bay and skerries where
he'd landed in July the year before to begin the campaign. This place was the
beginning and the end and it has all the romance necessary to be utterly convincing. Is that a French ship out there in the mist?

**1938 Glenfinnan** The place where he 'raised his standard' to rally the clans to the
Map 9 Jacobite cause. For a while on that August day in 1745 it had looked as if only
**J20** a handful were coming. Then they heard the pipes and 600 Camerons came
marching from the valley (where the viaduct now spans). That must have
been one helluva moment. Though it's thought that he actually stood on the
higher ground, there is a powerful sense of place and history here. The VC
has an excellent map of Charlie's path/flight through Scotland – somehow he
touched all the most alluring places! Tower can be climbed (NTS). Consider
also the monument from L Shiel itself (1680/JOURNEYS).

**Culloden** nr Inverness 1923/BATTLEGROUNDS.

## ROBERT THE BRUCE 1274-1329

**1939 Bruce's Stone** Glen Trool nr Newton Stewart   26km N by A714 via
Map 11 Bargrennan (8km to head of glen) which is on the S Upland Way (1997/LONG
**L29** WALKS). The fair Glen Trool is a celebrated spot in the Galloway Forest Park
(1635/GLENS). The stone is signed (200m walk) and marks the area where
Bruce's guerrilla band rained boulders down on the pursuing English in 1307
after they had routed the main army at Solway Moss. Good walking, incl
Merrick (1969/HILLS).

**1940 Bannockburn** nr Stirling The climactic battle in June 1314, when Bruce
Map 10 decisively whipped the English and got himself the kingdom (though
**N24** Scotland was not recognised as independent until 1328, just before his
death). The scale of the skirmish can be visualised at the heritage centre, but
not so readily 'in the field' (1929/BATTLEGROUNDS).

**1941 Arbroath Abbey** Not much of the Bruce trail here, but this is where the
Map 10 famous Declaration was signed that was the attempt of the Scots nobility
**R22** united behind him to gain international recognition of the independence
they had won on the battlefield. What it says is stirring stuff; the original is in
Edin (1922/ABBEYS). Gr interpretation centre.                                    HS

**1942 Dunfermline Abbey Church** Here, at last, some tangible evidence, his
Map 10 tomb. Buried in 1329, his remains were discovered wrapped in gold cloth,
**P25** when the site was being cleared for the new church in 1818. Many of the
other gr kings, the Alexanders I and III, were not so readily identifiable
(Bruce's ribcage had been cut to remove his heart). With gr national emotion
he was reinterred underneath the pulpit. The church (as opposed to the ruins
and Norman nave adj) is open Apr-Sept 10am-4.30pm. Gr café in Abbot
House thro graveyard (2228/MUSEUMS). Look up & see Robert carved on the
skyline.

**1943 Melrose Abbey** On his deathbed Bruce asked that his heart be buried here
Map 10 after it was taken to the Crusades to aid the Army in their battles. A likely lead
**R27** casket thought to contain it was excavated from the chapter house and it did
date from the period. It was reburied here and is marked with a stone. Let's
believe in this!                                                                 HS

# The Important Literary Places

**1944 Robert Burns (1759–96) Alloway, Ayr And Dumfries** A well-marked
heritage trail through his life and haunts in Ayrshire and Dumfriesshire. His
howff at Dumfries is v atmospheric. Best is at **Alloway** The Auld Brig o'
Doon and the Auld Kirk, where Tam o' Shanter saw the witches, dance are
evocative, & the Monument and surrounding gdns are lovely. 1km up the rd,
the cottage, his birthplace, has little atmos (now NTS so may improve), and
the Tam o' Shanter Experience – which has an auditorium and a café – has a
shop which is a bit of an embarrassment.

Map 9
L28
Map 11
N29
P30

**Ayr** The Auld Kirk off main st by river; graveyard with diagram of where his
friends are buried; open at all times. **Dumfries** House where he spent his
last yrs and mausoleum 250m away at back of a kirkyard stuffed with extravagant masonry. 10km N of Dumfries on A76 at **Ellisland Farm** (home
1788–91) is the most interesting of all the sites. The farmhouse with genuine
memorabilia e.g. his mirror, fishing-rod, a poem scratched on glass, original
manuscripts. There's his favourite walk by the river where he composed 'Tam
o' Shanter' and a strong atmos about the place. Open 7 days summer, cl
Sun/Mon in wint. **Brow Well nr Ruthwell** on the B725 20km S Dumfries
and nr Caerlaverock (1759/BIRDS), is a quiet place, a well with curative properties where he went in the latter stages of his illness. Not many folk go to
this one.

**Burns And A' That** festival in May is a major new development. I was the
director until 2005 so I would say it was good, wouldn't I? Now we'll see!
Report: 34/EVENTS.

**1945 Lewis Grassic Gibbon (1901–35) Arbuthnott nr Stonehaven** Although
James Leslie Mitchell left the area in 1917, this is where he was born and
spent his formative years. Visitor Centre (01561 361668; Apr-Oct 7 days
10am-4.30pm) at the end of the village (via B967, 16km S of Stonehaven off
main A92) has details of his life and can point you in the direction of the
places he writes about in his trilogy, *A Scots Quair*. The first part, *Sunset Song*,
is generally considered to be one of the gr Scots novels and this area, the
**Howe Of The Mearns**, is the place he so effectively evokes. Arbuthnott is
reminiscent of 'Kinraddie' and the churchyard 1km away on the other side of
rd still has the atmos of that time of innocence before the war which pervades the book. New, big film of *Sunset Song* on the way at TGP. His ashes are
here in a grave in a corner. From 1928 to when he died 7yrs later at the age
of only 34, he wrote an incredible 17 books.

Map 10
S21

**1946 Neil Gunn (1891–1973) Dunbeath nr Wick** Scotland's foremost writer
on Highland life, only recently receiving the recognition he deserves, was
brought up in this NE fishing village and based 3 of his greatest yarns here,
particularly *Highland River*, which must stand in any literature as a brilliant
evocation of place. The **Strath** in which it is set is below the house (a nondescript terraced house next to the Stores) and makes for a gr walk
(2014/GLEN AND RIVER WALKS). There's a commemorative statue by the harbour,
not quite the harbour you imagine from the books. The excl Heritage Centre
depicts the Strath on its floor & has a leaflet for you to foll. Gunn also lived
for many yrs nr **Dingwall** and there is a memorial on the back rd to
Strathpeffer and a wonderful view in a place he often walked (on A834, 4km
from Dingwall).

Map 6
P14

**1947 James Hogg (1770–1835) St Mary's Loch, Ettrick** 'The Ettrick Shepherd'
who wrote one of the great works of Scottish literature, *Confessions of a
Justified Sinner*, was born, lived and died in the valleys of the Yarrow and the
**Ettrick**, some of the most starkly beautiful landscapes in Scotland. **St
Mary's Loch** on the A708, 28km W of Selkirk: there's a commemorative
statue looking over the loch and the adj and supernatural seeming L of the
Lowes. On the strip of land betw is **Tibbie Shiels** pub (and hotel), once a
gathering place for the writer and his friends (e.g. Sir Walter Scott) and still a
notable hostelry (1332/PUBS). Across the valley divide (11km on foot, part of
the S Upland Way (1997/LONG WALKS), or 25km by rd past the Gordon Arms
Hotel is the remote village of **Ettrick**, another monument and his grave (and
Tibbie Shiels') in the churchyard. His countryside is stark and beautiful. The
James Hogg exhib is at Bowhill House Visitor Centre. Tel 01750 22204.

Map 10
R23
P27

**1948**
Map 10
R27

**Sir Walter Scott (1771–1832) Abbotsford, Melrose**  No other place in Scotland (and few anywhere) contains so much of a writer's life and work. This was the house he rebuilt from the farmhouse he moved to in 1812 in the countryside he did so much to popularise. The house, until only recently lived in by his descendants, is now run by Trustees. The library and study are pretty much as he left them, including 9,000 rare books, antiquarian even in his day. Pleasant grounds and topiary and a walk by the Tweed which the house o/look. His grave is at **Dryburgh Abbey** (1918/ABBEYS). House open daily 9.30am-5pm; Sun 2-5pm (in wint 10am).

**1949**
Map 1

**Robert Louis Stevenson (1850–94) Edinburgh**  Though Stevenson travelled widely – lived in France, emigrated to America and died and was buried in Samoa – he spent the first 30 yrs of his short life in.Edin. He was born and brought up in the New Town, living at **17 Heriot Row** from 1857-80 in a fashionable town house which is still lived in (not open to the public). Most of his youth was spent in this newly built and expanding part of the city in an area bounded then by parkland and farms. Both the **Botanics** (401/OTHER ATTRACTIONS) and **Warriston Cemetery** (1904/GRAVEYARDS) are part of the landscape of his childhood. However, his fondest recollections were of the **Pentland Hills** and, virtually unchanged as they are, it's here that one is following most poignantly in his footsteps. The 'cottage' at **Swanston** (a delightful village with some remarkable thatched cottages reached via the city bypass/Colinton t/off or from Oxgangs Rd and a br over the bypass; the village nestles in a grove of trees below the hills and is a good place to walk from), the ruins of **Glencorse Church** (ruins even then and where he later asked that a prayer be said for him) and **Colinton Manse** can all be seen, but not visited. Edinburgh has no dedicated Stevenson Museum, but **The Writers' Museum** at Makars' Court has exhibits (& of many other writers). The **Hawes Inn** in South Queensferry where he wrote *Kidnapped* has had its history obliterated by a brewery makeover.

**J.K. Rowling (we don't give a lady's birthdate)**  Scotland's most successful writer ever as the creator of Harry Potter, rich beyond her wildest dreams, was once (& famously) an impecunious single mother scribbling away in Edinburgh coffee-shops. The most-mentioned is opp the Festival Theatre & is now a Chinese restau (upstairs), but not listed. The **Elephant House** (282/COFFEESHOPS) was another & gives you the idea. Harry Potter country as interepreted by Hollywood can be found at **Glenfinnan** (1938/MARY, CHARLIE AND BOB) and **Glencoe** esp around the **Clachaig Inn** (1196/INNS). JKR lives nr Aberfeldy – you might see her in another coffee-shop, the one at the **House of Menzies** (2160/BEST SCOTTISH SHOPPING), tho' she no longer scribbles publicly.

**Irvine Welsh (c1958-)**  Literary immortality awaits confirmation. Tours (*that* toilet etc) likely any day. **Robbie's Bar** might suffice (344/'UNSPOILT' PUBS); you will hear the voices.

# The Really Spooky Places

**1950**
Map 9
J21

**Hidden Or Lost Valley** Glencoe  The secret glen where the ill-fated Macdonalds hid the cattle they'd stolen from the Lowlands and which became (with politics and power struggles) their undoing. A narrow wooded cleft takes you betw the imposing and gnarled '3 Sisters' Hills and over the threshold (God knows how the cattle got there) and into the huge bowl of Coire Gabhail. The place envelops you in its tragic history, more redolent perhaps than any of the massacre sites. Park on the A82 5km from the VC 300m W of 2 white buildings on either side of the rd (always cars parked here). Follow clear path down to and across the R Coe. Ascend keeping burn to left; 1.5km further up, it's best to ford it. Allow 3hrs. (1925/BATTLEGROUNDS.) 2-B-2

**1951**
Map 1
D4

**Under Edinburgh Old Town** Mary King's Close, a medieval st under the Royal Mile closed in 1753 (The Real Mary King's Close 08702 430160); and the Vaults under South Br – built in the 18th century and sealed up around the time of the Napoleonic Wars (Mercat Tours 0131 557 6464). History underfoot for unsuspecting tourists and locals alike. Glimpses of a rather smelly subterranean life way back then. It's dark during the day, and you wouldn't want to get locked in.

**1952** **The Yesnaby Stacks Orkney Mainland** A cliff top viewpoint that's so
Map 3 wild, so dramatic and, if you walk near the edge, so precarious that its super-
P10 naturalism verges on the uneasy. Shells of lookout posts from the war echo
the melancholy spirit of the place. ('The bloody town's a bloody cuss/No
bloody trains, no bloody bus/And no one cares for bloody us/In bloody
Orkney' – first lines of a poem written then, a soldier's lament.) Nr Skara Brae,
it's about 30km from Kirkwall and way out west.

**1953** **The Fairy Glen** Skye A place so strange, it's hard to believe that it's mere-
Map 7 ly a geological phenomenon. Entering Uig on the A855 (becomes A87) from
F17 Portree, there's a turret on the left (Macrae's Folly). Take rd on rt marked
Balnaknock for 2km and you enter an area of extraordinary conical hills
which, in certain conditions of light and weather, seems to entirely justify its
legendary provenance. Your mood may determine whether you believe they
were good or bad fairies, but there's supposed to be an incredible 365 of
these grassy hillocks, some 35m high – well, how else could they be there?

**1954** **Clava Cairns** nr Culloden, Inverness Nr Culloden (1923/BATTLEGROUNDS)
Map 7 these curious chambered cairns in a grove of trees nr a river in the middle of
M18 21stC nowhere. This spot can be seriously Blair Witch (1832/PREHISTORIC SITES
for details).

**1955** **The Clootie Well** On The Road betw Tore on the A9 & Avoch Spooky
Map 7 spooky place on the rd towards Avoch and Cromarty 4km from the r/bout at
M17 Tore N of Inverness. Easily missed, tho' now a marked carpark on the rt side
of the rd going E. What you see is hundreds of rags (actually pieces of clothing) hanging on the branches of trees around the spout of an ancient well.
They go way back up the hill behind and have probably been here for
decades. Don't wish you were here. This has what you'd call strange vibrations.

**1956** **Burn O' Vat** nr Ballater This impressive and rather spooky glacial curiosity
Map 8 on Royal Deeside is a popular spot and well worth the short walk. 8km from
Q20 Ballater towards Aberd on main A93, take A97 for Huntly for 2km to the car
park at the Muir of Dinnet nature reserve – driving thro' forests of strange
spindly birch. Some scrambling to reach the huge 'pot' from which the burn
flows to L Kinord. Forest walks, busy on fine weekends, but v odd when you
find it deserted.

**1957** **Crichope Linn** nr Thornhill A supernatural sliver of glen inhabited by water
Map 11 spirits of various temperaments (and midges). Take rd for Cample on A76
N29 Dumfries to Kilmarnock rd just S of Thornhill; at village (2km) there's a wood-
en sign so take left for 2km. Discreet sign and gate in bank on rt is easy to
miss, but quarry for parking 100m further on, on left, is more obvious. Take
care – can be very wet and very slippy. Gorge is a 10-min schlep from the
gate. We saw red squirrels!

**1958** **Sallochy Wood** Loch Lomond B837, N of Balmaha, look for Sallochy Wood
Map 9 car park on the left. Cross back over the rd, away from L Lomond, and follow
L24 the trail signs, up the hill. After the large cedar tree, the path takes you into
the woods. Slippery going (on the exposed tree roots) then an unexpected
clearing in middle of dense undergrowth. This is the ruined hamlet of Wester
Sallochy. Surrounded by gloomy conifers, the roofless buildings still stand,
awaiting the return of their long-dead tenants. Not a place to visit at night,
but some do, and they leave their mark ...

**The Necropolis** Glasgow 1903/GRAVEYARDS.

**Hamilton Mausoleum** Strathclyde Park 1868/MONUMENTS.

**Loanhead Of Daviot** nr Oldmeldrum, Aberdeenshire
1849/PREHISTORIC SITES.

# SECTION 9

*Strolls, Walks And Hikes*

# Favourite Hills

*Popular and notable hills in the various regions of Scotland but not including Munros or difficult climbs. Always best to remember that the weather can change v quickly. Take an OS map on higher tops. See p. 13 for walk codes.*

**1959**
Map 6
**K14**
✓✓ **Suilven** Lochinver From close or far away, this is one of Scotland's most awe-inspiring mountains. The 'sugar loaf' can seem almost insurmountable, but in good weather it's not so difficult. Route from Inverkirkaig 5km S of Lochinver on rd to Achiltibuie, turns up track by Achin's Bookshop (2172/SCOTTISH SHOPPING) on the path for the Kirkaig Falls; once at the loch, you head for the Bealach, the central waistline through an unexpected dyke and follow track to the top. The slightly quicker route from the N (Glencanisp) following a stalkers' track that eventually leads to Elphin, also heads for the central breach in the mt's defences. Either way it's a long walk in; 8km before the climb. Allow 8hrs return. At the top, the most enjoyable 100m in the land and below – amazing Assynt. 731m. Take OS map. 2-C-3

**1960**
Map 6
**J15**
✓✓ **Stac Pollaidh/Polly** nr Ullapool This hill described variously as 'perfect', 'preposterous' and 'gr fun', certainly has character and, rising out of the Sutherland moors on the rd to Achiltibuie off the A835 N from Ullapool, demands to be climbed. Route everyone takes is from the car park by L Lurgainn 8km from main rd. Head for the central ridge which for many folk is enough; the path to the pinnacles is exposed and can be off-putting. Best half day hill climb in the N. 613m. Allow 3-4hrs return. 2-B-3

**1961**
Map 9
**J27**
✓ **Goat Fell** Arran Starting from the car park at Cladach before Brodick Castle grounds 3km from town, or from Corrie further up the coast (12km). Worn path, a steady climb, rarely much of a scramble but a rewarding afternoon's exertion. Some scree & some view! 874m. Allow 5hrs. 2-B-2

**1962**
Map 9
**K24**
✓ **The Cobbler (Ben Arthur)** Arrochar Perennial favourite of the Glas hill walker and, for sheer exhilaration, the most popular of 'the Arrochar Alps'. A motorway path ascends from the A83 on the other side of L Long from Arrochar (park in lay-bys nr Succoth rd end; there are always loads of cars) and takes 2.5-3hrs to traverse the up'n'down route to the top. Just short of a Munro at 881m, it has 3 tops of which the N peak is the simplest scramble (central and S peaks for climbers). Way not marked; consult. 2-B-3

## FIVE MAGNIFICENT HILLS IN THE TROSSACHS

**1963**
Map 10
**L24**
✓ **Ben Venue & Ben A'An** 2 celebrated tops in the Highland microcosm of the Trossachs around L Achray, 15km W of Callander; strenuous but not difficult and with superb views. Ben Venue (727m) is the more serious; allow 4-5 hrs return. Start from Kinlochard side at Ledard or more usually from the L Katrine corner before L Achray Hotel. It's waymarked from new car park. Ben A'a (pron 'An')n (415m) starts with a steep climb from the main A821 above from the Tigh Mor mansions (just before the corner). Scramble at top. Allow 2 to 3hrs. 2-B-3

**1964**
Map 10
**M23**
**Benn Shian** Strathyre Another Trossachs favourite and not taxing. From village main rd (the A74 to Lochearnhead), cross bridge opp Monro Hotel, turn left after 200m then path to rt at 50m a steep start through woods. O/look village and views to Crianlarich & Ben Vorlich (*see below*). 600m. 1.5hrs. 2-B-3

**1965**
Map 10
**L24**
**Doon Hill** The Faerie Knowe, Aberfoyle Legendary hillock in Aberfoyle, only 1hr up and back, so a gentle elevation into faerie land. The tree at the top is the home of the 'People of Quietness' and there was once a local minister who had the temerity to tell their secrets (in 1692). Go round it 7 times and your wish will be granted, go round it backwards at your peril (well, you wouldn't, would you?). From main st take Manse Rd adj garden centre. 1km past cemetery & manse – then signed. 1-B-1

**1966**
Map 10
**M23**
**Ben Vorlich** The big hill itself is also approached from the S Lochearn rd; from Ardvorlich House 5km from A84. Enter 'East Gate' and follow signs for open hillside of Glen Vorlich. Track splits after 1.5km, take right then SE side of come to N ridge of mountain. Allow 5hrs ret. 2-B-3

**1967**
Map 9
**H24**
✓ **Dunadd** Kilmartin N of Lochgilphead  8km N on A816. Less of a hill, more of a lump, but it's where they crowned the kings of Dalriada for half a millennium. Stand on top when the Atlantic rain is sheeting in and ... you get wet like even the kings did. Kilmartin House Museum nearby for info & gr food (2238/MUSEUMS).  2-B-2

**1968**
Map 11
**N30**
**Criffel** New Abbey nr Dumfries  12km S by A710 to New Abbey, which Criffel dominates. It's only 569m, but seems higher. Exceptional views from top as far as English lakes and across to Borders. Granite lump with brilliant outcrops of quartzite. The annual race gets up and back to the Abbey Arms in under an hr; you can take it easier. Start 3km S of village, t/off A710 100m from one of the curious painted bus shelters signed for Ardwall Mains Farm. Park before the farm buildings and get on up.  2-A-2

**1969**
Map 11
**L29**
**Merrick** nr Newton Stewart  Go from bonnie Glen Trool via Bargrennan 14km N on the A714. Bruce's Stone is there at the start (1939/MARY, CHARLIE AND BOB). The highest peak in S Scotland (843m), it's a strenuous though straightforward climb in glorious scenery. 4hrs.  2-B-3

**1970**
Map 10
**R25**
**North Berwick Law**  The conical volcanic hill, a beacon in the E Lothian landscape. **Traprain Law** nearby, is higher, easy even if celebrated by rock climbers, but has major prehistoric significance as a hillfort citadel of the Goddodin and a definite aura. NBL is easy and rewarding – leave town by Law Rd, path marked beyond houses. Car park and picnic site. Views 'to the Cairngorms' (!) & along the Forth. Famous whalebone at the top.  BOTH 1-A-1

**1971**
Map 10
**R28**
**Ruberslaw** Denholm nr Hawick  This smooth hummock above the Teviot valley affords views of 7 counties, incl Northumberland. Millennium plaque on top. At 424m, it's a gentle climb taking about 1hr from the usual start at Denholm Hill Farm (private land, be aware of livestock). Leave Denholm at corner of Green by shop and go past post office. Take left after 2km to farm.  2-A-2

**1972**
Map 10
**N27**
**Tinto Hill** nr Biggar & Lanark  A favourite climb in S/Central Scotland with easy access to start from A73 nr Symington, 10km S of Lanark. Park 100m behind Tinto Hills farm shop. Good track, though it has its ups and downs before you get there. Braw views. 707m. Allow 3hrs.  2-A-2

**1973**
**Dumgoyne** nr Blanefield  Close to Glasgow & almost a mountain, so a popular non-strenuous hike. Huge presence, sits above A81 & Glengoyne Distillery (open to public). App from Strathblane War Memorial via Campsie Dene rd. 7km track, allow 3-4 hrs (or take the steep way up from the distillery). Refresh/replenish in Killearn (839/CENTRAL HOTELS, 1363/PUB FOOD). Take care on outcrops.  2-A-2

**1974**
Map 9
**L24**
**Conic Hill** Balmaha Loch Lomond  An easier climb than the Ben up the rd and a good place to view it from, Conic, on the Highland fault line, is one of the first Highland hills you reach from Glas. Stunning views also of L Lomond from its 358m peak. Ascend thro woodland from the corner of Balmaha car park. Watch for buzzards and your footing on the final crumbly bits. May be closed for lambing season Apr-May. 1.5hrs up.  2-A-2

**1975**
Map 10
**P23**
**Kinnoull Hill** Perth  Various starts from town (the path from beyond Branklyn Gdn on the Dundee Rd is less frequented) to the wooded ridge above the Tay with its tower & incredible views to S from the precipitous cliffs. Surprisingly extensive area of hill side common & it's not difficult to get lost. The leaflet/map from Perth TIC helps. Local lurv spot after dark.  1-A-1

**1976**
Map 8
**R19**
**Bennachie** nr Aberdeen  The pilgrimage hill, an easy 528m often busy at w/ends but never a let-down. Various trails take in 'the Taps'. Trad route from Rowan Tree nr Chapel of Garioch (pron 'Geery') signed Pittodrie off A96 nr Pitcaple. Also from Essons car park on rd from Chapel-Monymusk, which is steeper. Or from other side the Lord's Throat rd, a longer, more forested app from banks of the Don. All car parks have trail-finders. From the fortified top you see what Aberdeenshire is about. 2hrs. Bennachie's soulmate, **Tap O' Noth**, is 20km W. Easy app via Rhynie on A97 (then 3km).  2-B-2

**1977**
Map 5
**C20**
**Heaval** Barra  The mini-Matternorn that rises above Castlebay is an easy & rewarding climb. At 1250ft, it's steep in places but never over-taxing. You see the road to Mingulay. Start up hill thro' Castlebay, park behind the new-build house, find path via Our Lady of the Sea. 1.5hrs ret.

# Hill Walks

*The following ranges of hills offer walks in various directions and more than one summit. They are all accessible and fairly easy. See p. 13 for walk codes.*

**1978** **Walks On Skye** Obviously many serious walks in and around the Cuillins
Map 5 (1993/MUNROS, 2001/SERIOUS WALKS), but almost infinite variety of others. Can do no better than read a gr book, *50 Best Routes on Skye and Raasay* by Ralph Storer (avail locally), which describes and grades many of the must-dos.

**1979** **Lomond Hills** Fife nr Falkland The conservation village lies below a promi-
Map 10 nent ridge easily reached from the main st esp via Back Wynd (off which
P24 there's a car park). More usual app to both E and W Lomond, the main tops, is from Craigmead car park 3km from village towards Leslie trail-finder board. The celebrated Lomonds (aka the Paps of Fife), aren't that high (West is 522m), but they can see and be seen for miles. Also start from radio masts 3km up rd from A912 E of Falkland.               3-10KM CIRC XBIKES 2-A-2

An easy rewarding single climb is **Bishop Hill**. Start 100m from the church in Scotlandwell. A steep path veers left and then there are several ways up. Allow 2hrs. Gr view of L Leven, Fife and a good swathe of Central Scotland. Gliders glide over from the old airstrip below.

**1980** **The Eildons** Melrose The 3 much-loved hills or paps visible from most of
Map 10 the Central Borders and easily climbed from the town of Melrose which nes-
R27 tles at their foot. Leave main sq by rd to stn (the Dingleton rd), after 100m a path begins betw 2 pebble-dash houses on the left. You climb the smaller first, then the highest central one (422m). You can make a circular route of it by returning to the golf course. Allow 1.5hrs.          3KM CIRC XBIKES I-A-2

**1981** **The Ochils** Usual app from the 'hillfoot towns' at the foot of the glens that
Map 10 cut into their S-facing slopes, along the A91 Stirling-St Andrews rd. Alva,
N24 Tillicoultry and Dollar all have impressive glen walks easily found from the main streets where tracks are marked (2009/GLEN AND RIVER WALKS). Good start nr Stirling from the Sheriffmuir rd uphill from Br of Allan about 3km, look for pylons and a lay-by on the rt (a reservoir just visible on the left). There are usu-ally other cars here. A stile leads to the hills which stretch away to the E for 40km and afford gr views for little effort. Highest point is Ben Cleugh, 721m. Swimming place nearby is Paradise (1722/PICNICS).

2-40KM SOME CIRC XBIKES 1/2-B-2

**1982** **The Lammermuirs** The hills SE of Edin that divide the rich farmlands of E
Map 10 Lothian and the valley of the Tweed in the Borders. Mostly a high wide moor
R26 land but there's wooded gentle hill country in the watersheds of the south-ern rivers and spectacular coastal scenery betw Cockburnspath and St Abbs Head. (1778/WILDLIFE; 2043/COASTAL WALKS.) The eastern part of the S Upland Way follows the Lammermuirs to the coast (1997/LONG WALKS). Many moor-land walks begin at the car park at the head of Whiteadder Reservoir (A1 to Haddington, B6369 towards Humbie, then E on B6355 through Gifford), a mysterious loch in the bowl of the hills. Excellent walks also centre on Abbey St Bathans to the S – head off A1 at Cockburnspath. Through village to Toot Corner (signed 1km) and off to left, follow path above valley of Whiteadder to Edinshall Broch (2km). Further on, along river (1km), is a swing bridge and a fine place to swim. Circular walks possible; ask in village. Woodhall Dene a gr woody Lammermuir (foothill) option.

5-15KM SOME CIRC MTBIKES 1/2-B-2

**1983** **The Cheviots** Not strictly in Scotland, but they straddle the border and
Map 10 Border history. There are many fine walks starting from Kirk Yetholm (incl the
S27 Pennine Way which stretches 400km S to the Peak district and St Cuthbert's Way; 2000/LONG WALKS) incl an 8km circular route of typical Cheviot foothill terrain. See *Walking in the Scottish Borders* avail from all Border TICs (one of many excl guides). Most forays start at Wooler 20km from Coldstream and the border. Cheviot itself (2,676ft) a boggy plateau, Hedgehope via the Harthope Burn more fun. Or look for Towford (1721/RIVER PICNICS).

**The Campsie Fells** nr Glasgow  727/WALKS OUTSIDE THE CITY.

**The Pentland Hills** nr Edinburgh  413/WALKS OUTSIDE THE CITY.

# Some Great Starter Munros

✓ ✓ *There are almost 300 hills in Scotland over 3000ft as tabled by Sir Hugh Munro in 1891. Those selected here have been chosen for their relative ease of access both to the bottom and thence to the top. All offer rewarding climbs. None should be attempted without proper clothing (esp boots) and sustenance. You may also need an OS map. The weather can change quickly in the Scottish mts.*

**1984**  **Ben Lomond** Rowardennan, Loch Lomond  Many folk's first Munro, given
Map 9  proximity to Glas (soul and city). It's not too taxing a climb and has reward-
L24  ing views (in good weather). 2 main ascents: 'tourist route' is easier, from toi-
let block at Rowardennan car park (end of rd from Drymen), well-trodden all
the way; or 500m up past Youth Hostel, a path follows burn – the 'Ptarmigan
Route'. Circular walk poss. 974m. 3hrs up.

**1985**  **Schiehallion** nr Kinloch Rannoch  'Fairy Hill of the Caledonians' & a bit of
Map 10  a must. New path c/o John Muir Trust over E flank. Start Braes of Foss car
M22  park 10k from KR. 10km walk, ascent 750m. 6 hrs. 1083m.

**1986**  **Carn Aosda** Glenshee  One of the most accessible starting from Glenshee
Map 10  ski car park foll ski tow up. Ascent only 270m of 917m. So you can bag a
M21  Munro in an hr. The Grampian Highlands unfold.

**1987**  **Meall Chuaich** Dalwhinnie  Starting from verge of the A9 S of Cuaich ascent
Map 7  only 623m, total walk 14km. Foll aqueductto powerstation then L Cuaich. An
M20  easily bagged 951m.

**1988**  **An Teallach** Torridon  Sea-level start from Dundonnell on the A832 S of
Map 7  Ullapool. One of the most awesome Scots peaks but not the ordeal it looks.
J16  Path well trod; gr scrambling opportunities for the nimble. Peering over the
pinnacle of Lord Berkeley's Seat into the void is a jaw-drop. Take a day. 1,062m.

**1989**  **Beinn Alligin** Torridon  The other gr Torridon trek. Consult re start (path
Map 7  changed). Car park by br on rd to Inveralligin & Diabeg, walk thro woods over
J17  moor by river. Steepish pull up onto the Horns of Alligin. You can cover 2
Munros in a circular route that takes you across the top of the world. 985m.

**1990**  **Ben More** Mull  The 'cool, high ben' sits in isolated splendour, the only
Map 9  Munro, bar the Cuillins, not on the mainland. Sea-level start from lay-by on
G23  the coast rd B8073 that skirts the southern coast of L Na Keal at Dhiseig
House, then a fairly clear path through the bleak landscape.Tricky nr the top
but there are fabulous views across the islands. 966m.

**1991**  **Ben Wyvis** nr Garve  Standing apart from its northern neighbours, you can
Map 7  feel the presence of this mt from a long way off. N of main A835 rd Inverness-
L17  Ullapool & v accessible from it, park 6km N of Garve (48km from Inverness)
and follow marked path by stream and through the forest. Leave the plantations behind; the summit app is by a soft, mossy ridge. Magnificent 1,046m.

**1992**  **Lochnagar** nr Ballater  Described as a fine, complex mt, its nobility and
Map 10  mystique apparent from afar, not least Balmoral Castle. App via Glen Muick
Q20  (pron 'Mick') rd from Ballater to car park at L Muick (1660/LOCHS). Path to mt
well signed and well trodden. 18km return, allow 6-8hrs. Steep at top.
Apparently on a clear day you can see the Forth Br. 1,155m.

**1993**  **Bla Bheinn** Skye  The magnificent massif, isolated from the other Cuillins,
Map 7  has a sea-level start and seems higher than it is. The *Munro Guide* describes
G19  it as 'exceptionally accessible'. It has an eerie jagged beauty and – though
some scrambling is involved and it helps to have a head for exposed situa-
tions – there are no serious dangers. Take B8083 from Broadford to Elgol thro
Torrin, park 1km S of the head of L Slapin, walking W at Allt na Dunaiche
along N bank of stream. Bla Bheinn (pron 'Blahven') is an enormously
rewarding climb. Rapid descent for scree runners, but allow 8hrs. 928m.

**1994**  **Ben Lawers** betw Killin & Aberfeldy  The massif of 7 summits incl 6 Munros
Map 10  that dominate the N side of L Tay are linked by a twisting ridge 12km long that
M22  only once falls below 800m. If you're v fit, it's poss to do the lot in a day start-
ing from the N or Glen Lyon side. Have an easier day of it knocking off Beinn
Ghlas then Ben Lawers from the VC 5km off the A827. 4/5 hrs.

**1995**  **Meall Nan Tarmachan**  The part of the ridge W of Lawers (above), which
Map 10  takes in a Munro & several tops, is not arduous & is immensely impressive.
M22  Start 1km further on from NTS VC down 100m track & through gate.

# Long Walks

✓ ✓ *These walks require preparation, route maps, v good boots etc. But don't carry too much. Sections are always poss. See p. 13 for walk codes.*

**1996** **The West Highland Way** The 150km walk which starts at Milngavie 12km
Map 2 o/side Glas and goes via some of Scotland's most celebrated scenery to emerge in Glen Nevis before the Ben. The route goes like this: Mugdock Moor-Drymen-L Lomond-Rowardennan-Inversnaid-Inverarnan-Crianlarich-Tyndrum-Br of Orchy-Rannoch Moor-Kingshouse Hotel-Glencoe-The Devil's Staircase-Kinlochleven. The latter part from Br of Orchy is the most dramatic. The Br of Orchy Hotel (01838 400208; 1191/ROADSIDE INNS – not cheap!) and Kingshouse (01855 851259) are both historic staging posts, as is the Drover's Inn, Inverarnan (841/CENTRAL HOTELS). It's a good idea to book accom (allowing time for muscle fatigue) and don't take too much stuff. Info leaflet/pack from shops or Ranger Service (01389 722600).

**Start** Officially at Milngavie (pron 'Mull-guy') Railway Stn (reg service from Glas Central, also buses from Buchanan St Bus Stn), but actually from Milngavie shopping precinct 500m away. However, the countryside is close. Start from other end on Glen Nevis rd from r/bout on A82 N from Ft William. Way is well marked, but you must have a route map.                        2-B-3

**1997** **The Southern Upland Way** 350km walk from Portpatrick S of Stranraer
Map 11 across the Rhinns of Galloway, much moorland, the Galloway Forest Park,
**J30** the wild heartland of Southern Scotland, then through James Hogg country (1947/LITERARY PLACES) to the gentler E Borders and the sea at Pease Bay (official end, Cockburnspath). Route is Portpatrick-Stranraer-New Luce-Dalry-Sanquhar-Wanlockhead-Beattock-St Mary's L-Melrose-Lauder-Abbey St Bathans. The first and latter sections are the most obviously picturesque but highlights include L Trool, the Lowther Hills, St Mary's L, R Tweed. Usually walked W to E, the SU Way is a formidable undertaking ... (Info from Ranger Service: 01835 830281).

**Start** Portpatrick by the harbour and up along the cliffs past the lighthouse. or Cockburnspath. Map is on side of shop at Cross.                        2-B-3

**1998** **The Speyside Way** A long distance route which generally follows the val-
Map 8 ley of the R Spey from Buckie on the Moray Firth coast to Aviemore in the
**Q17** foothills of the Cairngorms (there are plans to complete the route to Newtonmore in the next couple of years), with side spurs to Dufftown up Glen Fiddich (7km) and to Tomintoul over the hill between the R Avon (pron 'A'rn') and the R Livet (24km). The main stem of the route largely follows they valley bottom, criss-crossing the Spey several times – a distance of around 100km, and is less strenuous than SU or WH Ways. The Tomintoul spur has more hill-walking character and rises to a gr viewpoint at 600m. Throughout walk you are in whisky country with opportunities to visit Cardhu, Glenlivet and other distilleries nearby (1539/1536/WHISKY). Info from Ranger Service: 01340 881266.

**Start** Usual start is from coast end. Spey Bay is 8km N of Fochabers; the first marker is by the banks of shingle at the river mouth.                        1-A-3

**1999** **Glen Affric** In enchanting Glen Affric and L Affric beyond (2007/GLEN AND
Map 7 RIVER WALKS; 1627/GLENS; 1714/PICNICS), some serious walking begins on the
**K18** 32km Kintail trail. Done either W-E starting at the Morvich Outdoor Centre 2km from A87 nr Shiel Br, or E-W starting at the Affric Lodge 15km W of Cannich. Route can include one of the approaches to the Falls of Glomach (1676/WATERFALLS).                        2-C-3

**2000** **St Cuthbert's Way** From Melrose in Scottish Borders (where St Cuthbert
Map 10 started his ministry) to Lindisfarne on Holy Island off Northumberland (where
**R27** he died) via St Boswells-Kirk Yetholm-Wooler. 100km but many sections easy. Bowden–Maxton and a stroll by the Tweed esp fine. Check local TICs. Leaflets/maps avail.                        2-A-3

# Serious Walks

✔ ✔ *None of these should be attempted without OS maps, proper equipment and preparation. Hill or ridge walking experience may be essential.*

**2001** **The Cuillins** Skye Much scrambling and, if you want it, serious climbing over
Map 7 these famously unforgiving peaks. The Red ones are easier and many walks
**G19** start at the Sligachan Hotel on the main Portree-Broadford rd. Every July there's
a hill race up Glamaig; the conical one which o/look the hotel. Most of the
Black Cuillins incl the highest, Sgurr Alasdair (993m), and Sgurr Dearg, 'the
Inaccessible Pinnacle' (978m), can be attacked from the campsite or the youth
hostel in Glen Brittle. Good guides are *Introductory Scrambles from Glen Brittle*
by Charles Rhodes, or *50 Best Routes in Skye and Raasay* by Ralph Storer both
available locally, but you will need something. Take extreme care! (2/BIG ATTRAC-
TIONS; 1173/1174/HOSTELS; 1643/WATERFALLS; 1993/MUNROS; 1706/PICNICS.)      3-C-3

**2002** **Aonach Eagach** Glencoe One of several poss major expeditions in the
Map 9 Glencoe area and one of the world's classic ridge walks. Not for the faint-
**J21** hearted or the ill-prepared. It's the ridge on your rt for almost the whole
length of the glen from Altnafeadh to the rd to the Clachaig Inn (rewarding
refreshment). Start from the main rd. Car park opp the one for the Hidden
Valley (1950/SPOOKY PLACES). Stiff pull up then the switchback path across.
There is no turning back. Scary pinnacles two-thirds over, then one more
Munro & the knee-trembling, scree-running descent. On your way, you'll
have come close to heaven, seen Lochaber in its immense glory and recon-
noitred some fairly exposed edges and pinnacles. Go with somebody good as
I did. (1666/SCENIC ROUTES; 1326/BLOODY GOOD PUBS; 1170/ HOSTELS; 1925/
BATTLEGROUNDS.)                                                            3-C-3

**2003** **Ben Nevis** Start on Glen Nevis rd, 5km Ft William town centre (by br opp
Map 9 youth hostel or from VC) or signed from A82 after Glen Nevis r/bout. both
**K21** lead to start at Achintee Farm & the Ben Nevis Inn (handy afterwards;
2332/FT WILLIAM). This is the main or tourist route which continues to the top
(many consider the tourist route to be v dull, but it is the safest). Allow the
best part of a day (and I do mean the best – the weather can turn quickly
here). For the more interesting arete route, consult locally. Many people are
killed every yr, even experienced climbers. It is the biggest, though not the
best; you can see 100 Munros on a clear day (i.e. about once a yr). You climb
it because ... well, because you have to. 1344m.                          2-B-3

**2004** **The Five Sisters Of Kintail & The Cluanie Ridge** Both generally started
Map 7 from A87 along from Cluanie Inn (1330/BLOODY GOOD PUBS) and they will keep
**J19** you rt; usually walked E to W. Sisters is an uncomplicated but inspiring ridge
walk, taking in 3 Munros and 2 tops. It's a hard pull up and you descend to a
point 8km further up the rd (so arrange transport). Many side spurs to van-
tage-points and wild views. The Cluanie or S ridge is a classic which covers 7
Munros. Starts at inn; 2 ways off back onto A876. Both can be walked in a
single day (Cluanie allow 9hrs). (1171/HOSTELS.)                          3-C-3

From the Kintail Centre at Morvich off A87 nr Shiel Br another long distance
walk starts to Glen Affric (1999/LONG WALKS).

**2005** **Glen More Forest Park** from Coylumbridge and L Morlich; 32km. (2) joins
Map 7 (3) beyond L Morlich and both go through the Rothiemurchus Forest
**N19** (2030/WOODLAND WALKS) and the famous **Lairig Ghru**, the ancient Rt of Way
through the Cairngorms which passes betw Ben Macdui and Braeriach.
Ascent is over 700m and going can be rough. This is one of the gr Scottish
trails. At end of June, the Lairig Ghru Race completes this course E-W in
3.5hrs, but generally this is a full-day trip. The famous shelter, Corrour Bothy
betw 'Devil's Point' and Carn A Mhaim, can be a halfway house. Nr Linn of
Dee, routes (1) and (2/3) converge and pass through the ancient Caledonian
Forest of Mar. Going E-W is less gruelling and there's Aviemore to look for-
ward to!

**Glen Affric** Or rather beyond Glen Affric and L Affric (2007/GLEN WALKS;
1627/GLENS), the serious walking begins (1999/LONG WALKS).

# Glen & River Walks

*See also* Great Glens, *p. 204. Walk codes are on p. 13.*

**2006** ✓ **Glen Tilt** Blair Atholl A walk of variable length in this classic Highland
Map 10 glen, easily accessible from the old Blair Rd off main Blair Atholl rd nr
**N21** Bridge of Tilt Hotel, car park by the (v) old bridge. Trail leaflet from park office
and local TICs. Fine walking and unspoiled scenery begins only a short distance
into the deeply wooded gorge of the R Tilt, but to cover the circular route you
have to walk to 'Gilbert's Br' (9km return) or the longer trail to Gow's Br (17km
return). Begin here also the gr route into the Cairngorms leading to the Linn of
Dee and Braemar, joining the track from Speyside which starts at Feshiebridge
or Glenmore Forest (2035/SERIOUS WALKS). UP TO 17KM CIRC XBIKE 1-B-2

**2007** ✓ **Glen Affric, Cannich** nr Drumnadrochit Easy short walks are marked
Map 7 and hugely rewarding in this magnificent glen well known as the first
**K18** stretch in the gr E-W route to Kintail (2004/SERIOUS WALKS) and the Falls of
Glomach (1638/WATERFALLS). Starting pt of this track into the wilds is at the end
of the rd at L Affric; there are many short and circular trails indicated here. Car
park is beyond metal rd 2km along forest track towards Affric Lodge (cars not
allowed to lodge itself). Track cl in stalking season. Easier walks in famous Affric
forest from car park at Dog Falls. 7km from Cannich (1714/PICNICS). Waterfalls
and spooky tame birds. Good idea to hire bikes at Drumnadrochit or Cannich
(01456 415251). Don't miss Glen Affric (1627/GLENS). 5/8KM CIRC BIKE 1-B-2

**2008** ✓ **Balquhidder to Brig O' Turk** Easy amble thro' the heart of Scotland via
Map 10 Glenfinglas (1659/LOCHS) with handy pubs (1367/GASTROPUBS) & tearms
**L23** (1457/TEAROOMS) at either end. Not circ so best to arrange transport. Usually
walked start ingat Rob Roy graveyard (1911/GRAVEYARDS), then Ballimore & past
Ben Vane to the reservoir & Brig o' Turk. 18KM XCIRC XBIKE 2-B-2

**2009** ✓ **Dollar Glen** Dollar nr Stirling The classic fairy glen in Central Scotland,
Map 10 positively hoaching with water spirits, reeking of ozone and euphoric after
**N24** rain, tho erosion has taken its toll & path no longer goes into the gorge. 20km
from Stirling by A91, or 18km from M90 at Kinross jnct 6. Start from top of tree-
lined ave on either side of burn or from further up rd signed Castle Campbell
where there are 2 car parks, the top one only 5mins from castle. The Castle at
head of glen is open 7 days till 6pm (Oct-Mar till 4pm), and has boggling views.
There's a circular walk back or take off for the Ochil Tops, the hills that surround
the glen. There are also first-class walks (the hill trail is more rewarding than
the 'Mill Trail') up the glens of the other hillfoot towns, Alva and Tillicoultry;
they also lead to the hills (1881/HILL WALKS). 3KM + TOPS CIRC XBIKE 1-A-2

**2010** ✓ **Rumbling Bridge** nr Dollar Formed by another burn off the Ochils, an
Map 10 easier short walk in a glen with something of the chasmic experience &
**N24** added delight of the unique double br (built 1713). At the end of one of the
walkways under the br you are looking into a Scottish jungle landscape as the
Romantics imagined. Nr Powmill on A977 from Kinross (jnct 6, M90) then
2km. Up the road is **The Powmill Milkbar** serving excellent home-made
food for 40 yrs. It's 5km W on the A977. Open 7 days till 5pm (6pm weekends) (1439/TEAROOMS). Go after your walk! 3KM CIRC XBIKE 1-A-1

**2011** ✓ **Glen Clova** Most dramatic of the Angus glens. Most walks from end at
Map 10 Acharn esp W to Glen Doll & the Loops of (Loch) Brandy walk. Enq at
**Q21** Glen Clova Hotel (1219/GET-AWAY-FROM-IT-ALL) & repair there afterwards (gr
walkers pub). Easy, rewarding walks! Check hotel for details.

**2012** **Falkland** Fife If you're in Falkland for the Palace (1792/CASTLES) or the tea-
Map 10 room (1458/TEAROOMS), add this amble up an enchanting glen to your day.
**Q24** Head thro vill then signed 'Cricket Club' for 'Falkland Estate' and School (an
activity centre) – car park just inside gate – & gdns are behind it. Glen & refurb
path are obvious. Gushing burn, waterfalls – you can even walk behind one of
them! Good café/restau in vill (903/FIFE RESTAUS). 3KM CIRC XBIKE 1-A-2

**2013** **The Big Burn Walk** Golspie A non-taxing, perfect glen walk through lush
Map 6 diverse woodland. Start beyond Sutherland Arms & Sutherland Stone works
**N15** off the A9 before Dunrobin Castle. Go past derelict mill & under aqueduct following river. A supernature trail unfolds with ancient tangled trees, meadows,
waterfalls, cliffs & much wildlife. 3km to falls, return via route to castle woods
for best all-round intoxication. 6KM CIRC XBIKE 1-B-1

**2014**
Map 6
**P14**
**The Strath at Dunbeath** The glen or strath so eloquently evoked in Neil Gunn's *Highland River* (1946/LITERARY PLACES), a book which is as much about the geography as the history of his childhood. A path follows the river for many miles. A leaflet from the Dunbeath Heritage Centre points out places on the way as well as map on its entire floor. It's a spate river and in summer becomes a trickle; hard to imagine Gunn's salmon odyssey. It's only 500m to the broch, but it's worth going into the hinterland where it becomes quite mystical (1913/GRAVEYARDS). 1-A-1

**2015**
Map 10
**Q27**
**Tweedside** Peebles The river side trail that follows the R Tweed from town (Hay Lodge Park) past Neidpath Castle (1712/PICNICS) and on through classic Border wooded countryside crossing river either 2.5km out (5km round trip), at Manor Br 6km out (Lyne Footbr, 12km). Pick up *Walking in the Scottish Borders* at local TIC. 5/12KM CIRC XBIKE 1-A-1
Other good Tweedside walk between Dryburgh Abbey & Bemersyde House grounds and at Newton St Boswells by golf course.

**2016**
Map 10
**L27**
**Failford Gorge** nr Mauchline Woody gorge of the R Ayr. Start from br at Ayr end of vill on B743 Ayr-Maucline rd (4km Mauchline). Easy, marked trail. Pub in vill but better is the Sorn Inn E of Mauchline (1348/GASTROPUBS). This is a v pleasant, bucolic part of Ayrshire. 3/5KM CIRC XBIKE 1-A-1

**2017**
Map 10
**M23**
**Glen Lednock** nr Comrie Can walk from Comrie or take car further up to monument or drive further into glen to reservoir (9km) for more open walks. From town take rt off main A85 (to Lochearnhead) at Deil's Cauldron restau. Walk and Deil's Cauldron (waterfall and gorge) are signed after 250m. Walk takes less than 1hr and emerges on rd nr Lord Melville's monument (climb for gr views back towards Crieff, about 25 mins). Other walks up slopes to left after you emerge from the tree-lined gorge rd. There's also the start of a hike up Ben Chonzie, 6km up glen at Coishavachan. BC (931m) is one of the easiest Munros, with good path & gr views esp to NW. 3/5KM CIRC XBIKE 1-A-1

**2018**
Map 8
**R17**
**Bridge Of Alvah** Banff Details: 2034/WOODLAND WALKS, mentioned here because the best bit is by the river and the br itself. The single span crossing was built in 1772 and stands high above the river in a sheer-sided gorge. The river below is deep and slow. In the rt light it's almost Amazonian.

**2019**
Map 10
**R21**
**The Gannochy Bridge & The Rocks Of Solitude** nr Edzell 2km N of village on B966 to Fettercairn. There's a lay-by after br & a wooden door on left (you're in the grounds of the Burn House). Thro' it is another world & a path above the rocky gorge of the R North Esk (1km). Huge stone ledges over dark pools. You don't have to be alone (well maybe you do). 2KM XCIRC XBIKE 1-A-1

**2020**
Map 9
**J23**
**Nr Taynuilt** A walk (recommended by readers) combining education with recreation. Start behind Bonawe Ironworks (2246/MUSEUMS) & go along the river side to a suspension br & thence to Inverawe Smokehouse (open to the public; café). Walk back less interesting but all v nice. Best not to park in Bonawe car park (for HS visitors, & it closes at 6pm). 10 KM CIRC BIKE 1-A-1

# Woodland Walks

**2021**
Map 9
**G21**
✓✓ **Ardnamurchan** For anyone who loves trees (or hills, gr coastal scenery & raw nature), this far-flung peninsula is a revelation. App from S via Corran ferry on A82 S of Ft William or N from Lochailort on A830 Mallaig–Ft William rd (1680/SCENIC ROUTES) or from Mull. Many marked & unmarked trails (see Ariundle below) but consult TIC & local literature. To visit Ardnamurchan is to fall in love with Scotland again. Woods esp around L Sunart.

**2022**
Map 8
**N17**
✓ **Randolph's Leap** nr Forres Spectacular gorge of the plucky little Findhorn lined with beautiful beechwoods and a gr place to swim or picnic (1713/PICNICS), so listen up. Go either: 10km S of Forres on the A940 for Grantown, then the B9007 for Ferness and Carrbridge. 1km from the sign for Logie Steading (2159/SHOPPING) and 500m from the narrow stone br, there's a pull-over place on the bend. The woods are on the other side of the rd. Or: take the A939 S from Nairn or N from Grantown and at Ferness take the B9007 for Forres. Approaching from this direction, it's about 6km along the rd; the pull-over is on your rt. If you come to Logie Steading in this direction you've missed it; don't – you will miss one of the sylvan secrets of the N. Trailboard at site & at Logie Steading.

**2023**
Map 9
**J24**

✓ **Lochaweside** Unclassified rd on N side of loch betw Kilchrenan and Ford, centred on Dalavich. Illustrated brochure available from local hotels around Kilchrenan and Dalavich post office, describes 6 walks in the mixed, mature forest all starting from car parking places on the rd. 3 starting from the Barnaline car park are trail-marked and could be followed without brochure. Avich Falls route crosses R Avich after 2km with falls on return route. Inverinan Glen is always nice. The 'timber trail' from The Big Tree/Cruachan car park 2km S of Dalavich takes in the loch, a waterfall & it's easy on the eye & foot (4km). The track from the car park N of Kilchrenan on the B845 back to Taynuilt isn't on the brochure, may be less travelled and also fine. There's a pub at Kilchrenan.          2-8KM CIRC XBIKE 2-A-2

**2024**
Map 9
**K25**

✓ **Puck's Glen** nr Dunoon Close to the gates of the Younger Botanic Garden at Benmore (1543/GARDENS) on the other side of the A815 to Stracher 12km N of Dunoon. A short, exhilarating woodland walk from a convenient car park. Ascend thro' trees then down into a faery glen, foll the burn back to the rd. Some swimming pools.          3KM CIRC XBIKE 1-A-1

**2025**
Map 7
**N19**

✓ **Rothiemurchus Forest** nr Aviemore The place to experience the magic and the majesty of the gr Caledonian Forest and the beauty of Scots pine. App from B970, the rd that parallels the A9 from Coylumbridge to Kincraig/Kingussie. 2km from Inverdruie nr Coylumbridge follow sign for L an Eilean; one of the most perfect lochans in these or any woods. Loch circuit 5km (1655/LOCHS). Good free brochure for all forest activities from TICs.

**2026**
Map 9
**H21**

✓ **Ariundle Oakwoods** Strontian. 35km Ft William via Corran Ferry. Walk guide brochure at Strontian TIC. Many walks around L Sunart and Ariundle: rare oak and other native species. You see how v different Scotland's landscape was before the Industrial Revolution used up the wood. Start over town br, turning rt for Polloch. Go on past Ariundle Centre, with good home-baking café and park. 2 walks; well marked.          5KM CIRC MTBIKE 1-A-2

**2027**
Map 7
**H18**

**Balmacarra, Lochalsh Woodland Garden** 5km S Kyle of Lochalsh on A87. A woodland walk around the shore of L Alsh, centred on Lochalsh House. Mixed woodland in fairly formal gdn setting where you are confined to paths. Views to Skye. A fragrant & verdant amble. Ranger service.          CIRC XBIKE 1-A-1

**2028**
Map 10
**N22**

**The Birks O' Aberfeldy** Circular walk through oak, beech and the birch (or birk) woods of the title, easily reached and signed from town main st (1km). Steep-sided wooded glen of the Moness Burn with attractive falls esp the higher one spanned by br where the 2 marked walks converge. This is where Burns 'spread the lightsome days' in his eponymous poem. Nice tearm back in town (1445/TEARMS)          3KM CIRC XBIKE 1-A-2

**2029**
Map 10
**P22**

**The Hermitage Dunkeld** On A9 2km N of Dunkeld. Popular, easy, accessible walks along glen and gorge of R Braan with pavilion o/look the Falls and, further on, 'Ossian's Cave'. Also uphill Craig Vean walks starts here to good view pt (2km). Several woody walks around Dunkeld/Birnam – good leaflet from TIC. 2km along river is **Rumbling Bridge**, a deep gorge, & beyond it gr spots for swimming (1709/SWIMMING HOLES).          2KM CIRC XBIKE 1-A-1

**2030**
Map 7
**N19**

**Glenmore Forest Park** nr Aviemore Along from Coylumbridge (and adj Rothiemurchus) on rd to ski resort, the forest trail area centred on L Morlich (sandy beaches, good swimming, water sports). Visitor centre has maps of walk and bike trails and an activity programme.

**2031**
Map 10
**M24**

**Above The Pass Of Leny** Callander A walk through mixed forest (beech, oak, birch, pine) with gr Trossachs views. Start from main car park on A84 4km N of Callander (the Falls of Leny are on opp side of rd, 100m away) on path at back, to the left – path parallels rd at first (don't head straight up). Way-marked and boarded where marshy, the path divides after 1km to head further up to crest (4km return) or back down (2km). Another glorious walk is to the **Bracklinn falls** – signed off E end of Callander Main St; start by the golf course (1km. See also 1718/SUMMER PICNICS.). Also loop to the Craggs (adding another 2km).          2 OR 4KM CIRC XBIKE 1-A-1

**2032**
Map 10
**N22**

**Loch Tummel Walks** nr Pitlochry The mixed woodland N of L Tummel reached by the B8019 from Pitlochry to Rannoch. Visitor centre at Queen's View (1698/VIEWS) and walks in the Allean Forest which take in some historical sites (a restored farmstead, standing stones) start nearby (2-4km). There are many other walks in area and the Forest Enterprise brochure is worth following (available from VC and local TICs). (1664/LOCHS.)

**2033** **The New Galloway Forest** Huge area of forest & hill country with every
Map 11 type of trail incl part of S Upland Way from Bargrennan to Dalry (1997/LONG
**L30** WALKS). VCs at Kirroughtree (5km Newton Stewart) & Clatteringshaws L on the
'Queen's Way' (9km New Galloway). Glen & L Trool are v fine (1635/GLENS);
the 'Retreat Oakwood' nr Laurieston has 5km trails. Kitty's in New Galloway
has great cakes & tea (1449/TEAROOMS). There's a river pool on the Raiders' Rd
(1719/PICNICS). One could ramble on … Get the TIC brochure.

**2034** **Duff House** Banff Duff House is the major attraction around here
Map 8 (2259/PUBLIC GALLERIES), but if you've time it would be a pity to miss the wood-
**R17** ed policies & the meadows & riverscape of the Deveron. To the Br of Alvah
where you should be bound is about 7km return. See also GLEN & RIVER WALKS.

**2035** **Torrachilty Forest & Rogie Falls** nr Contin & Strathpeffer Enter by old br
Map 7 just o/side Contin on main A835 W to Ullapool or further along (4km) at
**L17** Rogie Falls car park. Shame to miss the falls (1651/WATERFALLS), but the woods
and gorge are pleasant enough if it's merely a stroll you need. Ben Wyvis further up the rd is the big challenge (1991/MUNROS).

**2036** **Abernethy Forest** nr Boat of Garten 3km from village off B970, but hard
Map 8 to miss because the famous ospreys are signposted from all over
**N19** (1765/BIRDS). Nevertheless this woodland reserve is a tranquil place among
native pinewoods around the loch with dells and trails. Many other birdies
twittering around your picnic. They don't dispose of the midges.

**2037** **Fochabers** on main A98 about 3km E of town are some excellent woody and
Map 8 winding walks around the glen and Whiteash Hill (2-5km). Further W on the
**Q17** **Moray Coast Culbin Forest** – head for Cloddymoss or Kentessack off A96
at Brodie Castle 12km E of Nairn. Acres of Sitka in sandy coastal forest.

# Where To Find Scots Pine

*Scots pine, with oak and birch etc, formed the gr Caledonian Forest which once cov-*
*ered most of Scotland. Native Scots pine is v different from the regimented rows of*
*pine trees we associate with forestry plantations and which now drape much of the*
*countryside. It is more like a deciduous tree with reddish bark and irregular foliage;*
*no two ever look the same. The remnants of the gr stands of pine are beautiful to*
*see, mystical and majestic, a joy to walk among and no less worthy of conservation*
*perhaps than a castle or a bird of prey. Here are some places you will find them:*

**Rothiemurchus Forest** 2025/WOODLAND WALKS.

**Glentanar** Royal Deeside Nr Ballater, 10-15km SW of Aboyne.

Around **Braemar** and **Grantown-On-Spey**.

**Strathyre** nr Callander S of village on rt of main rd after L Lubnaig.

**Achray Forest** nr Aberfoyle Some pine nr the Duke's Pass rd, the A821 to
L Katrine, and amongst the mixed woodland in the 'forest drive' to L Achray.

**Blackwood Of Rannoch** S of L Rannoch, 30km W of Pitlochry via Kinloch
Rannoch. Start from Carie, fair walk in. 250-year-old pines; an important site.

**Rowardennan** L Lomond End of the rd along E side of loch nr Ben Lomond.
Easily accessible pines nr the loch side, picnic sites etc.

Shores of **L Maree**, **L Torridon** and around **L Clair**, **Glen Torridon**. Both
nr the **Beinn Eighe National Nature Reserve** (1780/GREAT WILDLIFE
RESERVES). Visitor Centre on A832 N of Kinlochewe.

**Glen Affric** nr Drumnadrochit 1627/GLENS. Biggest remnant of the
Caledonian Forest in classic glen. Many strolls and hikes poss. Try Dog Falls
(on main rd) for Affric introduction.

*Native pinewoods aren't found S of Perthshire, but there are fine plantation*
*examples in southern Scotland at:*

**Glentress** nr Peebles 7km on A72 to Innerleithen. Mature forest up the
burn side, though surrounded by commercial forest.

**Shambellie Estate** nr Dumfries 1km from New Abbey beside A710 at the
Shambellie House, 100yds sign. Ancient stands of pine over the wall amongst
other glorious trees; this is like virgin woodland. Planted 1775–80. Magnificent.

# Coastal Walks

**2038**  ✓✓ **Kintra** Islay   On Bowmore-Pt Ellen rd take Oa t/off: then Kintra
Map 9   signed 7km. Park in old farmyard by campsite (1231/HIGHLAND CAMP-
**F26**   ING). A fabulous beach (1611/BEACHES) runs in opp direction & a notable golf
course behind it (2070/GOLF IN GREAT PLACES). This walk leads along N coast of
the Mull of Oa, an area of diverse beauty, sometimes pastoral, sometimes wild,
with a wonderful shoreline. Many gr picnic spots.   ANY KM XCIRC XBIKE 2-B-2

**2039**  ✓✓ **The Bullers Of Buchan** nr Peterhead   8km S of Peterhead on
Map 8   A975 rd to/from Cruden Bay. Park and walk 100m to cottages. To
**T18**   the N is the walk to Longhaven Nature Reserve, a continuation of the dramatic cliffs and more sea bird city. The Bullers is at start of walk, a sheer-
sided 'hole' 75m deep with an outlet to the sea thro a natural arch. Walk
round the edge of it, looking down on layers of birds (who might try to dive-
bomb you away from their nests); it's a wonder of nature on an awesome
coast. Take gr care (& a head for heights).

**2040**  ✓✓ **Cape Wrath & The Cliffs Of Clo Mor**   Britain's most NW point
Map 6   reached by ferry from 1km off the A838 4km S of Durness by Cape
**K12**   Wrath Hotel; a 10min crossing then 40min minibus ride to Cape. Ferry holds
12 and runs May-Sept (check TIC at Durness for times: 01971 511259). At 280m
Clo Mor are the highest cliffs in UK; 4km round trip from Cape. MoD range –
access may be restricted. In other direction, the 28km to Kinlochbervie is one
of Britain's most wild and wonderful coastal walks. Beaches incl Sandwood
(1609/BEACHES). While in this NW area: **Smoo Cave** 2km E of Durness.

**2041**   **Old Man Of Stoer** nr Lochinver   The easy, exhilarating walk to the dramat-
Map 6   ic 70km sandstone sea stack. Start from lighthouse off unclassified rd 14km
**J14**   N Lochinver. Park and follow sheep tracks; cliffs are high and steep. 7km
round trip; 2/3 hrs.          1-B-2

**2042**   **Rockcliffe to Kippford**   An easy stroll along the 'Scottish Riviera' through
Map 11   woodland nr the shore (2km) past the 'Mote of Mark' a Dark Age hill ft with
**N30**   views to Rough Island. The better cliff top walk is in the other direction to
Castlehillpoint. Good teashop in Rockcliffe (1469/TEARMS).

**2043**   **St Abbs Head**   Some of the most dramatic coastal scenery in S Scotland, scary
Map 10   in a wind, rhapsodic on a blue summer's day. Extensive wildlife reserve & trails
**S25**   through coastal hills & vales to cliffs. Cars can go as far as lighthouse, but best
to park at VC nr farm on St Abbs village rd 3km from A1107 to Eyemouth and
follow route (1778/WILDLIFE). V nice caff here.   5-10KM CIRC XBIKE 1-B-2

**2044**   **Singing Sands** Ardnamurchan   2km N of Acharacle, signed for Arvegaig.
Map 9   3km to Arvegaig & park before wooden bridge (gate prob locked). Cross
**H21**   wooden br, following track round side of Kentra Bay. Follow signs for
Gorteneorn, and walk through forest track and woodland to beach. As you
pound the sands they should 'sing' to you whilst you bathe in the the beau-
tiful views of Rum, Eigg, Muck and Skye (and just possibly the sea). Check at
TIC for directions and other walks booklet.   10KM RET XCIRC BIKE 1-B-1

**2045**   **East From Cullen On The Moray Coast**   This is the same walk mentioned
Map 8   with reference to Sunnyside (1607/BEACHES), a golden beach with a fabulous
**R17**   ruined castle (Findlater) that might be your destination. There's a track E along
from harbour. 2hrs return. Superb coastline.   8KM XCIRC XBIKE 1-A-1

**2046**   **Cromarty, The South Sutor**   The walk, known locally as 'The 100 Steps' tho'
Map 7   there are a few more than that, from Cromarty village (1595/COASTAL VILLAGES,
**M17**   1473/TEAROOMS, 1021/RESTAU) round the tip of the S promontory at the narrow
entrance to the Cromarty Firth. E of vill; coastal path hugs shoreline then
ascends thro' woodland to headland. Good bench! Go further to top car park
and viewpt panel. Return by rd. There may be dolphins! 5KM CIRC XBIKE 1-A-1

**2047**   **The Chain Walk** Elie   Unique and adventurous headland scramble at the W
Map 10   end of Elie (and Earlsferry), by golf course. Hand- and footholds carved into
**R24**   rock with chains to haul yourself up. Watch tide; don't go alone.   2-B-2

**2048**   **Cock of Arran** Lochranza   This round trip starts in the moors but descends
Map 9   to breathtaking coastal trail past some interesting spots (see 2315/FANTASTIC
**J26**   WALKS IN THE ISLANDS)! Gr for twitchers, ramblers & fossils (strong boots need-
ed)! Approx 8km (5hrs) from village. Take a picnic.   2-B-2

# SECTION 10

*Sports*

# Scotland's Great Golf Courses

*Those listed open to non-members and available to visitors (incl women) at most times, unless otherwise stated. Handicap certificates may be required.*

## AYRSHIRE (MAP 9)

**2049**
**K28** ✓ ✓ ✓ **Turnberry** 01655 334032. Ailsa (championship) and Arran. Sometimes poss by application. Otherwise you must stay at hotel. (795/AYRSHIRE HOTELS.) Superb. Golf academy a gr place to learn.

**2050**
**K27** ✓ ✓ **Royal Old Course** Troon V difficult to get on. No wimmen. Staying at Marine Highland Hotel (01292 314444) helps. Easier is **The Portland Course** Across rd from Royal. Both 01292 311555. And 802/AYRSHIRE HOTELS for the adj Piersland House Hotel.

**2051**
**K27** ✓ **Glasgow Gailes/Western Gailes** 0141 942 2011/01294 311649. Superb links courses next to one another, 5km S of Irvine off A78.

**2052**
**L27** **Old Prestwick** 01292 477404. Original home of the Open and 'every challenge you'd wish to meet'. Hotels opp cost less than a round. North Beach best (2329/AYR). Unlikely to get on w/ends (Sat members only).

## EAST LOTHIAN (MAP 10)

*Note: There is a gr booklet available at the local TIC, entitled 'Golf in East Lothian'.*

**2053**
**R25** ✓ ✓ **Gullane No.1** 01620 842255. One of 3 varied courses surrounding charming village on links and within driving distance (35km) of Edin. Muirfield is nearby, but you need intro. Gullane is okay most days except Sat/Sun. (Handicap required for no.1 only – under 24 men, 30 ladies.) No.3 best for beginners. Visitor centre acts as clubhouse for non-members on nos. 2/3. Clubhouse for members/no.1 players only.

**2054**
**R25** ✓ ✓ **North Berwick East & West** E (officially the Glen Golf Club) has stunning views. A superb cliff-top course and is not too long, 01620 892726. W more taxing (esp the classic 'Redan') used for Open qualifying; a v fine links. Also has 9-hole kids' course, 01620 892135.

**2055**
**Q25** **Musselburgh Links** The original home of golf (really: golf recorded here in 1672), but this local authority-run 9-hole links is not exactly top turf and is enclosed by Musselburgh Racecourse. Nostalgia still appeals though. 0131 665 5438. **Royal Musselburgh** nearby compensates. It dates to 1774, fifth-oldest in Scotland. Busy early mornings and Fri-Sun, 01875 810139.

## NORTH EAST

**2056**
**Map 10**
**R23** ✓ ✓ **Carnoustie** 01241 853789. 3 good links courses; even poss (with handicap cert) to get on the championship course (though w/ends difficult). Every hole has character. Buddon Links is cheaper and rel quiet. Combination tickets available. A well-managed and accessible course, increasingly a golfing must.

**2057**
**Map 8**
**T19** ✓ **Murcar** Aberdeen 01224 704354. Getting on Royal Aber Course is difficult for most people, but Murcar is a testing alternative, a seaside course 6km N of centre off Peterhead rd signed at r/bout after Exhibition Centre. Handicap cert needed. Other municipal courses incl charming 9-hole at Hazlehead (part of excl 3-course complex).

**2058**
**Map 8**
**T18** ✓ **Cruden Bay** nr Peterhead 01779 812285. On A975 40km N of Aber. Designed by Tom Simpson and ranked in UK top 50, a spectacular links course with the intangible aura of bygone days. Quirky holes epitomise old-fashioned style. W/ends difficult to get on.

**2059**
**Map 7**
**N17** ✓ **Nairn** 01667 452787. Traditional seaside links course and one of the easiest championship courses to get on. Good clubhouse, friendly folk. Nairn Dunbar on other side of town also has good links. Hand cert reqd.

**2060**
**Map 6**
**N16** ✓ **Royal Dornoch** 01862 810219. Sutherland championship course laid out by Tom Morris in 1877. Recently declared 5th-best course in the world outside the US, but not busy or incessantly pounded. No poor holes.

Stimulating sequences. Probably the most northerly gr golf course in the world – and not impossible to get on. Sister course the **Struie** also a treat.

## FIFE (MAP 10)

**2061**
**R23**
✓ ✓ ✓ **St Andrews** 01334 466666. The home and Mecca of golf, v much part of the town (2340/HOLIDAY CENTRES) and probably the largest golf complex in Europe. Old Course most central, celebrated. Application by ballot the day before (handicap cert needed). For Jubilee (1897, upgraded 1989) and Eden (1914, laid out by Harry S. Holt paying homage to the Old with large, sloping greens), apply the day before. New Course (1895, some rate the best) easiest access. Less demanding are the new Strathtyrum and Balgove (upgraded 9-hole for beginners) courses. All 6 courses contiguous and 'in town'; the Dukes Course (part of Old Course Hotel) 3km away is a gr alternative to the links. Reservations (and ballot) 01334 466666. A whole lot of golf to be had – get your money out!

**2062**
**R24**
✓ **Kingsbarns** 01334 460860. Betw St Andrews & Crail. One of Fife's newest courses but already hailed as one of its best. Beautiful location – a secret coast & Cammo House grounds. Not chp.

**2063**
**Q24**
✓ **Ladybank** 01337 830814. Best inland course in Fife; Tom Morris-designed again. V well kept and organised. Good facs. Tree-lined and picturesque.

**2064**
**R24**
**Elie** Book 01333 330895. Splendid open links maintained in top condition; can be windswept. The starter has his famous periscope and may be watching you. Adj 9-hole course, often busy with kids, is fun. (01333 330955)

**2065**
**R24**
**Crail** 01333 450686. Balcomie Links originally designed by the legendary Tom Morris, or Craighead Links new sweeping course. All holes in sight of sea. Not exp; easy to get on.

**2066**
**Q24**
**Lundin Links** 01333 320202/ladies 320832. Challenging seaside course used as Open qualifier. Some devious contourings. There is a separate course for women. (01333 320832)

## ELSEWHERE

**2067**
Map 10
**N24**
✓ ✓ ✓ **Gleneagles** 0800 704705. Legendary golf the mainstay of resort complex in perfect Perthshire (hotel 01764 662231 report: 1127/CO-HOUSE HOTELS). 3 courses incl PGA centenary which will host Ryder Cup in 2014. No handicap certs reqd.

**2068**
Map 9
**L24**
✓ ✓ **Loch Lomond Golf Club** Luss 01436 655555. On A82 1km from conservation village of Luss. Exclusive American-owned club; membership expensive & the list's closed. We can buy a cheaper season ticket to see the annual Scottish Open (July; info: 01436 655559); but no access to plebs to clubhouse. 18 holes of scenic golf by the Loch. This is golfing for gold.

**2069**
Map 10
**S27**
✓ ✓ **Roxburghe Hotel Golf Course** nr Kelso 01573 450331. Only championship course in the Borders. Designed by Dave Thomas along banks of R Teviot. Part of the Floors Castle estate. Open non-res. Fairways bar/brasserie clubhouse. Report: 847/BORDER HOTELS.

# Good Golf Courses In Great Places

*All open to women, non-members and inexpert players.*

**2070**
Map 9
**F26**
✓ **Machrie** 01496 302310. Isle of Islay. 7km Pt Ellen. Worth going to Islay (BA's airstrip adj course or Calmac ferry from Kennacraig nr Tarbert) just for the golf. The Machrie (Golf) Hotel is sparse but convenient. Old-fashioned course to be played by feel and instinct. Splendid, sometimes windy isolation with a warm bar and restau at the end of it. The notorious 17th, 'Iffrin' (it means Hell), vortex shaped from the dune system of marram and close-cropped grass, is one of many gr holes. 18.

**2071**
Map 9
**G28**
✓ **Macrihanish** 01586 810213. By Campbeltown (10km). Amongst the dunes and links of the glorious 8km stretch of the Machrihanish Beach (1608/BEACHES). The Atlantic provides thunderous applause for your triumphs over a challenging course. 9/18.

**2072**   ✓ **Southerness** Solway Firth  01387 880677. 25km S of Dumfries by
Map 11   A710. A championship course on links on the silt flats of the Firth.
**N30**  Despite its prestige, visitors do get on. Start times avail 10-12pm and 2-4pm.
There are few courses as good as this at this price (under £50 a round). Under
the wide Solway sky, it's pure – southerness. 18.

**2073**   ✓ **Rosemount** Blairgowrie  01250 872622. Off A93, S of Blairgowrie. An
Map 10   excellent, pampered and well-managed course in the middle of green
**P22**  Perthshire, an alternative perhaps to Gleneagles, being much easier to get on
(most days) and rather cheaper (though not at w/ends). 18.

**2074**   ✓ **Boat Of Garten**  01479 831282. Challenging, picturesque course in town
Map 8   where ospreys have been known to wheel overhead. Has been called the
**N19**  'Gleneagles of the North'; certainly best around, tho not for novices. 18.

**2075**   ✓ **Tain & Brora**  01862 892314 & 01408 621911. 2 northern courses that
Map 6   are a delight to play on. Tain designed by Tom Morris in 1890. Brora
**M16**  stunning with good clubhouse & coos on the course. With Royal Dornoch
(above), they're a roving-golfer must.

**2076**  **Glencruitten** Oban  01631 562868. Picturesque course on the edge of
Map 9  town. Head S (A816) from Argyll Sq, bearing left at church. Course is signed.
**H23**  Quite tricky with many blind holes. Can get busy, so phone first. 18.

**2077**  **Gairloch**  01445 712407. Just as you come into town from the S on A832, it
Map 7  looks over the bay and down to a perfect, pink, sandy beach. Small clubhouse
**H16**  with honesty box out of hrs. Not the world's most agonising course; in fact,
on a clear day with views to Skye, you can forget agonising over anything. 9.

**2078**  **Harris Golf Club** Scarista, Isle Of Harris  01859 502331 (the captain, but no
Map 5  need to phone). Just turn up on the rd betw Tarbert and Rodel and leave £10
**E16**  in the box. First tee commands one of the gr views in golf and throughout
this basic, but testing course, you are looking out to sea over Scarista beach
(1614/BEACHES) and bay. Sunset may put you off your swing.

**2079**  **New Galloway** Local course on S edge of this fine wee toon. Almost all on a
Map 11  slope but affording gr views of L Ken & the Galloway Forest behind. No bunkers
**M29**  and only 9 short holes, but exhilarating play. Easy on, except Sun. Just turn up.

**2080**  **Minto** Denholm  01450 870220. 9km E Hawick. Spacious parkland in Teviot
Map 10  valley. Best holes 3rd, 12th & 16th. **Vertish** Hill Hawick  01450 372293. A
**R28**  more challenging hill course. Both among the best in Borders. 18. Best holes
2nd & 18th. An excl guide to all the courses in the Borders in avail from TICs
– 'Freedom of the Fairways'.

**2081**  **Taymouth Castle** Kenmore  01887 830228. Spacious green acres around
Map 10  the enigmatic empty hulk of the castle. Well-tended and organised course
**M22**  betw A827 to Aberfeldy and the river. Inexp, and guests at the Kenmore Hotel
(920/PERTHSHIRE HOTELS) get special rate. 18.

**2082**  **Gifford**  01620 810267. Dinky inland course on the edge of a dinky village,
Map 10  bypassed by the queue for the big E Lothian courses and a guarded secret
**R26**  among the regulars. Generally ok, but phone starter (above) for avail. 9.

**2083**  **Strathpeffer**  01997 421011. V hilly (and we do mean hilly) course full of
Map 7  character and with exhilarating Highland views. Small-town friendliness. You
**L17**  are playing up there with the gods and some other old codgers. 18.

**2084**  **Elgin**  01343 542338. 1km from town on A941 Perth rd. Many memorable
Map 8  holes on moorland/parkland course in an area where links may lure you to
**P17**  the coast (Nairn, Lossiemouth). 18.

**2085**  **Durness**  01971 511364. The most N golf course on mainland UK, on the wild
Map 6  headland by Balnakeil Bay, looking over to Faraid Head. The last hole is 'over
**L12**  the sea'. Only open since 1988, it's already got cult status. 2km W Durness.

**2086**  **Rothesay**  01700 503554. Sloping course with breathtaking views of Clyde.
Map 9  Visitors welcome. What could be finer than taking the train from Glas to
**J26**  Wemyss Bay for the ferry over (5/FAVOURITE JOURNEYS) and 18 holes. Finish up
with fish 'n' chips at the W End (1421/FISH AND CHIPS) on the way home.

**2087**  **Traigh** Arisaig  01687 450337. A830 Ft William-Mallaig rd, 2km N Arisaig.
Map 7  Pronounced 'try'- and you may want to. The islands are set out like stones in
**H20**  the sea around you and there are 9 hilly holes of fun.

# Best Of The Skiing

*In a good yr the Scottish ski season can extend from Dec (or even Nov) till the 'lambing snow' of late April. And on a good day it can be as exhilarating as anywhere in Europe. Here's a summary (**distances in kilometres**):*

| | GLENSHEE | CAIRNGORM | NEVIS RANGE | GLENCOE | THE LECHT |
|---|---|---|---|---|---|
| **DIST/EDIN** | 130 | 215 | 215 | 165 | 200 |
| **DIST/GLAS** | 170 | 235 | 200 | 150 | 160 |
| **NR CENTRE** | Perth 65 | Inverness 45 | Ft Will 10 | FT Will 40 | Aberdeen 95 |
| **NR TOWN** | Braemar 20 | Aviemore 15 | Ft Will 10 | Ballachul 20 | Tomintoul 11 |
| **NO OF RUNS** | | 38 | 19 | 35 | 19    21 |
| **EASY** | 10 | 3 | 7 | 4 | 7 |
| **INTERMED** | 13 | 6 | 12 | 6 | 7 |
| **DIFFICULT** | 13 | 9 | 11 | 7 | 6 |
| **ADVANCED** | 2 | 1 | 5 | 2 | 1 |
| **UPLIFTS** | 24 | 15 | 11 | 7 | 15 |
| **CAFÉS** | 3 | 2 | 2 + units | 2 | 1 + 1 unit |
| **GOOD FOR** | *Size* *Access from rd* *Views Glas Maol* *2 distinct areas* *Snowboarding* | *Size* *Non-skiing* *Views* *Intermediate* *Snowboarding* | *Uplift* *Access* *Views/Sunsets* *Ski School* *Café* | *Fewer crowds* *Nr road* *Views* *Most alpine* | *Fewer crowds* *Nr road* *Families* *Beginners* |

## 2088 GLENSHEE

Map 10
P21

**Base Station** 013397 41320. **School** 01250 885216 or 0870 443 0253 or 01339 741320.

### WHERE TO STAY

**Dalmunzie House Hotel** 01250 885224. 9km S. Country house. 9-hole golf adj. Family-run (recent change of ownership). 924/PERTHSHIRE HOTELS.
MED.EX

**Bridge Of Cally Hotel** 01250 886231. 36km S (1195/INNS). **Glenisla, Kirkton Of Glenisla** 01575 582223. 32km SE. INX

**Spittal Of Glenshee** 01250 885215. 8km S. Cheap 'n' cheerful. MED.INX

### WHERE TO EAT

**Cargill's Bistro Blairgowrie** 01250 876735 (935/PERTHSHIRE EATS).

**Dalmunzie/Bridge Of Cally Hotel/Glenisla** *as above.*

### APRÈS-SKI

**Blackwater Inn** 17km S on main rd. A good all-round pub. Occasional live music.

### SKI HIRE

**Base station** 01339 741320. **Cairnwell Ski School** 08704 430253 at Spittal of Glenshee.

## 2089 CAIRNGORM

Map 8
N19

**Base Station** 01479 861261. **School** 01479 810296. **Hire** 01479 811917.

### WHERE TO STAY

**Corrour House** 01479 810220. 11km W (1140/COUNTRY-HO HOTELS). INX

**Aviemore Bunkhouse** 01479 811181 (1158/HOSTELS).

**Hilton Coylumbridge Hotel** 01479 810661. 10km W. Nearest and best of modern Aviemore hotels. 2 pools/sauna. Ski hire. Okay restau. Comfort when you need it. MED.EX

**Cairngorm** Aviemore 01479 810630. Main st of main town. Busy bar. Rms not unreasonably priced and lots of them. INX

**The Cross** Kingussie 01540 661166. (977/HIGHLANDS HOTELS) . MED.INX

## WHERE TO EAT

**The Cross** Kingussie 01540 661166. See above.

**The Einich** Coylumbridge 01479 812334 (1025/INEXP HIGHLANDS RESTAUS).

**The Boathouse** Kincraig 01540 651394 (1027/INEXP HIGHLANDS RESTAUS).

**The Old Bridge Inn** Aviemore Welcoming, good atmos (1358/GASTROPUBS).

## Après-SKI

**The Winking Owl** Aviemore At end of main st. Owl's Nest.

●●●●●●●●●●●●●●●●●●●●●●●●●●●●●●●●●●●●●●●●●●●●●●●●●●●●●●●●●●●●●●●●

## 2090 THE NEVIS RANGE/AONACH MOR

Map 9
**K21** **Base Station** 01397 705825. **School** 01397 705825.

## WHERE TO EAT & STAY

See **Fort William**, *p. 311*

## APRÈS-SKI

No pub in immediate vicinity. Nearest all-in ski centre is **Nevis Sport, Fort William** 01397 704921. Bar (side entrance) till midnight. Self-serve café all day till 5pm (4.30pm Sun). Bookshop and extensive ski/outdoor shop on ground floor. Also ski hire.

## SKI HIRE

As above (01397 704921), also **Ellis Brigham** (01397 706220), and base stn.

●●●●●●●●●●●●●●●●●●●●●●●●●●●●●●●●●●●●●●●●●●●●●●●●●●●●●●●●●●●●●●●●

## 2091 GLENCOE

Map 9
**J21** **Base Station** 01855 851226. **School** 01855 851226.

## WHERE TO EAT & STAY

See **Fort William**, *p. 311*, and also:

**Isles Of Glencoe Hotel** Ballachulish 01855 811602. Modern development leisure centre incl pool. Good touring base (1142/KIDS).

**Clachaig Inn** Glencoe 01855 811 252. Famous 'outdoor inn' for walkers, climbers etc with pub (1326/BLOODY GOOD PUBS), pub food and inexp accom.

**Kingshouse Hotel** 01855 851259. The classic travellers' inn 1km from A82 through Glen and nr slopes (8km). Pub with food/whisky. Inexp rms but v basic, esp bunks.

## APRÈS-SKI

As above, especially Clachaig Inn and Kingshouse.

## SKI HIRE

At base stn.

●●●●●●●●●●●●●●●●●●●●●●●●●●●●●●●●●●●●●●●●●●●●●●●●●●●●●●●●●●●●●●●●

## 2092 THE LECHT

Map 8
**Q19** **Base Station** 019756 51440. **School** 019756 51412.

## WHERE TO STAY

Nearest town (28km S) with big choice of hotels is Ballater. But also:

**Glenavon Hotel** TomintouL 01807 580218. On sq in Tomintoul, the nearest town. The most ski- and hiking-friendly place in the zone. INX

**Richmond Arms Hotel** TomintouL 01807 580777. On sq. Trad hotel, log fires, local beers. A v good prospect. 24 rms. MED.INX

### WHERE TO EAT

**The Clockhouse** Tomintoul 01807 580378. Main St. Good rep. INX

**Green Inn** Ballater 01339 755701. Also has rms. 960/NE RESTAUS. MED.EXP

**Station Restaurant** Ballater 01339 755050. Converted from old station. Daytime only.

**Gordon Hotel** TomintouL 01807 580206. The local hotel with the most aspirational menu. INX

### APRÈS-SKI

**Glenavon Hotel** TomintouL 01807 580218. Good large bar for skiers, walkers (S end of Speyside Way is here) and locals.

**Allargue Hotel** Cockbridge 019756 51410. On rd S to Ballater 5km from slopes and o/look Corgarff Castle and the trickle of the R Don. Rms also.

### SKI HIRE

At base stn.

# The Best Sledging Places

*Locals will know where the best slopes are. Here's my suggestions for* EDIN/GLAS:

## EDINBURGH

2093 **The Braid Hills** The connoisseur's choice, you sledge down friendly and not-too-challenging slopes in a crowded L S Lowry landscape that you will remember long after the thaw. Off Braid Hills Drive at the golf course. Can walk in via Blackford Glen Rd. **Corstorphine Hill** Gentle broad slope with woodland at top and trails (412/CITY WALKS) and a busy rd at the bottom. App via Clermiston Rd off Queensferry Rd. **Queen's Park** The lesser slopes that skirt Arthur's Seat, and further in around Hunter's Bog for the more adventurous or less sociable sledger.

## GLASGOW

2094 **Kelvingrove Park** At Park Terr side. No long runs but a winter wonderland when the rime's in the trees. **Gartnavel Hospital Grounds** In W end (Hyndland) off Gr Western Rd. You can play safe sledging into the playing field, or more adventurously through the woodlands. **Queen's View** On A809 N of Bearsden 20km from centre. A v popular walk (734/BEST VIEWS) is also a gr place to sledge. Variable slopes off the main path. The Highlands can be seen on a clear day. **Ruchill Park** In N of city (735/BEST VIEWS) and **Queen's Park** in S.

# The Best Cycling

## EASY CYCLING

2095 **Speyside Way Craigellachie-Ballindalloch** The cycling part of the Way
Map 8 (1998/LONG WALKS), with gr views; flat and no cars. Goes past distilleries. Circ
Q18 by ret on minor rds. Start: Craigellachie by rangers' office. 20KM CAN BE CIRC

2096 **Forth & Clyde Canal Glasgow–Falkirk Wheel** E out of the city, urban at
Map 10 first then nice in the Kelvin Valley; Kilsyth Hills to the N. Falkirk Wheel must be seen (4/ATTRACTIONS) Start: The Maryhill Locks, Maryhill Rd. 55KM

2097 **Glentrool** nr Newton Stewart Two main routes from VC (1662/LOCHS,
Map 11 1939/MARY, CHARLIE & BOB). Deep in the forest and well signed. Briefly joins
L29 public rd. Start: Glentrool VC off A714. 15KM CAN BE CIRC

2098 **Edinburgh Trails** Edinburgh streets can be a nightmare for cyclists & there's lots of uphill graft. But there is a vast network of cycle & towpaths esp N of the New Town. Another gd run is to Balerno from Union Canal towpath in lower Gilmore Place. End at Balerno High School. 12KM/VARIOUS CIRC

**2099** **The Trossachs** nr Aberfoyle & Callander  Many low-level lochside trails.
Map 10  Consult TICs. Nice run is Loch Ard Circle from Aberfoyle going W (signed
Inversnade Scenic Route).                                                    11KM CAN BE CIRC

**2100** **Loch An Eilean** nr Aviemore  Lots of bike tracks here in the Rothiemurchus
Map 8  Forrest. This one goes past one of Scotland's most beautiful lochs
**N19**  (1433/LOCHS) and you can go further to Loch Insh via Feshiebridge and around
Glen Feshie. Prob best to get a route leaflet at VC (loch car park and
Coylumbridge). Start: signed from B970 at Coylumbridge.           20KM CIRC

**2101** **Cumbrae**  Take ferry from Largs to beautiful Cumbrae Island (1431/CAFÉS).
Map 9  Four or five routes around the island. One a stiff pull to a gr viewpoint. Others
**K26**  stick to sea level. Consult leaflet from TIC. All rds quiet.

## MOUNTAIN BIKING

**2102**  ✓ ✓ **7 Stanes, Borders & SW**  Hugely ambitious and hugely popular
network of bike trails in S of Scotland, some still under construction. Include **Glentress** (see below), **Newcastleton**, **Forest of Ae**,
**Dalbeattie**, **Maybie**, **Glentrool** (see above), and **Kirroughtree**. Routes at
all levels. Many challenges. Good signage and information available from
local TICs and 7stanes.gov.uk

**2103**  ✓ ✓ **Glentress Forest nr Peebles**  Specially built mt-bike trails. Well
Map 10  signed and well used in this hugely popular national cycling centre.
**Q27**  Gr café (1433/CAFÉS).Trails for all levels, plenty of flowing descents and drops.
7 Stanes cross-country route also starts nr by at Traqair.

**2104** **Clatteringshaws**  Nr **Glentrool** (see above). Various routes around
Map 11  Clatteringshaws Loch in the Galloway Forest and Hills. Most are easy, but
**M29**  some serious climbs and descents. VC has tearoom. Routes under construc-
tion as part of 7 Stanes Project.                                    25KM CIRC

**2105** **Glen Tanner Deeside**  Good way to encounter this beautiful glen in the
Map 8  shadow of Mount Keen. Quite difficult in places. Start: Tombae on the B976
**Q20**  opp jnct of A97 & A93.                                                25KM CIRC

**2106** **Great Glen, Fort William-Loch Lochy**  Easy at first on the Caledonian
Map 7  Canal towpath. Later it gets hilly with long climbs. Gr views. Start Neptune's
Staircase at Banavie nr Fort William.                                 NOT CIRC

**2107** **Perthshire & Angus, Glenfernate-Blair Atholl**  Beautiful Highland trail
Map 10  that takes in forests, lochs and Glen Tilt (2006/GLEN WALKS). Mainly rough
track. Follow directions from TIC leaflets. Start: On the A924 14km E of
Pitlochrie, 500m E of school.                                         25KM CIRC

# The Best Leisure Centres

**2108**  ✓ **Perth Leisure Pool**  01738 635454. A perfect example of the mega
Map 10  successful water-based leisure-land. Large, shaped pool with o/side
**P23**  section (open also in winter, when it's even more of a novelty); 2 flumes, 'wild
water channel', whirlpools etc. 25m 'training' pool for lengths (sessions).
Outdoor kids' area. Excellent facility. Daily 10am-10pm.

**2109**  ✓ **Aquadome Inverness**  01463 667500. Inverness's all-weather attrac-
Map 7  tion. Leisure waters; incl 3 flumes, wave machine and toddler area. Huge
**M18**  competition pool for serious swimming and luxurious health suites; mas-
sages, hydrotherapy and (ladies) that essential bikini line wax. All in all, a bigger splash. Mon-Fri 7.30am-10pm, Sat-Sun until 5pm.

**2110**  ✓ **Dunbar Pool**  01368 865456. Model of its kind, o/look old harbour
Map 10  (where folks used to swim on a summer's day) and castle ruins. Cool,
**R25**  modern design amidst the warm red sandstone. Flumes and wave machine
that mimics the sea o/side; lengths just possible in betw (though it's often v
crowded). Phone for opening hours.

**2111** **Magnum Centre Irvine**  01294 278381. From Irvine's throughway system,
Map 9  follow signs for Harbourside, then Magnum. Big shed still unalluring and
**K27**  looking rather tatty – well... established! This phenomenally successful plea-
suredrome provides every diversion from the monotony of my
namesake o/side. From soothing bowls to frenetic skating, pools (in season),
cafés, courses, you name it. Secrete endorphins and other hormones.

**2112** **The Time Capsule** Monklands 01236 449572. They say Monklands, but
Map 10 where you are going is downtown Coatbridge about 15km from Glas via M8.
**M26** Known rather meanly as the 'Tim Capture' (local joke – you don't want to
know!). Leisure (and 25m) pool and (refurbed) ice-rink. Even if you haven't
been swimming for yrs, this is the sort of place you force the flab into the
swimsuit. Cafés and view areas. Facs of the clean-up-your-act variety (e.g.
squash, health suite). 6.30am-9pm.

**2113** **Dollan Aqua Centre** Town Centre Park, East Kilbride 01355 260000. An
Map 10 excl family leisure centre. 50m pool, fitness facs, soft play area and
**M26** Scotland's first interactive flume, (aquatic pin ball machine with you as the
ball!) – there had to be a twist. Mon, Wed, Fri 7.30am-10pm; Tue, Thur 8am-
10pm; Sat & Sun 8am-5pm.

**2114** **Scotstoun Leisure Centre** 0141 959 4000. Clydeside expressway then
Map 2 A814, rt at Victoria Park lights, first left after r/about. Danes Drive. If 'moder-
**xA4** nity is suburban' this is state of the art. 10 lane pool, sports halls, health
suite, dance studio and gym. Outdoor footie and tennis – it's enormous.
Mon, Wed, Fri 7.30am-10pm, Tue & Sun 9am, Thu 10am, Sat 9am-5pm.

**2115** **East Sands Leisure Centre** St Andrews 01334 476506. From S St take rd
Map 10 for Crail then follow signs. About 2km from centre. Bright and colourful cen-
**R23** tre o/look the E Sands, the less celebrated beach of St Andrews. Mainly a fairly conventional pool with 25m lane area as well as 50m water slide, toddlers'
pool etc. Also 2 squash courts, gym with Pulsestar machines, 'remedial
suite', bar and café. 7 days. Hrs vary.

**2116** **Beacon Leisure Centre** Burntisland 01592 872211. On the front of quiet-
Map 10 ly-getting-on with-it Fife town nr Kirkcaldy. Family fun pool centre with
**P25** 'landmark' beacon thing and external flume tubes. It does work. Loadsa kids
and 'waves' do come. Latest swimming in area (9.30pm, but check). 7 days.

**2117** **Beach Leisure Centre** Aberdeen 01224 655401. Beach Esplanade across
Map 8 rd from beach itself. Multisports facility with bars and cafés. 'Leisure' Pool
**T19** isn't much use for swimming (Aber has many others, 2126/SWIMMING POOLS)
but it's fun for kids with flumes etc. Lynx Ice Arena is adj for skating, curling,
ice hockey. O/side is the long long beach and the N Sea. Call for times.

# The Best Swimming Pools
# & Sports Centres

*For* Edinburgh, *see p. 70; for* Glasgow, *see p. 109. And see* Leisure Centres, *p
266.*

**2118** ✔ **Stonehaven Outdoor Pool** Stonehaven The 'Friends of Stonehaven
Map 10 Outdoor Pool' won the day (eat your hearts out N Berwick) and they've
**S20** saved a gr pool that goes from length to strength. Fabulous 1930s Olympic-
sized heated salt-water pool. There are midnight swims in midsummer most
Wednesdays (is that cool, or what?). June-Aug only: 10am-7.30pm (10-6pm
w/ends). Heated saltwater heaven.

**2119** ✔ **Gourock Bathing Pool** 01475 631561. The only other open-air (prop-
Map 9 er) pool in Scotland that's still open! On coast rd S of town centre 45km
**K25** from central Glas. 1950s-style leisure. Heated, so it doesn't need to be a
scorcher (brilliant, but choc-a-block when it is). Open May-early Sep weekdays until 8pm.

**2120** ✔ **The Waterfront** Greenock 01475 797979. Easily spotted at the water-
Map 9 front at Customhouse Way – vast building resembling a modernist whale
**K25** carcass; a rather groovy one at that. Big leisure pool, proper swim pool, 65m
flume, ice rink, gym and more. Undeniably fun, by the way. Daily AYR. Hrs
vary, phone to check.

**2121** ✔ **Carnegie Centre** Dunfermline 01383 314200. Pilmuir St. Excellent all-
Map 10 round sports centre with many courses and classes. 2 pools (ozone-
**P25** treated), 25m, and kids' pool. Lane swimming lunch time and evenings.
Authentic Turkish and Aeretone Suite with men's, women's and mixed ses-
sions. Large gym with Pre-cor stations etc. Badminton, squash, aerobic
classes. Usually open till 9pm (including pool), but check. Keeping
Dunfermline fitter then most of us.

**2122**
Map 2
**xF1**
✓ **The Leisuredrome** Bishopbriggs 0141 772 6391. 147 Balmuildy Rd. At the N edge of Glas, best reached by car or 1km walk from stn; adj Forth and Clyde Canal walkway (724/CITY WALKS). Large, modern, efficient with 25m pool, multi gym, sauna, games hall, café etc. Mon-Fri 9am-10/10.30pm.

**2123**
Map 10
**N25**
✓ **Linlithgow Pool** 01506 846358. On edge of pleasant town off rd to Lanark. Modern light and airy sports centre with sauna and steam room at the pool side and W Lothian outside the windows. Excellent community facility, well designed and laid out. All towns should enjoy this quality of life. Daily till 9pm, gym 10pm.

**2124**
Map 6
**K15**
✓ **Lochbroom Leisure Centre** Ullapool 01854 612884. 2 streets back from waterfront, but central. Games hall & v nice pool, easy to get in & out, tiny sauna. Small-town friendly atmos. 7 days till 8pm (Sat/Sun 6pm).

**2125**
Map 10
**R27**
**Galashiels Pool** 01896 752154. An award-winning pool in the Central Borders on the edge of parkland with picture windows bringing the outside in. No leisurama nonsense, just a good deck-level pool (25m) (Teviotdale Leisure Centre). Modern pool in Hawick also good. Phone for opening hrs.

**2126**
Map 8
**T19**
**Aberdeen Baths** 01224 587920. City well served with swimming pools. 3 in suburbs are not esp easy to find, though Hazlehead (01224 310062) is signed from inner ring road to W of centre. Only open to public from 6pm weekdays, all day w/ends. Bon Accord Baths are a fine example of a municipal pool; recently refurbished, they're centrally situated behind the W end of Union St. Annie Lennox learned to swim here. The newer Beach Leisure Centre has just about thought of everything (2117/LEISURE CENTRES). Hrs vary.

**2127**
Map 9
**F26**
**MacTaggart Centre** Bowmore, Islay 01496 810767. Eco-friendly pool (heated by adj distillery) o/look bay. Interesting whisky cask shaped ceiling and good fitness suite. Laundry facs. Cl Mon.

# The Best Water Sports Centres

**2128**
Map 10
**R24**
✓ **Elie Watersports** Elie 01333 330962/077966 84532 (day) 330942 (night). Gr beach location in totally charming wee town where there's enough going on to occupy non-watersporters. Easy lagoon for first timers and open season for non-experienced users. Wind-surfers, kayaks, water-ski. Also mt bikes and inflatable 'biscuits'. (894/896/FIFE HOTELS, 1360/GASTROPUBS, 2064/GREAT GOLF).

**2129**
Map 9
**J22**
✓ **Linnhe Marine** 01631 730401 or 07721 503981. Lettershuna, Port Appin. 32km N of Oban on A828 nr Portnacroish. Established, personally run business in a fine sheltered spot for learning and ploutering. They almost guarantee to get you windsurfing over to the island in 2hrs. Individual or group instruction. Wayfarers, Luggers and fishing-boats. Moorings. Castle Stalker and Lismore are just round the corner, seals & porpoises abound; the joy of sailing. May-Sept. 9am-6pm.

**2130**
Map 9
**K26**
✓ **Scottish National Watersports Centre** Cumbrae 01475 530757. Ferry from Largs (centre nr ferry terminal so 5km Millport) then learn all about how to pilot things that float. You need to book – call them, then bob about 'doon the watter'. Gr range of courses. 2-bunkrm accomm avail.

**2131**
Map 10
**P25**
✓ **Port Edgar** South Queensferry 0131 331 3330. At end of village, under and beyond the Forth Road Br. Major marina and water sports centre. Berth your boat, hire dinghies (big range). Big tuition programme for kids & adults incl canoes. Home to Port Edgar yacht club.

**2132**
Map 10
**M26**
✓ **Strathclyde Park** 01698 266155. Major water sports centre 15km SE of Glas and easily reached from most of Central Scotland via M8 or M74 (jnct 5 or 6). 200-acre loch and centre with instruction on sailing, canoeing, windsurfing, rowing, water-skiing and hire facs for canoes, Lasers and Wayfarers, windsurfers and trimarans. Call booking office for sessions and times.

**2133**
Map 7
**N19**
✓ **Loch Insh Watersports** Kincraig 01540 651272. On B970, 2km from Kincraig towards Kingussie and the A9. Marvellous loch side site launching from gently sloping dinky beach into shallow forgiving waters of L Insh. Hire of canoes, dinghies (Mirrors, Toppers, Lasers, Wayfarers) and windsurfers as well as rowing boats; river trips. An idyllic place to learn. Watch the

others and the sunset from the balcony restau above (1089/INEXP HIGHLAND RESTAUS). Sports 9.30am-5.30pm, Apr-Oct.

**2134**
Map 7
**N19**
✓ **Loch Morlich Watersports** nr Aviemore 01479 861221. By Glenmore Forest Park, part of the plethora of outdoor activities hereabouts (skiing, walking etc). This is the loch you see from Cairngorm and just as picturesque from the woody shore. Canoes/kayaks/rowing boats and dinghies (Wayfarers, Toppers, Optimists) with instruction in everything. Evening hire poss. Good campsite adj (1241/CAMPING WITH KIDS).

**2135**
Map 10
**M22**
✓ **Croft-Na-Caber** nr Kenmore, Loch Tay 01887 830588. S side of loch, 2km from village. Purpose-built water sports centre with instruction and hire of windsurfers, canoes, kayaks, dinghies, motor boats as well as water-skiing, river rafting (down the Tay from Aberfeldy to white water at Grandtully: pure exhilaration), archery, clay shooting, quad biking. A v good all-round activities centre in a gr setting. Timeshare chalet accom avail (for short stays 01887 830236). Centre cl Mon/Tues.

**2136**
Map 11
**M30**
✓ **Galloway Sailing Centre** Loch Ken nr Castle Douglas 01644 420626. 15km N on A713 to Ayr. Dinghies, windsurfers, canoes, kayaks, tuition. Also the Climbing Tower so you can zip-wire & take the leap of faith! All this by a serene & forgiving loch by the Galloway Forest. Phone for times & courses. Open Mar-Nov.

**2137**
Map 7
**K20**
**Great Glen Water Park** 01809 501381. 3km S Invergarry on A82. On shores of tiny L Oich & L Lochy in the Gr Glen. Wonderful spot, with many other lochs nearby. Day visitors welcome with windsurfers, Wayfarers, kayaks, canoes & also mountain bikes & fishing rods for hire. Mainly, however, a chalet park with all the usual condo/timeshare facs (you can rent by the week).

**2138**
Map 9
**L26**
**Clyde Muirshiel Regional Park** Castle Semple Centre, Lochwinnoch 01505 842882. 30km SW Glas M8 jnct 29, A737 past Johnstone then A760. Also 20km from Largs via A760. Loch (nr village) is 3km x 1km and at the Rangers Centre you can hire dinghies and canoes etc (also mountain bikes). Bird reserve on opp bank (1782/WILDLIFE). Peaceful place to learn. Nov-Mar 10am-4pm, Apr-Oct 10am-8pm.

**2139**
Map 9
**K25**
**Kip Marina** Inverkip 01475 521485. Major sailing centre on Clyde coast 50km W of Glas via M8, A8 and A78 from Greenock heading S for Wemyss Bay. A yacht heaven as well as haven of Grand Prix status. Sails, charters, pub/restau, chandlers and myriad boats. Diving equipment and dinghies for hire.

**2140**
Map 10
**P24**
**Lochore Meadows** nr Lochgelly 01592 414300. From Dunfermline-Kirkcaldy motorway take Lochgelly t/off into town and follow signs for Lochore Country Park. Small, safe loch for learning and perfecting. Canoes and dinghies for hire. Equipped for disabled. Park contains 2 good adventure playgrounds for wide age range.

**2141**
Map 10
**M23**
**Lochearnhead Watersports** 01567 830330. On A85 nr jnct with A84 is a water sports centre specialising in anything that's pulled by a boat: skiing, boarding etc. Certainly the loch is wide open and (usually) gently lapping the sport is nice to watch. Café.

**2142**
Map 7
**G18**
**Raasay Outdoor Centre** nr Skye 01478 660266. Excl activity place! Day visits or holidays. Friendly, personal attention. A special place.

# The Best Diving Sites

*Scotland's seas are primal soup, full of life and world-class sites as hard core divers already know. The E coast can be tricky if the wind is blowing from the N or E, therefore the W coast is preferable (the further N the better). Thanks to the Gulf Stream it's not cold, even without a dry suit, and once you're down it's like flying thro the Botanics (says my friend Tim Maguire). So when you see all those crazies walking into the sea, remember, they may know something that you don't.*

## 2143 WEST COAST
Map 5

**The Outer Hebrides** excellent with fantastic visibility esp off the W coast of **Harris** where you can plop in virtually anywhere.

**St Kilda** offers the best diving in the UK, but it's the hardest to get to. On the edge of the Continental Shelf and the whale migration route, it has huge drop-offs and upwellings of life. Book boat and board well in advance.

**The Summer Isles** from Ullapool harbour. Wrecks, lee shores and unpolluted waters.

Map 9 **Oban** Scuba central with lots of sites in the neighbourhood and easy access to the isles. Charter a boat and search for scallops in **The Garvellach** or dive the wrecks in the **Sound Of Mull**. Somewhere off **Tobermory** there is reputedly, one of Scotland's most enigmatic wrecks, a Spanish galleon. Easier to find are dolphins off the coasts of **Islay & Tiree** and see 1777/DOLPHINS for other likely spots.

All W Coast sea lochs are good for general wildlife diving.

## 2144 EAST COAST
Map 10

✓ **St Abbs Head** Accessible from the shore (2043/COASTAL WALKS) or by boat from **Eyemouth**, a marine reserve, so leave the lobsters alone. The spectacular Cathedral Rock is encrusted with green and yellow dead men's fingers and in August /Sept is a sanctuary for breeding fish (this cathedral is as beautiful as St Giles and is distinctly non-denominational). Nearby shore-based diving at **Dunbar** is shallow, safe and simple.

Map 10
R24 **The Isle Of May** across the Forth is more advanced. Take a boat from Anstruther (1761/BIRDS). Main site is Piccadilly Circus, a central atrium fed by gullies, full of friendly seals.

## 2145 ORKNEY
Map 3
Q11

✓ ✓ **Scapa Flow** The world-famous underwater burial site where the Germans scuttled their fleet in 1918. Think Gaudalcanal, but colder. Although the scrappies have been in, 3 battleships & 4 light cruisers remain among other wrecks. Most lie in 20-40m deep, so not so dark & dangerous but plan carefully. Still majorly eerie!

## DIVE OPERATORS (Don't leave home without one).

**Edinburgh** Edinburgh Diving Centre 0131 229 4838. Shop only.

**Coldingham** Borders Scoutscroft Dive Centre 01890 771669.

**Oban** Puffin Dive Centre 01631 566088. Full diving services. Oban Dives 01631 562755. Shop only.

**Skye** Dive & Sea the Hebrides 01470 592219. Charter only.

**Mull** Seafare Chandlery & Diving 01688 302277.

**Ullapool** Atlantic Diving Services (Achiltibuie) 01854 622261. Charter only.

**Orkney** Diving Cellar 01856 850055. Sunrise Charters 01856 874425. Scapa Scuba 01856 851218. Scapa Flow Charters 01856 850879.

For wide network of v helpful local diving clubs around the country, contact Scottish Sub Aqua Club 0141 425 1021.

# The Best Windsurfing

## FOR BEGINNERS AND INSTRUCTION (*see also* WATER SPORTS).

**Croft-Na-Caber** Kenmore, Loch Tay 01887 830588.

**Linnhe Marine** nr Oban 01631 730401.

**Lochmore Meadows** Lochgelly, Fife 01592 414300. (No instruction.)

**Tighnabruaich Sailing School** Tighnabruaich 01700 811717.

**Scottish National Watersports Centre** Cumbrae 01475 530757.

**Strathclyde Park** nr Motherwell & Glasgow 01698 266155. Lots to do in this recreational zone of the conurbation. Water may not be so turquoise. 1572/COUNTRY PARKS.

**Elie** East Neuk Of Fife 01333 330962. Small, friendly windsurfing and water sports operation on the beach (beyond the Ship Inn).

## WINDSURFING SPOTS

### 2146 WEST COAST

**Map 9 L24** **Macrihanish** Wave-sailing, fabulous long beach (1608/BEACHES). Mainly at Air Force base end. Big waves, for the more advanced.

**K26** **Prestwick/Troon** Town beaches.

**L27** **Island Of Cumbrae** Millport beach.

**G28** **Milarrochy Bay** Loch Lomond 8km from Drymen (45km N of Glas). W/end centre run by 7th Wave. Second beach up from Balmaha. Picturesque.

### 2147 EAST COAST

**Map 8 T17** **Fraserburgh** Town beach. Also surfing.

**Map 10 R22** **Lunan Bay** 12km N of Arbroath. Also surfing.

**Map 10 R23** **Carnoustie** Town beach.

**Map 10 R23** **St Andrews** W Sands. Also surfing.

**Map 10 Q23** **Longniddry/Gullane** 25/35km E of Edin via A1 and A198.

**Map 10 R25** **Bellhaven Bay** Dunbar Leads to John Muir Country Park.

### 2148 NORTH COAST

**Map 6** **Thurso** Many beaches nr town and further W. (1621/BEACHES)

## FOR ENTHUSIASTS

**2149 Map 9 E22** ✓ **Isle Of Tiree** The windsurfing capital of Scotland. 40km W of Mull. Countless clean, gently sloping beaches all round island (and small inland loch) allowing surfing in all wind directions (2281/MAGICAL ISLANDS). Accom basic or self-catering (Oban TIC 01631 563122). Loganair fly every day except Sunday (0845 7733377) and Calmac run ferries from Oban every day (01475 650100).

## INFORMATION/BOARD HIRE:

| Glasgow | Boardwise 1146 Argyle St 0141 334 5559. |
| | Boardwise Royal Exchange Sq 0141 248 1179. |
| Edinburgh | Boardwise Lady Lawson St 0131 229 5887. |
| North Coast | Tempest Surf Thurso On harbour. 01847 892500. |

# The Best Surfing Beaches

*A surprise for the sceptical: Scotland has some of the best surfing beaches in Europe. Forget the bronzed beachboys and lemon bleached hair, surfing in Scotland is titanium-lined, rubber and balaclavas, and you get an ice-cream head even encased in the latest technology. The main season is Sept-Dec.*

## 2150 WEST COAST

Map 5
**F13**
✓✓ **Isle of Lewis** Probably the best of the lot. Go N of Stornoway, N of Barvas, N of just about anywhere. Leave the A857 and your day job behind. Not the most scenic of sites, but the waves have come a long way, further than you have. Derek at Hebridean Surf Holidays (01851 705862) will tell you when and where to go.

Map 9
**G28**
✓ **Macrihanish** Nr Campbeltown at the foot of the Mull of Kintyre. Long strand to choose from (1608/BEACHES). Clan Skates in Glasgow (0141 339 6523) usually has an up-to-date satellite map and a idea of both the W and (nearest to central belt) Pease Bay (*see below*).

## 2151 NORTH COAST

Map 6
**P12**
✓ **Thurso** Surf City, well not quite, but it's a good base to find your own waves. Esp to the E of town at Dunnet Bay – a 5km long beach with excellent reefs at the N end. They say it has to be the best right-hand breaking wave on the planet! When it ain't breaking, go W to...

Map 6
**N12**
✓ **Melvich & Strathy Bay** Nr Bettyhill on the N coast halfway betw Tongue and Thurso on the A836. From here to Cape Wrath the power and quality of the waves detonating on the shore have justified comparisons with Hawaii. And then there's **Brimsness**.

Map 6
**Q13**
**Wick** On the Thurso rd at Ackergill to the S of Sinclair's Bay (1267/HOUSE PAR-TIES). Find the ruined castle and taking care, clamber down the gully to the beach. A monumental reef break, you are working against the backdrop of the decaying ruin drenched in history, spume and romance.

## 2152 EAST COAST

Map 8
**T20**
**Nigg Bay** Just S of Aberdeen (not to be confused with Nigg across from Cromarty) and off the vast beach at Lunan Bay (1615/BEACHES) betw Arbroath and Montrose. There's 4 spots around **Fraserburgh** ('the broch').

Map 10
**S25**
✓ **Pease Bay** S of Dunbar nr Cockburnspath on the A1. The nearest surfie heaven to the capital. The caravan site has parking and toilets. V consistent surf here and therefore v popular.

### INFORMATION/BOARD HIRE:

| | |
|---|---|
| **Glasgow** | **Boardwise** 1146 Argyle St  0141 334 5559. |
| | **Clan Skates** 45 Hyndland St  0141 339 6523. |
| **Edinburgh** | **Boardwise** Lady Lawson St  0131 229 5887. |
| | **Momentum** Bruntsfield Pl  0131 229 6665. |
| **North Coast** | **Tempest Surf** Thurso  01847 892500. |

# SECTION 11

*Shopping*

# Best Scottish Shopping

_signifies_ **notable café**.

**2153**
Map 7
**N16**
✓ **Anta Factory Shop** Fearn nr Tain  01862 832477. Off B9175 from Tain to the Nigg ferry, 8km through Hill of Fearn, on corner of disused airfield. Shop with adj pottery. Anta also in Edin & London – it's a classy brand. Much tartan curtain fabric; many rugs, throws and pots. You can commission furniture to be covered in their material. Pottery tour by arr. Shop. AYR daily 9.30am-5.30pm (Sun 11-5pm, phone for wint hrs). Pottery Mon-Fri only.

**2154**
Map 7
**M16**
✓ **Tain Pottery** Off the A9 just S of Tain (opp side of A9 to rd signed for Anta at Fearn; see above). Big working pottery, big stuff & often big, perhaps OTT designs but v pop (they do the NTS). Daily in summer, 10am-5pm. Cl Sun in wint.

**2155**
Map 6
**J14**
**K15**
✓ **Highland Stoneware** Lochinver & Ullapool  On rd to Baddidarach as you enter Lochinver on A837; & in Mill St, Ullapool, on way N beyond centre. A large-scale pottery business incl a shop/warehouse & open studios that you can walk round (Lochinver is more _engagé_). Similar to the 'ceramica' places you find in the Med, but not too terracotta – rather, painted and heavy-glazed stoneware in set styles. Gr selection, pricey, but you may have luck in the Lochinver discount section. Mail-order service. Open AYR.

**2156**
Map 10
**R24**
✓ **Crail Pottery** Crail  At the foot of Rose Wynd, signposted from main st (best to walk). In a tree-shaded Mediterranean courtyard and upstairs attic is a cornucopia of brilliant, useful, irresistible things. Open 9am-5pm (w/ends from 10am). Don't miss the harbour nearby, one of the most romantic neuks in the Neuk. Pity there's nowhere decent in Crail for tea.

**2157**
Map 10
**N21**
✓ **MacNaughton's** Pitlochry  Station Rd on corner of main st, this the best of many. A vast old-fashioned family-owned outfitter with acres of tartan attire – incl obligatory tartan pyjamas & dressing gowns! Make their own cloth, and 9m kilts prepared in 6-8 wks. This really is the real McCoy. 7 days till 5.30pm (4pm Sun).

**2158**
Map 1
**xE1**
✓ **Kinloch Anderson** Edinburgh  Commercial St, Leith. A bit of a trek from uptown, but firmly on the tourist trail and rightly so. Experts in Highland dress and all things tartan; they've supplied _everybody_. They design their own tartans, have a good range of men's tweed jackets; even rugs. Mon-Sat 9am-5.30pm (5pm winter).

**2159**
Map 8
**N17**
✓ **Logie Steading** nr Forres  Courtyard in beautiful countryside 10km S of Forres signed from A940 Forres-Grantown rd. Nr pleasant woodlands & picnic spot. (Directions: 2022/WOODLAND WALKS.) Better than usual crafty courtyard. Art & ceramics from Highland artists & workshops. Second-hand books, even dresses! Tearoom (1467/TEARMS). Mar-Dec, 7 days 10.30am-5pm.

**2160**
Map 10
**N22**
✓ **House of Menzies** nr Aberfeldy  On Weem Rd Across river from Aberfeldy. Adj to Menzies Castle (1802/CASTLES) on rd to Glen Lyon. Mainly art (local & Edin's Wasp Studios) & wine (huge New World collection) on sale here & coffee shop in beautifully converted steading. The glen awaits.

**2161**
Map 10
**N21**
**House Of Bruar** Pitlochry  Courtyard emporia nay, mall and shopaholic honey pot on the A9 N of Blair Atholl esp for those who just missed Pitlochry. Self-s restau not as good as it was but retail food side well selected (good range of Scottish cheeses, Mackie's ice cream, MacSween's haggis, etc). Outdoor wear with big labels (Musto, Patagonia), golf shop & gdn centre, even antiques. They know what you want. Falls nearby for more spiritual sustenance (1678/WATERFALLS). 7 days 9am-5pm.

**2162**
Map 8
**N17**
**Brodie Country Fare** By main A96 betw Nairn and Forres, nr Brodie Castle (1790/CASTLES). Not a souvenir shoppie in the trad sense, more a drive-in one-stop shopping experience on the taste by-pass. Deli food, a fairly up-market boutique designer womenswear and every crafty tartanalia of note. The self-serve restau gets as busy as a motorway café. 7 days till 5.30pm.

**2163**
Map 7
**L17**
**Falls Of Shin Visitor Centre** nr Lairg  Self-serve café/restau in the VC and shop across the rd from the Falls of Shin on the Achany Glen rd 8km S of Lairg (1653/WATERFALLS). Good basic food in an unlikely emporium of all things Harrods (Mohammed al Fayed's estate is here). They come from miles around at Xmas for hampers etc. 9.30am-6pm AYR.

**2164** **Made In Scotland** Beauly  Station Rd on way out of town to Inverness.
Map 7  Large emporium & restau of things made in Scotland. Well... some are bet-
**L18**  ter than others. AYR 9.30am-5.30pm, Sun 10-5pm.

**2165** **Mortimer's & Ritchie's** Grantown-On-Spey  3 & 41-45 High St respectively
Map 8  of respectable Speyside holiday town where fishing gear is in demand (Ritchie's
**P18**  have stopped fishing). Mortimer's more exclusively angling for your custom,
but both with a big range of flies. Big-name outdoor clothing in every shade of
olive. Ritchie's also have guns if you want to kill something. Both cl Sun.

**2166** **Edinbane Pottery** Skye  500m off A850 Portree (22km) – Dunvegan rd.
Map 7  Long-established and reputable working pottery where all the various
**F17**  processes are often in progress. Earthy pots of every shape and size & for
every purpose imaginable. Open AYR 9am-6pm. 7 days (not w/ends wint).

**2167** **Skye Silver** Colbost, Skye  10km Dunvegan on B884 to Glendale. Long
Map 7  established and reputable jewellery made and sold in an old schoolhouse by
**F18**  the rd in distant corner of Skye, but 3 Chimneys restau nearby (2304/ISLANDS
RESTAUS). Well-made, Celtic designs, good gifts. Mar-Oct 7 days, 10am-6pm.

**2168** **Kiln Room Pottery & Coffee Shop** Laggan  On main A889 route to Ft
Map 7  William and Skye from Dalwhinnie. Simple, usable pottery (tho pottery itself
**M20**  no longer in use) with distinctive warm colouring. Selected knitwear and useful things. Home-made cakes and scones; 1446/COFFEE SHOPS. 10am-5.30pm,
7 days. Now with hostel out back v inx incl comfy lounge with gr vista and
unique seven-person hot-tub spa (01528 544231). ☕

**2169** **Glenelg Candles** Glenelg  Signed from glen rd which comes over the hill
Map 7  from Shiel Bridge (1667/SCENIC ROUTES) and hard to miss. Wooden cabin/cof-
**H19**  fee shop with multifarious candles and local art. Excl home-made food
(1446/COFFEE SHOPS). Easter-Oct 9.30pm-5pm daily. ☕

**2170** **Balnakeil** Durness, Sutherland  From Durness & the A836 rd, take Balnakeil
Map 6  & Faraid Head rd for 2km W. Founded in the 1960s in what one imagines was
**L12**  a haze of hash, this craft village is still home to 'downshifters'. Paintings, pottery, weaving & a bookshop in prefab huts where community members live &
work (the site was an early warning station). Lotte Glob *is* (01971 511354) v good
but opening own studio on L Eriboll where she lives at TGP. Bistro & restau.
Some businesses seasonal. All open in summer, daily 10am-6 pm (mostly).

**2171** **Skye Batiks** Portree, Skye  In centre near TIC. V original Sri Lanka 'batiks'-
Map 7  cotton fabrics of ancient Celtic designs in every shape and size. Mainly hand-
**G18**  made, majorly colourful; a unique souvenir of Skye. Island Outdoors adj has
outdoor 'fashion' & all-important midge helmets.

**2172** **Achin's Bookshop** Lochinver  At Inverkirkaig 5km from Lochinver on the
Map 6  'wee mad rd' to Achiltibuie (1673/SCENIC ROUTES). Unexpected selection of
**J14**  books in the back of beyond providing something to read when you've
climbed everything. Outdoor wear too and gr hats. The path to Kirkaig Falls
and Suilven begins at the gate (see 1879/MONUMENTS). Easter-Oct 7 days;
9.30am-6pm (wint Mon-Sat 10am-5pm). Adj café 10am-5pm, summer only.

**2173** **Iona Abbey Shop** Iona via Calmac ferry from Fionnphort on Mull. Crafts
Map 9  and souvenirs across the way in separate building. Proceeds support a wor-
**F23**  thy, committed organisation. Christian literature, tapes etc, but mostly artefacts from nearby and around Scotland. Celtic crosses much in evidence, but
then this is where they came from! Mar-Oct 9.30am-5pm.

**2174** **Octopus Crafts** nr Fairlie, nr Largs  On main A78 Largs to Ardrossan rd, S of
Map 9  Fairlie. Crafts, wines & cookshop an excellent restau (1400/SEAFOOD RESTAUS)
**K26**  & a seafood deli. An all-round road side experience – the sign says Fencebay
Fisheries. Everything here is hand-made and/or hand-picked. Even the wines
are well chosen. Good pots. Glass and wood. They also run courses. Cl Mon.

**2175** **Starfish Ceramics** Tobermory, Isle of Mull  Actually 7km from Tobermory
Map 9  in the steadings of Glengorm Castle (signed off rd to Dervaig) – 2326/MULL.
**G22**  Adj to gr café, this is a working studio/pottery with distinctive stripey useful
& decorative work – a cut above many of the more conventional pots on
these pages. Open Mon-Sat AYR.

**2176** **Borgh Pottery** Borve, Isle Of Lewis  On NW coast of island a wee way from
Map 5  Stornoway, but not much of a detour from the rd to Callanish where you are
**F13**  probably going. Alex and Sue Blair's pleasant gallery of handthrown pots with
diff glazes; domestic and gdn wear. Some knits. Open AYR 9.30-6pm. Cl Sun.

**2177  Galloway Lodge Preserves** Gatehouse Of Fleet  On main st of compact
Map 11  town. Packed with local jams, marmalades, chutneys and pickles. Scottish
**M30**  pottery by Scotia Ceramics, Highland Stoneware and Dunoon. Good presents
and jam for yourself. 10am-5pm Mon-Sat, and Sun afternoons in summer.

**2178  Crafts And Things** nr Glencoe Village  On A82 betw Glencoe village and
Map 9  Ballachulish. Eclectic mix of so many baubles that some are literally hanging
**J21**  from the rafters. Mind, body & mountain books (& this one) and reasonably
priced knit/outerwear. Good coffee shop, with local artist's work on walls.
All-round nice place. AYR, daily until 5.30pm. ☕

**2179  Harestanes Countryside Centres** nr Jedburgh  Off A68 at Ancrum the
Map 10  B6400 to Nisbet. Farm steading complex on Monteviot Estate (1560/GARDENS)
**R27**  with café/exhib/superior crafts incl the excl **Buy Design** showing furniture,
ceramics & glass. Easter-Oct 10am-5pm.

**2180  Drumlanrig Castle** nr Thornhill, nr Dumfries  A whole day out of things to
Map 11  do (1569/COUNTRY PARKS) including the craft centre in the old stable/courtyard
**N29**  to the side of the house. Studio-type shops with tartan, jewellery and 'bodg-
ing'! Hire a bike and ride while you decide.

**2181  Kirkcudbright High St**  A run of craft shops by the Tolbooth Arts Centre.
Map 11  Inc Jo Gallant textiles, Cranberries (general), Gill's jewellery and the High St
**M31**  Gallery. Browse on, then walk over to the Corner Gallery (2204/WOOLLIES).

# Where To Buy Art

*These galleries, outside the dealer & public-gallery concentrations in Edin & Glas,*
*cater also for tourists... but they're all a cut above the rest.* See also Small
Galleries Edinburgh *p. 72,* Glasgow *p. 110.*

**2182  McEwan Gallery** nr Ballater Deeside  A surprising place but for many years
Map 8  this cottage gallery has been dealing in 19th/20th century, mainly Scottish
**Q20**  art. They wrote the book! Summer exhibs, but open AYR 11am-5pm (Sun 2-
5pm). Wint hrs 01339 755429. 300m up A939 Tomintoul rd.

**2183  The Lost Gallery** Middle Of Nowhere, Aberdeenshire  Signed from
Map 8  Bellabeg on A944 nr Strathon vill. 3km up farm rd, then another 3km on
**Q19**  rough track to a fab studio/gallery in farmhouse in the Cairngorms with var-
ied work by contemp Scots & the owner Peter Goodfellow. AYR 11am-5pm. Cl
Tues. 01975 651287 if you get... lost.

**2184  Kilmorack Gallery** nr Beauly  01463 783230. On A831 for Struy & Cannich
Map 7  5km SW of town. Pleasant & serious gallery in converted church by the rd.
**L18**  Significant exhibs of mainly Highland artists. **The Beauly Gallery** 2km
nearer Beauly on same rd has art along with 'gifts' but some interesting photography.

**2185  Castle Gallery** Inverness  On rd up to castle amid many restaus, another
Map 10  Highland gallery that takes itself quite seriously. Changing exhibs. Mon-Sat
**N23**  9am-5pm.

**2186  Strathearn Gallery** Crieff  32 W St (on Main St). Accessible & affordable.
Map 10  The Maguires do know what you like. Fine and applied arts. 7 days till 5pm
**N23**  (Thu-Sat in wint).

**2187  Tolquhon Gallery** nr Aberdeen  01651 842343. Betw Ellon and Oldmeldrum
Map 8  and nr Haddo House (1851/COUNTRY HOUSES) & esp Pitmedden (1561/GARDENS)
**S18**  – follow signs for castle, an interesting ruin for kids to clamber. Art at realistic
prices & a pretty garden. (Pron 'T'hon'.) 11am-5pm, Sun 2-5pm. Cl Thu.

**2188  Just Art** Fochabers  64 High St, the A96 through Fochabers E of Elgin.
Map 8  Changing exhibs of serious and selected mainly Scottish artists. Good ceram-
**Q17**  ics. An interesting stop on this rd along the coast. Affordable art.

**2189  McIntosh Gallery** Kingussie  Main St. Crowded with pictures & also rugs.
Map 7  Across st, **Something Different** is a real treasure-trove of cool things.
**M20**

**2190  Solas Gallery** Gairloch  Flowerdale Bay by the Old Inn (1347/INNS) as you
Map 7  come into Gairloch from S. Original work – painting, ceramics – by W
**H16**  Highland artists. Nice space. Easter-Oct.

**2191** **Plockton Gallery** Plockton  Innes St opp Plockton Inn. 2 floors, lot of wall
Map 7  space for summer exhibs incl some significant artists. Summer only 10am-
**H18**  10pm.

**2192** **Browns Gallery** Tain  Off Main St. Surprising repository of gr contemp
Map 7  Scottish art with reg exhibs by notable artists like John Byrne, Calvin Colvin,
**M16**  Neil Macpherson. They must like this guy. Mon-Sat 10am-5pm.

**2193** **Finsbay Gallery** Golden Road, S Harris  Wonderful windy rd down E coast of
Map 5  S Harris. This cute gallery showing mainly Hebridean artists. Another gallery
**E16**  (Skoon)/café nearby (2325/HEBRIDES). Mon-Sat 10am-5pm (wint Thur only).

**2194** **St Andrews Fine Art**  Crowded walls of Scottish art from 1800-present.
Map 10  Includes some good work from kent contemporaries. Peploe-Redpath and
**R23**  their chums. Cl Sun.

**2195** **Kranenburg & Fowler Fine Arts** Oban  Star Brae & Stevenson St. 01631
Map 9  562303. Geoff & Jan source work from artists that ranges from the polite to
**H23**  the interesting. Small group of regular exhibitors and others. Mon-Sat
9.30am-5.30pm. Suns when exhib 12-4pm.

**2196** **Morven Gallery** Barvas, Isle Of Lewis  Coast rd just N of Barabhas 30km
Map 5  from Callanish and those stones. Janice Scott's excl farm steading kind of
**F13**  gallery with well-selected work, mainly local. Painting, tapestry, ceramics and
fab original knits. Baking. AYR Apr-Sept 10am-5pm. Cl Sun. 🍴

**2197** **Scottish Sculpture Workshops** Lumsden nr Alford & Huntly  01464
Map 8  861372. Main st of ribbon town on A97. Not a place to see work for sale (main-
**Q19**  ly commissions), but work being made. They also look after the sculpture gdn
at Alford end of st by the school. Workshops open AYR. Mon-Fri 9am-5pm.

**2198**  ✓ ✓ **The Glasgow Art Fair**  The Scottish market place for contempo-
Map 2  rary art. Mainly home-grown but London galleries with Scottish
**D3**  connections. Held in mid April in pavilions in George Square. 0141 552 6027
for details. 🍴

**The Degree Shows Edinburgh/Glasgow & Duncan of Jordanstone,
Dundee Art Schools**  Work from final-year students. Discover the Bellanys,
Howsons, Douglas Gordons & Simon Starlings of the future. 2-week exhibi-
tion after manic first night (mid June).

*Prints by many contemp Scottish artists available from:*

**Glasgow Print Studios**  22 King St, Merchant City/Tron area.

**Edinburgh Printmakers Workshop**  23 Union St off Leith Walk

**Peacock Visual Arts** Aberdeen  21 Castle St.

# Where To Buy Good Woollies

**2199**  ✓ ✓ **Belinda Robertson** Edinburgh  0131 557 8118. 13a Dundas St.
Map 1  Queen of the commissioned cashmere creations; you can only
**xA4**  choose from the *prêt-à-porter* collection in her showroom here (or in
London). Her team design and process the stock which is made up in Hawick.

**2200**  ✓ **Hilary Rohde Cashmere** Edinburgh  0131 225 3948. 22 Moray Pl. Posh
Map 1  address for this crème de la crème hand-knitted Scottish cashmere.
**A1**  Sweaters, accessories, off-the-peg or order some knitted bespoke. Appt only.

**2201**  ✓ **Judith Glue** Kirkwall, Orkney  Opp the cathedral. Distinctive hand-made
Map 3  jumpers, the runic designs are a real winner. Also the widespread but indi-
**Q10**  vidual Highland and Joker stoneware (jewellery and animal clocks v popular),
condiments and preserves. The landscape prints of Orkney are by twin sister,
Jane. Open AYR 7 days 9am-6pm (wint cl Suns).

**2201**  ✓ **Floraidh-Tweed & Wool Collection** Skye  01471 833421. In S on Sleat
Map 7  adj Eilean Iarmain Hotel (2294/ISLAND HOTELS). Small, packed & tasteful
**H19**  selection of woolly things for women, with some local crafts. Somebody here
has the 'good eye'. 7 days in season.

**2203** **Ragamuffin, Skye**  On Armadale Pier, so one of the first or last things you
Map 7  can do on Skye is rummage through the Ragamuffin store and get a nice knit.
**G19**  Every kind of jumper and some crafts in this Aladdin's cave within a new-
build shed; incl tweedy things and mad hats.

**2204**
Map 11
**M31**
**Corner Gallery** Kirkcudbright 75 St Mary's Street (01557 332020). Anne Chaudhry's resplendent knitwear shop with some very nice gear. Woollens not just for middle-aged blokes on the golf course, nor the wife. All carefully selected Scottish & the opportunistic Irish. Easter–Dec 10am-5pm daily (wint lunch break). Cl Feb.

**2205**
Map 8
**P17**
**Johnston's Cashmere Centre** Elgin Large Mill Shop kind of operation and full-blown visitor attraction nr the Cathedral (1813/RUINS). 'The only British mill to transform fibre to garment' (yarns spun at their factory in Elgin and made into garments in the Borders) and though this is more British High St than Bloomingdale's, New York, these mum-&-dad-like jumpers will keep you just as warm. Mon-Sat 9am-5.30pm, Sun 11am-5pm. Slight variations in winter.

**2206**
Map 10
**R27**
**Lochcarron Visitor Centre** Galashiels · If you're in Galashiels (or Hawick), which grew up around woollen mills, you might expect to find a good selection of woollens you can't get everywhere else; and bargains. Well, tough! There's no stand-out place, but L Carron is a big tourist attraction with mill tours (Open AYR 4 times a day), exhibits and an okay mill shop. Vivienne Westwood has been this way & well... Hawick did invent the Y-front.

**2207**
Map 10
**R28**
**Hawick Cashmere** Factory in Hawick since 1874, with VC beside the river on Duke St. Also shops in Kelso & Edinburgh. 'State-of-the-art colours and designs'. Not only, but mostly cashmere. Mon-Sat 9.30am-5pm; Sun 11am-4pm (in season).

## Harris Tweed

**2208**
Map 5
**Tweeds & Knitwear** 4 Plockropool, Drinishadder Organised operators (they even cater for coach parties) with weaving demonstrations & wool & knitwear for sale as well as tweed. Cl Sun.

**Joan McClennan No 1A**, Drinishadder Further down the Golden Rd (1671/SCENIC ROUTES). I don't know, but I've been told, this is where you find the real golden fleece. Go look for it.

**Luskentyre Harris Tweed** No 6, Luskentyre 2km off W coast on main rd S to Scarista and Rodel. Donald and Maureen Mackay's place is notable for their bright tartan tweed. 9.30am-6pm Cl Sun.

**Lewis Loom Centre** Stornoway Main St in the N, far from Harris but nr the tourists. Cloth & clothes. Weaving demo. Cl Sun.

## The Best Garden Centres

☕ signifies **notable café**. Others may have cafés not recommended.

**2209**
Map 10
**P25**
✓ ✓ **Dougal Philip's New Hopetoun Gardens** nr S Queensferry 01506 834433. The mother of all (Scottish) garden centres with 16 demonstration gardens (incl Oriental & Scottish). Everything you could ever grow or put in a Scottish garden. Acres of accessories. Orangery tea-room has commanding views and tasty home-made stuff. AYR 10am-5.30pm. Tearm closes 4.30pm. ☕

**2210**
Map 9
**J22**
✓ **Kinlochlaich House** Appin On main A28 Oban-Ft William rd just N of Pt Appin t/off, the West Highlands' largest nursery/gdn centre. Set in a large walled gdn filled with plants and veg soaking up the climes of the warm Gulf stream. Donald Hutchison and daughter nurture these acres enabling you to reap what they sow; with a huge array of plants on offer it's like visiting a friend's gdn and being able to take home your fave bits. Charming cottages for let 01631 730342. 7 days: 9.30am-5.30pm (10.30am Sun). Cl Sun in winter.

**2211**
Map 10
**S27**
✓ **Floors Castle** Kelso 3km outside town off B6397 St Boswells rd (gdn centre has separate entrance to main visitors' gate in town). Set amongst lovely old greenhouses within walled gdns some distance from house, it has a showpiece herbaceous border all round. First-class coffee shop and patio. 'V good roses'.Lovely kids' lawn. Centre is open AYR. 10am-5pm. (1859/COUNTRY HOUSES.) ☕

**2212**
Map 7
**N19**

✓ **Inshraich** nr Kincraig nr Aviemore   On B970 betw Kincraig and Inverdruie (which is on the Coylumbridge ski rd out of Aviemore), a nursery that puts others in the shade. John & Gunn Borrowman carrying on (& developing) the horticulture of Jack Drake (from 1930s) & John Lawson (1949). Specialising in alpines and bog plants, but with neat beds of all sorts in the grounds (and a wild gdn) of the house by the Spey and frames full of perfect specimens, this is a potterer's paradise. Tearm with squirrel- & bird-viewing gallery. Mar-Oct Mon-Fri 9am-5pm, Sat/Sun 10am-5pm. ☕

**2213**
Map 2
**xA1**

✓ **Dobbies** Milngavie, Glasgow   Formerly Findlay Clark's, the original home of the gdn centre chain in Campsie countryside N of city, 20km from centre via A81 or A807 (Milngavie or Kirkintilloch rds) or heading for Milngavie (pron 'Mullguy'), turn rt on Boclair Rd. Best of many Dobbies, a vast gdn complex and all-round visitor experience. 'Famous' coffee shop (the famous waitresses are local babes and what they turn into), saddlery with everything except horses. Books, clothes and piles of plants; and live pets. 9am-6pm (till 8pm Thurs). ☕

**2214**
Map 10
**P23**

✓ **Glendoick** Glencarse nr Perth   On A85, 10km from Perth, in the fertile Carse of the Tay. A large family-owned gdn centre notable esp for rhododendrons and azaleas, a riot of which can be viewed in the nursery behind (May only). Pagoda Garden (they practice what they preach). V popular coffee shop with superior home-baking. 7 days till 6pm, 5pm wint. ☕

**2215**
Map 7
**M18**

**Brin Herb Nursery** Flichity, nr Inverness   Off A9 S of Daviot, 12km S of Inverness, then 10km SW to Farr. An old school and playground dedicated to herbs, plants and all the potions and lotions that come from them. Tearoom in the school room. Mar-Oct 10am-6pm, Sun 12.30-5pm (summer only). ☕

**2216**
Map 9
**K24**

**The Tree Shop** Cairndow, Loch Fyne   A gdn centre specialising in trees & shrubs. Part of the Ardkinglas Estate nr (1km) the Woodland Garden (1563/GARDENS) with UK's tallest tree. The shop on the main A83 L Lomond-Inveraray rd also does houseplants & all the usual greeneries. Café. 7 days 9.30am-5pm (6pm in summer).

**2217**
Map 8
**Q17**

**Christie's** Fochabers   On A98 going into town from Buckie side. Huge gdn centre and forest nursery, with tearm/restaurant. An all-round shopping/recreational experience With some absolutely ghastly trinketry, but their outside plant section still sound. 9am-5pm, 7 days (from 10am Sun).

**2218**
Map 8
**R20**

**Raemoir Garden Centre** Banchory   On A980 off main st 3km n of town. A friendly family-run gdn centre & excl coffee-shop that keeps the fastidious gardeners hereabouts happy. And this is Deeside. If it's good enough for them... (1453/TEAROOMS) 7 days 9am-5.30pm. Tearm till 5pm. ☕

**2219**
Map 5
**D17**

**Keske Nurseries** Clachan North Uist   In the remote heart of wild and watery N Uist on main rd to Benbecula S of Lochmaddy and just after Clachan Stores and the t/off for Bayhead a cottage nursery. Idiosyncratic app, but certainly the Hebridean choice for trees, shrubs, veg and bedding plants. Go on, make a statement – plant a tree in this treeless tract. Open Apr-Aug 1pm-5.30pm. Cl Sun.

**2220**
Map 10
**R25**

**Smeaton Nursery & Gardens** East Linton   01620 860501. 2km from village on N Berwick rd (signed Smeaton). Up a drive in an old estate is this walled gdn going back to early 19th century. Wide range; good for fruit (and other) trees, herbaceous etc. Nice to wander round, an additional pleasure is the 'Lake Walk' halfway down drive through small gate in woods. 1km stroll round a secret finger lake in magnificent mature woodland. You're only supposed to go during gdn hrs Mon-Sat 9.30am-4.30pm; Sun 10.30am-4.30pm. Phone for wint hrs.

**2221**
Map 10
**M26**

**The Clyde Valley** The lush valley of the mighty Clyde is gdn centre central. Best reached say from Glas by M74, jnct 7, then A72 for Lanark. Betw Larkhall and Lanark there's a profusion to choose from and many have sprouted coffee/craft shops. Pick your own fruit in summer and your own picnic spot to eat it. Sandyholm at Crossford is rec.

**2222**
Map 10
**P25**

**Binny Plants** Ecclesmachan   01506 858931. Through village and up driveway past the big house (now a hospice). Down in dell this is run by a respected nurseryman, Billy Carruthers. Grasses, ferns and perennials flourishing here may also flourish for you. 7 days 10am-5pm.

# SECTION 12

*Museums, Galleries, Theatres And Music*

# Best History & Heritage

*For* Edinburgh Galleries, *see p. 72*; Glasgow, *see p. 110*. ☕ : **notable café**.

**2223**
Map 10
**R25**

✓ ✓ **Museum Of Flight & Concorde Experience** nr Haddington, E Lothian 01620 880308. 3km from A1 S of town. In the old complex of hangars and nissen huts at the side of E Fortune, an airfield dating to World War I (there's a tacky open-air market on Sundays), a large collection of planes from gliders to jets and esp wartime memorabilia has been respectfully restored and preserved. Inspired and inspiring displays; not just boys' stuff. Marvel at the bravery back then and sense the unremitting passage of time. From E Fortune the airship R34 made its historic Atlantic crossings. Recently installed Concorde raises the ante. Separate 'Boarding Pass'. Hugely impressive outside, claustrophobic in (especially queueing to leave as you do). But did David Frost & Joan Colllins ever? AYR 7 days; 10.30am-5pm (till 6pm Jul-Aug, 4pm wint). ☕

**2224**
Map 10
**R24**

✓ ✓ **The Secret Bunker** nr Crail/Anstruther 01333 310301. The nuclear bunker and regional seat of government in the event of nuclear war – a twilight labyrinth beneath a hill in rural Fife so vast, well documented and complete, it's utterly fascinating and quite chilling. Few 'museums' are as authentic or as resonant as this, even down to the 1950s records in the jukebox in the claustrophobic canteen. Makes you wonder what 300 people would have felt like incarcerated down there, what the Cold War was all about and what secrets They are cooking up these days for the wars yet to come. Apr-Oct 10am-5pm.

**2225**
Map 10
**Q23**

✓ ✓ **Verdant Works** Dundee 01382 225282. West Henderson's Wynd nr Westport. Award-winning heritage museum that for once justifies the accolades. The story of jute and the city it made. Immensely effective high-tech and designer presentation of industrial & social history. Excl for kids. Almost continuous guided tour. Café. 7 days 10am-6pm; wint Wed-Sun till 4.30pm. All Suns from 11am. ☕

**2226**
Map 5
**E13**

✓ ✓ **The Blackhouse Village** Gearrannan nr Carloway, Lewis 01851 643416. At the end of the rd (3km) from A858 the W coast of Lewis, an extraordinary reconstruction of several blackhouses, the trad thatched dwelling of the Hebrides. One is working Black House Museum (set 1955) with café. Another is a hostel & 4 of them are self-cat accom. Gr walk starts here with viewpts. Apr-Sept 11-5.30pm. Cl Sun. ☕ Also:

**2227**
Map 5
**F13**

✓ **The Blackhouse At Arnol** Lewis 01851 710395. The A857 Barvas rd from Stornoway, left at jnct for 7km, then rt through township for 2km. A single blackhouse with earth floor, bed boxes and central peat fire (no chimney hole), occupied both by the family and their animals. Remarkably, this house was lived in until the 1960s. Smokists may reflect on that peaty fug. Open AYR 9.30am-6.30pm (4.30pm in wint). Cl Sun.                    HS

**2228**
Map 10
**P25**

✓ **The Abbot House** Dunfermline Maygate in town centre 'historic area'. V fine conversion of ancient house demonstrating the importance of this town as a religious and trading centre from the beginning of this millennium to medieval times. Encapsulates history from Margaret and Bruce to the Beatles. One of the few tourist attractions where 'award-winning' is a reliable indicator of worth. Café and tranquil gdn; gate to the graveyard and Abbey. 7 days 10am-5pm. Excl coffeeshop by ladies who can cook & bake. ☕

**2229**
Map 9
**H23**

✓ **Easdale Island Folk Museum** On Easdale, an island/township reached by a 5min (continuous) boat service from Seil 'island' at the end of the B844 (off the A816, 18km S of Oban). Something special about this grassy hamlet of white-washed houses on a rocky outcrop which has a pub, a tearoom and a craft shop, and this museum across the green. The history of the place (a thriving slate industry erased one stormy night in 1881, when the sea drowned the quarry) is brought to life in displays from local contributions. Easter-Sept 11am-5pm.

**2230**
Map 6
**M13**

✓ **Strathnaver Museum** Bettyhill 01641 521418. On N coast 60km W of Thurso in a converted church which is v much part of the whole appalling saga: a graphic account of the Highland clearances told through the history of this fishing village and the Strath that lies behind it from whence its dispossessed population came; 2,500 folk were driven from their homes –

it's worth going up the valley (from 2km W along the main A836) to see (esp at Achenlochy) the beautiful land they had to leave in 1812 to make way for sheep. Detailed leaflet of Strath fo foll by car & foot. Elizabeth's Café on roadside for sustenance (esp fish 'n' chips). Museum: Apr-Oct Mon-Sat 10am-5pm (cl at lunchtime).

**2231** ✓ **Museum of Scottish Country Life** Kittochside by East Kilbride I
Map 10  have to admit I've never been to this rel new attraction in the S hinter-
**M26** land of Glas tho' not for want of trying. East Kilbride 'did my head in' so much that I gave up after an hour or two of trying to find a way out. However folk do say... & they have a big worthy prog for kids. It's in the middle of all those dual carriageways. The phone no., should you get lost, is 0131 (sic) 247 4377. 7 days 10am-5pm.

**2232** ✓ **Applecross Heritage Centre** Along the strand from the Applecross
Map 7  Inn (1222/GET-AWAY-FROM-IT-ALL) adj lovely church built on ancient
**H18** monastery, a well-designed building & lay-out of the story of this remarkable, end-of-the-world community. May-Oct 12-5pm.

**2233** ✓ **The Museum Of Scottish Lighthouses** Fraserburgh  At Kinnaird
Map 8  Head nr Harbour. A top attraction, so signed from all over. Purpose-built
**T17** and v well done. Something which may appear to be of marginal interest made vital. In praise of the prism and the engineering innovation and skill that allowed Britain once to rule the seas (and the world). A gr ambition (to light the coastline) spectacularly realised. *At Scotland's Edge* by Allardyce and Hood (or its follow-up) is well worth taking home. Gt patter from the 4 guides. Apr-Oct 10am-5pm, till 6pm July/Aug; wint closes at 4pm.

**2234** ✓ **Bright Water Visitor Centre & Gavin Maxwell House** Eilean Ban off
Map 7  Kyleakin, Skye 01599 530040. You don't have to be a Maxwell fan, *Ring of*
**H18** *Bright Water* reader or even an otter-watcher to appreciate the remarkable restoration of this fascinating man's last house on the island now under the Skye Bridge. Island itself is a natural haven & the Stevenson Lighthouse superb. Limited access only (12 per tour). Contact centre & book ahead. Apr-Oct.

**2235** ✓ **Surgeons' Hall Museum** Royal College Of Surgeons, Edinburgh  0131
527 1649. 18 Nicolson St. 2 separate small museums left out of the Edin section's 'attractions', but too good to miss. Displays of 'pathological anato-my' in the classic Playfair Hall in the main st (opp Festival Theatre; pre-booked tours only) & the History of Surgery round corner at 9 Hill Square. Includes permanent exhibits, Dental Museum and Sport & Exercise Medicine Museum. Extraordinary & somewhat macabre exhibits in 'the home of med-icine' which celebrated its 500th anniv in '05. Mon-Fri 12-4pm. Donations.

**2236** **West Highland Museum** Fort William  Cameron Sq off main st, listed
Map 9  building next to TIC. Good refurb yet retains mood; the setting doesn't over-
**K21** shadow the contents. 7 rms of Jacobite memorabilia, archeology, wildlife, clans, tartans, arms etc all effectively evoke the local history. Gr oil paintings line the walls, incl a drawn battle plan of Culloden. The anamorphic painting of Charlie isn't so bonny, but a fascinating snapshot all the same. Cl Sun except July/Aug (2-5pm).

**2237** **Mary-Ann's Cottage** Dunnet  On N coast off A836 from Thurso to John o'
Map 6  Groats, signed at Dunnet; take the rd for Dunnet Head. Lived in till 1990 by
**P12** Mary-Ann Calder, 3 generations of crofters are in these stones. But not nos-talgic or heritage heavy, just an old lady's house, the near present & past. Cf that other old lady's house 10 mins up the rd (Castle of Mey, 1793/CASTLES). Open summer 2.30-4.30pm. Cl Mons.

**2238** **Kilmartin House** N of Lochgilphead on the A816. 01546 510278. Centre for
Map 9  landscape and archeology interpretation – so much to know of the early peo-
**H24** ples and Kilmartin Glen is littered with historic sites. Intelligent, interesting, run by a small independent trust. Excellent organic café (1375/VEGN RESTAUS) & book-shop without usual tat. Some nice Celtic carvings. AYR 10am-5.30pm daily. ☕

**2239** **Pictavia** Brechin  01356 626241. S of Brechin on the Forfar rd at Brechin
Map 10  Castle. Centre opened summer '99 to give a multimedia interpretation of our
**R21** Dark Age ancestors. Sparse on detail, high on interactivity. Listen to some music, pluck a harp and argue about the Battle of Dunnichen – was it that important? AYR 7 days 9.30am-5.30pm. Wint: w/ends only.

**2240** **Cromarty Courthouse Museum** Cromarty 01381 600418. Church St.
Map 7 Housed in the 18th cent courthouse, this award-winning museum uses mov-
**M17** ing & talking models to bring to life a courtroom scene & famous Cromarty
figures to paint the varied history of this quite special little town. Entrance
includes multilingual taped tours of the town 7 days. 10am-5pm (winter 12-
4pm). Jan & Feb – by appoint.

**2241** **Summerlee Heritage Park** Coatbridge 01236 431261 Heritage Way. Follow
Map 10 signs from town centre. Here in the Iron Town is this tribute to the industry,
**M26** ingenuity & graft that powered the Industrial Revolution & made Glasgow
great. Anyone with a mechanical bent or an interest in the social history of the
working class will like it here; tots & bored teens may not. Tearm. 7 days, 10am-
5pm (Winter 10am-4pm). Cl part of '06 for major redevelopment.

**2242** **Skye Museum Of Island Life** Kilmuir on Uig-Staffin rd, the A855, 32km N
Map 7 of Portree. The most authentic of several converted cottages on Skye where the
**F17** poor crofter's life is recreated for the enrichment of ours. The small thatched
township includes agricultural implements as well as domestic artefacts, many
of which illustrate an improbable fascination with the royal family. Flora
Macdonald's grave is nearby (1866/MONUMENTS). Apr-Oct. Cl Sun.

**2243** **Auchendrain** Inverary 8km W of town on A83. A whole township recon-
Map 9 structed to give a v fair impression of both the historical and spatial relation-
**J24** ship betw the cottages and their various occupants. Longhouses and byre
dwellings; their furniture and their ghosts. 7 days. Apr-Sept 10am-5pm.

**2244** **Inverary Jail** 'The story of Scottish crime and punishment' (sic) told in
Map 9 'award-winning' reconstruction of courtroom with cells, where the waxwork
**J24** miscreants & their taped voices bring local history to life. Guided tours of
Peterhead can't be far off. Open AYR, 9.30am-6pm (wint 10am-5pm).

**2245** **Arctic Penguin aka Maritime Heritage Centre** Inverary 'One of the
Map 9 world's last iron sailing ships' moored so you can't miss it at the loch side in
**J24** Inveraray. More to it than would seem from the outside; displays on the history of Clydeside (the *Queens M* and *E* memorabilia etc), Highland Clearances,
the Vital Spark. Lots for kids to get a handle (or hands) on. And a 'puffer' for
nostalgic trips. 7 days 10am till 6pm; 5pm winter.

**2246** **Bonawe Ironworks Museum** Taynuilt At its zenith (late 18th-early 19th
Map 9 century), this ironworks was a brutal, fire-breathing monster, as 'black as the
**J23** Earl of Hell's waistcoat'. But now, all is calm as the gently sloping grassy
sward carries you around from warehouse to foundry and down onto the
shores of L Etive to the pier, where the finished product was loaded on to
ships to be taken away for the purpose of empire-building (with cannonballs).
Apr-Sept daily until 6.30pm; Oct-Nov daily until 4.30pm; cl Dec-Mar.

**2247** **Scottish Fisheries Museum** Anstruther 01333 310628. In and around a
Map 10 cobbled courtyard o/look the old fishing harbour in this busy East Neuk
**R24** town. Excellent evocation of trad industry still alive (if not kicking). Impressive
collection of models and actual vessels incl those moored at adj quay. Crail
and Pittenweem harbours nearby for the full picture (and fresh crab/lobster).
Open AYR 10am-5.30pm, Sun 11am-5pm (cl 4.30pm in winter).

**2248** **Robert Smail's Printing Works** Innerleithen 01896 830206. Main St. A
Map 10 trad printing works till 1986 and still in use. Fascinating vignettes/ history.
**Q27** Have a go at hand setting, then have a go at a Caldwell's ice-cream (1536/ICE
CREAM). Apr-Oct, Thur-Mon 12-5pm, Sun 1-5pm. W/ends in Oct. (Cl 1-2pm.)

**2249** **Myreton Motor Museum** Aberlady 01875 870288. On Drem rd, past
Map 10 Luffness Mains. Ideal 'little' museum in old barn w restored vehicles dating
**Q25** from 1896. Even for the Luddite, engineering seems an aesthetic here. Dr
Finlay's Casebook fans prepare yourselves. 7 days 11.30am-4pm; wint Suns
only 1-3pm.

**2250** **Shambellie House Museum Of Costume** New Abbey nr Dumfries
Map 11 Another obsession that became a museum. On 2 floors of this country house
**N30** set among spectacular woodlands. Fab frocks etc from every 'period'. Apr-Oct
10am-5pm. Accommodating tearoom staff.

**2251** **Wick Heritage Centre** Wick 01955 605393. On Bank Row. Amazing civic
Map 6 museum run by volunteers. Jam-packed with items about the sea, town and
**Q13** that hard land. Somebody should ensure these people get MBEs or some-
thing. Easter-Oct 10am-5pm. Cl Sun.

**2252**
**Map 8**
**T19**
**Aberdeen Maritime Museum** 01224 337700. Shiprow. Aberdeen faces the sea – and this place tells you the stories. Films, exhibits, photos & paintings, from sail to oil. Decent cafe. Mon-Sat 10am-5pm, Sun 12-3pm. ADM

**2253**
**Map 10**
**L25**
**Map 9**
**L25**
**K27**
**The Scottish Maritime Museum** Spread out over 3 sites, Irvine (01294 278283), Braehead (0141 886 1013) and Dumbarton (01389 763444). Dumbarton has the ship model experiment tank, Braehead (off J25A of the M8) has hands-on engines, while Irvine boasts a massive shed (Victorian engine shop) full of the bits that non-engineers never usually see, as well as the hulk of an old clipper at Irvine harbour. Completely fascinating. Irvine Easter-Oct, Braehead open daily AYR. Dumbarton AYR Mon-Sat. Hrs vary.

# The Most Interesting Public Galleries

For Edinburgh, see p. 63–64; Glasgow, p. 103.  ☕ : **notable café**.

**2254**
**Map 10**
**Q23**
✓✓ **Dundee Contemporary Arts** Nethergate (01382 432000). State of contemporary art gallery (by award-winning architect Richard Murphy) with great café (1091/DUNDEE RESTAUS), cinema facilities, etc. which has transformed the cultural face of Dundee. People actually come from Edin/Glas for the openings. Oft-quoted evidence of city's changing status. ☕

**2255**
**Map 8**
**T19**
✓ **Aberdeen Art Gallery** Schoolhill. Major gallery with temp exhibits and eclectic permanent collection from Impressionists to Bellany. Large bequest from local granite merchant Alex Macdonald in 1900 contributes fascinating collection of his contemporaries: Bloomsburys, Scottish, Pre-Raphaelites. Excellent watercolour rm. An easy and rewarding gallery to visit. 10am-5pm (Sun 2-5pm).

**2256**
**Map 10**
**P23**
✓ **The Fergusson Gallery** Perth Marshall Pl on corner of Tay St in distinctive round tower (former waterworks). The assembled works on two re-roofed floors of J D Fergusson 1874-1961. Though he spent much of his life in France, he had an influence on Scottish art and was pre-eminent amongst those now called the Colourists. It's a long way from Perth to Antibes 1913 but these pictures are a draught of the warm S. Mon-Sat 10-5pm.

**2257**
**Map 10**
**Q24**
✓ **Kirkcaldy Museum & Art Gallery** Nr railway stn, but ask for directions (it's easy to get lost). One of the best galleries in central Scotland. Splendid introduction to the history of 19th/20thC Scottish art. Lots of Colourists/McTaggart/Glasgow Boys. And Sickert to Redpath. Museum ain't bad. Kirkcaldy doesn't get much good press but this & the parks (1582/PARKS) are worth the journey (plus Valente's – 1412/FISH AND CHIPS). 7 days till 5pm.

**2258**
**Map 11**
**M31**
✓ **Hornel Gallery** Kirkcudbright Hornel's house now a fabulous evocation with collection of his work & atelier as was. 'Even the Queen was amazed'. The beautiful gdn stretching to the river is a real eye opener. House & garden Easter-Oct 11am-4pm (10am-5pm July/Aug). Garden only: Feb. NTS

**2259**
**Map 8**
**R17**
✓ **Duff House** Banff Nice walk and easy to find from town centre. Important outstation of the National Galleries of Scotland in meticulously restored Adam house with interesting history and spacious grounds. Ramsays, Raeburns, portraiture of mixed appeal and an El Greco. Maybe OTT for some, but major attraction in the area (go further up the Deveron, 2063/WOODLAND WALKS). Nice tearm. ☕

**2260**
**Map 11**
**N29**
✓ **Sculpture At Glenkiln Reservoir** nr Dumfries Take A75 to Castle Douglas & rt to Shawshead; into village, rt at T-jnct, left to Dunscore, immediate left, signed for reservoir. Follow rd along loch side & park. Not a gallery at all but sculpture scattered in the hills, woods & meadows around this reservoir in the Galloway Hills 16km SE of Dumfries. One or two are obvious, the others you have to find: Epstein, Moore, Rodin in the gr outdoors!

**2261**
**Map 3**
**Q10**
**The Pier Art Centre Stromness** Orkney Mainland 01856 850209. On main st (1594/COASTAL VILLAGES), a gallery on a small pier which could have come lock, stock & canvases from Cornwall. Permanent St Ives-style collection of Barbara Hepworth, Ben Nicholson, Paolozzi & others shown in a *simpatico* environment with the sea o/side. Reopening 2007 after major refurb.

**2262**
**Map 10**
**L26**
**Paisley Art Gallery & Museum** 0141 889 3151. High St. Permanent collection of the world famous Paisley shawls and history of weaving techniques. Other exhibs usually have a local connection and an interactive element. Notable Greek Ionic-style building. 10am-5pm, Sun 2-5pm. Cl Mon.

**2263** **Rozelle House** Ayr   In Rozelle Park and the only art in these parts.
Map 9 Temporary exhibs change every month (incl local artists' work). 4 galleries,
**L28** and additional 5 rms featuring the Alexander Goudie collection in Rozelle
Hse; craft shop. AYR Mon-Sat 10am-5pm, Apr-Oct also Sun 2-5pm.

# Great Theatres & Cinemas

*For* Edinburgh, *see p. 73; and* Glasgow, *see p. 112.*

**2264** ✓ **Dundee Rep** 01382 223530. Tay Sq. Cornerstone of Dundee's cultural
Map 10 ✓ quarter (with DCA 2254/GALLERIES). Houses Scotland's only rep co.
**Q23** Ambitious prog. Anyone into contem Scottish drama comes here. Good
café/restau.

**2265** ✓ **Mull Theatre Dervaig** Mull   01688 302828. 'The smallest theatre in
Map 9 ✓ Britain' is still there after more than 25 years but moving late 2006. At
**G22** TGP on edge of Dervaig but soon to take up residence on Aros estate by
Tobermory. Always an interesting programme. Phone in meantime.

**2266** ✓ **Eden Court Theatre** Inverness   01463 234234. An important theatre
Map 7 ✓ complex making a vital contribution to the cultural life of the Highlands.
**M18** Undergoing major refurb at TGP. Reopening Dec '06.

**2267** ✓ **Bowhill Little Theatre** Bowhill House nr Selkirk   01750 22204. Tiny
Map 10 ✓ (72-seat) theatre off the courtyard below Bowhill House with intermit-
**Q27** tent mixed programme (must phone), but always delightful, esp with supper
afterwards in Courtyard Restau (also phone to book).

**2268** ✓ **Eastgate** Peebles   01721 725777. Beautiful state-of-the-art wee the-
Map 10 ✓ atre clamped on to the back of a church (by eminent architect Richard
**Q27** Murphy) in Peebles Main St (Galashiels end). Eclectic, sometimes inspired
programming by director Mary Shiels. Expect everything! Caff & excl restau
adj (863/BORDERS RESTAUS). Phone or eastgatearts.com for prog.

**2269** ✓ **Pitlochry Theatre** 01796 484626. Modern rep theatre across river
Map 10 ✓ from main st performing usually 6 plays on different nights of the week.
**N21** Well-chosen programme of classics and popular works, the 500-seat theatre
is often full. V mixed Sunday concerts and foyer fringe events. Coffee bar and
restau menu. Also: Port-Na-Craig adj, by river & The Old Armoury (940/936/
PERTHSHIRE EATS), tho' both LO 8.30 ish.

**2270** ✓ **Byre Theatre St Andrews** 01334 476288. Abbey St or South St. A lot-
Map 10 ✓ tery-funded major reconstruction. Gr auditorium & café-bar (decent chef
**R23** at TGP). Major social hub for town & gown. Wills however has moved on (sob!).

**2271** **Cumbernauld Theatre** 01236 732887. Nr old part of this new town on a
Map 10 rise o/look the ubiquitous dual carriageway (to Stirling). Follow signs for
**M25** Cumbernauld House. Bar/café-restau and 258-seat theatre (in the round)
with a mixed programme of one-nighters and short runs of mainly Scottish
touring companies. Also concerts, drama workshops and kids' programmes.

**2272** **The Wynd** Melrose   01896 820028. 100-seater arts venue which regularly
Map 10 entertains locals and even Edin folk. From classic Ibsen and musicals to folk,
**R27** jazz, dance and film. Intimate atmos in an intimate town.

**2273** **Campbeltown Piture House** 01586 553899. Campbeltown, Argyll.
Map 9 Cinema Paradiso on the Kintyre peninsula. Lovingly preserved art deco gem;
**H28** a shrine to the movies. Opened 1913, closed 1983, but such was the tide of
nostalgic affection that it was refurbished and reopened resplendent in 1989.
Shows mainly first-run films. To see a film here and emerge onto the
esplanade of Campbeltown L is to experience the lost magic of a night at the
pictures. Prog: weepictures.co.uk

**2274** **The New Picture House** St Andrews   01334 473509. On North St. 'New'
Map 10 means 1931 and, apart from adding other small screens, it hasn't changed
**R23** much, as generations of students will remember with fondness. Mainly first-
run flicks; Oct-May, a prog of late-night cult/art movies.

✓ **Tolbooth** Stirling   01786 274000. See p. 317.

✓ **Lemon Tree** Aberdeen   01224 642230. 1075/ABERDEEN RESTAUS.

# SECTION 13

*The Islands*

# The Magical Islands

**2275**
Map 7
**G18**
✓✓ **Raasay** A small car ferry (car useful, but bikes best) from Sconser betw Portree and Broadford on Skye takes you to this, the best of places. The distinctive flat top of Dun Caan presides over an island whose history and natural history is Highland Scotland in microcosm. The village with rows of mining-type cottages is 3km from jetty. The Outdoor Centre (01478 660266) in the big hoose (once the home of the notorious Dr No who, like others before him, allowed Raasay to go to rack and ruin) has courses galore. They'll put you up if they've got rm (mostly bunkrooms). The views from the lawn, or the viewpoint above the house, or better still from Dun Caan with the Cuillins on one side and Torridon on the other, are quite brilliant (2312/ISLAND WALKS). Dolphin Café at the House is licensed. Long-awaited refurb on the way at TGP. The island hotel (15 rms, MED.EX) has bar but could do with some TLC. There's a ruined castle, a secret rhododendron-lined loch for swimming, seals, otters and eagles. Much to explore. Go quietly here. *Regular Calmac ferry from Sconser, but not Sun.*

**2276**
Map 9
**G25**
✓✓ **Jura** Small regular car ferry from Pt Askaig on Islay takes you into a different world. Jura is remote, scarcely populated and has an ineffable grandeur indifferent to the demands of tourism. Ideal for wild camping, alternatively the serviceable hotel and pub (2303/ISLAND HOTELS) in the only village (Craighouse) 15km from ferry at Feolin. Walking guides available at hotel and essential esp for the Paps, the hills that maintain such a powerful hold over the island. Easiest climb is from Three Arch Br; allow 6hrs. In May they run up all of them and back to the distillery in 3hrs. Jura House's walled gdn is a hidden jewel set above the S coastline; myriad wildflowers and Australasian trees with scenic walks to the shore (1564/GARDENS). The Corryvreckan whirlpool (2320/ISLAND WALKS) is another lure, but you may need a 4-wheel drive to get close enough, and its impressiveness depends upon tides. Orwell's house (Barnhill; where he wrote 1984) is not open, but there are many fascinating side tracks: the wild west coast; around L Tarbert; and the long littoral betw Craighouse and Lagg. (Also 1617/BEACHES; 1905/GRAVE-YARDS.) With one rd, no st lamps and over 5,000 deer the sound of silence is everything. *Western Ferries (01496 840681) regular 7 days, 5min service from Pt Askaig. Gemini Cruises (01546 830208) go from Crinan which is much quicker than Islay from central belt (& will go as & when, eg £60 per boatload to Ardlussa).*

**2277**
Map 9
**F23**
✓✓ **Iona** Strewn with daytrippers – not so much a pilgrimage, more an invasion – but Iona still enchants (as it did the Colourists), esp if you can get away to the Bay at the Back of the Ocean (1623/BEACHES) or watch the cavalcade from the hill above the Abbey. Or stay: **Argyll Hotel** best (01681 700334; 1217/GET-AWAY HOTELS) or B&B. Abbey shop isn't bad (2173/CRAFT SHOPS). Pilgrimage walks on Wed (10am from St John's Cross). Bike hire from Finlay Ross shop 01681 700357 & Seaview GH at Fionnphort 01681 700235. Everything about Iona is benign; even the sun shines here when it's raining on Mull. *Reg 15min Calmac service from Fionnphort till 6pm, earlier in winter (01681 700512).*

**2378**
Map 9
**F24**
✓✓ **Colonsay** Accessible to daytrippers in summer (on Weds you can do an overnight stay); this island haven of wildlife, flowers and beaches (1606/BEACHES) deserves more than a few hrs exploration. Recently re-opened & refurb hotel is congenial & convenient (2290/ISLAND HOTELS). Gr bar; self-catering units nearby. Some holiday cottages & many B&Bs (check Colonsay website), but camping discouraged. Bar meals & supper at the hotel and 'Pantry' at the pier. A wild 18-hole golf course & bookshop (sic) adj. Semi-botanical gdns adj to Colonsay House & fine walks, esp to Oronsay (2316/ISLAND WALKS). Don't miss the house at Shell Beach which sells oysters & honey. *Calmac from Oban (or Islay). Crossing takes just over 2hrs. Times vary.*

**2279**
Map 7
**G20**
✓✓ **Eigg** After changing hands, much to-do and cause célèbre, the islanders seized the time and Eigg is (in-fighting apart) theirs; and of course, ours. A wildlife haven for birds and sealife; otters, eagles and seal colonies. Scot Wildlife Trust warden does weekly walks around the island. Refurb tearoom at pier. Licenced and evening meals. Bicycle hire 01687 482432. 2 croft houses at Cleadale near Laig bay and the Singing Sands beach; contact Sue Kirk 01687 482405. She also offers full board accom and caters for vegn and other diets. 2,000 sheep on island. Gr walk to Sgurr an

*Eigg – an awesome perch on a summer's day. CalMac (from Mallaig) 01687 462403 or (better, from Arisaig) Arisaig Marine 01687 450224 every day except Thurs in summer. Phone for other timings. No car ferry; but motorbikes poss. Day trips to Rum and Muck.*

**2280**
Map 7
**F20**

✓ ✓ **Rum** The large island in the group S of Skye, off the coast at Mallaig. The Calmac ferry plies betw Canna, Eigg, Muck and Rum but not too conveniently and it's not easy to island-hop and make a decent visit (but *see below*). Rum the most wild and dramatic has an extraordinary time-warp mansion in Kinloch Castle which is mainly a museum (guided tours tie in with boat trips). Below stairs a hostel contrasts to the antique opulence above. Rum is run by Scottish Natural Heritage and there are fine trails, climbs, bird-watching spots. 2 simple walks are marked for the 3hr visitors, but the island reveals its mysteries more slowly. The Doric temple mausoleum to George Bullough, the industrialist whose Highland fantasy the castle was, is a 9km (3hr) walk across the island to Harris Bay. Sighting the sea eagles may be one of the best things that ever happens to you. Take a picnic. *Calmac ferry from Mallaig via Eigg (2hrs 15mins) or Canna at an ungodly hr. Better from Arisaig (Murdo Grant 01687 450224) Tues/Thur AYR plus Sat/Sun in summer (3hrs ashore).*

**2281**

✓ **Isle of Tiree** It is an isle, not just an island – it's flat, it has lovely sand & grass & the weather's usually better than the mainland. Bit of wind does keep away the midges. Lots of outdoor activities: windsurfing of course (2149/WINDSURFING), but kayaking, birdwatching & other gentle pursuits. The Scarinish Hotel (01879 220308) is friendly, so local & increasingly special Glebe House (01879 220758) is a manse with nice rms & a homely ambience. Tiree is different to the islands on this page – it's where we're going next. But you may long for trees. *Daily flights from Glasgow (0870 850 9850) & Calmac ferries from Oban (daily in summer).*

**2282**
Map 9
**G26**

✓ **Gigha** Romantic small island off Kintyre coast; with classic views of its island neighbours. Easy access to mainland (20min ferry trip) contributes to an island atmos that lacks any feeling of isolation. Like Eigg, Gigha was bought by the islanders so its fragile economy is even more dependent on your visit. The island currently remains a whole estate; with gdns open at the main house (1555/GARDENS), a tearm nr ferry and a hotel (2300/ISLAND HOTELS) providing comfortable surroundings. The locals are relaxed and friendly; with bike hire (07766 112619), 3 B&B options incl the big house (01583 505400), café-bar at the Boathouse & golf (9 holes). Best Walk: Left after golf course (9 hole), through gate and follow track (signed Ardailly) past Mill L to Mill and shore; gr views to Jura (1-B-2). See: Double Beach, where the Queen once swam off the Royal Yacht; two crescents of sand on either side of the N end of the isthmus of Eilean Garbh (seen from rd but path poorly marked). *Calmac ferry from Tayinloan on A83, 27km S of Tarbert (Glas 165km). One an hour in summer, fewer in winter. Cars exp and unnecessary.*

**2283**
Map 9
**F22**

✓ **Ulva** Off W coast of Mull. A boat leaves Ulva Ferry on the B8073 26km S of Dervaig. Idyllic wee island with 5 well-marked walks incl to the curious basalt columns similar to Staffa, or by causeway to the smaller island of Gometra; plan routes at boathouse 'interpretive centre' and tearoom (with Ulva oysters). 'Shiela's Cottage' faithfully restored. No accom. A charming Telford church has services 4 times a yr. Ulva is a perfect day away from the rat race of downtown Tobermory! *All-day 5min service (not Sat; Sun service summer only) till 5pm. Ferryman: 01688 500226.*

**2284**
Map 5
**D19**

✓ **Eriskay** Made famous by the sinking nearby of the SS *Politician* in 1941 & the salvaging of its cargo of whisky, immortalised by Compton Mackenzie in *Whisky Galore*, this Hebridean gem has all the 'idyllic island' ingredients: perfect beaches (1936/MARY, CHARLIE AND BOB), a hill to climb, a pub (called the Politician and telling the story round its walls; it sells decent pub food all day in summer), & a causeway to S Uist. There's only limited B & B and no hotel, but camping is ok if you're discreet. Eriskay & Barra together – the pure island experience. (Also 1888/CHURCHES *and see* THE OUTER HEBRIDES p. 298). *Ferry from Barra (Airdmhor) rn by Calmac (40 mins): 5 a day in summer, wint hrs vary.*

**2285**
Map 5
**C20**

✓ **Mingulay** Deserted mystical island nr the southern tip of the Outer Hebrides, the subject of one of the definitive island books, *The Road to Mingulay*. Now easily reached in summer by daily trip from Castlebay, Barra with 1.5hr journey and 3hrs ashore (enquire at TIC or Castlebay Hotel). Last inhabitants left 1912. Ruined village has the poignant air of St Kilda; similar spectacular cliffs on W side with fantastic rock formations, stacks and a huge natural arch – best viewed from boat. Mingulay was bought by NTS in '99. Only birds & sheep live here now.

**2286** **The Shiants** 3 magical, uninhabited tiny islands off E coast of Harris. Read
Map 5 about them in one of the most detailed accounts (a 'love letter') to any small
**F15** island ever written: 'Sea Room' by the guy who owns them, Adam Nicolson. There's a bothy & it is poss to visit by visiting first his website, but you'll have to find that for yourself.

**2287** **Lismore** Sail from Oban (car ferry) or better from Pt Appin 5km off main A828,
Map 9 the Oban-Ft William rd, 32km N Oban and where there's a seafood
**H22** bar/restau/hotel (1408/SEAFOOD RESTAUS), to sit and wait. A rd goes down the centre of the island, but there are many hill and coastal walks and even the nr end round Pt Ramsay feels away from it all. History, natural history and air. Bike hire on island from Mary McDougal 01631 760213 who will deliver to ferry or Port Appin Bikes 01631 730391. Alas no pub or tearoom! *Calmac service from Oban, 4 or 5 times a day (not Sun). From Pt Appin (32km N of Oban) several per day. 5mins. Last back 8.15pm 9.30 Fri & Sat, but check (6.15pm winter).*

**2288** **Staffa** For many a must, esp if you're on Mull. The geological phenomenon
Map 9 of Fingal's Cave and Mendelssohn's homage are well known. But it's still
**F22** impressive. Several boat-trip options, many incl the Treshnish Islands. *From Mull 0800 858786. From Iona/Fionnphort 01681 700338. From Oban 01631 566809.*

**CalMac** 08705 650000

# The Best Island Hotels

**2289** ✓ ✓ **The House Over-By At The Three Chimneys** Skye 01470
Map 7 511258. At Colbost 7km W of Dunvegan by the B884 to Glendale.
**F18** Eddie & Shirley Spear's quietly luxurious and tastefully decorated rms, adj or just over-by from their accolade-laden restau (in world's top lists) (2304/ISLAND RESTAUS). Separate dining rm for healthy buffet b/fast. Outside the sheep, the sea and the sky. Have set new standards for the Highlands, this is where to come for the pamper-yourself w/end.
6RMS JAN-DEC T/T PETS CC KIDS LOTS

**2290** ✓ **Colonsay Hotel** Colonsay 01951 200316. Long est but after lapse a newly
Map 9 refurb & potentially superb island hotel 100m from the ferry on this per-
**F24** fectly proportioned island for short stays (2278/ISLANDS). The laird (& the wife) & their partners seem determined to turn this into a contemp destination hotel. Rms refurb '05/06. Cool public rms & buzzy bar (esp Wed quiz nights). Mobiles only work in the garden. Stunning bench 5km. On your bike.
6RMS JAN-DEC T/T PETS CC KIDS MED.EX

**2291** ✓ **Kinloch Lodge** Skye 01471 833333. S of Broadford 5 mins, new rd in
Map 7 Sleat Peninsula, 55km Portree. The ancestral, but not overly imposing
**H19** home of Lord and Lady Macdonald with new build house adj – adding 5 v well appointed rms and spacious, country drawing rm. Lady Mac is Claire Macdonald of cookery fame, so her many books for sale in 'the shop', cook-ery courses thro' yr and her hand in all the wonderful things you eat (all meals in the Lodge itself). Some Lodge rms small and less exp.
9+5RMS JAN-DEC X/T XPETS KIDS LOTS
**EAT** At Lady Claire's table. 2305/ISLAND RESTAUS.

**2292** ✓ **Port Charlotte Hotel** Islay 01496 850360. Epitome perhaps of the
Map 9 comfortable, classy island hotel. Modern, discreet approach in this fine
**F26** whitewashed village (1598/COASTAL VILLAGES), good whisky choice & good, bistro-style food in dining rm; gr bar meals. Tourists in summer, hardcore twitchers in winter... and us anytime. 10RMS JAN-DEC T/T PETS CC MED.EX
**EAT** Best on Islay. 2306/ISLAND RESTAUS.

**2293** ✓ **Harbour Inn** Bowmore, Islay 01496 810330. 2 doors up from the har-
Map 9 bour in centre of main town on lovely, quite lively Islay. Rms contempo-
**F26** rary & comfy, lounge with views & notable restau. Bar with malts & bar meals (LO 8.45pm). 2 other rms across the st.
7RMS JAN-DEC T/T PETS KIDS MED.EX

**2294**
Map 7
**H19**
✓ **Eilean Iarmain** Skye  01471 833332. Isleornsay, Sleat. 60km S of Portree. Tucked into the bay this Gaelic inn with its gr pub and good dining provides famously comfortable base in S of the island. 6 rms in main hotel best value (6 are in house over-by). Also 4 suites over-by – plus. Environs superb.  12RMS + 4SUITES JAN-DEC T/T PETS CC KIDS EXP

**EAT** Especially in the bar.

**2295**
Map 5
**E15**
✓ **Scarista House** S Harris  01859 550238. 21km Tarbert, 78km Stornoway. On the W coast famous for its beaches and o/look one of the best (1614/BEACHES). Tim & Patricia Martin's civilised retreat & home from home. Fixed menu meals in dining rooms o/look sea. No phones (TV in kitchen), but many books. The golf course over the rd is exquisite. Check wint opening. Gd family hotel as well as couples on romantic break dining in.  5RMS JAN-DEC X/X PETS CC KIDS EXP

**EAT** Destination Harris. Fixed menu.

**2296**
Map 9
**G22**
✓ **Highland Cottage,** Tobermory 01688 302030. Breadalbane St opp fire stn. Trad Tobermory st above harbour (from r/bout on rd in from Craignure). 6 comfy rms named after islands (all themed, one called Nantucket). Their reputation grows and it's harder to get in but foodies should try hard. Everything here is small but perfectly formed – relaxed atmos with fine dining.  6RMS MAR-OCT T/T XPETS CC KIDS MED.EXP
**EAT** The fine-dining on Mull but not at all precious. 2307/ISLAND RESTAUS.

**2297**
Map 9
**F22**
✓ **Calgary Farmhouse** Mull 01688 400256. 7kms S of Dervany (30 mins Tobermory) nr beautiful Calgary Beach. Roadside bistro/restau (2310/ISLAND RESTAUS) with rms and gallery/coffee shop. Excl island hospitality – Matthew's furniture in public rms & 'Art in Nature' sculpture walking woods at back down to the beach. Bohemia in the bay. Get up early to see the otters (I never have). 2 self-cat suites above gallery. Good mod-Brit cooking.  9RMS MAR-NOV X/X PETS CC KIDS EXP

**EAT** Best informal ambience.

**2298**
Map 9
**J27**
✓ **Kilmichael** Brodick, Arran 01770 302219. On main rd to castle/ Corrie, take left at bend by golf course and you're in the country. 3km down track is this haven from Brodick & beyond. Country-house refined, so not gt for kids. Rms in house or garden courtyard – painstaking detail in food and environs.  6RMS EASTER-OCT T/T PETS CC KIDS EXP

**EAT** Best eats on Arran. 2308/ISLAND RESTAUS.

**2299**
Map 5
**C20**
✓ **Castlebay Hotel** Barra 01871 810223. Prominent position o/look bay and ferry dock. You see where you're staying long before you arrive. Old-style holiday hotel at the centre of Barra life with nice owners who are always there. Good restau and bar meals (2325/OUTER HEBRIDES). Adj bar one of the best bars for craic and car culture in Scotland and with more than a dash of the Irish (1328/BLOODY GOOD PUBS).  12RMS JAN-DEC T/T PETS CC KIDS INX

**2300**
Map 9
**G26**
**The Gigha Hotel** Isle Of Gigha 01583 505254. A short walk from the ferry on an island perfectly proportioned for a short visit; easy walking and cycling. Residents' lounge peaceful with dreamy views to Kintyre. Menu with local produce, eg Gigha prawns & scallops (in bar or dining rm) but ask what's fresh (not frozen)! Island life without the remoteness. Also self-cat cottages. 2282/ISLANDS.  13RMS FEB-NOV T/T PETS CC KIDS MED.EX

**2301**
Map 7
**G18**
**Viewfield House** Portree, Skye 01478 612217. One of the first hotels you come to in Portree on the rd from S (driveway opp gas stn); you need look no further. Individual, grand but comfortable, full of antiques and memorabilia, though not at all stuffy; this is also one of the best-value hotels on the island. Log fires, 4-course dinner. The Macdonalds like you to eat in as if you lived there.  12RMS APR-OCT T/X PETS CC KIDS MED.EX

**2302**
Map 7
**G17**
**Flodigarry** Skye 01470 552203. Staffin, 32km N of Portree. A romantic country house o/look the sea, with Flora Mac's cottage in the grounds. New owners at TGP. Reports please.  12RMS (+ 7COTT) JAN-DEC T/X PETS CC KIDS EXP

**2303**
Map 9
**G25**
**Jura Hotel** 01496 820243. Craighouse, 15km from Islay ferry at Feolin. Serviceable, basic hotel o/look Small Isles Bay; will oblige with all walking/exploring requirements. Pub is social hub of island. Rms at front may be small, but have the views.  17RMS JAN-DEC X/X PETS CC KIDS INX

✓ **Argyll Hotel** Iona 01681 700334 (1217/SEASIDE INNS).  MED

# The Best Restaurants In The Islands

**2304**  ✓ ✓ **The Three Chimneys** Skye  01470 511258. Colbost. 7km W
Map 7    Dunvegan on B884 to Glendale. Shirley and Eddie Spear's classic
**F18** restau in a converted cottage on the edge of the best kind of nowhere. They
shop local for everything (Skye supplies have hugely improved) so best ingredients. AYR. Lunch (except Sun & wint months). Dinner LO 9.30pm. It's a
long rd to Colbost, but you find out why Shirley's not in the kitchen so much
these days but overseeing everything, while chef Michael Smith will doubtless gather his own accolades. Best to stay, the wine-list is just too tempting.
EXP

**2305**  ✓ **Kinloch Lodge** Skye  01471 833333. In S on Sleat Peninsula, 55km S of
Map 7    Portree signed off the 'main' Sleat rd, along a characterful track. Lord
**H19** and Lady MacDonald's family home/hotel offers a taste of the high life without hauteur; a setting and setup especially appreciated by eg Americans,
starting with drinks in the dining rm 7.30pm for 8. Lady Claire's stints at the
stoves are renowned, as are the cookery books that result. Dinner almost a
theatrical event, (the dining rm: lined with oils, furnished with antiques,
glinting with silver). Fixed menu. Perfect cheeses but you simply must leave
rm for the puds.
EXP

**2306**  ✓ **Port Charlotte Hotel & Harbour Inn** Bowmore, Islay  01496 850360
Map 9    and 01496 810330. Both excl island inns, with dining rms & bar meals
**F26** using local produce that are as good as anything comparable on the mainland.
Both look over the western sea. Reports: 2292/2293 ISLAND HOTELS.

**2307**  ✓ **The Dining Room @ Highland Cottage** Tobermory  01688 302030.
Map 9    Jo Currie's down-to-earth fine dining; destination for foodies, a treat for
**G22** locals. Impeccably sourced. Nae nonsense!
MED

**2308**  ✓ **Kilmichael Hotel** Arran  01770 302219. 3km from seafront rd in
Map 9    Brodick, this is quite the place to go for dinner. Antony Butterworth
**J27** excels in the kitchen with best of local & national produce. Charming
Vietnamese waiting staff. Peacocks in the garden enliven the otherwise mel-
low soundtrack. Report: 2298/ISLAND HOTELS.
MED

**2309** **Castlebay Hotel** Castlebay  01871 810223. V decent plain cooking in infor-
Map 5 mal dining-rm or bar o/look castle and bay. Scores mainly when fresh from
**C20** the bay (lobster) or off the beach (cockles in garlic butter), but their sticky tof-
fee pudding is exactly as it ought to be.
MED

**2310** **Calgary Farmhouse & Dovecote Restaurant** Mull  01688 400256. 7km
Map 9 from Dervaig on B8073 nr Mull's famous beach. Roadside farm setting with
**F22** inexp light, piney bedrms and a bistro/wine bar restau using local produce.
For Mod-Brit cuisine. Gallery/coffee shop in summer. A quiet spot for most
ambient meal on Mull. No frills.
INX

**2311** **The Chandlery At The Bosville Hotel** Portree, Skye  01478 612846. Fine
Map 7 dining has come to Portree with John Kelly winning awards & more impor-
**G18** tantly, local approval. 2-choice menu well thought-out, sourced & present-
ed. Bistro menu in adj space is Portree's good deal/good food option.
EXP/INX

**Lochbay Seafood** Skye  12km N Dunvegan (2324/SKYE).
INX

**Creelers** Arran  01770 302810. Edge of Brodick (2322/ARRAN).
MED

**Digby Chick** Stornoway  01851 700026. (2325/OUTER HEBRIDES).

**Busta House** Shetland  01806 522506. 35km N of Lerwick (2328/SHETLAND).
MED

✓ **Argyll Hotel** Iona  01681 700334 (1217/SEASIDE INNS).
MED

✓ **Scarista House** Harris  01859 550238 (2295/ISLAND HOTELS).

# Fantastic Walks In The Islands

*For walk codes, see p. 13.*

*For walk codes, see p. 13.*

**2312** **Dun Caan** Raasay  Still one of my favourite island walks – to the flat top of
Map 7  a magic hill (1688/VIEWS). Take ferry (2275/MAGICAL ISLANDS), ask for route from
**G18**  Inverarish. Go via old iron mine; looks steep when you get over the ridge, but
it's a dawdle. And amazing.                                    10KM XCIRC XBIKE 2-B-2

**2313** **The Lost Glen** Harris  Take B887 W from Tarbert almost to the end (where
Map 5  at Hushinish there's a good beach, maybe a sunset), but go rt before the Big
**E15**  House (signed Chliostair Power Stn). Park here or further in & walk to dam
(3km from rd). Take rt track round reservoir & left around the upper loch.
Over the brim you arrive in a wide, wild glen; an overhang 2km ahead is said
to have the steepest angle in Europe. Go quietly; if you don't see deer &
eagles here, you're making too much noise on the grass.
                                                              12KM RET XCIRC XBIKE 2-B-2

**2314** **Carsaig** Mull  In S of island, 7km from A849 Fionnphort-Craignure rd nr
Map 9  Pennyghael. 2 walks start at pier: going left towards Lochbuie for a spectac-
**G23**  ular coastal/woodland walk past Adnunan Stack (7km); or rt towards the
imposing headland where, under the cliffs, the Nuns' Cave was a shelter for
nuns evicted from Iona during the Reformation. Nearby is a quarry whose
stone was used to build Iona Abbey and much further on (9km Carsaig), at
Malcolm's Pt, the extraordinary Carsaig Arches carved by wind and sea.
                                                              15/20KM XCIRC XBIKE 2-B-2

**2315** **Cock of Arran** Lochranza  Turn right at church & follow signs. 8/9km cir-
Map 9  cular walk into Glen Chalmadale and high into moorland (260m), then drops
**J26**  down to magnificent shoreline. Here eagles catch the updraft and peregrines
lose it. Divers and ducks share the shore with seals. About 1km from where
you meet the shore, look for Giant Centipede fossil trail. Futher on at opening of wall pace 350 steps and turn left up to Ossian's Cave. Path crosses Fairy
Dell Burn and eventually comes out at Lochranza Bay. Allow 5/6hrs & stout
boots (good walk desc from y hostel).                          11KM CIRC XBIKE

**2316** **Colonsay** (2278/MAGICAL ISLANDS). From hotel or the quay, walk to Colonsay
Map 9  House and its lush, overgrown intermingling of native plants and exotics
**F24**  (8km round trip); or to the priory on Oronsay, the smaller island. 6km to 'the
Strand' (you might get a lift with the postman) then cross at low tide, with
enough time (at least 2hrs) to walk to the ruins. Allow longer if you want to
climb the easy peak of Ben Oronsay. Tide tables at hotel. Nice walk also from
Kiloran Beach (1646/BEACHES) to Balnahard Beach – farm track 12km ret.
                                                              12+6KM XCIRC BIKE 1-A-2

**2317** **The Old Man Of Storr** Skye  The enigmatic basalt finger visible from the
Map 7  Portree-Staffin rd (A855). Start from car park on left, 12km from Portree.
**G17**  There's a well-defined path through woodland & then towards the cliffs and
a steep climb up the grassy slope to the pinnacle which towers 165ft tall. Gr
views over Raasay to the mainland. Lots of space and rabbits and birds who
make the most of it. Was the location of major environmental art event by
notable nva organisation in summer 2005.                      5KM XCIRC XBIKE 2-B-2

**2318** **The Quirang** Skye  See 1686/VIEWS for directions to start pt. The strange for-
Map 7  mations have names (e.g. the Table, the Needle, the Prison) and it's possible
**G17**  to walk round all of them. Start of the path from the car park is easy. At the
first saddle, take the second scree slope to the Table, rather than the first.
When you get to the Needle, the path to the rt betw two giant pinnacles is
the easiest of the 3 options. From the top you can see the Hebrides. This
place is supernatural; anything could happen. So be careful.
                                                              6KM XCIRC XBIKE 2-B-2

**2319** **Hoy** Orkney  There are innumerable walks on the scattered Orkney Islands
Map 3  and on Hoy itself; on a good day you can get round the north part of the
**Q11**  island and see some of the most dramatic coastal scenery anywhere. A passenger ferry leaves Stromness 2 or 3 times a day and takes 30mins. Make
tracks N or S from jnct nr pier and use free Hoy brochure from TIC so as not
to miss the landmarks, the bird sanctuaries and the Old Man himself.
                                                              20/25KM CIRC MTBIKE 2-B-2

**2320 Corryvreckan** Jura  The whirlpool in the Gulf of Corryvreckan is notorious.
Map 9  Betw Jura and Scarba; to see it go to far N of Jura. From end of the rd at
**H24**  Ardlussa (25km Craighouse, the village), there's a rough track to Lealt then a
walk (a local may drive you) of 12km to Kinuachdrach, then a further walk of
3km. Phenomenon best seen at certain states of tide. There are boat trips
from Crinan and Oban – consult TICs. Consult hotel (2303/ISLAND HOTELS) and
get the walk guide. (2276/MAGICAL ISLANDS)        6/24KM XCIRC XBIKE 2-C-2

**2321 Sgurr An Eigg**  Unmissable treat if you're on Eigg. Take to the big ridge. Not
Map 7  a hard pull, and extraordinary views & island perspective from the top.
**G20**  (2279/MAGICAL ISLANDS)

# The Best Of Arran

**2322**
Map 9

**Ferry** Ardrossan-Brodick, 55mins. 6 per day Mon-Sat, 4 on Sun. Ardrossan-Glas, train or rd via A77/A71 1.5hr. Claonaig-Lochranza, 30mins. 9 per day (summer only). *The best way to see Arran is on a bike.*

## WHERE TO STAY

✓ **Kilmichael House** Brodick  01770 302219. Period mansion 3km from the main rd and into the glens. Elegant interior & furnishings in house and courtyard rooms. V discreet hence no groups or kids. Still *the* place to eat on Arran, but book (2298/ISLAND HOTELS). Also has self-cat cottages.

6RMS JAN-DEC T/T XPETS CC XKIDS MED.EX

**Auchrannie House** Brodick  01770 302234. Once an old mansion now expanded all over & become a holiday complex. House still best rms & eats (Garden Restau) & even pool. But the 'Spa Resort' like a Holiday Inn Xpress in the country is best for families – in fact perfect for families – quite stylish modern rms. Another pool & leisure facs. Upstairs restau a bit Heathrow Airport but fits all sizes! Old house enlarged and recently refurbed. Somewhat overshadowed by the travelodge/spa. Burgeoning time-share in grounds.

29RMS(HOUSE), 36(SPA) JAN-DEC T/T XPETS CC KIDS MED.EX

**Argentine House** Whiting Bay  01770 700662. Seaside home on the front at Whiting Bay, a GH run by Swiss couple, the inimitable Baumgärtners. Cluttered, rather boho public rms but contemp, light bedrms. Mrs B does massage. You have been warned!5RMS MAR-JAN X/T PETS CC XKIDS MED.INX

**Burlington** Whiting Bay  01770 700255. Adj Argentine (above). The Lamonts' homely hoose. Pride themselves on their 'slow-food' menu (see below). 8RMS APR-OCT X/T PETS CC KIDS MED.INX

**Lochranza Hotel** 01770 830223. Small hotel with tranquil views across bay and 13thC castle. In village. Basic accom but home-spun hosp, soups, pâtés, scones & more (scones). Beer garden with food all day in season.

7RMS EASTER-DEC T/T PETS CC KIDS INX

**S.Y. Hostels** at Lochranza (01770 830631) and Whiting Bay (01770 700339). Both busy Grade 2s in picturesque areas (Mar-Oct), 25 and 15km from Brodick.

**Camping & Caravan Parks** at Glen Rosa (01770 302380) 4km Brodick; Lamlash (01770 600251), Lochranza (01770 830273). And Glen Rosa has idyllic river side camping.

## WHERE TO EAT

✓ **Kilmichael House** Brodick   01770  302219. (See above.) Unquestionably the best food on Arran. 8 choices & starter/main/pud. Report: 2308/ISLAND RESTAUS. MED

**The Lighthouse** 01770 850240. Restau bunkhouse at Pirnmill looking over to Kintyre. Maritime blue & pine room – wholesome menu of gr home-made food (1500/BEST TEAROOMS). Best place on island for sundowners & cappucinos. BYOB. 7 days. Feb-Nov 9am-8pm. INX

**Creelers** Brodick  01770 302810. Art, seafood & atmos (when you find the place open). Phone ahead – hrs a tad unpredictable but gr seafd, much v locally sourced – has own smokery. (1401/SEAFOOD RESTAUS). MED

**Burlington Hotel** Whiting Bay  01770 700255. Kitchen under the direction of Robin Gray (who also runs an organic produce business) & the likeable Lamonts. The food is 'slow', the vibe is green & organic. Nice for Arran, nice for you! Apr-Oct. Dinner only, daily. INX

**The Distillery Restaurant** 01770 830264. At the Distillery Visitor Centre, Lochranza. Good light menu in light even clinical rm with running water accompaniment although the new Americans are planning big changes at TGP. Daily 10am-6pm in season. Phone out of season. INX

**Brodick Bar** Best pub food in Brodick? Yes. Bar snacks, then turns into more of a bistro (they call it a 'brasserie', but it can feel like a camp canteen in summer) in the eve. Food until 10pm. Off N end of main st by Royal Mail. Bar open till midnight. CHP

**Corrie Golf Club Tearoom** Sannox Just outside vill (Sannox not Corrie) going N. Best cakes & light snacks on island in hut-like golfing situation. 7 days 9am-6pm tho' may open early evens for bookings. Cl in wint. INX

**Joshua's** Whiting Bay 01770 700738. Shoreline location with conservatory & contemp look. Home-made up-to-a-point burgers/steaks & snacks. Best book evens in summer. 10am-5pm, 6pm-8.30pm. Cl Sun. INX

## WHAT TO SEE

**Brodick Castle** 5km walk or cycle from Brodick. Impressive museum and gdns. Tearoom. Flagship NTS property. (1790/CASTLES.) NT

**Goat Fell** 6km/5hr gr hill walk starting from the car park at Cladach nr castle and Brodick or sea start at Corrie. Free route leaflet at TIC. (1961/HILLS.) 2-A-2

**Glenashdale Falls** 4km, but 2hr forest walk from Glenashdale Br at Whiting Bay. Steady, easy climb, silvan setting. (1641/WATERFALLS.) 1-B-1

**Corrie** The best village 9km N Brodick. Go by bike. (1604/COASTAL VILLAGES.)

**Machrie Moor Standing Stones** Off main coast rd 7km N of Blackwater Foot. Various assemblies of Stones, all part of an ancient landscape. We lay down there.

**Glen Rosa, Glen Sannox** Fine glens: Rosa nr Brodick, Sannox 11km N. 1-B-2

Tourist Info 01770 303774. CalMac 08705 650000.

# The Best Of Islay & Jura

2323  **Ferry** Kennacraig-Pt Askaig: 2hrs, Kennacraig-Pt Ellen: 2hrs 10 mins.
Map 9  Pt Askaig-Feolin, Jura: 5mins, frequent daily (01496 840681).

**By Air** from Glas to Pt Ellen Airport in S of island. BA 08457 733377.

## WHERE TO STAY

✓ **Port Charlotte Hotel** Port Charlotte 01496 850360. Restored Victorian inn and gdns on seafront of conservation village. Restful place, restful views. Good bistro-style menu, the best around. Eat in bar/conservatory or dining rm. Report: 2292/ISLAND HOTELS.
10RMS JAN-DEC T/T PETS CC KIDS MED.EX

✓ **Harbour Inn** Bowmore 01496 810330. Some yrs ago one Scott Chance transformed this into a contemp island/Highland gem. With Neil & Carol Scott it remains in good hands. An excl conservatory lounge, snug bar & stylish dining rm with Mod British menu. Bedrms vary but all mod & con. Report: 2293/ISLAND HOTELS.
7RMS JAN-DEC T/T PETS CC KIDS MED.INX

**Kilmeny Farm** nr Ballygrant 01496 840668. Margaret and Blair Rozga's top-class GH just off the rd S of Pt Askaig (the ferry). Huge attention to detail, great home-made food, house party atmos and a shared table. Tho small.
3RMS JAN-DEC X/X XPETS XCC KIDS MED.INX

**Glenmachrie** nr Port Ellen 01496 302560. On A846 betw Bowmore & Pt Ellen adj airport. Sister GH of Kilmeny Farm (above). Here it's Rachel's award-winning farmhouse with everything just so (fluffy bathrobes, toiletries supplied, fruit bowl & a sweet on the pillow) and gr meals, esp her famously good b/fast (must have the porridge). Farmers with a green sensibility. & see below.
5RMS JAN-DEC X/T PETS XCC XKIDS MED.INX

**Glenegedale House** The new venture by Rachel Whyte nr Glenmachrie & opp the airport. An ambitious project that augurs well (but will she have the same attention to detail in the much bigger place?). A v good bet! Open 2006. For now, same no. as Glenmachrie.

**The Machrie** Port Ellen 01496 302310. 7km N on A846. Restau and bar meals in clubhouse atmos. Restau in old byre and 15 lodges in the grounds. You'll likely be here for the golf – so you might overlook its rather bleak setting. Food, I'm told, is surprisingly good. The gr beach (1611/BEACHES) *is* over there.                    15RMS + 15(COTT) JAN-DEC T/T XPETS CC KIDS MED.INX

**Lochside Hotel** Bowmore  01496 810244. Probably best selection of Islay malts in the world; so gr bar & bar meals in lochside, actually seaside setting. Rms 50-50. Pub food standard.                                          MED.INX

**Bridgend Inn** Bridgend  01496 810212. Middle of island on rd from Pt Askaig, 4km Bowmore. Roadside inn with good pub meals & surprising no of rms. A reasonable stopover.          10RMS JAN-DEC T/T PETS CC KIDS MED.EX

**Jura Hotel** Craighouse  01496 820243. The best hotel on the island – well, the only one! But it does what you want. Situated in front of the distillery by the bay. Front rms best (not all en suite). There's craic in the bar. Report: 2303/ISLAND HOTELS.                      18RMS JAN-DEC X/X PETS CC KIDS INX

**Camping, Caravan Site, Hostel** at Kintra Farm. 01496 302051. Off main rd to Pt Ellen; take Oa rd, follow Kintra signs 7km. July-August B&B in farmhouse. Grassy strand, coastal walks. **Islay Youth Hostel** Pt Charlotte 01496 850385.

## WHERE TO EAT

✓ **Harbour Inn** Bowmore and **Port Charlotte Hotel**  *see above.*

✓ **Ardbeg Distillery Café**  5km E of Pt Ellen on the whisky rd. Gr local rep for food. Beautiful rm. Food home-made as are those Ardbegs. Most vintages & Ardbeg clothes to boot. AYR Mon-Fri (7 days June-Aug) 10am-LO4pm.                                                             INX

**Croft Kitchen**  Pt Charlotte. 01496 850230. Serviceable caff in fine vill where Port Charlotte Hotel is the food destination. The cheap, cheerful AYR option (except Jan). 7 days 10.30am-8.30pm. Book in season.          INX

**Ballygrant Inn**  01496 840277. S of Pt Askaig. Basic pub with dining rm & 3 rms upstairs. Like being in their home – & it is! Food home-made (gr soda bread). Over 80 whiskies. Reports vary but these are good people. Lunch & dinner (can be late) & bar can be v late. Nice family will welcome yours.  INX

## WHAT TO SEE

Islay:  **The Distilleries** esp Ardbeg (good café), Laphroaig and Lagavulin (classic settings), all by Pt Ellen; tours by appointment. Bowmore has regular glossy tour; Ardbeg, open daily, good cafe (1530/WHISKY); **Museum of Islay, Wildlife Info & Field Centre** (1786/WILDLIFE): all at Pt Charlotte; **American Monument** (1864/MONUMENTS); **Oa & Loch Gruinart** (1766/BIRDS); **Port Charlotte** (1598/COASTAL VILLAGES); **Kintra** (2038/COASTAL WALKS); **Finlaggan** The romantic, sparse ruin on 'island' in L Finlaggan: last home of the Lords of the Isles. Off A846 5km S of Pt Askaig, check TIC for opening.

Jura  (2276/MAGICAL ISLANDS): **The Paps of Jura**; **Corryvreckan, Barnhill** (2320/ISLAND WALKS); **Killchianaig, Keils** (1905/GRAVEYARDS); **Lowlandman's Bay** (1617/BEACHES); **Jura House Walled Garden**; utterly magical in the right light (1564/GARDENS).

**Tourist Info**  01496 810254. **CalMac**  08705 650000.

# The Best Of Skye

2324
Map 7 **The Bridge** the hump (which it gave to a lot of locals); unromantic but convenient – now free; from Kyle. **The Ferries** Mallaig-Armadale, 30mins. Tarbert (Harris)-Uig, 1hr 35mins (Calmac, as Mallaig). **The Best Way To Skye** is Glenelg-Kylerhea, 5mins. Continuous Apr-Oct 01599 511302. Wint sailings: check TIC.

## WHERE TO STAY

✓✓ **House Over-By** 01470 511258. Report: 2289/ISLAND HOTELS

✓ **Kinloch Lodge** 01471 833333. Report: 2291/ISLAND HOTELS

✓ **Eilean Iarmain** 01471 833332. 15km S of Broadford on A851. V Gaelic inn on bay with dreamy views, good food and gr pub. Main hotel best value (with cottage annexe); suites over rd are more ex (2294/ISLAND HOTELS).
12RMS (4SUITES) JAN-DEC T/X PETS CC KIDS EXP

**Viewfield House** Portree 01478 612217. One of the oldest island houses; it's been in the MacDonald family over 200 yrs. Unique and antique atmos. Highland hospitality. Gr dinner. (2301/ISLAND HOTELS.)
12RMS APR-OCT T/X PETS CC KIDS MED.EX

**Sabhal Mòr Ostaig** 01471 888000. Part of the Gaelic College in Sleat off A851 N of Armadale. Pron *Sawal More Ostag*. Excl inx rms in modern build o/looking Sound of Sleat. Penthouse spectac. B/fast in bright café. Best deal on the island; you could learn Gaelic. 80RMS JAN-DEC X/X XPETS CC XKIDS CHP

**Torvaig House** Sleat 01471 833231. Roadside hotel on A851, the speedy new rd to Armadale from Broadford & the br. Recently & totally refurb mansion with good views. Individ bedrms with good beds. Dining ok, and good choices nearby. 9RMS JAN-DEC T/T PETS CC KIDS EXP

**Cuillin HIlls Hotel** Portree 01478 612003. On the edge of Portree (off rd N to Staffin) nr water's edge. Secluded mansion house hotel with nice conservatory. Decor: a matter of taste (you may like leather-studded sofas and draped 4-posters) but gr views from most rms.
28RMS JAN-DEC T/T PETS CC KIDS MED.EX

**Skeabost** 01470 532202. 11km W of Portree on A850. Country house with 9-hole golf and salmon fishing on R Snizort. Latest of many owners (at TGP) have music biz background (hence photo library on walls) & unusual app to hotel management. There are v 6 rock 'n' roll suites. Locals say staying here is like a night at the Osbournes'. 23RMS JAN-DEC T/T PETS CC KIDS MED.EX

**The Stein Inn** Waternish 01470 592362. Off B886, the Waternish rd which is 5km Dunvegan on the rd to Portree. Distant but v Skye location in vill row on the water & nr Lochbay (see below). Ancient inn with atmos pub (1182/SEASIDE INNS) & 5 nice rms above. An excl retreat.
5RMS JAN-DEC X/X PETS CC KIDS CHP

**Flodigarry** 01470 552203. 30km N Portree on A855. Far-flung N of the island; the views exceptional. Country-house ambience. New owners still settling in at TGP. Bar & restau perhaps not what they were.
11RMS + 7(COTT) JAN-DEC T/X PETS CC KIDS EXP

**S.Y. Hostels** At Kyleakin (biggest, nearest mainland), Armadale (interesting area in S), Broadford, Glen Brittle (v Cuillin), Uig (for N Skye, ferry to Hebrides). **Independent Hostels** at Kyleakin & Staffin (1173/1174/HOSTELS). 2 (1 rel new) in Portree.

## WHERE TO EAT

✓✓ **Three Chimneys** 01470 511258. 7km W of Dunvegan on B884. Superb home cooking, best in the islands. Report: 2304/ISLAND RESTAUS.                                                                MED

✓ **Kinloch Lodge** 01471 833333. 13km S Broadford off A851. Classy food in almost theatrical atmos at Lady Claire's table(s). Report: 2305/ISLAND RESTAUS.                                                                EXP

**The Chandlery, Bosville Hotel & Bistro** 01478 612846. The Bosville is where to eat proper in Portree. Bistro & adj (same space), the 'fine-dining' Chandlery under 'award-winning' chef John Kelly haven't got much competition, but both menus are on the button. AYR. Bistro: lunch & dinner. Chandlery dinner only LO 9.45pm. Open Apr-Oct for lunch & LO 10pm.   MED

**Lochbay Seafood** 01470 592235. 12km N Dunvegan off A850. Small; simple fresh seafood in loch-side setting, Apr-Oct. Cl Sun & Sat (Sat dinner in July/Aug only). Report: 1397/SEAFOOD RESTAUS.   INX

**An Tuireann Café** 01478 613306. Nr Portree. Coffee shop/gallery. Good food and chat in a cultural caff. Cl Sun. Report: 1379VEGN RESTAUS.

**Harbour View** Portree 01478 612069. Bosville Terr on rd to Staffin and N Skye with harbour view at least from the door. Local seafood in intimate bistro dining rm. 7 days Easter-Oct lunch and dinner (not Sun lunch). LO 9.30pm.

**Creelers** Broadford 01471 822281. Just off A87 rd from Kyleakin & bridge to Portree as you come into Broadford. Small cabin seafood restau & t/away round back, but excl local rep. 4pm-10pm (& t/away till 10pm). Cl Wed.

**Pasta Shed** Armadale no number. On the quayside at Armadale where the Mallaig ferry comes in. A real pizza hut, but best to get Alistair MacPhail to knock you up some super-fresh seafood. Amazone teas & herbs from garden adj. 7 days in season 9am-5.30pm (7.30 high season).

**Café Arriba** Portree 01478 611830. Above/over Over the Rainbow on rd down to harbour. At last a cool caff on Skye. Some healthy food, some not. Good bread/coffee/vegn. Does the trick. 7 days. LO 9pm.

**The Stables** Coffee shop/restau of the Clan Donald Centre/Museum of the Isles on A851 1km N of Armadale. Decent self-serv comfort food & cakes for us tourists. Apr-Oct till 5.30pm.

## WHAT TO SEE

**The Cuillins** (2/BIG ATTRACTIONS); **Raasay** (2275/MAGICAL ISLANDS), (2312/ISLAND WALKS); **The Quirang** (1686/VIEWS), (2318/ISLAND WALKS); **Old Man Of Storr** (2317/ISLAND WALKS); **Dunvegan** (1800/CASTLES); **Eas Mor** (1643/WATERFALLS); **Elgol** (1691/VIEWS); **Skye Batiks** (2171/CRAFT SHOPS); **Skye Museum Of Island Life** (2242/MUSEUMS); **Flora Macdonald's Grave** (1866/MONUMENTS); **Skye Silver, Edinbane Pottery** and **Carbost Craft** (2167/2166/CRAFT SHOPS); **Fairy Pools** (1706/PICNICS).

**Tourist Info** 01478 612992. **CalMac** 08705 650000.

# The Best Of The Outer Hebrides

**2325**
Map 5
**Ferries** Ullapool-Stornoway, 2hrs 40mins, (not Sun). Oban/Mallaig-Lochboisdale, S Uist and Castlebay, Barra; up to 6.5hrs. Uig on Skye-Tarbert, Harris (not Sun) or Lochmaddy, N Uist 1hr 40mins. Also Leverburgh, Harris-Otternish, N Uist (not Sun) 1hr 10mins.

**By Air** BA 3 times daily (2 Sat; not Sun). Inverness/Glas/Edin. Local 01851 703240. BA Otter to Barra/Benbecula from Glas (1/2 a day). Linkline 08457 733377.

## WHERE TO STAY

✓ **Scarista House** S Harris 01859 550238. 20km S of Tarbert. Cosy haven nr famous but often deserted beach; celebrated retreat. Also self-catering accom. Report: 2295/ISLAND HOTELS.

✓ **Blue Reef Cottages** Scarista, S Harris 01859 550370. 1 km from Scarista House (above) & o/looking the same idyllic beach. I don't usually list self-cat cotts in StB but these 2 are exceptional. For couples only tho' the study could be another bedrm at a pinch. Stylish, good facs, amazing view. Gourmet meals from lady nearby or eat at Scarista Ho. 7-day stays. 2-day mins in wint.   EXP

**Rodel Hotel** S Harris 01859 520210. Hotel at the end of the rd, the A859, S of Tarbert, S of everywhere. Superb setting, you are truly away from it all. Recent makeover, so comfy & contemp (2 self-cat). Large front rms best. Restau gets mixed reception. 4(+2)RMS APR-DEC X/T PETS CC KIDS MED.EX

**Baile-Na-Cille** Timsgarry, W Lewis 01851 672241. Nr Uig 60km W of Stornoway. This is about as far away as it gets but guests return again & again to the Collins' house by the sea. Hospitable hosts allow you the run of their place – the books, the games rm, the tennis court & the most amazing beach. Gr value & esp good for families (1144/HOTELS KIDS). 7RMS APR-OCT X/X PETS CC KIDS MED.INX

**Castlebay Hotel** Castlebay, Barra 01871 810223. O/looks ferry terminal in main town. Excellent value. Decent food. Brilliant bar (2307/ISLAND HOTELS; 1328/BLOODY GOOD PUBS).

**Tigh Dearg (The Red House) Hotel** Lochmaddy, N Uist 01876 500700. Opening autumn '05 (after TGP). Gr things expected of this new venture. Reports please.

**Royal Hotel** Stornoway, Lewis 01851 702109. The most central of the 3 main hotels in town which are all owned by the same family co. HS-1 bistro and Boatshed (probably 'best' hotel dining). The **Cabarfeidh** 01851 702604 is the upmarket ie most exp option – prob the best bedrms. These hotels are the only places open in Lewis on Suns, although the **Caladh** (pron 'Cala') **Inn** & its caff '11', has recently been made over & seems best value. 26RMS JAN-DEC T/T PETS CC KIDS MED.INX

**Ardhasaig House** N Harris 01859 502066. 4km N of Tarbert just off A859 Stornoway rd. Neither this modern-build house nor its locally well-connect- ed chef/prop (her family owns everything hereabouts) are esp comfortable to be with but there are redeeming features. Nice location & convenient. While madame may not have gone to charm school, she did learn to cook (Andrew Fairley's kitchen has been mentioned). And there's a nice conservatory. 6RMS JAN-DEC X/X XPETS CC KIDS MED.EXP

**Harris Hotel** Tarbert 01859 502154. In the township nr the ferry terminal so good base for travels in N/S Harris. Variety of public rms & diverse range of bedrms (view/non-view, refurb/non-refurb, standard/superior), some of which are large & v nice. Friendly & well run. Food not a strong pt, but ade- quate. Also barmeals in pub next door. 24RMS JAN-DEC T/T PETS CC KIDS MED.INX/EX

**Pollachar Inn** S Uist 01878 700215. S of Lochboisdale nr small ferry for Eriskay/Barra (2199/ISLANDS) an inn at the end of the known world. Excl value, good craic and the view/sunset across the sea to Barra. New owners & planned major refurb should improve '06/07. 9RMS JAN-DEC T/T PETS CC KIDS MED.INX

**Hostels** Simple hostels within hiking distance. 2 in Lewis, 3 in Harris, 1 each in N and S Uist. Altogether an excellent hostelling holiday prospect with 2 exceptional (1240 & 1241/ HOSTELS) & Barra.

## WHERE TO EAT

**Digby Chick** Stornoway 01851 700026. 11 James St. Contemp café/restau with seafood speciality & good local rep. Mon-Sat, lunch & LO 8.30pm. MED

**The Thai Café** Stornoway 01851 701811. 27 Church St opp police stn. An unlikely find but prob the best place to eat in this town – Mrs Panida Macdonald's restau an institution here & you may have to book. Gr atmos, excl real Thai cuisine, though you couldn't be further in every respect from Bangkok. Lunch & LO 11pm. Cl Sun.

**The Boatshed At The Royal Hotel** Stornoway & '11' At The Caladh Inn (see above). Best hotel options (& open Suns).

**Tigh Mealros** Garynahine, Lewis 01851 621333. On A858 22km SW Stornoway. 2km S of Callanish. Unpretentious surf 'n' turf. Scallops (dived) a special. BYOB. Gr dry-stone stonework in progress at TGP. Open AYR. LO 9pm.

**Sunsets, Stornoway** 01851 705862. 26 Francis St, corner with Keith. Another rel recent addition to Stornoway's restau offering, this a more dis- creet, back-street bistro. Fine enough. Evens only 6-9pm. Cl Sun. INX

**Coffee Shops** at **An Lanntair Gallery** Stornoway and **Callanish Vistor Centre** Lewis. The latter esp good. Daytime hrs (1865/PREHISTORIC SITES). An Lanntair re-opening at TGP after moving & metamorphosing.

**Scarista House** Harris *(see above)*. Dinner possible for non-residents. A 20mins Tarbert, 45min Stornoway drive for best meal in the Hebrides. Fixed menu. Book.

**Skoon Art Café** S Harris 01859 530268. On stunning Golden Road (1671/SCENIC ROUTES) 12km S of Tarbert, this café in a gallery. All done well – interesting soups, gr home-baking. Open AYR Mon-Sat daytime only.     CHP

**First Fruits Tearoom** Tarbert, Harris Nr TIC and ferry to Uig. Home-cooking that hits the spot. Good atmos. Wide-ranging menu incl all-day b/fast. 10.30am-4.30pm Apr-Sept.

**Orasay Inn** Lochcarnan, S Uist 01870 610298. 3km from main, spinal A885, signed from rd. Small hotel apparently in the middle of nowhere, but with a conservatory & bar that's often packed with those that know. Esp good for seafood, from local halibut to razors & 'witches'. Milky seaweed jelly amongst extraord menu. Also 9 INX rms. Open AYR, lunch & LO 9pm.     INX

**Stepping Stones** Balvanich, Benbecula 01870 603377. 8 km from main A855. Nondescript building in ex- (tho' still operational) military air base. Serving the forces & the tourists – it aims to please. 7 days, lunch & LO 9pm (wint hrs may vary). Menu changes thro' day.     INX

**Tourist Info** 01851 703088. **CalMac** 08705 650000.

# The Best Of Mull

**2326**
Map 9

**Ferry** Oban-Craignure, 45mins. Main route; 6 a day. Lochaline-Fishnish, 15mins. 9-15 a day. Kilchoan-Tobermory, 35mins. 7 a day (Sun – summer only). Winter sailings – call TIC.

## WHERE TO STAY

✓ **Highland Cottage** Tobermory 01688 302030. Breadalbane St opp fire stn a street above the harbour. Like a co house, well... a gorgeous cottage in town. The top spot. Report: 2296/HOTELS.
6RMS MAR-OCT T/T XPETS CC KIDS EXP

✓ **Tiroran House** Mull 01681 705232: In S of Mull, a treat and a retreat way down the SW of Mull nr Iona. Light, comfy house in glorious gdns with excl food & flowers. See eagles fly over. Report: 1216/GET AWAY HOTELS.
6RMS + 2COTT JAN-DEC X/T XPETS CC KIDS EXP

✓ **Argyll Hotel** Iona 01681 700334. Nr ferry and on seashore o/looking Mull on rd to abbey. Laid-back, cosy accom, cottage rms, home cooking, good vegn. (1179/SEASIDE INNS)   15RMS FEB-NOV X/X PETS CC KIDS MED.INX

**Glengorm Castle** nr Tobermory 01688 302321. Minor rd on right going N outside town. Glen Gormenghast! Fab views over to Ardnamurchan from this baronial pile. Luxurious bedrms in family home – use the library & grand public spaces. Loads of art, lawn & gardens. Excl self-cat cotts on estate. B&B only.     5RMS JAN-DEC X/X PETS CC KIDS EXP

**Calgary Farmhouse** Calgary 01688 400256. Nr Dervaig on B8073 nr Mull's famous beach. Gallery/coffee shop and good bistro/restau. Report: 2297/ISLAND HOTELS.     9RMS MAR-NOV X/T PETS CC KIDS MED.INX

**Tobermory Hotel** 01688 302091. On waterfront. Creature comforts, gr outlook in the middle of Balamory bay. 10 rms to front. Restau ok & others nearby.     16RMS JAN-DEC X/T PETS CC KIDS MED.INX

**Ptarmigan House** Tobermory 01688 302863. Above the town (ask for golf course, it's adj clubhouse) & above all that. Modern, almost purpose-built GH. High-spec rms with gr views and... a swimming pool. Sue & Michael Fink have pushed the boat out since they left the Western Isles (quel demise!). Evening meals on request.     4RMS MAR-NOV X/T XPETS CC XKIDS MED.INX

**S.Y. Hostel** In Tobermory main st on bay (1168/HOSTELS).

**Caravan Parks** At Fishnish (all facs, nr Ferry) Craignure and Fionnphort.

**Camping** Calgary Beach, Fishnish and at Loch Na Keal shore. All fab.

## WHERE TO EAT

✓ **Highland Cottage** 01688 302030. As above and 2314/ISLAND RESTAUS. Only real-fire dining option. Also the local night out. Small so must book.
MED

✓ **Calgary Farmhouse** 01688 400256. Dovecote Restaurant. Local produce in atmospheric wine-bar setting. Mellow people, art/sculpture everywhere. (2310/ISLAND RESTAUS) Coolest dining rm on the island.    INX

✓ **Glengorm Farm Coffee-Shop** Excl daytime eats outside Tobermory. Report: 1455/TEAROOMS.

**Ulva House** Tobermory 01688 302044. Above the town (via Back Brae, past Western Isles Hotel). Excl seafood restau/dining rm, a conservatory-like space with only 16 covers. Spectacular seafood platter. Gr fresh produce & service. Awards in the post, methinks. AYR. Dinner only. Must book.    MED

**The Anchorage** Tobermory 01688 302313. Main St opp pier. Best on the bay. Seafood, steaks, specials, good vegn options. Homely and friendly & keen to impress. 7 days, lunch and LO 9pm. Winter hrs will vary.    INX

**Mull Pottery** Tobermory 01688 302592. Fun mezzanine café above working pottery just outside Tobermory on rd S to Craignure. Evening meals (best atmos) and usual daytime offerings tho' all home-baking. Locals do recommend. AYR. 7 days. LO 9pm.

**Meditteranea** Salen 01680 300200. In mid-vill on main Craignure-Tobermory rd. A real, & I mean *real* Italian restau run by Scottish guy & extended Italian family. Mama in kitchen pure Sicilian. So excl pasta, salads, puds & specials with Italian twist. All islands should have one of these. Mar-Oct. Dinner only LO 9pm.    INX

**Island Bakery** Tobermory 01688 302225. Main St. Bakery-deli with excl take-away pizza by Joe Reade, the son of the cheese people. Home-made pâtés, quiches, salads & old-fashioned baking. Buy your picnic here. 7 days LO 7.15pm (w/end only in wint).    CHP

**The Chip Van aka The Fish Pier** Tobermory 01688 302390. Tobermory's famous meals-on-wheels underneath the clock tower on the bay. Usual fare but fresh as... and usually a queue. The situation is unquestionably fine. Apr-Dec, noon-9pm. Cl Suns. (1425/FISH 'N' CHIPS)    CHP

**Javiers** Tobermory 01688 302365. Far corner of the bay above MacGochan's pub. Argentinian chef, mix-match & Mexican meals. Building local rep at TGP. Reports please. AYR. Lunch & LO 9.30pm.    INX

## WHAT TO SEE

**Torosay Castle** Walk or train (!) from Craignure. Fabulous gdns and fascinating insight into an endearing family's life. Teashop. (1799/CASTLES.) **Duart Castle** 5km Craignure. Seat of Clan Maclean. Impressive from a distance, homely inside. Good view of clan history and from battlements. Teashop. (1798/CASTLES.) **Eas Fors** Waterfall on Dervaig to Fionnphort rd. V accessible series of cataracts tumbling into the sea (1642/WATERFALLS). **The Mishnish** No mission to Mull complete without a night at the Mish (1324/BLOODY GOOD PUBS), MacGochan's over the bay no contest. **Wings Over Mull** (1752/KIDS). **Ulva & Iona** (many refs). **The Treshnish Isles** (Ulva Ferry or Fionnphort). Marvellous trips in summer (1760/BIRDS); walks from **Carsaig Pier** (2314/ISLAND WALKS); or up **Ben More** (1990/MUNROS); **Croig** and **Quinish** in N, nr Dervaig and **Lochbuie** off the A849 at Strathcoil 9km S of Craignure: these are all serene shorelines to explore. **Aros Park** forest walk, from Tobermory, about 7km round trip.

**Tourist Info** Craignure (AYR) 01680 812377. Tobermory 01688 302182.
**CalMac** 08705 650000.

# The Best Of Orkney

2327 **Ferry** Northlink (0845 6000449) Stromness: from Aber – Tue, Thu, Sat, Sun, takes 6hrs; from Scrabster – 2/3 per day, takes 1.5hrs. John O'Groats to Burwick (01955 611353), 40mins, up to 4 a day (May-Sept only). Pentland Ferries from Gill (nr J o'Groats) to St Margaret's Hope (01856 831226) – 3 a day, takes 1hr.

**By Air** BA (08457 733377) to Kirkwall: from Aber – 3 daily; from Edin – 2 daily; from Glas – 1 daily; from Inverness – 2 daily; from Wick – 1 daily (not w/ends).

## WHERE TO STAY

**Foveran Hotel** St Ola  01856 872389. A964 Orphir rd; 4km from Kirkwall. Scandinavian-style hotel is a friendly informal place serves trad food using local ingredients; separate vegn menu. Gr value. Comfortable light rms refurbished; gdn o/look Scapa Flow.

8RMS JAN-DEC T/T XPETS CC KIDS MED.INX

**Ayre Hotel** Kirkwall  01856 873001. Roy and Moira Dennison have spent years refurb their family hotel. They have the highest grading on the Orkney mainland. Situated on the harbour front, the whole place is well tidy and well established. It's where to stay in Kirkwall.

33RMS JAN-DEC T/T PETS CC KIDS MED.EX

**Cleaton House Hotel** Westray  01857 677508. Beautifully refurbished former Victorian manse. Panoramic seascapes, relaxed atmos & good food.

6RMS JAN-DEC T/T PETS CC KIDS MED.EX

**Merkister Hotel** Harray  01856 771366. A fave with fishers and twitchers; handy for archaeological sites and poss the Orkney hotel 'of choice'. À la carte or table d'hôte in the conservatory o/look the loch.

13RMS JAN-DEC T/T PETS CC KIDS MED.INX

**Stromness Hotel**  01856 850298. Orkney's biggest hotel, made over à la mode. Central and picturesque.    42RMS JAN-DEC T/T PETS CC KIDS MED.INX

**Woodwick House** Evie  01856 751330. Comfy country house and gdn, nr shore with views of those islets. A gr retreat. Home cooking, local produce. Good value.    7RMS JAN-DEC X/X PETS CC KIDS MED.INX

**S.Y. Hostels** At Stromness (excellent location, 01856 850589), Kirkwall (the largest, 01856 872243). Other hostels at: Hoy, N & S Ronaldsay, Birsay, Sanday.
**Peedie Hostel** Kirkwall  01856 875477. Ayre Rd; by the sea. Private bedrm, own keys.
**Bis Geos Hostel** Westray  01857 677420. Hostel with 2 self-catering cottages. Traditional features & some luxuries.
**The Barn** Westray  01857 677214. Four-star self-catering hostel in renovated stone barn. Gr views.

**Camping/Caravan** Kirkwall (01856 879900) & Stromness (01856 873535).

## WHERE TO EAT

**The Creel Inn & Restaurant** St Margaret's Hope  01856 831311. On S Ronaldsay, 20km S of Kirkwall. In the wild area where seals vie with the fishermen. Excl table (2 AA rosette) though fairly exp. Many sauces over meat or fish. Clootie for pud or Orkney cheeses. Popular with the islanders. Dinner only. Seal Rescue Centre nearby. Also well-appointed 3 rms; a good choice B+B.    3RMS MED

**Foveran Hotel** St Ola  01856 872389. 4km Kirkwall. *As above.*    MED

**Woodwick House** Evie  01856 751330. *As above.*    MED

**The Hamnavoe Restaurant** Stromness  01856 850606. 35 Graham Pl off main st. Seafood is their speciality, but they do haggis. Apr-Oct; Tue-Sun 6.30pm-late. Nov-Mar open w/ends only.    INX

**Julia's Café & Bistro** Stromness 01856 850904. Gr home baking, black-board & vegn specials. Internet. A favourite with the locals. Gets busy – fill yourself up before the ferry journey! Open AYR, 7 days 7.30am-10pm (cl 5-6.30pm). Phone for winter opening hrs. CHP

## WHAT TO SEE

**Skara Brae** 25km W Kirkwall. Amazingly well-preserved underground labyrinth, a 5,000-year-old village (1829/PREHISTORIC SITES).

**The Old Man Of Hoy** on Hoy; 30min ferry 2 or 3 times a day from Stromness. 3hr walk along spectacular coast (2319/ISLAND WALKS).

**Standing Stones Of Stenness, The Ring Of Brodgar, Maes Howe** Around 18km W of Kirkwall on A965. Strong vibrations (1830/PREHISTORIC SITES).

**Yesnaby Sea Stacks** 24km W of Kirkwall. A precarious cliff top at the end of the world (1952/SPOOKY – or spiritual – PLACES).

**Italian Chapel** 8km S of Kirkwall at first causeway. A special act of faith. (1883/CHURCHES).

**Skaill House** 01856 841501. At Skara Brae. 17th-century 'mansion' built on Pictish cemetery. Set up as it was in the 1950s; with Captain Cook's crockery in the dining-rm looking remarkably unused. Apr-Sep; 7 days 9.30am-6pm (or by appointment). Tearoom and VC and HS link with Skara.

**St Magnus Cathedral** (1883/CHURCHES); **Stromness** (1594/COASTAL VILLAGES); **The Pier Arts Centre** (2261/INTERESTING GALLERIES); **Tomb Of The Eagles** (1836/PREHISTORIC SITES); **Marwick Head** and many of the smaller islands (1767/BIRDS); **Scapa Flow** (1926/BATTLEGROUNDS; 2145/DIVING); **Highland Park Distillery** (1535/WHISKY); **Puffins** (1769/BIRDS)

**Craft Trail & Artists' Studio trail** Take in some of the trad arts & crafts in the isles. Lots of souvenir potential. TIC for details & maps.

**Tourist Info** 01856 872856.

# The Best Of Shetland

2328 **Ferry** Northlink (0845 6000 449), Aber-Lerwick: Mon, Wed, Fri – dep 7pm, 12 hrs. Tue, Thurs, Sat, Sun – dep 5pm (via Orkney, arr 11.45pm), 14hrs.

**By Air** BA (linkline 08457 733377, Shetland 01950 460345) sto Sumburgh: from Aber (4 a day, 2 Sat, 2 Sun). From Inverness (1 a day). From Glas (2 a day, 1 Sat). From Edin (2 a day).

## WHERE TO STAY

**Burrastow House** Walls 01595 809307. 40 mins from Lerwick. Most guides & locals agree this is the place to stay on Shetland. Peaceful Georgian house with views to Island of Vaila. Wonderful home-made/produced food. Full of character with food (set menu; order day before), service & rooms the best on the island. 5RMS MAR-DEC X/T PETS CC KIDS MED.EX

**Herrislea House Hotel** Tingwall 01595 840208. 7km NW of Lerwick. Refurbished country house in beautiful setting. Incorporating Starboard Tack café-bar, open daily till 11pm. Basic, good home cooking and useful children's play area. Family-run. 13RMS JAN-DEC T/T PETS CC KIDS MED.INX

**Busta House Hotel** 01806 522506. Historic country house at Brae just over 30 mins from Lerwick. Elegant & tranquil. High standards, gr malt selection. 20RMS JAN-DEC T/T PETS CC KIDS MED.EX

**Sumburgh Hotel** Sumburgh 01950 460201. Refurbished manor house in v S of mainland 42 km from Lerwick. Next to airport and Jarlshof excavations. Sea views as far as Fair Isle (50km S). Beaches and birds! Wide and relatively cheap menu. 32RMS JAN-DEC T/T PETS CC KIDS MED.INX

**Kveldsro Hotel** Lerwick 01595 692195. Pron 'Kel-ro'. Probably best proposition in Lerwick; o/look harbour. Reasonable standard at a price. Locals do eat here.                              16RMS JAN-DEC T/T X/PETS CC KIDS MED.EX

**Westings, The Inn On The Hill** Whiteness 01595 840242. 12 km from Lerwick. Breathtaking views down Whiteness Voe. Excellent base for exploring. Large selection of real ales and three different menus. Campsite alongside.                              6RMS JAN-DEC T/T PETS CC KIDS MED.INX

**Almara B&B** Hillswick 01806 503261. We don't usually venture into the world of the B&B in this book but, although we haven't stayed ourselves, couldn't ignore numerous good reports of Mrs Williamson's four-star establishment. Friendly family home with good food & nice vibes.

**S.Y. Hostel** in Lerwick, Isleburgh House: 01595 692114. Beautifully refurbished and v central. Also home of excl Isleburgh House Café. Open Apr-Sept.

**Camping Bods** (fisherman's barns). Cheap sleep in wonderful sea-shore settings. **The Sail Loft** at Voe; **Grieve House** at Whalsay; **Wind House Lodge** at Mid Yell; **Voe House** at Walls; **Betty Mouat's Cottage** at Dunrossness; **Johnnie Notions** at Eashaness. Remember to take sleeping mats. Check TIC for details.

**Camping/Caravan Clickimin** Lerwick 01595 741000. **Levenwick** 01950 422207. **The Garths** Fetla 01957 733227. **Westings** Whiteness 01595 840242.

## WHERE TO EAT

**Burrastow House** Walls **& Busta House Hotel** Brae (*see above*). The best meal in the islands.                              MED

**Sumburgh Hotel** Sumburgh (*see above*). The organically farmed smoked salmon 'possibly the best in the world' according to one local.
MED.INX

**Monty's Bistro** Lerwick 01595 696555. Mounthooley St nr TIC. Renovated building in light Med décor. Best bet in town. Good service and imaginative menu using Shetland's finest ingredients. Bistro: Cl Sun/Mon. Lunch and LO 9pm.                              MED

*Pub food also recommended at the following:*

**The Mid Brae Inn** Brae 32km N of Lerwick, 01806 522634. Lunch and supper till 8.45pm (9.30pm w/ends), 7 days. Big portions of the filling pub-grub variety.                              CHP

**The Maryfield Hotel** Bressay 01595 820207. 5 mins ferry ride from Lerwick to Bressay. Better known for its seafood rather than accommodation, both bar and dining rm menus worth a look. LO are for those off the 8pm ferry. Don't miss the return ferry at 10.30pm Sun-Thurs and 12.45am, Fri & Sat.                              INX.MED

**Havly** Lerwick 01595 692100. 9 Charlotte St. Norwegian-style café with family-friendly atmos. Gr homemade soup, baking, waffles. Open Mon-Fri 10am-3pm, Sat 10am-4.45pm.                              CHP

**Da Haaf Restaurant** Scalloway 01595 880747. Part of the North Atlantic Fisheries College, Port Arthur. Basically a canteen but fresh Shetland seafood overlooking the harbour at reasonable prices more than makes up for the plastic trays and fluorescent lights. Lunch & LO 8pm.                              INX

**The Castle Café & Takeaway (Scalloway Fish & Chip Shop)** New Rd, by the castle. Quite the freshest and best fish and chips in Shetland (if not Scotland, some say); can also sit in.                              CHP

**Osla's Café Lerwick** 01595 696005. Commercial St or Da St, just up from Monty's. Best café. Incredibly good value. Cosy & very child-friendly. Art exhibitions on walls. Upstairs La Piazza is a good bet for supper. LO 9.30pm. CHP

**The Peerie Shop Café** Lerwick 01595 692817. On the Esplanade. A local delicacy!                              CHP

## WHAT TO SEE

**Mousa Broch** and **Jarlshof** (1833/PREHISTORIC SITES), also **Clickimin** broch.

**Old Scatness**  01595 694688. A fascinating, award-winning excavation – site of one of the world's best-preserved Iron Age villages. Ongoing and accessible; climb the tower and witness the unearthing first-hand. Tours, demonstrations & exhibitions. 5 mins from airport. Open July-Aug only.

**St Ninian's Isle** Bigton  8km N of Sumburgh on W Coast. An island linked by exquisite shell-sand. Hoard of Pictish silver found in 1958 (now in Edin). Beautiful, serene spot.

**Scalloway**  7km W of Lerwick, a township once the ancient capital of Shetland, dominated by the atmospheric ruins of Scalloway Castle.

**Noup Of Noss** Isle Of Noss off Bressay  8km W of Lerwick by frequent ferry and then boat (also direct from Lerwick 01595 692577 or via TIC), May-Sept only. National Nature Reserve with spectacular array of wildlife.

**Up Helly Aa**  Festival in Lerwick on the last Tuesday in Jan. Ritual with hundreds of torchbearers and much fire and firewater. Norse, northern and pagan. A wild time. Permanent exhibition at St Sunniva Street, Lerwick.

**Sea Races**  The Boat Race every summer from Norway. Part of the largest North Sea international annual yacht race.

**Bonhoga Gallery & Weisdale Mill**  01595 830400. Former grain mill housing Shetland's first purpose-built gallery. Café.

**Island Trails**  Historic tours of Lerwick and the islands. Book through TIC or 01950 422408. Day trips, evening runs or short tours.

**Tourist Info**  01595 693434.

# SECTION 14

*Local Centres*

# The Best Of Ayr

## WHERE TO STAY

✓ **Lochgreen House**  01292 313343. Monktonhall Rd, Troon 12km N on way in from Ayr. White seaside mansion nr famous golf courses of Troon (2050/GREAT GOLF). Elegant setting; some tacky touches, eg dreadful pictures. Civilised wining and dining. (802/AYRSHIRE HOTELS)

40RMS (7 IN COURTYARD) JAN-DEC T/T PETS CC KIDS EXP

✓ **The Ivy House**  01292 442336. 3km from centre on rd to Alloway. Small but v well-appointed establishment, more a superior restau with rms. Esp good bathrms. New chef at TGP. (798/AYRSHIRE HOTELS)

5RMS JAN-DEC T/T PETS CC KIDS EXP

✓ **Savoy Park**  01292 266112. 16 Racecourse Rd. Period mansion run by the Hendersons for 40 yrs. V Scottish, v Ayrshire. Lovely grdn for summer b/fast (1256/SCOTTISH HOTELS). 15RMS JAN-DEC T/T PETS CC KIDS MED.INX

**Fairfield House**  01292 267461. Fairfield Rd. 1km centre on the front. Ostensibly the 'best' hotel in town. 'De luxe' facs incl pool/sauna/steam, conservatory brasserie and breakfast and refurb dining rm at TGP. Only 3 rms have seaview.          44RMS JAN-DEC T/T PETS CC KIDS MED.EX

**The Ellisland**  01292 260111. 19 Racecourse Rd. On rd towards Alloway of many hotels (see Savoy Park, above). A makeover by the Costley group who have Lochgreen (above) & Brig o' Doon (below). Rms vary but mostly large & well appointed. Decent restau.          9RMS JAN-DEC T/T PETS CC KIDS EXP

**Ramada Jarvis**  01292 269331. Dablair Rd. Centrally situated, best bedbox in town with facs incl pool. Café Mezzaluna opposite (see below) for more charming meals.          118RMS JAN-DEC T/T PETS CC KIDS MED.INX

**The Richmond**  01292 265153. 38 Park Circus. Best of bunch in sedate terrace nr centre. John and Anne are nice folk.

6RMS JAN-DEC X/T XPETS XCC KIDS CHP

**Piersland** Troon  01292 314747. 12km N of Ayr. (802/AYRSHIRE HOTELS)

**Brig O' Doon** Alloway  01292 442466. 5km S of Ayr. Romantic, many weddings, few rms.

**Enterkine House** Annbank  01292 521608. 10km town centre across ring rd. Country house comforts. (801/AYRSHIRE HOTELS)

**Sorn Inn** nr Mauchline  01290 551305. 25km E. Top gourmet pub with rms. (800/AYRSHIRE HOTELS)

## WHERE TO EAT

*These 7 places cover the range from seriously good to trad Scottish caff cuisine.*

✓ **Fouters**  01292 261391. 2 Academy St (810/AYRSHIRE RESTAUS). Long-established favourite Ayr restau changed hands at TGP. Reports please.

**The Tudor Restaurant**  8 Beresford St. Superb caff. They don't make 'em like this any more! Till 8pm. Report: 1444/TEAROOMS.

**Ivy House**  01292 442336. Restau of hotel above 798/AYRSHIRE RESTAUS. The best just outside town but menu und review at TGP.

**The Hunny Pot**  37 Beresford Terr. 01292 263239. Wholemeal-slanted, kid-friendly, GM-free café – good home baking and light meals. Mon-Sat 9am-9pm, Sun 10.30am-8pm.

**The Stables**  41 Sandgate, downtown location in courtyard of shops. Coffee shop/bistro with wine bar ambience; enlightened attitude. Till 5pm. Cl Sun. INX

**Carrick Lodge Hotel**  01292 262846. 46 Carrick Rd on main rd out of town in Alloway dir. At TGP prob the most pop dining rms in town. À la carte menu of wholesome pub food. They pack 'em in; book Fri/Sat. Lunch & 5.30-9pm.

**Mezzaluna**  01292 288598. Dablair Rd opp Ramada Jarvis. Contemp bistro with wide-ranging à la carte & specials. Exceptionally good value. Good pasta. 7 days LO 9.30/10.30pm. Sun 4-9pm.          INX

### THE REST ...

**Cecchini's** 01292 317171. 72 Fort St (also in Troon at 72 Fort St). Excl Italian & Med restau run by the estimable Cecchini family. Mon-Sat, lunch & LO 10pm.

**Scott's** Troon 01292 315315. Harbour rd within the Marina about 2km downtown Troon. Serving as a caff for the sailors & the less serious water-bound folk around here, a stylish, contemp bar/restau upstairs & o/looking the surprisingly packed marina. Same people have Elliots in Prestwick. Food ok, gr views & v well thought-out watering hole on the water. 7 days. All day LO 10/11pm.                                                                        INX

**The Rupee Room,** Ayr 01292 283002. Wellington Sq. Ordinary-looking restau on the sq serving the denziens of Ayr so they do fish 'n' chips but rather good Indian food that's exactly what you want. 7 days. Lunch & LO 11pm.                                                                                      INX

**Mancini's** Ayr Ice-cream & a' that. 1485/ICE CREAM.

## WHAT TO SEE & DO

**Culzean** (1791/CASTLES); **Heads Of Ayr** (1685/SCENIC ROUTES) and **The Electric Brae** nr (3km S Dunure on the A719); **Burns Heritage Trail** (1944/LITERARY PLACES); **Gailes/Troon/Prestwick/Turnberry/Belleisle** (*see* GREAT GOLF, *p. 260*); **Magnum** Irvine (2111/LEISURE CENTRES); **Kidz Play** (1740/KIDS); **Burns 'N' A' That** (34/EVENTS). **Swimming** V good pool com-plex at Beach Harbour Rd (01292 269793), and at Prestwick, off the road in from Ayr (01292 474015).

**Tourist Office** 01292 290300. Jan-Dec.

# The Best Of Dumfries

## WHERE TO STAY

*There's nowhere to recommend in Dumfries town centre. The following are the best bests. The nearest good hotel is* **Cavens** (816/SW HOTELS) *15 km S at Kirkbean.*

**Trigony House Hotel** Closeburn S Of Thornhill 01848 331211. Comfortable manor house just off A76 18km N of Dumfries. Restau does lunch & dinner. Nice gardens. Rms vary.

8RMS JAN-DEC T/T PETS CC KIDS MED.INX

**Redbank House** Dumfries 01387 247034. New Abbey Rd just beyond edge of town. Large suburban house with v suburban interior (wicker chairs in the conservatory kind of thing). Rec in Michelin. B&B only.

5RMS JAN-DEC T/T XPETS CC XKIDS INX

**Abbey Arms** 01387 850489 (862/SW HOTELS). **Criffel Inn** 01387 850305 both in **New Abbey** 12 km S of Dumfries A710. 2 decent old-style pubs on either side of the green in this lovely wee vill where Sweetheart Abbey is the main attraction (1920/ABBEYS). Criffel best for food & rms marginally nicer but both basic inx accom.          7/4RMS JAN-DEC X/T PETS CC KIDS INX

## WHERE TO EAT

✓ **The Linen Room** 01387 255689. 53 St Michael St. Only fine dining in the area. Report: 823/SW RESTAUS.

*The best Dumfries has to offer apart from the notable exception above are all Italians.*

**3 Stalwart Italians & A New One  Pizzeria Il Fiume** 01387 265154. In Dock Park nr St Michael's Br, underneath Riverside pub. Usual Italian menu but gr pizzas and best for cosy tratt atmos. 5.30-10pm daily.          INX

**Benvenuto** 01387 259890. 42 Eastfield Rd, off Brooms Rd – follow signs for Cresswell Maternity Hospital. Sort of surreal wooden hut setting next to owner's chippy. Local rep. 5pm-late. Tues-Sun.          INX

**Bruno's** 01387 255757. 3 Balmoral Rd, off Annan Rd. Well-established Italian eaterie beside **Balmoral** chippy (1424/FISH AND CHIPS). They are not related. 6-10pm, Cl Tue.                                                                    INX

**Casa Mia** 01387 269619. 53 Nunholm Rd (direction Edinburgh). The new kid. Hugely popular. 7 days lunch & LO 9pm.                              INX

**Hullabaloo** 01387 259679. At Robert Burns Centre which also houses local art-house cinema. Contemporary pasta/wrap/burger kind of place – good though. Opens from 11am for coffee, then lunch, then dinner. 7 days. Lunch & Tue-Sat dinner. LO depend on movie times.                            INX

**The Old Bank** 01387 253499. Tearoom in converted bank. Very old-school, but lovely cakes. Tue-Sat 10am-5pm.                                    INX

## WHAT TO SEE & DO

**Rockcliffe** (1599/COASTAL VILLAGES); **Rockcliffe To Kippford** (2042/COASTAL WALKS); **Southerness** (2072/GOLF IN GREAT PLACES); **Sweetheart Abbey** (1920/ABBEYS); **Criffel** (1968/HILLS); **Caerlaverock** (1759/BIRDS); **Caerlaverock Castle** (1810/RUINS); **Ellisland Farm** (1944/LITERARY PLACES). **Gardens** (all off A75): **Castle Kennedy Gardens** 75 acres laid out around 2 acre lily pond, 2 lochs; rare species. Apr-Sep 10am-5pm. **Glenwhan Gardens** Dunragit enchanting 12 acre hill side, tamed and lovingly hewn into lush over-flowing haven. Gr views and walks. Apr-Oct 10am-5pm. **Threave Garden** nr Castle Douglas for all seasons. AYR 9.30am-sunset. **Swimming** Modern pool on river side nr Buccleuch St Br (01387 252908).

# The Best Of Dunfermline & Kirkcaldy

2331

Map 10
P25
Q24

## WHERE TO STAY

**29 Bruce St** Dunfermline 01383 840041. V central (& adj main carpark) conversion of townhouse into Italian restau (see below) & contemp bou-tique-style rms. Bar/club adj. Well targeted to urban traveller, tho' what they're doing in Dunfermline... 17RMS JAN-DEC T/T XPETS CC XKIDS MED.INX

**Keavil House Hotel** Crossford, Dunfermine 01383 736258. 3km W of Dunfermline on A994 towards Culross (1596/COASTAL VILLAGES) and Kincardine. Rambling mansion house in grounds within a suburban edge of town, con-verted into modern business-type hotel with all facs incl separate leisure club (not bad pool). Best Western.     47RMS JAN-DEC T/T PETS CC KIDS MED.EX

**Dunnikier House** Kirkcaldy 01592 268393. 3 km centre in parkland area. Prob the only half-decent hotel hereabouts but not exp. We can say no more.
15RMS JAN-DEC T/T PETS CC KIDS MED.INX

**The Belvedere** W Wemyss nr Kirkcaldy 01592 654167. In the absence of competition this is worth the 8km trek E of town via A955 coast rd. At begin-ning of neat village, a curious mixture of dereliction and conservation. Views of bay and Kirkcaldy from comfortable rms in cottages and on the seafront, all white and with red-tiled roofs. Harmless pictures, decent menu.
20RMS JAN-DEC T/T PETS CC KIDS MED.INX

*No hostels (Burgh Lodge, Falkland, is miles away, but good; 1175/HOSTELS).*

## WHERE TO EAT IN & AROUND DUNFERMLINE

**Townhouse** 01383 432382. 48 East Port in centre. This is the credible restau in Dunfermline by the youngest of the Brown family who run the Bouzy Rouges (526/GLAS BISTROS) & the Roman Camp (832/CENTRAL HOTS), so they know what they're doing. Light, modern feel to room & menu. Open all day 12-LO9.30pm. Lunch, dinner or just grazing. Best in town no doubt. MED

**The Abbot House** Marygate. Interesting folk museum (2228/BEST HISTORY) & in the basement this excl coffee shop that spills into the Abbey garden. Friendly ladies whom you'd want as your mum cook & bake. Daytime only but easily better than all else around. Till 5pm (food 4pm).

**Il Pescatore Limekilns**  01383 872999. 7km from town via B9156 or to Rosyth, then Charlestown. Local favourite and the best pasta etc around. Now has 6 inexp rms above. Good for birthdays or a stroll after dinner. 7 days, LO 11pm. (No lunch.)                                                                               INX

**Luigi's**  01383 726666. Entrance of Kingsgate mall on Douglas St. The local choice for standard Italian fare. Cl Mon. Fri-Sun lunch, Tues-Sun dinner LO 11pm.                                                                                                                                       INX

**Ristorante Alberto**  01383 840044. 29 Bruce St. Part of hotel/club complex (above). Newish, fun Italian style. 7 days lunch & LO 10.30pm (Sun 9.30pm).                                                                                                                                       INX

**Oohla**  01383 841680. 8 High St (& t/away opp at 7). Latest high st arrival at TGP opp TO. Reasonable, contemp grazing restau with home-made pâtisserie. 7 days till 9/10pm.                                                                                                                     INX

**Noodle Bar**  01383 624222. 41 Carnegie Drive. Popular with locals. Noodles & other Chinese staples. 7 days LO 10.30-11pm.                                                                                                                  INX

## WHERE TO EAT IN & AROUND KIRKCALDY

**The Old Rectory** Dysart  01592 651211. 5km E (904/FIFE RESTAUS).

**La Gondola**  640085. N Harbour. The best, most lively Italian restau in town.                                                                                                                                                             INX

**Feuars Arms**  205025. 66 Commercial St. V good pub food west of town nr high flats. Best in town for informal meal and atmos. Lunch and dinner w/ends.                                                                                                                                        INX

**Bar lizd**  01592 204257. Main St E end. Café-bar with Tex-Mex menu & accoutrements. 7 days. LO 9.30pm.                                                                                                                                    INX

**Valente's**  01592 205774. Not sit-in, but *absolutely the best* fish and chips. Take them to Ravenscraig Park nearby, walk along the coves. 2 branches but Overton Rd (not central) best. Report: 1412/FISH 'N' CHIPS.

## WHAT TO SEE & DO

**Abbot House** Dunfermline (2228/MUSEUMS); **Pittencrieff & Ravenscraig Parks** Dunfermline (1581/TOWN PARKS) and **Beveridge Park Kirkcaldy** (1582/TOWN PARKS); **Carnegie Centre** Dunfermline (2121/SWIMMING POOLS); **Dunfermline Abbey** (1942/MARY, CHARLIE AND BOB); **Kirkcaldy Art Gallery** (2257/PUBLIC GALLERIES).

### Tourist Offices

**Dunfermline**  1 High Street. 01383 720999. Jan-Dec.
**Kirkcaldy**  339 High St. 01592 267775. Jan-Dec.

# The Best Of Fort William

## WHERE TO STAY

✓ ✓ **Inverlochy Castle** 01397 702177. 5km out on A82 Inverness rd. In the forefront of hotels in Scotland. Victorian elegance, classically stylish & impeccable service. (971/HIGHLANDS HOTELS)

17RMS JAN-DEC T/T XPETS CC KIDS LOTS

✓ **The Grange** 01397 705516. Grange Rd o/looks loch & the main rd S. Don't know how I missed this place in previous editions. Joan & John Campbell have been running a top, contemp B&B in bereft Ft William for yrs. Anyone: my pleaseure to bring it to your attention. Gr views, fab rms. No dinner.

4RMS MAR-NOV X/T XPETS CC XKIDS MED.EX

**Lime Tree Studios** 01397 701806. Achintore rd as you come in along the loch from S, last 'hotel' of many almost at end of main st. Unassuming, but at TGP all about to change – major refurb into regional art-gallery space with rms above. Understated, tasteful art everywhere: these are prob the best inx rms in town.

5(+5NEW)RMS JAN-DEC X/T PETS CC KIDS INX

**The Moorings** 01397 772797. Banavie (follow signs), 5km out on A830 Corpach/Mallaig by the Caledonian canal by 'Neptune's Staircase' (some rms o/look). Good location, pub dining best. Serviceable enough.

29RMS JAN-DEC T/T PETS CC KIDS MED.INX

**Waterfront Lodge** 01397 703786. On the N Lochside nr Morrisons supermarket etc. Rms for the dive school but inx & serviceable. Like a chain lodge thing without the chain. Adj the best restau in town (see below). Loch views (ish!).

20RMS JAN-DEC X/X XPETS CC XKIDS INX

**Lodge On The Loch** 01855 821237. In Onich, quite stylish peace and quiet. Rms to high standard. (985/HIGHLAND HOTELS)

**Onich Hotel** 01855 821214. At Onich 16km S on A82. Loch side; good value (991/HIGHLANDS HOTELS).

**S.Y. Hostel** Glen Nevis 01397 702336. 5km from town by picturesque but busy Glen Nevis rd. The Ben is above. Grade 1. Fax poss. Many other hostels in area (ask at TIC for list) but esp **FW Backpackers** 01397 700711, Alma Rd.

**Achintee Farm** 01397 702240. On app to Ben Nevis main route & adj Ben Nevis Inn (see below). GH/self/c & bunkhouse. A walkers' haven.

**Camping/Caravan Site** Glen Nevis 01397 702191. Nr hostel. Well-run site, mainly caravans (also for rent). Many facs incl restaus & much going on.

## WHERE TO EAT

✓ ✓ **Inverlochy** (as above): cf the rest, think Ben Nevis.

✓ **Crannog At The Waterfront aka The Seafood Restaurant** 01397 705589. The Crannog moved its room & its reputation to another room also o/looking the water. Less conspicuous site but still the best restau in town. Gr views. Gr seafood. AYR. 7 days lunch & LO 9pm.

**No 4** 01397 704222. Cameron Sq behind the TIC. Best bet in main st area tho mixed reviews. À la carte and daily specials. Lunch and LO 9.30pm.     MED

**Café Beag Glen Nevis** 01397 703601. 5km along Glen Nevis rd; past VC. New owners at TGP. Alpine-looking cabin, ok atmos; open fires, books. Restau, bar & coffee-stop. (Prob) AYR till 6pm (9pm Jun-Aug).     INX

**Pier Café** 01397 708666. Sticking out on the lochside mid ring rd – can't miss what was Ft William's most notable restau (now moved – see Crannog, above). Same owners now running a seafront/seafood caff. Nonetheless interesting. AYR. All day. LO 9pm.

**Café 115** 01397 702500. Av caff in av main st – but you know, it's what there is & it ain't bad: Ft William's finest. BYO. 7 days LO 9.30pm.     INX

**Ben Nevis Inn At Achintee** On main app to the Ben iself. Reach across river by footbridge from VC or by rd on rt after Inverlochy/Glen Nevis r/bout on A82 (3km). Excl atmos inn in converted farm building. Good grub/ale & walking chat. LO 9pm. W/ends only in wint.

**The Moorings** 01397 772797. 5km by A830. Pub best.

## WHAT TO SEE & DO

*Most of the good things about Ft William are outside the town, but these incl some v big items esp the Ben and the Glens (Glens Nevis as well as Coe):*

**Glencoe** 30km S (1666/SCENIC ROUTES; 2002/SERIOUS WALKS; 1925/BATTLE-GROUNDS); **Glen Nevis** (1629/GLENS); **Ben Nevis** 6km E on Glen Nevis rd (2003/SERIOUS WALKS); **West Highland Way** (1996/LONG WALKS); **Steall Falls**, Glen Nevis (1645/WATERFALLS); **Glencoe Skiing** (2091/SKIING); **Aonach Mor Skiing** (2090/SKIING) **Museum** (2236/MUSEUMS). **Nevis Range Gondola** Aonach Mor (01397 705825). 12km via A82. Scotland's most modern ski resort (2090/SKIING). Gondola goes up in summer for the view. Open AYR, it's a big attraction. Go up for the incredible view and the air and the Ben over there. **Mountain Bike World Cup/Ben Nevis Race** (53/54/EVENTS). **Swimming/Sports** Lochaber Centre (01397 704 359). Beyond main st and Alexandra Hotel. Squash, sauna, 2 gyms, climbing wall, swimming (with flume).

**Tourist Office** Cameron Square. 01397 701801. Jan-Dec.

# The Best Of The Border Towns

## WHERE TO STAY

✓ **Roxburghe Hotel** Kelso 01573 450331 (847/BORDERS HOTELS).  LOTS

✓ **Burts** Melrose 01896 822285 (850/BORDERS HOTELS).  MED.EX

✓ **The Townhouse** Melrose 01896 822645 (851/BORDERS HOTELS).

✓ **Cringletie** Peebles 01721 730233 & **Philipburn** Selkirk 01750 20747 (848/855/BORDERS HOTELS).  MED.EX

✓ **Edenwater** Ednam nr Kelso 01573 224070 (852/BORDERS HOTELS).  MED.EX

✓ **Clint Lodge** nr St Boswells 01835 822027 (858/BORDERS HOTELS).  INX

✓ **Fauhope** Gattonside 01896 823184 (860/BORDERS HOTELS).  INX

**Jedforest Country Hotel** Jedburgh 01835 840222 (856/BORDERS HOTELS).

**Ednam House Hotel** Kelso 01573 224168 (857/BORDERS HOTELS).

**Dryburgh Abbey Hotel** nr St Boswells 01835 822261 (854/BORDERS HOTELS).

**Hundalee House** Jedburgh 01835 863011. 1km S. Jedburgh off A68. Lovely 1700 manor house in 10 acre gdn. Brilliant value, gr base, views of Cheviot hills. Nr the famously old Capon Tree.
5RMS MAR-OCT X/T XPETS XCC KIDS CHP

**Allerton House** Jedburgh 01835 869633. Up the rd by the swimming baths. Pleasant small mansion GH in gardens but no gr views. Contemp facs incl good disabled. 6RMS JAN-DEC X/T XPETS CC KIDS MED.INX

**S.Y. Hostels** V good in this area (1162/HOSTELS).

## WHERE TO EAT

✓ **Marmions** Melrose 01896 822245 (861/BORDERS RESTAUS).

✓ **Cringletie** Peebles 01721 730233 (848/BORDERS HOTELS); **Philipburn** Selkirk 01750 20747 (855/BORDERS HOTELS); **Edenwater** Ednam nr Kelso 01573 224070 (852/BORDERS HOTELS).

✓ **Roxburghe Hotel** and **Fairways** Adj brasserie in the clubhouse o/look the course (Fri/Sat only, dinner: 01573 450331). 847/BORDERS HOTELS

✓ **Burt's Hotel** Melrose, **Townhouse Hotel** Melrose and **King's Arms** (850/851/BORDER HOTELS) Local faves (864/BORDERS RESTAUS).

✓ **Auld Cross Keys** Denholm 01450 870305; **Horseshoe Inn** nr Peebles 01721 730225; **Wheatsheaf** Swinton 01890 860257 (1374/1357/GAS-TROPUBS). **Craw Inn** Auchencrow 01890 761253 (1269/ROADSIDE INNS).

✓ **Chapters** nr Melrose 01896 823217 (862/BORDERS RESTAUS).

**Lazels** Peebles 01721 720602 (869/BORDERS HOTELS).

**The Nightjar** Jedburgh 01835 862552. Corner of Abbey Close and Canongate 100m up from sq. Small even restau with local rep. Thai/Scottish props so usually a green curry on menu & Thai nights every last Tue of month. Evens only.                                                                          INX

**Brydons** Hawick 01450 372672. 16 High St. Once Brydons were bakers, now they have this oddly funky family caff-cum-restau. Home cooking, good folk – this is a totally Hawick experience. All day and dinner Fri/Sat.

**Damascus Drum Café & Books** Hawick 0786 7530709. 2 Silver St nr TO. Surprising contemp, laid-back 2nd-hand bookshop & caff in this cultural backwater. Comfy seats. Home-made soups, quiche & bagels. Let's hope they're not driven out by the locals! Mon-Sat 10am-5pm.                    CHP

**Oblo's** Eyemouth 01890 752527. Italian plus good vegn. Glossy & fun. All day till late (1422/FISH AND CHIPS).

## WHAT TO SEE & DO

**Thirlestane Castle** Lauder (1861/COUNTRY HOUSES); **Tweed Fishing**; **Peniel Heugh** (1869/MONUMENTS); **Mary Queen Of Scots' House** (1931/MARY, CHARLIE AND BOB); **Ancrum** (1910/GRAVEYARDS; 1720/PICNICS); **Abbeys** (1917/JEDBURGH; 1918/DRYBURGH; 1921/MELROSE); **Priorwood** (1588/GARDENS); **Monteviot/Woodside** (1560/GARDENS); **Abbotsford** (1948/LITERARY PLACES); **Eildon Hills** (1980/HILL WALKS); **Ruberslaw** (1971/HILLS); **Scott's View/Irvine's View** (1694/1695/VIEWS); **Lilliard's Edge** (1927/BATTLE-GROUNDS); **Lochcarron** and **Chas Whillans** (2206/2207/WOOLLIES); **Swimming** V good leisure facs both in and around Hawick and Galashiels. Galashiels Pool (01896 752154).

**Tourist Info** 0870 608 0404.

**Jedburgh** Murray's Green. Jan-Dec;
**Kelso** The Square. Jan-Dec; **Hawick** Tower Knowe. Apr-Oct;
**Melrose** Adj Abbey. Jan-Dec.

# The Best Of Oban

## WHERE TO STAY

✓ ✓ **Dun Na Mara** Benderloch 01631 720233. A GH off main A828 Oban-Ft William rd at Benderloch 12km n of Oban. Gorgeous setting with beach adj for fab contemp conversion of seaside mansion. This place shows how it can be done! (780/BEST ARGYLL)

7RMS JAN-DEC X/T XPETS CC KIDS MED.INX

✓ **Manor House** 01631 562087. Gallanach Rd. On S coast rd out of town towards Kerrera ferry, o/look bay. Quiet elegance in contemp style, and a restau that serves (in an intimate dining-rm) prob the most 'fine-dining' dinner in town. Bedrms also prob the cosiest (tho' the competition ain't great). More delightful than de-luxe. Nice bar. In summer dinner is part of the deal.

11RMS JAN-DEC T/T PETS CC KIDS EXP

✓ **Glenburnie Hotel** 01631 562089. Corran Esplanade. Run by the inimitable Strachan family. From tea & shortbread on arrival & the bowl of good-looking apples, it's clear this is a superior bed for the night & def the best prospect in this seafront of hotels & GH. Home-made muesli & personal attention to detail & yr needs. Plus the view!

12 RMS MAR-OCT X/T PETS CC KIDS MED.INX

✓ **Caledonian Hotel** 01855 821582. Lashings of money a bit of & style spent on this refurbed seafront hotel. Can't beat the captain's rooms – comfort & urban facs. Restau & café. 59RMS JAN-DEC T/T PETS CC KIDS EXP

**The Kimberley** 01631 571115. Dalriach Rd above the town centre (2 mins main st). Solid Victorian mansion converted quite tastefully by Austrian folk. Nice public rms incl restau & with contemp bedrms & bathrms it's a cut above the rest. 14RMS JAN-DEC T/T PETS CC KIDS MED.EX

**Barriemore Hotel** 01631 566356. Corran Esplanade. The last in the long sweep of hotels to N of centre & better than most, a rep est yrs ago – many changes of owners later it's still a nice GH with gr views.

13RMS MAR-OCT X/T PETS CC KIDS INX

**S.Y. Hostel** 01631 562025. On Esplanade (ie on the front). Good location.

## WHERE TO EAT

✓ **Coast** 01631 569901. 104 George St. Middle of the main st on corner of John St, a site that has seen a few restaus come & go. Let's hope this creation of Richard (in the kitchen) & Nicola (out front) Fowler lasts the course since it brings the best food yet to Oban. Mod Brit menu by a pedigree chef in contemp, laid-back rm. Excl value for this quality & no fuss. Open AYR. 7 days lunch & LO 9.30pm. MED

✓ **Ee-Usk** 01631 565666 & **Piazza** 01631 563628. North Pier. You can't miss these 2 adj identical contemp steel & glass houses on the corner of the bay, both the ambitious creation & abiding passion of the Macleod family. Père Macleod runs a tight ship at Ee-usk, a bright, modern seafood café with gr views. Wild halibut tho' frozen haddock/cod, hand-cut chips; all home-made starters & puds. Piazza run by Macleod Fils purveys standard tho' good standard Italian fare. Both address perfectly what people want – Oban just got a whole lot better. 7 days lunch & LO 9.30pm. MED

✓ **The Waterfront At The Pier** 01631 563110. In the port, by the station, right on the dock of the bay, the place that's serious about seafood. 'From pier to pan' is about right. Blackboard menu & monkfish à la carte. Locals fill this airy upstairs diner with a fishmonger & a boat-charter office below – you are on the waterfront.Open L and LO 9pm ish, Mar-Nov. MED

**The Manor House** (*see above*). The best hotel dining-rm in town. Creative sauces on fresh seafood and other good things from long-est chef team, Patrick & Sean. Booking essential. EXP

**Café 41** 01631 564117. 41 Combie St. Before the big church on the Campbeltown rd out of town. Small, informal, always-busy bistro/caff where chef Vilas Roberts produces a no-fuss with best ingredients menu from a tiny kitchen. Regulars swear by the place. BYOB. Dinner only LO 8.45pm (9.30 Fri/Sat). Cl Mon/Tue. MED

**Julie's Coffee House** 01631 565952. 33 Stafford St opp Oban Whisky Visitor Centre. Only 10 tables, so fills up. Nice approach to food (snacky, with home-baking) & customers. Best coffee shop in town. Tue-Sun 10am-5pm. INX

**The Studio** 01631 562030. Craigard Rd off main st at Balmoral Hotel. Up the hill to find this here forever, candle-lit restau. Way beyond time for a makeover but who needs it? Surprising menu. Often have to book. Apr-Oct, 5-10pm. INX

**The Kitchen Garden** 01631 566332. 14 George St. Deli-café that's often busy & you may have to queue to go upstairs to the small gallery caff. Not a bad cup of coffee & ciabatta sandwich. Aimed at local gastros & visiting yachties. Gt whisky selection & a plethora of cheese. 7 days 9am-5pm (Suns from 10.30am).

## WHAT TO SEE & DO

**Dunollie Castle** On rd to Ganavan (1819/RUINS); **Glen Lonan** Gr wee glen starting 8km out of town (1634/GLENS); **Sealife Sanctuary** 16km N on A28 (1754/KIDS); **Rare Breeds Farm** 4km S from Argyll Sq (1755/KIDS); **Oban Inn**; **McCaig's Tower or Folly** You can't miss it, dominating the skyline. A circular granite coliseum. Superb views of the bay. Many ways up, but a good place to start is via Stevenson St, opp Cally Hotel. Free, Open AYR (1874/MONUMENTS). **Kerrera** The island in the Sound reached by regular ferry from coast rd to Gallanach (4km town). Ferries at set times, but several per day – check TIC. A fine wee island for walking, pack your lunch but look for the tea gdn (adj lovely small bunkhouse: 01631 570223). **Lismore** The other, larger island (2287/MAGICAL ISLANDS). Ferry from Oban (Calmac) or Pt Appin (passengers only). **Dunstaffnage Castle** Signed and visible off A85 betw Oban and Connel (7km). 13th-century. V early type of castle, more of a ft, really. Unoccupied, except for the odd Clan McDougall spectre rattling around in the dungeons. Pity about the post-industrial approach rd, but there is a chapel in the woods. **Ardchattan** 20km N via Connel. Along N shore of L Etive, a place to wander amongst ruins and gdns. Tearoom. If you're along that way, go to the end of the rd at Bonawe where the famous granite that cobbled the world was (and still is) quarried. Ironworks open as a museum is a tranquil place (2246/MUSEUMS). **Swimming** Atlantis Leisure Centre at Dalriach Rd (01631 566800).

**Tourist Office** Argyll Sq. 01631 563122. Jan-Dec.

# The Best Of Perth

Map 10
P23

## WHERE TO STAY

✓ **Ballathie House** Kinclaven 01250 883268. 20km N of Perth via Blairgowrie rd A93/left follow signs after 16km just before the famous beech hedge; or A9 and 4km N, take B9000 through Stanley. Former baronial hunting lodge beside the R Tay. Relaxed and informal atmos in definitive country house. New riverside rms. Kevin MacGillivray's award-winning food. Fishing by arrangement with Estate office.

42RMS JAN-DEC T/T PETS CC KIDS LOTS

**Huntingtower Hotel** 01738 583771. Crieff rd (1km off A85, 3km W of ring route A9 signed). Elegant, modernised mansion house o/side town. Good gdns with spectacular copper beech & other trees. Subdued, panelled restau with decent menu (esp lunch) and wine list. Business-like service.

34RMS JAN-DEC T/T PETS CC KIDS MED.EX

**Parklands** 01738 622451. 2 St Leonards Bank nr stn o/look expansive green parkland of N Inch. Reasonable town mansion hotel on the up. 2 restaus with rep for food. 14RMS JAN-DEC T/T PETS CC KIDS EXP

**Royal George** 01738 624455. Tay St by the Perth Br over the Tay to the A93 rd to Blairgowrie and relatively close to Dundee rd and motorway system. Br is illuminated at night. Georgian proportions and some faded elegance. Mums and farmers and visiting clergy seem happy here.

39RMS JAN-DEC T/T PETS CC KIDS MED.EX

## WHERE TO EAT

✓ ✓ **Let's Eat** 01738 643377. 77 Kinnoull St. The place to eat (929/PERTHSHIRE RESTAUS).

✓ ✓ **63 Tay Street** 01738 441451. 63 Tay St on riverside. The other seriously good bistro. Report: (930/PERTHSHIRE EATS).

✓ **Deli-cious** 46 Methven St. Small, cheery take-away and sit-in coffee shop. Some hot dishes. Excl s/wiches. 7.30am–evening, Sun 11am–7pm. INX

**Keracher's** 01738 449777. Corner of South St & Scott St. Seafood corner run by notable local supplier monger (fish). Downstairs and smart upstairs dining. Excl ingredients and service. Cl Mon. Lunch & LO 9.30/10pm.

INX(BAR)/MED

**Metzo** 01738 626016. 33 George St. Bistro-style diner/dining: a local favourite. Lunch & dinner daily, LO 9.30pm (10pm Fri). INX

**Exceed** 01738 626000. 65 Main St in Bridgend, on the N side of the Tay. Very suave, very classic Franco-Scottish eats in unlikely location. Long may they thrive over there. Mon-Sat, lunch and LO 10pm INX

**Krungthai** 01738 633090. 161 South St. Authentic fare offered by proper Thai chefs has earned good local rep. Open late daily, lunch Tues-Sat only. INX

**Paco's** 01738 622290. Now a bit mega. Still the happy burger 'n' pasta 'n' Mex restau in Mill St (behind M&S) and a newer t/away. Also St John's Place by the city hall & church (daily until 7pm, 5pm Sun). Young atmos in both, LO in restau 11pm. INX

**That Bar (The Loft)** 01738 634523. 147 South St. Perthshire trendy, designery bar (with pool table & big TV). Predictable food upstairs. Somewhere to watch more TV. INX

**Marcello's** 143 South St. Pizza pasta pitstop (eek... and kebabs). T/away only. Noon–11pm (midnight Fri/Sat). Good-looking guys knead the dough. INX

**Holdgate's Fish Teas** South St. A classic (for over 100 yrs)! INX

## WHAT TO SEE & DO

**Kinnoull Hill** (1975/HILLS); **Fergusson Gallery** (2256/PUBLIC GALLERIES); **Glendoick** (2214/GARDEN CENTRES).

**LOCAL CENTRES** • 2335

**Bell's Cherrybank Centre/Branklyn Gardens** Cherrybank is off Glasgow Rd, 18 acres of formal gdns around the offices of the whisky company, notable esp for heathers. Open May-Oct 10am-5pm (Sun 12-5pm); wint hrs 01738 472800. Branklyn is signed off Dundee Rd beyond Queen's Br; park and walk 100m. A tightly packed cornucopia of typical gdn flowers & shrubs. Open Mar-Oct 7 days 9.30am-6pm.

**Perth Theatre** 01738 621031. Established 1935 and Scotland's most successful repertory theatre (Ewan MacGregor got his first break here). Bar/coffee bar and restau. Essential all-round centre even for non-theatregoers.

**Swimming** Excellent large leisure centre with flumes pool and 'training' pool for lengths. Part of it is outdoors. Best app via Glasgow Rd (01738 492410) (2108/LEISURE CENTRES).

**Tourist Office** Lower City Mills. 01738 636103. Jan-Dec.

# The Best Of Stirling

## WHERE TO STAY

2336
Map 10
N24

**Stirling Highland** Stirling 01786 475444. Reasonably sympathetic conversion of former school (with modern accom block) in the historic section of town on rd up to castle. Serviceable businessy hotel in prime location; light 17m pool. Scholars restau ok. None of this is partic good value for what you get.                    98RMS JAN-DEC T/T PETS CC KIDS MED.EX/EXP

**Royal Hotel** Bridge Of Allan 01786 832284. Middle of main st of the civilised (almost suburb) adj town. Stately mansion with good service & notable restau. Also 100m same st the **Royal Lodge** (01786 834166). Both a civilised billet. Best Western. 33/11RMS JAN-DEC T/T PETS CC KIDS MED.INX-EXP

**Park Lodge** 01786 474862. 32 Park Terrace off main King's Park Rd, 500m from centre. Posh-ish hotel in Victorian/Georgian town (they say 'country') house nr the park and golf course. Objets and lawns. French chef/prop.
9RMS JAN-DEC T/T PETS CC KIDS MED.EX

**Portcullis Hotel** 01786 472290. Castle Wynd, no more than a cannonball's throw from the castle & one of the best locations in town. Pub & pub food (hearty, v popular, may be noisy); upstairs only 4 rms, but 3 have brilliant views of Castle/graveyard/town & plain.   4RMS JAN-DEC T/T PETS CC KIDS MED.INX

**Stirling Management Centre** 01786 451666. Not strictly speaking a hotel, but is as good as. Fully serviced rms on the univ campus (7km from centre in Br of Allan – & v good restau choice). Excl leisure facs nearby. No atmos but a business-like option. 76RMS JAN-DEC T/T XPETS CC KIDS MED.INX

**Queen's Hotel** Bridge of Allan 01786 833268. 5km Stirling centre but B of A is the best place to be. Report: 836/CENTRAL.

**S.Y. Hostel** 01786 473442. On rd up to castle in recently renovated jail is this new-style hostel, tho still very SYH (1231/HOSTELS). The **Willy Wallace Hostel** 01786 446773 at 77 Murray Pl (corner with Friars St) is more funky. Upstairs in busy centre with many caffs & pubs nearby. Unimposing entrance but bunkrms for 56 backpackey folk.

## WHERE TO EAT

✓ **The Tolbooth** 01786 274010. Jail Wynd betw 2 streets leading to castle (250m). Stirling's bright, but no longer new, arts centre & auditorium has gr café-bar (11am-late) & restau (6-9.30pm). Italian-Scottish 'fusion' in stylish rms.                                               CHP/MED

**Hermann's** 01786 450632. Mar Place House on rd up to (& v close to) Castle. Hermann Aschaber's (with Scottish wife, Kay) corner of Austria where schnitzels and strudels figure along with trad Scottish fare. 2 floor, ambient well run rms. LO 9.30pm.                                    MED

**The Cottage** 01786 446124. 52 Spittal St on rd up to castle. Tearm/caff with home-made aft tea-type fare but hot mains with Scottish no-nonsense approach. Upstairs and down. Lunch & dinner. Cl Mon.              CHP

**Alexander The Great** 01786 446277. Baker St in centre. Genuine Greek restau such a long way from Athens you just want them to succeed. Plenty grills & familiars to please those who don't know their loukanika. 7 days. Dinner only LO 9/10pm.  INX

**Papa Joe's** 01786 446414. Nr TIC in town centre. Popular, big Tex-mex/Italian/everything kind of menu. Woody ambience. LO 10/11pm.  INX

**The East India Company** 01786 471330. 7 Viewfield Pl. Yrs on it still proclaims to be the best Indian in town tho a bit shabby now. Good atmos in woody basement rm. Open 7 days till 11pm.  INX

**Corrieri's** 01786 472089. On rd to Br of Allan at Causewayhead. For 70 yrs this excl café/restau nr busy corner below the Wallace Monument. Pasta/pizza & ice-cream as it should be. 7 days, LO 9.30pm. Cl Tues.  CHP

**Italia Nostra** 01786 473208. 25 Baker St. Gr name. The tratt to try. Busy atmos. Decent wine list. Usual but decent pastas. 7 days. 10.30 (12 w/ends). CHP

**Birds & Bees** 01786 473663. Betw Stirling & Br of Allan at Causewayhead, Easter Cornton rd. Gr pub & pub grub worth finding. A roadhouse which is the Scottish *pétanque* (French *boules*) centre. Good for kids. 7 days. LO 9.15/10pm.

INX

**Allan Water Café** Bridge Of Allan 8km up the rd in Br of Allan main st nr br itself. Great café, the best fish 'n' chips 'n' ice cream (1477/CAFÉS).  CHP

**Clive Ramsays** Gt deli & café/restau in Bridge of Allan main st. V cool caff with snack & graze menu. LO 8/9pm.  INX

## WHAT TO SEE & DO

**Stirling Castle** (1788/CASTLES); **Wallace Monument/The Pineapple** (1865/1871/MONUMENTS); **Bannockburn/Sheriffmuir** (1929/BATTLE-GROUNDS); **The Ochils** (1981/HILL WALKS; 2008/GLEN AND RIVER WALKS); **Logie Old Kirk** (1912/GRAVEYARDS); **Paradise** (1722/PICNICS); **Dunblane Cathedral** (1892/CHURCHES).

**Stirling Old Town Jail** St John's St on rd up to Castle. Guided tour and put-up job, but rather well done. Live actors. Kids will be quiet or simply tortured. Open AYR 5.30pm (3.30pm winter).

**The Ghost Walk** A stroll through old part of the town nr the castle: 'a world of restless spirits and lost souls' (sound familiar?). Info: TIC or 01592 872788.

**Rainbow Slides** Nr Railway Stn. A leisure centre with good 25m pool and gym (Pulsestar) and for kids 3 water slides of varying thrill factors. Open 7 days (Sat and Sun till 4pm). Check times: 01786 462521.

**Tourist Office** 01786 479901. Jan-Dec.

# The Best Of Wick & Thurso

2337

## WHERE TO STAY

Map 6
P12
Q13

✓ **Portland Arms** Lybster 01593 721208. On main A9 20km S of Wick and 45km S of Thurso by A895. A coaching inn since 1851; still hospitable tho' recently swallowed like so many hotels in the N. Small rms are a bit, well, small but this is a homely hotel with decent food in a choice of settings. Log fires. Feels part of the community. While in Lybster, pop down and see Waterlines (nice restoration, poignant story).

22RMS JAN-DEC T/T PETS CC KIDS MED.INX

**Borgie Lodge Hotel** nr Bettyhill 01641 521332. A836 12km E of Tongue. Secluded trad huntin', shootin', fishin' sort of a place: 20 hill lochs and 2 rivers with salmon and trout. Shooting on the adj 12,000 acre estate and Jacqui's acclaimed cooking to come home to. Getaway people may like it too. Another MacGregor establishment – Peter's brother has Forss House (below).

8RMS JAN-OCT X/T PETS CC KIDS MED.INX

**Pentland Hotel** Thurso  01847 893202. Princes St nr centre. Not the most wonderful but the most wonderful of what's on offer. Public rms are fine incl No 23, a café-bar with Caithness flagstone floor that's a pleasure to eat & drink in. Rms vary.                    41RMS JAN-DEC T/T PETS CC KIDS MED.INX

**Quayside B&B** Wick  25 Harbour Quay. 01955 603229. Brenda Turner's great little establishment, right on the harbour across from the boats. Basic, economical and friendly – with parking & summer barbies in the back yard.
                    6RMS (2SELF-CAT) JAN-DEC X/X XPETS CC KIDS CHP

**Forss House** nr Thurso  01847 861201. 8km W to Tongue off A836. Best in the NW. 984/HIGHLAND HOTELS.    41RMS JAN-DEC T/T PETS CC KIDS MED.INX

**Ackergill Tower** nr Wick  01955 603556. A rare treat. ( 1267/HOUSEPARTIES)

**S.Y. Hostel** 01955 611424. At Canisbay, John O'Groats (7km). Wick 25km. Regular bus service. The furthest-flung youth hostel on the mainland. Thurso has **Sandra's** at 24-26 Princes St. Cheap 'n' cheerful with snack bar adjacent. 01847 894575.

## WHERE TO EAT

✓ ✓ **Captain's Galley** Scrabster  01847 894999. The best on this coast. Seafood with simplicity & integrity. Report: 1389/SEAFOOD RESTAUS. INX

✓ **Forss House Hotel, Portland Arms, Borgie Lodge Hotel**  (*all as above*)

✓ **La Mirage** Helmsdale  60km S so a fair drive, but Viva Las Vegas! (1024/INEXP HIGHLAND RESTAUS).                    INX

**The Ferry Inn** Scrabster  01847 892814. 3km W of Thurso in busy pt area o/look BP and ferry terminal for Orkney. Nr Captain's (above). Surf but mainly turf. 7 days. Lunch & 6-9pm.                    INX

**Bord de L'Eau** Wick  01955 604400. Market St by the br, v much on the waterside. Passably French bistro (menu in French as well as English) where locals might go for big night out. Lunch Tue-Sat, dinner Tue-Sun.    MED

**The Tempest Café** Thurso  On harbour adj Tempest Surf shop (2149/SURF). Laid-back, surfee, kind of waiting on the wave place. Nice home-made soup, butties, cakes etc. LO 4.30pm. Cl Mon.

## WHAT TO SEE & DO

**Dunbeath** 32km S of Wick (1946/LITERARY PLACES; 2014/GLEN AND RIVER WALKS); **Cairns Of Camster** 15km S of Wick (1840/PREHISTORIC SITES); **Bettyhill Museum** 50km W of Thurso (2230/MUSEUMS); **North Coast Beaches** (1660/BEACHES); **Castle of Mey** (1793/CASTLES).

**Waterlines** Lybster harbour. 01593 721520. Sympathetically restored VC telling Lybster's tale & its harbour. Good history – the big contrast between then and now. Tearoom! May-Sep, daily, 11am-5pm.

**The Trinkie** A walk along the rocky coast E of Wick or drive through housing scheme from harbour until cliff rd appears (ask locals). Flat rocks, an open-air pool; a good spot. 2km further for the 'Brig O'Trams'. (1726/SWIMMING HOLES.)

**Whaligoe Steps** On A9 N of Lybster; down track nr cottages and septic tank, by Cairn O' Get sign. Infamy regained after Billy Connolly's visit; 318 (my friend Keith counted) stone cliff steps to sea where herrings used to be landed and cured. Unsignposted so ask locally for directions if lost, and go carefully.

**Wildlife Cruise, John O' Groats** 01955 611353. June-Aug; 90min trips to sea stacks, birds and **John O' Groats-Orkney** May-Sept day trips. White water adventures and 'nature shows', try **North Coast Marine Adventures**, Easter-Oct. 07867 666273.

**Swimming** Wick (01955 603711), Thurso (01847 893260). Both central.

**Tourist Info** 01847 893155.

**Wick** Whitechapel Rd. Jan-Dec; **Thurso** Riverside. Apr-Oct.

# Holiday Centres

2338
Map 10
N21

## PITLOCHRY

### WHERE TO STAY

**East Haugh House** 01796 473121. 3km S from A9. (918/PERTHSHIRE HOTELS).
MED.EX

**Killiecrankie House** 01796 473220 (919/PERTHSHIRE HOTELS). MED.EX

**Pine Trees** 01796 472121. Off Main St (917/PERTHSHIRE HOTELS). MED.EX

**Craigatin House** 01796 472478. Main rd N just beyond shops. V contemp GH & 'courtyard' that clearly aspires to the 'Hip Hotels' lifestyle. Big beds, flat screens, cool colours. B&B only. This place a first in the teuchter tourist towns. 3RMS JAN-DEC T/T XPETS CC XKIDS MED.INX

### WHERE TO EAT

**The Old Armoury** 01796 474821. (936/PERTHSHIRE EATS). INX

**Prince Of India** 01796 472275. Off main st by McNaughton's. Unusually good Indian and good late bet (LO 10.30pm). MED

**Moulin Inn** 01796 472196. Notable for pub food & gr atmos (1338/REAL ALE). 5km uphill from main st. LO 9.30pm. CHP

**Portnacraig** 01796 472777. By theatre, on river. An insider choice. Cl Mon & LO 8.30pm. INX

**Old Smithy** 01796 472356. Main St. Ok coffee/restau. 7 days. LO 9pm. INX

### WHAT TO SEE & DO

**The Salmon Ladder** From Main St and across dam to see 34-pool fish ladder (salmon leaping May-Oct, if you're lucky) and Hydro Board displays (sic); **Ben Vrackie** Local fave with fab Trossachs views climbed from Moulin (2km from town). Rd behind Moulin Inn. Car park. 734m. Scree at top; and goats; **Faskally Woods/Linn Of Tummel Walks** Well-marked woodland walks around L Faskally and Garry R. Can incl the Linn (rapids) and Pass of Killiecrankie (1928/BATTLEGROUNDS). Start: town/Garry bridge/visitor centre; **Woollen Shops** Many major chains and local shops in one small area/the main st. **Pitlochry Theatre** (2269/THEATRES); **Queen's View** (1698/VIEWS); **Edradour Distillery** (1534/WHISKY); **MacNaughton's** (2157/OUTDOOR SHOPS); **Moulin Inn** (1338/REAL ALE).

2339
Map 9
J24

## INVERARAY

### WHERE TO STAY

**George Hotel** 01499 302111. On main st & in the Clark family for centuries (really - 1790). Gr value: ales, good pub food, fires. 783/ARGYLL HOTELS CHP

**Loch Fyne Hotel** 01499 302148. On A83 rd out of town towards W, o/look loch. Big hotel, personally run. Good bar meals. 788/ARGYLL HOTELS. MED.INX

### WHERE TO EAT

✓ **The George/Loch Fyne Hotels** Bar meals esp. (*See above.*) CHP

**Loch Fyne Oyster Bar** 01499 600236. 14km E on A83. INX

**Creggans Inn** 01369 860279. 32km E and S via A83/A815. On opp bank of L Fyne, but 35mins by rd. Bar meals/restau. MED

### WHAT TO SEE & DO

**Inverary Castle** Home of the Duke of Argyll and clan seat of the Campbells. Spectacular entrance hall; chronicle of Highland shenanigans unfurls in the gilded apartments. Fine walks in grounds esp to the prominent hill and folly

320 LOCAL CENTRES • 2338-2339

(45mins up). Apr-Oct. **Ardkinglas Woodland** 17km E on A83 (1563/GAR-DENS). **Crarae Gardens** (1549/GARDENS). **Auchindrain** 8km S on A83; **Inverary Jail** (2244/MUSEUMS).

# *ST ANDREWS*

## WHERE TO STAY

√√ **Old Course Hotel** 01334 474371 (889/FIFE HOTELS). LOTS

√ **Rufflets** 01334 472594 (891/FIFE HOTELS). MED.EX

√ **St Andrews Bay** 01334 837000 (892/FIFE HOTELS). MED.EX

√ **Old Station** 01334 880505 (893/FIFE HOTELS). MED.INX

**Rusacks** 01334 474321. Long-standing golfy hotel nr all courses and over-looking the 18th of the Old. Nice sun-lounge and b/fast o/looking the greens. Reliable & quite classy for a Macdonald Hotel, the recent new owners.
78RMS JAN-DEC T/T PETS CC KIDS MED.EX

**2 Good Guest Houses 18 Queens Terrace** 01334 478849. Address as is. Family home run by the enthusiastic Jill Hardie. Her lounge, gardens, v indi-vid bedrms & lovely b/fast are yours. You'll become friends (or not).
4RMS JAN-DEC X/X XPETS CC XKIDS MED.INX

**5 Pilmour Place** 01334 478665. Address as is. Adj 18th green of Old Course. Contemp-style GH with own lounge. 6RMS JAN-DEC X/T XPETS CC KIDS MED.EX

## WHERE TO EAT

√√ **The Peat Inn** 01334 840 206. 15km SW (907/RESTAU). EXP

√ **The Seafood Restaurant** 01334 479475. Top seafood, top view. Report: 1391/SEAFOOD RESTAUS.

√ **Grange Inn** 01334 472670. 4km E off Anstruther rd A917. V popular country pub in several rms with local rep. Report: 1352/PUB FOOD. INX

**The Vine Leaf** 01334 477497. 131 South St. Inauspicious entrance belies civilised St Andrews fav restau with menu that covers all bases, good vegn, good wines. Morag & Ian Hamilton know how to look after you and what you like esp for pud. Tues-Sat dinner only. MED

**The Doll's House** 01334 477422. Church Sq. V central café/restau that caters well for kids (and teenagers). Eclectic range, smiley people and tables outside in summer. Same people have **The Grill House**; this is better. INX

**Balaka Bangladeshi Restaurant** 01334 474825. 'Best Curry in Scotland' winner. Certainly as good as many in Edin or Glas. Celebrated herb & spice gdn out back which supplies other restaus in St Andrews. MED

**Janetta's** 31 South St. Known for ice-cream (1487/ICE-CREAM), but pop caff. Open 7 days till 5/5.30pm.

**Old Course & Rufflets** Top end, top dining rms (*see above*).

**Inn On North St** 01334 474664.

## WHAT TO SEE & DO

**The Town Itself** The lanes, cloisters, gdns and the University halls and col-leges; the harbour and the botanic gdns. Perfect lawns; **The Castle Ruins** Founded in 13th cent on promontory; good for clambering over. 'Escape tun-nel' to explore (if not tall). Spooky by night along this shore; **British Golf Museum** Sophisticated audio-visual exhibition illustrating history and allure of the game. Even non-players will enjoy. **The Himalayas** the most brilliant putting green; piles of fun, near the beach. Apr-Oct till 8pm, 7 days. Many **Golf Courses** (2061/GREAT GOLF); **West Sands/Kinshaldy Beach** (1620/BEACHES); **Leuchars Church** 9km by A91 N (1889/CHURCHES); **Tentsmuir** 20km by A91/A919 N (1784/WILDLIFE); **New Picture House** (2274/THEATRES); **Janetta's** (1487/ICE CREAM); **St Andrews Fine Art**; **Cathedral** (1822/RUINS); **East Sands** (2115/LEISURE CENTRES).

# ROYAL DEESIDE: BALLATER & BANCHORY

## WHERE TO STAY

✓ ✓ **Raemoir** Banchory 01330 824884. Large mansion in secluded grounds 3km town by Raemoir Rd off A93. Relaxed and discreet. 9-hole golf and tennis. Growing rep for food. LOTS

✓ ✓ **Darroch Learg** Ballater 01339 755443. Town mansion above/off (at tight bend) A93 on way in from Braemar. Excellent nosh. (943/NE HOTELS.) MED

**Lys-Na-Greyne** Aboyne 01339 887397. Small GH, person touch, gr gardens. 950/NE HOTELS.

**Tor-Na-Coille** Banchory 01330 822242. Town mansion above/just off main A93 on way in from Ballater. Nr golf. Antiques in tasteful/individual rms. EXP

## WHERE TO EAT

✓ ✓ **Darroch Learg** Ballater 01339 755443. The other Deeside hoteliers aspire to. (*see above*).

**The Oak Room** Ballater 01339 755858. EXP

✓ **The Black-Faced Sheep** Aboyne 01339 887311. Near main rd. Coffee shop/gift shop with excellent home-baking. Daytime hrs (1442/TEA-ROOMS).

✓ **Milton Restaurant** 01330 844566 (958/NE RESTAUS). MED

**Falls of Freugh** Banchory 01330 822123. Report: 1443/TEARMS.

**The Candlestick-Maker** Aboyne 01330 822123.

**White Cottage nr Aboyne** 01398 85757. Report: 961/NE RESTAUS.

**The Green Inn** Ballater 01339 755701. Report: 960/NE RESTAUS.

**Raemoir Garden Centre (Tearoom)** Report: 2218/GARDEN CENTRES.

## WHAT TO SEE & DO

**Craigievar/Drum** (1805/1806/CASTLES); **Fasque** (1853/COUNTRY HOUSES); **Crathes** (1545/1863/GARDENS/COUNTRY HOUSES); **Balmoral** (1807/CASTLES); **Lochnagar** (1992/MUNROS); **Albert Memorial** (1875/MONUMENTS); **Glen Muick** (1660/LOCHS); **Cambus O' May** (1723/PICNICS); **Golf** Well-managed/picturesque courses, open to visitors at both Ballater (013397 55567), and Banchory (01330 822447). Both 18 holes; **Fishing** Difficult, not impossible, on Dee or on R Feugh (N bank only) – permits from Feughside Inn (01330 850225); **Walks** Walks down both sides of the Dee, esp Ballater to Cambus O'May, 7km; **Viewpoints** Up Craigendarroch, the Hill of the Oaks, Ballater, from Braemar Rd (45mins). Scolty Hill and Monument, Banchory. Ask for directions; **Raemoir Garden Centre** (2218/GARDEN CENTRES); **Burn O' Vat** (1956/SPOOKY PLACES); **MacEwan Gallery** (2182/WHERE TO BUY ART); **Braemar–Linn Of Dee, Ballater–Tomintoul** (1676/1677/SCENIC ROUTES).

**Tourist Info** 01330 822000.

# CALLANDER

## WHERE TO STAY

✓ ✓ **The Roman Camp** 01877 330003. Secluded riverside location off main st. Best in the region. 832/CENTRAL HOTELS.

**3 Great Guesthouses Leny House** 01877 331078. Edge of town in own estate. **The Priory** 01877 330001. **Arden House** 01877 330235.

**Callander Meadows** 01877 330181. 3 rms above restau (see below) in main st. Nicely appointed.                    INX

## WHERE TO EAT

✓ ✓ **The Roman Camp** 01877 330003. As above.

**Atrium** 01877 331611. Main St. 846/CENTRAL RESTAUS.

**Dun Whinny** Daytime café. 1474/TEARMS.                    EXP

**Callander Meadows** 01877 330181. Decent dining in Main St. At last a restau to speak of on the tartan strip. Thur-Mon. Lunch & LO 9pm.

**The Lade Inn** Kilmahog 01877 330152. Just outside the town on Trossachs rd. Roadhouse pub that brews its own. Good local rep. Lunch & dinner LO 9pm.                    INX

**The Conservatory** Ballachallan 01877 339190. 2 km E on A84 for Stirling. Serious seafood restau (with rms). Haven't tried but everybody talks about it locally. Reports please.

**Old Bank** 01877 330651. Café/restau in lofty rm at N end of Main St. Notable for home-baking esp cakes. Decent coffee. 7 days. LO 9pm in summer, earlier in wint.

**The Ben Ledi Café** Fish 'n' chips, ice cream, etc. 1434/CAFÉS.

## WHAT TO SEE & DO

**The Trossachs** All around; **Scotch Oven** (1479/BAKERS); **Bracklinn Falls** (1718/SWIMMING HOLES); **Ben Venue, Ben A'An, Ben Shian** (1963/1964/HILLS).

# A few things the Scots gave the world

*The population of Scotland has never been much over 5 million and yet we discovered, invented or manufactured for the first time the following quite important things.*

The decimal point

Logarithms

The Bank of England

The overdraft

Cannabis (the active principle)

Documentary films

Colour photographs

Encyclopaedia Britannica

Postcards

The gas mask

The theory of combustion

The advertising film

The bus

The steam engine

The locomotive

The fax machine

The photocopier

Video

The telephone

Television

Radar

Helium

Neon

The telegraph

Street lighting

The lawnmower

Kinetic energy

Electric light

The alpha chip

The Thermos flask

The hypodermic syringe

Finger-printing

The kaleidoscope

Anaesthesia

Antiseptics

Golf clubs

The 18-hole golf course

Tennis courts

The bowling green

Writing paper

The thermometer

The gravitating compass

The threshing machine

Insulin

Penicillin

Interferon

The pneumatic tyre

The pedal bicycle

The modern road surface

Geology

Artificial ice

Morphine

Ante-natal clinics

Bovril

Marmalade

The fountain pen

The Mackintosh

Gardenias

Dolly, the cloned sheep

*Auld Lang Syne*

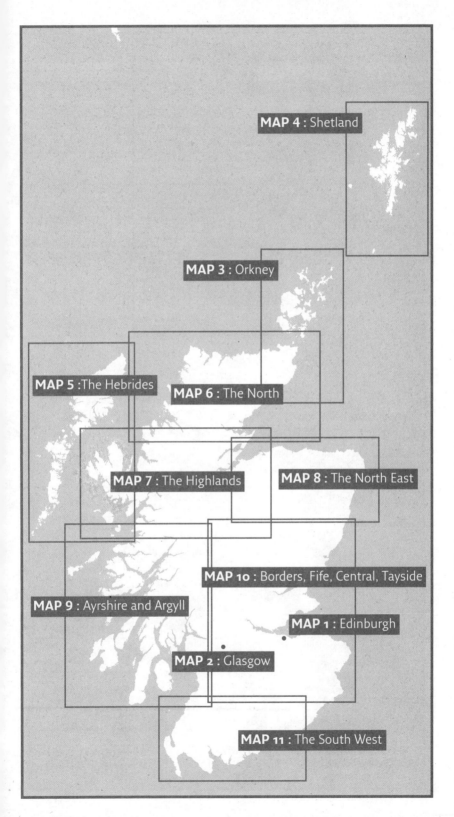

MAP 4 : Shetland

MAP 3 : Orkney

MAP 5 :The Hebrides

MAP 6 : The North

MAP 7 : The Highlands

MAP 8 : The North East

MAP 10 : Borders, Fife, Central, Tayside

MAP 9 : Ayrshire and Argyll

MAP 1 : Edinburgh

MAP 2 : Glasgow

MAP 11 : The South West

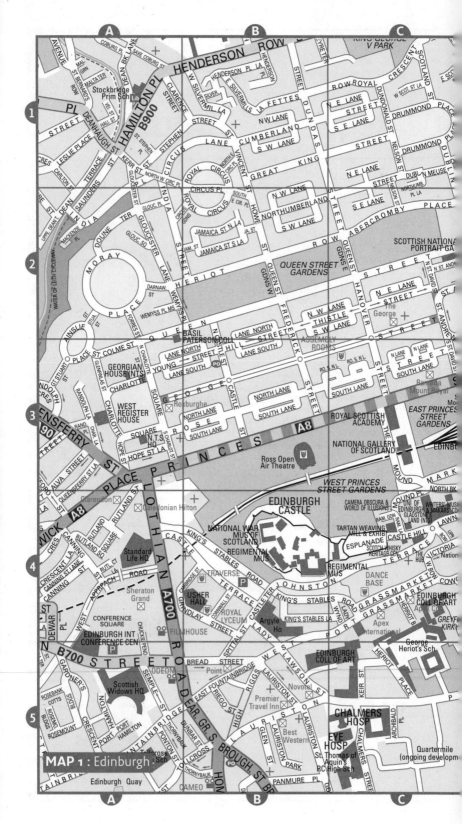

MAP 1 : Edinburgh

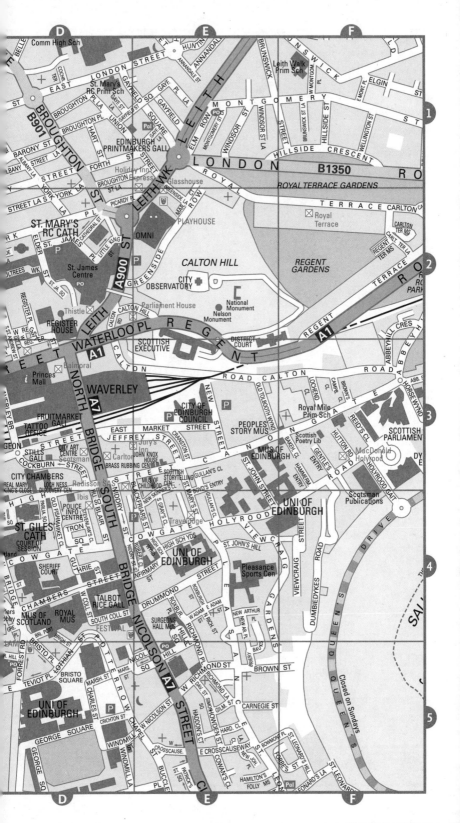

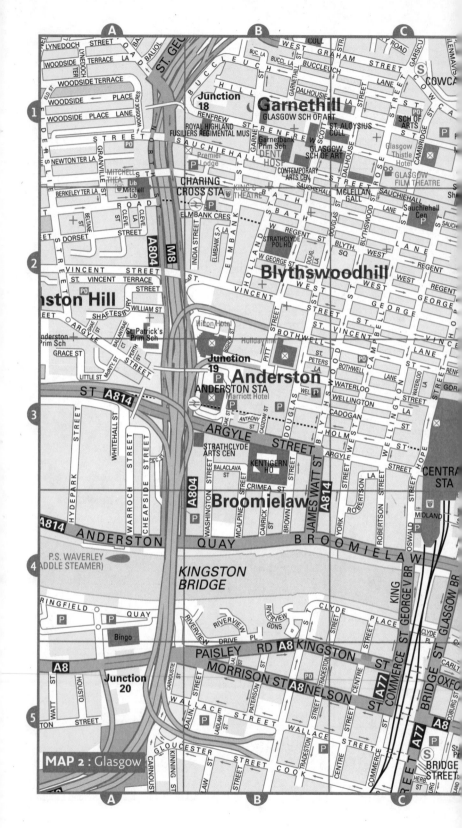

MAP 2 : Glasgow

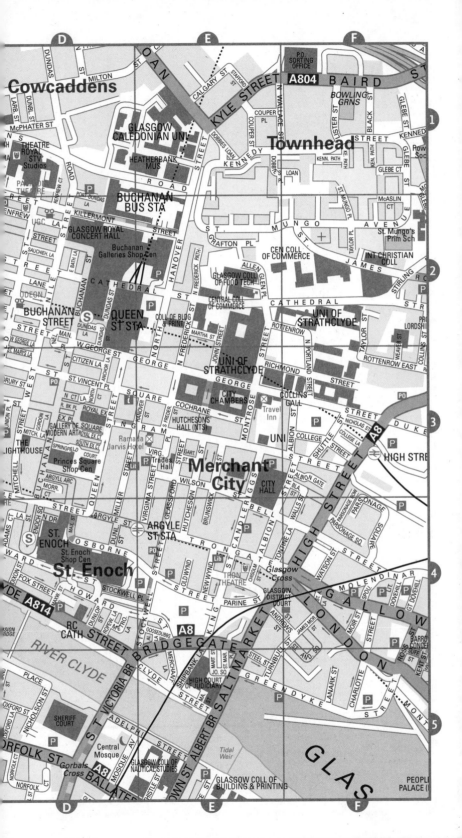

Cowcaddens

Townhead

Merchant City

St. Enoch

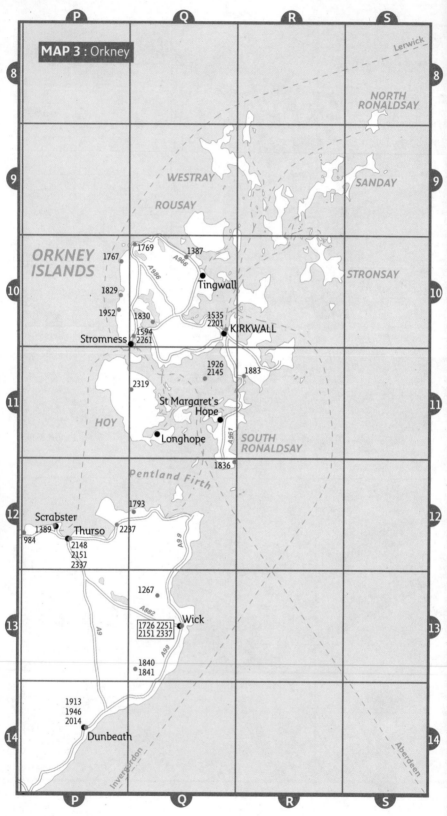

MAP 3 : Orkney

Lerwick

NORTH
RONALDSAY

WESTRAY

ROUSAY

SANDAY

ORKNEY
ISLANDS

1769

1387

1767

A966

STRONSAY

A986

1829

Tingwall

1952

1830

1535
2201

1594
2261

KIRKWALL

Stromness

2319

1926
2145

1883

St Margaret's
Hope

HOY

Longhope

A961

SOUTH
RONALDSAY

1836

Pentland Firth

1793

Scrabster

A99

1389

Thurso

2237

984

2148
2151
2337

1267

A882

1726 2251
2151 2337

Wick

A99

A9

1840
1841

1913
1946
2014

Dunbeath

Invergordon

Aberdeen

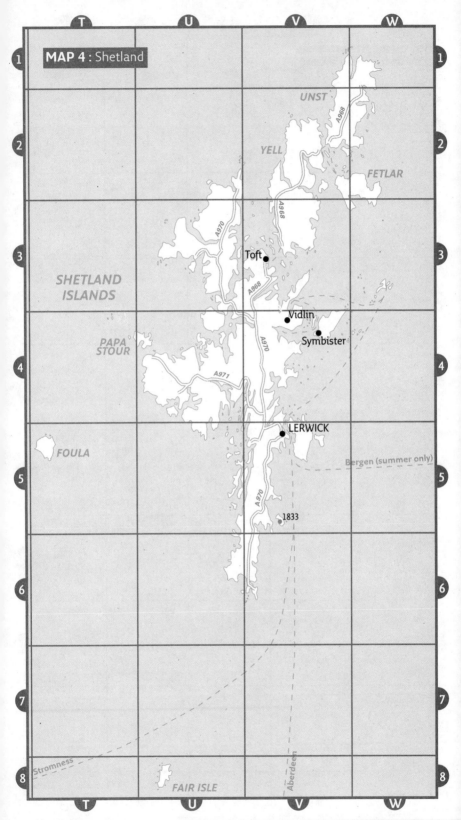

MAP 4 : Shetland

UNST

YELL

FETLAR

A968

SHETLAND
ISLANDS

Toft

Vidlin

Symbister

PAPA
STOUR

A970

A971

FOULA

LERWICK

Bergen (summer only)

1833

Stromness

Aberdeen

FAIR ISLE

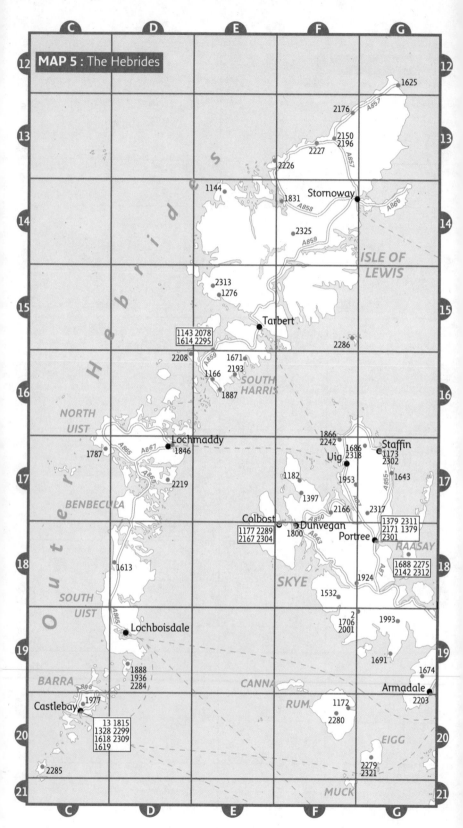

MAP 5 : The Hebrides

Outer Hebrides

ISLE OF LEWIS

1625
2176          A857
2150
2196          A857
2227
2226

1144
1831      Stornoway
          A858

2325
          A858

          A866

2313
1276

Tarbert

1143 2078
1614 2295

2286

2208
1671
1166  2193
    1887

SOUTH
HARRIS

NORTH
UIST

1787    A865  A867   Lochmaddy
                     1846

1866
2242
        1686
        2318   Staffin
Uig            1173
               2302
1182
        1953           1643
    1397
        2166   2317
Colbost         1379 2311
1177 2289  Dunvegan  2171 1379
2167 2304  1800      2301
           Portree
                     RAASAY

1613                 1688 2275
                     2142 2312

A865  2219

BENBECULA

SOUTH
UIST

Lochboisdale

1888
1936
2284

SKYE

1924
1532

2
1706
2001
          1993

          1691
               1674
Armadale
2203

CANNA

BARRA
    1977
Castlebay    RUM   1172
                   2280
13 1815
1328 2299           EIGG
1618 2309
1619

2285                2279
                    2321

MUCK

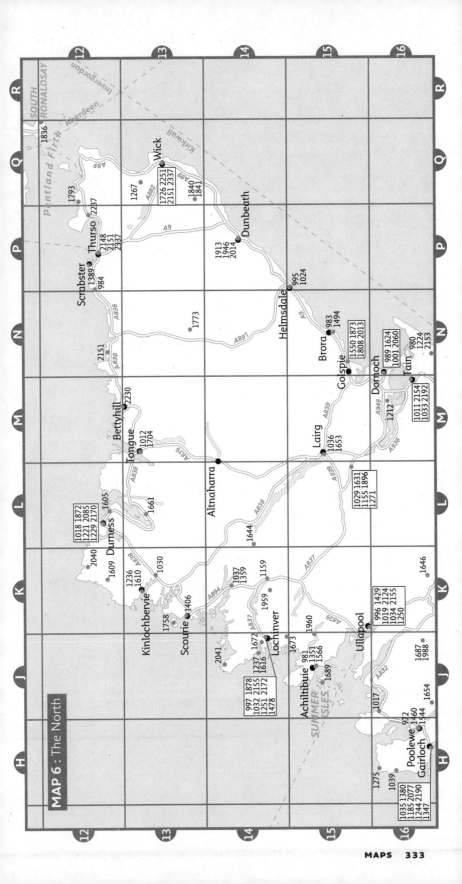

MAP 6: The North

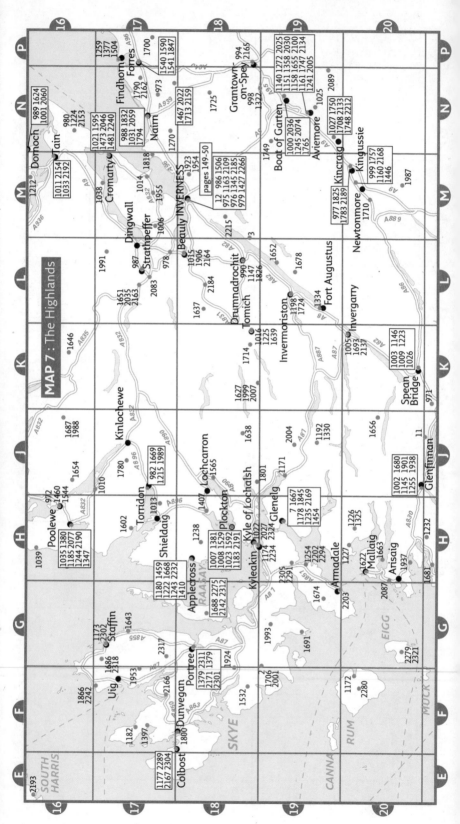

MAP 7: The Highlands

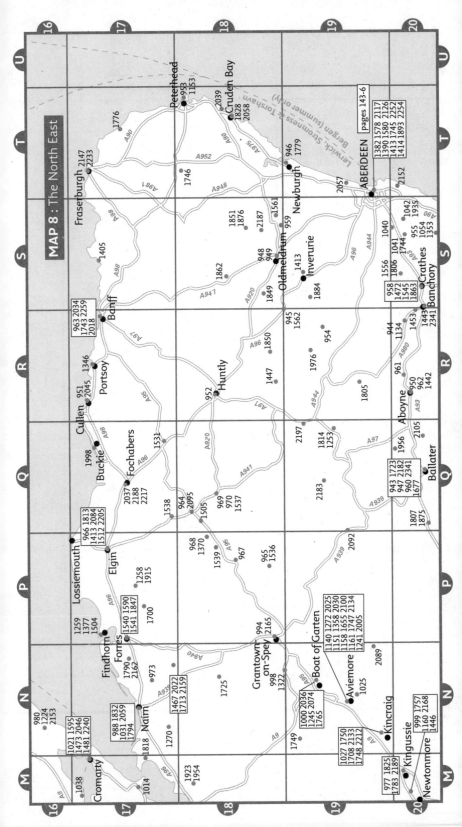

MAP 8 : The North East

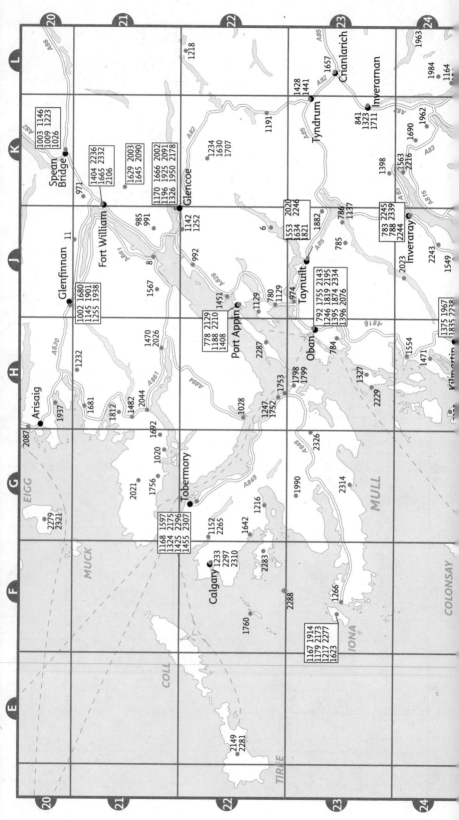

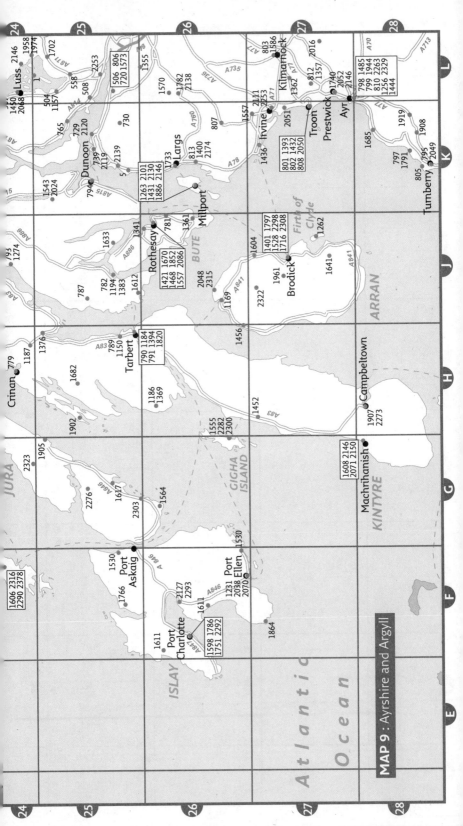

MAP 9 : Ayrshire and Argyll

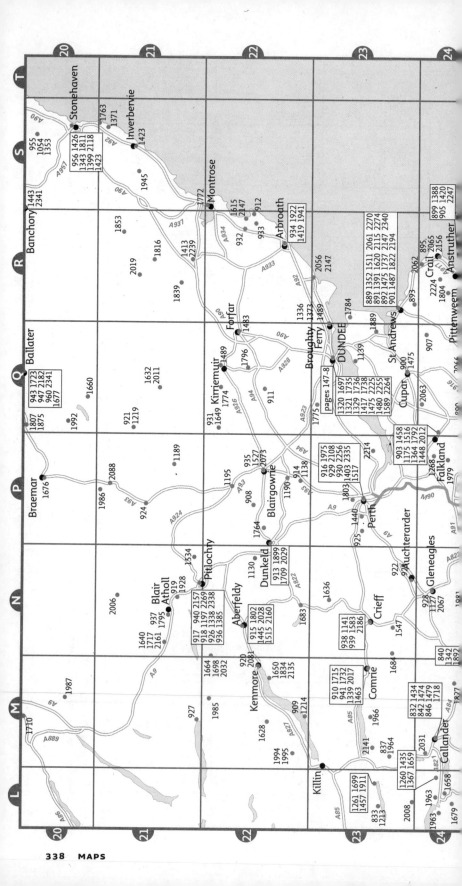

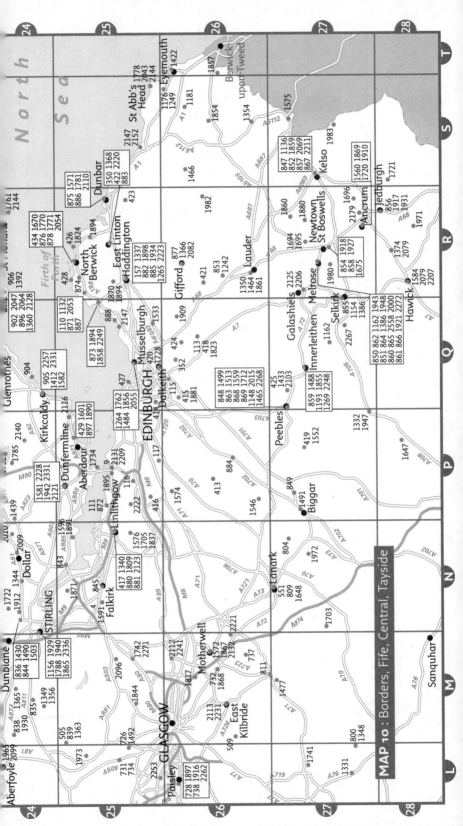

MAP 10 : Borders, Fife, Central, Tayside

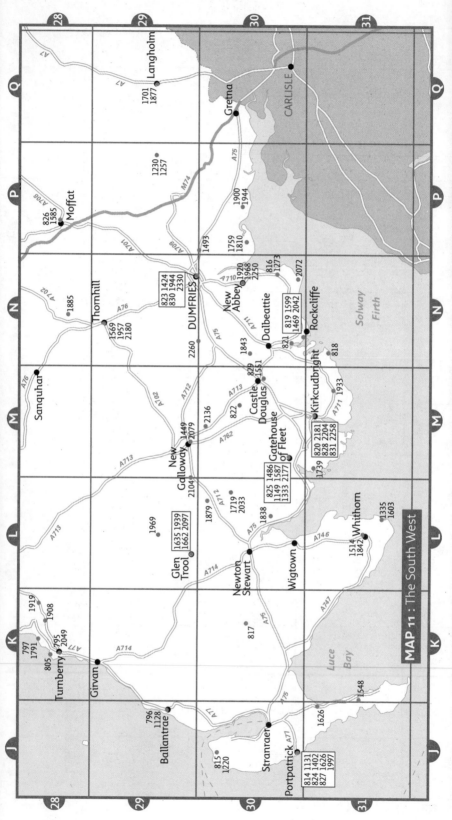

MAP 11 : The South West

# INDEX

**Note:** the numbers listed against index entries refer to the page number on which the entry appears and not the entry's item number.

# A Declaration

*Scotland the Best* is a handbook of information about all the 'best' places in Scotland. 'Best', you will understand, is a subjective term; it means 'best' according to what I think, but it's intended to be obvious that I am conveying opinions and impressions. We believe in what we are saying. We take no bribes and have no vested interest in any of the places recommended, other than that we do talk things up and shamelessly proclaim the places we like or admire.

Along with observations, every 'item' conveys factual information; I hope it is plain where the facts end and the opinions begin. In guide books, this is not always the case. However, it's with the 'facts' that inconsistencies may appear. We try to give accurate and clear directions explaining how to find a place and basic details that might be useful. This information is gleaned from a variety of sources and may be supplied by the establishment concerned. We do try to verify everything, usually by visiting, but the process of acquiring and transcribing information is tricky when there's so much of it. Things change and because nowhere we mention has solicited their inclusion (or if they have, it has made little difference), nor been invited to check what we say – well, mistakes can be made. With this density of information, it's impossible to run it past proprietors, and they might well not like what we say because it's our opinion, not theirs. So I'm sorry if we get something wrong. Please let us know if there are any mistakes, so we can fix them.

This admission is therefore made in advance. My cringing excuse is that we are merely human. This guide is made by fallible humans, of which I hope you are one. However, be clear on one thing; this book is more than about trying to get it right. As with many of the people we celebrate in these pages, we do strive for perfection.

# Your Help Needed

### (and win good whisky)

*Scotland the Best* wouldn't be the best if I didn't receive feedback and helpful suggestions from so many people. It really has become an interactive book because so many of you seem to know what sort of places are likely to fit. With each new edition I believe I get closer to the definitive best guide including everywhere in Scotland that's any good. It bothers me if I miss something – a new restaurant might be forgiveable, but there may be an established one that I've omitted from this edition. There are pubs for example that have been doing great food for years and as each edition passes I get closer to knowing all of them. This completeness is because people write to tell me. And I hope very much that they will continue to do so. *Scotland the Best* is supposed to follow the inside track to Scotland and you who live here, or are experiencing it as a visitor, are on it. Send me the word!

Write and let me know whether you have found the information helpful and accurate and whether you agree or disagree with my selections. Have places lived up to your expectations and, in particular, are there any superlative places that ought to have been mentioned? Even if it's your own place and you think it deserves wider attention, let me know. Everywhere you recommend will be checked out for the next edition in 2006/2007. Please send your comments or suggestions to:

Peter Irvine/*Scotland the Best*
Reference Department
HarperCollins Publishers
Westerhill Rd
Bishopbriggs
Glasgow
G64 2QT

For sharing this information, HarperCollins will be happy to share out some good whisky and cheese. A bottle of malt together with a drum of Tobermory cheddar will be presented at the launch of the next edition, to the best three suggestions received by 30 September 2007. Recommendations can be for any category or for any number of categories, and anywhere that you recommend will be included next time, if it checks out. Please give reasons for your recommendation and specific directions if it is difficult to find.